Entering the 21st Century

World Development Report 1999/2000

Published for the World Bank
Oxford University Press

Oxford University Press

OXFORD   NEW YORK   ATHENS   AUCKLAND   BANGKOK   BOGOTA
BUENOS AIRES   CALCUTTA   CAPE TOWN   CHENNAI   DAR ES SALAAM
DELHI   FLORENCE   HONG KONG   ISTANBUL   KARACHI
KUALA LUMPUR   MADRID   MELBOURNE   MEXICO CITY   MUMBAI
NAIROBI   PARIS   SÃO PAULO   SINGAPORE   TAIPEI   TOKYO
TORONTO   WARSAW

and associated companies in

BERLIN   IBADAN

Published by Oxford University Press, Inc.
200 Madison Avenue, New York, N.Y. 10016

Cover and chapter opener design by W. Drew Fasick, ULTRAdesigns.
Illustration/calligraphy by Jun Ma. The cover and chapter openers depict
the Chinese character for *gate* or *door*.
Inside design and typesetting by
Barton Matheson Willse & Worthington, Baltimore.

Manufactured in the United States of America
First printing August 1999

ISBN 0-19-521125-1 clothbound
ISBN 0-19-521124-3 paperback
ISSN 0163-5085

Text printed on recycled paper that conforms to the American Standard
for Permanence of Paper for Printed Library Material Z39.48-1984.

Foreword

he *World Development Report 1999/2000,* the 22nd in this annual series, addresses the changing development landscape of the early 21st century. Development thinking has evolved into a broad pragmatism, realizing that development must move beyond economic growth to encompass important social goals—reduced poverty, improved quality of life, enhanced opportunities for better education and health, and more. Experience has also taught that sustainable progress toward these goals requires integrated implementation and must be firmly anchored in processes that are open, participatory, and inclusive. In the absence of a strong institutional foundation, the outcomes of good policy initiatives tend to dissipate. These lessons and insights are incorporated into the Comprehensive Development Framework, recently initiated by the World Bank to address the challenges of development in a more holistic, integrated way by bringing in aspects such as governance, legal institutions, and financial institutions, which were too often given short shrift earlier.

Looking ahead, this report explores the environment in which the major issues of the 21st century—poverty, population growth, food security, water scarcity, climate change, cultural preservation—will be faced. Many powerful forces, both glacial and fast-paced, are reshaping the development landscape. These include innovations in technology, the spread of information and knowledge, the aging of populations, the financial interconnectedness of the world, and the rising demands for political and human rights. The report focuses in particular on two clusters of change—globalization and localization—because of their immense potential impact. They open up unprecedented opportunities for growth and development, but they also carry with them the threats of economic and political instability that can erode years of hard-earned gains.

Given their already present implications, it is not surprising that globalization and localization are a central preoccupation of policymakers around the world. Globalization is praised for bringing new opportunities for expanded markets and the spread of technology and management expertise, which in turn hold out the promise of greater productivity and a higher standard of living. Conversely, globalization is feared and condemned because of the instability and undesired changes it can bring: to workers who fear losing their jobs to competition from imports; to banks and financial systems and even entire economies that can be overwhelmed and driven into recession by flows of foreign capital; and, not least, to the global commons, which are threatened in many ways with irreversible change.

Localization is praised for raising levels of participation and involvement, and providing people with a greater ability to shape the context of their own lives. By leading to decentralized government where more decisions happen at subnational levels, closer to the voters, localization can result in more responsive and efficient local governance. National governments may use a strategy of decentralization to defuse civil strife or even civil war. However, when poorly designed, decentralization can result in overburdened local governments without the resources or the capacity to fulfil their basic responsibilities of providing local infrastructure and services. It can also threaten macroeconomic stability, if local governments, borrowing heavily and spending unwisely, need to be bailed out by the national government.

This report seeks neither to praise nor to condemn globalization and localization. Rather it recognizes them as forces that bring new opportunities but also raise new or greater challenges in terms of economic and political instability. Containing this instability and providing an environment in which a development agenda can be implemented to seize the opportunities will be a major institutional challenge in the coming decades. The discussion in the report focuses on three main aspects of globalization: trade in goods and services, international flows of capital, and global environmental issues, such as the dangers of climate change and destruction of biodiversity. The focus of the discussion then shifts to three aspects of localization: the decentralization of political power to subnational levels of government, the movement of population and economic energy in developing countries toward urban areas, and the provision of essential public services in these growing cities of the future.

In discussing the appropriate institutional responses to the challenges and opportunities of globalization and localization, the report draws on a vast array of national examples and cross-country empirical evidence, including both development success stories and episodes of failure. There is no simple answer to dealing with globalization and localization. Instead, the insights are rooted in pragmatic judgments about how the existing conditions of society will affect which policy choices make sense, or how one sequence of policies is preferable to another, or how certain policies can complement and sustain each other. The commitments and actions of the national government remain central to any workable development strategy. However, the forces of globalization and localization imply that much of the institution-building for development will be taking place at either the supranational or the subnational levels. In both cases, countries will need to focus on development strategies that are implemented through mutual consent, whether through international agreements between countries, or through constitutional and institutional arrangements between different levels of government and components of civil society within a country. At both the global and local levels, institutions based on partnership, negotiation, coordination and regulation would provide the basis for sustainable development.

Globalization and localization are not likely to disappear, or even to diminish in intensity. They are driven by powerful underlying forces like the new capabilities of information and communication technologies, and a rising sense among people all over the world that they are entitled to participate openly in their government and society. As globalization brings distant parts of the world functionally closer together, and localization multiplies the range of policy environments, it may well be that successful development policies will achieve results more quickly, while failed policies will have their consequences exposed more quickly and painfully as well. In such a world, exploring the institutional responses to globalization and localization, and disseminating the insights broadly, offers enormous potential for advances in development strategy—advances that can be of great and lasting benefit to the poorest people of the world.

James D. Wolfensohn
President
The World Bank

August 1999

This report has been prepared by a team led by Shahid Yusuf and comprising Anjum Altaf, William Dillinger, Simon Evenett, Marianne Fay, Vernon Henderson, Charles Kenny, and Weiping Wu. The team was assisted by Mohammad Arzaghi and Stratos Safioleas. The work was carried out under the general direction of Joseph Stiglitz. Throughout the preparation of this report Lyn Squire provided valuable advice and contributions. Timothy Taylor was the principal editor.

The team was advised by a distinguished panel of experts comprising Alberto Alesina, Masahiko Aoki, Richard Cooper, John Dixon, Barry Eichengreen, Jon Elster, Alan Harold Gelb, Harry Harding, Gregory K. Ingram, Christine Kessides, Jennie Litvack, Wallace Oates, Anthony J. Pellegrini, Guillermo Perry, David Satterthwaite, Paul Smoke, Paul Spray, T.N. Srinivasan, Jacques Thisse, and John Williamson.

Many others inside and outside the World Bank provided helpful comments, wrote background papers and other contributions, and participated in consultation meetings. The preparation of some background papers and the convening of several workshops was supported by the Policy and Human Resources Development Fund financed by the Japanese Government and a grant from the Government of the United Kingdom Department for International Development. These contributors and participants are listed in the Bibliographical Note. The Development Data Group contributed to the data appendix and was responsible for the Selected World Development Indicators.

Rebecca Sugui served as executive assistant to the team, and Maribel Flewitt, Leila Search, and Thomas A.J. Zorab as team assistants. Maria D. Ameal served as administrative officer.

Book design, editing, and production were coordinated by the Production Services Unit of the World Bank's Office of the Publisher.

Contents

Overview

The frontiers of development thinking 2

Globalization and localization 4

Supranational issues. 5

Subnational issues 8

Translating policies into actions 11

Introduction   New Directions in Development Thinking

Building on past development experiences 14

The many goals of development. 18

The role of institutions in development 21

The record and outlook for comprehensive development. 24

A changing world 28

Chapter 1   The Changing World

International trade. 33

International financial flows. 34

International migration 37

Global environmental challenges 40

New political tendencies in developing countries 43

Emerging subnational dynamics. 44

Urban imperatives. 46

Implications for development policy. 49

Chapter 2   The World Trading System: The Road Ahead

How the global trading system benefits developing countries. 52

WTO mechanisms for promoting and maintaining liberal trade regimes 53

Sustaining the momentum for trade reform 55

International trade and development policy: the next 25 years. 60

Chapter 3   Developing Countries and the Global Financial System

The gathering pace of international financial integration 70

Toward a more robust and diversified banking system. 75

The orderly sequencing of capital account liberalization 79

Attracting foreign investment. 81

Revitalizing international macroeconomic cooperation 84

Chapter 4   Protecting the Global Commons

The link between national and global environmental issues. 90

Moving from national to international action 93

The ozone treaties: a success story 94

Climate change   97
Biodiversity   102
Exploiting the links between global environmental problems   103

Chapter 5   Decentralization: Rethinking Government

What is at stake?   107
From centralized to decentralized governance   111
Balancing political power between central and local interests   112
The structure, functions, and resources of subnational governments   114
Making subnational governments accountable   121
Policies for the transition   122
What lessons for the future?   124

Chapter 6   Dynamic Cities as Engines of Growth

What makes cities grow?   126
The national government's role in urbanization   130
Local policies for urban economic growth   132

Chapter 7   Making Cities Livable

The unfinished urban agenda   140
Learning from the past   142
Service provision in developing countries   144
Looking ahead   152

Chapter 8   Case Studies and Recommendations

Making the most of trade liberalization: Egypt   157
Reforming weak banking systems: Hungary   160
Macromanagement under fiscal decentralization: Brazil   163
Improving urban living conditions: Karachi   166
Cultivating rural-urban synergies: Tanzania   169
The shifting development landscape at the dawn of the 21st century   172

Bibliographical Note   175
Appendix Selected Indicators on Decentralization, Urbanization, and the Environment   213
Selected World Development Indicators   223
Index   292

Boxes

1   Lessons from East Asia and Eastern Europe   17
2   Social capital, development, and poverty   18
3   Explaining power project outcomes in Sub-Saharan Africa   18
4   The Comprehensive Development Framework   21
5   A holistic approach to development in past *World Development Reports*   22
6   Institutions, organizations, and incentives   23
7   Trends in disease and health care   27
8   Sustainable development   28
9   The growing threat of water scarcity   29
1.1   The global macroeconomics of aging   35
1.2   The international Chinese network   40

2.1   Regional trading arrangements and the global trading system: complements or substitutes?   54
2.2   Building technical expertise on trade policy: the Integrated Framework for Trade
      and Development in the Least-Developed Countries   58
2.3   Child labor: how much? how damaging? and what can be done?   62
3.1   A continuing role for aid   73
3.2   What causes financial contagion?   75
3.3   Subnational governments face commitment problems too   83
3.4   Mitigating the commitment problem: the role of the World Bank   83
4.1   Global environmental issues   88
4.2   Preserving the ocean commons: controlling overfishing   92
4.3   The Global Environment Facility   94
4.4   NGOs and efforts to preserve the international environment   96
4.5   Falling costs for renewable energy   98
4.6   Taxes and quotas to reduce emissions   99
4.7   Trade measures in international environmental agreements   104
5.1   Decentralization as the devolution of powers   108
5.2   South Africa and Uganda: unifying a country through decentralization   108
5.3   Bosnia-Herzegovina and Ethiopia: decentralization as a response to ethnic diversity   109
5.4   India: a decentralizing federation?   110
5.5   Decentralization in China   113
5.6   Financing intermediate tiers of government   118
5.7   The cart before the horse: decentralization in Russia   123
6.1   Cities and urban areas: some definitions   127
6.2   Rural-urban linkages   128
6.3   The dispersal of industry in Korea   129
6.4   Africa: urbanization without growth   130
6.5   City development and land markets   135
6.6   Regionalism and local economic development: lessons from Europe   137
6.7   Know thy economy: the importance of local economic information   138
7.1   A spatial mismatch: Jakarta's kampung residents   147
7.2   Haiphong: partnering with consumers   148
7.3   Manila: a positive corporate image as an incentive to reduce pollution   151
7.4   Shenyang: social welfare in a struggling industrial city   152
7.5   Bangalore: citizens' report cards   154
8.1   Five case studies   158
8.2   The Arab Republic of Egypt at a glance   159
8.3   Hungary at a glance   161
8.4   Brazil at a glance   163
8.5   Pakistan at a glance   167
8.6   Tanzania at a glance   170

Figures

1   Computers are linking the world   4
2   All but a few democracies have decentralized some political power   4
3   Trade is growing much faster than national income in developing countries   5
4   Countries are joining the WTO in increasing numbers   6
5   Private capital flows to developing countries have increased dramatically   7
6   There are more countries and more democracies   9
7   Urban population is growing—primarily in developing countries   10

8   The incomes of rich and poor countries continue to diverge   14

9   Investment alone cannot account for variation in growth   15

10   Infant mortality fell in most developing countries from 1980 to 1995,
      even where income did not increase   19

11   The number of poor people has risen worldwide, and in some regions the proportion
      of poor has also increased   25

12   Life expectancies have risen greatly in some countries, but others have suffered setbacks   26

1.1   Exports of commercial services have surged in most regions since 1990   34

1.2   An increasing number of developing countries is committed to trade reform   34

1.3   Nonperforming loans can account for up to 50 percent of all bank loans at the peak
      of a banking crisis.   36

1.4   Resolving bank crises can cost up to 40 percent of GDP   37

1.5   Foreign direct investment was less volatile than commercial bank loans
      and total portfolio flows, 1992–97   37

1.6   Temperatures are rising as concentrations of greenhouse gases increase   41

1.7   More countries are becoming democratic   43

1.8   Most urban dwellers reside in developing countries   47

1.9   Asia and Africa are just beginning the urban transition   47

1.10 The largest increase in urban populations during 1980-2020 will occur in Africa and Asia   48

2.1   Foreign trade has increased in most developing countries since 1970   52

2.2   More of the world's exports are covered by WTO disciplines, especially exports from
      developing countries   53

2.3   More regional trading arrangements (RTAs) came into force in the 1990s than ever before   54

2.4   Many developing countries started liberalizing before the end of the Uruguay Round   56

2.5   Equal players? African representatives at the WTO   57

2.6   The composition of many developing countries' exports was transformed in just over 10 years . .   59

2.7   New users initiated an increasing number of antidumping suits during 1987–97   60

2.8   When filing antidumping investigations, industrial and developing countries target
      each other almost equally   61

2.9   Many countries bound their tariffs on agricultural products in the Uruguay Round at levels
      well above estimated actual tariffs in 1986–88   63

2.10 Exports of commercial services increased in every region from 1985 to 1997   64

3.1   Since 1980 net flows of foreign direct and portfolio investment to developing economies
      have grown enormously   70

3.2   Firms from developing countries are issuing more international debt than before   71

3.3   A growing pool of institutionally managed funds is invested abroad   71

3.4   A few developing countries received the lion's share of FDI invested outside industrial countries
      in 1997   73

3.5   Bank intermediation typically accounts for a larger share of the financial sector in developing
      countries   76

4.1   Climate change jeopardizes crop yields, especially in developing countries   89

4.2   Atmospheric concentrations of ozone-depleting substances rose, then began to fall   95

4.3   A 1-meter rise in sea level would cut Bangladesh's rice production approximately in half   100

4.4   Energy consumption in developing countries is forecast to outstrip industrial country
      consumption   100

4.5   High-income countries use energy more intensively than countries in low-income regions   101

5.1   Subnational expenditures are a small share of public expenditures, except in industrial countries
      and large federations   111

5.2   Local governments never control a large share of public resources 112
6.1   Urbanization is closely associated with economic growth. 126
6.2   Most of the world's urban population lived in small and medium-size cities in 1995 128
6.3   Small cities had the fastest growing populations, and megacities the slowest, from 1970 to 1990 . 130
6.4   As countries develop, central governments' share of public investment falls 133
7.1   Even low-income countries can achieve high levels of basic water and sanitation services 140
7.2   Housing affordability varies significantly at low levels of income 141
8.1   The population in Tanzania is increasingly urbanized 141

Tables
1.1   World foreign direct investment stock, 1997 38
1.2   Political and functional decentralization in large democracies, 1997. 45
2.1   Reported antidumping actions by members of the GATT and WTO, 1987–97 60
2.2   Share of parts and components in exports, 1995. 66
5.1   The structure of subnational governments in large democracies. 116
5.2   Subnational borrowing controls in selected countries 119
7.1   Infant mortality rate, Bangladesh, 1990 142

Definitions and data notes

The countries included in regional and income groupings in this report are listed in the Classification of Economies table at the end of the Selected World Development Indicators. Income classifications are based on GNP per capita; thresholds for income classifications in this edition may be found in the Introduction to Selected World Development Indicators. Group averages reported in the figures and tables are unweighted averages of the countries in the group unless noted to the contrary.

The use of the word *countries* to refer to economies implies no judgment by the World Bank about the legal or other status of a territory. The term *developing countries* includes low- and middle-income economies and thus may include economies in transition from central planning, as a matter of convenience. The term *advanced countries* may be used as a matter of convenience to denote the high-income economies.

Dollar figures are current U.S. dollars, unless otherwise specified. *Billion* means 1,000 million; *trillion* means 1,000 billion.

The following abbreviations are used:

AIDS	Acquired immune deficiency syndrome
CDF	Comprehensive Development Framework
FDI	Foreign direct investment
GATT	General Agreement on Tariffs and Trade
GDP	Gross domestic product
GNP	Gross national product
NIE	Newly industrializing economy
NGO	Nongovernmental organization
OECD	Organisation for Economic Co-operation and Development
PPP	Purchasing power parity
WTO	World Trade Organization

Overview

The development landscape is being transformed, presenting policymakers with new challenges at the global and local levels. This report charts the way forward by analyzing the contours of the new landscape and distilling lessons from the past. It examines the unfolding dynamic at the supranational and subnational levels. And it proposes new rules and structures to serve as a foundation for development policy in the 21st century.

Fifty years of development experience have yielded four critical lessons. First, macroeconomic stability is an essential prerequisite for achieving the growth needed for development. Second, growth does not trickle down; development must address human needs directly. Third, no one policy will trigger development; a comprehensive approach is needed. Fourth, institutions matter; sustained development should be rooted in processes that are socially inclusive and responsive to changing circumstances.

These insights are central to how the World Bank envisions its work in the 21st century and to the way in which it proposes to tackle the principal development challenges ahead. In addition to reducing poverty, these challenges include issues of food security, water scarcity, aging populations, cultural loss, and environmental degradation.

These challenges must be confronted even as many forces reshape the development terrain: innovations in technology, the spread of knowledge, the growth of population and its concentration in cities, the financial integration of the world, and rising demands for political and human rights. Some of these forces, like population growth, will work their way gradually, giving policymakers time to respond. Others, such as financial contagion, could batter apparently healthy economies without warning unless preemptive measures are in place. Some will give rise to challenges, like social welfare funding, that most nation-states can cope with on their own. Others, such as global climate change, will be beyond the reach of any one state and will call for international agreements.

If they are managed well, these forces could revolutionize the prospects for development and human welfare. However, the same forces are also capable of generating instability and human suffering that are beyond the ability of individual nation-states to remedy.

This report views the changes that have been set in motion as contributing to—and as manifestations of—two phenomena: globalization and localization. Globalization, which reflects the progressive integration of the world's economies, requires national governments to reach out to international partners as the best way to manage changes affecting trade, financial flows, and the global environment. Localization, which reflects the growing desire of people for a greater say in their government, manifests itself in the assertion of regional identities. It pushes national governments to reach down to regions and cities as the best way to manage changes affecting domestic politics and patterns of growth. At both the supranational and subnational levels, institutions of governance, negotiation, coordination, and regulation will play a critical role in promoting a new equilibrium between and within countries—and in abetting the creation of the stable environment that will make possible the implementation of development programs.

The frontiers of development thinking

As the 20th century draws to a close, mainstream development thinking has evolved toward a broad pragmatism. As with many subjects, a deeper understanding of development involves a recognition that sweeping beliefs are often incomplete, that layers of complexity are buried not far beneath the surface, and that wisdom is often contingent on the particular conditions of time and place. In recent decades both experience and intellectual insight have pushed development thinking away from debates over the role of states and markets, and the search for a single, overarching policy prescription.

Investment in physical and human capital, for example, should encourage economic growth, and as a general rule, empirical evidence supports this proposition. But in a number of cases, high rates of investment and education have not been enough to deliver rapid growth. A similar lesson holds true for industrial policies. Many countries decided, after experimenting with export subsidies, that the subsidies enriched business owners but did little to speed economic growth. They saw well-intended industrial subsidies turn into a costly form of corporate welfare, an expensive way of providing taxpayer support for private jobs in a narrow range of industries. Yet East Asian economies, making active use of export subsidies and credit allocation, experienced the most powerful sustained surge of economic development the world had seen in decades. And China, which alone includes 40 percent of all the inhabitants of low-income countries in the world, has had remarkable economic success with a development strategy that involves only a limited dose of market liberalization and privatization.

The failure of centrally planned economies to keep pace with their market-oriented counterparts has demonstrated clearly enough that planning entire economies at the central government level is not a productive path to long-term development. But the experiences of Japan, East Asia, and China make clear that it is possible for a country to have an interventionist government and still enjoy extremely rapid economic growth over a period of decades.

Brazil also grew very rapidly in the 1960s, in part by making widespread use of import-substitution policies. These policies certainly appeared helpful to Brazil at the time—at a minimum, they did not prevent a surge of rapid growth—but this success does not mean that similar policies would make sense in other countries, or even in Brazil three decades later. Similarly, certain policies that helped Japan develop in the 1950s and 1960s, generated growth in East Asia in the 1970s and 1980s, and sparked China's economic boom in the 1980s and 1990s were specific to the time and place. They may not have worked well in other countries, nor are they likely to be appropriate in the opening decades of the 21st century.

In any given country, progress depends on a constellation of factors, and on shifts in their configuration that take place over time. What is required is to step beyond the debates over the roles of governments and markets, recognizing that they need to complement each other, and to put to rest claims that any particular policy intervention—in education, health, capital markets, or elsewhere—is the magic formula that will inspire development in all times and places. This shift in development thinking can be summarized in four propositions:

Sustainable development has many objectives. Raising per capita incomes is only one among many development objectives. Improving quality of life involves more specific goals: better health services and educational opportunities, greater participation in public life, a clean environment, intergenerational equity, and more.

Development policies are interdependent. No single development policy can make much of a difference in an unfavorable policy regime. Countries need integrated policy packages and institutional environments that reward good outcomes, minimize perverse incentives, encourage initiative, and facilitate participation.

Governments play a vital role in development, but there is no simple set of rules that tells them what to do. Beyond generally accepted rules, the role of government in the economy varies, depending on capacity, capabilities, the country's level of development, external conditions, and a host of other factors.

Processes are just as important as policies. Outcomes of policies based on consensual, participatory, and transparent processes are more easily sustained. Institutions of good governance that embody such processes are critical for development and should encompass partnerships among all elements of civil society.

Creating new guidelines for development

In light of these propositions, the World Bank is introducing a comprehensive development framework to serve a number of purposes: to sharpen the focus on the major goals of development, to highlight the integrated nature of policymaking, to emphasize the institutional processes required to sustain development, and to coordinate development efforts.

The framework underscores the growing realization that the many elements that make up the development process must be planned together and coordinated in order to obtain the best results—and sometimes in order to arrive at any results at all. A school-building project is a good example. Physically putting up the building is only a start. Raising educational levels will depend on many other things, such as effective mechanisms for selecting, training, and remunerating teachers adequately and sufficient resources to buy enough textbooks and supplies.

What is true of a school-building project is also true of privatization programs, social safety nets, and sustainable energy programs. The complementarities between projects and processes are vital to success. A comprehensive framework makes these complementarities explicit by emphasizing the relationships among the human, physical, sectoral, and structural aspects of development.

The human and physical aspects of development are well known. Sectoral aspects stress the importance of cross-cutting elements such as coordination, management, and maintenance of an effective enabling environment for private business and community initiatives. Structural aspects focus on the need for good governance, transparent decisionmaking, efficient legal and judicial processes, and sound regulatory systems. This identification of rules and processes as a critical foundation for sustained development adds a new dimension to mainstream development thinking.

These items do not constitute an exhaustive list of all the concerns development should embrace. Issues of gender and equity are integral to every part of the framework. Moreover, as mentioned earlier, macroeconomic stability is a necessary condition for the success of development initiatives. How important each of these concerns is to individual countries depends on the particulars of time and place. Every country will benefit from identifying and prioritizing its needs—an exercise that reveals the economic or governmental weaknesses and institutional failures that stand in the way of full development.

Building institutions and partnerships

Effective development requires partnerships among different levels of government, the private sector, donor groups, and civil society. A comprehensive strategy is simply too demanding for any one level or area of government or for a single donor. National governments need to provide the guidance that agencies and organizations require to coordinate their efforts to remove bottlenecks to development.

A solid foundation of effective organizations and enabling institutions is a necessary precondition to development. In this context "institutions" are sets of rules governing the actions of individuals and organizations, and the interaction of all relevant parties and the negotiations among the participants. Specifically, countries need institutions that strengthen organizations and promote good governance, whether through laws and regulations or by coordinating the actions of many players, as international treaties and public-private partnerships do. Rule-based processes increase the transparency of policies designed to create desired outcomes and of organizations used to implement them.

The message of this report is that new institutional responses are needed in a globalizing and localizing world. Globalization requires national governments to seek agreements with partners—other national governments, international organizations, nongovernmental organizations (NGOs), and multinational corporations—through supranational institutions. Localization requires national governments to reach agreements with regions and cities through subnational institutions on issues such as sharing responsibility for raising revenues. Both globalization and localization often require responses that are beyond the control of a single national government. Yet national governments will remain pivotal in shaping development policies in an environment that circumscribes, constrains, and redefines their role. In an interconnected world in which countries may continue to fragment, development agendas must respond to both global and local imperatives.

Globalization and localization

Technological advances in communication have made it possible to know in an instant what is happening in a household or factory or on a stock market half a world away. The growing importance of services and information in the world economy means that an increasing proportion of economic value is weightless—that is, it can be transmitted over fiber-optic cable rather than transported in a container ship. At the same time improvements in transportation networks and technology are reducing the costs of shipping goods by water, ground, and air, and improvements in information technology have made it easier to manage the new interconnections (figure 1). Multinational companies now rely on production chains that straddle many countries. Raw materials and components may come from two different countries and be assembled in another, while marketing and distribution take place in still other venues. Consumers' decisions in, say, London or Tokyo become information that has an almost immediate impact on the products that are being made—and the styles that influence them—all over the globe.

Figure 1
Computers are linking the world

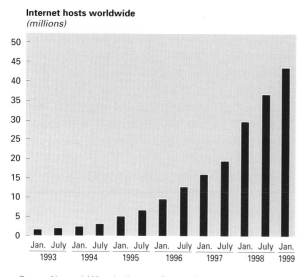

Internet hosts worldwide
(millions)

Source: Network Wizards, *Internet Domain Survey*, January 1999 (*www.nw.com.*).

Figure 2
All but a few democracies have decentralized some political power

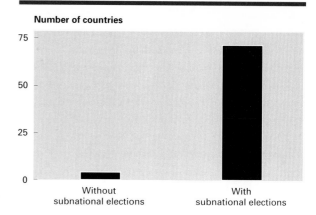

Number of countries

Note: Figure shows all countries classified as multiparty democracies for which data were available.
Source: Freedom House, *Freedom in the World*, 1998; appendix table A.1.

Rising educational levels, technological innovations that allow ideas to circulate, and the economic failure of most centrally planned economies have all contributed to the push for localization. National governments have responded to this push in various ways. More countries have become democracies, and political participation through elections has expanded at both the national and subnational levels. National governments are increasingly sharing responsibilities and revenues with subnational levels of government that are closer to the people affected by policy decisions (figure 2). People are also forming NGOs to pursue objectives such as political reform, environmental protection, gender equality, and better education.

Globalization and localization are terms that provoke strong reactions, positive and negative. Globalization is praised for the new opportunities it brings, such as access to markets and technology transfer—opportunities that hold out the promise of increased productivity and higher living standards. But globalization is also feared and often condemned because it sometimes brings instability and unwelcome change. It exposes workers to competition from imports, which can threaten their jobs; it undermines banks and even entire economies when flows of foreign capital overwhelm them.

Localization is praised for raising levels of participation in decisionmaking and for giving people more of a chance to shape the context of their own lives. By decentralizing government so that more decisions are made at subnational levels, closer to the voters, localization nourishes responsive and efficient governance. But it can also jeopardize macroeconomic stability. Local governments that have borrowed heavily and spent unwisely, for example, may have to be bailed out by the national government.

This report does not praise or condemn globalization and localization. Rather, it sees them as phenomena that no development agenda can afford to ignore. While national governments remain central to the development effort, globalization and localization require that they engage in essential institution-building at both the supra- and subnational levels in order to capture the benefits of growth in the 21st century.

Supranational issues

National governments will inevitably face frustrations in dealing with globalization, and these frustrations will be magnified for small developing economies. But such countries stand to gain more from international trade and finance than their larger counterparts, since they face tighter resource and market-size constraints. At the same time these economies may feel any disruption the global economy generates far more intensely. An economic shock that may feel like only a ripple to an enormous economy like the United States, or even to a relatively large developing economy like Brazil, is a tidal wave for an economy the size of Ghana or Bangladesh. When it comes to environmental issues, national governments can strike their own balance on domestic problems by, for example, determining how to apply pollution standards to regions that lie entirely within the country. But unless developing countries work through international agreements, they have little ability to address global environmental problems like the threat of climate change. This report considers three dimensions of globalization: trade, financial flows, and environmental challenges.

Trade

Foreign trade has grown more quickly than the world economy in recent years, a trend that is likely to continue (figure 3). For developing countries, trade is the primary vehicle for realizing the benefits of globalization. Imports bring additional competition and variety to domestic markets, benefiting consumers, and exports enlarge foreign markets, benefiting businesses. But perhaps even more important, trade exposes domestic firms

to the best practices of foreign firms and to the demands of discerning customers, encouraging greater efficiency. Trade gives firms access to improved capital inputs such as machine tools, boosting productivity as well. Trade encourages the redistribution of labor and capital to relatively more productive sectors. In particular, it has contributed to the ongoing shift of some manufacturing and service activities from industrial to developing countries, providing new opportunities for growth.

The creation of the World Trade Organization (WTO) in 1995 built on the General Agreement on Tariffs and Trade (GATT) and is the latest multilateral step toward creating an environment conducive to the exchange of goods and services (figure 4). A number of other important measures must follow, so that the momentum for reform is not lost.

Future trade talks will require a forward-looking agenda for broader trade liberalization if they are to repeat their past successes in opening markets. The Millennium Round, which is scheduled to start in November 1999 under WTO auspices, may be the first test of such an agenda. Reducing trade barriers in agriculture and services should be high on the list of priorities. Trade in agricultural products is one area that offers many developing economies real opportunities—if these opportunities are not blocked by trade barriers in wealthy countries. Trade in services is another issue that must be

Figure 3
Trade is growing much faster than national income in developing countries

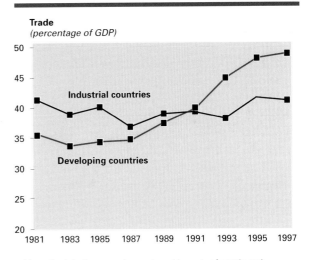

Note: Trade is the sum of exports and imports of goods and services.
Source: World Bank, *World Development Indicators*, 1999.

Figure 4
Countries are joining the WTO in increasing numbers

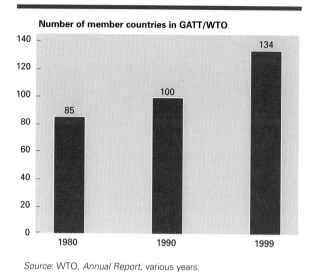

Number of member countries in GATT/WTO

Source: WTO, *Annual Report*, various years.

addressed. Driven by advances in information and communications technology, it is growing explosively— 25 percent between 1994 and 1997 alone. This type of trade offers another opportunity for developing countries, which can readily supply many sought-after services.

Countries must make greater use of WTO mechanisms. For example, a country that wants to strengthen its commitment to reducing (and maintaining) low trade barriers can "bind" its tariffs by incorporating the decision to lower them into its international obligations at the WTO. The more countries view the WTO and international trade rules as mechanisms for advancing national goals (rather than as obstacles to self-determination), the greater will be the support for such institutions.

Public policies must take into account the plight of workers displaced by the forces of trade. These policies must address the concerns of displaced workers in general, since many workers will blame foreign trade for job losses and wage cuts whether it is responsible or not. Augmenting trade liberalization with labor market policies that ease workers' adjustment to the effects of global trade will reduce pressure to close domestic markets to foreign goods.

Governments must change policies that are still allowed under existing trade rules but that hinder rather than promote trade. For example, antidumping laws are allowed under the WTO. They are intended to ensure that prod-

ucts are not sold below what is considered a "fair" price on domestic markets. But such rules can easily be turned into barriers to imports, diluting market access and reversing the gains from previous trade agreements. One solution is to treat the pricing decisions of importers and domestic firms according to the same criteria. Under this approach only antitrust issues such as predation are remedied directly.

Financial flows

Financial flows across national borders have risen far more quickly than trade in recent years. These capital flows can be divided into foreign direct investment, foreign portfolio investment, bank loans, and official development flows. Foreign direct investment is made up of flows intended to purchase a stake in the management of a company or factory. Foreign portfolio investment includes purchases of "paper" assets like equities and bonds (below the threshold required to give owners managerial control of physical assets). The increase in foreign direct investment and portfolio flows is particularly striking (figure 5).

Flows of foreign capital offer substantial economic gains to all parties. Foreign investors diversify their risks outside their home market and gain access to profitable opportunities throughout the world. Economies receiving inflows of capital benefit in many ways. Initially, inflows raise the level of investment. When foreign direct investment is involved, management expertise, training programs, and important linkages to suppliers and international markets often accompany the capital. Yet international capital flows, especially flows of volatile short-term investments, also expose developing countries to certain dangers. Among these are sharp changes in investor sentiment and waves of speculation that can upset exchange rate regimes, imperil banks and large firms, and wreak havoc on economies. Putting the genie of foreign capital back in the bottle is not possible—and ultimately not desirable. But such capital comes with a challenge: to devise policies and institutions that tip the balance so that capital mobility benefits developing economies rather than injuring them.

Governments of developing countries can begin this process by reforming their banking sectors and nurturing capital markets. The paucity of mutual and pension funds and the weakness of stock and bond markets in developing countries make banks the primary providers of financial intermediation. Creating a robust banking regulatory framework offers a substantial economic

Figure 5
Private capital flows to developing countries have increased dramatically

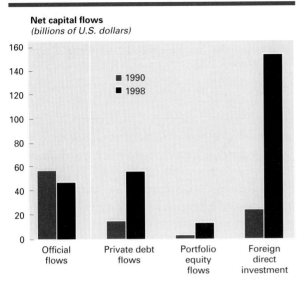

Net capital flows
(billions of U.S. dollars)

- ■ 1990
- ■ 1998

Note: Private debt flows include bank loans and bonds. The Republic of Korea is included in the figures for developing countries.
Source: World Bank, *Global Development Finance*, 1999.

payoff. An effective regulatory regime creates an environment that encourages prudent risk-taking. A regulatory structure for banking also sets out the conditions for establishing banks, the services they can provide, the level of capital they must hold, and the amount of information they must disclose. And a sound regulatory framework specifies the prudential steps regulators are required to take if these standards are not met.

Increased competition in the financial sector improves incentives for both banks and their customers. Competition increases as the domestic financial sector develops and securities, stock markets, and other intermediaries begin playing larger roles. Allowing foreign banks to enter a country, especially when their home countries have sound regulatory systems in place, boosts regulation by importing high-quality risk-management standards, regulatory practices, and trained managers.

Banks in developing countries must balance two risks. Banks often raise short-term money on global markets in one currency, such as U.S. dollars or Japanese yen, and then loan that money out for longer periods in domestic currency. These banks run the risk of losing their supply of short-term foreign money if the market dries up, as well as the risk of losing much of the value of their assets if the exchange rate depreciates.

Countries can hedge these risks to some extent, but regulations are needed to moderate the demand for short-term foreign borrowing in the first place. One such measure could require that a part of all capital inflows not intended to purchase productive physical assets be set aside for a specified period, thereby raising the cost of short-term borrowing from abroad.

In a world where financial markets continue to "go global," developing countries need to work toward becoming good homes for long-term foreign investment. Building an investment-friendly environment requires a commitment to a transparent regime of investors' rights and regulations, a legal system that offers equal treatment and protection to foreign and domestic investors, sound macroeconomic fundamentals, and investment in human capital. When investment is integrated into a well-functioning local economy, other investors will always be ready to step in should one investor decide to withdraw.

International institutions have a role to play in helping developing countries promote financial stability and investment. International banking agreements such as the Basle Accords can serve as models for local bank accounting standards. The International Monetary Fund (IMF) can monitor economic performance and coordinate short-term relief for liquidity problems, dampening the severity of a financial crisis. Trade agreements can help keep responses to financial shocks from turning into a beggar-thy-neighbor cycle of protectionism. Regional and international talks on coordinating macroeconomic policies can seek ways to avoid actions that favor one economy at the expense of its neighbors.

Global environmental challenges

Just as a country's economy can be swamped by global economic forces it has little power to control or deflect, its environment can be threatened by activities taking place beyond its borders and its control. In some low-income countries the threats may be severe enough to jeopardize further sustainable development. Climate changes, for example, could raise ocean levels, swamping the homes of millions of people in low-lying countries like Bangladesh. Governments acting alone, and even regional organizations, cannot respond effectively to this kind of environmental problem. The response must be global. Industrial countries are responsible for most of the existing global environmental problems—especially man-made greenhouse gases—but developing countries are catching up rapidly. Their capacity to contribute to future environmental damage increases as they grow.

The world has already seen one genuine environmental success story in the Montreal Protocol of 1987, which brought all countries together to address a common environmental threat. The Montreal Protocol attempts to solve the problem of chlorofluorocarbon emissions, which reduce ozone concentrations in the upper atmosphere. In the 1980s scientists realized that allowing these emissions to continue unchecked would dangerously increase ultraviolet radiation in the higher latitudes, raising rates of skin cancer and cataracts and damaging the environment. Thanks to the Montreal Protocol and follow-on agreements, global international production of chlorofluorocarbons has fallen steeply, and global cooperation to reduce ozone depletion appears to be succeeding.

The world faces a number of other pressing environmental problems that threaten the global commons. Perhaps the best known is climate change, which is associated with increasing emissions of carbon dioxide into the atmosphere. Others include biodiversity loss, which is occurring at an alarming rate; desertification; the depletion of fish stocks; the spread of persistent organic pollutants; and threats to the ecology of Antarctica.

The ozone success story provides a model for future international agreements on global environmental issues. The scientific case for addressing the risk of environmental damage needs to be made forcefully in open and robust public debate. The world's peoples and their governments must share the belief that the costs of environmental damage are heavy enough to justify immediate action. Alternatives to current behavior must be technically feasible and reasonably inexpensive, and all countries must be willing to participate in international accords. Sometimes this willingness will come at a price, with high-income countries paying low-income economies to comply with an agreement and groups of signatories imposing penalties on countries that fail to meet the standards the agreement sets. Finally, the standards themselves must be flexible, because very rarely is there a "one size fits all" solution to global problems.

The conditions surrounding biodiversity and climate change suggest that reaching international agreement on these issues will be more complex than it was with ozone depletion. But the international community has already begun seeking solutions. The Convention on Biological Diversity and the Framework Convention on Climate Change created at the 1992 Rio Earth Summit form a basis for moving forward. The Global Environment Facility (GEF) is a joint initiative of the United Nations Development Programme, the United Nations Environment Programme, and the World Bank. The GEF provides grants and concessional funds to cover additional costs countries incur when a development project also targets one or more of four global environmental issues: climate change, biodiversity loss, the pollution of international waters, and depletion of the ozone layer. National governments can take a number of actions that improve domestic welfare while helping preserve the global commons. Removing fuel subsidies and improving public transportation, for example, not only are in the best interest of individual economies but also contribute to reducing global carbon dioxide emissions that affect other countries.

Subnational issues

Even as globalization directs the attention of national governments to events, forces, and ideas outside their borders, localization highlights the opinions and aspirations of groups and communities at home. Two aspects of localization receive particular attention in this report: decentralization and urbanization.

Political pluralism and decentralization

Localization has generated political pluralism and self-determination around the world. One of its manifestations is the increase in the number of the world's countries, which has climbed as regions win their independence. Another is the change in countries' choice of governments. As recently as 25 years ago, less than one-third of the world's countries were democracies. In the late 1990s that proportion has risen to more than 60 percent (figure 6).

The ability of people to participate in making the decisions that affect them is a key ingredient in the process of improving living standards—and thus in effective development. But political responses to localization, such as decentralization, can be successful or unsuccessful, depending on how they are implemented. The following are several important lessons for governments to consider when embarking upon decentralization.

Decentralization is almost always politically motivated. Often its primary objective is to maintain political stability and reduce the risk of violent conflict by bringing a wide range of groups together in a formal, rule-bound bargaining process. Arguing about whether decentralization should happen is largely irrelevant; the way it is implemented will determine how successful it is.

Devising a successful decentralization strategy is complex because decisionmakers do not always fully control the decentralization process. Decentralization requires changing the system of governance and establishing new political, fiscal, regulatory, and administrative institutions. It involves not simply the decision to permit local elections but also a series of choices about electoral rules and party practices that will affect the options available to voters. It involves more than a decision to devolve a certain type of responsibility—for education, say—to the local level. It requires deciding which level of government will be responsible for financing education (particularly in poor regions), which level will establish curricula and develop instruction materials, and which level will be responsible for the day-to-day management of the schools, including hiring, promoting, and dismissing teachers. So that decentralization does not occur at the expense of equity, it requires granting revenue sources to subnational authorities and designing a system of intergovernmental fiscal transfers to complement local resources. It demands rules governing subnational borrowing. And finally, it must include steps to build the capability of subnational governments to carry out their new responsibilities.

The elements of reform must be synchronized. The political impetus that is often behind decentralization prompts central governments to make concessions hastily, and granting local elections is a relatively fast and easy step to take. But devising new regulatory relationships between central and subnational governments is a slow and difficult task, as is the transfer of assets and staff from the central to the local level. Equally difficult is the conversion of a system based on annual budgetary transfers between units of a centralized administration to one based on the assignment of taxes and expenditures at different levels of government.

National governments need to demonstrate their commitment to the new rules of the intergovernmental relationship at the very outset. Precedents matter, because they affect expectations. One of the most important precedents a central government can set for newly democratized subnational governments is to keep the central budget constraint hard. Local governments must know that if they overspend, the national government will not bail them out and that local taxpayers and politicians will bear the burden of adjustment.

Urbanization

More and more of the world's population is moving from rural to urban areas. Twenty-five years ago less than 40 percent of the world's population lived in urban areas; 25 years in the future this share could reach nearly 60 percent. Of the urban dwellers of the future, nearly 90 percent will be living in developing countries. Half a century ago just 41 of the world's 100 largest cities were in developing countries. By 1995 that

Figure 6
There are more countries . . .   **. . . and more democracies**

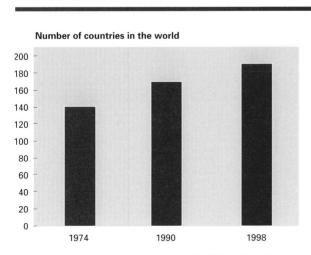

Number of countries in the world

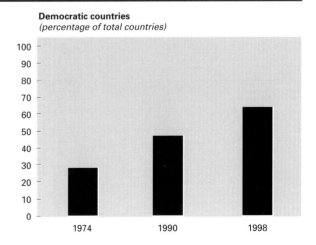

Democratic countries
(percentage of total countries)

Source: Freedom House, *Freedom in the World,* 1998; Larry Diamond, "Is the Third Wave Over?" *Journal of Democracy,* 1996.

number had risen to 64, and the proportion keeps rising (figure 7).

Some national governments tax rural areas or place restrictions on the prices of rural products as a way of supporting cities, on the grounds that such policies encourage a "modern" economy. Other governments, concerned about the growing population of urban poor, have tried to discourage rural-urban migration, sometimes by requiring official permission to move to a city. Neither course of action has worked especially well. Preventing individuals from moving in response to incentives generally fails, as national governments have not proven adept at deciding where households and firms should locate. Governments will be better off if they pursue development policies that benefit both urban and rural areas, recognize that the process of development will spur urbanization over time, and plan accordingly.

Local governments can take steps to make their cities more hospitable venues for economic development. One important step is to maintain a sufficient level of investment in essential infrastructure, including water, sanitation, roads, telephones, electricity, and housing. Increasingly, local governments are working with the private sector, which has an important role to play in housing, on-site infrastructure, and municipal utilities. But municipalities will still be required to raise substantial sums to finance capital investment, particularly during the rural-urban transition. Private capital markets are a promising source, but they require an ad-

equate legal framework and a firm central government commitment against bailouts. Land use planning is an important and useful tool, but the rules need to be specific to local circumstances.

Countries do not need to wait until they become wealthy to improve urban services. Innovative institutional arrangements can result in much better service provision, even at low levels of income. Recent trends in providing essential services point to the potential of public-private partnerships.

■ *Housing.* Private developers, voluntary agencies, community organizations, and NGOs need to provide an increased share. For its part, the public sector must focus on property rights, financing and subsidies, building regulations, and trunk infrastructure.
■ *Water.* Large cities are moving to private sector provision. Private concessions have already replaced public providers in Buenos Aires, Jakarta, and Manila. The role of government is to regulate this industry and foster competition.
■ *Sewerage.* Governments are often unable to fund the heavy initial investment required for citywide solutions. But communities are managing, with the assistance of NGOs, to implement affordable solutions, providing a model for future efforts.
■ *Transportation.* Public education and creative partnerships can reduce air pollution. But the greatest payoff is likely to come from channeling urban

Figure 7
Urban population is growing—primarily in developing countries

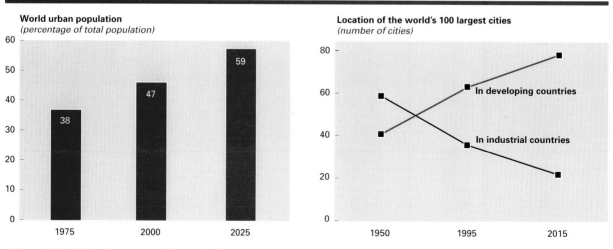

Source: United Nations Department of International Economics and Social Affairs, *World Urbanization Prospects*, 1998.

growth along public transit routes to create more efficient transportation corridors.

It is sometimes argued that poverty alleviation is purely the national government's responsibility. While the national government should play a prominent role in providing subsidies to the poor, many services that affect the poor most—water, health, education, and transportation—are best managed at the local level in ways that respond effectively to local needs.

Translating policies into action

Globalization and localization offer exceptional opportunities, but can also have destabilizing effects. This report identifies some steps governments can take, singly and together, to minimize potential crises. National governments have a leading role, but international organizations, subnational levels of government (including urban governments), the private sector, NGOs, and donor organizations all play vital supporting parts. These organizations are building the institutions—the formal and informal rules—that shape the way the

processes of globalization and localization will evolve. The report presents five case studies that illustrate how governments and organizations can capture some of the benefits of these two phenomena and respond to potential disruptions. The studies cover trade liberalization in the Arab Republic of Egypt; the reform of Hungary's banking sector; Brazil's efforts to structure the fiscal relationships between regional and national government; efforts of community groups and local developers to improve living standards in Karachi, Pakistan; and the creation of an urban-rural synergy in Tanzania.

The challenges for development are many: poverty, hunger, ill health, lack of housing, and illiteracy, to name a few. Much progress has been made, so that people in some regions such as East Asia are far better off than they were several decades ago. Even in Sub-Saharan Africa, where economic performance has been dismal in recent decades, life expectancies and educational levels have risen. Still, the number of people living on less than $1 per day is rising. This trend can be reversed, to the benefit of the world's people, by harnessing the forces of globalization and localization in the 21st century.

New Directions in Development Thinking

The principal goal of development policy is to create sustainable improvements in the quality of life for all people. While raising per capita incomes and consumption is part of that goal, other objectives—reducing poverty, expanding access to health services, and increasing educational levels—are also important. Meeting these goals requires a comprehensive approach to development.

The last half-century has been marked by a mix of pessimism and optimism about prospects for development. The Green Revolution held out the prospect of overcoming the Malthusian threat, and countries like India succeeded in achieving food security. But the world's burgeoning population, combined with relatively slow growth in the productivity of food grains in the 1990s, is once again raising fears of food shortages. Some development approaches, such as Brazil's import-substitution policies, appeared to work for a while but then failed. The more recent downturn in the most remarkable economic success story of all—East Asia—has raised new questions about development policies, as has the slow response to market reforms shown by the economies in transition.

Yet a consensus is emerging on the elements of future development policy.

- *Sustainable development has many objectives.* Insofar as raising per capita income improves people's living standards, it is one among many development objectives. The overarching aim of lifting living standards encompasses a number of more specific goals: bettering people's health and educational opportunities, giving everyone the chance to participate in public life, helping to ensure a clean environment, promoting intergenerational equity, and much more.

- *Development policies are interdependent.* When a policy does not work well, what is involved may be more than just the individual strategy. Policies require complementary measures in order to work best, and a policy failure can occur because these complements are not in place.

- *Governments play a vital role in development, but there is no simple set of rules that tells them what to do.* There is consensus that governments should adhere to the policy fundamentals, but beyond that, the part the government plays depends on its capacity to make effective decisions, its administrative capabilities, the country's level of development, external conditions, and a host of other factors.

■ *Processes are just as important as policies.* Sustained development requires institutions of good governance that embody transparent and participatory processes and that encompass partnerships and other arrangements among the government, the private sector, nongovernmental organizations (NGOs), and other elements of civil society.

The idea that development has multiple goals and that the policies and processes for meeting them are complex and intertwined has provoked an intense debate on the wisdom of traditional development thinking. This introduction draws on the threads of that debate to review perspectives and lessons from past development experiences. It emphasizes the need to reach beyond economics to address societal issues in a holistic fashion. The chapter then turns to the role of institutions in development and points to the institutional changes that will be necessary to ensure sustainable development in the 21st century. While development still faces many challenges, the opportunities waiting to be grasped in the new century hold out just as many exciting prospects.

Building on past development experiences

The evidence of recent decades demonstrates that while development is possible, it is neither inevitable nor easy. The successes have been frequent enough to justify a sense of confidence in the future. But while these successes may be replicable in other countries, the failure of many development efforts suggests that the task will be a daunting one.

One measure of development is per capita GDP, which is often correlated with other indicators of well-being and so serves as a convenient starting point. The average level of per capita GDP in developing countries for which data are available rose at a rate of 2.1 percent per year from 1960 to 1997—a growth rate that, if it kept rising, would double average per capita GDP every 35 years or so.

But such aggregate data invariably mask an array of variations across times and places. For example, the growth rate of per capita income in developing countries rose relatively quickly in the 1960s and 1970s and leveled out in the 1980s. An optimist might see signs of a return to rapid growth in the first half of the 1990s, but such signs have been less apparent in the aftermath

of the East Asian financial crisis that began in 1997. In addition, East Asia is the only region of the world where incomes in low- and middle-income countries are converging toward incomes in richer countries.

Compared to this regional success, the broad picture of development outcomes is worrisome. The average per capita income of the poorest and middle thirds of all countries has lost ground steadily over the last several decades compared with the average income of the richest third (figure 8). Average per capita GDP of the middle third has dropped from 12.5 to 11.4 percent of the richest third and that of the poorest third from 3.1 to 1.9 percent. In fact, rich countries have been growing faster than poor countries since the Industrial Revolution in the mid-19th century. A recent estimate suggests that the ratio of per capita income between the richest and the poorest countries increased sixfold between 1870 and 1985.[1] Such findings are of great concern because they show how difficult it is for poor countries to close the gap with their wealthier counterparts.

Standard economic theories predict that, other things being equal, poor countries should grow faster than rich ones. For instance, developing countries arguably have an easier task in copying the new technology and production processes that are central to economic development than industrial countries have in generating them. Capital, expertise, and knowledge should flow from

Figure 8
The incomes of rich and poor countries continue to diverge

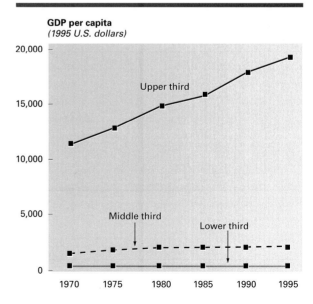

GDP per capita
(1995 U.S. dollars)

Source: World Bank, *World Development Indicators,* 1999.

wealthier countries that have these resources in abundance to those developing economies in which they are scarce—and where they should be even more productive.

Both past and present development thinking has devoted much effort to uncovering explanations for why low-income countries have difficulties in following this pattern.[2] A number of studies show that low-income countries can grow faster than high-income countries (by about 2 percent per year), thus catching up gradually over time, if they implement an appropriate mix of growth-enhancing policies.[3] And increasing experience with development outcomes is providing insight into the complexity of the process and the multifaceted approach needed to achieve this growth.[4]

The complexity of the development process has long been recognized. Arthur Lewis's classic 1955 study *The Theory of Economic Growth* includes chapters on profit incentives, trade and specialization, economic freedom, institutional change, the growth of knowledge, the application of new ideas, savings, investment, population and output, the public sector and power, and politics.[5] But over the years, various development processes have been singled out as "first among equals" in terms of their impact. The conceptual frameworks for development of the last 50 years, especially in their popularized versions, tended to focus too heavily on the search for a single key to development. When a particular key failed to open the door to development in all times and places, it was set aside in the search for a new one.

Development models popular in the 1950s and 1960s drew attention to the constraints imposed by limited capital accumulation and the inefficiency of resource allocation.[6] This attention made increasing investment (through either transfers from abroad or savings at home) a major objective. But the experience of recent decades suggests that a focus on investment misses other important aspects of the development process. Investment rates and growth rates for individual countries between 1950 and 1990 varied considerably (figure 9). Some low-investment countries grew rapidly, while a number of high-investment countries had low growth rates.[7] Although investment is probably the factor that is most closely correlated with economic growth rates in these four decades, it does not fully explain them.[8]

Early theories of development, especially those associated with Simon Kuznets, also argued that inequality generally increases during the early stages of development. Evidence from recent decades has not validated these theories, and it now appears likely that growth,

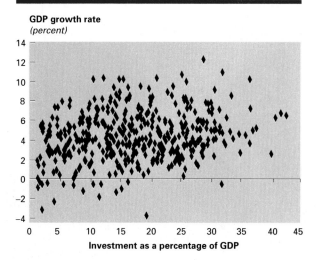

Figure 9
Investment alone cannot account for variation in growth

GDP growth rate
(percent)

Investment as a percentage of GDP

Note: Figure shows decade-average investment rates against decade-average GDP growth rates from 1950 to 1990 for a 160-country sample.
Source: Kenny and Williams 1999.

equality, and reductions in poverty can proceed together, as they have in much of East Asia. Many policies promote growth and equality simultaneously. For example, improving access to education builds human capital and helps the poor, and providing land to poor farmers increases not only equality but also productivity. The East Asian countries also showed that countries can have high savings rates without high levels of inequality.

Development theorists of the 1950s and 1960s also offered a wide variety of rationales explaining why open economies and limited intervention would not suffice to spur growth. Many development economists focused on planning as at least a partial solution to the prevailing problems of low investment and slow industrialization, especially as memories of the Great Depression made many policymakers skeptical about the virtues of unconstrained market forces. Two other factors seemed to argue for an aggressive government role in development: the U.S. government's close management of production during World War II, and the investment and GDP levels of the Soviet Union, which was then surging forward under communism despite enormous human costs.

Over time, however, it became clear that while governments do have a vital role in the development process, only a few governments have run state enterprises efficiently. Returns to investment in the Soviet Union fell almost to zero. Governments padded public sector payrolls and the overstaffing, combined with inefficiency, produced large deficits that imposed a fiscal burden and diverted needed revenues. Concerns were also mounting that governments of developing countries were making poor decisions in the macroeconomic sphere, leading to problems such as inflation and the debt crises in Latin America.[9]

In the late 1960s the attention of policymakers began to shift toward an emphasis on human capital, which is often measured in terms of school enrollment (as a proxy for education) and life expectancy (as a proxy for health status). In the last two decades investment in human capital has shown impressive results. Rates of return on primary education in low-income countries have been as high as 23 percent per year.[10] But like investment in physical capital, investment in health and education alone does not guarantee development. In Sub-Saharan Africa, for example, life expectancy and school enrollment rates have increased dramatically in recent decades, but as a group the economies in the region have had slow and even negative growth since the early 1970s.

By the 1980s the intellectual climate had shifted again. Confidence in government planning as a solution had diminished dramatically. The primary concerns of the day were, in fact, government-induced price distortions (such as those associated with tariffs) and inefficiencies arising from government production.

Still, governments continued to be recognized as central to the development process. As the 1991 *World Development Report* noted: "[M]arkets cannot operate in a vacuum—they require a legal and regulatory framework that only governments can provide. And markets sometimes prove inadequate or fail altogether in other regimes as well. The question is not whether the state or market should dominate: each has a unique role to play."[11] At the same time, research was showing that the market imperfections central to the discussion in the 1950s and 1960s were (at least theoretically) more widespread than had been previously believed. However, as a response to public sector inefficiency, policy discussion nonetheless focused on market-conforming solutions: eliminating government-imposed distortions associated with protectionism, subsidies, and public ownership. A solution to the problem of excessive debt accumulation was also put forward that involved adjusting the fiscal, monetary, and external imbalances adversely affecting price stability and growth. Like government intervention and investment in education and

health in previous decades, reduced distortions and greater austerity had become the central elements of the development agenda.

The evidence of the last two decades continues to support the need for macro stability and sector reform. Once again, however, an exclusive focus on these issues proved insufficient. Some countries followed policies of liberalization, stabilization, and privatization but failed to grow as expected. Several African countries implemented sound macroeconomic policies but still reached an average growth rate of only 0.5 percent per year.[12] Low-inflation countries with small budget deficits face many alternate sources of economic instability, including weak and inadequately regulated financial institutions, as East Asia discovered.

The lessons of small versus big government performance were also less clear than expected. In the Russian Federation the move from inefficient central planning and state ownership to decentralized market mechanisms, private ownership, and a profit orientation should have increased output, perhaps in tandem with a slight increase in inequality. Instead, Russia's economy has shrunk by up to one-third, according to some estimates, and income inequality has increased dramatically. Living standards have deteriorated along with GDP, and health indicators have worsened.[13]

Other countries intervened to a relatively large extent in markets and enjoyed rapid growth. The governments of East Asian countries failed to follow many of the tenets of liberalization in the early stages of development, yet their societies have been transformed in the last several decades.[14] Even with a few years of zero or negative growth in the late 1990s, their per capita GDP at the turn of the century is many times what it was a half-century ago and far higher than those of countries that pursued alternative development strategies. The East Asian governments often pursued industrial policies that promoted particular sectors. They intervened in trade (although more to promote exports than to inhibit imports). They regulated financial markets, limiting the investment options available to individuals, encouraging savings, lowering interest rates, and increasing the profitability of banks and firms.[15] Their policies placed heavy emphasis on education and technology in order to close the knowledge gap with more advanced countries. More recently, China has forged its own version of an East Asian–style development path. Its transition strategy for replacing the centrally planned economy with a market-oriented regime has resulted in extraordinary gains for hundreds of millions of the poorest people in the world.

The twists and turns of development policy and the nature of the successes and failures around the world illustrate the difficulty of interpreting the development drama. The situations in which success and failure occur differ so much that it is sometimes not apparent which lessons should be extracted or whether they can be applied in other countries. For example, the role the government plays depends on a range of factors, including administrative capacity, the country's stage of development, and the external conditions it faces.

Despite the difficulty of drawing clearly applicable lessons from development history, current development thinking has been able to draw on country experiences to suggest a range of complementary policies. These policies, if implemented together and in a way that takes into account the situations of individual countries, are likely to encourage development. Several factors that

played a part in the most impressive development success story of the last 50 years—East Asia—undoubtedly contribute to growth and development in general: high savings, strong returns to investment, education, trade, and sound macroeconomic policy. At the same time, development failures point to the importance of institutional structures, competition, and control of corruption (box 1).

Studies of World Bank projects illustrate the many elements necessary for successful development.[16] These studies show that projects in countries that adhere to the macroeconomic fundamentals of low inflation, limited budget deficits, and openness to trade and financial flows are more successful than projects in closed countries with macroeconomic imbalances. But the projects need more than a stable macroeconomy in order to succeed. For example, social projects are more likely to succeed if they emphasize beneficiary participation and are responsive to gender concerns. Studies

Box 1
Lessons from East Asia and Eastern Europe

The success of East Asia provides some notable lessons on successful development strategies.

- *Savings.* All the East Asian countries had much higher savings rates than other developing countries. From 1990 to 1997, for example, gross domestic savings in the countries of East Asia and Pacific were 36 percent of GDP, compared with 20 percent in Latin America and the Caribbean and 17 percent in Sub-Saharan Africa.
- *Investment.* The East Asian countries managed to invest these savings productively, so that the return on capital investment remained higher than in most other developing countries (at least until the mid-1990s).
- *Education.* These economies invested heavily in education—including female education. The investments paid off in contributions to growth.
- *Knowledge.* The East Asian countries managed to narrow the knowledge gap with high-income countries by investing heavily in science and engineering education and by encouraging foreign direct investment.
- *Global integration.* The experience of East Asia's economies shows that developing countries have a greater ability to enter global markets for manufactured goods than many believed possible several decades ago.
- *Macroeconomic policy.* The East Asian countries implemented sound macroeconomic policies that helped contain inflation and avoid recessions. Indonesia and Thailand had positive real GDP growth from 1970 until 1996. Over that same time period Malaysia and the Republic of Korea each had only one year of negative real GDP growth.

Each of these points opens up a number of new issues. For instance, the high savings rate might have been generated by personal preferences, government policies, or a combination of the two. And while these countries invested their savings well, many others do not. Nonetheless these elements of overtly successful policies point the way toward a partial development agenda.

Failures as well as successes can provide positive lessons for development. Among the most recent (and sometimes spectacular) examples of such failures are Russia, some of the economies in transition in Central and Eastern Europe, and several East Asian countries affected by the economic and financial crisis of the mid-1990s. Their experiences point to other factors that can influence economic growth, including corporate and public governance and competition.

- *Legal frameworks.* A sound legal framework helps ensure that managers and majority shareholders in the corporate realm focus on building firms rather than on looting them.
- *Corruption.* Reducing corruption in the public sphere makes a country more attractive to investors. Many privatization efforts have been racked by corruption, undermining confidence in both the government and the market economy. The loans-for-shares scheme in Russia was so widely perceived as raising corruption to new heights that much of the resulting wealth is considered illegitimate.
- *Competition.* Competition is essential. It encourages efficiency and provides incentives for innovation, but monopolies may try to suppress it unless the government steps in.

also find that government "ownership" of projects is essential and that measures of government credibility are closely correlated with returns on the projects. In low-income countries stronger institutions are associated with a 20 percent increase in the likelihood that a project will receive a "satisfactory" rating.[17] The role of social capital in project success has also been highlighted—indeed, it is hard to overemphasize the importance of networks of trust and association for sustainable development (box 2). Finally, the studies emphasize the importance of coordinated development efforts among governments and donors.[18]

Overall, the impact of World Bank projects depends on a host of factors extraneous to the projects themselves. A recent review of World Bank energy projects in Sub-Saharan Africa offers some vivid examples of these factors, including governance, human capital, and a good policy framework (box 3). What is true of energy projects in Sub-Saharan Africa is equally true of privatization programs. The outcome of privatization projects is heavily dependent on governance structures, macroeconomic and structural factors, the competitiveness of the market, social sustainability, regulatory regimes, corporate and commercial law, financial sector reforms, and the state of business accounting.[24] In turn, what is true of power and privatization projects is just as true of efforts to create social safety nets, build schools, or improve the environment.

The many goals of development

The World Bank's experience with large dam projects highlights the importance of taking a broad view of the outcomes of projects. In the 1950s and 1960s large dams were almost synonymous with development. But more recent evidence of their effects on the environment and on the welfare of groups displaced by construction suggests that these projects must be handled with great care if they are to have a positive impact on

Box 2
Social capital, development, and poverty

Social capital refers to the networks and relationships that both encourage trust and reciprocity and shape the quality and quantity of a society's social interactions.[19] The level of social capital has a significant impact on a range of development processes. For example:

- In education, teachers are more committed, students achieve higher test scores, and school facilities are better used in communities where parents and citizens take an active interest in children's educational well-being.[20]
- In health services, doctors and nurses are more likely to show up for work and to perform their duties attentively where their actions are supported and monitored by citizen groups.[21]
- In rural development, villages with higher social capital see greater use of credit and agrochemicals and more village-level cooperation in constructing roads.[22]

Social capital serves as an insurance mechanism for the poor who are unable to access market-based alternatives. It is therefore important to facilitate the formation of new networks in situations where old ones are disintegrating—as, for example, during urbanization.

Social capital can have an important downside, however. Communities, groups, or networks that are isolated, parochial, or counterproductive to society's collective interests (for example, drug cartels) can actually hinder economic and social development.[23] This has led some to make a distinction between vertical social capital (generally negative, as in gangs) and horizontal social capital (generally positive, as in community associations).

Box 3
Explaining power project outcomes in Sub-Saharan Africa

Until the mid-1990s the record of World Bank power projects in Sub-Saharan Africa was comparatively weak. Out of 44 such projects completed in the region between 1978 and 1996, 64 percent were rated satisfactory, compared with a worldwide average of 79 percent. A recent study analyzing the causes of this poor performance suggested that a wide range of factors influenced project outcomes and sector performance, including:

- *External factors,* such as rising fuel prices, international interest rates, and terms-of-trade shocks
- *Regulatory and legal structures,* including lack of transparency in regulatory processes
- *Low technical capacity,* especially a limited human resource base
- *Lack of private sector involvement,* through either ownership or service contracting
- *Limited government ownership* of reform processes
- *Weak coordination* among donor agencies and little overall government direction.

This list indicates just how complex and intertwined the development process can be in practice.

Source: Covarrubias 1999.

sustainable development. They require a participatory approach that allows all the potential costs to be aired openly and fully.[25] This approach is appropriate for other projects as well. In order to be effective, all projects must be implemented with an awareness of their social, civil, environmental, political, and international implications.

Similar lessons can be drawn from experience with development at the macroeconomic level. While increased income is clearly an important component of an improved standard of living, its relationship to other measures of well-being is complex. For example, those living on less than $1 per day are five times more likely to die before age five than those living on more than $1.[26] Nonetheless, recent studies suggest that rates of economic growth over the last 30 years reveal little about the rates of improvement in vital measures of development such as political stability, education, life expectancy, child mortality, and gender equality. Reductions in the mortality rate of children under the age of five, for example, appear to have little to do with the speed of economic growth (figure 10). While economic performance was poor in many developing countries in the 1980s and early 1990s, only one country in the sample used here (Zambia) saw an increase in infant and child mortality.

One likely reason for this weak relationship is that countries and communities place different priorities on education and health. For example, public expenditures on health care are 63 percent of GDP in Latin American and Caribbean countries and 5 percent of GDP in South Asia, but they account for just 2.7 percent of GDP in Sub-Saharan Africa. Sri Lanka is often cited as an example of a poor country that has invested wisely in primary health care and has reaped the benefits. In 1997 life expectancy averaged 59 years in the world's low-income countries, and infant deaths averaged 82 per 1,000 live births. But despite its low level of GDP per capita, Sri Lanka's life expectancy was 73 years, and infant mortality was just 14 per 1,000 live births—not quite the levels of the high-income countries of the world, but not far short either.[27]

Further, like all development endeavors, achievements in health and education are interrelated, and they may also affect other government programs. Countries that pursue egalitarian growth strategies— for example, education or land reform—are more likely to perform well on indicators of human well-being. So,

Figure 10
Infant mortality fell in most developing countries from 1980 to 1995, even where income did not increase

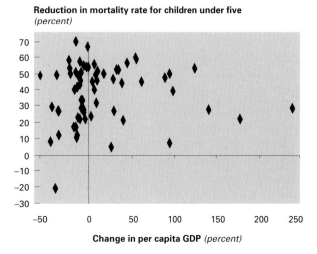

Note: Calculations for this figure are based on a developing country sample taken from the World Bank's *World Development Indicators,* 1998. *Per capita GDP* was adjusted for purchasing power parity.
Source: World Bank staff calculations.

the most effective way to obtain improved health outcomes may be direct spending that improves nutrition and discourages smoking, drugs, and alcohol, rather than direct expenditures on health care. In some areas the most effective way to improve educational outcomes for children may not involve increased expenditure on books or teachers but instead may involve building a rural road or a bridge across a river to facilitate access to schools. Countries that pay attention to such linkages may discover unexpected improvements in their indicators of human well-being.

Improving health is itself one clear case where targeting broad goals is likely to have dramatic spillover effects. Studies suggest that as much as 30 percent of the estimated per capita growth rate in the United Kingdom between 1870 and 1979 might be associated with improvements in health and nutritional status. Microstudies support such findings—in Indonesia, for example, anemia reduced male productivity by 20 percent.[28]

Improvement in gender equality is another important example of a development goal that reinforces other elements of the development agenda. Low levels of education and training, poor health and nutritional status, and limited access to resources depress women's quality of life throughout the developing world. And gender-based discrimination can also be significantly deleterious to other elements of a sustainable development agenda. Women are a major part of the workforce in developing countries—they comprise about 60 percent of Africa's informal sector and 70 percent of the region's agricultural labor, for example. Discrimination reduces their productivity. Estimates from Kenya suggest that if women had the same access to factors and inputs as men, the value of their output would increase nearly 22 percent. Discrimination also has a negative effect on a range of other development indicators. One study has found that a 10 percent increase in female literacy rates reduces child mortality by 10 percent (increased male literacy had little effect).[29] Throughout the developing world, gains in the educational level of women in the 1960–90 period might account for as much as 38 percent of the decline in infant mortality over that time, and for 58 percent of the drop in total fertility rate.[30] Improving gender equality is likely to produce dramatic results, and it is a goal that can be targeted at any level of development.

While the level of income is not necessarily correlated with a higher standard of living, economic growth is linked with some negative outcomes—particularly carbon dioxide and sulfur dioxide output and the production of waste.[31] This suggests the importance of trade-offs in a comprehensive development strategy. Policymakers must sometimes make hard choices when a project or policy supports one development goal while damaging the prospects for another. Such trade-offs are not limited to those involving projects with high economic returns and adverse environmental impacts. In education, for instance, primary schooling may offer the most benefits in terms of increasing equity, but tertiary education may offer the most in terms of closing the knowledge gap with industrial countries.

Hence, development must pursue a range of outcomes, such as equality, education, health, the environment, culture, and social well-being, among others. Furthermore, the linkages between these outcomes—both positive and negative—need to be fully understood.[32] In cooperation with the World Bank and the United Nations, the Development Assistance Committee (DAC) of the OECD has produced indicators that set global targets for the wider goals of development to be reached by 2015 or earlier. These goals are to:

- Reduce extreme poverty by one-half
- Ensure universal primary education and eliminate gender disparity in education
- Reduce infant and child mortality by two-thirds and maternal mortality by three-quarters, while providing universal access to reproductive health services
- Implement worldwide national strategies for sustainable development and reverse trends in the loss of environmental resources.

These DAC development goals represent an important step toward recognition of the need for a holistic approach. More recently, the World Bank has begun piloting a strategy—the Comprehensive Development Framework—to help operationalize a multifaceted development agenda (box 4).

Economic history and lessons drawn from World Bank projects reinforce a number of conclusions. Sustainable development is a multifaceted process, involving multiple instruments and goals. In some cases the goals and instruments of successful development are one and the same—as in the case of gender, health, and education, for example. Strong interlinkages connect these goals, so that progress toward one is frequently dependent on progress toward others. The role of government and the participation of civil society are vital, as are the importance of sequencing and the complementarities among development projects. These lessons point to the importance of identifying bottlenecks—the economic or governmental weaknesses that stand in the way of a wide range of development objectives. Such lessons are humbling and have come at great cost over the last 50 years. They alter the framework in which the development enterprise should be approached, and they cannot be ignored.

Since 1990 a number of *World Development Reports* have examined many of the elements of a broad-based development strategy and have made recommendations for improving the provision of structural, physical, human, and sectoral services (box 5). While some details may have changed in light of recent experiences, the tried and effective mechanisms for removing development bottlenecks presented in these reports remain a useful starting point. All of the reports have discussed linkages among parts of the development process—poverty, education, health, gender issues, the environment, and service provision, for instance. This report and future reports (specifically the 2000/2001 report on poverty) will continue that tradition, providing

Box 4
The Comprehensive Development Framework

The World Bank has been evolving the Comprehensive Development Framework (CDF) in an attempt to operationalize a holistic approach to development. The framework is designed to serve as both a planning and a management tool for coordinating the responses aimed at overcoming bottlenecks and meeting development goals. Implementing this strategy in any country would involve consulting with and winning the support of a range of actors in civil society, as well as NGOs, donor groups, and the private sector. Under the overall direction of the government, different agencies and organizations could coordinate their efforts to overcome constraints on development. The framework could enable the government to develop a matrix of responsibilities in each area showing what each group must do to fight poverty and encourage growth.[33]

The CDF is designed to be a means of achieving greater effectiveness in reducing poverty. It is based on the following principles:

- The country, not assistance agencies, should own its development strategy, determining the goals, timing, and sequencing of its development programs.
- Governments need to build partnerships with the private sector, NGOs, assistance agencies, and the organizations of civil society to define development needs and implement programs.
- A long-term, collective vision of needs and solutions should be articulated that will draw sustained national support.
- Structural and social concerns should be treated equally and contemporaneously with macroeconomic and financial concerns.

It is important to note that the CDF is meant to be a compass, not a blueprint. The way the principles are put into practice will vary from country to country, depending on economic and social needs and the priorities of the stakeholders involved. Further, the CDF is only at the pilot stage and is very much a work in progress. The mixed record of development programs in the past suggests the need for both caution in application and realism about expected results. Nonetheless, the CDF might allow participants in a country's development program to think more strategically about the sequencing of policies, programs, and projects. It could help to improve sectoral balance, encourage the efficient use of resources, and foster transparency when trade-offs need to be made and complementarities taken into account in the macroeconomic and social spheres.

The proposed new framework is based on four areas of development—structural, human, physical, and sectoral.

- *Structural* elements include honest, competent governments committed to the fight against corruption; strong property and personal rights laws supported by an efficient and honest legal and judicial system; a well-supervised financial system that promotes transparency; and a strong social safety net.
- *Human* development includes universal primary education and strong secondary and tertiary systems, and a health system that focuses on family planning and child care.
- *Physical* concerns center around the efficient provision of water and sewerage; expanded access to reliable electric power; access to road, rail, and air transportation and to telecommunications; preservation of the physical environment; and a commitment to preserving cultural and historical sites and artifacts that buttress indigenous cultures and values.
- *Sectoral* elements include an integrated rural development strategy, a strong urban management approach, and an enabling environment for the private sector.

The CDF does not seek to be exhaustive. A stable macroeconomy, shaped by prudent fiscal and monetary policies, is an essential backdrop to the development efforts the CDF proposes. This stable macroeconomic environment occupies the "other half of the balance sheet," complementing the CDF. And the pressing issues of poverty, gender inequality, knowledge and information gaps, and overpopulation are incorporated into virtually all of its components. Gender, for example, is central to all aspects of a comprehensive framework. Additionally, each country is likely to have its own unique priorities that would need to be included in a matrix that evolves over time. The priority each country gives to trade issues, the labor market, and employment concerns, for example, will depend on the conditions specific to the economy and the results of a national dialogue about development priorities and the programs needed to address them.

practical advice on implementing the many strands of broad-based development.

This report extends past analysis in a number of ways. It looks at governance reform in the context of urbanization and decentralization. It discusses regulatory reform and examines financial systems in a global context. Human elements permeate the discussion of the impact of trade and the need for sustainable urban development, and the section on urbanization emphasizes the importance of infrastructure provision. The report addresses environmental concerns at both the global and local levels. It also provides up-to-date lessons from experience and recommendations for successful development strategies.

The role of institutions in development

A strong network of effective organizations and enabling institutions is central to holistic development.

Box 5
A holistic approach to development in past *World Development Reports*

Macroeconomic policy and trade. *World Development Report 1991: The Challenge of Development* laid out the importance of a stable macroeconomic framework and an open trade regime for development, a message that has been repeated in reports since then. For example, *World Development Report 1997* noted the role of the WTO in fostering world trade (a topic this report will discuss at greater length).

Government, regulation, and corruption. *World Development Report 1996: From Plan to Market* pointed out the potential economic consequences of corruption and looked at policies that tend to increase or to mitigate its effects. Among other things, the report emphasized the need for a strong and independent judiciary and discussed methods for strengthening financial systems in transition economies through banking reform and the development of capital markets. It also examined mechanisms that increase the effectiveness of government, including expenditure control, budget management, and tax policy reform. *World Development Report 1997: The State in a Changing World* further explored issues of government reform and regulation, looking at the institutions that are needed in a capable public sector, discussing restraints on corruption, and outlining ways of bringing the state closer to the people.

Social safety nets. *World Development Report 1990: Poverty* discussed the need for transfers and safety nets to complement a market-oriented policy agenda that favors the poor. It emphasized the importance of efficient targeting, discussed methods of improving formal social security systems, and suggested complementary mechanisms for food-based interventions. *World Development Report 1995: Workers in an Integrating World* revisited these issues, addressing income security measures in the formal sector and methods of equipping workers for change and of facilitating labor mobility.

Health. *World Development Report 1993: Investing in Health* reviewed cost-effective mechanisms for providing government support for improved health care. The broad agenda covered female education and women's rights, increased and retargeted expenditures, improved management, and decentralized public-private partnerships. In all areas the mechanisms included delivering information, providing protection against infectious diseases, and ensuring universal access to essential clinical services.

Education. *World Development Report 1998/99: Knowledge for Development* suggested strategies for improving the quality of education from the primary to tertiary levels by decentralizing, improving information flows, and targeting support.

Infrastructure. *World Development Report 1994: Infrastructure for Development* focused on the urgent need to make the provision of infrastructure more efficient through commercial management (public-private partnerships or privatization), competition, and stakeholder involvement. The 1998/99 report studied the role of reform and government support in improving access to telecommunications.

Environment. *World Development Report 1992: Development and the Environment* analyzed the linkages among economic policy, poverty, and environmental outcomes and discussed methods of providing cost-effective interventions that ensure sustainable development. It examined self-enforcing policies and standards, the role of local participation, and improved know-how and technology. The 1998/99 report focused on the links between information and environmental degradation.

Rural strategy. In its study of poverty, the 1990 *World Development Report* presented an effective strategy for improving access to government services for the rural poor. In particular it focused on providing social services and access to infrastructure, credit, and technology.

Private sector strategy. The 1996 *World Development Report* presented a framework for creating institutions to support the private sector. It discussed the need for clearly defined property rights and laws governing corporations, contracts, competition, bankruptcy, and foreign investment and outlined methods of privatization. The 1997 *World Development Report* took another look at the roles of liberalization, regulation, and industrial policy in fostering markets.

Gender. *World Development Report 1990* noted the high rates of return to women's education and the role of community-based health care and family planning services in ensuring safe motherhood. These issues were explored in the 1993 report, which also discussed the broader agenda for equality. Last year's report emphasized the important role of microcredit schemes for women.

The term *institutions,* as it is used here, refers to sets of formal and informal rules governing the actions of individuals and organizations and the interactions of participants in the development process (box 6). The institutional infrastructure of an economy embraces two primary areas. The first includes social capital and norms—the unwritten rules of behavior that allow cooperation and dispute resolution, with low transaction costs. The second includes formal legal rules, which en-

sure that contracts are enforced, property rights honored, bankruptcies settled, and competition maintained.

The efficacy of markets, which are themselves institutions, depends on the strength of supporting institutions that help align the expectations of agents regarding the procedures that govern their transactions. Institutions affect the modes of participation and negotiation among groups and, through their incentive effects, shape the nature of agents' reactions and responses.

Box 6
Institutions, organizations, and incentives

This report follows the notion of institutions introduced in the new institutional economics, in which institutions are viewed as rules.[34] Rules can be formal, taking the shape of constitutions, laws, regulations, and contracts. Or they can be informal, like values and social norms. Institutions simultaneously enable and constrain the actions of individuals or organizations. Institutional reforms specify new rules or alter old ones with the intention of changing the behavior of individuals and organizations in desirable directions. For example, markets require social norms that offer at least a degree of respect for contract and property rights and a system of law that can quickly and inexpensively resolve disputes over such matters. Markets also require rules that eliminate unnecessary delays in processing cases and the biased decisions that make investors nervous about contributing to increased investment and growth. For this reason, judicial reform is a high priority for many countries.

Organizations themselves are characterized by internal rules that define for their members prerequisites for eligibility, responsibilities, sanctions, and rewards. How effectively and faithfully members pursue the organization's objectives depends on these rules. Large corporations are continuously adapting their internal rules, centralizing some functions, decentralizing others, adding discretion where advantageous, and modifying the criteria for rewards when doing so is likely to improve performance. In many countries civil service reforms that put in place internal rules of monitoring and accountability are an important item on the policy agenda. Similar reforms of local institutions aim to improve the delivery of urban services and their regulation.

Much remains to be learned about the determinants of institutional change. Institutions change slowly but constantly, either in response to shifts in outside circumstances or as a result of group conflict and bargaining.[35] Even so, it is possible to posit institutions that can help stabilize the global economy and improve the prospects for development—and to suggest mechanisms that facilitate their implementation by aligning incentives with desirable outcomes. In this report institutional reform typically implies changing and specifying formal rules that determine the objectives and incentives for the behavior of individuals and organizations.

A vital role for effective institutions of governance and regulation arises across the range of activities encompassed by a broad-based approach to development—including the structural, human, physical, and sectoral elements included in the CDF.[36]

Institutions at the structural level

A well-run civil service and an efficient judiciary are prerequisites for efficient government action. When a government provides goods directly, it is often a monopoly supplier. As such, it must not take advantage of its monopoly position to provide a suboptimal level of service to the public. Rather, it must structure itself in a way that provides incentives for efficient production and for ongoing gains in productivity. *World Development Report 1997: The State in a Changing World* outlined methods of improving the operations of policymaking and executive agencies that reduce opportunities for politicians and civil servants to exploit public ownership and control over supplies. The report found that countries with stable governments, predictable methods of changing laws, secure property rights, and a strong judiciary saw higher investment and growth than countries lacking these institutions.

A strong regulatory policy is of central importance across a range of sectors. This year's report discusses its role in the provision of essential urban public services at the local level, in resolving global environmental problems, and in imparting stability to the financial sector. For example, without appropriate accounting and regulatory standards, neither bank depositors nor outside investors are well positioned to monitor the degree of risk that banks take when making loans. Last year's *World Development Report* noted that similar problems plague the relationship between investors and companies in stock markets more generally, and regulations addressing these information issues offer substantial benefits.

Institutions and the provision of human development services

Governance institutions are also of primary importance in determining how society addresses human development. In the area of education, for example, the forces of consumer choice that provide such strong incentives for providers in other markets are limited in various ways. Students and even parents are rarely in a position to assess the quality and relevance of education, and it is costly for students to change schools. Institutional reforms center around empowering teachers and schools and improving access to information for both parents and students. In Minas Gerais, Brazil, the reforms implemented since 1991 have increased school autonomy and parental participation and improved student evaluation. These reforms, coupled with efforts to build capacity and professional development in school staff, have increased student test scores.[37]

Providing a social safety net that effectively targets the poor requires efficiently designed programs that benefit those most in need. *World Development Report 1998/99* noted a study carried out in Jamaica which found that food stamps distributed through health clinics reach 94 percent of malnourished children. Over 30 percent of the total benefits of targeted food stamps go to the poorest 20 percent of Jamaican society, while universal food subsidies provide greater benefits to the rich than the poor.

Institutions and the provision of physical services

A central feature of utilities and infrastructure is network externality—that is, the average costs of providing services tend to decrease and the usefulness of the service tends to increase as the system grows. For example, a telephone network with only two connections is costly to set up on a per-person basis and is of little use even to the two parties, since they can call only each other. But a network with many connections costs less and provides greater benefits per user. Network externalities create situations that tend toward monopoly ownership; in the absence of competition, however, firms often overcharge users and operate inefficiently. The telecommunications sector needs regulation to enforce competition, including rules requiring operators to connect each other's customers at an efficient price. A well-run regulatory regime has had a dramatic effect on line rollout in Chile, for example, where a decade of regulated competition has seen a tripling of the number of telephone lines per capita.[38]

The physical dimension of development concerns also includes the environment. Without some form of regulation, companies would not pay for the health and environmental damage manufacturing processes inflict. Individuals and organizations will often pollute indiscriminately if they are allowed to, leaving others to pay the costs. In some cases institutions can have a sizable impact on pollution simply by collecting information about what is happening and making that information widely available. One model is the Indonesian Clean Rivers program, which used to good advantage firms' concern for their public image in inducing them to limit the release of pollutants. By publicizing information on plant emissions, the program lowered the total discharges of 100 participating plants by one-third between 1989 and 1994.

Institutions and sectoral issues

Rural areas often suffer because traditional formal markets fail to provide them with adequate services such as

banking. But innovative institutional structures can overcome this problem, as was discussed in *World Development Report 1998/99*. In Bangladesh the Grameen Bank's group lending program has given rural women access to credit. The bank grants loans to members of a group, who are held collectively responsible, creating incentives for members to monitor each other.

Cities present a wide range of positive and negative externalities. They require efficient institutions if they are to benefit from the positive externalities associated with agglomeration economies and mitigate the negative externalities of congestion and environmental damage that concentrated populations generate. *World Development Report 1997: The State in a Changing World* touched on the subject of efficient city government, and this report examines the topic in greater detail.

Sustainable development is a complex task in which appropriate institutions will play a central role. But such institutions will not necessarily emerge spontaneously. Institutions grow and change over time, but the process of evolution does not necessarily produce socially optimal institutions. Institutional change is more often the result of conflicts over the allocation of societal resources than of planning designed to maximize social welfare. Thus, while institutions are central to implementing broad-based development, understanding which institutional changes will ensure sustainable development in the new century is equally important. It requires having a clear conception not only of the progress that has already been made but also of the challenges the new century will present. The next two sections look at these issues.

The record and outlook for comprehensive development

What has been the record to date of development? And what does the future hold? Answering these questions involves looking at a range of indicators of economic, human, and environmental welfare. The evidence suggests that while remarkable progress has been made in some areas, in others development has fallen behind. Current trends suggest that even the gains achieved could prove short-lived in the absence of new policies and institutions.

Some parts of the developing world have enjoyed levels of growth high enough to reduce poverty in recent decades. Even in parts of the world where poverty rates remain high, the percentage of the poorest—those living on less than $1 per day (a frequently used poverty line)—has declined. In South Asia, for example, the proportion of the population below the poverty line declined from 45.4 percent in 1987 to 43.1 percent in 1993. But the proportion is rising in some regions. In Latin America it rose from 22.0 percent of the population in 1987 to 23.5 percent in 1993, and in Sub-Saharan Africa it increased from 38.5 percent to 39.1 percent (figure 11).

The ongoing increase in population levels means that the absolute number of those living on $1 per day or less continues to increase. The worldwide total rose from 1.2 billion in 1987 to 1.5 billion today and, if recent trends persist, will reach 1.9 billion by 2015.

With the recent East Asian crisis, poverty rates have risen again, even in this successful developing region. If the poverty level is set at $2 per day, Thailand is projected to see poverty increase by 19.7 percent between 1997 and 2000.[39] Inequality typically does not reverse itself quickly, so that if average levels of income change,

Figure 11
The number of poor people has risen worldwide, and in some regions the proportion of poor has also increased

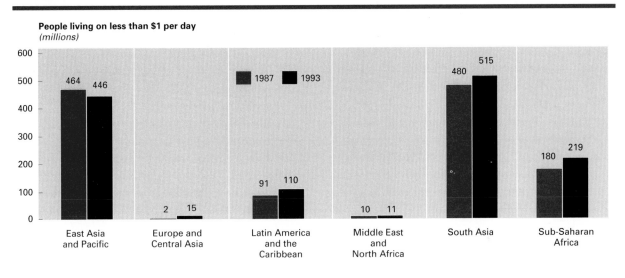

People living on less than $1 per day
(millions)

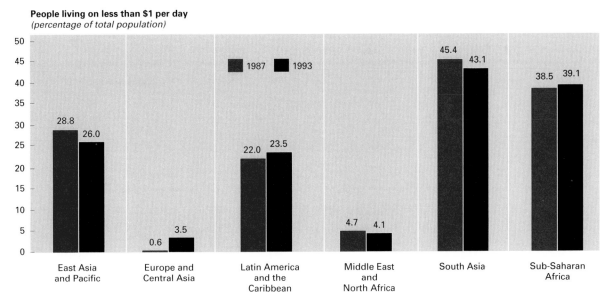

People living on less than $1 per day
(percentage of total population)

Source: World Bank, *World Development Indicators*, 1998.

the number of individuals at the bottom—those in poverty—will not move in tandem. An informal rule of thumb is that a per capita growth rate of 3 percent or more is considered the minimum for reducing poverty rapidly.[40] But the average long-term growth rate of developing countries is below that level. Between 1995 and 1997 only 21 developing countries (12 of them in Asia) met or exceeded this benchmark rate. Among the 48 least-developed countries, only 6 exceeded it.[41]

Measures of health and education offer another perspective on development and living standards. By and large, income increases over the last 50 years have been accompanied by improvements in a variety of indicators of human well-being—life span, infant mortality, and educational level. Even many low-income countries with very slow economic growth have been able to manage some significant improvements in the quality of life of their citizens. In the group of low-income countries as a whole, rates of infant mortality have fallen from 104 per 1,000 live births in 1970–75 to 59 in 1996, and life expectancy has risen by four months each year since 1970. Primary school enrollments have shown significant increases, and adult literacy has risen from 46 to 70 percent. Gender disparities have narrowed, with the average ratio of girls to boys in secondary school rising from 70:100 in 1980 to 80:100 in 1993. These trends testify to the enormous gains that have been made in the length and quality of life for billions of the poorest people around the world.[42]

However, some of these gains are proving fragile. A number of factors—notably prolonged economic crises and slumps—have begun to erode previous advances in life expectancy. In African countries burdened with slow economic growth and an increasing number of people with AIDS, life expectancy declined in 1997 to pre-1980 levels. Lower life expectancies are also apparent in countries of the former Soviet Union and in Eastern Europe (figure 12).

A number of other fundamental indicators, including adequate calorie intake, reasonable shelter, and access to basic services, remain deeply unsatisfactory. Of the 4.4 billion people in developing countries, nearly three-fifths lack basic sanitation; a third have no access to clean water; a quarter lack adequate housing; and a fifth have no access to modern health services. About 20 percent of children do not complete five years of school, and a similar percentage does not receive enough calories and protein from their diet.

Progress on countering infectious diseases over the last 40 years has been dramatic. While the worldwide eradication of smallpox is perhaps the best-known success, polio is also on the retreat. The last-known case of polio caused by wild poliovirus in the Western Hemisphere was on August 23, 1991, and that in the western Pacific was in March 1997. Sadly, the majority of African countries are still exposed to the poliovirus, as well as to malaria and tuberculosis. New diseases such as AIDS have also spread with alarming speed (box 7).[43] In 1995

Figure 12
Life expectancies have risen greatly in some countries, but others have suffered setbacks

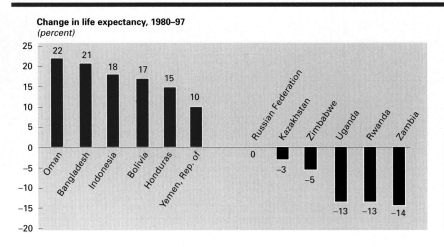

Change in life expectancy, 1980–97 (percent)

	1980	1997
Oman	60	73
Bangladesh	48	58
Indonesia	55	65
Bolivia	52	61
Honduras	60	69
Yemen, Rep. of	49	54
Russian Federation	67	67
Kazakhstan	67	65
Zimbabwe	55	52
Uganda	48	42
Rwanda	46	40
Zambia	50	43

Source: World Bank, *World Development Indicators*, 1999.

Box 7
Trends in disease and health care

Standards of health profoundly influence economic performance and quality of life. The past 50 years have witnessed enormous gains in medical science and health care in developing countries. However, on the threshold of a new century, the epidemiological statistics present a mixed picture. Many infectious diseases are on the retreat because of improved sanitation, nutrition, drugs, and vaccines and life expectancies are rising.[44] Urbanization could decrease the incidence of waterborne and parasitic diseases if it improves access to clean water and better sewerage. And the urban environment remains reliably inhospitable to certain insect vectors.[45] But the virulence of old infectious scourges such as tuberculosis (TB) and malaria has resisted modern science, and in recent years AIDS has emerged as a sizable cause of death and disability among adults in the 15–59 age group.[46] Moreover, in middle- and many low-income countries, the toll exacted by infectious diseases is increasingly overshadowed by that of noncommunicable diseases such as cancer, injuries, and neuro-psychiatric conditions. The future contribution of health to sustainable development will depend on successful action on these several fronts.[47]

Using the concept of disability adjusted life years (DALY)—which expresses years of life lost to premature death and years lived with a disability—injuries account for 16 percent of all DALYs, followed by psychiatric conditions (10 percent), noncommunicable diseases (10 percent), and HIV/AIDS, TB, and maternal conditions (7 percent). Major childhood conditions caused by diarrheal and respiratory infections and by malaria comprise another major component of DALYs.[48]

As countries urbanize and further embrace automobility, the risks from injury are likely to increase—road traffic accidents are already the ninth leading cause of DALYs worldwide, and the fifth highest in industrial countries.[49] With longer life expectancies and older populations, many middle-income and some low-income countries will see an increase in the incidence of chronic diseases and psychiatric disorders. This will lead to rising expenses on diagnoses and curative treatment. Furthermore, the concentration of populations in urban areas could exacerbate the spread of infectious diseases such as TB and HIV/AIDS, and possibly dengue fever, whose vector, the *aedes* mosquito, thrives in urban environments.[50]

In many developing countries, injuries, HIV/AIDS, and TB[51] could shave several points off the GDP growth rate by winnowing the number of prime age adults. Together with increased outlays on those suffering from chronic and psychiatric ailments, these diseases could also substantially raise expenditures on health care. Estimates of the effect of HIV/AIDS on the worst-hit African countries,[52] where the rate of infection continues to spiral upward, suggest that potential GDP could be reduced by 10–15 percent over the course of a decade by this one disease alone.[53]

Although research on vaccines that offer effective protection against HIV/AIDS[54] and malaria continues to move forward (with encouraging progress in the case of the latter),[55] in other areas ground is being lost because of the emergence of multi-drug resistant (MDR) strains of the tuberculin bacillus and of plague,[56] and strains of strep and staph bacteria that are beginning to defy even the most powerful antibiotics such as vancomycin.[57] In 1997, TB caused 2.9 million deaths.[58] Under conditions of poverty and crowding in urban areas, this toll could rise further, especially when health services are unable to cope. The problem is not likely to be limited to low-income countries because in an integrated world in which population mobility is high, new pathogenic strains diffuse rapidly, turning local outbreaks into global problems.[59] The speed with which new strains of influenza and cholera have spread throughout the world testifies to this aspect of globalization.

At the national level, low- and middle-income countries will need to pursue a multi-track strategy, with the priorities dictated by levels of income, financing, age profile, social circumstances, and organizational capacity. Preventive measures propagated by educational campaigns are likely to be the most cost effective against HIV/AIDS, smoking, maternal complications, and conditions affecting children. Simple but highly effective technologies such as vitamin A and zinc supplements[60] and insecticide-treated bednets,[61] propagated by well-designed campaigns, could be the most effective medium-term measures against malaria, whose diffusion to higher latitudes and altitudes could increase with climate change.[62]

Controlling infectious diseases such as TB will require a broader effort that embraces housing and the infrastructure of health services. In a decentralized milieu, this will require coordination between subnational entities, with some centralized oversight and funding. At the very least, a simpler, shorter duration regimen of drugs—as well as the organization to identify the infected, administer treatment over a period of weeks, and keep track of patients—will be necessary for significant gains.[63] In the process of treating diseases such as TB, medical personnel will have to husband the potency of available antibiotics through careful use, so as to contain the threat from resistant strains of bacteria.

Over the longer haul, the answer to many old and new diseases, including possibly heart disease, could lie in new DNA-based vaccines, better drugs that draw on advances in genetic engineering, and ingenious new ways of targeting and destroying pathogens inside the body.[64] But chronic conditions, injury, and poor mental health, which will be responsible for a growing share of the DALYs, will be best held in check by sustained educational efforts to influence living and eating habits and by controlling environmental hazards.

Greater effort at the national level must be strongly reinforced by well-orchestrated action at the international level, with a coordinated division of labor among international organizations and other bodies. This will ensure both the requisite provision of public goods and the management of health-related externalities, whose likelihood has been greatly magnified by globalization.[65]

alone more than 9 million children under the age of five in developing countries died from preventable causes.

Population growth is also connected with the success or failure of a sustainable development agenda. Long-term projections show that the world's population may level off around the middle of the 21st century. But before it does, the number of people could rise from the current level of 6 billion to more than 10 billion. This growth will pose difficult issues involving education, worker training, cultural stability, retirement programs, political majorities, and much more.

In parts of the world with fragile ecological systems that are already threatened by water stress and land degradation, increased population pressure could lead to environmental catastrophes. Global food supplies will need to double over the next 35 years because of population (and economic) growth. While food supplies have actually doubled in the last 25 years, agronomists warn that the next doubling will be far more difficult—especially if it is to be environmentally sustainable. In Nepal, for instance, where population growth is reducing average farm size, farmers have been pushed into clearing and cropping hillsides in an attempt to maintain their income, and erosion is becoming an increasingly serious problem.

The doubling of food production will have to occur at a time when 800 million people worldwide are already malnourished, 25 billion tons of topsoil are lost annually, and nearly three-quarters of the ocean's fish stocks are overexploited. The current costs of environmental damage, including such things as erosion and the health and other effects of pollution, have been estimated at 5 percent or more of GNP worldwide—a figure that will increase rapidly if the world does not move toward a sustainable development agenda (box 8).

Water scarcity also threatens the potential for continued improvements in the quality of life of the world's poorest people. Today, about one-third of the world is living under moderate or severe water stress, with at least 19 countries dependent on foreign sources for more than 50 percent of their surface water. By 2050 the proportion of people living at or above moderate water stress could double (box 9). The great majority will be in developing countries where technical, financial, and managerial limitations will complicate attempts to respond.[66] Under conditions of water scarcity, agricultural yields will fall as irrigation supplies dry up, and health will suffer as more people are reduced to using unsafe water sources for drinking and washing. The potential for conflict over riparian rights among states is also likely to increase.

Box 8
Sustainable development

Any sustainable development agenda must be concerned with intergenerational equity—that is, with ensuring that future generations have the same capability to develop as the present generation. A development path is sustainable only if it ensures that the stock of overall capital assets remains constant or increases over time. These assets include manufactured capital (such as machines and roads), human capital (knowledge and skills), social capital (relationships and institutions), and environmental capital (forests and coral reefs). The environment matters not just because of its effect on psychic and noneconomic welfare but also because of its impact on production over the long term.

Environmental sustainability is also closely connected with intragenerational equity. While the wealthy consume more resources overall, the poor tend to rely more heavily on the direct exploitation of natural resources than the rich. If they have no access to nonenvironmental resources—and so have limited capacity to adapt—they may have no choice but to engage in unsustainable uses of environmental resources.

Source: Pearce and Warford 1993; Watson and others 1998.

Economic stagnation or collapse, new health crises, continued population growth, and a range of environmental issues all threaten the gains that have been made in the development agenda over the last half century and will be a continuing challenge for development in the new millennium. These issues will have to be faced in a world that is very different from what it is today—a world that will create a new set of challenges and opportunities.

A changing world

The only thing that can be said with certainty about the future is that it will differ from the present. Any list of the most significant changes that the world will undergo in the next few decades is to some degree arbitrary. However, such a list might include the following possibilities.

The spread of democracy. The proportion of countries that are considered democratic has more than doubled since 1974. In a worldwide shift, people are demanding a larger say in the way their governments are run. In addition, demands for increased decentralization of power often accompany democratic trends.

Urbanization. Agriculture accounts for a larger share of production in low-income countries than it does in high-income economies. In Sub-Saharan Africa, for example, agriculture today is about one-quarter of GDP—not very different from the level of U.S. GDP in agri-

Box 9
The growing threat of water scarcity

Global population has doubled since 1940 but fresh water usage has risen fourfold. Estimates of the upper limit of usable freshwater suggest a second quadrupling of world water use is unlikely.[67] The prospect of water scarcity is very real with implications for regional peace, global food security, the growth of cities, and the location of industries. The problem is exacerbated by a very uneven distribution. Most available fresh water is found in industrial countries which have one-fifth of the world's population. However, nearly all of the 3 billion increase in global population expected by 2025 will be in developing countries where water is already scarce.

Slowing population growth rates are providing some reprieve, dramatically lowering the projections of people who will be living in countries subject to water stress or scarcity (defined as fresh water resources of under 1,700 and 1,000 cubic meters per person per year, respectively) in 2050—from 3.5 billion (more than tenfold the number in 1990) to 2 billion. But, the problem of water scarcity is expected to get worse before it gets better. Currently, only 166 million people in 18 countries are suffering from water scarcity, while almost 270 million more in 11 additional countries are considered water stressed.

The consequences will be felt most acutely in arid and semi-arid areas, in rapidly growing coastal regions and in the megacities of the developing world. Urbanization will enlarge the claims on available supplies because of higher per capita water consumption in urban areas. Twenty-five years ago less than 40 percent of the world's population lived in urban areas; 25 years in the future this share could reach 60 percent. The ability to supply safe, clean water and adequate sanitation, already stretched, will be severely tested.

One major outcome, with regional and even global consequences, is the greater likelihood of conflicts over water, in large part because of the imperatives of geography. Nearly 47 percent of the land area of the world, excluding Antarctica, falls within international water basins shared by two or more countries. There are 44 countries with at least 80 percent of their total areas within international basins. And the number of river and lake basins shared by two or more countries are now more than 300.

Water shortages will be especially adverse for agriculture, which takes 70–80 percent of all available fresh water in the world. Food security could be a casualty since the growth in food supply in recent decades has largely been fuelled by irrigation—both the expansion in area and productivity increases. Under current best practice coefficients, it will take 17 percent more water to feed the world's population in 2025. But agriculture is already competing for available water resources with urban and industrial uses and the competition will only intensify with time. Although technological advances are making desalination a feasible option for municipal and industrial usage in coastal areas, the costs remain much too high for agricultural purposes.

Preventing crises, regional disputes and their spillover effects calls for a mix of economic and institutional measures. The growing competition for water indicates that there will be benefits from treating and pricing it as an economic good. And the geography of river basins makes unavoidable the effort to search for cooperative arrangements. Both within and across countries, allocation and usage of water within a framework of clearly defined laws and policies and joint development of infrastructure for storing and distributing water would avoid economic inefficiencies associated with autarkic solutions. More importantly, only strategies involving basin-wide rather than national solutions will prove sustainable and advantageous for the majority of riparians.

---

culture at the beginning of the 20th century. However, two characteristics of economic development are working together to encourage migration away from rural areas and into cities: increased agricultural productivity (which allows fewer farmers to produce more food) and expanded economic opportunities in the manufacturing and service sectors. The world's urban population is set to rise by almost 1.5 billion people in the next 20 years, and in developing countries the share of the population living in urban areas is likely to rise from one-half to about two-thirds by 2025. This growth will have a significant effect on the political clout of cities and will make getting policy right at the municipal level even more important than it is today.

Demographic pressures. The world's population is likely to increase by at least another 4 billion by 2050—a huge number of people who will need to be fed, sheltered, and absorbed into the workforce. The age composition of the population will also shift as birthrates decline and life expectancies increase. The transition will be particularly rapid in the industrial world, where in 30 years one in four people will be over 65—up from one in seven today.[68] This shift will strongly influence global financial flows as an increasing number of retirees stop saving and instead begin to draw down their accumulated assets.

The revolution in information and communications technology. Economic output has traditionally been visualized as commodities and goods—wheat, coffee, shirts, or automobiles. This economic vision grows less accurate each year. In industrial economies the service sector has accounted for more than half of all output for decades, and a similar shift toward services is under way in developing countries. The growing importance of services means that knowledge—how to do things, how to communicate, how to work with other people—is becoming ever more important, overshadowing the natural resource base. It means that investment in human capital, including health and education, might become more urgent than investment in physical capital. It implies that economic output is becoming more "footloose," since many services and information can be shipped over phone wires or fiber-optic cable or even through the radio spectrum, increasing the range of choices for locating production. Improved communications technology—and continued improvements in the efficiency of international transport—have also facilitated the rapid increase in global trade and financial flows.[69]

Threats to the environment. A number of environmental problems will become significant threats to sustainable development if they are not addressed. Climate change from atmospheric concentrations of greenhouse gases and the growing rate of global species extinction are two of the most pressing, but others also demand attention, including disease, water shortages, and land degradation.

This report argues that the changes the world is already experiencing will greatly increase the importance of global and local (or supra- and subnational) institutions. In many cases the responses to economic, social, and environmental changes will require international cooperation under enhanced or completely new institutional structures. At the same time, governments will increasingly decentralize, devolving greater power to city and regional authorities. While the central authorities will continue to play an important role in coordinating and enforcing cooperative outcomes, decisions affecting people's lives will increasingly be taken at the international and local levels.

The movement toward a globalized and localized world with many more important players and voices from both above and below the national government level offers new opportunities for development and new challenges for governments. Grasping the opportunities and meeting the challenges requires building institutions that will shape and channel the forces of change to best serve the cause of sustainable development.

• • •

Development thinking has followed a circuitous path over the last 50 years. At various times it has emphasized market failures and market successes, governments as active interventionists or passive enablers, openness to trade, saving and investment, education, financial stability, the spread of knowledge, macroeconomic stability, and more. The list of policies accepted as relevant to sustainable development is now longer than it was even 10 years ago, and some of the emphases have changed. Inflation remains a concern, for instance, but little evidence exists showing that low to moderate rates of inflation have significantly adverse effects on growth. On the other hand, increasing recognition is being given to the importance of strong financial institutions, and in the regulatory sphere the focus has shifted from deregulation to building an effective regulatory framework.

It would be presumptuous to predict which of these items will be high on policy agendas one or two decades from now. But even as the general understanding of development grows and evolves, one lesson remains. Understanding the process of development requires acknowledging both its complexity and the context in which it operates. Simple solutions—investments in physical and human capital, for instance, and unfettered markets—will not work in isolation. Governments, the private sector, civil society, and donor organizations need to work together in support of broad-based development.

1

The Changing World

Policymakers in the 21st century will find themselves pursuing development goals in a landscape that has been transformed economically, politically, and socially. Two main forces will be shaping the world in which development policy will be defined and implemented: globalization (the continuing integration of the countries of the world) and localization (the desire for self-determination and the devolution of power).

At the end of the 20th century, globalization has already demonstrated that economic decisions, wherever they are made in the world, must take international factors into account. While the movement of goods, services, ideas, and capital across national borders is not new, its acceleration in the last decade marks a qualitative break with the past.[1] The world is no longer a collection of relatively autonomous neighborhoods that are only marginally connected (by trade, for example) and are generally immune to events in other neighborhoods. Information and ideas can be accessed in all corners of the globe at the push of a button. The international economic order is

evolving into a highly integrated and electronically networked system. So close are its ties that a retailer in one country can describe the products consumers want to producers in several other countries, setting in motion immediate revisions in design and production. So closely interwoven are financial markets that exchange rates, interest rates, and stock prices are intimately linked, and the amount of private capital circulating in financial markets dwarfs the resources of many countries.

At the same time that globalization is gathering the world's countries together, the forces of localization are tilting the balance of power within them. The demand for self-determination can take a number of forms, including the replacement of authoritarian or single-party rule by multiparty politics, greater autonomy of subnational political units, and the involvement of community groups and nongovernmental organizations (NGOs) in governance. Even as private businesses consolidate to gain leverage on the global market, many countries are moving in the opposite direction, fragmenting, questioning established authority, and groping for mechanisms to coordinate their internal activities.

At first glance, globalization and localization may look like countervailing forces, but in fact they often stem from the same source and reinforce each other. For example, the same advances in information and communications technology that have been so important in the spread of global economic forces often allow local groups to bypass central authorities in the search for information, visibility, and even financing. Together, these global and local pressures are revolutionizing traditional forms of centralized governance and dramatically affecting development thinking.

Development economics, born after World War II, came into being in an era when strong and autonomous states were the chief decisionmakers. But that autonomy is gradually being eroded. Markets, for instance, have developed the potential to discipline states, punish their mistakes and call their bluff. Globalization has circumscribed the ability of many central governments to raise revenues by taxing corporations, which now have the option of moving part or all of their economic activity to low-tax venues. As central governments find themselves looking for other sources of revenue, regional and urban communities are coming together to assert their own interests, putting yet more pressure on the traditional forms of governance. The result has been new ways of thinking about how to manage the world's economies and a corresponding need to create new institutions to do so. These institutions will be needed at three levels: supranational, national, and local.

At the supranational level some institutions for shaping and channeling the forces of globalization are already in place. The World Trade Organization (WTO), the Basle Accords, and the Montreal Protocol, which affect, respectively, trade, banking systems, and the release of ozone-depleting chemical agents worldwide, are representative of the kinds of institutions the world will need in the 21st century. The events of the 1980s and 1990s have shown that existing institutions are far from sufficient to address the economic and environmental issues of the future: many more are needed. Economic catastrophes like the Latin American debt crises of the 1980s and the meltdown of the East Asian economies in the late 1990s may continue to occur, perhaps in even more dramatic forms. And while countries have begun initiating responses to important environmental issues

like climate change and preservation of biodiversity, these actions are but the first of many that must be taken to protect the global commons (see chapter 4). The lack of consensus on many vital issues and the difficulties inherent in protracted negotiations stand in the way of meaningful international institution-building.

At the national level many countries are learning which policies work well and which should be avoided for the purposes of macroeconomic stability. Many industrial economies learned of the potential boom-and-bust dangers of capitalism from events like the Great Depression and thus have put in place a bevy of national policies and institutions. These policies seek to moderate economic volatility through countercyclical macroeconomic actions designed to minimize the potential instability of capital flows; regulate the conduct of private agents; protect investors, depositors, and consumers; disclose the information necessary to assess risks and make prudent decisions; and provide social insurance to ride out temporary crises. Such institutions have become integral parts of the capitalist system in industrial countries, shaping expectations and fundamentally altering private sector decisionmaking. As developing economies are increasingly exposed to the new global economy, they build similar institutions in their own countries. They are likely to find that some policies in particular offer exceptional payoffs. A stable macroeconomic environment, a liberalized domestic business services sector, and a legal framework that induces transparency and protects investors' rights is advantageous. Conversely, deficiencies in financial policies and business practices are a recipe for disaster—a bitter lesson learned from the banking and currency crises of the late 20th century.

At the subnational level localization has led many central governments to grant political, fiscal, and administrative powers to local governments. But arrangements aimed at maintaining workable intergovernmental relations have not kept pace with the speed of decentralization. Ideally, decentralization rests upon effective institutions that determine voting procedures, provide for the disclosure of information, ensure accountability at the local level, and define a system of allocating resources and responsibilities to subnational authorities. But the devolution of central government authority and functions has often proceeded at its own pace—with elements not only of learning by doing but of suffering by stumbling. There are vitually no good models of decentralization. Recent macroeconomic instability arising in part from tensions between the central government and subnational entities (although the cases are very different) in Brazil and Russia show how important harmonious relations between central and local authorities are in creating and sustaining market confidence. Governments at all levels have also begun to understand the importance of due process and inclusive, participatory, and consensual modes of public sector decisionmaking and resource allocation.

This chapter sets the stage for later chapters by defining the forces of globalization and localization. It explores issues such as trade, capital flows, and the implications of urban growth. And it looks at the institutional changes that will be needed to keep development sustainable, providing the groundwork for a more detailed examination in later chapters of the report.

International trade

International trade flows are penetrating deeper into the workings of developing economies, affecting the overall economic structure in general and income distribution, employment practices, and productivity growth in particular.[2] Trade in goods and services has grown twice as fast as global GDP in the 1990s, and the share attributable to developing countries has climbed from 23 to 29 percent. These aggregate numbers do not reflect the important compositional changes of the last 10 years, which offer developing economies new opportunities for growth. Chapter 2 addresses these challenges and opportunities in depth.

The compositional shifts in trade have created a new pattern in the international exchange of goods, services, and ideas. Trade in components is one part of that new pattern. "Sourcing" such components from abroad is an increasingly common practice, and use of the Internet is sure to expand the process, encouraging entry by new producers throughout the developing world. While precise numbers are difficult to come by, in the early 1990s one-third of all manufactures trade (approximately $800 billion) involved parts and components. This type of trade has generated an ever-spreading web of global production networks that connect subsidiaries within transnational firms to unrelated designers, producers, and distributors of components. These networks offer their con-

stituent firms access to new markets and commercial relationships and facilitate technology transfer. Advances in information technology help to link firms from developing countries into global production networks. General Electric, for instance, posts information on its components requirements on the Internet, and firms from all over the globe bid to supply them.

The tremendous growth of trade in services and, more recently, of electronic commerce is also a part of the new trade pattern. Exports of commercial services have been growing on every continent (particularly Asia) throughout the 1990s (figure 1.1). This change has its own special significance, as services are frequently used in the production of goods and even other services. Enhanced international competition in services means reductions in price and improvements in quality that will enhance the competitiveness of downstream industries. Both industrial and developing economies have much to gain by opening their markets. Developing countries would derive large gains from an easing of barriers to agricultural products and to labor-intensive construction and maritime services.[3] Over the longer term, electronic business will loom large as an area where expanding opportunities for trade require an expanding framework of rules.[4]

Underpinning this surge in trade flows is the growing commitment developing economies have shown to liberalizing their trade regimes. Their resolution has taken many forms: membership in the WTO (110 of 152 developing countries were members in 1999), participation in regional trade agreements, and unilateral reforms (figure 1.2).[5] But this push for trade reform is meeting with increased resistance, especially in industrial economies, where adjustment to the competitive pressure of the international marketplace can be a painful process. Successful trade reform requires reallocating resources among economic groups, and that adjustment can be costly for some. Increasingly, governments are recognizing that successful trade reform requires flexible labor market institutions, a point developed in chapter 2. Import-competing firms are also resisting further trade reform by using antidumping laws to reverse the gains in market access previous reforms have secured. At least 29 countries were applying such laws by 1997, and many more had them on their books.

Although the 1990s saw impressive progress in liberalizing trade regimes, sustaining that momen-

Figure 1.1
Exports of commercial services have surged in most regions since 1990

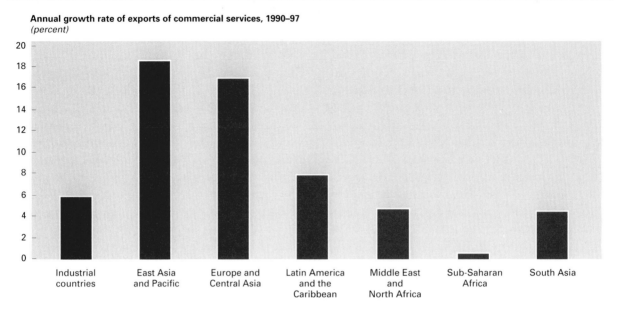

Annual growth rate of exports of commercial services, 1990–97
(percent)

Note: The annual growth rate for the European Union was zero in 1997. Figures for the European Union exclude intra–European Union trade.
Source: WTO, *Annual Report,* various years.

tum over the next 25 years will be more difficult. The Millennium Round commencing in November 1999 will provide the international community with an opportunity to meet the challenge. For the developing countries it will be important to be fully engaged and to use the technical expertise at their disposal to arrive at favorable outcomes in areas such as liberalization of agricultural trade and of trade in those services of greatest relevance to their future development. Recognizing that trade reform creates both winners and losers (and more of the former than the latter) is the starting point. The real test will be persuading the winners to forgo some of their gains in order to compensate influential losers who could otherwise stymie the process of reform.

International financial flows

The financial crises of 1997–99 have put the growing interdependencies among countries in the spotlight and led to their intense scrutiny. International capital flows to developing countries, though still concentrated in a dozen or so host economies, are rapidly becoming a major force, making the effective development, regulation, and liberalization of finan-

cial markets a top priority. Financial flows soared in the 1990s, spurred by the greater readiness of countries to liberalize capital account transactions. Even though they slipped in 1998, such flows are resum-

Figure 1.2
An increasing number of developing countries is committed to trade reform

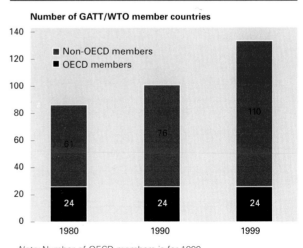

Number of GATT/WTO member countries

Note: Number of OECD members is for 1999.
Source: WTO, *Annual Report,* various years.

ing their upward trend.[6] Much has rightly been made of the technological developments in computing and telecommunications that are reducing transactions costs. In addition, considerable attention has been given to the possibility that hedge funds and the use of new derivatives instruments could increase the volatility of capital flows.[7] At the same time, financial innovation has done much to contain the newly emergent risks and create a rich menu of investment possibilities—another trend that will not be arrested, simply because the potential rewards are so attractive.[8] More significant, the supply of financial resources will expand over the next two decades, fed by pension and mutual funds in industrial societies (box 1.1). The value of global pension assets rose from $6 trillion in 1992 to $9.7 trillion in 1997. Although

the rate of growth of pension assets in the United Kingdom and the United States could drop to 6–7 percent a year over the medium term, the projected value of global assets for 2002 is a hefty $13.7 trillion. These resources will be aggressively seeking high returns throughout the world.

Increases in demand for funds will match, if not exceed, any increase in supply. Some 85 percent of the world's people reside in developing countries, half of them in cities. Large numbers of them (close to 1.5 billion in 2000) live on less than $1 a day (a widely used poverty line). To modernize, industrialize, and urbanize, developing countries will need huge injections of capital. Most of it will come from domestic savings, but well-run developing countries offering solid returns can expect to supplement their

Box 1.1
The global macroeconomics of aging

The aging of populations in industrial countries and some industrializing East Asian economies could seriously reduce the international supply of capital by 2025. Three factors will determine exactly how serious the reduction will be: the effect of aging and rising dependency ratios on household savings, the ages at which people retire, and the coverage provided by social security systems.

The bleakest scenario projects a substantial drop in household savings in industrial and East Asian economies as the number of people over 65 continues to climb. It points to an increasing tendency for people to retire in their fifties, as many already do in Europe. And it indicates that unreformed, pay-as-you-go social security schemes will go bankrupt or at least come under great pressure.

The median age of the population in northeast Asia will rise from 28 years to 36 years between 1995 and 2015.[9] Just 12.5 percent of the U.S. population and 11.8 percent of the Japanese population were over 65 in 1990, proportions that will rise to 18.7 and 26.7 percent by 2025. Between 1990 and 2025 rapid aging will raise the share of the 65-plus cohort from 6 to 13.3 percent in China and from 5 to 15 percent in the Republic of Korea.

As countries begin to gray, the number of men between the ages of 60 and 64 who are still in the labor force is dropping precipitously. In the 35 years leading up to 1995 the percentage of men in this age group who were still working fell from 80 to 55 percent in the United States, from 80 to 20 percent in Italy, and from 70 to 15 percent in France. This scenario suggests a severe global capital shortage that raises interest rates and depresses growth, trade, and commodity prices—a gloomy prospect.

A second and much brighter scenario suggests that a savings crunch can be avoided. Household surveys show that aging may not lead to the steep decline in savings some cross-

country studies predict. The growing numbers of women joining the labor force will partially offset the decreasing number of older male workers. And policies and institutions can narrow (if not close) the savings gap in some industrial countries and prevent shortages in developing economies.

Research on Japan and East Asia supports the view that savings could decline as populations age but that diminishing rates of investment will more than offset lower savings.[10] Furthermore, as fertility declines in South Asia and Central and South America, dependency ratios will fall during the next two decades, savings could climb—and countries in the region could gradually become capital exporters, like Japan.[11] In fact, some recent research on the United Kingdom and the United States points to the likelihood of higher savings rates as baby boomers approach retirement in the next two decades.[12]

Some sociologists believe that the retirement age will stop falling in the next two decades and may even begin to climb.[13] If it does—and there are plenty of opposing views that stress the attractiveness of retirement and the declining price of recreation—a savings shortfall in industrial countries would be a less pressing problem.[14] But even if this favorable scenario becomes more likely, industrial and developing countries with aging populations need to accelerate reform. Pay-as-you-earn social security schemes in industrial countries will run out of money in the next two or three decades unless governments increase funding, shave benefits, and maintain or raise the age of retirement. Raising contributions or cutting benefits will generate resistance, but this adjustment is unavoidable. The total bill over the next 30 years for pensions and medical care for the aged is estimated at $64 trillion.[15] To meet their share of these expenses, industrial countries need to create an institutional framework that minimizes the threat of inadequate savings by ensuring that social security schemes are fully funded and by discouraging early retirement.[16]

savings with resources from all over the globe.[17] Developing countries are also the fastest-growing markets for the products of multinational corporations.[18] As these markets expand they will attract ever-greater amounts of foreign direct investment, which provides jobs and managerial and technical expertise, as well as capital. But the governments of developing countries must take measures to attract such investment, since it will not automatically find its way to them. In 1996 investors sent only one-quarter of their money to the developing world.[19]

The globalization of financial markets affects development because finance plays such an important role in economic growth and industrialization.[20] Financial globalization affects growth in two ways: by increasing the global supply of capital, and by promoting domestic financial development that improves allocative efficiency, creates new financial instruments,[21] and raises the quality of banking services.[22] Competition comes not only from other domestic banks but also from foreign banks and from thriving nonbank financial intermediaries. Both complement banks and, in the case of stock markets and other monitoring agencies, enhance discipline by continuously assessing information on portfolios and performance.[23] Moreover, experience suggests that foreign financial institutions do not undermine domestic banking systems; they are rarely dominant and tend to exhibit a long-term commitment.[24]

The financial performance of emerging markets in the 1990s made capital account liberalization an attractive option for developing countries. Markets seemed broadly stable and fairly disciplined, and many countries began to view the recommended sequence of liberalization (starting with the building of regulatory capabilities and the strengthening of banking and financial markets) as less important than research had indicated it was.[25] Several developing countries, urged by the weight of opinion in some industrial countries, began loosening controls on inflows and outflows of capital, and while most retained some constraints, a few abolished all of them.[26] Furthermore, openness remained the most popular option as containing outflows became increasingly difficult and the advantages of inflows grew ever more evident.

The crisis in East Asia in 1997 made policymakers apprehensive about further financial globalization. Several of the most successful emerging economies have been badly bruised by financial turbulence associated with the East Asian meltdown. In fact, the costs of the crisis have been much higher than those associated with other recent financial debacles (figure 1.3). But the fiscal costs pale in comparison with the forgone growth and increased poverty and inequality these crises can create, especially in urban areas (figure 1.4).[27] The East Asian crsis has abruptly pushed the issue of sequencing liberalization measures to the top of the policy agenda. Several questions need to be answered. What role can capital controls play in minimizing exposure to sudden changes in the sentiment of portfolio investors? Are controls on capital outflows desirable, or even possible? And, given the increasing number of international transactions of goods and services, how easily can these controls be sidestepped?

Like earlier crises, the East Asian meltdown has enhanced the attractiveness of long-term capital investment, with one difference. Until recently, governments preferred debt to equity financing or to foreign direct investment, both because they did not want foreign interests controlling major segments of the economy and because domestic owners of major corporations feared losing control.[28] The mood began shifting as countries recognized that foreign direct investment brings with it not only capital but also tech-

Figure 1.3
Nonperforming loans can account for up to 50 percent of all bank loans at the peak of a banking crisis

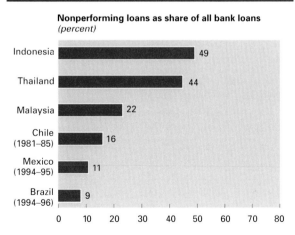

Source: Figures for Indonesia, Malaysia, and Thailand are from official sources; figures for other countries are from *Wall Street Journal*, December 9, 1998.

**Figure 1.4
Resolving bank crises can cost
up to 40 percent of GDP**

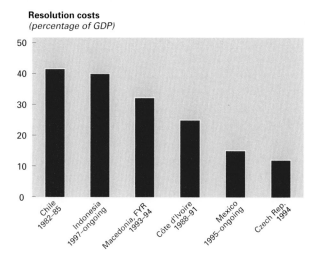

Resolution costs
(percentage of GDP)

Note: *Resolution costs* include the government's direct costs as well as quasi-fiscal costs such as exchange rate subsidies, as defined by the IMF.
Source: Caprio and Klingebiel 1999.

**Figure 1.5
Foreign direct investment was less volatile
than commercial bank loans and total portfolio
flows, 1992–97**

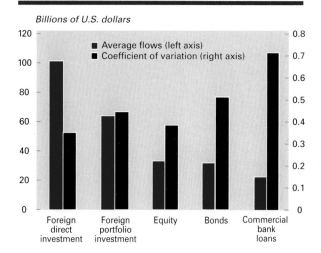

Billions of U.S. dollars

■ Average flows (left axis)
■ Coefficient of variation (right axis)

Source: UNCTAD, *World Investment Report*, 1998.

nology, market access, and organizational skills.[29] Studies of recent episodes of financial turmoil have focused on the volatility of certain private financial flows and the ways in which it helps create an unstable environment and hurts economic development. An analysis of the period 1992–97 shows that foreign direct investment was less volatile (as measured by the coefficient of variation) than commercial bank loans and foreign portfolio flows (figure 1.5).

In 1997 developing countries accounted for 30 percent of the foreign direct investment stock, or $1.04 trillion, 90 percent of which originated in industrial countries (table 1.1). Five countries—Argentina, Brazil, China, Mexico, and Poland—received half the total for developing countries.[30] Multinational corporations account for much of this investment. Their investment stimulates export-led growth in well-positioned economies through spillovers arising from the sourcing of their products, and distribution of their production facilities.[31] Philips Electronics, for instance, employs more workers in China than in the Netherlands. Alliances between multinationals continue to fuse markets as corporations take advantage of scale and scope economies and cope with the rising cost of technological innovation.[32] Chapter 3

details how developing countries can reform their institutions and policies to attract more foreign direct investment.

The East Asian crisis also raised the issue of whether coordinated macroeconomic and regulatory actions could have averted or mitigated the crisis and lessened the contagion effects. A number of institutional possibilities are explored in chapter 3. Closer policy coordination among the principal economies in the Asia-Pacific region might have kept the exchange rate and associated interest rate fluctuations within reasonable bounds, leading to earlier concerted action to contain the crisis.[33] Coordination and some degree of uniformity could also have extended to financial regulation. Regional and possibly international bodies could have reviewed national banking practices to determine their compliance with the basic prudential rules for banks established by the Basle Accords. (In principle, countries can adopt unilateral or regional standards higher than those in the Basle Accords, including the changes in the accords proposed in 1999.)[34]

International migration

Along with goods, services, and investment, people are crossing borders in record numbers. Each year between 2 million and 3 million people emigrate, with

Table 1.1
World foreign direct investment stock, 1997

Region	Amount (billions of U.S. dollars)	Percentage of total
World	3,455.5	100.0
Industrial countries	2,349.4	68.0
Western Europe	1,276.5	36.9
North America	857.9	24.8
Other industrial countries	215.1	6.2
Developing countries	1,043.7	30.2
Argentina, Brazil, and Mexico	249.2	7.2
Other Latin America	126.2	3.7
China (includes Hong Kong)	244.2	7.1
Southeast Asia[a]	253.1	7.3
Other Asia	96.3	2.8
Africa	65.2	1.9
Other developing countries	9.4	0.3

a. Indonesia, the Republic of Korea, Malaysia, Philippines, Singapore, Taiwan (China), and Thailand.
Source: UNCTAD, *World Investment Report,* 1998.

the majority of them going to just four host countries: the United States, Germany, Canada, and Australia, in that order.[35] At the beginning of the 21st century, more than 130 million people live outside the countries of their birth, and that number has been rising by about 2 percent a year. In relative terms the number of migrants is a modest 2.3 percent of world population. But they are concentrated in just a few regions—North America, Western Europe, Oceania, and the Middle East.[36] In North America and Western Europe the migrant stock grew at 2.5 percent a year between 1965 and 1990, far outstripping growth among indigenous populations. If Oceania is included in this group, 1 in every 13 people living in these regions is foreign born.[37] While the net benefits are positive for the receiving countries and for many of the originating countries as well, the resulting ethnic and labor market tensions in urban areas have led to tighter immigration restrictions in some countries.

Conflict and natural disasters have dramatically increased the number of refugees. By 1975 a total of 2.5 million refugees had crossed national borders, but by 1995 the total had risen to 23 million.[38] To that figure must be added the more than 20 million internally displaced persons who have migrated within their own countries.[39] The effects of such displacement are

not temporary, and they extend beyond those who moved. For example, the substantial displacement of people from southwestern Afghanistan caused considerable damage to the pattern of cultivation practiced there.[40] So many people left the area that the population fell below the levels needed to maintain the country's basic agricultural infrastructure.

Cross-border migration, combined with the "brain drain" from developing to industrial countries, will be one of the major forces shaping the landscape of the 21st century, for at least three reasons. First, migration is causing dramatic shifts in the demographic profiles of both industrial and developing countries. Second, the movement of highly skilled people from the developing world affects low-income countries and recipient countries alike. Third, the international diasporas have tremendous business potential.

In the next few decades many countries will see profound changes in their population growth rates and demographic profiles. Indigenous populations are declining in most industrial and East European countries, where fertility rates are low. But population growth rates remain high in Asia and Sub-Saharan Africa, although they have begun to slow. Shortages of agricultural land and urban unemployment are two important concerns, and through migration they could lead to problems for other economies. In Africa, parts of the Middle East, and South Asia, intense competition for jobs could create an additional incentive to emigrate. Shrinking and aging populations in Europe, Japan, and the United States might also boost the demand for migrant workers, as it did in Western Europe between the mid-1950s and the mid-1970s.[41]

In a positive scenario, policy reforms in developing countries, greater financial and trade integration, short-term migration generated by the liberalization of construction services, and increased possibilities for emigrating to industrial countries could enable low-income countries to cope with population pressures during the demographic transition. Foreign investment and trade also have a role to play in developing countries, where they accelerate growth, expand employment opportunities, and thus reduce incentives to emigrate.[42] This optimism must be tempered, however, by the fact that new, low-skilled migrants face serious hurdles as they enter labor markets in industrial countries.[43]

In other, less attractive scenarios, globalization slows, developing countries have less access to international capital and markets, and cross-border migration becomes more difficult because industrial countries are reluctant to liberalize trade in services that entail short-term cross-border labor movement and adopt policies to significantly reduce immigration. While a few low-income countries may respond decisively—reducing fertility and promoting growth by mobilizing domestic resources and fostering innovation—most are likely to experience ever-greater instability and slow income growth.

A second concern is the emigration of skilled workers from developing economies, especially from Africa and South Asia. A brain drain can impair a developing country's capacity to harness modern agricultural and industrial technology. Some countries in Sub-Saharan Africa, the Caribbean, Central America, and South Asia have, in fact, lost one-third of their skilled workers.[44] But recent research also points to the benefits of outward migration. The most important of these is the money migrants send to their countries of origin. These sums can be substantial: foreign workers remit about $75 billion to their home countries each year, 50 percent more than total official development assistance.[45] Those remittances are used to support family members, or they may be invested (primarily in housing), thus stimulating other expenditures.[46]

Of all the potential overseas investors in a country, emigrants are likely to be the best informed about business and employment practices and legal norms. A country that adopts measures to enhance foreign direct investment and integrates with global production networks by maintaining low and predictable trade barriers will find that doing so generates additional benefits. If the quality and technological sophistication of a developing country's exports increases, highly skilled emigrants may decide to return. Several East Asian economies have benefited from this reflux.

However, experience suggests that returning emigrants do not always benefit a country. A study of reverse migration in Turkey notes that only half of the returned migrants were economically active in 1988.[47] Of those, 90 percent were self-employed, and many had used funds saved abroad to establish new businesses. The few returnees who did have educational qualifications found little demand for their skills in Turkey. National governments can take a number of measures to increase the benefits of re-

verse migration, however. Among the most important are encouraging emigrants to maintain their links with the home country and supplying information and advice both before and after their return.

The market for highly skilled workers will become even more globally integrated in the coming decades, and increasing returns to skilled people might continue to favor spatial concentration. Knowledge workers will cross borders freely, facilitating the circulation of technology, inducing the growth of technology-intensive industries (as in Israel), and helping to create a truly global marketplace of skills.[48] Because development requires a highly skilled workforce, primary and secondary education will continue to be important. Countries unable or unwilling to create such a workforce, compete for skilled workers, and build a technology-friendly environment will find themselves stuck on the lower rungs of the income ladder. In order to narrow the gap with rich countries, developing economies must also put in place policies to nurture, through tertiary-level training, and effectively employ skilled workers, as the Republic of Korea and Taiwan (China) have done. Without such policies, manufacturing and service activities with high value added will not take root in the countries where the need is most urgent.

A third facet of international migration in the 21st century will be the expansion of far-flung diasporas from developing countries—another source of global interconnection (box 1.2). Diasporas serve as informal channels for the flow of information, market intelligence, capital, and skills. They may supplement formal channels that rely on market institutions, providing a way for migrants to conduct transactions in an atmosphere of trust. In this way they act to offset information asymmetries and other market failures. Modern diasporas, like their Mediterranean predecessors, expedite business transactions by resolving monitoring problems, reducing opportunism, and building reputations and ethnic trust based on networking.[49] As migration continues, diasporas will expand, tying together regions and continents. Even if governments attempt to slow the process, communications, technology, and human relationships will maintain this trend.

Governments in South Asia, Central and South America, and Sub-Saharan Africa have made limited efforts to exploit the potential of overseas networks

Box 1.2
The international Chinese network

The Chinese diaspora embraces more than 50 million people, commands enormous resources, and is a force behind the development of the Asia-Pacific region.[50] This community, with its interlaced informal social and business ties and its formal overseas Chinese associations, is a source of dynamism for many East Asian economies. It has bridged market failures, created markets where there were none, and helped emerging economies become competitive in a remarkably short time. These successes are the result of collaboration with local communities and governments in the region. The cross-hatching of formal and informal business linkages will persist and perhaps eventually dwarf official linkages.

In addition to producing, assembling, and distributing goods through extensive manufacturing chains in the Asia-Pacific region, the Chinese diaspora has acquired widespread property holdings and citizenship rights. Citizenship rights are an elaborate mechanism for hedging against the risk of abrupt changes in economic conditions, political regimes, and regulations. That risk falls when developing economies in the region adopt rules-based regimes for trade, investment, and other policies, inducing members of the diaspora to shift their investment portfolios toward direct investment and away from risk-hedging devices.

Indeed, the diaspora's response to emergent rules-based regimes could be much faster and, at least initially, stronger than the response from non-Chinese multinational corporations. Chinese investors have an edge over other investors, who do not have an intimate knowledge of the region's economic conditions and businesses. But an important caveat must be added here. Subnational governments must participate in building rules-based institutions in order to encourage continued investment. Only if every important level of government enhances the predictability of its laws and regulations will the countries of the Asia-Pacific region realize the many benefits the Chinese diaspora offers.

In the meantime, ethnic Chinese have been making substantial investments in Europe and the United States, particularly in the computer industry. In 1997 Taiwanese (Chinese) firms invested in 55 manufacturing projects throughout Europe, 44 of them in the computer industry.[51] The desire to be close to product and process development has also fueled an increase in the number of ethnic Chinese firms in California's Silicon Valley. At the same time, other migrant communities are increasing their business and commercial orientation. The South Asian diaspora, with a network reaching from Southeast Asia to the Middle East, the United Kingdom, and North America, has a net worth of between $150 billion and 300 billion. Its potential remains to be tapped in the early 21st century. And throughout the Americas, Hispanics are developing networks that profoundly affect industrial development and trade.

to further development. The push to form partnerships may come from local governments, as in China, with the central authorities working to create an environment conducive to such interaction. The main hurdles in this process relate to openness and regulation. As long as economies remain inwardly oriented, predisposed to regulating business activities, and prone to arbitrary actions, diasporas may not be able to evolve into business networks that strengthen markets and prod development. In the next few decades, however, countries with large and growing emigrant communities scattered throughout the world will have the opportunity to tap into the development potential of their diasporas.

Global environmental challenges

Environmental concerns have long been the subject of international interest, in part because of the burgeoning world population. But at the end of the 20th century, global concerns have acquired a new urgency. Over the past 20 years the content and quality of the discourse on the environment have been completely transformed. By its sheer volume, the authoritative scientific evidence available on environmental problems commands the attention of governments and the public alike. Moreover, along with globalization has come a new recognition of a shared responsibility for the environment. Numerous organizations—international, governmental, and nongovernmental—with a deep interest in this issue have appeared on the scene. These bodies have made full use of the United Nations system and the abilities of new communications technology to reach people all over the world.[52]

Climate change, the loss of biodiversity, and other issues related to the global commons are slowly being recognized as problems that the community of nations must take on collectively. Left unattended, they will worsen as the planet becomes more crowded and overpopulation puts increasing pressure on natural resources. Many of these issues are closely linked to the potential success of development efforts in poor countries, and the growing awareness of these linkages is part of the continuing shift in the development perspective. Only 10 years ago the development community often brushed environmental concerns aside, emphasizing instead the primacy of growth, stability, and poverty reduction. Central to the discussion of environmental sustainability at the start of the 21st century is the problem of how to devise mechanisms that distribute the burdens of reform equally without discouraging the participation of every country that has the capacity to cause environmental damage. This challenge is particularly pressing because developing economies must sometimes balance environmental concerns with their people's desire to advance economically. Chapter 4 examines the preconditions for international agreements that support environmental sustainability. Two areas in particular require concerted international effort: climate change and biodiversity loss.

Climate change

Climate change is occurring at unprecedented rates because huge quantities of carbon dioxide, methane, and other greenhouse gases are being released into the atmosphere daily (figure 1.6). Global temperatures have been rising slowly since 1800. The 20th century has been the warmest century in the past 600 years, and 14 of the warmest years since the 1860s occurred in the 1980s and 1990s. Temperatures in 1998 were higher than the mean temperatures for

the 118 years on record, even after the effects of El Niño are filtered out.[53] Satellite readings now confirm a similar elevation of temperatures in the upper atmosphere.[54] Moreover, wintertime temperatures of seawater north of 45° latitude have risen by 0.5° Celsius since the 1980s. As a result, the incidence of sea ice in the Grand Banks shipping lanes has declined, and in 1999, for the first time since the sinking of the *Titanic* in 1912, the International Ice Patrol did not report a single iceberg south of 48° latitude.[55] The concentration of carbon dioxide in the atmosphere has risen from 280 particles per million (ppm) in 1760 to 360 in 1990 and is expected to reach 600 ppm in 2100. Average temperatures could then rise by some 2° Celsius.[56] The source of the increase in carbon dioxide thus far, like the entire increase in atmospheric chlorofluorocarbons responsible for depleting the ozone layer, is anthropogenic.[57]

These facts are now widely accepted. Other information is less well understood: how severe fluctuations in weather will be in a warming world, how the effects of climate change on agriculture and living conditions will be distributed globally, the rapidity of the change, and how people displaced by rising sea levels in countries such as Bangladesh will be accommodated else-

Figure 1.6
Temperatures are rising as concentrations of greenhouse gases increase

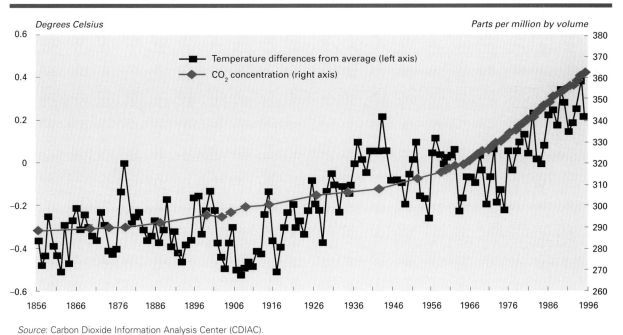

Source: Carbon Dioxide Information Analysis Center (CDIAC).

where.[58] These unknowns make precise measurement of the economic impact of climate change very difficult. Nonetheless the impact will be huge, and it will be felt primarily in developing countries.[59]

An international agreement to contain climate change faces many hurdles. There is uncertainty about the scale of possible benefits and the scope for adaptation. There is resistance to incurring the costs involved in bringing about a drastic flattening of long-run trends. And there is concern about the difficulty of monitoring compliance with emissions rules and enforcing adherence through credible sanctions. Distributional considerations also play a part. Industrial countries account for 60 percent of all energy-related carbon dioxide emissions, with the United States alone responsible for 25 percent in 1998. But in the absence of corrective policies, developing countries will be emitting a higher proportion of all greenhouse gases within 20 years, with China pulling ahead of the United States by 2015.[60] Until the early 1990s little progress was made in moving toward an agreement that embraced the concerns of both developing and industrial countries. In particular, developing countries argued that because greenhouse gases were the result of industrialization in wealthy countries, those countries must take responsibility for the ensuing problems. Developing countries also faced an uphill battle to build the regulatory capacity to control the release of gases and other pollutants.[61] This impasse has extended to other environmental issues, such as efforts to slow the loss of biodiversity. But some progress is being made on the international front to cope with climate change, with increased awareness of the long lags in arresting trends that are already apparent, such as the accumulation of greenhouse gases, and a greater sensitivity to the risks they pose.

There have been two international agreements to reduce emissions of greenhouse gases, in Rio in 1992 and in Kyoto in 1997. In the first, industrial countries undertook voluntary commitments to reduce their level of emissions in 2000 to the level in 1990. The 1997 agreement set more ambitious goals, and more binding commitments (though it too lacked effective enforcement measures). Developing countries have resisted entering into binding commitments, and without their agreement several industrial countries, such as the United States, are reluctant to impose binding commitments upon themselves. Moreover, without adequate global enforcement (including monitoring) countries with stronger legal structures would wind up bearing inequitable burdens once treaties were ratified.

The Rio Convention defined emissions levels for countries relative to their past history; thus, countries that polluted more were allowed to continue to pollute more. For developing countries, this seemed unjust: why allow industrial countries to emit higher levels of emissions per capita (albeit lower levels of emissions per unit GDP) simply because they had done so historically?

While these equity issues were not effectively addressed at Kyoto, the Kyoto convention made an important step forward in trying to ensure efficiency in reducing emissions, through the Clean Development Mechanism. That scheme would allow industrial countries to help developing countries lower their emissions, while granting the industrial countries some "credit" for these lower emissions. Chapter 4 explores such issues and the possible course of institution-building.

Protecting biodiversity

The evidence on biodiversity loss is growing. The United Nations Environment Programme (UNEP) estimates that about 22 million species exist at the end of the 20th century. About 1.5 million have been described. Some 7 million species, or more than four times the number described, risk extinction in the next 30 years. Among higher animals, three-fourths of the world's bird species are declining, and some observers claim that nearly one-fourth of the world's mammal species are threatened with extinction.[62] In agriculture, crop plant varieties disappear every year, but few of these crops are represented in world collections of genetic material. Wild varieties are even more poorly represented. Only 12 of the 38 base collections of rice listed in the International Board for Plant Genetic Resources (IBPGR) directory of genetic material include wild species, and only 5 collections have long-term storage facilities.[63]

The major causes of biodiversity loss are modern farming techniques, deforestation, and the destruction of wetland and ocean habitats, all of which are closely linked to development activities. Of all the world's countries, developing countries are richest in biodiversity, in part because many are in tropical climes. The pressure on these countries to protect biodiversity is severe. Just one-fifth of the earth's original forests remains in large, relatively natural ecosystems, or frontier forests. Seventy-six countries have lost all of their frontier forest, and 70 percent of what is left is found in just three countries—Brazil, Canada, and Russia. Ninety percent of the remaining crop species are in Africa, Asia, and Latin America.[64] Despite these worrying trends, however, international agreement on preserving biodiversity is only beginning. Nonetheless, the Convention on Biological Diversity and the Global Environment Facility are important first steps in the process of preserving biodiversity.

New political tendencies in developing countries

Along with the wave of globalization in trade, finance, and environmental issues, another worldwide force is reshaping development efforts everywhere—localization. Localization is the push to expand popular participation in politics and to increase local autonomy in decisionmaking. The impetus toward local autonomy stems in part from another global trend—urbanization.

What are the main elements of the new local landscape? One is the replacement of authoritarian or single-party rule by plural politics and the increase in citizen participation through community groups and NGOs. Another is a growing demand for substantial power and autonomy on the part of subnational units. Central governments have responded to this demand by devolving power and responsibility to local levels.

Plural politics and broad-based popular participation are rapidly becoming features of modern governance. The proportion of countries with some form of democratic government rose from 28 percent in 1974 to 61 percent in 1998. (figure 1.7). A majority of governments have made legally binding commitments to respect the civil and political rights of their citizens. Thus far, 140 countries have ratified the International Covenant on Civil and Political Rights, and 42 have signed the optional protocol of the covenant, recognizing the authority of the United Nations Human Rights Committee to consider claims from those alleging violations of their rights.

As people's participation in society grows, so does the number of organizations that give it voice. NGOs and civic movements are on the rise, assuming an ever-larger role in articulating people's aspirations and pressuring governments to respond. This swelling of participation promises to be of even greater

Figure 1.7
More countries are becoming democratic

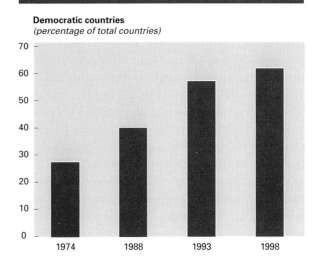

Democratic countries
(percentage of total countries)

Source: Diamond 1996; Freedom House, *Freedom in the World*, 1998.

significance than elections. It will affect the process of institution-building and the types of policies that are likely to be effective. With power decentralized and the central government less able to impose its own solutions, the demand for socially oriented policies will grow.

What will the push for increased citizen participation and plural politics mean for development? Four changes are likely. First, vigorous political activity involving many organized groups rooted in assertive societies will substantially reduce the scope for autonomous government action. The central government will have to engage and negotiate with society, field claims and pressures from diverse quarters, and seek legitimacy by winning public approval for its performance. There will be less room for close business dealings, more calls for accountability, and a continuing move away from the authoritarianism practiced in various parts of the world between the 1960s and the 1980s.

However, this change has far-reaching implications. Taking swift policy action to adjust to shocks may become increasingly difficult. Efforts to promote strategic sectors that also benefit special interests will come under close scrutiny—and not only from the electorate. The business community, labor unions, and others may serve as checks on the central government's authority. The Korean government learned of the power of these groups when it tried to push through a new labor code in 1997 and attempted to restructure large industrial conglomerates in 1998–99.

Recent events underscore the significance of the new political landscape and the difficulties international financial organizations face in negotiating agreements that can have adverse consequences for segments of a country's population, at least in the short term. The Russian and Brazilian parliaments refused to go along with international pledges made by their presidents during the East Asian crisis. Their reaction prompted U.S. Treasury Secretary Robert Rubin to remark that when it comes to saving countries from economic implosion, "the ultimate key is not economics or finance, but politics." Governments must learn to muster support for strong policies, especially when those policies require sacrifices by present generations for the generations yet to come.[65]

Second, political openness will highlight the disclosure of information and the emergence of the private monitoring, regulatory, and information-processing entities that are vital to a dynamic economy. These entities may include private mechanisms for enforcing public laws like those suggested for the countries of the former Soviet Union.[66] Authoritarian regimes tend to become predatory and, except in rare cases, have not succeeded in creating efficient, technocratic bureaucracies or in single-mindedly pursuing development. These failures are partly attributable to the temptations offered by patronage, political interference in the operations of public agencies, and the politicizing of bureaucrats at all levels. Plural politics and civic participation can reverse those forces, preventing the worst excesses of authoritarian systems. But good intentions are no guarantee of rapid progress, as India's situation illustrates.[67] Whether opportunities exist for institutional reforms that will encourage these reversals remains to be seen.

Third, participatory politics, by giving more voice to people, will hasten decentralization in some countries. This trend is most likely to be felt in large countries and those with marked ethnic divisions and deeply rooted local identities. Strong urban regions could accelerate the redistribution of central authority to subnational entities, requiring the central government to pursue major, long-term development

goals by consensus. And more responsibility for development may devolve to subnational governments.

Fourth, participatory politics and limited international labor mobility could increase calls for policies that address social dislocation.[68] Until regional and global governents begin coordinating policies to reduce the risks posed by shocks with potentially long-term consequences, national governments will be responsible for buffering their populations against extreme economic hardship. This situation will create a number of dilemmas. In order to finance safety nets, governments will have to adjust the composition of public spending, possibly dampening growth in the short term. Attempts to mobilize additional resources could meet with resistance from taxpayers who mistrust the government's ability to deliver services and are accustomed to a culture of tax avoidance.[69] Chapters 5 and 6 review the preliminary evidence on mobilizing financial and fiscal resources at the local level.

What about the differences among countries? Economic and social instability of the kind that exists in Russia and Ukraine could dampen the desire for change. In Sub-Saharan Africa the small size of the middle class, ethnic friction, and the region's recent history of clientelistic politics hinder the spread of pluralism and the pursuit of development objectives. Demographic pressure is testing African and Middle Eastern countries. In the next 20 years these countries will have to cope with large numbers of young people seeking jobs. Ethiopia's population, for example, is likely to double to 120 million by 2030, and already, more than half the people in Iran are under the age of 25. To sustain economic growth, political and social institutions will need to adapt rapidly to these changes. While the trend toward participatory politics is strong in the 1990s, the institutional reforms vital to future stability may not be keeping pace.

Emerging subnational dynamics

As the 20th century draws to a close, people in subnational units such as provinces and states are demanding the right to self-determination and self-government. Such demands are part of the process known as localization. They may originate in dissatisfaction with a central government, reluctance to subsidize other parts of a country, or conflict between ethnic groups. Whatever its cause, localization generally results in the redistribution of power within a country. It can, under certain circumstances (as in southeastern Europe and Central Asia), lead to the creation of new states.[70] The number of countries has more than doubled in the last three decades, rising from 96 in 1960 to 192 in 1998. And the number of countries with fewer than 1 million people has almost tripled, growing from 15 to 43. When accommodated in a democratic setting, localization involves a shift in the locus of decisionmaking, the structure and quality of governance, and modes of policy implementation. For this reason it is expected to have a significant effect on the future of development.

Localization and decentralization

Governments have responded to demands for increased self-government by sharing power with and devolving authority to lower tiers of government. The action has been grudging at times, more forthcoming at others (especially when financially strapped central governments want to shed expenditure responsibilities). But the trend is clearly continuing, and the numbers speak for themselves. In 1980 national elections had taken place in 12 of the world's 48 largest countries, and local elections had been held in 10 of them. By 1998, 34 of these countries had held elections at both the national and local levels. Half the countries that decentralized politically also decentralized major functional responsibilities (table 1.2).[71] Poland has devolved responsibility for primary and secondary education, for example, while the Philippines has decentralized primary health care and local road maintenance. Decentralization often translates into substantial increases in the subnational share of public expenditure. In Mexico this share increased from 11 percent in 1987 to 30 percent in 1996, and in South Africa from 21 to 50 percent.[72]

Decentralization is not limited to large, wealthy countries. In the Middle East and North Africa, Jordan, Lebanon, Morocco, and Tunisia all have elected local governments. In Europe and Central Asia, the constitutions of Albania, Bosnia, Bulgaria, Croatia, Georgia, Hungary, Kazakhstan, Russia, Tajikistan, and Ukraine address the rights and responsibilities of subnational governments, although this does not automatically guarantee autonomy. The Baltics and the Kyrgyz Republic have also taken significant steps to strengthen local governments.[73] In Africa, 25 of the 38 countries that held national elections in the 1990s also had local elections—and that includes a

Table 1.2

Political and functional decentralization in large democracies, 1997

Decentralizing politically only	Decentralizing politically and functionally
Bangladesh	Argentina
Iran, Islamic Rep.	Brazil
Kenya	Colombia
Korea, Rep. of	Ethiopia
Morocco	Mexico
Nepal	Philippines
Nigeria	Poland
Pakistan[a]	Russian Federation
Romania	South Africa
Thailand	Uganda
	Ukraine
	Venezuela

Note: Sample includes all countries that had populations of 20 million or more in 1997 and that introduced competitive multiparty elections at the subnational level between 1980 and 1995.
a. Local elections have not been held regularly in Pakistan, so local governments have mostly been run by administrators.
Source: Freedom House, *Freedom in the World*, 1996; U.S. Central Intelligence Agency, *The World Factbook*, 1998; country-specific sources.

number of very small countries such as Cape Verde, Mauritius, and Swaziland. In Latin America, every country has elected mayors. Excluding Argentina, Brazil, Colombia, and Mexico (all large federations), local governments account for 20 percent of government expenditures in the countries for which data are available.[74]

The end of the Cold War has been a key factor in the recent wave of decentralization. In the former Soviet Union, dissolution of the party monopoly on national political power has led subnational governments to step up demands for increased local authority. In Eastern Europe the collapse of communism removed the external military support that had been propping up unpopular governments. Local governments rebounded—both in reaction to former regimes' policy of forced centralization and as a bulwark against the return of authoritarianism. The declining threat of a major international conflict, combined with increased openness to trade, has made the advantages of being part of a large federation less attractive to smaller economies.[75]

The end of the Cold War has had effects that are less direct but no less important in other regions. In Latin America the declining threat of leftist violence (the initial grounds for military takeovers) has contributed to the demise of authoritarian regimes throughout most of the region. (In Peru, where the threat of leftist violence did not decline, most spending decisions continue to be made by the presidency.) In Africa and parts of East Asia (Korea and the Philippines), both the United States and Russia have ended their support for authoritarian governments. In a number of African countries, reduced external support combined with domestic economic collapse have undermined authoritarian governments' ability to use public spending to maintain the support of key interest groups. Ruling elites have been forced to concede some power, though often they have relinquished just enough to permit them to retain their hold.[76]

The pace of decentralization and the kinds of reforms that have been implemented vary from country to country. India, a multiparty democracy at the federal and state levels, has relatively weak local governments (see box 5.4). China is still officially a centralized state with a dominant party, though provincial governors and mayors have had considerably more autonomy and managerial authority since the reforms initiated in 1978 (see box 5.5). In a number of countries decentralization has not resulted in the center relinquishing much control.[77] Ghana, Malawi, and Zambia have each created local councils, but the central government continues to direct almost all spending and management decisions. Similarly the ruling national party in Tanzania holds almost all subnational offices. Pakistan convenes local elections, but so infrequently that the country has only rarely had sitting, elected local governments.[78]

Institutional challenges

Localization raises complex institutional and policy issues that governments will have to resolve in coming decades. The expanded power of subnational governments has implications not only for growth and macroeconomic stability but also for governance, coordination, and regulation. It will affect (and be affected by) the availability of international financing, the delivery of public services, the management of social safety nets, and the reduced ability to redistribute that could result in increasing inequality. Rules must be designed that apportion responsibility, manage relations among tiers of government, and strike an acceptable trade-off between central and local authority. The types of rules discussed in chapter 5 are intended to help keep governments ac-

countable and efficient—and to lessen the risk that excessive borrowing and fiscal deficits at the subnational level will cause economic instability.[79]

Development will succeed in localized economies only if subnational units provide sound, effective governance. Good local governance gives people a voice and incorporates rules that ensure the accountability of public employees. By providing citizens with the opportunity to express their views, encouraging them to monitor the workings of local government, and calling on them to participate, an effective system of governance creates a willingness to obey laws and pay taxes.[80] Over time, sound governance builds trust and social capital. Whether in Tanzania or northern Italy, well-governed communities are rich in social capital and adequately furnished with revenues.

In many cases local governments need to develop the skills and resources to provide high-quality services that meet constituents' demands.[81] These services (along with adequate fiscal and financial resources) are what allow cities to perform well economically and to offer their residents a good standard of living. In most cases the private sector will need to be involved in providing services, especially in countries with weak access to international capital resources.[82] But encouraging the private sector to participate requires governments to have in place regulatory structures that minimize transactions costs and barriers to entry but also ensure that private providers deliver with respect to quality, cost, and volume. The good news is that increasing administrative and regulatory capacity and improving governance will allow subnational units to reap the benefits of market-led growth.

Urban imperatives

At the beginning of the 21st century, half the world's population will be living in areas classified as urban. As recently as 1975 this share was just over a third, but by 2025 it will rise to almost two-thirds. The most rapid changes in urban demographics will occur in developing countries (figure 1.8). While the rate of urbanization has passed its peak in relatively high-income countries in Latin America, Eastern Europe, and the Middle East, the transition is just beginning in Asia and Africa (figure 1.9). Urban populations are expected to increase by almost 1.5 billion people in the next 20 years (figure 1.10). The speed of urbanization and the enormous numbers

Figure 1.8
Most urban dwellers reside in developing countries

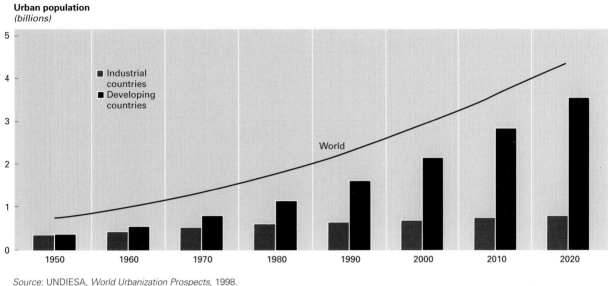

Source: UNDIESA, *World Urbanization Prospects*, 1998.

involved make it one of the major development challenges of the 21st century.

Despite the challenges it presents, urbanization should be a positive trend. In industrial countries economic growth and structural transformation accompanied urbanization. As agricultural sectors modernized, mechanized, and became more efficient, the number of agricultural jobs declined. Workers went looking for jobs in nonagricultural industries, which are generally located in areas with much higher population densities than farming communities—that is, in cities. Wealthy societies in the late 20th century are four-fifths urban and derive less than 3 percent of their GDP from agriculture, while in low-income countries agriculture still accounts for 30 percent or more of GDP.

Can this pattern repeat itself in developing countries, given that urbanization and economic growth in industrial countries took place over a fairly long period and involved much smaller numbers of people? These economies were pioneers, their growth unconstrained by external standards and codes pertaining to labor, human rights, or the environment. The conditions in which developing countries are attempting the transition to urban societies are now dramatically different and, with continuing advances in communications technology, will continue to alter.

The East Asian experience with sustained economic growth and successful rural development suggests that the pattern can be repeated. Korea took just 40 years to transform itself from a society that was 80 percent rural to one that is 80 percent urban.

Figure 1.9
Asia and Africa are just beginning the urban transition

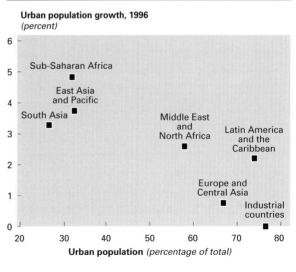

Source: World Bank, *World Development Indicators*, 1998.

Figure 1.10
The largest increase in urban populations during 1980–2020 will occur in Africa and Asia

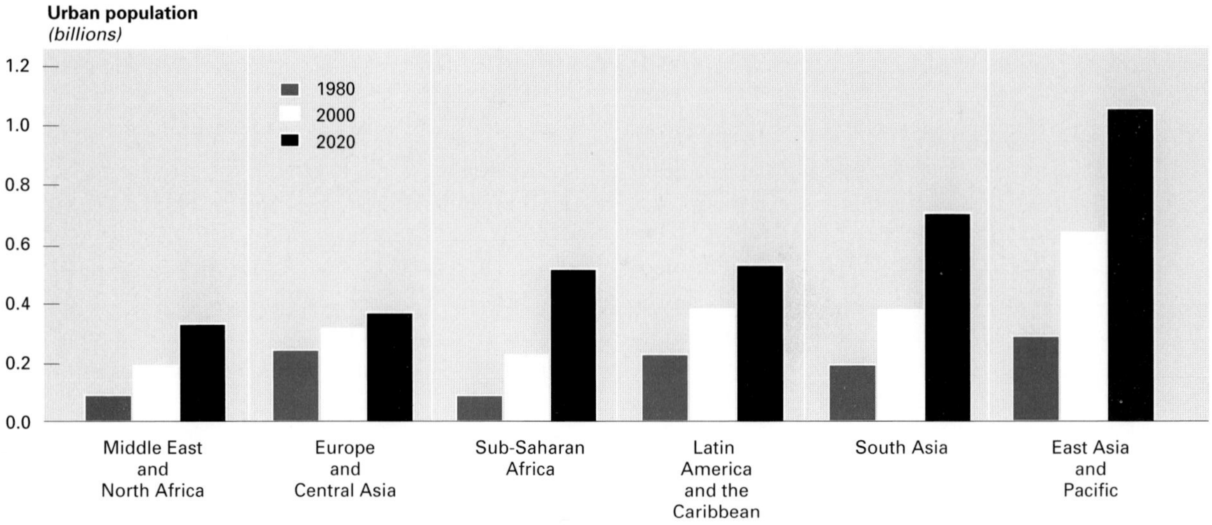

Urban population
(billions)

	1980
	2000
	2020

Middle East and North Africa   Europe and Central Asia   Sub-Saharan Africa   Latin America and the Caribbean   South Asia   East Asia and Pacific

Source: UNDIESA, *World Urbanization Prospects,* 1996.

As it did, the share of agriculture in GDP fell from a high of 37 percent in 1965 to 6 percent in 1996. But elsewhere, the link between urbanization and growth has been less obvious. Famines, civil wars, ethnic conflicts, stagnant agriculture, the absence of rural development, or merely the removal of constraints on mobility can push people to urban areas, which may lack the resources to absorb them productively. Regions such as Sub-Saharan Africa and South Asia, where per capita GDP growth has been slow or flat, have had the most difficulty in absorbing urban newcomers. The relationship between economic growth and urbanization is covered in detail in chapter 6.

Urban centers are expected to offer better access than rural areas to such essentials as water and sewerage and to health care and educational services. The quality of urban living conditions has traditionally been reflected in reduced morbidity and infant mortality rates and increased life expectancies. But since the mid-1980s the advantages urban areas (especially big cities) have enjoyed have been declining. In Sub-Saharan Africa mortality rates are nearly the same in rural areas and small cities—90 per 1,000—and rates in large Latin American cities have risen to those of smaller urban areas.[83]

Access to shelter in urban areas is, if anything, worsening. About 100 million people—including large numbers of children—have no permanent home and simply make use of whatever urban spaces they

can find. More than 700,000 people sleep on Mumbai's pavements.[84] The growth of *favelas* in Rio de Janeiro and São Paulo is typical of what is happening in other large cities in the developing world.[85] Increasing violence is linked to the growing inequality evident in urban areas, most notably in Latin America, but also in South Asia.[86] Immigration may exacerbate this trend.[87] The well off live in fortified enclaves, abandoning entire neighborhoods to the poor—an increasingly common characteristic of cities where the decline in public services and life chances has created an increasingly differentiated urban environment.[88]

In many respects these patterns are a replay of the decline in urban living conditions that occurred in Western Europe during the rapid industrialization of the first half of the 19th century.[89] The second half of the century witnessed a remarkable turnaround. Can historically similar reform strategies help reverse the trends in developing countries, or will urban decay become a permanent feature of municipal areas?

The development community has long been aware of the challenges rapid urbanization poses.[90] But decentralization, globalization, and industrialization will heap new challenges on the old.[91] Some of the most important issues for the 21st century are subnational borrowing for public infrastructure, the coordination of interregional infrastructure, and the location of lumpy investments. Competition for global capital is another issue local authorities will have to contend with, learning, as they do, that probusiness policies must not take precedence over social welfare. National policies that inhibit the mobility of capital and labor are another significant issue. Governments will need to consider revising those policies in order to promote efficient industrialization that allows firms in mature industries to relocate from large to small cities.

During the three decades of development between 1960 and 1990, the concentration of economic activities in urban areas coincided with the rise of per capita GDP. But this trend was merely noted and did not leave a mark on policies or institutional design.[92] Now that globalization and decentralization are reshaping geographic as well as economic landscapes, the relationship between growth and urbanization can no longer be ignored.

Rapid urbanization also has social and political implications. The institutions, social capital, and politics that served a stable, dispersed rural population do not transfer well to cities. Much social capital is lost and needs to be replaced, reconstituted, and augmented. The moral economy of a hierarchical rural society, which provided a measure of insurance against risks, needs to be replaced by urban safety nets, both formal and informal.[93] Middle classes emerge and expand in cities and are subject to demonstration effects from industrial countries.[94] Second- and third-generation urban residents often begin to organize and voice their demands with more assertiveness. Governments need new political and social mechanisms in order to meet rising expectations.

Implications for development policy

If governments do not establish the policies and institutions needed to manage urbanization and provide complementary infrastructure, urban areas could experience slow economic growth and social unrest, and valuable resources will be wasted. Mismanaged cities with inadequate resources and ineffective political processes are unattractive to new industries. They cannot raise the quality of life, and they do not build human capital or attract fresh talent. In addition, unless governments provide a level playing field, small and medium-size cities cannot compete effectively with their larger urban counterparts for manufacturing activity.

The absence of appropriate regulation in rapidly growing urban areas can create inefficient land-use patterns that encourage reliance on private automobiles. Well-designed urban transportation systems not only affect land use but also improve growth prospects by better integrating the urban labor market.[95] Quality of life, which is often measured by the availability and efficiency of public services, is also a major issue.[96] Inadequate investment in sewers and sanitation systems can create serious health problems. Weak land market institutions that fail to clarify and strengthen tenure and ownership rights can hurt the quality of shelter. Karachi, Pakistan, and Lagos, Nigeria, which are experiencing a decline in the volume and quality of infrastructural and social services, are typical of cities where the public sector is on the verge of collapse. These problems require innovative solutions, including public-private partnerships, selective privatization of local functions, and community involvement in regulation.

Cities also face new industrial challenges. Expanded export opportunities and the emergence of "industry clusters" require careful planning to provide the necessary infrastructure and the skilled workforce modern high-technology industries require.[97] The poor quality of urban training facilities has hindered the growth of such industries in Latin America. But skills are only one part of the equation. Industrialization in Kerala, which has the most educated workforce in India, is inhibited by labor militancy, land tenure constraints, and power shortages.[98]

Institutional and regulatory reform in domestic financial markets must reflect not just national and global imperatives but urban infrastructure and housing investment requirements as well. Newly empowered state and local governments must find the means to finance these investments.[99] At the same time, they will need to develop new measures to cope with unemployment, poverty, and inequality. Avoiding urban poverty traps will require building industrial skills and creating a competitive urban economy. Skilled workers could move in search of employment, an important consideration because mobility is sometimes the only recourse for workers in towns where the industrial base is narrow and has been declining. Many urban areas in China, Eastern Europe, and the former Soviet Union, for example, are saddled with failing industries and rising unemployment.

Cities that want to compete for foreign direct investment need to meet world production standards. Being second best can also mean being saddled with high unemployment and increasing poverty.[100] The ease of international sourcing in a competitive milieu with many specialized suppliers has changed labor markets. Because tasks can be combined flexibly, urban production centers worldwide are increasingly segmented between those that can meet the exacting standards of a global production system and those with too few skills to do so. This open production environment mercilessly weeds out those centers with below-par macroeconomic environments, services, and labor-market flexibility.

Urban dwellers also need formal safety nets. In rural villages kinship ties or patron-client relations often performed this function, but as people move to cities, their ties to their home villages weaken. Providing basic services and some income insurance will be a priority for governments in the 21st century. Local authorities and communities may be required to take the initiative in helping build safety nets. But success is predicated on organizational capacity, accountability, and trust. As with the Friendly Societies in Britain in the early 20th century, private and community provision can play a significant role, but only with adequate government support. Community efforts, abetted by responsive local governments, can supplement government resources in other areas as well.[101]

Developing countries enter the 21st century in a world that is being transformed by the forces of globalization and localization. It is a world subject to the wide-ranging effects of demographic change and the movement of populations across countries and to urban areas. It is also a world that confronts an ongoing shift in the climate and loss of biodiversity. These forces are modifying the roles and obligations of national governments. However, developing countries need not and should not be passive respondents to these forces. The discussion in the chapters that follow, along with the specific case studies presented in chapter 8, suggest a number of strong institutional measures that can be taken to benefit from the opportunities offered by these trends, and to limit the risks. In this process, unilateral responses by national governments will not suffice. Instead, there must be a continuing interplay of commitments and responsibilities. Subnational governments will take on responsibilities but will be monitored by the central government. The central government will make commitments, which will be monitored by both the subnational governments and relevant international organizations. Market forces will play a central and vital role, both in providing the engine of economic growth and in responding to the incentives and constraints decided upon by different levels of government. Perhaps most important of all, the citizens of developing countries will partner with governments and nongovernmental organizations and work through open and participatory institutions to shape their own future.

2

The World Trading System: The Road Ahead

Many aspects of globalization have captured worldwide attention in the 1990s, including capital flows, migration, and environmental issues. But for more than a century, the driving force behind globalization has been the expansion of trade in goods and services. And throughout the early decades of the 21st century, trade will continue to drive global integration, especially among developing countries.

Trade is important to developing countries for four reasons. First, it is frequently the primary means of realizing the benefits of globalization. Countries win when they gain market access for their exports and new technology through international transfers, and when heightened competitive pressure improves the allocation of resources. The rising share of imports and exports in gross domestic product (GDP) for Latin American and Southeast Asian countries in 1980–97 attests to a growing exposure to international trade (figure 2.1). African economies have also felt the effects of international trade for some time. Although the continent's share declined during the 1980s, it fell from a high starting point.[1]

Second, the continuing reallocation of manufacturing activities from indus-

trial to developing countries offers ample opportunity to expand trade not only in goods, but also in services, which are becoming increasingly tradable. In a few decades global trade in services may well exceed that in goods.

Third, trade is intertwined with another element of globalization: the spread of international production networks. These networks break up sequential production processes, which traditionally have been organized in one location, and spread them across national borders. This dynamic will result in further geographic dispersion of production and increased trade among cities, regions, and countries. Increasingly, the fortunes of the new production venues are bound together by trade.

Fourth, the growth of trade is firmly buttressed by international institutions of long standing. The World Trade Organization (WTO), built on the legacy of the General Agreement on Tariffs and Trade (GATT), is the latest step in creating a commercial environment more conducive to the multilateral exchange of goods and services.[2] The GATT and WTO have served as the means of securing past gains through multilateral trade liberalization. But more important, the

Figure 2.1
Foreign trade has increased in most developing regions since 1970

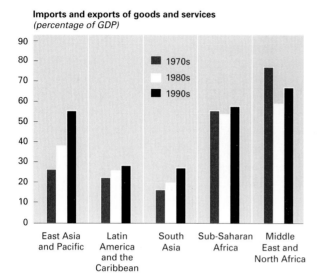

Imports and exports of goods and services
(percentage of GDP)

Note: Data are averages over each decade.
Source: World Bank, *World Development Indicators*, 1999.

WTO can function as the point of departure for future rule-making to promote still greater openness to trade. If trade is to continue expanding as rapidly as it has in the past, and if it is to be of greater benefit to developing countries, the international community must engage in further liberalization and institutional reforms.

This chapter starts by outlining how the global trading system benefits developing countries, and reviewing the impressive record of trade liberalization during the last 15 years. However, the lack of attention given to the social consequences of reform has threatened a backlash against trade, which has the potential to stall this momentum toward reform. The chapter then describes how further trade liberalization in two sectors—agriculture and services—can especially benefit developing countries. The rise of global production networks and cities will also have profound implications for the world trading system—broadening participation in the system and fusing its participants closer together. The chapter ends by analyzing how the pace of and support for liberalized trade in developing countries will be affected by these developments.

How the global trading system benefits developing countries

Trade liberalization benefits economies in two important ways. First, when tariffs are lowered and relative prices change, resources are reallocated to production activities that raise national incomes. The tariff reductions implemented after the Uruguay Round raised national incomes by 0.3–0.4 percent.[3] Second, much larger benefits accrue in the long run as economies adjust to technological innovations, new production structures, and new patterns of competition. These gains will continue to be as important in the future as they have been in the past.

Trade liberalization has other powerful effects. First, it strongly influences the way firms perform. The evidence of its effects on domestic enterprises highlights the benefits developing economies gain from access to world markets.

- Increased imports have been found to discipline domestic firms in Côte d'Ivoire, India, and Turkey by forcing incumbent firms to bring prices closer to marginal costs, thereby reducing the distortions created by monopoly power.[4]
- Trade liberalization can permanently raise the productivity of firms by providing access to up-to-date capital equipment and high-quality intermediate inputs at relatively low prices. Some firms in the Republic of Korea and Taiwan (China), for instance, raised productivity by diversifying their use of intermediate inputs.[5]
- Firms' productivity levels also rise when businesses are exposed to demanding international clients and the "best practices" of overseas competitors. Domestic firms may also benefit from the opportunity to re-engineer foreign firms' products. Indeed, the differences in the productivity levels of exporting and nonexporting firms often diminish once previously nonexporting firms begin selling products abroad, as studies from Colombia, Mexico, Morocco, and Taiwan (China) show.[6]

Second, trade liberalization can set off a chain of events that concentrates economic activity in a city or region.[7] When costs fall as output rises, businesses have an incentive to locate production activities in a few locations, laying the groundwork for "agglomerations" of economic activity. As demand from overseas purchasers boosts output in these locations, average costs fall and profits rise. The rising profits attract new firms that produce similar goods and thus provide a new source of agglomeration. The increase in final goods producers then encourages the entry of new intermediate input producers with products (such as nontradable services) tailored specifically to the needs of the final goods producers. The new inputs make the production of final goods yet more efficient, lowering costs and raising quality (and possibly revenues). Final goods production becomes still more profitable, attracting more producers. The cycle continues until it is curtailed by congestion—that is, when output grows faster than the capacity of local infrastructure. These cumulative processes lead to the higher productivity that characterizes urban areas (see chapter 6).[8]

WTO mechanisms for promoting and maintaining liberal trade regimes

The international trading system owes its robust development to successful institutions that straddle international and national levels—for many decades the GATT and now its successor, the WTO. An effective WTO serves the interests of developing countries in four ways:

- It facilitates trade reform.
- It provides a mechanism for settling disputes.
- It strengthens the credibility of trade reforms.
- It promotes transparent trade regimes that lower transactions costs.

These benefits explain the willingness of developing countries to join the WTO in increasing numbers. In 1987, 65 developing countries were GATT members.[9] In 1999, 110 non-OECD countries were members of the WTO, accounting for approximately 20 percent of world exports (figure 2.2).[10]

Facilitating trade reform

Countries benefit from unilateral reductions in their own barriers to imports. But in a classic dilemma for policy reform, the costs of unilateral trade liberalization are concentrated among a few import-competing interests, while the benefits are distributed thinly across many consumers. The would-be beneficiaries of trade liberalization have little incentive to lobby against the opponents. The WTO exists to overcome this problem—that is, to facilitate trade reform by changing the political equation to generate support for multilateral trade agreements. These agreements create a set of concentrated "winners" in member states—the exporting firms, which benefit from lower tariffs in potential export markets, and which therefore have an incentive to oppose import-competing firms. To maximize the number of winners, multilateral trade negotiations tend to cover many sectors and countries.

Multilateral trade negotiations are not the only means of tilting the political balance to favor trade lib-

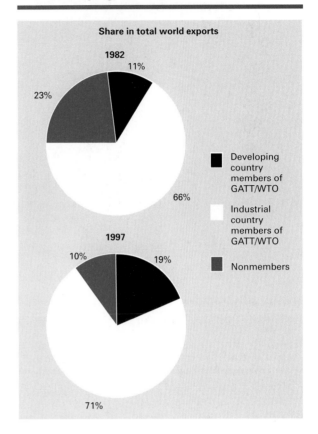

Figure 2.2
More of the world's exports are covered by WTO disciplines, especially exports from developing countries

Source: WTO, *Annual Report,* 1997.

eralization. Growing numbers of industrial and developing countries are signing regional trading arrangements (RTAs), often, but not always, with neighboring countries. Regional agreements have proliferated since 1990, covering not only trade in goods but also trade in services, investment regimes, and regulatory practices (figure 2.3). This regionally based liberalization has increased intraregional trade and investment flows.[11] In some cases the regional concentration of trade has become pronounced. In 1992 trade among the members of the Andean Community—Bolivia, Colombia, Ecuador, Peru, and Venezuela—was 2.7 times higher than their economies' national incomes and geographic separation would typically generate (box 2.1).[12]

Encouraging countries to resolve their disputes through negotiation

The dispute settlement mechanism of the WTO benefits developing economies.[13] Initially, members of the

Figure 2.3
More regional trading arrangements (RTAs) came into force in the 1990s than ever before

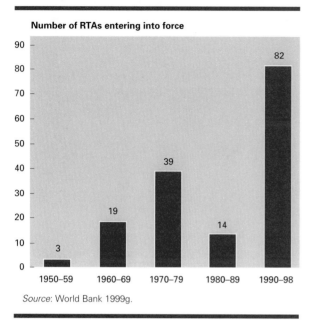

Source: World Bank 1999g.

WTO undertake to settle disputes bilaterally. But if this process fails, a dispute can be referred to an international panel for adjudication. If the panel votes to uphold the complaint, it can recommend that the offending measure be removed.[14] If the country against which the complaint has been lodged does not comply with the panel's ruling, the complainant can apply for permission to retaliate by withdrawing trade concessions.

In principle, the dispute settlement mechanism makes it easier to enforce the numerous trade agreements that fall under the WTO umbrella. But due to the costs and expertise required to mount a case, and the limited leverage gained by shutting a trade partner out of a small market, more often than not the dispute settlement mechanism is of greatest benefit either to large developing countries or to several small countries acting in concert. Still, in certain areas the mechanism particularly benefits developing economies. For instance, many of the liberalizing measures affecting the textile trade that were agreed to during the Uruguay Round will be implemented in the first decade of the

Box 2.1
Regional trading arrangements and the global trading system: complements or substitutes?

The growing popularity of regional trading arrangements (RTAs) has ignited concerns that these agreements may undermine the global trading system by discriminating against imports and investments from nonmembers. Critics of regional arrangements argue that this practice would violate a core principle of the World Trade Organization (WTO): that all imports from member states should face the same barriers to trade. Furthermore, eliminating tariffs on imported goods from some countries but not others can be counterproductive. If imports from high-cost producers inside the agreement replace goods from low-cost producers outside the agreement, the importing country will not only lose tariff revenue but will wind up with imports that cost nearly as much as before.

Supporters of RTAs maintain that these agreements have enabled countries to liberalize trade and investment barriers to a far greater degree than multilateral trade negotiations allow. Proponents also argue that regional agreements have gone beyond trade liberalization, taking important steps toward harmonizing regulations, adopting minimum standards for regulations, and recognizing other countries' standards and practices—trends that enhance market access. Some empirical evidence supports each view. Thus, a recent survey concluded that regional arrangements "seem to have generated welfare gains for participants, with small, possibly negative spillovers onto the rest of the world."[15]

Should future research suggest that RTAs are having adverse effects on the world trading system, the arrangements will have to be aligned with the nondiscrimination principle of the global trading system. One response is to pursue further multilateral trade liberalization to limit the margin of preference regional agreements create. Policymakers who believe that their country is suffering because of the rise of RTAs elsewhere thus have a further incentive to support multilateral trade liberalization.

A second response is to alter the WTO's agreement on regional trading arrangements to commit members to phase out any preferential market access within a certain time frame. Such a provision ensures that preferential market access is only a temporary feature of any regional initiative. To make this approach more attractive to members of a regional initiative, they could be offered credit for the reduction in trade barriers, which could be used in future multilateral trade negotiations.

A third response is to negotiate a "model accession clause" for the principal types of RTAs. Such clauses contain a set of conditions nonmembers must meet in order to become members. Meeting the conditions automatically triggers a negotiation for accession to the regional agreement. These clauses could also ensure that the trade barriers nonmembers face do not rise when an RTA is established or when new members are admitted.

Source: Baldwin and Venables 1995; Bhagwati 1991; Fernandez and Portes 1998; Frankel 1997; Panagariya 1999; Panagariya and Srinivasan 1997; Primo Braga, Safadi, and Yeats 1994; Schiff and Winters 1998; Serra and others 1998; Wei and Frankel 1996; World Bank 1999g; Yeats 1996.

21st century.[16] In this case the dispute resolution mechanism can play a significant role in ensuring that developing countries are still able to expand their textile exports. The dispute settlement mechanism can also be used to protect developing countries from the imposition of banned market-closing measures, such as pressure to agree to "voluntary" restraints on their exports, or the improper use of permitted market-closing measures, such as the use of sanitary standards as a barrier to trade rather than a protection for public health.[17]

Reinforcing the credibility of trade liberalization

Countries that have a history of import substitution policies—that is, of imposing barriers to imports with the intention of producing the same goods domestically—may want to signal that they have switched to a more liberal trade policy. In this case the WTO's tariff-binding option may prove particularly useful.[18] A WTO member can unilaterally reduce its trade barriers to some new level and then promise that future trade barriers to imports from all other WTO members will be no higher than this new, lower level. This promise, known as a "binding," is incorporated into the country's obligations at the WTO. Binding reinforces the political will to maintain a more liberal trade policy, even in the face of attempts by import-competing firms to reverse the reforms. If a country reneges on its obligations, WTO rules require that it offer compensation to trading partners whose interests have been adversely affected.[19]

In the past 15 years, largely because of the environment created by the GATT and WTO, many developing economies have unilaterally reduced their trade barriers. The trend toward outward-oriented trade policies is not confined to any one continent or region, and it predates the completion of the Uruguay Round (figure 2.4). For example, between 1988 and 1992 Kenya reduced its average tariff rate from 41.7 to 33.6 percent. The credibility of such unilateral trade reforms plays a crucial role in their success. The private sector and international investors react less favorably to an announced trade liberalization if they believe that the reforms are likely to be reversed at the first sign of import surges, current account difficulties, or recession.

Only a few countries have bound their unilateral trade reforms, typically during a subsequent multilateral trade round.[20] An additional incentive for binding unilateral reforms might be to give explicit credit in subsequent multilateral trade negotiations to developing countries that "bind" their unilateral reforms before those negotiations begin. The advantage of these inducements was apparent in the Uruguay Round negotiations, when credit was given informally for such bindings. Developing economies that bound substantial unilateral reforms received $1.50 of tariff concessions for every $1 they offered, significantly more than the $1.10 received by countries that had not undertaken unilateral reforms.[21] Codifying this informal system would reduce uncertainty about the benefits of using this commitment mechanism.

Promoting transparent trade policy regimes

The WTO's Trade Policy Review Mechanism, created in 1989, is designed to enhance the transparency of trade policy regimes worldwide. Depending on a country's share of world trade, its trade policy regime is reviewed every two, four, or six years. Representatives from member states discuss the results of these reviews in a forum that provides a nonconfrontational atmosphere for discussing trade practices.[22] This process reduces the incentive for governments to adopt and retain trade policy measures that contravene international rules, especially those countries with the largest shares of world trade. Such mechanisms not only nudge governments to comply with WTO commitments but also lower tensions among members.

Building technical capacity in trade matters in least-developed countries

The growing number and complexity of the issues negotiated at the WTO have prompted questions about the adequacy of the technical expertise available to developing countries in their national capitals and at their missions in Geneva.[23] In 1997 industrial countries deployed an average of 6.8 officials to follow WTO activities in Geneva. Developing countries sent an average of 3.5 (figure 2.5). Because they are not as well represented, developing countries may have difficulty negotiating the most favorable trade agreements and using the dispute settlement mechanism effectively. To tackle this problem, the World Bank, in conjunction with other multilateral institutions, has developed the Integrated Framework for Trade and Development in the Least-Developed Countries. The aim of the framework is to prepare developing countries to participate effectively in the WTO (box 2.2).

Sustaining the momentum for trade reform

The successful completion of the Uruguay Round of multilateral trade negotiations and the growing popu-

Figure 2.4
Many developing countries started liberalizing before the end of the Uruguay Round

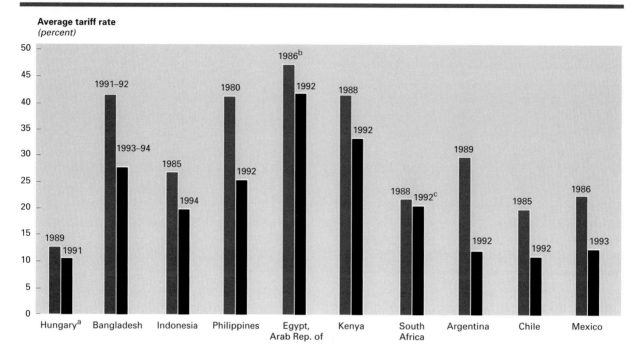

Note: This figure focuses on pre-1994 tariff rates because reductions in the average tariff rate after 1994 could be due to the implementation of the Uruguay Round.
a. Data are from the European Commission's Market Access database.
b. Trade-weighted average.
c. Manufacturing-sector average.
Source: Drabek and Laird 1998.

larity of RTAs have created considerable momentum for integrating countries further into the global trading system. Policymakers in developing and industrial countries now confront the task of maintaining this momentum. Concerns about the effects of trade have received much attention in recent years, including worries over inequality, poverty, the environment, and the financing of social safety nets.[24] Even though the empirical evidence almost always fails to validate these concerns, policymakers have become increasingly sensitive to them.

Recent concerns about the pace of trade reform

Developing countries are indeed exporting more to their industrial counterparts. As early as 1990, many industrial countries had seen substantial increases in the ratio of their merchandise imports to merchandise output, leading to even greater competition for sales in their markets.[25] The composition of developing countries' ex-

ports has changed, too, creating increased competition in manufactured products, especially in medium- and high-technology goods. For example, the share of high-technology products exported by East Asian economies increased substantially between 1985 and 1996. Meanwhile, Latin American countries and India have shifted their exports from resource-based manufactures to low- and medium-technology exports (figure 2.6). The quality of exports from the Czech Republic, Hungary, Poland, and the former Yugoslavia in engineering, clothing, textiles, and footwear products has also improved in the 1990s.[26]

These heightened competitive pressures enhance overall national welfare, but they are not well received by import-competing firms. These firms are already leading a reaction against trade liberalization in both developing and industrial countries. In addition to lobbying policymakers, import-competing firms use antidumping laws—which are still permitted by WTO

Figure 2.5
Equal players? African representatives at the WTO

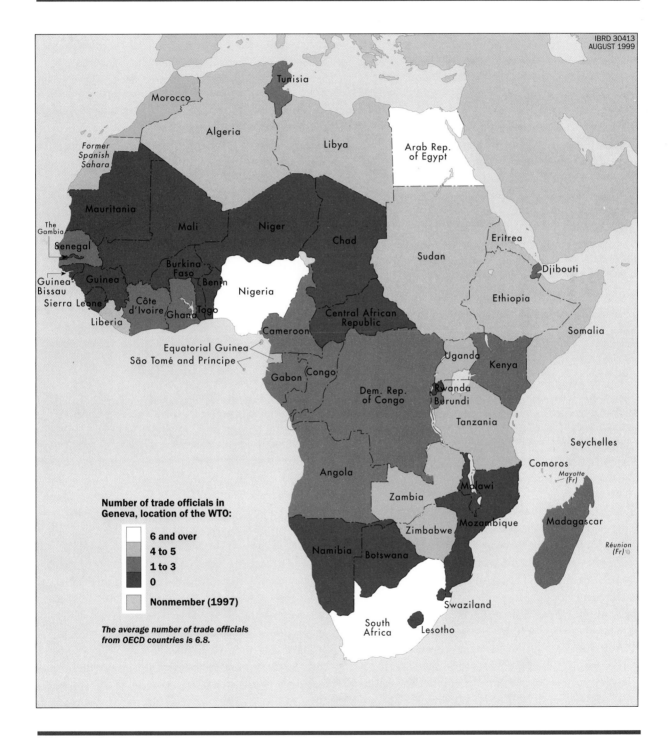

Note: Data are for 1997. Mauritius, which is not pictured, had four officials in Geneva.

Box 2.2
Building technical expertise on trade policy: the Integrated Framework
for Trade and Development in the Least-Developed Countries

The Integrated Framework for Trade and Development in the Least-Developed Countries, a partnership among multilateral agencies and least-developed countries, provides assistance in integrating these countries into the global economy. The framework was initiated by the 1996 World Trade Organization (WTO) Ministerial Declaration, which asked WTO member countries to provide enhanced market access for the least-developed countries. The declaration also requested that the multilateral institutions involved—the WTO, the World Bank, the International Monetary Fund, the United Nations Development Programme, the United Nations Conference on Trade and Development, and the International Trade Center—provide an integrated framework for trade-related assistance.

The framework includes initiatives to build infrastructure, streamline the business environment, ensure the efficiency and transparency of customs administration, increase governments' capacity to develop effective trade policies, and enhance the private sector's ability to identify and operate in export markets. The framework also aims to enhance least-developed countries' participation in the WTO so that they can take a more active role in the day-to-day workings of the organization and help set the agenda for the next round of multilateral negotiations.

In establishing the framework, the WTO invited each least-developed country to submit a needs assessment for trade-related assistance, including for physical infrastructure, human resource development, and institutional capacity building. In their assessments of the major obstacles to trade expansion, most countries identified supply-side constraints and a lack of technical capacity. The countries will update and rank their needs to produce multiyear programs of trade-related assistance that will be presented at donor consultations on trade matters. For each participating country, this consultation will produce concrete pledges constituting a firm program of trade-related assistance.

Of the 48 least-developed countries, 40 have already presented their needs assessments. Uganda has already implemented its program of trade-related assistance, and 16 other countries have been preparing similar programs for a 1999 donor consultation on trade matters. The discussion of the multiyear program at the Consultative Group meeting in Kampala in December 1998 raised the profile of the Integrated Framework. Several donors are prepared to support aspects of the program, including the U.S. Agency for International Development and the U.K.'s Department for International Development. Country teams from multilateral agencies assist the least-developed countries whenever requested.

Uganda's experience demonstrates just how much this framework can contribute to a developing country. Uganda presented its multiyear program of trade-related assistance at the Consultative Group in 1998. The World Bank's resident mission in Uganda created the operational process for the program, using existing sector investment projects in education, health, and roads. A steering committee led by the trade ministry reviewed the needs assessment, ranking items according to the country's general priorities. The presence of donors and private sector representatives on the steering committee facilitated a consensus and ensured full financing of the priorities the program had identified.

---

rules—to allege unfair trade practices by foreign competitors. A good is said to be dumped if its export price is less than either the price in its home market or the average cost of production. Antidumping laws enable countries to impose offsetting duties on the products of foreign firms found to be both dumping products on the domestic market and causing "material injury" to a domestic industry.[27]

Until the early 1990s the main users of these laws were Australia, Canada, the European Community (as it was then), New Zealand, and the United States. However, these countries have been joined by a number of new users, primarily developing economies such as Argentina, Brazil, India, Korea, Mexico, and South Africa (table 2.1). In the late 1980s developing countries initiated less than 20 percent of all antidumping actions. By the late 1990s they accounted for around 50 percent (figure 2.7). Developing countries have also become the targets of antidumping actions at close to the rate of industrial countries (figure 2.8). Antidumping actions are becoming a widespread phenomenon, diluting market access and the gains from trade liberalization.[28]

The reaction against increased competition from imports is not limited to antidumping suits. Concerns have been raised that rising import competition is adversely affecting labor market outcomes and, in particular, causing the widening income inequality observed in some industrial economies.[29] These concerns have led to calls to slow, halt, or even reverse trade liberalization in industrial economies—actions that would directly affect the number and size of export markets open to developing countries.

The link between increases in imports and rising income inequality is highly controversial. With a few exceptions, empirical research has found that imports from developing countries have relatively limited effects on wages and employment in industrial countries.[30] This research does not deny that income inequality is

Figure 2.6
**The composition of many developing countries'
exports was transformed in just over 10 years**

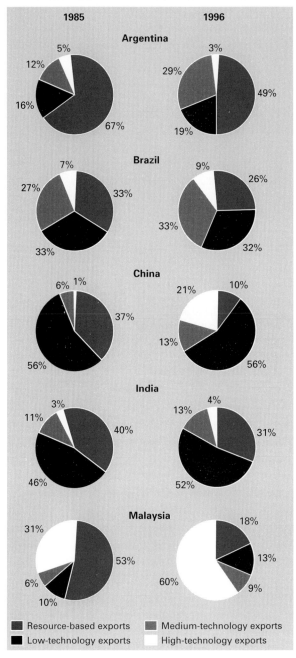

1985   **1996**

Argentina

Brazil

China

India

Malaysia

■ Resource-based exports   ▨ Medium-technology exports
■ Low-technology exports   ☐ High-technology exports

Note: Export groups are based on the use of scientists and engineers
in production and on the amount of research and development activity
required. *Resource-based exports* are unfinished raw products. *Low-
technology exports* are typically labor-intensive manufactures with low
worker-skill requirements, such as textiles, garments, and footwear.
Medium-technology exports are products that entail fast-moving production technologies and some design effort, such as automobiles, chemicals, industrial machinery, and consumer electronics. *High-technology
exports* are products that combine intensive use of highly skilled employees with substantial research and development; examples include fine
chemicals and pharmaceuticals, aircraft, and precision instruments.
Source: Lall 1998.

increasing, but it does suggest that, because increased
trade is not a primary cause, erecting new trade barriers is unlikely to solve this pressing problem.[31]

Sustaining reform by treating import competition on a par with domestic competition

The widening use of antidumping actions against foreign firms threatens to undermine one of the key benefits of global trade rules: stable and predictable access
to foreign markets.[32] Even though there is no economic
rationale for doing so, antidumping laws treat the effects of competition from foreign firms differently from
those of competition from domestic firms. The parity
between foreign and domestic firms could be restored
by an international agreement to eliminate antidumping laws and to apply national competition policy laws
to import competition. That is, if an antitrust issue
exists—such as predation—deal with it, but otherwise
leave pricing decisions to individual firms.

Sustaining reform by easing the adjustment to trade liberalization

Supporters of trade liberalization should give greater attention to developing social safety nets and to education and retraining policies that facilitate labor market
adjustment to internal and external shocks.[33] Augmenting trade liberalization policies with complementary
labor market policies that ease adjustment will reinforce
social cohesion and help offset pressures to close domestic markets to foreign goods.[34]

Research into innovative public policies that reduce
the costs of economic adjustment continues. "Income
insurance," for instance, would compensate workers in
the short term for part of any income they lose because
of economic adjustment to liberalization. Such a program reduces the pain of job loss while preserving the
incentive to look for employment.[35] However, there is
little economic justification for treating workers affected by trade competition differently from workers
affected by domestic competition, macroeconomic
shocks, the adoption of new technology, or any other
form of economic adjustment. Economic adjustment
policies should aim to reduce the adverse impact of all
shocks, irrespective of their source.

Sustaining reform by directly tackling labor conditions in developing countries

Labor practices in developing countries have received
much publicity recently, thanks largely to the efforts of
nongovernmental organizations (NGOs). Multinational

Table 2.1
Reported antidumping actions by members of the GATT and WTO, 1987–97

	1987	1988	1989	1990	1991	1992	1993	1994	1995	1996	1997
New users	24	17	19	20	48	70	162	114	83	148	115
Traditional users	96	107	77	145	180	256	137	114	73	73	118

Note: Traditional users of antidumping laws are Australia, Canada, the European Community (and its successor, the European Union), New Zealand, and the United States. This classification is taken from the source. New users are Argentina, Brazil, India, the Republic of Korea, Mexico, and South Africa.
Source: Miranda, Torres, and Ruiz 1998.

corporations are particularly in the spotlight. Damaging reports have emerged of workers laboring for a fraction of the minimum wage in industrial countries in facilities that fall far short of the safety standards of high-income countries. This publicity has generated strong demands for incorporating international labor standards into the WTO, with trade sanctions to enforce them.[36] The debate on the merits of this proposal is intense, but the evidence that lower labor standards boost export

performance is weak.[37] Moreover, imposing trade sanctions on imports from developing countries—especially in labor-intensive industries—will lower wages and worsen working conditions in those countries, not improve them. Better alternatives to imposing trade sanctions exist, including aid programs to improve labor conditions. In addition, developing economies can take steps themselves to improve the conditions of working people, including children (box 2.3).

Sustaining reform by preserving the legitimacy of global trade rules

The number of disputes among WTO members is likely to increase in the future, thanks to growing competition in the services and goods markets and the wider scope of multilateral trade rules. NGOs, subnational governments, and even private sector firms will want to be included as participants in the dispute settlement mechanism.[38] If this pressure is not handled well, the legitimacy of global trade rules will be called into question.

A first step in maintaining the legitimacy of global trade rules is to make more resources available for the WTO to implement its dispute resolution mechanism. Several other reforms are also worth considering.[39] Dispute panels could be allowed to take evidence from groups other than governments so that all interested parties can be heard. In addition, regular WTO ministerial meetings can review the ongoing case law that will result from the dispute resolution mechanism, resolving the inconsistencies that disputes might reveal in the provisions of WTO agreements.

International trade and development policy: the next 25 years

International trade institutions and liberal trade policies are a means to an end. They boost trade in existing and new products, enhancing competition in markets, stim-

Figure 2.7
New users initiated an increasing number of antidumping suits during 1987–97

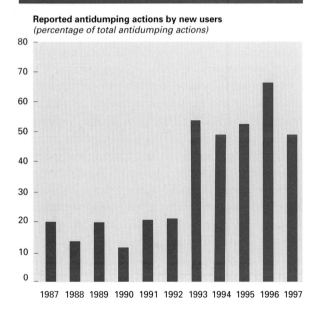

Reported antidumping actions by new users
(percentage of total antidumping actions)

Note: Traditional users of antidumping laws are Australia, Canada, the European Community (and its successor, the European Union), New Zealand, and the United States. This classification is taken from the source. New users are Argentina, Brazil, India, the Republic of Korea, Mexico, and South Africa.
Source: Miranda, Torres, and Ruiz 1998.

Figure 2.8
When filing antidumping investigations, industrial and developing countries target each other almost equally

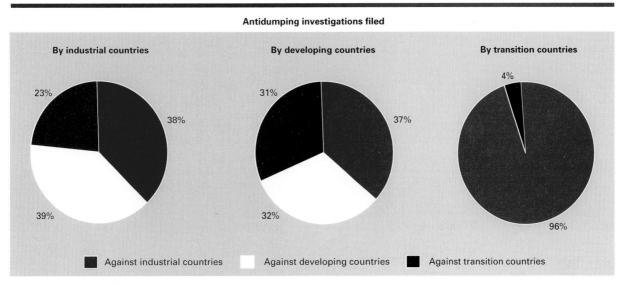

Antidumping investigations filed

By industrial countries

23%
38%
39%

By developing countries

31%
37%
32%

By transition countries

4%
96%

■ Against industrial countries   □ Against developing countries   ■ Against transition countries

Source: Miranda, Torres, and Ruiz 1998.

ulating productivity, and fostering technology transfer. All these developments in turn increase social welfare. The experience of the last 50 years demonstrates that global trade rules enhance the benefits of unilateral trade liberalization by reinforcing incentives to lower trade barriers and avoid policies that constrain trade.

The global trade regime does face challenges (as discussed above) that must be tackled in order to make further gains. Should these challenges be overcome, what are some of the growth-inducing possibilities? Four such possibilities are likely to be uppermost in the early decades of the 21st century: agricultural trade, foreign investment and trade in services, international production networks, and commerce arising from urban development.[40] Other possibilities have been discussed elsewhere. For example, devising the appropriate intellectual property rights regime for developing countries was discussed in *World Development Report 1998/99: Knowledge for Development*.[41] The World Bank is not alone in analyzing these issues, as the OECD's 1998 study *Open Markets Matter* shows.

Stimulating trade in agricultural products
In developing countries, agriculture offers opportunities not only for expanding export trade but also for improving the livelihoods of many rural populations, as

the case study on Tanzania in chapter 8 makes clear. The Uruguay Round of trade talks realized only a small part of the feasible gains from liberalized trade in agriculture because countries were reluctant to scale down barriers.[42] Likely opportunities will arise from a variety of sources: changes in consumer habits, reductions in air transportation costs, advances in biotechnology, and the liberalization of global trade rules.

Rising consumer incomes and declining demand for frozen, canned, and other processed food are creating a need for high-value-added products rather than homogeneous bulk goods. Falling surface and air transportation costs enable firms to supply new markets with fresh products. By increasing the variety of available agricultural products, advances in biotechnology may become particularly relevant for developing countries whose climates sustain only a narrow range of basic agricultural crops. These developments expand the range of potential exports as well as the markets to which products can be sold. But exports can be constrained if a country's domestic infrastructure and trade regulations do not permit speedy delivery. Fears about product safety that lead to calls for banning imports of certain foods can also constrain export growth. The long-standing dispute between the European Union and the United States over hormones used in cattle feed is but one example of this

Box 2.3
Child labor: how much? how damaging? and what can be done?

In developing countries about 250 million children between the ages of 5 and 14 work, at least 120 million of them full time. In Asia 61 percent of all children work full time; in Africa, 32 percent; and in Latin America, 7 percent. Around 70 percent of all child laborers are unpaid family workers. Fewer than 5 percent are employed in export-related production. The vast majority of children working in rural areas are engaged in agricultural activities, while urban children tend to work in services and manufacturing.

Though official statistics suggest that more boys work than girls, the main difference is that boys tend to work in more visible types of employment (in factories, for instance), while girls perform unpaid household tasks or work as domestics. When this difference is taken into account, boys and girls work in similar proportions. The intensity of work boys and girls perform may differ, however, with girls working longer hours. This fact is consistent with the common observation that girls in developing countries generally have lower school enrollment rates than boys.

Not all child labor is harmful. Working children who live in a stable environment with their parents or under the protection of a guardian can benefit from informal education and job training. Many working children are also studying, and their wages help their siblings attend school. However, some forms of employment, in particular prostitution and forced or bonded labor, involve working conditions that are hazardous to the children's health, both physical and mental.

The rate of children's participation in the labor force declines as a country's per capita GDP rises. While as many as half of all children in the poorest countries work, the numbers begin falling rapidly as per capita GDP reaches around $1,200. The incidence of child labor also tends to decline as educational enrollment rises and school quality improves, although the cross-country variations in these relationships are large.

Policies that reduce child labor have strong support on purely economic grounds. When children are sent to work at very young ages for extended periods, they do not develop the skills necessary to earn higher wages later in life, and society loses needed human capital. As adults these individuals have low productivity levels that become a drag on economic growth.

Several approaches to reducing child labor have been suggested. They are not mutually exclusive and probably work best in combination.

■ *Reducing poverty*. Poverty is a major cause of harmful child labor. In poor households, children's wages may be essential to the family's survival. Even though poverty reduction is a long-term process, programs that improve the earnings of the poor, address capital market constraints, and provide safety nets can help reduce child labor in the short term.

■ *Educating children*. Increasing primary school enrollments tends to decrease child labor. Making it easier for children to attend school and work simultaneously may be the best approach in rural areas. The school year must be carefully scheduled in these areas in order not to conflict with the peak agricultural season, however. Reducing the cost of education through subsidies, direct payments, and school feeding schemes also gives households an incentive to send children to school rather than to work.

■ *Providing support services to working children*. These services can include meals, basic literacy classes, and night shelters. Since these programs usually concentrate on children working visibly on the street, their scope is somewhat limited.

■ *Raising public awareness*. This approach covers a wide spectrum: improving the general awareness of hazards to working children, raising parental awareness of the loss of human capital associated with child labor, and involving employers, unions, and civil society in efforts to reduce child labor.

■ *Enforcing legislation and regulations*. Most countries have laws and regulations governing child labor, but enforcement is weak. In fact stricter, across-the-board enforcement may end up hurting those it intends to protect by reducing the income of poor families and forcing children into more dangerous and hidden forms of employment. The alternative is to focus legislation on the most intolerable forms of child labor. A new International Labour Organization (ILO) convention targeting the worst forms of child labor—including slavery, prostitution, forced labor, bonded labor, and illegal and hazardous work—was adopted in June 1999.

Many other proposals for reducing child labor—including trade sanctions, consumer boycotts, social clauses and certification, and labeling schemes—are fraught with problems. For example, exports produced in the formal sector are the products hit hardest by trade measures, and one effect can be to force workers (including child laborers) into the informal sector, where working conditions are typically worse. Trade sanctions, which may be little more than a cover for the introduction of protectionist measures, may be implemented in ways that have little to do with child labor. Finally, labeling schemes and social clauses are often impossible to monitor.

The World Bank has taken steps to reduce harmful child labor through its ongoing poverty reduction efforts and the child labor program established in May 1998. The program is the focal point for Bankwide child labor activities and supports initiatives such as child labor reduction evaluations. It draws upon the international experience of labor experts from academia, nongovernmental organizations, and other multilateral and bilateral organizations such as the United Nations Children's Fund (UNICEF) and the ILO.

Source: Fallon and Tzannatos 1998; Grootaert and Kanbur 1995; ILO 1993; World Bank 1999f.

problem. The debate over agricultural trade policy, then, is likely to encompass not just market access but methods of production as well.[43]

The Uruguay Round agreement on trade in agricultural products laid the foundation for future liberalization. Countries agreed to convert nontariff agricultural barriers into tariff barriers and to set their tariffs at or below a certain level (the "bound" tariff rate). Similar maximums were agreed to for export subsidies and domestic subsidies. The advantage of this approach is that it converts a wide range of trade distortions into three observable trade policies, with maximum levels that can be negotiated down over time.[44] Unfortunately, many countries took advantage of this opportunity to convert their nontariff barriers into extremely high maximum tariffs. For three widely traded commodities—rice, coarse grains, and sugar—many governments chose to set their maximum permitted tariff in the Uruguay Round well above the actual tariff collected in 1986–88 (figure 2.9).

There are several reasons why these tariffs are highly damaging. First, by raising domestic prices above world prices, they raise the cost of food to consumers. Second, they increase costs for domestic food processing firms, harming their export competitiveness. Third, the artificial expansion of the domestic agricultural sector increases the demand for resources, making them more expensive for the rest of the economy.[45] These economic costs must be added to those created by export subsidies for agriculture and the taxes that finance these subsidies. Thus, the next round of trade negotiations should seek to negotiate substantial reductions both in agricultural trade barriers and in those market barriers created by state-owned monopolies that trade in agricultural products.[46]

Since agricultural trade barriers distort the allocation of national resources, their removal will induce adjustments that may include migration from rural to urban areas. Moreover, reform may lead to fears about dependence on foreign sources for food. Recognizing the dislocation induced by trade reform reinforces the case for enhanced flexibility of domestic labor markets and for a robust social safety net. Furthermore, during 1996–97 the World Bank provided loans to over 20 countries to smooth the adjustments created by reform. In addition, assistance was offered to countries facing food shortages and other agricultural emergencies.[47]

Advances in biotechnology have introduced a new factor into agricultural trade policy—sanitary and phytosanitary regulations. Sometimes these regulations are

Figure 2.9
Many countries bound their tariffs on agricultural products in the Uruguay Round at levels well above estimated actual tariffs in 1986–88

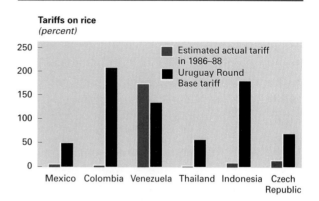

Tariffs on rice
(percent)

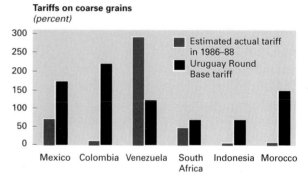

Tariffs on coarse grains
(percent)

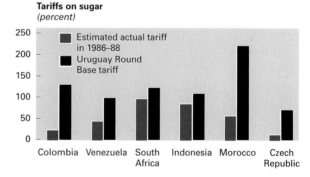

Tariffs on sugar
(percent)

Note: Figure shows selected commodities to which tariffication was applied and that are subject to safeguards.
Source: Hathaway and Ingco 1996.

particularly blunt instruments, imposing restrictions on imports that go well beyond what is needed to protect human health.[48] However, governments often have legitimate concerns about protecting the well-being of their citizens. The Agreement on Sanitary and Phytosanitary Measures that resulted from the Uruguay Round seeks to strike a balance between these concerns and unnecessary restrictions by ensuring that sanitary and phytosanitary regulations do not deliberately discriminate against foreign suppliers. A core requirement is that domestic standards be based on scientific evidence, and nothing prevents those standards from being above international norms.[49] But even seemingly unobjectionable regulations based on scientific evidence can be disputed, and the implementation of the agreement will place further burdens on the WTO's dispute settlement mechanism. Those hearing the cases may well have to assess each protagonist's scientific case as well as the implications for international trade.[50]

Liberalizing trade and foreign investment in services
Changes in technology, demand, and economic structure will make the exchange of services an increasingly important form of trade in the 21st century (figure 2.10). Falling communication costs and the use of common international standards for some professional services contributed to the large jump in service trade that took place in the mid-1990s. Developing countries stand to gain considerably from the liberalization of trade in services, especially in labor-intensive sectors such as construction and maritime activities.[51] The liberalization of services will also promote competitiveness in sectors that use services as inputs to production.

During 1994–97, world exports of services grew by more than 25 percent. Forecasts of the growth in U.S. trade in services suggest that this pace will resume in the early part of the 21st century, after the macroeconomic effects of the East Asian crisis have abated. Much of this growth will come from developing countries in Asia and from Brazil, challenging the dominance of North American and European firms.[52] In addition, the rise of electronic commerce has created new possibilities for trade in services. For example, a leading Ukrainian manufacturer of wind turbines now contracts out all of its administrative and financial reporting to an accounting firm in southern England.[53]

The stakes in service liberalization are high because most industries use services as inputs to production. Manufacturing industries need cheap and reliable access to global communication and transportation networks to maintain export performance. With products becoming increasingly time-sensitive—the result of shorter product lives and the use of "just-in-time" production—foreign buyers must be assured that a supplier can deliver needed goods on time. Inefficient transportation systems (see the case study on the Arab Republic of Egypt in chapter 8) can prevent domestic industries from joining global production networks.

Figure 2.10
Exports of commercial services increased in every region from 1985 to 1997

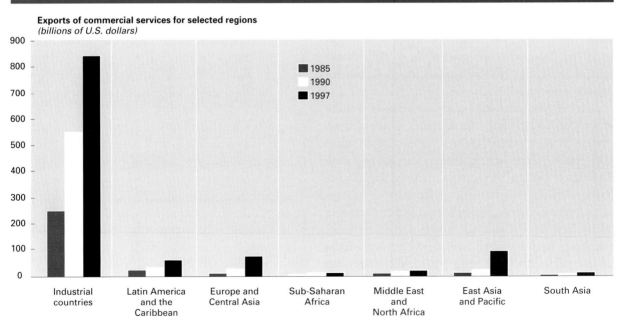

Source: WTO, *Annual Report,* 1996, 1998.

When service firms receive trade protection from foreign competition, they can raise the prices they charge to purchasers, which increases the purchasers' costs. In this case protecting service sectors effectively reduces any protection received by their purchasers—as happened in Egypt in 1994, undermining industrial performance in chemicals, crude petroleum and natural gas (where the services purchased accounted for 89 percent of input costs), and iron and steel.[54]

The same core principle underlies trade policy reforms in both services and goods. Measures that give foreign firms increased access to domestic markets will enhance competition, lower prices, raise quality, and improve social welfare. But trade policy for services must take into account an important issue that does not affect trade in goods. Trade in services generally involves the movement of people or capital across national boundaries, often in the form of new subsidiaries. As a result, opening services to international competition may require changes in policies on border measures (as with tariffs), foreign direct investment (see chapter 3), or migration, both temporary and permanent. Future trade negotiators, like those in the Uruguay Round, face the challenge of refining global trade rules for services that take into account the interactions among these policies.

The Uruguay Round produced an agreement on reducing barriers to trade in services, the General Agreement on Trade in Services (GATS). The principal contribution of the agreement lies in the framework it defines, which mandates the application of certain trade rules across service sectors. These include rules governing most favored nation (MFN) treatment and prohibitions against certain restrictions on suppliers.[55] The framework also defines four supply modes for services: cross-border, which does not require the physical movement of producer or consumer; movement of consumer to producer; permanent movement of the producer (including establishing subsidiaries); and temporary movement of people.

But the agreement leaves a substantial amount of room for future liberalization. The coverage of service sectors and supply modes is limited. The agreement covers only 47 percent of sectors (including the key telecommunications and financial sectors) in industrial countries and 16 percent in developing countries, with numerous exceptions. A revealing measure of the limits of liberalization under this agreement is the percentage of service sectors that will experience full international competition: 25 percent in industrial countries and a paltry 7 percent in developing countries.[56]

Industrial countries tend to have more restrictions on services that require the temporary entry of people or the temporary establishment of businesses—for example, construction services, which is one sector where developing countries have a comparative advantage.[57] Looking forward, there is substantial room for the further liberalization of numerous service sectors in both developing and industrial economies. Since the competitiveness of these sectors differs across countries, negotiations that encompass a wide range of sectors, rather than a few sectors in which one country (or group of countries) has a competitive advantage, offer the most room for trade-offs and mutually beneficial agreements.[58]

Fusing domestic firms into global production networks

The fragmentation of production processes across international borders is an important new trend, particularly for developing economies. This "slicing up the value chain" involves separate stages of production being conducted in different countries.[59] Declining communication costs and improved transportation systems permit just-in-time delivery and the coordination of production across borders.[60] Developing economies can expedite their integration into the new production systems by liberalizing and improving their telecommunications and transportation sectors. Global trade rules have fostered global production networks, and an associated rise in intrafirm trade, by progressively lowering trade barriers and reducing the likelihood of unpredictable increases.[61]

International trade data are useful indicators of the rise in global production networks.[62] More than half the exports of foreign affiliates of Japanese and U.S. firms go to other members of the firms' production networks, and close to 40 percent of the parent firms' exports go to their foreign affiliates. In total, about one-third of world trade in the mid-1990s took place within global production networks. In certain industries the trend is even more impressive. In 1995 components accounted for more than one-third of all transportation and machinery imports to Honduras, Indonesia, Mexico, the Philippines, and Thailand.[63] Similarly, parts and components accounted for more than one-third of total transportation and machinery exports from Barbados, Brazil, the Czech Republic, Hong Kong (China), Nicaragua, and Taiwan (China) (table 2.2).

Table 2.2
Share of parts and components in exports, 1995

Economy	Percentage of parts and components in:		
	Total exports	Exports of manufactures	Exports of transportation and machinery
Singapore	18.2	21.7	27.8
Taiwan (China)	17.4	18.8	36.3
Malaysia	14.3	19.1	25.9
Hong Kong (China)	13.6	14.5	46.2
Mexico	13.0	16.8	24.9
Thailand	10.9	15.0	32.5
Barbados	10.9	18.5	61.6
Czech Rep.	10.6	13.0	36.2
Korea, Rep. of	10.0	11.0	19.1
Slovenia	7.7	8.6	24.5
Philippines	6.6	16.0	29.7
Brazil	6.4	12.1	33.9
China	6.0	7.2	28.8
Croatia	5.4	7.3	32.1
Nicaragua	5.0	24.6	81.6

Source: Yeats 1998.

The creation of these global production networks, either as formal corporations or as part of ethnic diasporas (see chapter 1), helps foster an open trading system. Their supporters can be expected to push for continued liberalization on three main fronts. First, they will argue for the removal of tariffs on parts and semi-finished goods because when these goods cross national borders several times, even small tariffs can accumulate and undermine profitability. Second, proponents will push for improvements in domestic and international transportation systems because substandard communication and transportation act as a tax on profitability.[64] Third, the new production networks thrive on—indeed, they expect—stable, predictable trade and investment policies. For this reason alone, multinational corporations will support effective enforcement provisions in regional and multinational trade agreements.[65]

Developing countries can benefit substantially from their firms' participation in global production networks. However, they must also beware of possible adverse fiscal implications. A large portion of the trade these networks generate happens within firms that are able to realize profits in countries with low tax rates. Countries with high corporate tax rates may attract foreign direct investment but will realize lower profits than they expected.[66] The benefits of these networks to the economy are then partly offset by a smaller national corporate tax base, resulting in increased pressure to raise taxes on incomes that are less internationally mobile, such as labor. Such pressure could in turn undermine political support for open markets. Multinational corporations may appear to be the primary beneficiaries of liberalization, while contributing little to the infrastructure that encourages production networks in the first place.

In response to these concerns and others about the environmental consequences of some types of production and the competitive consequences of mergers by some of the largest corporations, multinationals may face more constraints on their activities. A farsighted approach would be for leading multinational corporations to develop a code of practices on tax and environmental measures that includes enforcement mechanisms similar to those in international trade agreements. Alternatively, a long-term goal could be a unitary tax system that distributes corporate tax revenues among countries according to a prearranged formula.[67]

Urban development, trade flows, and the world trading system

The expected growth of cities is emphasized throughout this report (especially in chapters 6 and 7) as a key factor shaping the future of developing economies. Urban growth, geographic and economic, will affect both trade flows and the international system governing them. One challenge that has already been mentioned requires accommodating more views in international trade forums—including those of urban policymakers—while retaining the rights of national governments to initiate, participate in, and conclude trade negotiations. But many other issues will arise as well.

First, the economic strength of cities is built on agglomeration economies, which enable producers to function more efficiently in proximity to a dense network of information, employees, suppliers, and customers. These agglomeration economies can generate more specialized urban production structures. As a result, urban policymakers also have an interest in preserving market access abroad and at home—abroad for their cities' exports, and at home for intermediate inputs that improve productivity and for consumption goods that may be cheaper elsewhere. The rise of cities as economic and political powers, then, is likely to reinforce support for an open world trading system.

Second, to exploit agglomeration economies, cities will increasingly recognize the need to make progress in several policy areas, not just trade liberalization. For example, the effectiveness and cost of transportation and communications services clearly affect cities' capacity to import and export goods and services.[68] Cities may become a force advocating the simultaneous negotiation of liberalization in many sectors, counteracting the interests of producers who support a sector-by-sector approach to negotiation. Because the number of potential trade-offs across sectors in international trade negotiations is greater than those within sectors, cities may offer increased support for broad-based trade liberalization in the WTO.

Third, while integration into the world trading system offers numerous opportunities for urban producers and consumers, cities will have to bolster their capacity to absorb external trade shocks, such as a collapse in export prices. The range of employment opportunities in cities is wider than in rural areas (where production is often concentrated in a few goods and services) and thus helps absorb some of the effects of shocks on the labor market. However, ensuring that urban labor markets are not overburdened with regulations that prevent them from performing this function is essential to avoiding permanent increases in unemployment. The speed at which information about profitable urban economic opportunities reaches investors can increase cities' capacity to absorb shocks. Again, capitalizing on this advantage requires urban policies that ease the exit and entry of firms, including foreign firms. Ultimately, the rise of cities—especially cities that take measures to minimize the damage wrought by external shocks—may quicken the pace of trade liberalization and the integration of developing economies into the world trading system.

• • •

The impressive trade reforms developing countries have undertaken in recent years have yielded substantial economic benefits. But sustaining the momentum of trade reform will be a key challenge for the next 25 years. The continued liberalization of the agricultural and service sectors, in particular, will deliver considerable benefits to developing economies.

The social consequences of the new openness to trade have been associated with a series of economic adjustments, such as regional and sectoral disparities and internal migration to cities. Labor market institutions, including schemes to enhance labor mobility and raise skills, need to be strengthened in order to smooth the adjustment to trade reform. Policymakers must work to ensure that the considerable gains from trade reform are widely shared among the population, reassuring those who initially suffer from reform that their long-term welfare is secure.

Maximizing the opportunities for development offered by expanding international trade will require a stable and predictable framework of institutions. Codifying the rights, responsibilities, and policies of all parties in broad-based institutions will smooth the path of trade liberalization and development reform over the next 25 years. The upcoming Millennium Round of trade negotiations provides an excellent opportunity to pursue such a wide-ranging approach to trade policy reform.

3

Developing Countries and the Global Financial System

The 1990s saw a huge upsurge in flows of private capital from industrial to developing countries. At the beginning of the decade, private and official flows were about the same, but only five years later private flows dwarfed official flows. Not since the late 19th century have international capital flows assumed such prominence.[1] But there are marked differences between the movement of capital at the end of the 20th century and the movement of capital a century earlier. These differences have important policy implications for developing countries as they integrate into the global financial system.

At the end of the 19th century capital flows financed infrastructure projects such as railroads and direct investment in foreign companies. A hundred years later foreign direct investment is channeled primarily through multinational corporations that are establishing plants and service operations throughout the world. These investments bring with them more than money. They open access to markets, make new technologies available, and provide workers with training. But another type of capital has

appeared—a huge pool of highly mobile money channeled through mutual funds, pension funds, and wealthy individuals that is ready to move across borders at a moment's notice in search of the highest short-term returns.

Countries that open themselves up to these short-term capital flows are discovering that such investments have their costs. Rapid changes in investor sentiment can cause enormous instability, particularly in developing economies. This realization has led to a reexamination of the international economic architecture, raising some important questions: Are the benefits of liberalizing capital accounts worth the costs? Can developing countries find ways to capture the gains from financial globalization without running such enormous risks, which often jeopardize the poorest individuals? The policy response is to calibrate a sequential approach to financial reform that both ensures stability in developing countries and captures the benefits of integration into world capital markets.

This chapter emphasizes the four key components of that approach:

- Developing countries need to strengthen banking regulations and, where possible, build complementary and well-regulated securities markets, if the benefits of domestic financial liberalization are to materialize.
- While banking regulation is being strengthened, policies should be directed to reducing the demand for—and volatility of—short-term foreign borrowing.
- Further international cooperation in setting and implementing fiscal, monetary, and exchange rate policies should be considered.
- Long-term foreign investment should be attracted by cultivating a healthy economic environment—including investing in human capital, allowing domestic markets to work without unnecessary distortions, and committing to a strong regime of investors' rights and obligations—and not by offering subsidies or other inducements.

The chapter examines the mixed record to date of developing countries' integration into the international financial system. It draws from a variety of experiences to identify the principal benefits and risks of global financial integration. Even more important, it proposes national and global responses that can further development goals without jeopardizing financial stability.

The gathering pace of international financial integration

Rapid improvements in technologies for collecting, processing, and disseminating information, along with the opening of domestic financial markets, the liberalization of capital account transactions, and increased private saving for retirement, have stimulated financial innovation and created a multitrillion-dollar pool of internationally mobile capital. At the same time, consolidation in the global banking industry and competition from nonbank financial institutions (including hedge and mutual funds) have lured new players to the international financial arena. These trends accelerated in the 1990s, expanding investment opportunities for savers and offering borrowers a wide array of sources of capital.[2] The same trends can be expected to continue well into the 21st century.

The growing pool of international financial capital

Over the last two decades, the financial markets of leading industrial countries have melded into a global financial system, permitting ever-larger amounts of capital to be allocated not only to their economies, but also to

developing and transition economies.[3] Since 1980 the amount of net foreign direct investment in developing countries has climbed more than twelvefold (figure 3.1).[4] In contrast, net portfolio investment flows have been far more volatile throughout the 1990s, exceeding $100 billion in 1993 and 1994 and falling considerably since then.

Firms in developing and industrial countries alike are raising more funds from international securities markets. Multinational corporations are registering their equity on more than one country's stock exchange and are raising funds from financial markets in different economies. Since 1993 the amount of outstanding international debt issued by all firms has risen by 75 percent, reaching $3.5 trillion in early 1998. Although financial and nonfinancial companies headquartered in industrial countries issue most of this debt, firms in countries such as Brazil, Mexico, and Thailand have also begun to tap the global market for capital—a path others will surely follow (figure 3.2).

This rising number of international capital transactions, together with the substantial growth in interna-

Figure 3.1
Since 1980 net inflows of foreign direct and portfolio investment to developing economies have grown enormously

Source: IMF, *Balance of Payments Statistics Yearbook,* 1998.

Figure 3.2
Firms from developing countries are issuing more international debt than before

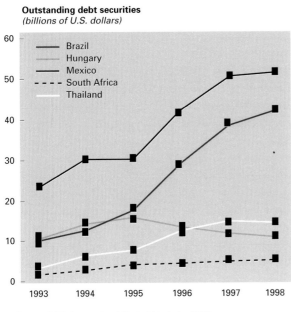

Source: IMF, *International Capital Markets*, 1998.

Figure 3.3
A growing pool of institutionally managed funds is invested abroad

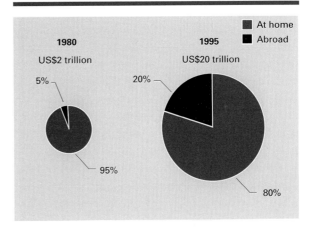

Source: IMF, *International Capital Markets*, 1998.

tional trade in goods and services, has increased turnover on foreign exchange markets eightfold. In 1998 the daily total stood at around $1.5 trillion, an amount equal to around one-sixth of the annual output of the U.S. economy. Financial instruments with very similar risks pay similar returns no matter where they are issued, providing further evidence of the integration of national capital markets. The returns on these instruments varied widely across countries as recently as 10 or 20 years ago.

Mutual funds, hedge funds, pension funds, insurance companies, and other investment and asset managers now compete with banks for national savings. Although thus far this phenomenon has been confined primarily to industrial economies, the consequences for developing countries could be far-reaching. Institutional investors have taken advantage of the easing of restrictions in many industrial countries to diversify their portfolios internationally, enlarging the pool of financial capital potentially available to developing and transition economies. In 1995 these investors controlled $20 trillion, 20 percent of it invested abroad. This figure represents a tenfold increase in the funds and a fortyfold increase in such investments since 1980 (figure 3.3).

Liberalizing capital flows in developing and transition economies

The 1990s have seen a consistent trend toward more flexible exchange rate regimes and the liberalization of capital account transactions. The latter involves changes in policies toward different types of private capital flows, such as foreign direct investment, foreign bond and equity investment, and short-term borrowing from abroad. Developing countries in Asia and the Western Hemisphere, and the transition economies, have moved toward having a single exchange rate, rather than trying to have one rate for those who are exchanging their currency because of foreign trade and an alternative rate for those who exchange currency in order to invest.[5] Old-style rules that used to require exporters to exchange their earnings of foreign currency with the nation's central bank have been relaxed by developing countries on every continent, particularly in the Western Hemisphere and Eastern Europe.

The speed and depth of capital account liberalization have varied across countries, however. Most countries have moved toward capital account convertibility as part of a wide-ranging, gradual economic reform program that includes measures to strengthen the financial sector. But Argentina, the Baltic countries, Costa Rica, El Salvador, Jamaica, the Kyrgyz Republic, Mauritius, Singapore, Trinidad and Tobago, and Venezuela have opened important parts of their capital accounts in one stroke.[6]

In addition to moves toward capital account convertibility, other policies have made many developing countries a more attractive destination for foreign investment: macroeconomic stabilization and structural reforms, privatization policies, relaxed rules on foreign direct investment, and lower interest rates in industrial countries. Rising confidence in the economic prospects of developing countries in the 1990s was reflected in the fact that foreign direct investment accounted for a greater proportion of capital inflows, which signals a commitment to invest over a longer time horizon than portfolio investments like equity holdings.[7]

By 1997 approximately half of all capital flows to developing countries was foreign direct investment.[8] These investments fell slightly in 1998 in response to the East Asian crisis, a change that may prompt many countries to reevaluate their policies toward such investments—and the recommendations developed later in this chapter provide a framework for action. Developing countries are also becoming foreign investors themselves. In 1996 they invested $51 billion abroad, raising their share of global foreign direct investment outflows to 15 percent. Like industrial countries, they invest predominantly in economies in the same region or continent.

Foreign direct investment in service industries accounts for close to two-thirds of such capital flows, while the share of such investment in manufacturing has been falling. Although these aggregate figures conceal differences across countries, the shift toward services is significant. Traditionally, service industries have been less exposed to international trade and so lacked this stimulus to control costs, develop products, and innovate. Foreign direct investment offsets this deficiency by enhancing the degree of competition in domestic service markets and by transferring best practices from abroad (see chapter 2). In addition, firms in developing countries have become more involved in cross-border partnerships with foreign firms—joint ventures with or without equity stakes, franchises, licensing, and subcontracting or marketing agreements. Since 1990 more than 4,000 such agreements have been signed, complementing the flows of foreign investment.[9]

The continuing liberalization of national regulatory frameworks for foreign investment has fostered these capital inflows and interfirm agreements. In 1997 at least 143 nations had frameworks for foreign direct investment in place. Some 94 percent of the regulatory changes since 1990 have actually helped create more favorable environments for foreign direct investment.[10]

A proliferation of bilateral investment treaties reinforced these domestic reforms. Between 1990 and 1997 developing countries were parties to 1,035 bilateral investment treaties, which protect the rights of foreign investors and engender a regulatory environment that promotes investment. Other treaties also reduce investor exposure to double taxation by authorities in the home country of the investor and in the destination of the investment.[11] Argentina, China, the Arab Republic of Egypt, the Republic of Korea, and Malaysia have signed the most treaties, followed by Central and East European countries. More recently, Latin American countries have also begun signing such treaties, starting, as is traditional, with their regional neighbors. By reinforcing commitments to stable national investment regimes, these treaties are encouraging greater international investment flows. In addition, these bilateral treaties are being reinforced by a growing set of regional and sectoral investment accords.[12]

A small group of developing countries has consistently attracted most foreign investment (figure 3.4).[13] Brazil, Indonesia, Malaysia, Mexico, and Thailand have been among the top 12 recipients in each of the past three decades. China (including Hong Kong) joined this group in 1990 and by 1998 had received $265.7 billion in foreign direct investment, making it the most sought-after destination among developing countries. A few African and Middle Eastern countries have been very successful in attracting foreign investment as well, but as a group Africa and the Middle East have received less than 10 percent of foreign direct investment flows. In 1997 the stock of such investment in Africa was less than 2 percent of the world total. For this reason many Sub-Saharan countries will continue to rely on multilateral and bilateral aid to finance investment projects (box 3.1).

Although multinational corporations typically invest in foreign countries in order to sell in domestic markets or to create new bases for exporting, international firms have long shown an interest in exploiting developing countries' natural resources, including oil, minerals, and lumber. Investment in natural resources is often enclave investment. It brings needed capital into a country but offers few of the other benefits—new technologies, new markets, and increased human capital—that are usually associated with manufacturing investment. In many cases, the economic activities such investments entail are located in relatively remote areas, far from other areas of economic activity.

The benefits to developing countries of foreign investment in natural resource exploitation have been

Figure 3.4
A few developing countries received the lion's share of FDI invested outside industrial countries in 1997

Worldwide stock of FDI in 1997 ($3,456 million)

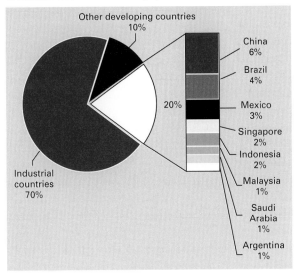

Source: UNCTAD, *World Investment Report*, 1998.

ambiguous, for several reasons. First, the benefits to a developing country may be smaller than GDP indicators initially suggest, as these indicators do not take into account the wealth the country loses when resources are extracted. Second, the resulting economic growth may not be sustainable. In some cases the legacy may be more negative than in others. If gold extraction technologies lace the surrounding environment with cyanide, the costs of restoration can be enormous. In contrast, companies can replant hardwood forests that have been logged.

The kinds of foreign direct investment that are most likely to provide useful benefits and sustainable, long-term growth are associated with manufacturing producer services. Unfortunately even those African countries with a five-year record of good economic policies have found it difficult to attract this kind of investment, in spite of evidence showing that the overall returns in these economies may be just as good as elsewhere.

Financial interruptions to development: banking and currency crises
Even though it is widely accepted that developing countries have substantially benefited from large inflows of foreign direct investment, the far more controversial aspect of capital account liberalization has concerned poli-

Box 3.1
A continuing role for aid

Among least-developed countries, the smallest and most resource poor are the least likely to receive substantial private capital flows. These countries still need official aid flows to finance investments in health, education, the environment, and basic infrastructure. In 1998 net official flows worldwide totaled approximately $51.5 billion.

Aid can be highly effective in promoting growth and reducing poverty. But aid is also a scarce resource that needs to be used well, and using it well requires good decisions by governments and donors alike. Whether aid increases economic growth, for instance, depends on a country's policy and institutional environment. Good macroeconomic management, sound structural policies and public sector administration, and measures that increase equity are all important. They promote growth themselves, and they support the growth-enhancing effects of development assistance.

Development assistance, like so many other economic inputs, is subject to diminishing returns. Even countries with excellent policies are limited in their capacity to absorb such aid. Once official assistance reaches around 12 percent of GDP, its potential contribution to growth is usually exhausted. But few countries receive such high levels of aid, so that only a country's policy environment limits its capacity to absorb development assistance.

While the governments of developing countries determine the effectiveness of aid in the growth process, donors determine how effective aid is in global poverty reduction. For it is donors, not recipient governments, that decide which countries receive assistance. In making this decision, donors need to keep in mind two factors:

■ The extent to which assistance will raise the growth rate, a factor that depends on the policy and institutional environment and thus differs considerably across countries
■ The existing level and distribution of income in the recipient country, since income growth in a country like Chile, where poverty is low, tends to reduce poverty less than it would in a country with mass poverty, like India.

Three-quarters of the world's poor (those living on less than $2 per day) now live in countries where the policy environments are such that additional aid would raise the growth rate. The challenge is to allocate the assistance available in order to take advantage of the favorable climate for growth.

Source: Collier and Dollar 1998; World Bank 1998a, 1999i.

cies (or lack thereof) toward foreign portfolio investment and short-term foreign borrowing.[14] These kinds of flows have been closely linked with the financial and currency market volatility of the late 1990s. Countries with high levels of short-term debt are vulnerable to sudden changes in investor sentiment. The resulting massive shifts in the direction of flows are often too much for even strong financial systems and are certain to have disastrous consequences for weaker ones. The economic crises resulting from such vacillations have imposed enormous costs on the countries involved—costs that have affected not only borrowers but also huge numbers of innocent bystanders. In some cases workers have seen unemployment soar and wages fall by one-fourth or more.[15] Small businesses with prudent levels of debt have found themselves either cut off from access to credit or facing astronomical interest rates few can afford. Bankruptcies have soared, contributing to the economic havoc and destroying information and organizational capital that will not be recovered for years.

In considering the risks inherent in the ebbs and flows of international capital, governments will want to differentiate between liberalizing domestic financial institutions and liberalizing the capital account. Although they involve different policy instruments and pose different risks, both types of liberalization can result in financial instability if they are poorly managed. The past two decades should leave no doubt about the heavy costs of global banking crises. Between 1977 and 1995, 69 countries faced banking crises so severe that most of their bank capital was exhausted.[16] Recapitalizing these banks was extremely expensive, with budgetary costs reaching approximately 10 percent of GDP in Malaysia (1985–88) and 20 percent of GDP in Venezuela (1994–99). These crises can retard the progress of economic growth for years. As the Mexican crisis of 1994 and the East Asian crisis of 1997–98 made clear, banking and currency crises often come as a pair.[17]

Liberalizing the capital account also influences domestic financial stability because portfolio investment can be volatile.[18] Latin America has seen its foreign capital flows rise and fall sharply. Net inflows were $60 billion in 1993, but in the wake of the Mexican crisis in 1995, net outflows reached $7.5 billion. Access to a growing pool of global capital can mean more volatility in emerging financial markets and greater exposure to changes in sentiment by institutional investors in industrial countries, too. Many empirical studies have demonstrated the sensitivity of portfolio flows of foreign capital to interest rates in industrial economies.

Increases in interest rates in industrial countries raise the probability of a banking crisis in developing and transition countries, for three reasons.[19] First, to retain investments from industrial country investors who can now realize higher returns at home, banks in develop-

ing countries must raise their rates. The higher costs are passed on to domestic borrowers, increasing the likelihood of defaults. Second, many firms in developing countries borrow from overseas banks. When such borrowing is widespread, increases in interest rates in industrial countries create a common macroeconomic shock, leaving firms unable to repay their loans to domestic as well as to foreign banks.[20] Balance sheets deteriorate even further when a jump in industrial countries' interest rates leads to a depreciation in a developing country's exchange rate, so that domestic borrowers need more domestic currency to repay their foreign currency debts.

Third, speculative attacks can seriously jeopardize the stability of a developing economy's banking system.[21] A speculative attack on a currency occurs when foreign and domestic depositors suddenly shift their funds out of domestic banks into foreign currency, often leaving the domestic banking system facing a bank run. These attacks take place because investors receive new information that affects the attractiveness of keeping money in a country. And financial contagion tends to occur when a country's economic characteristics resemble those of another country that is known to be in severe macroeconomic difficulties (box 3.2).[22]

Fears of a banking or currency run may be self-fulfilling, creating a macroeconomic crisis that would not otherwise have occurred.[23] During the banking crisis in Argentina in 1995, deposits fell by one-sixth in the first quarter of the year, and the central bank lost $5 billion in reserves. The crisis was attributed in part to the collapse in confidence in Latin American financial markets that followed the Mexican crisis in December 1994.[24] The two recent financial crises in East Asia and Latin America suggest that geographic proximity is an important determinant of financial contagion. "Institutional proximity," or similarities in legal and regulatory systems, and exposure to the same shocks may also be factors. Countries thus have an interest in ensuring that the financial systems and macroeconomic policies of neighboring countries do not increase the likelihood of a financial crisis and induce contagion. Potential spillovers across countries provide a compelling rationale for regional cooperation and coordination in macroeconomic policy, banking standards, and the enforcement of bank regulations—a proposal explored later in this chapter.[25]

Recent cross-country studies find that imposing capital controls has little effect on economic growth.[26] One

Box 3.2
What causes financial contagion?

During a financial crisis elsewhere, contagion is said to have occurred when a country succumbs to a financial crisis for reasons other than a change in its fundamentals. The crises that began in Mexico during 1994 and Thailand in 1997 spread rapidly around the world. These crises had a major effect on financial markets, labor markets, and output in a range of other countries in different regions—even half a world away.

What causes financial contagion?[27] The series of events could begin with a country that experiences a currency devaluation, perhaps as the result of a combined bank and currency run by foreign investors. That country's export goods become cheaper for foreign consumers to buy, and other countries that export the same goods find themselves at a competitive disadvantage. The latter countries then come under pressure to devalue their exchange rates. In 1997 and early 1998 many feared that East Asian countries, in an attempt to shore up export sectors against regional competition, would engage in rounds of "competitive devaluations" that would damage the economic prospects of every country involved.

These sorts of trade and exchange rate effects emanated from the Thai devaluation in 1997 and helped spread the East Asian crisis. But they cannot explain the depth or breadth of financial contagion. An alternative cause, which is disseminated through the attitudes of investors worldwide, is the response of mutual fund managers to country crises. Fund managers can spread financial volatility in several ways:

- Emerging market fund managers often allocate their portfolios across different countries according to percentages specified beforehand. When the value of investments in one country drops, one manager's response might be to sell stocks in other emerging markets to rebalance the portfolio, depressing stock prices and putting pressure on currencies in all the countries in which the manager invests.
- Fund managers facing losses from investments in one country may have liquidity problems, forcing the sale of investments in other markets.
- Investors, especially in emerging markets, find information on the prospects of a company or a country costly to collect. This difficulty encourages herd behavior: the disposal of stock by one investor is assumed to be based on news that is not yet widely known, so other investors interpret this action as a signal to sell their own holdings. The lack of information also encourages investors to take news of poor performance in one emerging market as a signal that bad news is imminent in similar markets.

plausible interpretation of this finding is that the benefits of having access to a global pool of capital—like the opportunity for adding to investment capital or diversifying risks—have been offset by the costs of the crises financial liberalization causes. While cross-country regressions are always open to scrutiny, they do underscore the difference between the evidence on the effects on economic growth of trade liberalization and capital account liberalization. A wealth of studies exists on trade liberalization, all of them suggesting that it has many benefits, but the evidence on capital account liberalization is much more mixed. The challenge is to devise policy and institutional responses attractive enough to lure investments that will have a significant positive impact on growth and, at the same time, to reduce the potential for costly financial crises. The rest of this chapter presents an integrated program to do just that.[28]

Toward a more robust and diversified banking system

Banking systems are especially important for raising and allocating capital in developing countries, where the banking sector typically accounts for a larger share of total financial intermediation than it does in industrial economies (figure 3.5).[29] Cross-country studies point to the beneficial effects of a healthy banking sector on capital accumulation, productivity, and economic growth.[30] This evidence and the frequent banking crises developing countries experience suggest that a robust banking regulatory framework offers substantial payoffs. Such a framework would ensure that bank managers and owners balance the costs and benefits of risk-taking behavior.

Striking the appropriate balance in designing bank regulations is difficult, however. Lax regulation raises the risk that lending will move from the realm of measured risk-taking to foolhardiness. But excessive bank regulation is likely to send funds flowing to the more lightly regulated nonbank financial sector.[31] This sector is less likely to be associated with systemic failures than banks, since severe bank failures lead to difficulties with the payment mechanism. Yet this sector can also breed financial instability, suggesting that at least some regulations may need to extend beyond the banking system to other financial entities.

The growing complexity and diversity of banking activities are straining bank regulatory resources everywhere, but especially in developing countries where these resources are scarce. Private monitoring of banks can complement formal regulations, and only a judicious combination of public and private oversight will allow developing economies to reap all the possible benefits of financial liberalization.

Figure 3.5
Bank intermediation typically accounts for a larger share of the financial sector in developing countries

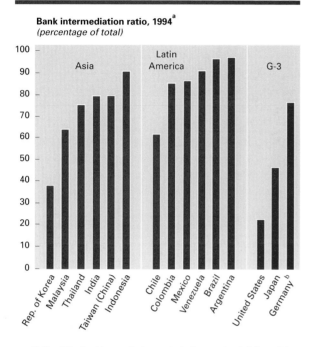

Bank intermediation ratio, 1994[a]
(percentage of total)

a. Ratio of the banking sector's assets to the assets of all financial institutions.
b. The Universal banking system in Germany accounts for its very high bank intermediation ratio.
Source: World Bank 1997c.

In industrial countries an extensive legal and regulatory structure underpins banking operations. Laws protecting the rights of creditors permit banks to lend confidently and to collect deposits. Laws regulate bankruptcy and the recovery of assets and collateral, and judicial proceedings implement such laws quickly and impartially.[32] Accounting and auditing standards help in comparing investment projects and are prerequisites for building efficient bond and stock markets. The rise of international bank lending increases the importance of global accounting standards.[33] And because these legal and professional institutions take years to build, it is important to begin constructing them now. In the meantime governments can develop regulatory frameworks that address some of the special problems of banking activities in developing countries.

Why are deposits insured?
Banks borrow money on a short-term basis from depositors and lend it out for longer periods. Depositors con-

cerned about the security of their money must try to gauge the quality of their bank's lending practices, which determine whether the bank is solvent enough to return deposits on demand. If many depositors—for good reasons or bad, based on good information or poor—demand their deposits back at the same time, banks face a liquidity problem. When banks lend large sums to each other, the resulting financial commitments can put pressure on a number of entities. If depositors cannot differentiate between them, a run on one bank may lead to runs on others, threatening the stability of the entire financial system. To limit this possibility, governments often insure deposits, guaranteeing depositors that they will get their money back and thereby reducing the incentive to start a bank run in the first place. Central banks may also act as lenders of last resort to help banks deal with short-term liquidity problems.

Deposit insurance has been criticized as contributing to the fragility of the banking system, and without the appropriate regulatory structure this can well be the case. With deposit insurance, depositors simply put their money in the bank offering the highest return. A variant of Gresham's law—with bad banks driving out good banks—can occur; a bank that is willing to take greater risks with higher expected returns can offer higher depositor rates; as funds flow to that bank, the profitability of more conservative banks that invest in low-risk, low-return activities declines.[34] Actually, the problem is not formal deposit insurance, as governments will bail out any large bank because the risks of systemic crisis are simply too great. Financial crises have afflicted countries with and without formal deposit insurance, as Sweden's recent crisis bears testimony. In short, the moral hazard problem arises whenever there are large banks, and in most developing and transition economies the concentration of banking activity is sufficiently high that it is implausible that government would not intervene.

Not all deposit insurance schemes are alike, however.[35] Some are more efficient than others, incorporating practices that could usefully be emulated elsewhere. Some governments limit deposit insurance coverage, setting a ceiling on the size of deposits or the number of accounts that can be insured. Some collect premiums from all banks on a regular basis, rather than imposing levies on surviving banks after a crisis. This last practice is particularly pervasive, since leaving the survivors to pick up the tab gives banks no incentive to avoid collapse in the first place. Theoretically, deposit insurance premiums can be linked to the risk level of a bank's portfolio or to the proportion of nonperforming loans. But to date, no government has tried this idea.

Regulatory incentives to reduce risk-taking

A banking regulatory structure deals with many aspects of bank operations: the requirements for setting up a bank, the services banks can provide, the levels of capital they must hold, the reserves they need to protect themselves against nonperforming loans, and the liquidity levels they must have to handle withdrawals. The regulatory structure defines the terms for disclosing a nonperforming loan, governs the portfolio composition of banks, and specifies remedial measures in the event of deteriorating loan portfolios or bank runs. As the number and variety of services banks offer increase, regulators need to respond to the possibility that problems can occur simultaneously in many areas.

The reluctance of ever-hopeful regulators to control risk-taking or to preemptively close banks with deteriorating loan portfolios has made many banking crises worse.[36] For this reason, creating mechanisms that limit such "regulatory forbearance"—the term for putting off tough actions in the hope that the bank will recover on its own—is another important step governments must take to make bank regulations more effective.[37] Some governments have already begun to remedy this problem by insisting on independent audits of banks' balance sheets, punishing failures to disclose nonperforming debt in a timely fashion, and fining (or closing) banks that do not meet their capital adequacy requirements. After its banking crisis in 1982, Chile introduced reforms specifically intended to reduce regulatory forbearance by increasing regulators' autonomy and mandating public disclosure of the activities of both regulators and banks. Chilean law also proscribes links between insured banks and business conglomerates.[38]

The growing number of banking crises calls into question the merits of certain other government policies. For example, governments have tried to encourage lending to targeted industries either by guaranteeing loans or by simply directing banks to make loans.[39] Some commentators on the East Asian crisis argue that these initiatives have created implicit or explicit government guarantees.[40] In these situations banks have little incentive to carefully screen loan applications for favored projects, a lapse that often results in widespread default.

Banks are also sometimes restricted in the types of loans they can make. Often these restrictions permit lending only to certain industries or regions. To the extent that they prevent a bank from maintaining a well-diversified loan portfolio that balances risks in one industry or region against risks in others, such restrictions should be avoided. This concern is particularly important for banks that lend in only one geographic region and where most borrowers are in the same industry. In such situations a collapse in prices that threatens the industry's solvency will also affect the solvency of the banks.

Two other challenges faced in designing appropriate bank regulation are worth noting: competing jurisdictions over banks, and close links between provincial banks and subnational governments.[41] To avoid duplication of subnational and national regulatory resources, subnational pressure for regulatory forbearance, and the offer of implicit guarantees by subnational governments, there is a strong case for executing bank regulation at the national level.

Establishing private incentives to reduce risk-taking

Private incentives that complement the framework of government regulation can help align the costs and benefits of the risks banks take. Banks can, for instance, periodically issue a special category of subordinated debt that is not guaranteed by the government. Since those holding subordinated debt lose their capital if a bank defaults, they have a powerful incentive to monitor the riskiness of bank lending practices.[42] But unlike holders of bank equity, holders of subordinated debt do not see higher returns if a bank increases its revenues by making high-risk loans, since the market sets the initial rate of return on subordinated debt.[43]

Banks wanting to reduce high interest payments to those holding subordinated debt (especially because high interest rates send a signal to depositors and government regulators) have an incentive to establish monitoring and disclosure practices that regularly report on the quality of the bank's lending portfolio. Chile and Argentina have adopted some of these practices.[44]

Credible banking reform

A new bank regulatory system may well face credibility problems, especially in countries with histories of directed government lending, regulatory corruption, and recurrent banking crises. Arm's-length relationships between regulators and regulated may well be a novel idea, along with the notion that strong interventions occur automatically and without regulatory discretion when a bank fails to meet its legal obligations. Developing countries can improve the credibility of new bank reforms by adopting and enforcing international banking standards. The various accords of the Banking Regulations and Supervisory Practices Committee of the Bank for International Settlements, more widely known as the "Basle Accords" or "Basle Standards," can provide such standards.

Many argue that the current Basle Accords do not go far enough and in fact are now being revised.[45] Critics say they do not do enough to discourage directed lending, promote transparency (through the publication of regulatory standards), or minimize the risks of regulatory discretion. The standards have also been criticized for recommending relatively low capital standards for developing countries that may face significant external shocks.[46] But developing countries can draw up a memorandum of understanding with international financial bodies like the World Bank and the International Monetary Fund (IMF) adopting standards stronger than those in the Basle Accords. Or, given the risks of regional contagion, neighboring countries can create stronger voluntary banking standards for the region.

Adopting internationally recognized banking standards does more than just stabilize the banking system. There are other payoffs, such as reduced borrowing costs for domestic banks, which will be considered safe risks. Realizing the payoffs is likely to require some external monitoring of the country's compliance with the new standards. For example, if a group of neighboring countries agrees to a set of voluntary standards, the agreement can include a mechanism for periodically investigating compliance. This mechanism may be similar to the Trade Policy Review Mechanism of the World Trade Organization (WTO). An impartial body conducts an investigation and, after a nonconfrontational discussion among the countries involved, publishes a report on its findings. The country under investigation can produce a rejoinder that includes commitments for further reforms. These reports are available to investors, enabling them to better differentiate among countries. Ultimately, such a system reduces the likelihood of banking crises and financial contagion by inducing countries to conform to higher banking standards.

A role for foreign banks

Allowing foreign banks to enter a country can disrupt the domestic banking sector in the short term. But the presence of foreign banks also offers long-term benefits in the form of additional pressure for appropriate risk-taking by domestic banks. Admitting foreign banks is no panacea, but if it is carefully timed and the economy can withstand the short-term disruptions, the benefits can be considerable.

Governments can foster the transfer of skills and best practices to their countries by allowing high-quality international banks with impeccable reputations to supply domestic markets with financial services.[47] This step requires governments to give foreign banks the right to establish themselves and to permit the immigration of skilled banking personnel. These international banks inevitably recognize that local bankers have a better knowledge of the domestic economy, business practices, and customs—and so offer them employment. Over time, local bankers will learn from the practices of the international banks and acquire skills that they retain when they move back to domestic banks.

The benefits of admitting foreign banks are not limited to the transfer of skills and technology. Foreign banks can stimulate competition, encouraging all banks to lower margins and overhead costs. A recent study of the effects of foreign banks on the banking systems of 80 countries found that in economies with relatively large numbers of foreign banks, domestic banks have lower expenses. However, domestic banks also have lower profitability.[48] The findings suggest that the timing of foreign bank entry should be considered carefully. It would be highly undesirable if a rise in foreign competition caused domestic banks to expand their portfolio of high-risk loans in a desperate attempt to stave off default.[49]

Foreign banks are generally more diversified than domestic banks and can better withstand the effects of internal shocks. A severe macroeconomic downturn can push a domestic bank into default. But if a foreign bank has assets in healthy economies, a macroeconomic shock in the host country is likely to be less damaging. Of course, this benefit works only if the business cycles of the various countries differ. Economic shocks can be region-specific, continent-specific, or industry-specific. In such cases developing economies can expect little benefit from diversification if their foreign banks are from the same region or continent or from countries with similar production structures. Another warning concerning the admission of foreign banks: events abroad will affect the banks' willingness to lend in the new host country. For example, lower real estate and stock prices in Japan in the 1990s led to reduced lending by Japanese banking subsidiaries in the United States.[50] In general, however, the risks posed by an undiversified banking system overshadow this possibility.

A final benefit of admitting foreign banks is that the presence of these banks conserves on scarce administrative and bank regulatory resources in developing countries. Foreign banks are traditionally regulated by authorities in their home country. If foreign banks are allowed to take over domestic banks—or to buy domestic banks in privatization sales—regulatory responsibilities are transferred abroad, and domestic regulators can concentrate their resources on the remaining domestic banks. This scenario highlights the need for a clear allocation of regulatory responsibilities across international borders.

The orderly sequencing of capital account liberalization

Improving bank regulation would be an important policy step even if world financial markets were not becoming increasingly interconnected. However, the safety and security of a developing country's banking system matters even more in light of the volatility of international capital flows. The question then becomes one of finding a way to fit bank regulation into national strategies to liberalize the capital account. The macroeconomic crises in Mexico and East Asia following the liquidation of short-term capital holdings by foreign investors has rekindled interest in proposals for a measured, sequential approach to capital account liberalization.[51]

This discussion identifies a number of pitfalls developing countries face as they consider liberalizing their capital accounts. Each of these pitfalls must be sidestepped in order to minimize the risk of a financial crisis. Of course, developing countries differ substantially in the nature of their legal institutions, corporate governance practices, banking regulations, capital market development, and macroeconomic conditions.[52] A unique recipe for sequencing capital account liberalization is therefore unlikely to exist. Instead, the formula will vary across countries, dictated in part by how quickly countries can correct macroeconomic imbalances and enforce credible financial regulations.

A key element of the sequential approach involves devising policies that control the demand for short-term foreign debt.[53] This type of foreign capital is the most likely to flee, destabilizing the banking sector and the entire economy. Policies affecting short-term debt are best implemented before the inflows occur. In part,

restraint in short-term foreign borrowing is a matter of government will. In the Mexican crisis, for example, state entities were heavy foreign borrowers.[54] Private demand for short-term foreign debt should not be encouraged with preferential tax treatment, as happened in Thailand with borrowing through the Bangkok International Banking Facility.

A more aggressive way to limit short-term foreign borrowing is to directly influence capital inflows.[55] This discussion focuses on controls on inflows because controls on outflows are typically ineffective.[56] One method of circumventing outflow controls has multinational firms selling goods to overseas parent companies at very low bookkeeping prices, transferring value out of the country. Foreign investors wanting to circumvent the controls also sometimes swap their funds for the overseas assets of a domestic resident.

A scheme that provides disincentives for short-term capital inflows has been in place in Chile since 1991.[57] This scheme imposes a one-year unremunerated reserve requirement on all foreign inflows that do not increase the stock of physical capital, such as foreign loans, fixed income securities, and equity investments. A portion of any such inflows must be held in a non-interest-bearing account for one year. The amount was initially set at 30 percent, but it was lowered to 10 percent in June 1998 and subsequently to zero. The requirement remains on the statute book and can be reinstated, however. This experience demonstrates that such a requirement can be varied in order to stabilize the level of capital inflows. Rather than targeting specific types of capital inflows— a measure investors can easily circumvent by relabeling—this scheme provides a sharp disincentive to investing for less than one year.[58] Empirical studies suggest that the effect of this tax has been to alter the composition of capital inflows toward less "footloose" foreign direct investment, although evidence on the overall impact on the level of capital inflows is mixed.[59] Countries may be able to reduce their exposure to changes in the sentiments of foreign portfolio investors without banning such investment outright. Then, as governments strengthen their bank regulation systems, they can gradually lower the nonremunerated deposit requirement. This approach reduces an economy's vulnerability to capital outflows by limiting certain of the original inflows.

In addition to modulating short-term foreign borrowing, governments must decide how to treat foreign currency deposits in their domestic financial systems.

Such deposits often account for a substantial percentage of the broad money supply in developing countries and in fact exceeded 30 percent in 18 countries in 1995.[60] While so-called dollarization undoubtedly has many implications for macroeconomic management, the focus here is on its effects on financial stability and the implications for capital account liberalization.[61]

In a fractional reserve banking system, a rapid expansion of foreign currency deposits increases the liabilities of domestic banks' loan portfolios. The risk involved stems from the fact that the amount of net foreign currency in the economy is much lower than the total volume of foreign currency–denominated assets and liabilities. Faced with a run on foreign currency deposits in the domestic banking system, the central bank may come under pressure to act as lender of last resort and provide substantial loans in foreign currency to domestic banks. [62] But these loans require the central bank to hold a relatively high level of costly foreign currency reserves. In addition, the liquidation of foreign currency deposits may affect the exchange rate and the solvency of domestic firms that have borrowed in foreign currency. These factors argue for discouraging holdings of foreign currency deposits in banking systems with rudimentary regulatory oversight, by means of taxation or higher bank capital-adequacy requirements.

Developing countries can also reduce the risk of financial and economic crises from capital outflows by maintaining high levels of foreign currency reserves.[63] The necessary level of reserves will depend on the country's level of international trade and on the amount of footloose capital invested in the economy. Countries with enough reserves send a signal to investors, who know they can convert their assets into foreign currencies at the prevailing exchange rates. This knowledge reduces the risk that investors will all stampede for the exits at the same time because they fear a currency crash.[64] But accumulating reserves comes at a price. Usually, domestic consumption and investment must be limited so that exports exceed imports and the net receipts are retained. Alternatively, reserves can be borrowed by issuing long-term bonds, in which case the cost equals the difference between short-term and long-term interest rates.

The choice of exchange rate regime is another important element affecting the sequencing of liberalization. Of course, which exchange rate regime best serves a country's interests depends on many considerations other than the regime's compatibility with capital account liberalization. However, different types of exchange rate regimes do provide different incentives to potential borrowers of foreign short-term capital. In particular, a fixed exchange rate regime offers what some interpret as an implicit guarantee to borrowers that they can ignore the risk of changes in the exchange rate. Coupling fixed exchange rate regimes with deposit insurance is tantamount to relieving foreign depositors of much of their credit risk.[65] Such guarantees encourage capital inflows, potentially exacerbating an economy's dependence on short-term foreign debt. More troublesome still, when investors call these guarantees into question, substantial capital outflows are likely. The exchange rate regime is then in jeopardy unless the country has enough foreign reserves to cover the outflows. Apparently, the preconditions for successfully maintaining a fixed exchange rate are more stringent than was previously thought.

In contrast, flexible exchange rate regimes provide incentives for investors to take exchange rate risk into account and offer no protection against a fall in the exchange rate. As the experiences of Mexico in 1995, Thailand in 1997, and Indonesia in 1998 show, the viability of a national banking system can be threatened when corporate borrowers face insolvency because a devaluation of the national currency substantially increases their foreign currency exposure. Financial crises are certainly possible in flexible exchange rate regimes, but these regimes create more incentives for investors to take account of exchange rate movements than fixed exchange rate regimes. Exchange rate regimes also differ in the options available to policymakers when facing a surge of capital inflows—an issue discussed in the World Bank's *Global Economic Prospects 1998/99*.

The extent of macroeconomic instability and imbalances suggests that other considerations are important in determining the appropriate pace of capital account liberalization. Although the consequences of liberalization may depend on the exchange rate regime, removing barriers to capital flows at a time when a massive inflow or outflow of funds seems likely is imprudent. For example, an outflow can be precipitated if capital account liberalization occurs during a period of high inflation, when domestic investors prefer stable returns overseas.

The objective of a measured policy of sequential capital account liberalization is to gradually increase a national financial system's tolerance for external disruptions. While governments are building domestic capital market institutions (like bank regulation), they can also focus on ways of reducing exposure to changes in the sentiments of holders of foreign debt instruments— so long as the methods chosen do not scare off too much long-term foreign investment.

Attracting foreign investment

Long-term foreign investment will continue to provide developing countries with important benefits. Public sector infrastructure projects will be in ever-greater demand in expanding cities, and governments and domestic savers need not be the sole sources of financing. In the private sphere the benefits of long-term foreign investment begin with the expansion of the host country's capital stock. However, since multinational corporations are responsible for most foreign direct investment, there are other benefits as well. This investment enhances competition in domestic markets, so resources are allocated more efficiently and domestic firms invest more. Foreign direct investment that involves joint ventures or licensing arrangements between local and foreign firms often transfers technology[66] and best practices to the host nation, stimulating productivity growth.[67] (The importance of foreign direct investment to Egypt and Tanzania is taken up in two case studies in chapter 8.)

How can countries attract foreign investment? This discussion presents several of the most effective methods: adopting complementary human capital policies, liberalizing the trade policy regime, avoiding inducements for foreign investors, creating a stable set of rights and responsibilities for those investors, and developing stock markets as alternative funding sources.

Adopting complementary human capital policies

One recent study found that countries with low levels of education and low rates of foreign direct investment grow much more slowly than countries with high education rates and levels of inflow.[68] Countries whose working populations have less than an average of five months of secondary schooling and whose levels of foreign investment are less than 0.1 percent of GDP have annual growth rates of less than 1 percent. But countries whose workers have an average of more than one year of secondary schooling and inflows worth more than 0.2 percent of GDP enjoy, on average, annual growth rates of 4.3 percent. Countries with high educational levels but low foreign direct investment, or with low educational levels but high foreign investment, do little better than countries that score low on both measures. These results may in part reflect the fact that if labor is to facilitate continuous transfers of in-

vestment and technology, workers must be sufficiently well educated—often with industry-specific skills— and able to continue to learn.[69] And as foreign investors increasingly discriminate between regions and cities within countries, the payoff to subnational governments of improving local systems of education and training increases still further.

Liberalizing the trade policy regime

Foreign direct investment has a more profound impact on growth in countries that pursue policies promoting exports than it does in countries that follow import-substitution policies.[70] The reason may be that foreign-owned companies aiming for global competitiveness and international markets have a greater incentive to bring in technology and training—with the accompanying spillover benefits. In East Asian countries, foreign direct investment has played an important role in bolstering advanced manufacturing exports and output. In Korea, for example, foreign affiliates accounted for between 65 and 73 percent of output in the electrical and electronics sector.[71]

An open trade policy is also important for attracting foreign direct investment. Surveys of Japanese firms which had decided to invest abroad found that a positive perception of policies governing such investments was a strong determinant of plans to invest in a country and that low trade barriers made it more likely that multinational companies would enter a country.[72] When first-rate information technology systems reinforce liberal market access, a country is further integrated into the world economy and becomes still more attractive as a destination for investment. A survey of international firms in Hong Kong (China), Singapore, and Taiwan (China) found that the presence of advanced infrastructure was the most important consideration in choosing to locate regional headquarters and service and sourcing operations in a country, and the second most important factor in siting production. Foreign direct investment is increasingly connected more with trading opportunities than with local market exploitation.[73] For example, the huge increase in foreign direct investment in Mexico after the North American Free Trade Agreement (NAFTA) came into force is evidence that the country is seen as a desirable base for supplying the U.S. market.

Export-oriented development means that investment decisions depend less on the scale of home markets, since firms are looking to sell in the global marketplace. Because multinational corporations are no longer tied to domestic markets, they have more flexibility in choosing locations. Both points suggest that stable and attractive economic policies have become much more important. In fact, foreign direct investment seems to be responding faster to economic factors than it has in the past.[74]

Avoiding inducements for foreign investors

Not all measures to attract foreign direct investment have enhanced national welfare. In an assessment of 183 foreign direct investment projects in 30 countries over the past 15 years, one recent study found that between 25 and 45 percent of projects had a negative net impact on national welfare.[75] This unwelcome and unexpected finding reflects the fact that foreign direct investment is often accompanied by distortive policies. Such policies include requirements that producers use a specified number of domestic inputs; trade protection against imports that compete with the goods produced by foreign investors; financial inducements, subsidies, or tax holidays; and mandated joint ventures and technology licensing arrangements. At least some of these policies may encourage investment, but for society as a whole the losses all too often outweigh the gains. Yet another problem arises when urban centers and other subnational entities compete for investment, often engaging in inefficient beggar-thy-neighbor competition to provide public subsidies and incentives. National governments can play a role here in restricting the types of inducements that subnational governments can offer foreign investors.

Creating a stable set of rights and responsibilities for foreign investors

National policies and regulatory institutions help foster a climate conducive to foreign direct investment by multinational corporations. Taking steps to clearly define the rights and obligations of multinational investors is a start. Many developing countries are taking steps to create such legal frameworks and to simplify bureaucratic procedures. This sort of institutional reform is especially attractive to investors considering investing in countries plagued by political risk and corruption, since these practices are negatively associated with foreign direct investment.[76] Countries that reduce red tape and bureaucratic delays not only make themselves more attractive to investment but help their own producers as well.[77]

Two other types of domestic regulations and commitments have particularly important ramifications for foreign direct investment. The first is privatization policy, which can be designed to induce foreign investment. Chapter 8 describes Hungary's successful efforts to attract foreign buyers for its formerly state-owned banks. The second involves a country's obligations under the WTO's General Agreement on Trade in Services. These obligations may include commitments to allow foreign firms access to certain domestic service markets, as chapter 2 notes.

Even if a nation implements sound macroeconomic policy, market liberalization measures, and clear legal rules, it is not always possible to ensure that successor governments, including subnational governments and their agencies, will honor the commitments of their predecessors over the long term. This risk can limit the attractiveness of investments with high set-up costs and long payback periods, such as urban infrastructure projects. The growing activities of subnational governments may exacerbate this problem (box 3.3).

A dispute settlement mechanism can help resolve the issue of commitment. International arbitration is often the preferred option. Arbitration clauses can be included in investment agreements with subnational entities. In certain situations arbitration under the auspices of the International Centre for Settlement of Investment Disputes (ICSID) can be made available to subnational governments that contract with foreign investors. Almost 1,000 bilateral investment treaties and 4 multilateral investment treaties contain clauses providing for binding arbitration under the ICSID. Some of the bilateral treaties explicitly state that their provisions cover acts and omissions of local governments in states signing the agreements.

In the end, long-term investment agreements that are balanced and mutually beneficial may be the most lasting safeguards. Providing specialized training to increase local governments' capacity to negotiate fair agreements in the first place can advance this objective. The International Development Law Institute in Rome trains developing country lawyers to deal effectively with foreign investors and lenders, and a number of World Bank initiatives also work to ameliorate this commitment problem (box 3.4).

The collapse of negotiations on a multilateral investment agreement in 1998 suggests that a global treaty on investment rules is still some way off. However, the number of bilateral and regional investment agreements and treaties has increased. Signatories to these agreements realize that extending protections to foreign investors provides an incentive to cosignatories not to renege on long-term deals with their own foreign investors. Since most

Box 3.3
Subnational governments face commitment problems, too

A U.S. company agreed to build the Dabhol Power Project, which would supply the Indian state of Maharashtra with 2,000 megawatts of power over a 20-year period.[78] After the agreement was signed in 1993, the foreign investor began to incur heavy expenses for the construction of the power station. The state government officials who signed this contract lost the 1995 election, in which the investment project had become a contentious political issue. The new state government canceled the project, and only after 10 months of negotiations and several concessions by the foreign investor was a new agreement signed. Many argued that the original agreement was too generous to the investor, and the fact that the company did not abandon the project but instead chose to renegotiate offers some evidence for this view. With renegotiation, the formal cost of construction fell from $1.3 million per megawatt to $0.9 million per megawatt.[79] Canceling a project the previous administration had agreed to was clearly not the best way of attracting further foreign investment to the sector. The investor reported that the delay cost approximately $250,000 a day, and the international financial press gave the crisis extensive coverage.

This case shows how the proliferation of assertive subnational entities, which this report identifies as one of the chief political reactions to localization, can complicate the efforts of national governments to make binding commitments. If foreign investors cannot discriminate among subnational entities in a given nation, the actions of one entity may be seen as reflecting the behavior of all others. This kind of spillover is a serious concern for national governments keen on attracting foreign direct investment.

Box 3.4
Mitigating the commitment problem: the role of the World Bank

The World Bank has provided loans to host governments to fund their obligations under political risk guarantees that are in turn issued to foreign investors. The Bank also offers lenders a guarantee that covers the risks of debt service defaults resulting from the failure of host governments to perform specified obligations in respect of the project. When issuing this guarantee, the Bank requires that host governments sign a counterguarantee to reimburse the Bank for any compensation the Bank pays the foreign investor(s). Unless the host government plans to default on its obligations to the Bank (jeopardizing its entire relationship with the World Bank Group), this counterguarantee diminishes the government's incentive to break its contractual obligations.

The Multilateral Investment Guarantee Agency (MIGA) provides foreign investors with insurance against losses from war and civil disturbances, expropriations, and currency inconvertibility. When a foreign investor cannot enforce a contract with a host government in that country's courts, MIGA can insure it against losses caused by the breach of contract. Between 1991 and March 1996, MIGA issued 30 contracts involving approximately $3.5 billion in infrastructure projects. These contracts are in addition to those supplied by private insurers, which now offer contracts for "breach of undertaking."

In 1992, at the request of the Development Committee, the World Bank Group issued a set of guidelines embodying commendable approaches to the legal framework for the treatment of foreign investment. The guidelines cover the main areas dealt with in investment protection treaties: the admission, treatment, and expropriation of foreign investments and the settlement of disputes between governments and foreign investors. By their terms the guidelines are not binding and are intended to complement applicable international agreements. Moreover, by their terms they are intended to apply to both states and any of their constituent subdivisions.

foreign direct investment is intraregional—with developing countries now investing substantial amounts abroad and so recognizing the need to protect their investments—an even greater role for regional investment agreements is likely to emerge.

When these investment accords include commitments to maintain domestic reforms, the reforms are more credible. Reversing the reforms once the accords are signed would do more than wreak domestic havoc; it would also invite retaliation by foreign governments. NAFTA's investment provisions in effect "locked in" Mexico's domestic regulatory and institutional reforms. Similarly, the Mercado Común del Sur (MERCOSUR) preferential trade agreement reinforced reforms in Brazil and Argentina and stimulated foreign direct investment from other countries, principally the United States.[80]

Regional foreign investment agreements can also include constraints on the use of subsidies, tax inducements, and regulatory competition. The initial agreement can identify accepted forms of favoritism, quan-

tify them, and negotiate common guidelines for their use. Signatories can then negotiate additional constraints later on, in much the same way as signatories to international trade agreements have renegotiated tariff levels. These agreements also reduce incentives to engage in beggar-thy-neighbor policies to attract capital. They allay fears that countries may be tempted to reduce environmental and other important protections in return for the promise of an investment project (the so-called "race to the bottom" syndrome).

Developing stock markets as alternative funding sources

Although foreign portfolio investment does not offer the same opportunities for technology transfer and increased competition as foreign direct investment, it can also be very useful to developing countries. Opening stock markets to foreign participation increases liquidity by deepening the pool of buyers and sellers. Price-earnings ratios rise as liquidity increases, making the market a far more attractive source of equity financing.[81] As the stock market develops and strengthens, it benefits other parts of the financial sector as well as the wider economy—foreign direct investment accompanies stock market purchases, for instance. Stock market development and banking development have a strong positive relationship, as do stock market liquidity and economic growth.[82]

The potential volatility of a stock market is an ongoing concern. Many policies for reducing volatility in the banking sector can help reduce the volatility of bourses, however, and approaches to sequencing capital account liberalization can be applied to portfolio equity flows as well. But as with other parts of the financial sector, the cause of stock market volatility is often a lack of reliable, up-to-date information. Accurate information from independent sources makes an emerging market attractive to foreign equity investors and increases the stability of capital flows. Rules mandating the regular public reporting of financial positions in key areas such as investment, property and equipment, foreign currency operations, and long-term contracts reduce uncertainty.[83] Financial markets develop best in the presence of legal codes that stress the rights of shareholders (especially minority holders) and regulatory systems that encourage the disclosure of corporate information.[84]

During the next 25 years the flow of foreign investment to and from developing economies will increase substantially. Developing countries will have a growing interest in establishing secure and stable regimes that protect their overseas investors—and that clearly delineate their responsibilities. As the supply of capital grows, subnational and central government entities will increase their demands for capital to fund urban infrastructure projects. Developing economies can take action to attract and maximize the benefits of long-term foreign investment by participating in regional agreements that enhance investor security and by maintaining stable macroeconomic, trade, and regulatory policies.

Revitalizing international macroeconomic cooperation

This sketch of international financial integration has deliberately avoided placing the entire burden of reform

on individual countries. The contributions of regional and global agreements to foreign direct investment and financial supervision have already been discussed. But a corollary to the growing trend toward a globalized economy exists. As economies become increasingly interdependent, the effects of national policy decisions spread, with ramifications—including potentially disruptive ones—for other countries.[85] Although the interdependencies are typically strongest among neighboring countries, macroeconomic conditions in industrial economies have distinct consequences for the rest of the world.

Fluctuations in interest rate differentials between industrial countries alter the flow of capital to and from developing countries, potentially destabilizing their financial systems. A variety of vehicles for international cooperation could be considered that would enable industrial countries to meet their own goals without buffeting the outside world.

The growing links among countries in the same region also suggest a motivation for regional networks to prevent and fight financial crises.[86] Because of the growing trade and financial links among regional economies, one economy's poor performance can profoundly effect its neighbors. This fact argues for close monitoring and mutual support among countries in the same region. However, the growing strength of regional linkages will cause national economic cycles within a region to move more closely in phase. In this case the IMF's function as an extraregional crisis management body will take on added importance, as countries in the same region are likely to enter downturns together, reducing the resources they have available to help their regional partners.

One promising approach builds on the steps some countries are already taking toward regional economic monitoring. The Association of Southeast Asian Nations (ASEAN) agreed to implement an economic monitoring mechanism in November 1997. The mechanism aims to monitor policies in "vulnerable" sectors, to improve economic policy coordination among members, and to assist members during a crisis.[87] But doubts have been raised about this mechanism, with skeptics questioning not only whether enough resources have been devoted to it, but whether governments will actually be willing to release timely information or to criticize each other's domestic policies.[88] This points to the difficulty of sustaining cooperation in regional initiatives such as this and the Manila Framework.

When a regional grouping does establish a credible monitoring scheme to certify that members have implemented commendable regulatory and macroeconomic practices, members can extend cooperation to include pooling funds to deter speculative currency attacks. This "seal of approval" helps investors differentiate among member states. This pool of regional funds can be used to augment the national reserves of what might otherwise become the "trigger economy" for a regional crisis. If these additional reserves reduce the likelihood of a future devaluation of a country's currency, foreign and domestic investors will be less inclined to liquidate their portfolio investment in that country, possibly preventing a currency run altogether.

Countries can also explore opportunities for cooperation with regional partners during a financial crisis. Crisis management accords can be signed in advance, providing investors with the expectation of a coordinated response to shocks and helping allay the most pessimistic expectations. These accords can then serve as a framework for a coordinated fiscal policy of tax cuts and spending increases that provides a safety net for those most affected by shocks and stimulates the regional economy.[89] The accords can also lay the groundwork for commitments not to engage in competitive devaluations or impair market access by raising existing tariff and nontariff barriers.

• • •

Internationally mobile capital is here to stay. Growing trade links, new communications technologies, and increasingly sophisticated financial products are making national borders more porous to financial flows. The challenge facing policymakers in developing countries is how to navigate through this financially integrating world. Since 1997, when the East Asian crisis began, the world has learned that poorly managed financial liberalization can lead to a protracted economic downturn and a renewed cycle of poverty. But the potential upside of international capital flows is enormous, as the positive contribution of foreign direct investment to boosting productivity in recipient countries demonstrates.

The discussion in this chapter has highlighted four essential and related measures for developing economies wishing to integrate into global financial markets. First, even if an economy is completely isolated from foreign financial flows, the benefits of domestic financial liberalization cannot be assured without strong banking regulation. Second, strengthening those regulations takes years, and in the interim governments must develop policies that reduce the volatility of short-term foreign inflows. Third, developing countries will want to increase their attractiveness to long-term foreign investment. The rise of global production networks (discussed in chapter 2) shows that multinational firms are slicing up production processes, distributing them across economies. Large domestic markets are likely to become less important to multinationals looking for new locations, creating opportunities for smaller developing countries with suitable infrastructure and education. Finally, efforts to coordinate aspects of financial and regulatory policies can be advantageous to developing economies. Financial crises in developing countries are not always homegrown. Fluctuating interest rate differentials between industrial countries have increased the volatility of global capital flows, which can be ameliorated by policy coordination among industrial countries.

4

Protecting the Global Commons

At the end of the 20th century, environmental problems are a matter of both national and global concern. Many of them create spillovers that impose heavy costs not only on those close to the source of the problem but on society as a whole and on future generations. Individual countries have strong economic and social reasons for aggressively protecting their environments by creating incentives to reduce and manage such spillovers.[1] However, an important subset of environmental problems is global in scope. Many countries have contributed to these problems, and no individual country can effectively address them by acting alone. These are the problems of the "global commons," which will place all countries at risk if no collective action is taken. There are many such issues, including desertification, persistent organic pollutants, the fate of Antarctica, and the environmental health of the high seas and the seabed (box 4.1), but this chapter focuses on three in particular: ozone depletion, global climate change, and threats to biodiversity.

Effective responses to these problems are vital to the struggle for sustainable development. Climate change, for example, is likely to raise sea levels, threatening island economies and low-lying countries such as the Maldives and Bangladesh. Climate change also jeopardizes agricultural production in developing countries. The Russian Federation and parts of Africa could see dramatic reductions in their crop yields by 2050 (figure 4.1). The overall impact of a doubling of carbon dioxide in the atmosphere would be to reduce the gross domestic product (GDP) of developing countries by an estimated 2–9 percent (compared with 1.0–1.5 percent of GDP in industrial economies).[2] Within developing countries, the price of inaction is likely to fall particularly on the poorest, who have the fewest resources for responding to climate change. And because of the concentration of biodiverse areas in developing countries, failure to preserve biodiversity would also disproportionately affect poorer nations.

Despite the urgency and importance of environmental issues, building cooperation to address global environmental problems is not simple; it involves contentious issues such as the division of responsibilities and differing capabilities to respond. Industrial countries have cre-

Box 4.1
Global environmental issues

Beyond the three cases discussed in detail in this chapter—ozone depletion, climate change, and biodiversity protection—a range of other environmental issues calls for action on a global scale. These issues include desertification and land degradation, Antarctica, persistent organic pollutants (POPs), and the high seas and seabed.

Desertification and land degradation
Today 900 million people in about 100 countries are affected by desertification and drought. By 2025 that number will double, and 25 percent of the earth's land area will be degraded. Land degradation, which is closely linked to issues of population, poverty, water use, and biodiversity, increases as growing numbers of people overexploit fragile ecosystems.

By mid-1998 almost 150 countries had ratified the United Nations Convention to Combat Desertification. The convention is a significant first step that will benefit millions of people if it is properly implemented. The convention's thrust is not to set up a separate program to counter desertification but to mainstream efforts toward this objective into a country's overall development strategy, with the support of bilateral and multilateral donors.[3]

Antarctica
Since the negotiation of the Antarctic Treaty in 1959, countries that had laid claim to territory on the continent have "frozen" their claims. Under Article IV no signatory nation is allowed to assert its claims or make new ones. Furthermore, signatories are not allowed to deploy military units (except in support of scientific missions), dump radioactive waste, or explode nu-

clear devices on the continent or in the surrounding seas. Since then, two conventions and one protocol to the treaty have aimed to protect seals, the region's unique marine living resources, and the Antarctic environment in general.[4]

Persistent organic pollutants
Twelve of these pollutants are currently the subject of international negotiation. POPs are chemical substances used in a variety of activities (including agricultural and industrial production and disease control) that do not break down naturally and that accumulate in the fatty tissues of animals at different levels of the food chain. Because POPs are long-lasting and are frequently able to travel long distances in the atmosphere, they have spread all over the world, even to areas where they have never been used. POPs harm both human and animal populations—in humans, for example, they can cause cancer, diseases of the immune system, and reproductive disorders. The United Nations Environment Programme is leading the development of a global, legally binding agreement to minimize the release of POPs into the environment, with negotiations scheduled to conclude in 2000.[5]

The high seas and the seabed
The United Nations Convention on the Law of the Sea (UNCLOS), which incorporated a number of earlier agreements, was adopted in 1982 and entered into force in 1994. Beyond creating exclusive economic zones (box 4.2), UNCLOS stipulates that states must take action to control marine pollution from both land-based sources and vessels at sea. It also sets up a global authority responsible for the environmental health of the seabed.

---

ated much of the current stock of many transnational environmental problems. In the pursuit of economic advance, they have destroyed much of their own biodiversity and have overexploited fisheries worldwide. They also have the highest levels of energy use and thus bear the overwhelming responsibility for the present level of manmade greenhouse gases in the atmosphere. At the same time, developing countries are unlikely to become actively involved in addressing global environmental problems if the price is slower economic progress. The United Nations Framework Convention on Climate Change and the Convention on Biological Diversity (both agreed at the 1992 Rio Earth Summit) specifically recognized that economic and social development and poverty eradication are developing countries' overriding priorities.[6] For this reason the need for flexible mechanisms that transfer resources from rich to poor countries are central to any solution of global environmental problems.

Even though industrial countries have played a disproportionately large role in causing global environmental problems and should pay the lion's share of the costs of addressing them, developing countries are vital to any long-term solution to these problems and have accepted that they also have a role, under a system of common but differentiated responsibilities.[7] Developing countries are already doing damage to the global commons. Rain forests and coral reefs are rapidly being destroyed in many developing countries. Urbanization, industrialization, and growing numbers of automobiles worldwide mean yet more greenhouse gases in the atmosphere. And overfishing has spread to seas controlled by developing nations. Moreover, regardless of who has done the damage to the global commons, developing countries have a strong interest in ensuring that cooperative steps are taken to address these issues, which will have the greatest effect on their citizens.

Figure 4.1
Climate change jeopardizes crop yields, especially in developing countries

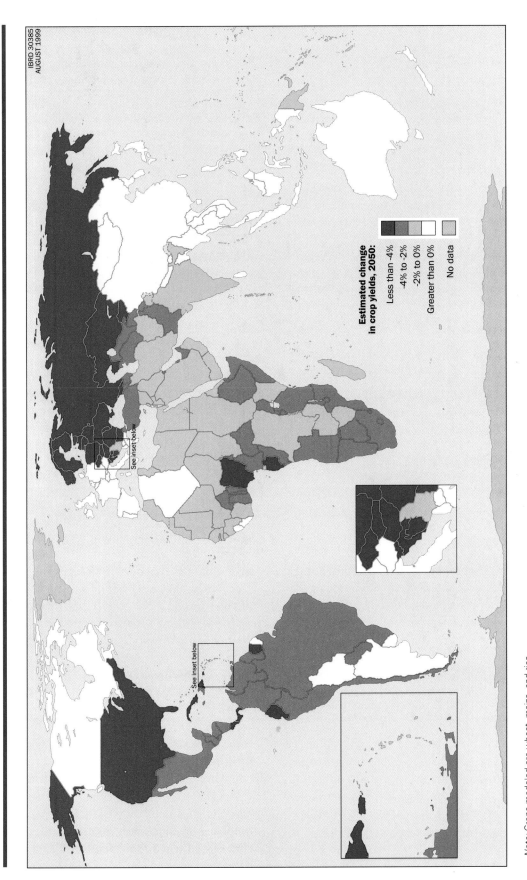

**Estimated change
in crop yields, 2050:**

Less than -4%
-4% to -2%
-2% to 0%
Greater than 0%

No data

See inset below

See inset below

IBRD 30385
AUGUST 1999

Note: Crops modeled are wheat, maize, and rice.
Source: Parry and Livermore 1997.

Already, developing countries are taking steps to combat environmental degradation, including some environmental problems that have global implications. Kazakhstan and Uzbekistan have been taking measures to prevent rapid deforestation, and China has crafted an ambitious set of environmental plans based on the agenda that emerged from the Rio Earth Summit.[8] These efforts have overlapped with a growing movement to tackle global environmental problems in a multinational framework. Since the 1972 Stockholm Conference on the Human Environment, governments have signed more than 130 environmental treaties, with increasingly substantive regulatory provisions.[9] These treaties have contributed to many positive developments, such as reduced water pollution in the Mediterranean and stronger protection for the Antarctic environment.

This chapter begins by discussing national initiatives aimed at improving the local economy or environment that also have some role in slowing climate change and biodiversity loss. Such initiatives illustrate the importance of the complementarities that can emerge from a comprehensive development strategy. Policies designed to improve economic efficiency, for instance, can sometimes have a significant and positive impact on rates of deforestation or energy use. The chapter moves on to a discussion of the need for further international initiatives that address regional and global environmental problems. Although the measures employed to tackle ozone depletion were based in part on circumstances particular to that case, they suggest guidelines for designing global measures that address the complex problems of greenhouse gas emissions and biodiversity preservation. The chapter concludes with a look at the linkages between biodiversity and greenhouse gas emissions, pointing out how these links can be exploited to negotiate more effective international agreements.

The link between national and global environmental issues

Autonomous, self-interested state actions can improve both the environment and economic performance, as emphasized in *World Development Report 1992*. In some fortuitous cases, protecting the local environment will also contribute to addressing a global environmental problem. Exploiting these synergies is vital. Linking actions that have short-term payoffs (such as controlling air pollution) to those with longer-term results (such as controlling the release of carbon dioxide) improves the economic efficiency and political viability of reforms designed to promote sustainable development. For example, the domestic environmental benefits of maintaining forest resources—including reduction of river sedimentation and soil erosion and preservation of water resources and fishing areas—greatly outweigh any economic benefits that might be gained by transforming the forest into poor-quality farmland. Similarly, governments can justify preserving coral reefs solely on the basis of their value to national economies.[10] Preservation, then, supports both the national environment and the national economy. But in both cases, efforts to protect national resources also benefit the global commons by preserving biodiversity and reducing carbon dioxide output.

Governments often take measures to promote economic efficiency (on both the national and international levels) that also reduce environmental degradation. Eliminating subsidies and tax credits for cutting timber and for building roads in forests is economically advantageous. But this policy has another benefit: it significantly reduces deforestation rates, preserving biodiversity and a valuable "carbon sink" that cuts carbon dioxide levels in the air.[11] Similarly, doing away with energy subsidies and imposing taxes on fuel reduces both global carbon dioxide emissions and local pollution such as acid rain and smog. Studies in Mexico suggest that a 1 percent increase in gasoline prices is associated with a 0.8 percent decline in gasoline consumption.[12]

Eliminating energy subsidies could reduce carbon emissions dramatically. If Western Europe and Japan abolished their coal production subsidies and their import restrictions on foreign coal by 2005, global carbon dioxide emissions would drop 5 percent. If the major developing countries simultaneously raised the price of coal to international market levels, the combined effect would be an 8 percent reduction in global emissions.[13] Removing subsidies is often difficult for political reasons, but it is important to note that subsidies rarely benefit the most deserving, especially in the developing world.[14] For example, subsidizing the electricity bills of rich consumers connected to the grid—or the gasoline of those who own cars—certainly does not help the poor in developing countries. A recent World Bank study found that in Malawi rich consumers receive $6.60 a year in electricity subsidies, while poor consumers receive just $0.04. Of course, those not connected to the electricity grid receive no subsidy at all.[15]

Even if the complete removal of subsidies is politically impossible, there may be a strong case for better targeting. The cost of protecting a German coal-mining job with per-ton subsidies reached $79,800 per job in 1995.[16] Much of the value of these subsidies went to the mine owners and operators, not to the workers. If the rationale for a subsidy is to protect jobs or workers' incomes, a per-worker subsidy is a more efficient choice. In Germany switching to a per-worker subsidy would have raised the price of coal closer to market levels (reducing coal consumption) and decreased the overall cost of the subsidies while protecting the mine workers' jobs and incomes.

Beyond national policies, local governments also have a role in countering global problems while tackling local issues. Automobile-related pollution does far more damage in cities than in the countryside because of the high concentration of both cars and people in urban areas. A recent U.S. study estimated that every gallon of gasoline consumed imposed a $0.10 cost on the country as a whole in terms of the damage caused by increased air pollution but that in Los Angeles the amount can run as high as $0.62 per gallon.[17] Such differentials suggest that local (and especially urban) governments have an important part to play in tackling pollution issues (see chapter 7). By investing in effective public and nonmotorized transportation networks and providing people with the incentives to use them, cities can reduce the economic and environmental costs of traffic congestion and motorized vehicle use. In the process, they also reduce greenhouse gas emissions.[18]

Preserving the environment involves not only eliminating subsidies that encourage polluting activities and supporting more environmentally efficient alternatives but also ensuring that polluters pay for the environmental damage they cause. These policies can frequently be implemented in ways that help protect the global as well as the local environment and that minimize the economic costs of environmental protection. Carbon taxes, which are applied to energy sources according to the amount of carbon dioxide they produce, have been suggested as one way for industrial and developing countries to reduce greenhouse gas emissions. Controversy often surrounds energy taxes. But proponents argue that such taxes sometimes have a broader base than other taxes commonly imposed in developing countries (such as those on trade) and so can be more economically efficient.[19] Proponents also argue

that a carbon tax that applies to energy imports and local sources of carbon-based energy such as coal mines and oil refineries might also be relatively easy to implement, as only a limited number of industrial operations require monitoring.

Another policy tool that can have a positive effect on both the national and the global environment is the imposition of market discipline on the exploitation of natural resources.[20] For example, making fishing quotas tradable helps create a market that promotes the efficient and sustainable use of fisheries resources (box 4.2). Market-based approaches are likely to be particularly important in international environmental agreements, as discussed later in this chapter.

By removing or reforming subsidies, fostering markets, and confirming property rights, countries acting alone can improve their own environments. To the extent that these unilateral actions also reduce cross-border pollution and environmental damage, they improve the welfare of other countries as well. But if such actions are so advantageous, why have more countries not taken them, and why are they not enough?

Entrenched producer interests account for the political difficulty in removing subsidies. Even better-targeted subsidies may meet resistance from workers. They may feel, for instance, that wage subsidies are demeaning to them in a way that price supports (which are far less efficient) are not.[21] This problem reinforces a point made in chapter 2: that a primary policy concern in the coming decades will be to help regional labor markets adjust to the economic changes caused by reform. It also suggests that international agreements might play a role in stimulating domestic support for environmental reform, much like the role the World Trade Organization (WTO) assumes in encouraging freer trade.

But even if national-level environmental concerns are fully addressed, international market failures call for an international response. Despite the sometimes positive effects of national efforts on international well-being, a focus on local environmental issues frequently leaves global concerns inadequately addressed. For example, catalytic converters can significantly reduce emissions of local pollutants, cutting hydrocarbon emissions by an average of 87 percent, carbon monoxide emissions by 85 percent, and nitrogen oxides by 62 percent. But depending on the type, these converters often have a minimal or negative effect on carbon dioxide output,

Box 4.2
Preserving the ocean commons: controlling overfishing

The imposition in the late 1970s of exclusive economic zones (EEZs) that stretch 200 miles from the coastlines of many countries has dramatically reduced the problem of fisheries as an international common pool resource, exploited by many and protected by none. Yet overfishing remains a significant issue. At the international level, regulating the stocks of migratory fish that traverse the EEZs of several countries still presents problems. But since 90 to 95 percent of fish are found within EEZs, such problems cannot account for global overfishing. In fact the most important causes of overfishing are national subsidies, overcapacity in the fishing industry, and governments' inability to enforce fishing limits in their economic zones.

In the underpatrolled waters off the coasts of some African nations, ships from both Europe and Asia fish illegally—and at rates that cannot be sustained.[22] But even legal fishing often depletes local fish populations. Technological advances such as advanced sonar and drift nets have made large boats much more effective. The Food and Agriculture Organization (FAO) estimates that the number of fishing boats more than doubled between 1970 and 1990, reaching some 1.2 million (although many of these are small fishing boats). The European Union alone has about 40 percent more boats than it needs to catch sustainable levels of fish. And as a result of overfishing, fish catches in recent years have not increased, despite the larger fleets. As stocks are exhausted, the fleets actually become less profitable.

Clearly, enforcing national rights, removing subsidies, and implementing national programs to counter overfishing are very important. Some countries have introduced individual transferable quotas—tradable rights to land a percentage of the annual catch—which, when well implemented, can ensure a sustainable catch for the most efficient fishermen.

Aquaculture may provide a technological solution for overfishing. While marine harvests still account for 80 percent of world seafood supplies, aquaculture is one of the fastest-growing food production industries. Farmed fish production doubled between 1990 and 1996, reaching 26 million tons, and output could reach 39 million tons by 2010. Aquaculture, however, is no panacea: it takes an estimated 5 kilograms of oceanic fish reduced to fish meal to raise a single kilogram of farmed shrimp, and the 300 to 1,000 kilograms of solid waste produced by each ton of farmed fish can cause problems with water quality, including overnutrification and algae blooms. But freshwater aquaculture at least can be made sustainable.

For transnational or highly migratory stocks of fish or stocks that stray into the high seas, international agreements still play an important part in controlling overfishing. The 1995 United Nations agreement on straddling fish stocks and highly migratory fish stocks struck a careful balance in determining the rights of coastal and distant-fishing states and strengthened the role of regional fishing organizations in controlling fishing on the high seas. Parties to regional agreements have been given powers to board and inspect vessels from any nation, although they have no power to impound the vessels or arrest the crews.[23] Another regional solution is a register of foreign vessels like that set up by the South Pacific Forum Fisheries Agency. Ships must be on this register in order to obtain fishing licenses from any member country, and they can be removed from the list for failure to pay fines.[24] This type of cooperation among states reduces the cost of enforcement.

With the EEZs and the 1995 United Nations agreement in place, is broader international action needed to preserve fisheries? The United Nations Convention on the Law of the Sea stipulates that countries have a duty to conserve fisheries within their EEZs, although the obligations are not clearly spelled out.[25] Some countries have apparently decided to allow overfishing, thus placing a low value on future fish stocks. International sanctions or transfers might change the incentives of the countries that continue to overfish. But for most developing countries, support for more effective fisheries management combined with voluntary sustainable fisheries labeling is likely to be more appropriate. A certification mechanism could also encourage sustainable fishing practices, an idea that has been taken up by the new Marine Stewardship Council. A future international agreement could also call for phasing out fishing subsidies, which clearly stimulate global overfishing.

Aquaculture's role in the production of fish and shellfish is growing

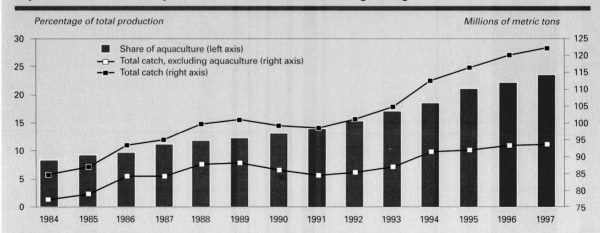

Source: FAO, *Fishery Statistics*, various years; FAO, *Aquacultural Production Statistics*, 1999.

the source of so much concern because of its relationship to climate change.[26]

Thus, national environmental policies are designed to benefit individual countries, not the rest of the world, and are likely to fall far short of global environmental goals. For international cooperation in the environmental arena to succeed, governments must consider the implications of domestic environmental policy decisions for other countries. Recognition of the effect that each nation's policies might have on other nations' welfare is an essential precondition for effective international environmental cooperation.

Moving from national to international action

Every environmental issue involves a unique configuration of scientific factors, stakeholders, costs, benefits, and policy implications. But all global environmental problems have one thing in common: individual countries do not have sufficient incentives to act on them because countries cannot capture all the rewards of doing so. In economic terminology, global environmental resources are public goods that are nonexcludable and nonrivalrous across borders. The atmosphere is a particularly good example. No individual or group can be prevented (excluded) from consuming or using the atmosphere. Furthermore, clean air does not benefit one nation at the expense of others, so countries are not rivals when it comes to consuming these goods. An opposite example is the sea: it can be divided into zones with boundaries that can be enforced, and at least in the case of fishing, one nation's use can be at the expense of another's.

Biodiversity poses a slightly different problem from that presented by the atmosphere. We cannot separate what might be considered the global common resource elements of biodiversity from the ecosystems in which they reside, and these are highly valuable at the national level. Forests and coral reefs both have usage values at this level that far exceed any value that might be gained by destroying them. A recent study in West Kalimantan, Indonesia, found that 95 percent of the forests in the province have an agricultural opportunity cost of less than $2 per hectare per year.[27] This figure compares poorly with estimates of the benefits of forest preservation that can be captured at the national level. These benefits include extractive values of minor forest products (fruits, latex, medicines, and so on) that average around $70 per hectare per year, hunting and fishing values of between $1 and $16 per hectare per year, and

recreational values (including tourism) of around $12 per hectare per year. Estimates of the value of the vital ecological functions of forests also overshadow agricultural opportunity costs. These functions include watershed protection (around $10 per hectare per year), erosion prevention ($2–$28), fisheries protection (approximately $14), and flood prevention ($2).[28] These figures suggest that the most important method of preserving global biodiversity is to ensure that the functioning of markets and institutions at the national level reflects the value of the services ecosystems provide. Technical assistance and knowledge transfer can support this goal and are already a focus of international efforts to preserve biodiversity under the Global Environment Facility (box 4.3).

Nonetheless, at least some elements of biodiversity can be seen as nonexcludable and nonrivalrous, in common with the atmosphere. Genetic material is arguably a global common resource, yet pharmaceutical companies in industrial countries rarely pay for the genetic material they have extracted from plants in developing countries. A recent cost-benefit analysis of a preservation program for Cameroon's Korup National Park rain forest found that while many benefits of preserving the forest could be captured at the national level, only around 10 percent of the genetic value of the forest's biological resources (including research material for pharmaceuticals, chemicals, and agricultural crop products) could be obtained by Cameroon through existing licensing structures and institutions. The rest would benefit others outside Cameroon. Furthermore, the study did not include the value of carbon storage (reducing carbon dioxide emissions) that forest preservation provides to the global community. Carbon storage is both a useful example of the linkages among global environmental issues (since preserving forests supports climate stability and slows biodiversity loss) and another example of the nonrivalrous, nonexcludable nature of some forest services.[29]

No system has ever been set up to pay for the "existence value" of species in other countries—the value of diversity independent of any expected economic returns from factors such as genetic material or ecological function. This scenario persists unchanged, even though studies conducted in the United States suggest a willingness to pay for the preservation of individual native species at prices that range from $2 to $150 per household per year.[30]

When environmental resources have the features of a global public good, it becomes very difficult for pri-

Box 4.3
The Global Environment Facility

The Global Environment Facility (GEF) provides grants and concessional funds to cover the additional costs incurred when a development project also targets global environmental objectives in four focus areas: biological diversity, climate change, international waters, and depletion of the Earth's ozone layer. The GEF is the interim financial mechanism of both the Convention on Biological Diversity and the United Nations Framework Convention on Climate Change. The GEF leverages its resources through cofinancing and cooperation with other donor groups and the private sector.

The GEF is involved in a range of innovative projects worldwide, including support for the management of protected areas, conservation programs, biomass and energy efficiency projects, solar home systems, and phaseout programs for chlorofluorocarbons (CFCs). In the Czech Republic, for example, GEF support was central to the phaseout of production and use of ozone-depleting substances such as CFCs and their replacement with alternative technologies. In a group of Caribbean countries, a GEF project backed the implementation of the International Convention for the Prevention of Pollution from Ships, which included new legislation, regional cooperation among countries and with cruise lines, and improved port waste management systems. Later in this chapter we discuss a project in Poland designed to improve forest management systems.

The GEF was never intended to cover all of the international financing needs of global environmental programs. As of September 1998, approximately seven years after its establishment, the GEF had allocated a total of just under $2 billion—less than the maximum allowed for carbon credit transfers under the Kyoto Protocol. On the other hand, where it is involved, the GEF is playing an important role in supporting a range of measures to ensure global environmental sustainability.[31]

vate market forces or national governments acting alone to set prices for them that reflect their value, since anyone can use a nonexcludable good without paying for it and the cost of additional nonrivalrous users enjoying such a good is essentially zero. Because neither markets nor national laws are likely to fully reflect the value of public goods that are shared globally, only international agreements can fully protect these resources. But the costs and benefits of protecting natural resources differ from country to country, as do the levels of resources available for countering environmental degradation, creating a need for effective transfer mechanisms. The Global Environment Facility is one model for such transfers.

Nonetheless, critics often argue that the agreements on biodiversity and climate change signed in the latter half of the 20th century fall short of attaining the full benefits of global cooperation. The Kyoto agreement is a solid first step away from "business as usual" and toward adaptive management. However, calculations by the Intergovernmental Panel on Climate Change (IPCC) show that emissions reductions well beyond the levels agreed at the Kyoto meeting would eventually be needed if governments wished to stabilize atmospheric concentrations of greenhouse gases at today's levels over the very long term.[32] Specifically, a reduction in emissions of approximately 60 percent from current levels would be required for stabilization. At present, the members of the Organisation for Economic Co-operation and Development (OECD) and the transition economies have agreed to reductions of around 5 percent.[33] This suggests that, if major climate change is to be avoided, there will at some point need to be an agreement with stricter emissions targets encompassing more countries. The situation is much the same with biological diversity loss. While the Convention on Biological Diversity provides a strong framework for future agreements, it has had little effect on forestry practices and coral reef degradation. Unsustainable forestry practices have slowed only marginally since the convention was signed, and coral reef degradation may have increased.

The rest of this chapter focuses on the conditions and mechanisms that determine the success of international agreements designed to counter global environmental problems. International treaties are based on bargaining, financial incentives, and, under some circumstances, limited controls on trade and finance. International funding based on the kinds of transfer mechanisms discussed here can help resolve two of the major problems that hold up such agreements: what kinds of environmental controls the agreements should include, and who should pay for those controls.

The ozone treaties: a success story

Concern about declining ozone levels in the upper atmosphere gained worldwide attention in the early and mid-1980s. Scenarios predicting huge increases in the rates of skin cancer and cataracts were widespread. Then, in 1987, the Montreal Protocol emerged as a cooperative effort to slow ozone depletion by reducing output of chlorine and bromine ozone-depleting substances. Twelve years later, thanks to the Protocol and follow-on agreements, concerns over ozone depletion are largely behind us. Global production of CFCs has fallen dramatically, and atmospheric concentrations of

Figure 4.2
Atmospheric concentrations of ozone-depleting substances first rose, then began to fall

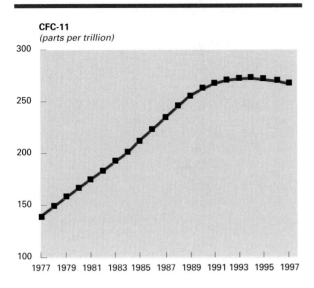

CFC-11
(parts per trillion)

Note: Figure reports ground-level concentrations of CFC-11 at seven monitoring stations (in Alaska, Hawaii, American Samoa, the South Pole, Canada, the continental United States, and Tasmania). *Source*: Elkins 1999.

these chemicals have not only stabilized but are beginning to drop (figure 4.2).[34] Not all the problems relating to ozone have been resolved. The black market in CFCs, while declining, is estimated at 20,000 to 30,000 tons per year.[35] But global cooperation to reduce ozone depletion can be broadly declared a success.

The key factors that allowed the negotiators in Montreal to reach a strong international agreement were:

- A consensus that the risks of ozone depletion as a result of CFCs and other substances containing chlorine and bromine had high costs, and that there was the technological and institutional ability to find cost-effective, environmentally benign substitutes.
- The involvement of all parties with a significant role to play in solving the problem, brought about by using both payments and penalties, along with flexibility in setting conditions for meeting the treaty's goals.

Consensus on high net benefits

At the time of the Vienna Convention for the Protection of the Ozone Layer in 1985, a consensus on the impact of chlorine and bromine ozone-depleting sub-

stances did not yet exist. So, although the Vienna talks created a framework for future agreements, they did not contain a protocol limiting the use of CFCs. The discovery of an ozone hole over the Antarctic in the winter of 1985 pushed the issue into the news and helped create consensus on the need for international action.[36] Six months after the 1987 Montreal meetings, the International Ozone Trends Panel report heralded the first occasion on which the link between CFCs and ozone depletion, along with evidence of depletion occurring over the populated mid- and high latitudes of the Northern Hemisphere, was reported by the scientific community and accepted by policymakers from key CFC-producing countries.[37] This stronger acceptance led to agreements being signed at the London meeting of the parties in 1990 that greatly accelerated the timetable for abandoning ozone-damaging chemicals. This agreement and its successors covered 97 ozone-depleting chemicals—far more than the 8 covered by the Montreal Protocol.

When the first treaty limiting CFC production was signed in Montreal in 1987, little or no evidence existed that ozone had thinned anywhere but over the Antarctic—nor that CFCs had caused the ozone hole, nor that increased ultraviolet radiation was already starting to reach the earth.[38] Montreal was the first significant treaty to accept the "precautionary principle," which holds that scientific uncertainty should not delay an international policy response if the delay might result in irreversible damage.[39] Nonetheless, growing scientific consensus on the costs of continued CFC production and possible substitutes was vital to the passage of the treaties. The process of coming to such a consensus was hastened by the Assessment Panel mechanism created as part of the Montreal treaty. These international panels of economic, scientific, and technical experts described the advancing status of scientific understanding and technical response options in the run-up to meetings of the parties.[40]

The high ratio of expected benefits to costs also helped the passage of the CFC agreements. One reason the costs were relatively low was that research into alternate technologies had been under way for some time. In response to earlier public pressure, some countries had begun introducing restrictions on CFCs in aerosol sprays in the late 1970s.[41] The United States, which had begun regulating CFCs in 1977, banned all nonessential CFC aerosol sprays in 1978, giving CFC producers time (and the incentive) to research alternative production methods before all uses of CFCs were banned.[42] At the same time, the costs of policing compliance with CFC-reduction targets were relatively low because the production of CFCs was largely concentrated in a few countries and was controlled by relatively few companies. This, combined with the large potential benefits of an international agreement to limit CFC production, gave OECD countries a strong incentive to negotiate. This was especially so given that the threat of skin cancer as a result of exposure to increased ultraviolet radiation was far greater in OECD countries than elsewhere.

Nongovernmental organizations (NGOs) also played a role by helping to put pressure on governments to negotiate deals. By raising public awareness of the possibly catastrophic dangers of ozone depletion and the links with chlorine- and bromine-containing substances, NGOs worked with the scientific community to create popular support for an agreement (box 4.4). The role of NGOs is in line with one of the themes of this report: that civil society can have an important place in the international policymaking arena.

Global participation

A vital element in the success of the ozone treaties was the participation of all countries that produced or consumed (or seemed likely to produce or consume) significant amounts of ozone-depleting substances—including developing countries. The post-Montreal consensus on ozone damage served as a dramatic testimonial to the importance of including developing countries in an agreement. The World Resources Institute estimated that if Brazil, China, India, and Indonesia alone increased CFC production to the levels allowed in the Montreal Protocol, global production of ozone-depleting substances would double from the 1986 base level. The impact of such an increase on ozone levels would be profound.[43] Not involving developing countries, especially in the more stringent targets set at London, would have also threatened the treaty with "leakage"—that is, companies moving CFC factories from OECD sites to developing countries with higher production limits.

But developing countries needed an incentive to agree to tighter restrictions. They feared that substitutes for ozone-depleting substances would be more expensive, and they felt in a poor position to bear such costs.[44] Questions of international equity took center stage. To secure their cooperation, developing countries were of-

---

Box 4.4
NGOs and efforts to preserve the international environment

Nonstate actors are playing an increasingly important role in the negotiations surrounding international agreements. Groups such as nongovernmental organizations (NGOs) often make an enormous contribution by serving as conduits for information on the environmentally damaging activities of countries and governments.

The Montreal Protocol negotiations were open to representatives from NGOs representing business and science. The World Meteorological Organization, with the United Nations Environment Programme (UNEP), played an important role in presenting numerous reports by the scientific community that illustrated the linkages between chlorine- and bromine-containing substances and ozone depletion.[45] Outside the formal negotiating process, Friends of the Earth UK led a boycott of CFC aerosol products that lasted until 1987. The boycott resonated with the public and put pressure on the U.K. government to push for a strong treaty.

NGOs are also essential players in efforts to support best environmental practices and to discourage unsustainable behavior. *World Development Report 1998/99* cited the role of the West African Newsmedia and Development Center, a regional NGO based in Benin, in disseminating environmental information through print and broadcast media.[46] NGOs are also working with industry to create and advertise standards for areas such as fishing and forestry. NGOs and representatives from the timber trade and forestry profession have formed the Forest Stewardship Council, an international association aimed at promoting sustainable forestry practices. The council's international labeling scheme for forest products provides a credible guarantee that the products bearing the labels come from forests meeting the standards laid out in the council's Principles and Criteria for Forest Stewardship.

---

fered a grace period of exclusion from controls on chlorine and bromine ozone-depleting substances. They would also have access to a fund set up to cover adjustment costs and finance technical assistance.[47] The initial fund introduced at the London meeting provided $160 million (paid for by OECD countries) and an additional $80 million if China and India signed the protocols.[48]

The Montreal agreement also banned international trade between signatories and nonsignatories of CFCs, products containing CFCs, and CFC technology. The significance of this provision was made clear when the threat of trade sanctions (combined with increased funding from a number of OECD countries and the Global Environment Facility) encouraged Russia to agree to meet its commitments to phase out CFC production by

2000.[49] Payments and trade mechanisms to support compliance, along with flexibility in treaty restrictions, were vital in creating a strong global agreement. But the payments and flexibility were possible and the trade sanctions credible only because eliminating CFCs would provide industrial countries with substantial net benefits. The potential benefits, plus the threat of sanctions gave these countries an incentive to sign the treaties, despite the financial burden the agreements imposed.[50]

Finally, restrictions on CFC production were made as flexible as possible. For example, Japan was reconciled to the treaty despite a high reliance on CFC-113 for cleaning computer chips by a mechanism that set a limit on total production of ozone-depleting chemicals and allowed countries to use any combination of CFCs within their overall limit.[51]

Climate change

Why have attempts to cut global greenhouse gas emissions been less successful so far than efforts to halt production of ozone-depleting substances? The contrast between the progress that has been made in tackling these two global environmental concerns highlights the importance of a consensus that actions to address the problems have clear net benefits.

Costs and benefits

At the global level the benefits of stabilizing or reducing carbon emissions are potentially substantial. As noted above, the IPCC estimates that a doubling of carbon dioxide in the atmosphere would result in costs for developing countries equal to 2–9 percent of GDP.[52] The quantifiable costs are lower as a percentage of GDP for industrial countries but are still around 1.0–1.5 percent of GDP. These estimates include only costs that can be easily quantified, omitting the effects of factors (such as species extinction) for which it is hard to assign a monetary value.

While the benefits of controlling greenhouse gases appear lower for industrial countries, estimates of the costs of controlling emissions suggest the reverse—that costs are higher in industrial economies than in developing countries. Holding carbon dioxide output in the United States at 1990 levels until 2010 will reduce the country's GDP by an estimated 0.2–0.7 percent. Lowering output by 20 percent will cost 0.9–2.1 percent of GDP. The costs are certainly far lower for developing countries. One recent study suggests that the cost of re-

ducing carbon dioxide emissions in the Arab Republic of Egypt and Zimbabwe by 20 percent would actually be negative, since the government would only have to remove inefficient subsidies—a net gain.[53]

The benefits of efforts to prevent climate change will become apparent only in the long term, while the costs of such mitigation must be paid today. And while controlling climate change offers potentially significant benefits, the costs of reducing carbon dioxide emissions are also significant—far greater than the costs of controlling ozone-depleting substances. With climate change, then, the costs of prevention are higher and the relative scale of benefits is lower, especially for industrial countries. While mechanisms such as carbon trading will reduce this disparity, it does suggest a reason for the greater political complexity of negotiating strong greenhouse gas accords: unlike the relatively narrow range of activities that affect the ozone layer, the major sources of greenhouse gas production are ubiquitous, including power generation, industrial energy use, transportation, and farming.[54] These activities account for a huge share of global GDP and are deeply entrenched in the production structures of industrial and developing economies alike.

Moreover, much of the technology required to make the switch to cleaner production methods is comparatively expensive, suggesting a greater economic and political burden in technology switching than in the case of ozone-depleting substances. In the long term, renewable energy sources may play a more important role in production, but wind and solar energy are not yet feasible economic substitutes for fossil fuels on a large scale. Even in areas where they are economically feasible today, market distortions and entry barriers limit their use (box 4.5). It should be noted, however, that economic reform and funding for research could make renewable energy sources more attractive.

Indeed, increased support for research on new technologies can lower the long-term costs of complying with stricter carbon emissions limits worldwide. Three of the most successful technologies supported by the U.S. Department of Energy—heat-reflecting windows, electronic ballasts for fluorescent lights, and variable-capacity supermarket refrigeration units—are now saving enough energy to justify the department's entire efficiency research budget.[55] Despite such remarkable results, "efficiency and renewables" research received only about 23 percent of the rapidly shrinking U.S.

Box 4.5
Falling costs for renewable energy

Renewable energy resources offer enormous potential for producing electricity, particularly in developing countries, which often have an abundant supply of sun, water, wind, biomass, and other energy sources. This potential remains largely untapped, mainly because of lack of familiarity with renewable energy technologies and because of their relatively high up-front costs. But two trends indicate that the future may be brighter for renewable energy sources in developing countries.

First, in certain niche areas, the costs of renewable energy are already competitive with conventional energy resources, even at the low fossil fuel prices of the late 1990s. Conventional power generation has two less costly competitors: mini-hydropower sites and biomass cogeneration facilities. These facilities are located close to population centers or to transmission lines (into which they feed their power). A number of solar photovoltaic systems are feasible for off-grid power generation. These systems are most useful in rural areas far from the main power grid and in sparsely populated areas where low demand makes the cost of extending the grid prohibitive.

Second, it has become clear that creating competitive, market-type conditions significantly reduces the costs of using renewable energy technologies. In Indonesia, once it became known that the World Bank and the GEF would finance a large renewable power project, potential vendors began to cut prices to secure their position in the emerging market. Competition also reduced the costs of wind-generated power under the United Kingdom's Non–Fossil Fuel Obligation (NFFO) scheme. Under the NFFO, renewable energy projects are selected in competitive bidding and receive an output subsidy financed by a levy on electricity generated with fossil fuels that applies to all electricity consumers. By November 1998, five NFFO bidding rounds had taken place. As the figure shows, bid prices—the lowest as well as the average bid—for wind energy de-

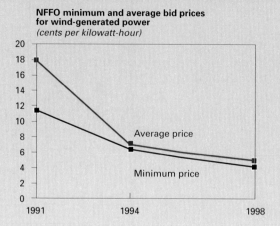

Competition has reduced the cost of wind-generated power in the United Kingdom

NFFO minimum and average bid prices for wind-generated power *(cents per kilowatt-hour)*

Source: World Bank data.

clined dramatically, falling from an average of around 18 cents per kilowatt-hour in 1991 to 5.1 cents per kilowatt-hour in 1998. (Declining prices for fossil fuels during this period meant that the relative costs of renewable technology fell more slowly.)

Although technological progress is clearly essential to reducing the costs of using renewable energy technologies, sector reform, including the removal of subsidies on fossil fuels and open competition, can also be an important factor. Whether managed, as in the United Kingdom, or spontaneous, as in Indonesia, reform has helped drive technological advance and has encouraged the efficient use of technology.

budget for energy research and development in 1997.[56] Redirected and increased expenditure on research, better coordinated at the international level, is a win-win international response to climate change.

Governments can take several steps to encourage private sector investment in alternative energy research, as well. Early and concrete moves toward carbon emissions limits will push firms to start looking at other energy sources. Turning from subsidizing carbon-based fuels to taxing them instead (or raising such taxes gradually) while offering support for research on alternative energy sources can change incentives. The recent commitment of some of the world's major oil companies to reducing their carbon emissions is a hopeful sign that the early negotiations on greenhouse gases have already encouraged private sector responses that will lower the cost of future emissions compliance. Even so, the chicken-and-egg problem—progress toward energy

alternatives requires emissions treaties, and treaties only happen when costs of agreement are lower—seems likely to plague greenhouse gas negotiations for some time to come.

The long-term approach of reaching an international agreement on reducing greenhouse gas output might include agreements on common policies and measures, such as fuel efficiency standards for cars. But it is also likely to involve negotiating either an internationally coordinated tax or a system of quotas on carbon emissions, which might be tradable between countries. Either approach will face many practical difficulties (box 4.6). This is one more reason that the perceived benefits of treaty making will have to rise far above the costs to create the flexibility needed to sign such a tough agreement.

In short, a number of reasons suggest that coming to an international agreement on greenhouse gas emis-

Box 4.6
Taxes and quotas to reduce emissions

Two competing mechanisms are frequently suggested for use in a global agreement on reducing greenhouse gas output. The first, which was used in the Kyoto agreement, sets caps on each country's output of greenhouse gases. Many economists favor auctioning off emissions permits, up to the quantity of the cap, that can be traded both within a country and across national boundaries. The second main approach would involve implementing national carbon taxes at globally agreed levels.

The mechanics of incorporating either approach into an international agreement are complicated, however, because the costs and benefits of reducing greenhouse gases vary considerably across countries. Energy taxes and energy efficiency also differ vastly across countries, raising the question of how to set a baseline for either tax rates or output.

With a globally agreed tax on emissions applied equally, countries with low marginal benefits from emissions would spend more on abatement measures than those with high marginal benefits. While the tax system would also generate healthy revenues for governments (and especially in the developing world, carbon taxes may be more efficient than the present tax regime), an equal tax regime would probably lead developing countries to abate more than those industrial countries with higher marginal costs of abatement. To equalize the pain of reducing output, tax rates might have to vary across countries. But that would create incentives for leakage, with high-polluting industries moving to countries with the lowest tax rather than reducing their greenhouse gas output. A global carbon tax agreement would also have to specify exactly which emissions were to be taxed. Certain emissions, such as those from livestock, paddy fields, and wood-burning stoves, are regarded as largely "untaxable." These types of emissions differ dramatically across countries, which adds to the difficulties of allowing certain activities to be exempt from an emissions tax. Finally, nations would have to agree whether the emissions taxes would be kept by each nation or shared to some extent across nations.

Under a global binding agreement on national emissions levels, the added flexibility of being able to negotiate national quotas could allow a more equitable distribution of the costs of treaty compliance than a tax agreement. Quotas could also be used to transfer resources from industrial to developing countries. This "cap and trade" system does present problems, however. Assigning quota allocations is not a simple process. For example, the Kyoto Protocol is based on the assumption that countries will make broadly similar percentage reductions, starting from 1990 levels. Future, more encompassing agreements will have difficulty with the assumption of broadly equal reductions from treaty-start levels; developing countries will find such reductions unacceptable because they expect to consume more energy as they develop. A mixed approach would be needed that sets quotas according to several factors, including present absolute output, output per capita, and level of development. Quotas could also be based on a target rate of improvement in energy intensity (use of energy per unit of GDP). Further problems remain, however:

- If developing countries are to be enticed into the system, the net quota trade would need to run from the developing to the industrial world, which creates the potential for large economic transfers. The political viability of this transfer mechanism is questionable, however, since transfers would be made without regard to the political and economic activities of recipient countries.[57]
- What has been termed the problem of "low-hanging fruit" might also affect the carbon-trading mechanisms proposed at Kyoto. This arises when developing countries have traded away the cheapest methods of reducing carbon emissions, and have to pay for more costly measures in order to meet their international obligations.
- Certifying that countries have met their obligations is likely to prove a major challenge, both in enforcing the Kyoto agreements and beyond. As has been mentioned, many activities contribute in some way to climate change. And issues such as how to measure carbon sequestration (if that is to be included as part of the treaty mechanism) are still far from settled.

sions as comprehensive as those on ozone will be a much more complex task. And it is not surprising that in many developing countries there are mixed feelings about controlling emissions. The Alliance of Small Island States (AOSIS) and some other low-lying countries such as Bangladesh give the most urgent priority to curbing climate change, for understandable reasons. A 1-meter increase in the sea level would force about 70 million people to move and would have a dramatic effect on food security in Bangladesh (figure 4.3). But even most developing countries would still rank such activities as burning forests for agriculture (releasing carbon dioxide and removing a carbon sink), raising livestock and growing rice (releasing methane), and

burning fossil fuels (releasing carbon dioxide) as more beneficial social priorities than reducing emissions of greenhouse gases. Thus while the AOSIS, for example, has adopted unilateral carbon abatement measures, until the coalition is larger, this first step is unlikely to translate into stronger multilateral accords.[58] Nonetheless, the world is moving toward increased global cooperation on climate change.

Increasing participation
Industrial countries are responsible for most of the increase in man-made greenhouse gases in the atmosphere. But before the middle of the next century, energy consumption in developing countries is projected

Figure 4.3
A 1-meter rise in sea level would cut Bangladesh's rice production approximately in half

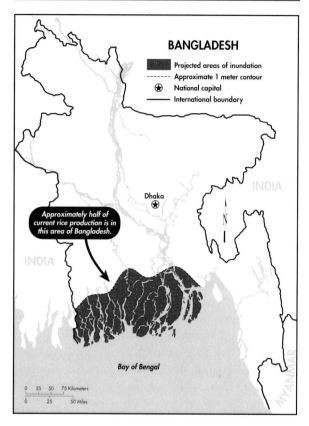

Source: World Bank 1998f.

Figure 4.4
Energy consumption in developing countries is forecast to outstrip industrial country consumption

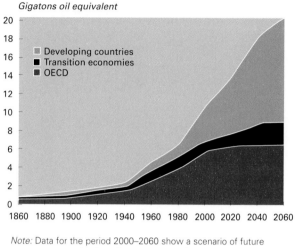

Note: Data for the period 2000–2060 show a scenario of future energy consumption based on current trends.
Source: World Energy Council; World Bank.

- Current and historical emissions of greenhouse gases in developing countries are much lower than in either industrial or transition economies. Per capita emissions are also likely to remain lower for the foreseeable future.
- Industrial countries have greater economic, technical, and institutional capacity to address the issue.
- The imperatives of social and economic development argue for increasing energy use in developing countries.

to be more than twice that of OECD countries, even though per capita consumption will remain much lower, as it is now (figures 4.4 and 4.5). Developing countries must be included in global greenhouse gas agreements, both because of the likelihood that they will someday bear the responsibility for most greenhouse gas emissions and because without their cooperation, any progress could be offset by leakages to developing countries (box 4.6). For example, if a steel plant tries to avoid emissions limits by moving its operations from a relatively energy-efficient industrial country to an energy-inefficient country not covered by an agreement, total greenhouse gas output could rise.[59]

But although drawing developing countries into binding agreements on greenhouse gas emissions is vital, industrial countries are still expected to take the lead on such an agreement, for several reasons:

The Kyoto Protocol encompasses transition economies and involves developing countries through a system of limited and voluntary cooperation. Industrial countries can meet their commitments for lower emissions not only by reducing emissions within their countries but also by trading obligations with countries that have committed to targets or by funding emissions reduction projects in developing countries. For transition economies that have agreed to emissions targets, the treaty allows for commitment trading, while the Joint Implementation scheme enables industrial countries to acquire emissions trading permits in return for supporting emissions reduction projects in those economies.[60] After 2000, the Clean Development Mechanism may allow industrial nations to buy project-based emissions

Figure 4.5
High-income countries use energy more intensively than countries in low-income regions

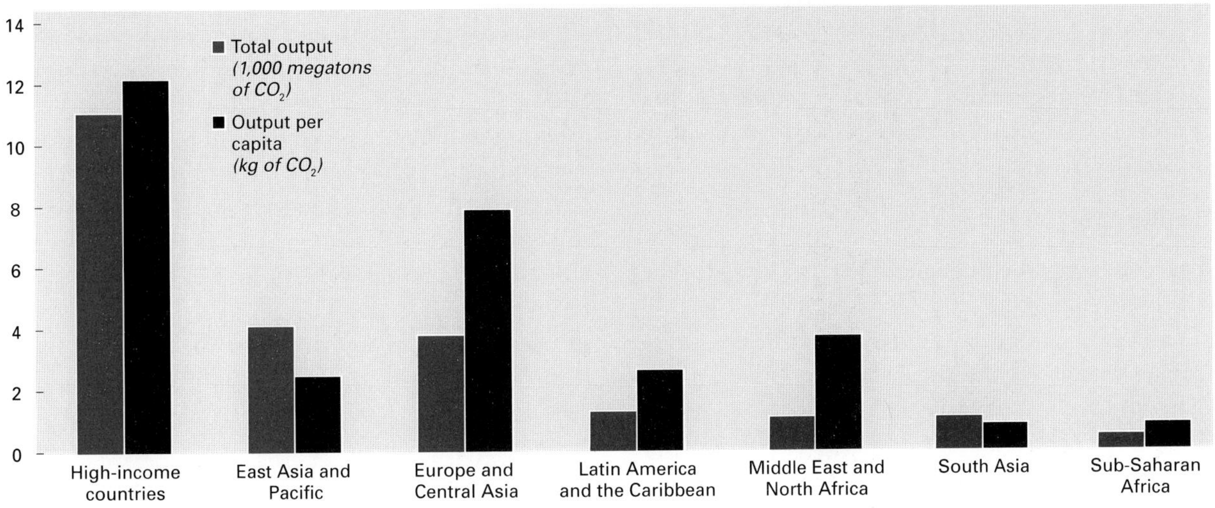

Total output
(1,000 megatons
of CO_2)

Output per
capita
(kg of CO_2)

High-income countries · East Asia and Pacific · Europe and Central Asia · Latin America and the Caribbean · Middle East and North Africa · South Asia · Sub-Saharan Africa

Source: World Bank, *World Development Indicators*, 1998.

rights from developing countries that have not agreed to binding emissions targets, with a portion of the proceeds being used for administration costs and to help particularly vulnerable developing countries meet the costs of adapting to climate change.

These limited trading mechanisms should have a significant effect on the costs of emissions reductions. Estimates vary, but one model suggests that the marginal tax or quota price for the United States to meet the Kyoto target (93 percent of 1990 levels by 2012) would be about 72 percent lower if quota trading were allowed among industrial and transition economies. Adding some key developing countries to the trading network would reduce permit prices even further, to an estimated 12 percent of the autarky price.[61]

The scale of trading—and thus of transfers among countries—is likely to be large. The OECD countries emit about 3 billion tons of carbon a year. The Kyoto agreement alone will reduce the emissions these countries would have produced without the agreement by at least 30 percent. If carbon is valued at $23 a ton, and only half the reductions are met through quota trading, the global quota market will be worth $11.5 billion a year—more than the total U.S. aid budget.

In the long term, the Kyoto Protocol's Clean Development Mechanism is not a full solution to the greenhouse gas problem, in part because it does not solve the

problem of leakage. It could also create perverse incentives for carbon trading among industrial and developing countries (see box 4.6). Still, it is an important first step toward global involvement in the reduction of greenhouse gas output.[62] As noted, involving developing countries at some level and as early as possible is very important for controlling future greenhouse gas emissions. The demand for electric power in developing countries is rising rapidly and is projected to climb by up to 300 percent between 1990 and 2010, outpacing by far the 20 percent rise expected in industrial countries.[63] Joint Implementation and the Clean Development Mechanism can be used to ensure that a significant proportion of the projected generating capacity in developing countries is based on low-carbon-dependent technology.[64]

To further the goal of reducing greenhouse gas output in developing countries, the World Bank has begun a series of projects under the pilot phase of Activities Implemented Jointly established at the Rio Summit. The Ilumex project in Monterrey and Guadalajara in Mexico has replaced some 200,000 ordinary incandescent light bulbs with compact fluorescent light bulbs. Because the new bulbs use far less energy than conventional lighting, power stations need to provide less electricity, permanently reducing the demand for fuel. The project should also help Mexico reach its own goals for reducing emissions of sulfur dioxide and nitrogen oxides. In Burkina Faso a sustainable energy management project will promote solar power systems and kerosene cooking stoves while supporting community-based sustainable forestry management and efficient carbonization techniques. The project will abate more than 300,000 tons of carbon emissions a year for just $2.5 million, or $8.30 per ton of carbon.[65]

Biodiversity

The Convention on Biological Diversity signed at the Rio Earth Summit in 1992 has been ratified by 169 countries. Signatories to the convention are obliged to conserve and ensure the sustainable use of their own biological diversity.[66] Those countries with the greatest biodiversity are concentrated in the developing world. Only one of the eight countries that are home to the largest number of native mammal species is industrial. Of the countries with more than 10,000 species of higher plants, 18 out of 20 are developing countries, and 12 of the 17 countries with more than 500 threatened species of higher plants are developing countries.[67] Developing countries are thus key to meeting the goals set at Rio, and the Convention on Biological Diversity was passed with widespread support from these countries.

Like the Framework Convention on Climate Change, the Biodiversity Convention recognized economic and social development as the top priorities for developing countries. It also stated that the extent to which developing country parties would effectively implement their commitments to preserve biodiversity would depend on industrial country commitments related to financial resources and transfer of technology.

The benefits of biodiversity and the costs of preservation

As we have seen, the ecosystems (and the species) in which genetic material resides provide valuable services at the national level. For this reason, the primary role of international agencies and bilateral support in the area of biodiversity should be to transfer knowledge and provide technical assistance to help overcome national market failures and create national markets for ecological benefits.

The GEF was chosen as the formal interim financing mechanism for the Convention on Biological Diversity. Total GEF financing for biodiversity projects comes to over $800 million and has already been used to support a range of technical and institutional proj-

ects. In Poland, for example, the Forest Biodiversity Protection Project has provided institutional support to the country's environment ministry, funded pilot investments in air- and soil-monitoring equipment and a forest gene bank, and supported farmers in the Bialowieza Primeval Forest who are making the transition to "ecological agriculture." In Algeria the El Kala National Park and Wetlands Management Project introduced actions to stop degradation within the complex and supported assessment activities that included surveys, studies, and public education programs aimed at bolstering long-term preservation efforts.

While such support may form the backbone of international efforts to preserve biodiversity, the global commons issues connected with existence value and exploitation of genetic resources remain. The economics of these issues is complicated by disagreement on what exactly is being valued—whether it is the right of plants or animals to exist, the material benefits that diversity offers, or the just the pleasure that the existence of many living organisms brings to people. Even basic facts such as the total number of species on earth and the rate of species extinction worldwide are not fully clear. The UNEP's Global Biodiversity Assessment estimates the number of species on the planet at 7 million–20 million and the expected loss of species over the next 25 years at between 140,000 and 5 million. Combining the lower-bound estimates suggests that 2 percent of all species are at risk; combining the upper-bound estimates produces an estimate of 25 percent (although it should be noted that even the lower rate of extinction is approximately 1,000 times the natural rate).[68]

Many of the benefits of preserving genetic material are also difficult to quantify in monetary terms. How is a dollar value to be placed on the rights of organisms to exist or on the pleasure people derive from their existence? Among the more quantifiable benefits is the medicinal use of genetic resources. The United Nations has estimated that medicines originally developed from plant material are worth about $43 billion a year.[69] The rosy periwinkle from Madagascar's rain forest, for example, provided a rare genetic trait that was used in developing pharmaceuticals to treat childhood leukemia. Two of the drugs one company has developed from this plant have sales worth $100 million a year. (None of these proceeds, it should be noted, goes to Madagascar.)[70] But even calculating the marginal benefit of the genetic material in a species is no easy task. The drugs developed from plants must be collected, refined, tested, and developed for the market, and sharing the profits along this value chain is clearly a complex issue. Genetic materials are also likely to be present in more than one species. This fact helps explain why estimates of the marginal value of species existence (put another way, the marginal value of preventing species extinction) are so uncertain. They have been put at anywhere from $44 to $23.7 million for an untested species.[71]

Expanding participation

Even if the value of genetic material is hard to estimate, it is certainly true that the international community continues to exploit it without paying—a scenario that constitutes a market failure. As a result, biodiversity may be undervalued in developing countries. An additional mechanism for promoting the preservation of genetic resources would be the extension of property rights to a country's genetic material. This subject was raised at the Convention on Biological Diversity, but no agreement was reached on what should be done about the situation.[72] One model for resource transfer might be that of Costa Rica's private, nonprofit National Biodiversity Institute (INBio), which struck a deal with U.S.-based pharmaceutical firm Merck and Company to help underwrite INBio's biodiversity prospecting plans.[73] The Merck deal will pay INBio $1.1 million plus royalties for any product Merck develops from Costa Rican resources. In return INBio provides Merck with samples from all over Costa Rica. Ten percent of the up-front money and 50 percent of any royalties are allocated to inventory, bioprospecting, and conservation.[74]

A number of doubts have been raised about such mechanisms. The Costa Rica–Merck agreement, for example, does not involve enough resources to pay for significant increases in protected reserves. The scheme might also not be widely replicable. One recent estimate suggests that even in western Ecuador, one of the areas richest in endemic species, the per-hectare value of genetic material to drug companies is only about $20.[75] Furthermore, by claiming royalties on products developed from plants and animals that may be found in more than one country, INBio is effectively reducing the incentive of neighboring countries to take similar measures to protect their genetic diversity. This problem is likely to be widespread: the rosy periwinkle was not endemic to Madagascar, for example. Moreover, it is unclear how such a scheme could work to protect areas that have already been explored for genetic material. Thus, while establishing limited property rights to genetic material may encourage developing countries to participate in preservation efforts, they represent only a partial solution. If industrial countries feel that additional incentives to preserve genetic material are required (to cover, as it might be, the existence value of species, regardless of their economic uses) the simplest method would be to expand direct international support for this purpose.

Biodiversity covers many different activities, including farming, forestry, coral reef protection, and others. This diversity calls for great flexibility in approach toward agreements on different biodiversity issues, at both the regional and global levels.[76] Technical and institutional support and flexible transfer payments are two such approaches. Sanctions have also been used. When biodiverse habitats are exploited in order to produce a tradable good—including tropical fish, tropical timber, and many of the animals covered by the Convention on International Trade in Endangered Species (CITES)—formal trade limits or certification schemes with strong penalties for noncompliance can play an important role. One way to protect coral, for example, might be to ban trade in fish caught by using cyanide, a significant source of coral degradation. Similar incentives have been widely used in a range of environmental treaties. Although questions remain about the risk of overusing trade measures to counter environmental threats (and thus using the environment as an excuse to strangle trade as a wealth-creating force), trade measures can be a very effective method of pursuing environmental goals under some circumstances (box 4.7).

Exploiting the links between global environmental problems

Climate change and biodiversity are not only serious issues in their own right but are also linked with each other and with a wide range of other environmental concerns. Depending on the rate of climate change, forest species may be unable to adapt fast enough to avoid severe population declines.[83] Aquatic ecosystems such as mangroves and coral reefs adapt even more slowly.[84] The loss of species and genetic material can increase the vulnerability of ecosystems to other environmental stresses, such as pollution.[85] To complete the circle, the destruction of forests has a dramatic impact on climate change because forests release significant quantities of carbon dioxide as they burn.[86]

Box 4.7
Trade measures in international environmental agreements

The earliest environmental treaty to use trade measures was the International Convention Respecting Measures to be Taken against the Phylloxera Vastatrix, which in 1881 banned trade in torn vines and dried shoots to prevent relocating the plant louse to other vineyards.[77] Other environmental agreements with trade measures include:

- CITES, which allows trade in listed species or products made from them with nonparties to the agreement only when competent authorities in the nonparty country issue documentation comparable to that required of treaty members. The convention also allows members to impose trade bans on other members that do not comply with the restrictions. In 1991 the CITES standing committee recommended that all trade with Thailand in flora and fauna species covered by the convention be stopped because of noncompliance.
- The United Nations agreement on the Conservation and Management of Straddling Fish Stocks and Highly Migratory Fish Stocks, which allows members to prohibit the landing or transshipment of fish caught using methods that undermine the effectiveness of conservation and management measures.[78]
- The Montreal Protocol, which requires parties to ban the import of controlled ozone-depleting substances from nonsignatories unless the nonsignatories are found to be in full compliance with the protocol regime.[79]

Trade measures can be an appropriate tool for addressing global environmental problems because they, like the problem, are global in nature. They can also be justified on the grounds that free trade is considered a global good because it maximizes welfare. If trade is instead causing serious environmental damage, then, it can be argued, it must be limited. Trade may be especially intertwined with certain environmental risks: damage from relocation; insect infestation of previously unexposed crops from imported infected fruit; negative disposal effects like those posed by imports of toxic waste; negative transport effects such as oil spills; and negative profit effects—as when trade ends up financing a decline in biodiversity.[80]

Three recent international trade rulings suggest that international trade agreements allow little flexibility on the unilateral introduction of environmental trade bans: the WTO's ruling against U.S. laws banning the import of shrimp caught in nets that also trap turtles, and two rulings by the General Agreement on Tariffs and Trade (GATT) dispute panel on tuna caught in nets that also trap dolphins. But the WTO ruling does support the right of states to impose sanctions as part of an international treaty. Distinguishing between unilateral and multilateral trade bans keeps environmental sanctions from being used as a cover for protectionist interests.[81]

Trade bans should also be limited to areas in which they can be effective. The international ivory trade (as well as mismanagement of elephant stocks) must be seen as an important reason for the drastic decline in elephant populations between 1979 and 1989.[82] In situations in which trade is the dominant outlet for production, as it is for ivory, sanctions can have a major effect. Often, however, trade sanctions are too far from the source of the problem to be effective—which might limit the effectiveness of trade bans to counter greenhouse gas emissions.

Exploiting such links can greatly reduce the cost of environmental protection. For example, whether land use activities should be eligible under the Clean Development Mechanism is an issue being decided by the parties to the Kyoto Protocol. But counting the preservation of developing country carbon sinks against emissions commitments could provide powerful synergies with local environmental and biodiversity protection needs.[87]

Costa Rica has already begun trading Certified Tradable Offsets (CTOs)—carbon credits priced at $10 a ton—in ways that exploit such links. The profits from these credits are designed to support sustainable forestry practices on private land or to finance the conservation of land as national parks and bioreserves.[88] So far, sustainable practices have been introduced on 3,000 farms covering 150,000 hectares. The bioreserve project has conserved another 530,000 hectares.[89] Although there have been few early takers for the credits, Costa Rica's experiences with the system, combined with continued international research, could lead to greater exploitation of this synergy between biodiversity preservation and the prevention of climate change.

These links across global environmental issues suggest that the international community needs to move beyond simply negotiating separate agreements for each environmental issue. As agreements such as CITES demonstrate, treaties are often agreed to only because complex problems are broken up into smaller units. But in some cases, agreements that cover many areas are easier to negotiate because of the potential for trade-offs or synergies between related issues. This pattern has prevailed in multilateral trade negotiations, for example, when countries that feel strongly about certain provisions have offered concessions in areas that concern them less. Global environmental protection can also be hastened by improving coordination between treaty and convention secretariats, including integration of meetings, scientific assessments, reporting requirements, publicity, training, and capacity-building efforts and improved coordination under the UNEP.

· · ·

The world's countries have come far in cooperating to address global environmental issues, and the ozone accords provide a model for future agreements. Although drawing up international agreements on biodiversity and climate change that are as effective as the ozone agreements has been difficult, the basic mechanics of successful international environmental agreements are becoming clearer. Moreover, even taking preliminary steps toward a partial agreement encourages private actors to prepare for stricter agreements and thus lowers the cost of future actions to resolve environmental concerns. Consensus on biodiversity, climate change, and other global environmental issues will only expand over time. Furthermore, the growing understanding of linkages among environmental concerns will create more opportunities to exploit both synergies and trade-offs, helping to foster coalitions that support concerted global action.

5

Decentralization: Rethinking Government

People around the world are demanding greater self-determination and influence in the decisions of their governments—a force this report has labeled *localization*. Some 95 percent of democracies now have elected subnational governments, and countries everywhere—large and small, rich and poor—are devolving political, fiscal, and administrative powers to subnational tiers of government (box 5.1).[1] But decentralization is often implemented haphazardly. Decisionmakers do not always fully control the pace or genesis of the decentralization process. Even when they do, models of decentralization are often exported from one country to another without regard for local political traditions, regulatory frameworks, or property rights.

Decentralization itself is neither good nor bad. It is a means to an end, often imposed by political reality. The issue is whether it is successful or not. Successful decentralization improves the efficiency and responsiveness of the public sector while accommodating potentially explosive political forces. Unsuccessful decentralization threatens economic and political stability and disrupts the delivery of public services.

This chapter argues that the success of decentralization depends on its design. It reviews developing countries' experience with decentralization and shows that the stakes are high. Drawing on this experience, it offers guidelines for improving the political, fiscal, and administrative institutions of decentralization. This advice is not only relevant to countries that have already decentralized. It can also help the many countries now embarking on this path avoid some of the major hurdles that have confronted their predecessors.

What is at stake?

The experience of the last 15 years shows that the devolution of powers affects political stability, public service performance, equity, and macroeconomic stability.[2]

Political stability

A primary objective of decentralization is to maintain political stability in the face of pressures for localization. When a country finds itself deeply divided, especially along geographic or ethnic lines, decentralization provides an institutional mechanism for bringing opposition groups into a formal, rule-bound

Box 5.1
Decentralization as the devolution of powers

Decentralization entails the transfer of political, fiscal, and administrative powers to subnational units of government. A government has not decentralized unless the country contains "autonomous elected subnational governments capable of taking binding decisions in at least some policy areas."[3] Decentralization may involve bringing such governments into existence. Or it may consist of expanding the resources and responsibilities of existing subnational governments. The definition encompasses many variations. India, for example, is a federal state, but the central government has considerable power over subnational governments. Political power in China is officially centralized, but subnational units have substantial de facto autonomy in what can be described as "decentralization Chinese style."

Central governments can devolve their powers in other ways. *Deconcentration* increases the autonomy of staff in regional offices, while *privatization* moves responsibility out of the public sector altogether. The policy implications differ. Deconcentration preserves the hierarchical relationship between field staff and the central government. Privatization eliminates it altogether, introducing the profit motive instead. Decentralization shifts the focus of accountability from the central government to constituents, usually through local elections.

Box 5.2
South Africa and Uganda: unifying a country through decentralization

South Africa and Uganda have adopted ambitious decentralization programs and, despite some difficulties with implementation, are emerging as two important models for devolving centralized power.[9] The models operate in different contexts: a middle-income and predominantly urban country (South Africa), and a low-income, predominately rural country (Uganda). But both have the same goal: to reunify the country.

South Africa. Apartheid fostered a dual structure of government based on race. For whites, it promoted accountability, political involvement, and effective service delivery. But blacks, spatially segregated in "homelands" and "townships" on the fringes of urban areas, had limited access to public goods and services. To reverse this racial system, the new constitution provides for a comprehensive decentralization policy, which the leadership has been implementing.

The racial jurisdictions were formally abolished along with the system of apartheid. The country was subdivided into 9 provinces, 5 metropolitan areas, and 850 municipalities, all racially mixed and with democratically elected governments. The central government retains primary fiscal responsibility for expenditures that have a major redistributive impact, such as health and education, but metropolitan governments have been restructured to implement policies at the local level. Some difficulties remain—for example, how to divide responsibility for health and education between the central government and the provinces. But decentralization has succeeded in becoming one of South Africa's main instruments of unification.

Uganda. The task President Museveni faced when he assumed power in 1985 was to reunite a country that had splintered into hostile factions during years of turmoil. The broad-based politics of "resistance councils" and committees that had been developed during the years of civil war helped pacify most parts of the country. This system—which entails giving power to the people of a village (the council) to freely choose their leaders (committees)—served as the basis for the local government policy enshrined in the 1995 constitution. The 46 districts, which are subdivided into smaller units down to the village level, have taken on substantial responsibilities for education, health, and local infrastructure. They now account for 30 percent of overall government spending.

Uganda still faces problems with implementing decentralization. Limited local capacity and resistance from central ministries have hobbled the transfer of responsibilities. The revenues local governments control (primarily user charges and local taxes) have not increased as much as expected, and grants still account for 80 percent of local resources. Despite increased participation, local services and management have not become significantly more responsive to local preferences—although this is now improving. Even with these difficulties, however, decentralization has been much more successful in maintaining national unity than the previous policies of centrally imposed controls.

bargaining process.[4] In South Africa and Uganda decentralization has served as a path to national unity (box 5.2). In Sri Lanka it offers a potential political solution to the civil war. It is an instrument for deflating secessionist tendencies in Ethiopia and Bosnia and Herzegovina (box 5.3). In Colombia centralized party elites relied on decentralization to gain grassroots support, particularly in areas under rebel control.[5] And Russia's transformation into a decentralized federal system can be seen as a means of conceding enough power to regional interests to forestall their departure from the republic.[6]

Public service performance

The classic argument in favor of decentralization is that it increases the efficiency and responsiveness of government.[7] Locally elected leaders know their constituents better than authorities at the national level and so should be well positioned to provide the public services local residents want and need. Physical proximity makes it easier for citizens to hold local officials accountable for their performance.[8] Finally, if the population is mobile and citizens can "vote with their feet" by moving to another jurisdiction, decentralization can create

Box 5.3
Bosnia and Herzegovina and Ethiopia: decentralization as a response to ethnic diversity

Ethiopia and Bosnia and Herzegovina illustrate the tension between political imperatives and economic efficiency that emerges in countries with ethnic tensions.

Bosnia and Herzegovina. The possibilities for instituting "efficient" federalism and equalization in an ethnically polarized society are limited. The Dayton Peace Agreement, which addressed the challenges of governing Yugoslavia's successor states, had the potential to solidify relations among the three ethnic groups that ratified it. But the agreements had to compromise on some key principles of fiscal federalism to reach a politically acceptable solution. The Dayton agreement limited the state's authority to international relations (including customs and trade policies, debt service, and debt management), central banking (through a currency board), and telecommunications and national transport infrastructure. The national government's only revenues are now passport fees and transfers from its two constituent entities, the Federation and the Republika Srpska. It has few spending powers and no redistributive functions. All taxing powers belong to the two entities, which are responsible for all other spending, including defense, pensions, health, and local roads. The entities are divided further into local governments that are responsible for education, housing, social transfers, and public services. There are no cross-subsidies across the two entities and very few across local governments.

The state faces challenges in carrying out even its minimal responsibilities, since it relies on transfers from the entity governments. Moreover, since economic conditions differ substantially across the country, large inequalities are likely to develop among and within the entities.

Ethiopia. Ethiopia's system of intergovernmental relations is designed to accommodate the rights of citizens to ethnic self-determination within a common political and economic community. The 1994 constitution, which establishes subnational boundaries and mechanisms for intergovernmental fiscal relations, stipulates that regions shall be formed on the basis of ethnic settlement patterns, language identity, and the consent of the people concerned. Subgroups within the member states have the right to establish their own states, and states have the right to secede from the federation.

The Ethiopian system differs from the Bosnian federalist structure in one key way: in Ethiopia the central government retains control of most tax revenues and has a strong redistributive role. Central transfers consist of block grants determined according to population, development indicators, and revenue performance. The poorer regions receive as much as 75 percent of their revenues through these grants. But the capital, Addis Ababa—which is the richest region—receives no central government support. State-level spending is kept under control by federal regulations on domestic borrowing and by a block grant formula that reduces regional transfers in proportion to external borrowing and donor grant flows. States are free to spend their block grants as they choose, subject only to federal auditing.

Ethiopia faces two challenges in its decentralization model. One is to develop stronger state revenue sources to deflect ethnic tension — especially resentment from ethnic groups in richer regions that receive less in government transfers. The second is to strengthen local governments, which are responsible for delivering most services but do not have the necessary capacity.

Source: Fox and Wallich 1997; World Bank 1999b.

competition among local governments to better satisfy citizens' needs.[10]

But evidence supporting these arguments is scanty—not because there is evidence to the contrary, but rather because the causal relationships are difficult to prove. Governments perform a variety of functions under vastly different circumstances, which complicates comparisons of performance in a country before and after decentralization, or across countries between centralized and decentralized systems. Moreover, efficiency and responsiveness can be hard to measure, and indicators are seldom readily available.[11]

How decentralization affects access to and quality of public services depends on the way it is designed and implemented. What local governments can achieve depends on the resources and responsibilities they are granted and on the power of national governments to override their decisions, as happens in India (box 5.4) and Zambia. Even within a particular sector, the mode of decentralization makes all the difference. In Central America, decentralizing management responsibilities from the central government to provincial and local levels had little effect on the primary education sector. But decentralizing management responsibility directly to the schools did improve educational performance.[12]

Decentralization can also lower the quality of public services, as it has in Latin America and Russia.[13] Conceding power to local governments is no guarantee that all local interest groups will be represented in local politics. It may simply mean that power is transferred from national to local elites. In India, for instance, local participation depends on social caste, and the poor have little influence.[14]

Equity

Whether decentralization exacerbates income differences among regions or becomes a positive force in efforts to alleviate poverty depends on two factors. The

Box 5.4
India: a decentralizing federation?

India has a federal constitution that gives its states substantial fiscal and regulatory powers. But three elements undercut those powers. First, the constitution also has strong unitary features, enabling the central government to dissolve state governments and take over their administration. Second, central planning—which until recently governed India's economy—blunted the economic powers of states. Third, national parties traditionally dominated subnational politics. Thus state budgetary outcomes were the result of centrally defined development policies and, in practice, state-level regulatory powers had little meaning.

The relative centralization of India's federalism is changing, however. The gradual weakening of central planning and the growing strength of regional parties in national coalition governments are strengthening state governments and allowing them a larger role in defining their development priorities. But most states are having difficulties growing into their new role. Many are saddled with excessive debt and unsustainable wage and pension bills and have few incentives to mobilize their own resources. A few states, including Andhra Pradesh, Uttar Pradesh, Orissa, and Haryana, are improving their financial situation and are making increasing use of the powers constitutionally granted to them.

The trend toward greater decentralization in India was reinforced in 1992 by the passage of the 73rd and 74th Amendments, which offered constitutional recognition to local governments. Until then, the constitution had made no mention of local governments, which were effectively creatures of the states. States were not under any obligation to hold regular local elections, and state-run agencies controlled most local functions, including urban planning and local infrastructure. Under the amendments states continue to define local governments' powers and resources and name their chief executive officers. They also retain the power of supersession—that is, the right to dissolve a local government and take over its powers. However, the amendments suggest a list of local responsibilities for inclusion in state constitutions and call for the creation of state-level financial commissions to oversee fiscal relations between states and local governments. Most important, states are required to hold elections within six months of superseding a local government.

Implementing the amendments has been a slow process, and some states have progressed more than others. With one exception, all states have held local elections and are observing the supersession rule. The proposed local functions are now part of most states' legislation, and a number of states have set up finance commissions that have submitted recommendations. However, state governments have been slow to implement these recommendations and to enable local bodies to execute the newly devolved functions. Recent assessments show that Gujarat, Karnataka, Kerala, Madhya Pradesh, Maharashtra, and West Bengal have made the most progress in devolving powers to local governments.

Source: Hemming, Mates, and Potter 1997; Mathur 1999; Mohan 1999; World Bank 1998i.

---

first is *horizontal equity*, or the extent to which subnational governments have the fiscal capacity to deliver an equivalent level of services to their population.[15] The second can be described as *within-state equity*, or the ability or willingness of subnational governments to improve income distribution within their borders. An additional complication springs from the fact that responsibilities for social services and direct income redistribution are typically shared across different tiers of government that have access to different sets of information and may have different objectives.[16]

Horizontal equity. Tax bases vary substantially from region to region and city to city, but tax rates cannot. A local government with a relatively small tax base cannot compensate by imposing much higher tax rates without losing businesses and residents to jurisdictions with lower taxes. The costs of providing public services may also vary because of regional characteristics such as population density and geographic location. To correct for such variations, most decentralized fiscal systems include equalization grants. In Vietnam the per capita tax revenues of low-income provinces are only 9 percent of those of wealthier provinces, but expenditures are 59 percent as a result of transfers from the central government.[17] In Australia, Canada, and Germany grants guarantee a minimum level of per capita expenditures for essential services in all regions. In other countries the goal is to ensure similar levels of service.[18] A difficulty with equalization grants is that subnational governments may differ in their willingness to raise taxes. Furthermore, the grants create an incentive for subnational authorities to understate their tax bases or relative wealth in order to maximize transfers.[19]

Within-state equity. In most countries income inequality is due more to differences among individuals within a state or province than to differences among the states or provinces themselves.[20] Providing poorer regions with additional resources, then, affects only one aspect of the equity problem. Evidence from India and Indonesia shows that even dramatic redistribution across regions will have limited results unless targeting is improved within regions themselves.[21] This, in turn, depends on the ability and willingness of the local government to engage in redistribution.

Recent studies have shown that local officials and community groups are better placed to identify and reach the poor than central authorities. In Albania, for example, local officials had considerable success in targeting the poor—far better than expected, given available statistical information on income and family characteristics.[22] In Uzbekistan elected neighborhood committees were able to increase both the efficiency and the cost-effectiveness of targeting.[23] Their success suggests that local officials have access to social networks that help them identify the truly needy. But this may not be the case in very large jurisdictions, such as China's provinces.

Subnational governments differ in their responsiveness to the needs of the poor. A recent review of an Argentine social program that is funded by the central government but implemented by provinces found that poverty targeting varied substantially across provinces. When reforms were introduced to improve the program's reach to the very poor, most of the improvements were due to reforms in intraprovincial targeting and better national monitoring of provincial performance.[24] Similarly, in Bolivia it was only when decentralization gave communities more power to influence their local governments that the composition of local public expenditures shifted in favor of the poor.[25]

Success in targeting the poor requires, therefore, a combination of national and subnational efforts. In general, the bulk of the funding needs to remain a central government responsibility, but the better information available to local officials can be tapped by involving local governments in the delivery and management of social services. Central government needs to retain a monitoring role, however, to ensure that redistributive goals are satisfied.

Macroeconomic stability

Decentralization, if handled poorly, can threaten macroeconomic stability.[26] Fiscal decentralization reduces the central government's control over public resources. The government of the Philippines, for example, is required to share nearly half its internal tax revenue with subnational governments, limiting its ability to adjust the budget in response to shocks. Deficit spending by local governments can also thwart central government efforts to cool the economy by restraining public expenditure.

When revenues are decentralized before expenditure responsibilities, central governments are forced to maintain spending levels with a smaller resource base.

The result—seen in many Latin American countries—is large central government deficits. More generally, separating taxing and spending powers allows subnational governments to incur only a fraction of the political and financial costs of their expenditures, especially when most local resources are funded out of a common national pool of tax revenues.

The threat of macroeconomic instability is a serious issue only in countries where subnational governments control substantial resources—usually, large federations or very decentralized wealthy countries (figures 5.1 and 5.2).[27] But even in these cases the evidence connecting decentralization and macroeconomic instability is mixed. Several studies suggest that decentralization has not undermined stability in the United States or in Western European countries. In Latin America subnational governments' contribution to the national deficit was negligible in most countries, except federal ones.[28]

From centralized to decentralized governance

A decentralization program needs to be adapted to a country's prevailing conditions. However, the experience of the past 15 years has yielded some universal

Figure 5.1
Subnational expenditures are a small share of public expenditures, except in industrial countries and large federations

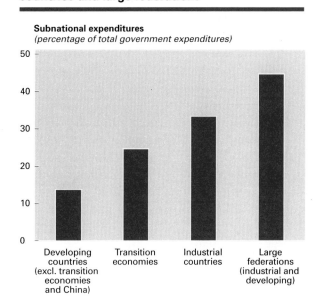

Subnational expenditures
(percentage of total government expenditures)

Note: Graph shows median values rather than averages. *Subnational expenditures* are most recent available observations after 1990. Large federations are Argentina, Brazil, Canada, India, Mexico, the Russian Federation, and the United States.
Source: Appendix table A.1.

Figure 5.2
Local governments never control a large share of public resources

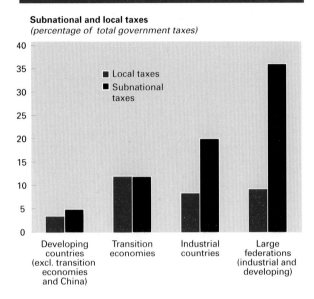

Subnational and local taxes
(percentage of total government taxes)

Developing countries (excl. transition economies and China) | Transition economies | Industrial countries | Large federations (industrial and developing)

■ Local taxes
■ Subnational taxes

Note: Graph shows median values rather than averages. *Local taxes* and *subnational taxes* are most recent available observations after 1990. Large federations are Argentina, Brazil, Canada, India, Mexico, the Russian Federation, and the United States.
Source: Appendix table A.1.

lessons, which countries currently decentralizing can use to their advantage. One such lesson is the need for a coherent set of rules to replace the hierarchical system of governance characteristic of centralized systems.

A major challenge of decentralization is to institutionalize the balance of power between the national and local governments. This requires rules that both protect and limit the rights of subnational governments. Such rules come in a variety of forms. Some are unwritten. No law prohibits the United States government from providing relief to states in default, for example. Nor does Turkish law require the national government to bail out its defaulting municipalities. Yet in both cases these are well-established practices that influence the expectations of lenders and borrowers.

Making the rules of decentralization explicit and reasonably permanent reduces uncertainty and provides a common ground for all players in the political process. Informal, negotiation-based decentralization is difficult to manage, as illustrated by China's experience (box 5.5). Rules enable subnational governments to coordinate a defense against an overassertive central government while restricting their ability to bargain.[29] The lit-

erature on constitutionalism makes a strong case for establishing the most fundamental of these rules—choosing the heads of state and government, electing members of the legislature, distributing power among branches of government—in a form that can be altered only by exceptional majorities or complicated amendment procedures.[30] To be sustainable, such rules must be "self-enforcing"—that is, all parties must believe they have more to gain by adhering to the rules than they do by breaking them.[31]

Rules should be explicit, stable, and self-enforcing. But how should a country decide what their substance should be? The answer involves three broad areas of analysis: the division of national political power between national and subnational governments; the structure, functions, and resources assigned to subnational governments; and the electoral rules and other political institutions that bind local politicians to their constituents.

Balancing political power between central and local interests

The rules that govern relations between the central and subnational levels are almost always established at the national level, generally by the central government.[32] Even when these rules are incorporated into constitutions or treaties, they are still subject to renegotiation and to varying interpretations as to appropriate implementation.[33] The balance of powers between national and subnational governments will therefore depend on the influence of regional interests on the national government. And the stability of this balance of powers hinges upon the design of institutions that make it in the interest of national and subnational political elites to cooperate with each other.

Moderating regional influence on the national government

The influence of subnational interests on the national government depends on two factors. The first is the way regional interests are incorporated in the national legislature, which determines a subnational government's ability to pressure the national government to change rules. The second factor is the strength of the national executive, which influences the central government's ability to withstand such pressure.

Regional interests and the legislature. Seats in parliament may be allocated to give equal representation to states or provinces, thereby favoring norms of territor-

Box 5.5
Decentralization in China

China is formally constituted as a unitary state, and the dominant political party—the Chinese Communist Party—recommends candidates for the posts of governor and mayor for ratification by the People's Congress.[34] But political and economic power has dispersed markedly in recent years, particularly since the reforms of 1978. The number of posts controlled directly by the central organization of the party declined from 13,000 to 5,000, and central planning has largely been abandoned. Under such conditions, local leaders have more incentives to generate local economic prosperity than to follow some nationally determined economic goal, and they have acquired substantial autonomy in designing and implementing policy. China's central government can no longer unilaterally recapture the powers it has conceded and may not even want to. In February 1999, when a township elected its leader directly for the first time, the outcome was broadcast on national television, signaling official support for this event.

China's approach to decentralization relies on negotiations rather than rules to define relations between the central government and the four subnational tiers—provinces, prefectures/cities, counties, and towns. The allocation of responsibilities across tiers of government remains unclear except for health and education, which are controlled by the provinces. On the revenue side, until the early 1990s local governments were responsible for administering and collecting a large proportion of central government taxes, but their loyalty shifted away from the national government to the subnational level. Provincial tax officers often used the tax administration system to establish tax autonomy. They entered into direct negotiations with enterprises for payments (in lieu of the central

government's enterprise income tax) and transferred tax funds that would otherwise have been shared with the central government into local extrabudgetary accounts.

In 1994 new reforms created separate tax administrations for national and local taxes, a step that increased the central government's share of tax revenues but remains highly unpopular. Five years later the principle that taxes belong to the central government unless specifically assigned to localities is still widely contested at the local level. Further, subnational governments continue to rely on extrabudgetary funds—some of them illegal—for the largest share of revenues. These funds, combined with frequent (and also illegal) provincial deficits, confer substantial fiscal independence on provincial administrations.

Decentralization Chinese-style does allow for considerable subnational autonomy. It creates incentives for local officials to work toward local prosperity and has also been an effective tool for instituting market reforms. But over time, the absence of clear rules may threaten its successes. Decentralization has accentuated a prereform tendency toward a fiefdom mentality that hampers efforts to unify the national market and periodically threatens central control over macroeconomic stability. Moreover, while administrative discretion has helped preserve the momentum for growth and reform, it has also created opportunities for rents that can be appropriated through financial corruption or political patronage. Official statistics show that by the end of 1998, 158,000 officials had been penalized by the Party's Commission for Discipline Inspection, and corruption was one of the main themes of the National People's Congress, China's parliament, in March 1999.

---

ial representation over norms of population (or citizen) representation. In bicameral systems the upper house commonly gives equal weight to states and thus represents regional interests in the national legislature. Senates in Argentina and Mexico award an equal number of seats to each state or province regardless of population, giving small units of government disproportional voting power. In the Argentine senatorial elections, one vote in Tierra del Fuego is worth 180 votes in Buenos Aires; in Mexico one vote in Baja California is worth 31 votes in the state of Mexico. And in Brazil, senators representing less than 13 percent of the electorate control 51 percent of the votes. In most bicameral countries, however, senates have limited powers, so the effect of territorial representation is much greater if it is applied to the lower house.[35]

When members of the upper house are chosen to represent regional interests, they can be elected directly by the people of that region, or they may be selected by

the regional governments themselves, as they are in Germany, India, Pakistan, and South Africa.[36] In Russia provincial governors and prime ministers serve in the upper house on an ex officio basis. In principle, such explicit representation renders the upper house a tool of regional governments. Again, however, the impact on the national legislature depends on the powers granted to the upper house.

Finally, electoral arrangements matter. For example, electoral districts based on regional boundaries reinforce political cleavages along regional lines. For this reason, the approach is seldom used.[37] Among the large democracies, Argentina, Brazil, Colombia, Italy, and Spain are the only ones defining legislative districts solely along regional lines. Others rely on smaller subregional districts or have a number of legislators elected at large to represent the whole country, rather than a specific region.

The power of the executive. A central government's ability to withstand regional pressure depends on the strength of the chief executive and on whether a clear majority emerges in parliament. Whether the executive is chosen by parliament or by direct popular vote (that is, whether the regime is parliamentary or presidential) matters less than the powers of the executive in relation to the legislature. These powers include vetoes and the ability to control the legislative agenda or to legislate by decree. The degree to which the chief executive depends on the support of a political party is also a factor. Thus the United States is a presidential regime, but the constitutional division of powers forces presidents to rely on their party's support.[38]

The electoral system also influences the vulnerability of the executive to pressure groups. Proportional representation, which allocates seats in proportion to the share of votes received by each party, tends to produce governments that require a coalition of parties to govern.[39] Such coalition governments are inherently less stable and more vulnerable to demands by interest groups than majoritarian governments.[40] But proportional representation does allow disparate regional and ethnic interests to have a distinct voice in government. Combined with a parliamentary system of government, as in most Western European countries, proportional representation imposes the need to govern by consensus. Conventional political theory advocates such a system for new democracies precisely because it ensures a voice even for smaller groups, giving them a stake and presence in the new democracy rather than shutting them out.[41] But proportional representation combined with a presidential regime, as in Latin America, tends to produce executive-legislative deadlock.[42]

Creating incentives for national and subnational governments to cooperate

For the balance of powers to be stable, a commonality of interests must develop between national and subnational political elites.[43] Political parties play a crucial if often underestimated role in this process.[44] In the United States and Germany, national parties control the state legislatures, whereas in Canada regional parties compete with each other in subnational elections. As a result, Canada's subnational politicians are often elected on platforms explicitly framed in opposition to the national government and hardly ever move from provincial to national elected office. In contrast, in the United States and Germany opposition between national and subnational politicians is likely to be purely partisan, and often national leaders in both countries start their careers as subnational elected leaders.

Institutions can be designed to promote a commonality of interests. The electoral system and the resulting party structure determine the degree to which the political system is nationally integrated. Holding national and local elections concurrently creates incentives to nurture the meaning of party labels and to develop nationwide parties.[45] Legislative bodies that explicitly represent regions tend to promote integrated party structures.[46] The executive authority of the central government relative to the regional government matters, since it determines whether the central government needs to govern by consensus or fiat. Similarly, the strength of the chief executive's powers determines the extent to which the executive must rely on regional support.

There is no single best way to divide national political power between central and subnational governments. Nor can a single constitutional provision ensure that central and subnational political elites will find it in their interest to cooperate. But whatever system is adopted, it must not make the central government a prisoner of subnational interests.

The structure, functions, and resources of subnational governments

The second major category of rules deals with the way subnational governments are structured, what they do at each level, and how they are funded. These rules need to be determined as a system, taking into account the interactions among fiscal, political, and administrative institutions.

Structure and functions

What is the best structure for subnational governments? The traditional approach of public finance economists to decentralization, known as "fiscal federalism," calls for a subnational government structure with several tiers, with each tier delivering those services that provide benefits to those residing in the jurisdiction.[47] Experience shows that this model, while useful, has some limitations and that governments should seek instead to develop a regulatory framework that allows for the sharing of responsibilities.[48]

The fiscal federalist framework and its practical limits. The fiscal federalist model identifies three roles for the public sector: macroeconomic stabilization, income redistribution, and resource allocation (in the presence of market failure). The model assigns the stabilization role to the central government because it controls monetary policy and has more scope to use fiscal policy than subnational governments. The model also assigns income redistribution to the center, since local attempts at taxing the rich and redistributing wealth to the poor would result in inefficient population movements—high-income groups would move to areas with low taxes, and low-income groups would concentrate in areas offering high benefits.[49]

More recently the literature has recognized that while the central government should continue funding and designing redistribution efforts, local governments are often in a good position to implement and administer standardized national policies.[50] In addition, local governments usually administer services that have important redistributive implications, such as primary health care, education, child care, housing, and public transportation. In poorer countries such services are often the only vehicle for providing in-kind transfers to poor households.

The fiscal federalist approach assigns a significant role to subnational government in allocating resources. This is because when the benefits of particular services are largely confined to local jurisdictions, the appropriate levels and mix of services can be set to suit local preferences. Local consumers can express their preferences by voting or by moving to other jurisdictions.[51] In this respect, local politics can approximate the efficiencies of a market in the allocation of local public services.

This approach faces two practical obstacles, however. First, in developing countries where land and labor markets may not function well and the democratic tradition is in its infancy, it is not realistic to assume that people can move easily between jurisdictions or make their voices heard through the political process.[52] Second, establishing separate tiers of government for each service is costly and poses serious coordination problems.[53]

The structure of subnational governments. The appropriate number of tiers of government and of jurisdictions in each tier varies depending on a country's physical characteristics, its ethnic and political makeup, and possibly its income level. But all countries face the same trade-off between representation and cost. The local government of Midnapur in India may have difficulties managing local services in a way that is representative of the preferences of all its 8.3 million people. But very small local governments—like those of Armenia, the Czech Republic, Hungary, Latvia, and the Slovak Republic, which have an average population of less than 4,000—are likely to use up most of their meager resources in fixed administrative costs.[54]

Trends in mature decentralized countries suggest that costs are an important consideration. Most countries of the Organisation for Economic Co-operation and Development (OECD) have a limited number of subnational tiers and jurisdictions (table 5.1). Some countries have recently been reducing the number of subnational units, largely on grounds of efficiency and cost.[55] But in a number of developing countries, subnational governments are proliferating. In 1992 Morocco increased the number of its municipalities from 859 to 1,544 and made regions the third tier of subnational government.[56] Even among very poor countries such as Madagascar, Malawi, and Zambia, the trend is toward a constant, if gradual, increase in the number of local governments—perhaps in part because a block grant available to each local government creates an incentive to divide jurisdictions.[57]

Clarifying the allocation of functions and allowing for shared functions. Some services can be provided less expensively on a larger scale, or their benefits may spill over across districts. Providing these services centrally creates economies of scale and captures externalities, but at the cost of imposing a common policy on populations with varied preferences and priorities.[58] This trade-off, which is the basis of the fiscal federalist approach, guides some of the choices that must be made in allocating functions. The services central governments provide should benefit the entire economy or exhibit substantial economies of scale—for example, national defense, external relations, monetary policy, or the preservation of a unified national market. Correspondingly, subnational units should provide local public goods. This model, which most established democracies have adopted, is also common to most countries that have recently decentralized, with the notable exception of Bosnia-Herzegovina (see box 5.3).

Such responsibility-sharing arrangements are complex. But they work well when they are clear, when each tier's responsibilities are relatively well defined, and when the regulatory framework anticipates that local governments are sometimes agents of the central government and sometimes principals acting on their own. Without clarity and an appropriate regulatory framework, there can be no accountability. In South Africa the central government and the provinces have joint responsibilities for health and education, but the exact responsibilities of each are not defined. The result is that provinces receive transfers to fund these services but use them for other purposes, knowing full well that

Table 5.1
The structure of subnational governments in large democracies

Country	Intermediate	Local	Country	Intermediate	Local
Industrial countries			Kenya	39 county councils	52 municipal, town, and urban councils
Canada	10 provinces, 2 territories	4,507 municipalities	Korea, Rep. of	6 special cities, 9 provinces	67 cities, 137 counties
France	22 regions, 96 departments	36,772 communes	Malaysia	13 states	143 city, municipal, and district councils
Germany	13 states, 3 city-states	329 counties, 115 county-free cities, 14,915 municipalities	Mexico	31 states, F.D.	2,412 municipios
Italy	22 regions, 93 provinces	8,100 municipalities	Mozambique	10 provinces	33 municipalities
Japan	47 prefectures	655 cities, 2,586 towns	Nepal	75 districts and town panchayats	4,022 village panchayats
Spain	17 autonomous communities	50 provinces, 8,097 municipalities	Pakistan	4 provinces	15 municipal corporations, 457 municipal and town committees, 40 cantonment boards, 4,683 union and district councils
United Kingdom	Counties	540 rural districts, metropolitan districts, and London boroughs			
United States	50 states, F.D.	39,000 counties and municipalities, 44,000 special-purpose local authorities	Philippines	76 provinces	64 cities, 1,541 municipalities, 41,924 barangays
			Poland	16 provinces, 307 poviats	2,489 gminas
Other countries			Russian Federation	21 republics, 17 territories or autonomous areas, 49 provinces (oblasts), 2 cities of federal status	1,868 raions, 650 first-tier cities, 26,766 secondary cities, townships, and villages
Argentina	23 provinces	1,617 municipios			
Bangladesh	—	4 city corporations, 129 pourashavas (smaller municipalities), 4,500 union parishads (which group 85,500 villages)			
Brazil	27 states, F.D.	4,974 municipios	South Africa	9 provinces	850 local authorities
Colombia	32 departments, F.D.	1,068 municipalities	Thailand	75 changwats, Bangkok	6,397 districts, 148 municipalities and cities
Ethiopia	9 regions, plus 2 special city administrations, 66 zones	550 woredas	Turkey	74 provinces	2,074 municipalities
India	25 states, 7 union territories	3,586 urban local bodies (95 municipal corporations, 1,436 municipal councils, 2,055 nagar panchayats), 234,078 rural local bodies	Uganda	45 districts, 13 municipalities	950 subcounties, 39 municipal divisions, 51 town councils
			Ukraine	24 regions (oblasts), 1 autonomous republic, 2 municipalities	619 districts
Iran, Islamic Republic of	25 provinces	720 districts and municipalities	Venezuela	23 states, F.D.	282 municipalities

—Not applicable.
F.D. Federal district.
Source: Appendix table A.1.

the central government will intervene to provide the needed service.

Assigning and controlling resources

The question of which tier of government controls which resources is perhaps the thorniest issue of decentralization. The ability of subnational authorities to act independently of the central government depends on whether they have access to independent tax bases and sources of credit.[59] Experience provides two lessons in this area. First, subnational governments need resources commensurate with their responsibilities. Second, subnational authorities must operate under firm budget constraints, so that they do not spend or borrow excessively in the expectation of a central government bailout.[60]

The guiding principle of revenue assignment is straightforward: finance should follow function. This is so not only because resources must be commensurate with what they fund, but also because the type of revenues used affects consumer behavior and results in different patterns of incidence. User charges, such as bus fares or water bills, affect the amounts consumed by users and are borne only by those who actually consume the service. Overall, the appropriate structure of subnational finance—the mix of user charges, taxes, and transfers—depends on the functions that have been assigned to each tier of government.

Certain forms of taxation are appropriate for financing local services with benefits that cannot be confined to individual consumers, such as local roads. Such taxes must fall on the residents of the jurisdiction and must be direct—that is they must directly target individuals or personal property so that their burden is local. Good examples are the property tax, the personal income tax, and capitation or head tax. Indirect taxes such as the value added tax (VAT) or corporate income tax, which can be built into the price of the goods and passed on to consumers outside the taxing jurisdictions, are not generally appropriate as local taxes.

But direct taxation in developing countries often yields limited revenues. The income tax is of limited use where most of the economy operates informally. In many countries the capitation tax, which was one of the main forms of taxation in colonial times, is politically unacceptable. And the property tax, which requires good information systems, is usually poorly administered.[61] To compensate, most municipalities rely on various forms of business taxation. Jordan imposes a business license fee, Brazil has taxes on services, and

some Indian states rely on the octroi (a tax on goods circulating across regional or municipal boundaries). Although efficient, such taxes are politically easier to impose, since their effects are hidden in the price of goods. As a result, even mature decentralized democracies such as Germany and the United States resort to them. Overall, subnational taxes are seldom a large share of subnational revenues (see figure 5.2), although there is scope, particularly in developing countries, for improving local revenue collection.[62] For intermediate levels of government, the problem of matching taxes to the jurisdiction is even more complicated (box 5.6).

The role of transfers. Since transfers account for a large part of subnational finances everywhere, their design is a critical factor in the success of decentralization.[63] Transfers are needed to fund the services local governments provide on behalf of the central government (while local revenues should ideally cover local expenditures). And transfers are essential to ensure that decentralization does not occur at the expense of equity, particularly if the central government relies on programs administered at the subnational level to redistribute income or if there are large income differences across districts. Finally, governments can use transfers to influence the sectoral pattern of local expenditure by earmarking transfers or disbursing them in the form of matching grants.

Although transfers are almost always necessary, they should not be so large as to eliminate the need for local taxes.[64] Local taxes ensure that subnational governments face, at least to some degree, the political consequences of their spending decisions. And political necessity sometimes imposes the need for relying heavily on local taxes. Tax sharing was one of the more contentious issues in the Yugoslav federation, where wealth differed greatly across ethnic groups and redistribution issues were embroiled in ethnic tensions. Similarly, the search for a good regional tax is of paramount importance in Ethiopia, where regions are defined on the basis of ethnic identity (see box 5.3).

Transfers have three variables.[65] The first variable is the amount to be distributed. This can be fixed as a percentage of national taxes, or it can be an ad hoc decision, sometimes to reimburse preapproved expenditures. The second variable is the criteria for distributing transfers among jurisdictions. In Argentina, for example, a predetermined formula is used to allocate a fixed percentage of certain national taxes, whereas in India the central government periodically determines, on the

Box 5.6
Financing intermediate tiers of government

Intermediate tiers of government, such as states and provinces, often have substantial responsibilities that cannot be funded solely through user fees.[66] Yet direct taxes have limited yields in developing countries and tend to be allocated to local governments. Indirect taxes are generally more appropriate for the national government, since the burden of such taxes can be passed on to consumers outside the taxing jurisdiction (a problem referred to as tax exporting). No perfect solution exists for the problem of financing the intermediate tier of government, and in practice large federal countries typically use a combination of two approaches.

The first approach consists of granting exclusive rights to a broad-based tax, such as an income tax or a value added tax (VAT), to the intermediate tier. The income tax has the advantage of affecting only residents of the state or region, avoiding the tax-exporting problem, but is of limited yield in poor countries. A VAT like that used in Brazil, Russia, and Ukraine provides substantial resources but raises issues of interstate smuggling and tax exporting. In fact, subnational VATs are so complex to administer that they should only be considered in countries with efficient tax administrations. State corporate income taxes also present administrative difficulties, notably the problem of determining in which state a company has realized its profits.

The second approach is to share national taxes. This can be implemented in a variety of ways. One is to let the states set a surcharge on a nationally administered and collected tax—which does present the advantage of making state government bear at least part of the political burden of a tax. Another is pure tax sharing, in which the central government remits a part of its tax revenues to the jurisdiction in which they were collected. Mexico, for example, imposes a national VAT which it redistributes to states on the basis of what they would have received by imposing this tax themselves. Argentina uses a similar system. Pure tax sharing has no advantage over surcharges except for preserving a uniform tax rate. Revenue sharing, which relies on a formula for allocating the proceeds of a national tax across different regions, is similar, although it can be used to equalize revenues across jurisdictions regardless of their tax base.

basis of need, both the levels of the transfers and the method of distribution. The third variable concerns the conditionalities imposed on the use of transfers. Transfers can be earmarked for specific uses, such as paying teachers' salaries, or left unrestricted.

Transfers should be designed according to their objectives. Those intended to finance functions that the municipal government is performing on behalf of the central government should be earmarked. Transfers intended as substitutes for local taxes should not, but

their amount needs to be equivalent to the tax base they are replacing. In practice, however, most transfers take the form of block grants. This tendency may reflect a search for administrative simplicity, or it may reflect the reluctance of subnational governments to accept any restrictions on the use of transfers. In countries where subnational interests are well represented in national parliaments—France, Germany, Japan, and the United Kingdom, for example—block grants account for the bulk of intergovernmental transfers.

Some basic principles are applicable across all countries and all types of transfers. Transfers should be determined as openly, transparently, and objectively as possible. They should be kept reasonably stable from year to year so that local governments can plan their budgets. And they should be distributed on the basis of predetermined rules, which need to be kept as simple as possible.[67] Simplicity, transparency, and predictability would help eliminate one of the worst problems of decentralization: the uncertainty and bargaining that often plague intergovernmental fiscal relations.

Controlling subnational debt. Subnational borrowing has emerged as one of the thorniest issues for decentralization. In principle, it is a private transaction between borrower and lender. But the national government is often drawn reluctantly into the transaction because of its responsibility for the stability of the financial system. As a result, subnational borrowing is almost always subject to the assumption that the central government will fund a bailout if necessary—an assumption that leads banks to lend to uncreditworthy local governments.

An alternative to the private financing of subnational borrowing is for the central government to provide long-term credit, lending either directly or through intermediaries. In most countries—particularly those with shallow financial systems—this remains the principal source of subnational credit and largely dominates private financing. But the repayment record for centrally sponsored financial intermediation is poor (see chapter 6). Loan allocation tends to become politicized, while debt collection is often lax, with national taxpayers ultimately bearing the financial burden of bad loans.

In general, however, private financing is either already the primary source of subnational credit or is meant to eventually replace central government financing. This requires developing means to protect the central government and the national financial system from exposure to excessive subnational debt. As shown in table 5.2, short of outright prohibition, four ap-

Table 5.2
Subnational borrowing controls in selected countries

	Market discipline		Cooperative control		Administrative control		Rule-based control		Borrowing prohibited	
	Overseas	Domestic	Overseas	Domestic	Overseas	Domestic	Overseas	Domestic	Overseas	Domestic
Industrial countries										
Australia			•	•						
Austria					•	•				
Belgium			•	•						
Canada	•	•								
Denmark			•	•						
Finland	•	•								
France	•	•								
Germany							•	•		
Greece					•	•				
Ireland					•	•				
Italy							•	•		
Japan						•			•	
Netherlands							•	•		
Norway					•	•				
Portugal	•	•								
Spain					•	•				
Sweden	•	•								
Switzerland							•	•		
United Kingdom					•	•				
United States							•	•		
Developing countries										
Argentina			•	•						
Bolivia			•	•						
Brazil			•	•						
Chile			•	•						
Colombia			•	•						
Ethiopia						•			•	
India					•	•				
Indonesia					•	•				
Korea, Rep. of					•	•				
Mexico						•			•	
Peru					•	•				
South Africa			•	•						
Thailand									•	•
Transition economies										
Albania									•	•
Armenia									•	•
Azerbaijan									•	•
Belarus									•	•
Bulgaria									•	•
China									•	•
Estonia					•	•				
Georgia									•	•
Hungary					•	•				
Kazakhstan									•	•
Kyrgyz Republic									•	•
Latvia					•	•				
Lithuania					•	•				
Poland									•	•
Romania									•	•
Russian Federation	•	•								
Slovenia									•	•
Tajikistan									•	•
Ukraine									•	•
Uzbekistan									•	•

Note: Classifications attempt to capture the predominant form of control. In most countries, the approach used involves a combination of several techniques. For detailed country-by-country explanatory notes, see Ter-Minassian and Craig (1997).
Source: Ter-Minassian and Craig 1997.

proaches are used to control subnational borrowing. The first approach relies on market discipline; the second relies on cooperation between the central and subnational governments to decide what constitutes an appropriate level of indebtedness; and the other two directly regulate subnational borrowing. In practice, countries use a combination of all four approaches.

In principle, central governments can simply refuse to intervene in transactions between subnational governments and their creditors, relying on market discipline to control subnational debt. This is the most important restraint on subnational borrowing in Canada, France, and Portugal, for example. But to be effective, a laissez-faire approach requires that a number of conditions hold—the most important being the credibility of the central government's commitment not to intervene.[68] Establishing this credibility requires time, particularly where bailouts have occurred in the past. It also requires avoiding situations in which the central government would be forced to intervene—for example, where a default threatens the national banking system or the country's international credit rating. Regulation can help prevent such situations.

Some types of regulation are better than others.[69] Direct government controls, like annual limits on borrowing or administrative authorization for loans, are subject to political bargaining and are generally at odds with the trend toward decentralization. Further, they may make it even more difficult for the central government to refuse to intervene and rescue a subnational government. But administrative controls are appropriate for external borrowing because a subnational government's behavior on the international market could have contagion effects on the ratings of other national borrowers and because managing the external debt is part of the macroeconomic responsibilities of a central government.

Rule-based controls like ceilings on debt-service ratios or constraints on the type or purpose of borrowing are more transparent and less subject to political interference. They function best when they set global limits that mimic the markets—for example, by establishing ceilings on debt service as a share of revenues—and rely on a global definition of what constitutes debt. Detailed regulations are hard to monitor and will encourage behavior aimed at circumventing them.

Fundamentally, however, rules and controls will be ineffective unless accompanied by market discipline and a credible "no-bailout" pledge by the central government. Brazil has just completed the third restructur-

ing of state debt in 10 years. Each debt crisis arose despite a blanket ceiling on subnational borrowing and a web of restrictions and controls on various forms of debt. Regulation, it seems, failed to withstand the pressure from strong regional interest groups. Even in industrial countries with sophisticated credit markets, borrowing controls are subject to slippage.[70] In the United States, for example, regulations are less important than market discipline. Bonds must be floated, and the federal government neither guarantees subnational debt nor bails out subnational governments.[71]

Central regulation of subnational governments

Rules are needed to govern relationships among tiers of government. But central governments in decentralizing countries tend to compensate for their loss of direct control by stepping up their regulation of subnational governments. This tendency can be counterproductive if central governments with only a limited knowledge of local conditions begin micromanaging local functions, or if they impose costs they are not prepared to finance.

Personnel matters are one area in which central regulation is generally undesirable. Since wages are often a very large part of local budgets, centrally mandated wage increases can cause a local fiscal crisis. The central regulation can prevent subnational governments from responding to local conditions by increasing or decreasing staff size or by keeping wages at market levels. In Turkey the central government creates the staff list for each municipality, along with the corresponding salary scale. The central government must approve any changes in a long process that involves the Ministry of the Interior, the state personnel organization, and the Council of Ministers. In Sri Lanka the central government determines the wage bill for provincial governments.

If a central government is concerned about nepotism or overstaffing at local levels, it can address them in other ways. For example, it can provide suggested hiring levels and salary scales and require subnational governments to publish their employment rolls. But central government involvement in personnel matters also reflects the power of public sector unions and their ability to organize nationally. This force has not been easy to counter, whether in developing or in industrial countries.[72]

Central government regulation remains appropriate in a wide range of other circumstances. When subnational governments act as agents of the central government, regulation and monitoring are needed to enforce national mandates and standards. Even countries that have granted substantial autonomy to subnational governments require that centrally financed welfare payments be distributed according to criteria the central government establishes. Regulation is also essential to ensure the validity of the local electoral process and to address conflicts between units of subnational government. But a free press, improved access to information, and the growth of democracy at subnational levels are decreasing the need for central regulation. Local interest groups are increasingly able to monitor the performance of local governments.

Making subnational governments accountable

The third major set of constitutional rules consists of those governing relations between local officials and their constituents. The degree to which local officials are accountable to their constituents determines whether decentralization produces the intended benefits—that is, more efficient and responsive services, and greater local self-determination. The process for electing governors, mayors, and members of the subnational legislature takes center stage in determining accountability. But elections in and of themselves are not sufficient to ensure that local governments are truly responsive to people's needs and wants. Three sets of complementary measures should be pursued. First, electoral rules need to encourage participation and representation and, at the same time, allow an effective majority to emerge. Second, civil society can be drawn upon to complement formal political processes. Finally, an effective local administration needs to develop.

Adopting effective electoral rules

Electoral rules affect whether local politics reflect the interests of the local population or are captured by local elites. Of course, rules interact with certain characteristics of civil society, such as education, access to information, and the existence of groups that have a voice in government. But making elections highly visible events, facilitating participation, and demonstrating that votes matter will affect electoral outcomes in any society.

Rules to improve visibility, participation, and expected payoffs. The size of electoral districts can influence the outcome of an election. Electing council members by ward or neighborhood rather than at large ensures that all geographically defined interest groups will have seats on the local council. This method also reduces the costs of running for office. Since candidates need to campaign only in a single ward rather than in an entire city

or province, minorities and low-income candidates are more likely to run and to win seats. In turn, the presence of such candidates shows minorities and the poor that they can play a role in the political decisionmaking process and encourages them to mobilize and vote.[73]

The visibility of an election also influences participation. In general, the more local an election is, the lower the participation.[74] As voter turnout drops, the chances increase of narrowly focused special-interest groups gaining power. This problem suggests that there is a trade-off between full representation, which requires small districts, and participation, which is encouraged by the relatively high levels of visibility that come with elections in larger districts.

Two measures can help increase visibility without requiring an increase in the size of local electoral jurisdictions. One is to hold concurrent local and national elections, although this approach carries with it the risk that national issues will overshadow local concerns. Another is for the mayor or governor to be elected directly by the whole constituency, while state assembly members or municipal councilors are elected by district or neighborhood. Together, these measures help ensure higher voter participation and better representation across social or income groups.[75]

Rules that promote effective governance. Effective governance requires stable coalitions and an executive with reasonably strong and clear powers. The probability that elections will produce a stable coalition is higher with majority voting than with proportional representation, as explained earlier. Local governments composed of stable coalitions govern better than unstable partnerships—for instance, they are better able to take the measures needed to adjust to shocks.[76]

Separating the executive and the legislative branches of local government and electing the chief executive directly may also yield more effective governance.[77] Mayors elected directly are more likely than appointees to challenge the status quo. The vast majority of major municipal reforms around the world have been initiated by strong mayors. But too much authority concentrated in the executive may not be appropriate, particularly in new democracies. The mayor of Moscow had enough power to modify the city's electoral laws against the wishes of the legislative assembly.

Harnessing civil society

A multitude of actors outside the public sector—grassroots organizations, unions, universities, philanthropic foundations, user groups, nongovernmental organizations (NGOs), and neighborhood associations—influence public performance. Among other things, they can help hold local governments accountable. Such groups, known collectively as "civil society," can also complement local administration in the search for more responsive and effective governance.

Civil society and formal political participation. How can governments encourage the participation of civil society in governance? Much depends on the strength of community organizations and their ability to organize. Local officials must also be willing to tap into these groups. But examples abound of collaboration between civil society and local governments. In Colombia local governments and community associations work together to provide infrastructure for the poor. In Brazil, Chile, Mexico, and Venezuela many municipalities have adopted participatory budgeting and hold open meetings to consult the population on its priorities. Donors everywhere have initiated projects to mobilize community resources and encourage participation.[78]

The formal participation of civil society in public life has limits. Active civic organizations cannot be created in a vacuum but instead need to draw on local traditions. In Bolivia, for example, the neighborhood associations that report municipal mismanagement to the national senate are built on traditional customs.[79] Further, civic organizations are not always effective and may only reflect the views of a narrow segment of the population.[80] But where civic organizations are weak, local governments can use other mechanisms to give the public a voice, such as polling or collecting data from user groups.[81]

Civil society and political parties. Democratic revolutions are often driven by a popular upsurge and the resurrection of civil society. In Latin America's move toward greater democratization, trade unions, grassroots movements, religious groups, intellectuals, and artists supported each other's efforts, coalescing into a whole that identifies itself as "the people." [82] In a number of African societies, popular respect gave religious leaders a status and influence that autocratic regimes could not ignore. And the activities of trade unions were crucial in many countries. Strikes prompted by industrial grievances, such as late payment of wages, against the government in its role as dominant employer rapidly exploded into demands for political reform.[83]

Once democratic movements achieve their immediate goals, the civic energy that fueled them often dissi-

pates. This was the case in the democratic revolutions of Africa, Eastern Europe, and Russia. Political parties can help maintain a continuing link between civil society and government. Parties aggregate the demands of a dispersed population, represent political interests, recruit and train new candidates for office, ensure electoral competition, and form governments. They can help organize minorities and the poor and facilitate their participation in the formal electoral process.[84] Party systems thus improve legitimacy and governability by making the democratic process more inclusive, accessible, representative, and effective.[85]

Developing an effective local administration

Improving local services requires an effective local administration. Even a well-meaning political team cannot overcome incompetent administration. In fact, lack of capacity at the local level and the need for a massive increase in skilled staff are the arguments most frequently invoked against decentralization.

Both central and local governments can take measures to improve the effectiveness of local administration.[86] First, when a central government has decentralized responsibilities, it can also devolve the appropriate staff, as the Ugandan government did. Second, local governments should be free to hire, fire, and offer appropriate incentive packages so that they can attract capable local officials. Third, privatization can reduce the number of skilled administrators needed by local governments, since the privatized services require only monitoring and regulation rather than actual management.

While problems of capacity constraints are surmountable, they deserve serious attention. Central governments need to provide technical support to local governments as part of the process of decentralization. Decentralization itself, by giving subnational governments greater responsibilities and control over resources, will then increase their incentives to invest further in their own administrative capabilities.

Policies for the transition

Decentralization typically takes place during periods of political and economic upheaval. Euphoria at the fall of an authoritarian regime, an economic crisis that precipitates a regime's collapse, the jockeying for power of new interest groups—all these conditions create an environment in which a careful, rational, and orderly process of decentralization is highly unlikely. Even when decentralization occurs in a less dramatic context, questions of strategy and timing still arise. The recent experiences of decentralizing countries can help answer them.

Synchronizing the elements of reform

The most compelling lesson of recent decentralization experiences is that all elements of reform must be synchronized. The political impetus behind decentralization prompts central governments to make concessions hastily. Granting local elections is a step that can be taken rapidly. But making decentralization a success requires taking a number of slow and difficult steps that create new regulatory relationships between central and subnational governments, transfer assets and staff to local levels, and replace annual budgetary transfers with a system of tax assignment and intergovernmental transfers. The recent history of decentralization illustrates the dangers of not sequencing appropriately.

Put expenditure and revenue rules in place before political liberalization. Russia liberalized politically while the fiscal structure of the former Soviet system was still in place (box 5.7). Subnational governments had historically acted as tax collectors for both the provinces and the central government. Once the provincial governments gained political autonomy, they began refusing to send tax revenues to the central government. Fiscal relations stabilized only after 1994, when fixed rules were established for dividing taxes among tiers of government. In contrast, Chile and Poland established fiscal rules before political liberalization and were spared a Russian-style fiscal crisis.

Decentralize a function and its corresponding revenue source simultaneously. Many African countries facing economic collapse devolved a broad range of government services to subnational governments without providing the necessary revenues. Not surprisingly, the quality of the decentralized services declined sharply. In much of Latin America the opposite occurred: governments decentralized revenues without offloading corresponding responsibilities. In Colombia central transfers to municipalities increased by 60 percent without a matching increase in responsibilities.

Decentralize the needed management controls. Governments have sometimes crippled local governments' ability to perform new functions by failing to decentralize management controls. In Colombia, for example, the central government continued to set the salaries of public school teachers even after the management of primary and secondary schools had ostensibly been decentralized to the provinces. The central government's

---

Box 5.7
The cart before the horse: decentralization in Russia

Under the Soviet system, subnational governments were merely extensions of the central government under the authority of the Communist Party. The central government controlled activities of national importance, such as transportation and defense. The republics were responsible for light industries. Provinces (oblasts) were responsible for health care, housing, utilities, and education. Although each tier of government was assigned a given tax base, the central government determined subnational budgets through central planning and closed-door negotiations. Revenue sharing and intergovernmental transfers were merely accounting devices used to bring each subnational budget into balance.

The party's monopoly on power was officially abolished in 1990. Following the breakup of the Soviet Union in 1991, a new constitution (adopted in 1993) declared Russia a democratic federal state. The new constitution recognized 89 subnational units (republics, autonomous regions, and oblasts) and mandated the election of governors (presidents in the republics) and legislatures in each jurisdiction.

However, Russia continued to struggle with its old system of intergovernmental fiscal relations for several years. Despite an attempt to establish a system based on separate tax assignments, subnational finances continued to depend on negotiations with Moscow. These talks soon became hostile, and the newly autonomous regional governments threatened to withhold the tax revenues they owed to the federal government or to secede from the federation entirely if their demands were not met.

Since 1994 Russia has been moving toward a rule-based system of intergovernmental fiscal relations. The 1994 reforms divided revenues from each of the major taxes among central and regional governments and established a formula-based equalization system to assist poorer regions. However, the reforms did not entirely resolve the fiscal conflicts between levels of government or settle the division of responsibilities for social expenditures. Moreover, the federal government still runs considerable risk from potential defaults on loans to subnational governments.

Source: Freinkman 1998; Le Houerou 1996; Martinez-Vasquez 1998.

---

subsequent decision to grant a major increase in salaries prompted a fiscal crisis at the provincial level that was resolved only though the creation of a special compensation fund.[87] In Poland the public housing stock was transferred to municipal governments, but the central government continues to control the rents.

The recent decentralization of education in Mexico followed a more balanced approach. The federal government transferred full management responsibility for preschool, primary, and secondary education to the state governments in 1992, along with funding that equaled spending on federal facilities in the previous year. Since then, funding has been based on a formula that gradually shifts the distribution from its historic pattern to one that provides an equal amount per pupil across all states. The experience of the Philippines has been similar.[88]

Demonstrating the hard budget constraint

Central governments must demonstrate early on that they are committed to imposing a hard budget constraint on subnational governments. The mere possibility of a central government bailout can prompt excess spending and deficit financing at the subnational level. Brazil, where the federal government has assumed over $100 billion in state debt, is a clear example (see chapter 8). Argentina, in contrast, succeeded in enforcing a hard budget constraint. From the outset, the current administration has refused to provide any significant debt relief to the provincial governments. It has also minimized its potential exposure in two ways. First, provinces may not borrow directly from the federal treasury. Second, loans that provincial banks make to their governments are not eligible for central bank discounts. After the 1994 Mexican economic crisis temporarily dried up funding sources all over Latin America, Argentina's provincial governments were forced to adjust rather than rely on federal relief.

What lessons for the future?

Decentralization is a work in progress. Many experiments are under way, and only limited evidence on final outcomes is yet available.[89] Nonetheless, some lessons have emerged from recent experiences. Perhaps the most important is that a system that is based on rules produces better results than one that is not. Explicit rules setting out the division of functional responsibilities among levels of government reduce ambiguity and increase political accountability. They also provide a framework within which interest groups can compete and negotiate without resorting to violence.

Some rules work better than others. Revenues need to be decentralized at the same time as expenditures, so that finance follows function. A "hands-off" attitude when subnational governments default on their loans may be more important in controlling debt than the most comprehensive set of regulations and controls. Ward-based local politics combined with direct elections for mayors and governors, and concurrent national and local elections, improve participation and representation. Subnational governments with multiple tiers and many small units are likely to have high administrative overhead costs.

Strategies to stop decentralization are unlikely to succeed, as the pressures to decentralize are beyond government control. The emergence of modern economies, the rise of an urban, literate middle class, and the decline of both external and domestic military threats have created nearly insurmountable pressure for a broader distribution of political power in Latin America, Eastern Europe, Russia, and parts of East Asia. This same pressure is likely to affect the rapidly urbanizing economies of South Asia and parts of Africa early in the 21st century. Rather than attempt to resist it, governments should face decentralization armed with lessons from countries that have gone before them.

Chapter

6

Dynamic Cities as Engines of Growth

As countries move through the development process, agriculture declines as a share of gross domestic product (GDP), and manufacturing and services begin to dominate the economy. Goods and services are often produced most efficiently in densely populated areas that provide access to a pool of skilled labor, a network of complementary firms that act as suppliers, and a critical mass of customers. For this reason sustained economic growth is always accompanied by urbanization (figure 6.1).

Globalization and localization have not diminished the importance—or the pace—of the urbanization process. Globalization promotes economic growth, which is the driving force behind urbanization. But communication and information technologies now allow firms to market their goods in distant countries and to incorporate into their production chain firms located halfway around the world. If globalization is lauded precisely because of its ability to make great distances seem much smaller, why does urbanization remain such an important trend?

Although globalization opens up new possibilities for linkages around the

world, it also reinforces certain advantages of proximity. Firms competing in the global economy (and their suppliers) still benefit considerably from access to a sizable pool of labor, materials, services, and customers. As a result, globalization is likely to contribute to further urbanization. This is particularly true in developing countries, where access to the opportunities offered by globalization is much greater in cities.

The growth of urban populations in both large capital cities and smaller municipalities feeds demand for increased localization of political power. It puts pressure on national institutions of governance and encourages them to take the steps toward decentralization discussed in chapter 5. It makes the success of decentralization perhaps even more important. When urban governments have the power and ability to enact a development agenda, they can help the citizens of their cities hook up with the global economy. These cities then become reliable links in the global production chain and attractive destinations for foreign investment.

Urbanization is integral to development, but it also presents difficult chal-

Figure 6.1
Urbanization is closely associated with economic growth

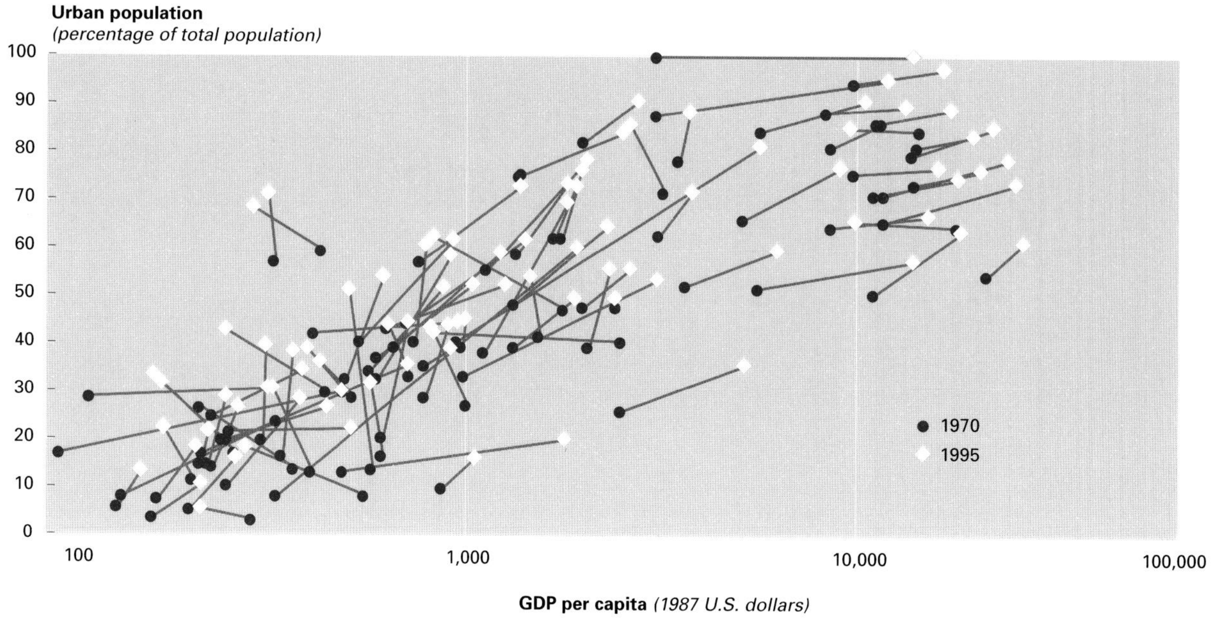

Urban population
(percentage of total population)

GDP per capita *(1987 U.S. dollars)*

Note: Sample includes industrial and developing countries for which data are available. The figure shows progress from 1970 to 1995 in each country. *GDP per capita* is on a log scale.
Source: World Bank, *World Development Indicators,* 1998.

lenges. This chapter reviews the economic forces underlying urbanization and discusses what national governments can do—and should not do—if they want to foster urban economic growth. Chapter 7, in turn, focuses on what makes cities livable, including essential services like housing, sanitation, and infrastructure.

What makes cities grow?

Healthy, dynamic cities are an integral part of sustained economic growth (box 6.1).[1] As countries develop, cities account for an ever-increasing share of national income. Urban areas generate 55 percent of gross national product (GNP) in low-income countries, 73 percent in middle-income countries, and 85 percent in high-income countries. The growth sectors of the economy—manufacturing and services—are usually concentrated in cities, where they benefit from agglomeration economies and ample markets for inputs, outputs, and labor, and where ideas and knowledge are rapidly diffused.[2]

The way cities manage development, including the arrival of industries, goes far in determining the rate of economic growth. Urban governments can foster economic development, or they can slow it down. Exam-

ining the urbanization process—the agglomerative forces and locational inducements that shape cities—is a useful way of identifying what role governments should play.

Agglomeration economies—the source of urban efficiency

Why is economic activity concentrated in urban areas, where land prices are often 50 to 100 times higher than they are 30 or 40 miles away? Why do so many individuals and firms settle in large metropolitan areas where the cost of living is typically twice as high as it is in smaller urban areas?[3] The answer must be that these costs are more than offset by the economic benefits cities offer—benefits that are generally the result of agglomeration economies.

Agglomeration increases the productivity of a wide array of economic activities in urban areas. Productivity rises with city size, so much so that a typical firm will see its productivity climb 5 to 10 percent if city size and the scale of local industry double.[4] Urban wages are also higher than rural wages—two to four times as high in middle-income countries—reflecting the higher

Box 6.1
Cities and urban areas: some definitions

This report uses the terms *cities* and *urban areas* interchangeably. The formal definition of urban areas describes them as concentrations of nonagricultural workers and nonagricultural production sectors. Most countries call settlements with 2,500–25,000 people urban areas. The definition varies from country to country and has changed over time. If the criteria China used in its 1980 census had been applied to its 1990 census, the country's urbanization rate for the 1980s would have been more than 50 percent—far more than the 26 percent produced by the more rigorous approach used in 1990. A city has a certain legal status (granted by the national or provincial government) that is generally associated with specific administrative or local government structures. In most countries large urban areas are referred to as *metropolitan areas* because they encompass a geographic area of human settlement (that may include legally defined cities) within which residents share employment opportunities and sets of economic relations.

Source: Mills 1998; UNCHS 1996.

productivity levels obtained from urban agglomeration economies.[5]

Urban areas have historically been more efficient than rural areas because cities had markets for inputs and outputs big enough to support good-sized plants and thus could take advantage of economies of scale. In smaller towns the economies of scale such plants provided were offset by high transportation costs to consumers or from input sources. The relationship between plant size and city size has all but disappeared, however. Transportation costs have also declined (and become much less important) as services and light industries increasingly dominate the world economy.

In a modern economy the benefit of the kind of proximity urban areas offer is that firms, regardless of size, are able to experience economies of scale and scope. The presence of a common pool of labor, materials, and services allows large and small firms alike to profit from scale economies. Economies of scope emerge when the presence of one activity makes carrying out a complementary activity cheaper by fostering diversity in supply and specialization among firms.[6] Proximity also facilitates the diffusion of knowledge. Firms operating in proximity to each other benefit from information spillovers, in some cases by observing what neighboring firms are doing. Evidence from patent citations shows that information flows actually deterio-

rate with distance.[7] When firms are concentrated in cities, transaction costs also fall, most notably the search costs involved in matching workers with employment opportunities.

Agglomeration economies come in various forms. Benefits that derive from firms locating close to firms in the same industry are known as *localization economies*. Benefits that derive from proximity to many different economic actors are known as *urbanization economies*. Evidence from Brazil and the Republic of Korea shows the benefits of localization economies. If a plant moves from a location shared by 1,000 workers employed by firms in the same industry to one with 10,000 such workers, output will increase an average of 15 percent, largely because the pool of specialized workers and inputs deepens.[8] Whether an industry benefits most from urbanization or localization economies depends on how innovative it is. New, dynamic industries are likely to locate in large urban centers where they can benefit from the cross-fertilization provided by diverse actors. Older, mature industries concentrate in smaller, more specialized cities, where congestion costs are low and localization economies can be high.

A final benefit of agglomeration in large urban areas is that these locales are less vulnerable to economic fluctuations because of their diversified economic base. Employment can flow from one sector to another, keeping average unemployment low.[9] The number and variety of consumers offer firms some protection, allowing them to apply the law of large numbers to inventory management (a practice that results in substantial savings). For consumers, large cities provide a variety of services and shopping and entertainment opportunities. Rural areas can tap into these benefits by building links to the urban sector (box 6.2).

Systems of cities

Although productivity is higher in large metropolitan areas, almost 65 percent of the world's urban residents continue to live in small and medium-size cities (figure 6.2). This pattern reflects the degree of agglomeration that works best for firms and industries and the kinds of benefits agglomeration provides. Large metropolitan areas provide some firms with enough benefits to justify the high labor and land costs. But other industries find smaller cities more lucrative bases. Economies can support a range of cities of different sizes and the accompanying variations in production patterns. And the effects of city size on workers are often minimal. A typ-

Box 6.2
Rural-urban linkages

Thinking on the links between urban and rural development has changed in the past 50 years. In the 1950s urbanization was considered a desirable alternative to rural overcrowding, particularly in densely populated areas where the prospects of raising agricultural productivity seemed limited. Manufacturing was seen as a key to growth. But manufacturing often failed to produce enough jobs for rural migrants to cities. As a result, governments worried about the rising number of underemployed in large cities and sometimes tried to restrain rural-urban migration—a policy that had the effect of lowering the migrants' welfare.

In principle, urban and rural economies can enjoy a symbiotic relationship. Cities benefit when agricultural productivity increases. Growing rural areas provide new, important markets for urban services and manufactured goods. Mechanization and the use of fertilizers, pesticides, and herbicides spur demand for these products. A boom in commercial agriculture boosts demand for marketing, transportation, construction, and finance, which urban centers often provide. In Africa every $1 of additional output in the agricultural sector generates an extra $1.50 of output in the nonfarm sector. In Asia that figure is $1.80.[10]

Rural areas also benefit from the growth of cities. Nearby cities provide ready markets for agricultural products such as vegetables and dairy products and for rural nonfarm output. Rural industries often supply parts and components to nearby urban manufacturers. Urbanization can also help raise rural productivity through technology transfers, educational services, and training.

Figure 6.2
Most of the world's urban population lived in small and medium-size cities in 1995

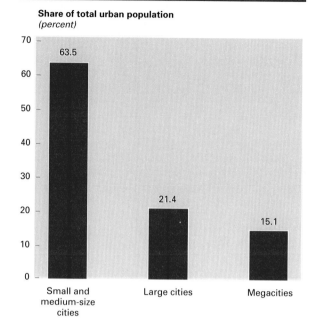

Share of total urban population
(percent)

Note: Megacities are cities with populations over 5 million. *Large cities* are cities with populations between 1 million and 5 million. *Medium-size cities* are cities with populations between 0.5 million and 1 million. *Small cities* are cities with populations less than 0.5 million.
Source: UNDIESA, *World Urbanization Prospects,* 1998.

ical worker is generally as well off in a small city with low wages and low living costs as a worker in a large urban area where wages and living costs are as much as 100 percent higher.[11]

The biggest metropolitan areas provide a large, diverse economic base for modern service and other innovative industries that derive important benefits from such an environment. In contrast, small and medium-size metropolitan areas tend to specialize in the production of goods that are exported outside the city, focusing on a single standardized manufacturing or service area such as primary metals, food processing, textiles, pulp and paper, machinery, or transportation. By specializing in one set of activities, smaller metropolitan areas exploit localization economies while conserving on the congestion costs that affect larger cities. Specialized cities grow with the economies of scale and local intermediate input linkages their activities generate, and with the size of regional markets and city-specific amenities.

The dynamics of city formation

The relationship between a country's industrial organization and its system of cities helps explain emerging patterns of urbanization. During the early stages of industrialization in most developing countries, modern industries—particularly in sectors that are influenced primarily by the location of consumers—often cluster in one or two large metropolitan areas. The first site for agglomeration is usually the national capital (Bangkok, Bogotá, Jakarta, Mexico City, Seoul, and Suva, Fiji) or a large city near the coast (Calcutta, São Paulo, and Shanghai). This clustering saves on scarce resources and helps industries cope with initial shortages of skilled labor, technical knowledge, business and financial services, and modern telecommunications and transportation infrastructure. For foreign investors and industrial exporters, the national capital may be a prime location for entering the country and the best place to find modern services. Capitals have the added advantage of proximity to government decisionmakers and regulators.[12]

As industrialization proceeds, manufacturing activities begin to move to smaller cities outside the capital. This shift occurs because congestion costs increase and because, to some extent, the benefits of agglomeration decrease as production standardizes in mature plants. The spread of effective telecommunications and transportation, the devolution of bureaucratic processes to local governments, and the opening of capital markets also encourage the movement of industries out of major cities (box 6.3).

In the future, the forces of globalization, including trade liberalization and financial integration, will continue to reinforce the importance of urban agglomeration economies. Because international firms and investors seek low-cost, accessible locations for their plants, localized production networks will be essential to a country's global competitiveness.[13] Manufacturing is placing increasing emphasis on high effective capital-labor ratios and light, high-tech materials, often in connection with intermediate service inputs such as software, programming, and engineering services that can be supplied at a distance. Sydney's transformation into a global city between 1971 and 1991 translated into a 25 percent increase in employment creation as well as a radical shift toward financial and business services.[14]

Openness to the world economy will increase the volatility of urban economies and heighten competition among cities within the same country. Cities that are able to exploit a comparative advantage in global tradables will thrive, but those that have depended on protected industries will struggle.

Technological change has enhanced agglomeration economies in the past and should continue to do so in the future. Commuter rail transportation, automobiles, and metropolitan highway systems have all contributed to urban growth in industrial economies during the 20th century. In the future, local human capital and the accumulation of knowledge will also affect city size. Estimates for 1940–90 suggest that an increase of one standard deviation in the percentage of college-educated residents in a U.S. city is associated with a 20 percent increase in size, even after accounting for growth trends and specific city characteristics.[15] Recent evidence suggests that telecommunications is a complement to, rather than a substitute for, face-to-face interaction.[16] In a world of extraordinary technological gains, one of the most effective mechanisms for transmitting knowledge and conducting business may still be geographic proximity.

Box 6.3
The dispersal of industry in Korea

Urbanization in Korea has meant that the proportion of the population living in Seoul has grown steadily. But this statement does not take into account the decline in Seoul's primacy in the country's system of cities and its manufacturing structure (see table). Seoul is growing, but other Korean cities are growing faster. Even more dramatic is the exodus of manufacturing employment from metropolitan Seoul to surrounding suburban areas. In 1970 three-quarters of provincial manufacturing employment was in metropolitan Seoul, but by 1993 the percentage had fallen to one-third. Industry began moving out of Korea's major metropolitan areas—Seoul, Pusan, and Taegu—and their satellite cities in the mid-1980s. The share of other cities and rural areas in national manufacturing employment rose from 26 to 42 percent between 1983 and 1993.

Policy changes were responsible for this trend. In the 1970s the government initiated policies designed to encourage the decentralization of industry from metropolitan Seoul. Key elements of these policies included financial incentives to relocate, direct relocation orders, and the construction of industrial parks. Despite the natural market forces that were encouraging firms to leave Seoul (including high wages and rents), these initial policies had little immediate effect. Strong government regulation and the associated red tape made plants unwilling to locate more than a 45-minute drive from the capital. Within that zone, only a few successful industrial parks existed.[17]

Ultimately, three developments sparked the move out of Seoul, Pusan, and Taegu. First, Korea liberalized its economy in the early 1980s, reducing the red tape tying industries to Seoul. Second, the government reinstated local government autonomy in 1988, enabling local authorities to hold elections and assess and collect taxes. Third, the government invested heavily in communications infrastructure and roads outside Seoul and Pusan—and has continued to do so.

The primacy of metropolitan Seoul
(Seoul as a percentage of national total)

	1960	1970	1980	1990
National urban population	34	41	38	33
National population	9	17	22	25
Manufacturing	..	..	21	14

.. Not available.

Source: Henderson, Lee, and Lee 1998; Henderson 1998.

Most of the world's urban population will remain in small and medium-size cities, since they are growing faster than large urban areas (figure 6.3). But sizes are relative. In 1970 a medium-size city was defined as one with a population of anywhere from 250,000 to

Figure 6.3
Small cities had the fastest growing populations, and megacities the slowest, from 1970 to 1990

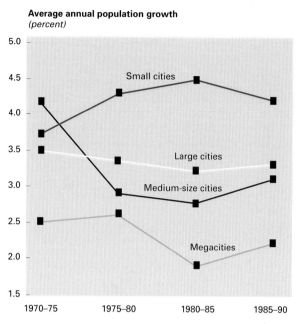

Average annual population growth
(percent)

Note: Megacities are cities with populations over 5 million. *Large cities* are cities with populations between 1 million and 5 million. *Medium-size cities* are cities with populations between 0.5 million and 1 million. *Small cities* are cities with populations less than 0.5 million.
Source: UNDIESA, *World Urbanization Prospects,* 1998.

500,000. Today a medium-size city is defined as one with a population closer to a million. The same is true for large cities. In 1950 the average population of the world's 100 largest cities was 2.1 million, but by 1990 it had reached more than 5 million. In 1800 it was only about 200,000.[18]

The number of cities will also continue to grow. In 1900 the United States had 75 metropolitan areas, which were defined as areas with a population of over 50,000. Today the number of metropolitan areas has reached almost 350. As these urban centers grow, the number of very large agglomerations will also increase. In 1970 some 163 metropolitan areas worldwide had more than 1 million people. Today there are about 350 such areas. Having more metropolitan areas in a country means having more centers of political power that feed the forces of localization and raise the stakes for good urban governance.

The national government's role in urbanization

National governments have often tried to influence the pace or location of urbanization. Often these efforts

consisted of shifting resources from agriculture to finance the expansion of "modern" economic sectors—usually manufacturing—which were concentrated in cities. Urban workers in the formal sector benefited from food and housing subsidies and government-sponsored unemployment and pension schemes, while rural populations received low prices for their crops and had little access to government support. Such misplaced efforts are part of the reason Africa has seen urbanization with very little economic growth (box 6.4).

In other cases governments, alarmed at the growing population of ill-housed and underemployed citizens living on the periphery of cities, have attempted to halt urbanization. In Indonesia squatters were rounded up and trucked back to the countryside. In China, the Soviet Union, and Vietnam a system of permits restricted rural-urban migration. And in India industrial

Box 6.4
Africa: urbanization without growth

Urbanization is typically associated with rising per capita income. This pattern has held true in Europe, Latin America, and—more recently—much of Asia. Africa has been the exception.

Between 1970 and 1995 the average African country's urban population grew by 4.7 percent annually, while its per capita GDP dropped by 0.7 percent a year. This negative correlation between urbanization and per capita income is unique, even among poor countries and economies with low growth rates. Industrialization did not accompany the boom in urban growth. Only 9 percent of Africa's labor force is employed in industry, compared with 18 percent in Asia, which has seen comparable rates of urbanization. Cities in Africa are not serving as engines of growth and structural transformation. Instead, they are part of the cause and a major symptom of the economic and social crises that have enveloped the continent.[19]

Africa's pattern of "urbanization without growth" is in part the result of distorted incentives that encouraged migrants to move to cities to exploit subsidies rather than in response to opportunities for more productive employment. African cities were the beneficiaries of food pricing and trade policies that favored urban consumers over rural producers. While the structural adjustment programs initiated in the mid-1980s removed many of these distortions, they have already contributed to excessive levels of rural-urban migration over prior decades. Worsening physical or economic security in rural areas may also be pushing the migration to the relative safety of cities. Over the years, wars and civil unrest have led millions in Angola, Liberia, and Mozambique to flee to cities. In Mauritania, Nouakchott's population doubled during one drought year in the mid-1980s.

firms were essentially prohibited from locating new plants in or near large cities.

Policies to stem urban population growth have largely failed. Indonesia's effort to evict migrants did not succeed and was later abandoned. Substantial internal migration occurred in China, the Soviet Union, and Vietnam despite controls on population movements. These efforts did, however, impose significant costs on both migrants and the economy. An overwhelming body of evidence shows that when the poor migrate, they are responding efficiently to economic incentives—notably higher wages—and generally are better off after they move. Attempts to stop migration prevent the poor from improving their economic situation and can impose other costs on migrants. Limits on migration to Dar es Salaam, for example, made the poor more susceptible to extortion by corrupt officials.[20]

Governments have also distorted urban growth through their choice of locations for state-owned industries and by creating special economic zones—decisions that are often influenced by political rather than economic considerations. The state-owned portion of the Brazilian iron and steel industry was placed near politically influential São Paulo and Rio de Janeiro rather than near the source of raw materials in the state of Minas Gerais (where private iron and steel producers have chosen to locate). Brazil's choice to put the heavily polluting iron and steel industries in the middle of the country's largest concentration of people (Grande São Paulo) not only raised transportation costs but had high human costs as well.[21]

Countries that set up special development zones offering relaxed tariffs encourage economic activity to settle in one privileged area at the expense of others. For example, if trade liberalization is introduced in the coastal area of a country first, inland regions may find themselves permanently disadvantaged. Such policies foster dual societies, with cosmopolitan cities on the coast and disadvantaged areas in the hinterland. The coastal cities that were the early beneficiaries of China's "open door" policy have maintained their advantage, even though their special status was abolished long ago.[22] Similarly, if the spread of technology or the liberalization of capital markets is confined to certain areas, these areas will have a permanent advantage over others in the country.

Bureaucratic centralization is another, more subtle form of the government-induced distortions that can influence the choice of new sites for production. Government regulations, especially rules governing import and export licenses and capital markets, affect the economic life of firms. Central government bureaucrats like to keep tight control over the process of allocating licenses or loans. But an overly centralized allocation process causes distortions when firms are deciding where to locate production. Producers tend to locate in capital cities and other bureaucratic centers in order to be able to deal effectively with red tape.[23] In the early 1980s Indonesia liberalized capital and export-import markets, creating new opportunities for small and medium-size firms. But the dispensing functions remained highly centralized, and the concentration of small and medium-size firms in larger metropolitan areas increased.[24]

The unhappy record of past government efforts to prevent rural-urban migration or to steer urban growth to particular locations leads to a straightforward conclusion: governments are not skilled at deciding where households and firms should locate. National governments can perform a more useful function by working to provide an environment conducive to economic growth regardless of location. Macroeconomic policies that promote price stability and national institutions that enable firms and households to make binding contracts may be the most important factors in creating a growth-oriented environment, and national governments can provide them.[25] In matters of location the ideal government policy is to provide a level playing field so that large and small cities and rural areas can compete fairly with each other.

Pursuing such a policy involves more than just eliminating subsidies and tax breaks, however. Many government decisions have unavoidable spatial implications, especially decisions on siting large-scale public infrastructure investments, military bases, and public enterprises. As urbanization spreads within a country, investments in public infrastructure must follow. Industrial producers in remote cities and areas outside of cities require interregional telecommunications, roads, and electricity if they are to produce competitively, move products to major markets, and communicate with buyers and sellers. The national government plays a key role in determining whether and when such investments take place. One difficulty is that centralized state-owned industries or established businesses may resist hinterland infrastructure investment for fear of competition. Another complication may be that the central government fails to understand the needs of hinterland areas. Industries in Korea began decentralizing in the late 1980s after the government made massive investments in communications and transportation in regions outside urban centers and restored local government autonomy.

In principle, a centralized government can create a level playing field for locational decisions. In practice, however, resisting pressure to concentrate investment in the primary city requires institutional mechanisms that give other regions a voice in the allocation process. Central governments are now under pressure to decentralize decisionmaking power and resources to subnational governments, as chapter 5 discusses. In a decentralized system the central government's role with respect to urban development no longer involves eliminating spatial biases in a centrally managed system of investment allocation. Instead, the role of central governments is to provide the institutional structure for decentralization and coordination across all levels of government.

Local policies for urban economic growth

If cities are to exploit the benefits of agglomeration, they must provide an efficient and attractive place to do business. This section focuses on three cross-sectoral elements of this strategy: financing for infrastructure investment, land use policy, and municipal entrepreneurship. Chapter 7 analyzes sector-specific policies for water, sanitation, and housing.

Financing capital investment

Cities need to invest in infrastructure if they are to provide the basic services necessary for economic growth. Pressure for investment will be particularly heavy during a country's urban transition—the years of rapid urban population growth fueled by rural-urban migration. In recent decades a boom in infrastructure spending has paralleled urban growth. Absorbing the 2.4 billion new urban residents expected over the next 30 years will require further investment in housing, water and sanitation, transportation, power, and telecommunications. The need for these new infrastructure investments comes on top of the backlog that already plagues the world's cities. Providing universal coverage for water and sanitation alone in the cities of developing countries will cost nearly 5 percent of those countries' GDP.[26]

Public or private? Not all the necessary investment financing need come from government, as several alternative sources are available. Housing, which accounts for about 30 percent of gross capital formation in many poor countries (including the on-site costs of water, sanitation, power, and access), is often funded by pri-

vate sources.[27] In industrial countries developers are frequently required to provide on-site infrastructure. These costs are incorporated into the price of finished housing and are ultimately financed through the mortgage market. In developing countries poor and low-income households have to finance housing from current income, adding space and infrastructure as their means allow. In both cases capital is mobilized and allocated independent of the government. The private sector can also finance off-site costs of power, water, and telecommunications. In fact, private firms are increasingly signing contracts to build such infrastructure and in many instances agree as part of the deal to finance the future expansion or upgrading of networks.

Publicly financed infrastructure will still be needed, however. In the case of streets, cost recovery is difficult. In the case of social infrastructure, it is undesirable. Recent estimates for India suggest that urban investments will require public funding equal to nearly 2 percent of GDP—even though the private sector's share of infrastructure funding is expected to increase from its present level of 25 percent to 45 percent by 2006.

Central or local? In most developing countries, central governments have traditionally mobilized the resources for public infrastructure through domestic taxation and borrowing, forced savings schemes, external debt, and donor assistance. These funds have been spent directly by central government ministries or government-owned enterprises. But pressure for decentralization is changing this pattern to allow subnational politicians to make investment decisions. Sound economic arguments exist for pushing these infrastructure investment decisions to the subnational level. Centrally determined spending can produce arbitrary allocations across cities and tends to sever the links among investment, operation, and maintenance.[28] In contrast, municipalities that have control over investment decisions can respond to local priorities. High-income countries have apparently found this argument persuasive. The central government's share of public investment spending is generally below 50 percent in countries with a per capita GDP of more than $5,000. Growth in GDP per capita is generally associated with a declining share of central government spending in public investment (figure 6.4).

Local governments can finance their new responsibilities in several ways. Development fees, connection charges, and local tax revenue can all generate funds that can be used for investment.[29] While such resources can make a significant contribution to investment fi-

Figure 6.4
**As countries develop, central governments'
share of public investment falls**

Share of central government expenditures in total
government expenditures on public investments
(percent)

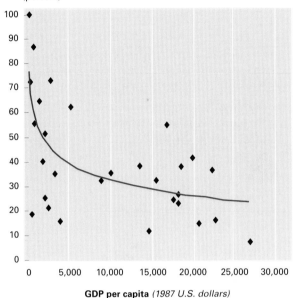

GDP per capita *(1987 U.S. dollars)*

Note: Sample includes all developing and industrial countries for
which calculations could be made of the share of central government
investment in total government investment in the mid-1980s and
mid-1990s.
Source: IMF, *Government Finance Statistics Yearbook,* 1998; World
Bank, *World Development Indicators,* 1998.

nancing, particularly in slow-growing cities, they may
not be enough to finance all infrastructure investments
at the peak of the urban transition. In this case debt financing may be required and can make financial sense.
Roads, schools, and pipelines have long useful lives,
and debt spreads out the costs over their lifetimes. But
what options do local governments have for borrowing?
The experience of industrial countries suggests two:
municipal bonds and municipal funds.

Municipal bonds. In the United States and Canada,
subnational governments rely on the bond market.
Bond debt issued by subnational governments in the
two countries now totals more than $7.4 trillion.[30]
Bond financing is possible because both countries have
well-developed capital markets, and their history of
macroeconomic stability has made private investors
willing to make the long-term financial commitments
infrastructure investment requires. Investors are famil-
iar with and have confidence in the laws and proce-

dures governing defaults and bankruptcies. Public disclosure guidelines and market intermediaries (such as
credit-rating agencies and bond insurers) help investors
process information on the risk of their investments.
And local governments have both well-established financial track records and the autonomy to respond to
changing financial circumstances rather than simply
defaulting.

In many developing countries, few of these conditions exist. Long histories of macroeconomic instability make long-term financial commitments extremely
risky. Information on potential borrowers is unreliable.
The legal framework needed to provide investors with
recourse in cases of default is underdeveloped and often
untested. Municipal governments in these countries are
viewed—often correctly—as particularly unattractive
borrowers because they lack the autonomy to raise revenues or reduce spending, particularly on personnel.
Moreover, local governments often have no credible political commitment to long-term financial obligations.
Under these conditions, even if long-term private capital is available, local governments generally can borrow
only at a very high rate of interest, if at all.

Despite these shortcomings, municipal bond markets are emerging in many developing countries. In
Latin America 52 municipalities and provinces accessed
capital markets between 1991 and 1998.[31] Asia's local
bond market is estimated at $477 billion. All Czech
cities with more than 100,000 people have issued municipal bonds, enabling the investment share of Czech
municipalities to remain at more than 38 percent of
their budgets, despite deep cuts in central government
capital transfers. Standard and Poor's has given Prague
and Ostrava "A" ratings for foreign currency bonds.
Poland, Russia, South Africa, and Turkey also have municipal bond markets.

Emerging municipal bond markets have an indifferent track record. Much like the U.S. bond market in
the 19th century, the initial years have been marked by
defaults. Ankara and Istanbul have both defaulted on
their bond debt, and many Brazilian states have either
defaulted or had their debts taken over by the national
government (see the case study on Brazil in chapter 8).
However, governments are taking measures to increase
investor confidence. Poland, for example, is considering both legislation on a municipal bankruptcy law and
controls on the volume of subnational debt.

Municipal funds and banks. The other source of long-
term financing in industrial countries is the munici-

pal bank or the municipal development fund (MDF). These have a long and successful history in Western Europe. European MDFs (Crédit Local de France, the Spanish Banco de Crédito Local, and the British Public Works Loans Board) were founded to address the unwillingness of private capital markets to provide long-term credit to small municipalities. In their initial years, many such funds were financed by the central government. In effect, central governments used their excellent credit ratings to raise money cheaply in capital markets and then lent the proceeds to municipalities through MDFs. More recently, MDFs have sprung up throughout the developing world.

Under an MDF the central government bears the ultimate risk of municipal default. Some governments have responded to this risk by behaving as diligent investors, insisting on prudent lending standards and strict repayment schedules. When central governments do not impose such standards, levels of default are high. One mechanism for encouraging governments to act as prudent investors is to dilute their exposure with some private participation. Under Colombia's FINDETER program, private banks originate all municipal loans and bear the full risk of default. The government functions as a second-tier bank, providing liquidity without assuming risk. As a result the government is exposed only to the risk that the originating bank itself will fail. The Czech Republic operates a program along similar lines.[32] And many of the European MDFs have shifted to market sources to finance their operations and are now in the process of privatizing.

Conditions in individual countries determine whether the bond or the bank approach makes more sense. Both can operate simultaneously, as they do in the United Kingdom. The challenge is not to choose between them, but rather to establish an environment that gives local governments the opportunity and incentive to become worthy borrowers. Such an environment emphasizes a stable macroeconomy, a legal framework that defines the rights and remedies of lenders and borrowers, and the creation of a supply of creditworthy borrowers. Central governments especially need to concentrate on the legal framework affecting municipal borrowing, including bankruptcy procedures for municipalities. They need to take measures to forestall pressure for government bailouts (see chapter 5). Finally, they need to do their part to enhance municipal creditworthiness by stabilizing intergovernmental transfers and scaling back unfunded mandates and regulations that limit local governments' flexibility in making spending decisions.

Local governments, for their part, can improve their attractiveness to borrowers by instituting accounting, auditing, and disclosure practices that are compatible with international standards. They can also improve the quality of their collateral by allowing central governments to deduct debt service directly from intergovernmental transfers or by using a specific tax or other revenue source to pay debt service. Loan contracts can specify that debt service will receive priority, prohibit new borrowing backed by the same revenue source until the debt is retired, or both. Actions, however, are more persuasive than words. The most convincing evidence a local government can offer potential lenders is a long, unblemished credit history.[33]

Land use

Firms and households must be able to make efficient decisions about where to locate within cities. Freedom of mobility, or the lack of it, profoundly affects urban economic growth. Agglomeration economies, by definition, require proximity—firms to firms, households to places of employment. The ability of firms and households to sort themselves into efficient location patterns requires an active real estate market in which land prices reflect the different economic values of various sites (box 6.5).

Governments regulate the operation of land markets in several ways. The most extreme approach is to ban the real estate market entirely and make location decisions by fiat. Cities in the former Soviet Union and in Eastern Europe were laid out in this manner. In market economies, zoning is the most common mechanism for controlling land use. Zoning typically assigns various uses—residential, retail, commercial, industrial, and mixed—to land in different parts of the city. It may also dictate the intensity of use by imposing maximum or minimum limits on lot sizes, floor space, or floor-area ratios. Zoning is intended to coordinate private configurations of land use with the public portion of the market, where the roads and ports are. It is also intended to minimize externalities across uses by, for example, isolating landfills from residential areas.

Even zoning can be taken too far, however. If manufacturing is isolated from residential areas, commuting becomes difficult and expensive for industrial workers. Excessively high standards for residential development drive up housing costs and force low-income households to locate far from job centers. Zoning can also be too static. Cities change, but redrafting land use plans can be a slow process. In the mid-1970s Malaysia

Box 6.5
City development and land markets

Most cities of the world have a common spatial pattern of economic activity. Most of the activity is densely packed near the city center and declines with distance. Commercial activity agglomerates at the city center in skyscrapers because of scale economies (from information exchanges and spillovers) and low transaction and transportation costs. Public transportation systems and utilities also operate more efficiently in high-density areas. Some households, especially those without children, cluster near the city center in high-rise apartments to minimize commuting time to work and downtown entertainment. Land prices reflect these density patterns, decreasing as the distance from the city center increases. High land prices near the city center mirror the many advantages of living there and the corresponding demand for office, housing, and retail space. Low land prices further out reflect the comparative disadvantages of reduced benefits from economies of scale and the long commuting times. Market forces thus tend to push cities toward an efficient pattern of land use, one that is (in the ab-sence of geographic obstacles) less intense as the distance from the city center grows.

In Paris residential population density declines steadily with distance from the city center. Land prices follow the same pattern. However, Moscow appears to violate the common pattern: its density gradient is upward, not downward. But Moscow's densities were determined not by market forces but by planned allocations that did not recognize either the benefits of central locations or the demand for them.

Market pricing is likely to change the pattern of land use in socialist cities. The price gradient for land in Moscow, which was relatively flat in the first quarter of 1992, had already begun to steepen two quarters later. Krakow, having opened land to market pricing somewhat earlier, has a considerably steeper land price gradient. As market forces take hold, both cities are likely to take on the steeply sloped density gradients of efficient Western cities, where economic activity clusters at the core areas.

In Paris population densities fall as the distance from the city center increases; in Moscow, densities increase

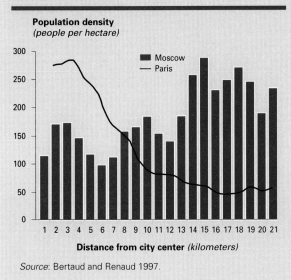

Source: Bertaud and Renaud 1997.

Land prices in Moscow and Krakow are beginning to look like those in the West

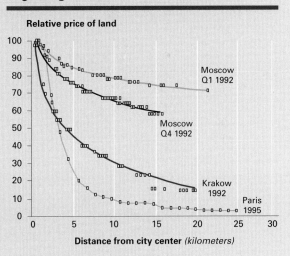

Source: Bertaud and Renaud 1997.

adopted the Town and Country Planning Act of Britain and Wales, imposing a rigid planning system developed for a slow-growing country on a fast-growing economy. The impact was immediate. The supply of housing in Kuala Lumpur became inelastic, and housing prices climbed at two to three times the rate of economic growth, reaching five to six times the average annual income. In Bangkok, where zoning regulations are more liberal, housing prices are only two to three times the average annual income.[34]

Governments also influence the location of economic activity through their control over public land and transportation systems. Up to half of urban land is in the public domain, including roads, highways, sidewalks, parks, and public buildings and facilities. The way the government chooses to use the public portion of urban land determines the spatial configuration of a city: where industry locates, how congested the city is, how dense neighborhoods are, and how the city will develop. Cities expand through progressive additions of

transportation corridors and ring roads that allow economic activity to spread out in more or less concentric
circles. Failure to expand transportation facilities delays
the movement of people and industry from city centers
to suburbs, resulting in exceedingly dense core cities
with poor living conditions and noncompetitive land
and wage costs. When Jakarta finally built toll roads
into the immediate surrounding countryside in the late
1980s, population density in the city center fell from
42,000 people per square kilometer in 1980 to 30,000
in 1990. Meanwhile, the suburbs around Jakarta, where
wage costs were 25 percent lower than in the city center, increased their share of the metropolitan area's formal manufacturing employment from 44 percent in
1985 to 65 percent in 1993.

Governments influence the efficiency of land use in
a third way: through their role as a repository of claims
to land ownership. Well-functioning land markets require clear title arrangements and a well-kept land registry, so that ownership rights are clearly established and
all transactions are recorded. The lack of such arrangements hinders private (re)development by jeopardizing
the gains developers and individuals expect when they
improve land. When a city has an informal sector where
land use rights are insecure, redevelopment becomes
even more difficult. Finally, urban planners need up-to-
date information on land use and transactions in order
to design and implement effective land use plans.

Municipal entrepreneurship

In 1996 senior officials of the Indian state of Gujarat
went to the World Economic Forum and wooed the
chief executive officer of General Motors, convincing
him that Gujarat was a suitable location for a plant. At
the beginning of the 1980s two U.S. states had trade offices abroad; by the end of the 1980s, 40 did. Today more
U.S. states have trade offices in Tokyo than in Washington.[35] In a world characterized by increased globalization
and urbanization, subnational governments are marketing their jurisdictions abroad, aiming to catalyze opportunities for innovation and cooperation. Can city governments become strategic brokers that influence their
city's—and even their country's—position in the global
urban hierarchy? With appropriate planning and support, the answer seems to be yes (box 6.6).

Some argue that cities need this kind of municipal entrepreneurship in order to seize the new opportunities
offered by globalization and localization and to cope
with the attendant challenges. But others fear that in-

creased competition within regions is causing cities to
enter a race they cannot win, in which urban governments offering lavish and costly incentives to "footloose"
investors force other local governments to follow suit.
Such corporate welfare is estimated to cost several billion
dollars annually in the United States, where examples
abound of states and cities providing massive subsidies
that seldom lead to new jobs. In Philadelphia, Pennsyl-
vania, the city and state have provided $426 million in
subsidies to Europe's largest shipbuilder just to retain existing jobs. In Ohio one city government spent $156,000
for each of the 180 jobs a General Motors plant created.

One intellectual justification for such subsidies is the
infant industry or scale economy argument, which supports subsidizing a line of industrial activity until it
achieves sufficient local scale to be viable. But if all cities
in a region adopt this strategy and begin offering excessive subsidies, they may well wind up with the same industrial base they would have had without the subsidies. An obvious policy solution is a national agreement
to harmonize or cap subsidies. Although such agreements are rare, they may become more common, given
the recent bad press on local subsidies in the United
States and related debates in the European Union.

Even without regional agreements to limit industrial
incentives, international trade agreements are limiting
the scope for such incentives.[36] The agreement on subsidies and countervailing measures adopted as part of
the General Agreement on Tariffs and Trade (GATT)
in 1993 prohibits any domestic subsidy that could displace imports in domestic markets or other countries'
exports in international markets. Subsidies are defined
according to the benefits they confer and the geographic
area or industry they target. This agreement may keep
local governments from offering subsidies to specific industries within their jurisdiction or using tax breaks to
attract particular firms. By connecting local economies
more fully to the global economy, globalization may
expand the ability of trade agreements to limit such
local industrial subsidies. Recent cases such as the one
brought against Nova Scotia, Canada, for incentives it
offered to a tire plant show how the GATT agreement
has made state and local governments vulnerable to re-
taliatory actions initiated by foreign countries.

In the debates over subsidizing industry, both politicians and the public too often forget that the inputs most
relevant to economic development are often beyond the
control of local governments—labor costs and skills, natural resources, climate, and energy prices.[37] Business sur-

Box 6.6
Regionalism and local economic development: lessons from Europe

The 1980s saw the demise—at least in Europe—of top-down industrial policies and their spatial correlate, regional economic development policies. By the early 1990s not a single national industrial policy initiative could be identified in Europe, and nationally determined regional policies were scarce.

Two factors explain the demise of centrally issued regional policies. First, they had a record of picking industrial lame ducks. Second, regional governments resented national policies aimed at their economies, complaining that local authorities were rarely consulted. The result has been a drop in spending on local development initiatives but greater regional input on how such funding is used.

The increased involvement of regions in development initiatives did result in some bidding wars to attract firms, but it also led to strategic improvements. Ireland is a good example of these changes. The Irish program emerged from the national economic crisis of the mid-1980s, which was characterized by severe long-term unemployment and attendant social ills. The central government's efforts to deal with the crisis were clearly not working, and budgetary pressure was forcing a reconsideration of social policies.

Out of this dilemma came the new Irish "social partnership," which created decentralized centers for the unemployed managed by boards composed of representatives of local governments, training agencies, and the office of the prime minister. The centers serve as vehicles for retargeting social assis-

tance to focus on the most vulnerable groups, increasing the resources available for economic development. To complement the centers, the government fostered partnerships in the same areas (and in rural areas) with a mandate to enhance the competitiveness of local firms by making residents more employable. Finally, with the support of the European Union, the government created county enterprise boards that allocated project grants locally using criteria set at the national level.

Despite some weaknesses, the Irish partnerships are generally considered successful. The keys to their success are:

- Their ability to draw directly on local resources, so that the experience of local businesspeople provides the foundation for enterprise creation and the unemployed themselves set up programs targeting the jobless
- Their ability to adapt the objectives and resources of state agencies to local needs
- Their capacity for improving the targeting of social welfare—and thus the cost-effectiveness of providing it.

Part of the reason for the success of Ireland's local partnerships is that they developed in a period of economic expansion. But their successes are proof that practical, positive area-based programming and public-private partnerships can work.

Source: Cooke and Morgan 1998; Sabel 1998.

---

veys suggest that entrepreneurs care about operating costs and conditions most, followed by quality of life. Transportation costs and wages are generally cited as the most important, followed by utility and occupancy costs. Among the public services that matter are transportation and safety. Taxes matter only at the margin in choosing among similar locations.[38] A municipality's economic development efforts should focus on efficiently providing the services it is responsible for and easing red tape and excessive regulation.

A possible role for municipal activism does remain, however. The efforts of local governments to promote industrial development can be successful and cost-effective if they focus on broad policies designed to form a critical mass for specific industries and not on firm-specific benefits. Sectorwide strategies are more likely to create a competitive advantage because they "cluster" activities that can lead to agglomeration economies. For example, local governments can develop training initiatives adapted to local economic conditions and comparative advantages. France and Italy are decentralizing vocational training on the theory that local governments are best suited to working with local

firms and workers' unions to identify needs and create potential partnerships. Arrangements among local governments, employers, and unions aimed at providing vocational training facilitate these efforts. In Penang, Malaysia, the Penang Skills Development Center brings together representatives of industry, state and local government, and academia to bridge the gap between formal education and the job skills the area's top investors require. Similarly, the Skill Development Councils of Karachi and Lahore (Pakistan), composed of provincial and federal government representatives, employers, and workers' representatives, are successful forums that serve as links between industry and training providers.[39]

What institutional arrangements are most likely to produce successful local development policies? Leadership is important, but it can emerge from many sources, either private or public.[40] A forum is needed within which the private and public sectors can communicate with each other and define a common goal or vision for a city. Such a forum requires the support of a common base of information (box 6.7). Different cities have different forums and institutional arrangements that range from formal chambers of commerce

Box 6.7
Know thy economy: the importance of local economic information

A city can judge the appropriateness of regulations only if it has reliable information on its economy and spatial organization. This lesson holds true whether the issue is deciding which growth-hampering regulations to eliminate or which growth-friendly regulations to implement during the urban transition. For example, the spatial organization implicit in a zoning plan is often hidden because zoning is usually the result of parcel-by-parcel negotiations. Few cities have an overall schematic zoning map. When Krakow conducted an overall review of its city zoning plan, it found that while the stated objective was to promote a compact city with few suburbs, the plan's constraints on land use and its tendency to reinforce existing land use patterns were actually blocking this goal. [41]

Regional analysis can help identify infrastructure investments that will improve integration between cities and nonurban areas, increase access to national and global markets, and contribute to regional prosperity. A regional economic analysis pointed out that for more than 30 years investment in Senegal's river delta had focused on rice farming—apparently because many believed that rice farming was the source of the region's growth. Yet rice farming has never generated more than 4 percent of the region's gross local product despite absorbing three times that amount in foreign aid in the 1990s. Meanwhile, the regional capital stagnated (along with the region) because its port and local transportation infrastructure were never properly developed.

A common base of facts promotes a constructive debate on municipal development and facilitates consensus around a local development strategy. Without a common factual base, the debate can be frustrating and inconclusive. At a conference organized by Durban, South Africa, to design an economic development strategy, all the speakers had been hampered by the paucity of data, and each had spent precious time gathering information that was often outdated and not always consistent or comparable. Unsurprisingly they found it difficult to place their work in context and to establish cross-sectoral priorities. [42]

In most countries the needed information is available through completed censuses and surveys, and the amount of work required to compile the information is manageable and affordable. A modest investment of time and money supported the collection of information for estimating and analyzing regional accounts in several West African regional capitals. Data came from the national census office, trade bureaus, and elementary surveys. [43] New technology has made it easier and cheaper to process data and understand its spatial implications.

If the information exists, why is it so difficult to access? Most cities have local planning offices or economic bureaus whose role is to collect and process statistical information about the city. But the census and survey data routinely collected at the national level are typically not available to local offices, at least not in a readily usable form. In other cases local offices collect basic demographic and production statistics. But these data are transmitted directly to the national capital and are not analyzed locally, either because local economic officers do not have the skills or resources or because the city's decisionmakers do not demand the information.

The key is to establish a structure to ensure that local development strategies and investment plans are based on good information. Regions can contract out the tasks of analyzing and compiling data or develop partnerships with groups that can help collect the necessary information, such as local universities, national statistical institutes, chambers of commerce, and trade institutes.

---

and municipal commissions to informal ad hoc commissions organized around a single vision or project. Whatever its structure, the forum needs to have the powers and means necessary to collect and process reliable information on the local economy.

• • •

In economic terms, what is good for a country is good for its cities. If the political, legal, and macroeconomic conditions for nationwide economic development are in place, urban economies are likely to grow. National governments will find it best not to attempt to stop or direct internal migration, since such efforts inevitably fail. Local governments can facilitate urban economic growth in their areas by investing in trunk infrastructure and fostering an open land market. But the key role of local government in economic development is to provide the basic infrastructure and public services needed to create an attractive environment for both businesses and households.

7 Making Cities Livable

As long as it is environmentally and socially sustainable, economic growth will in time lead to better living conditions. But cities need not wait for the slow compounding of aggregate growth rates to improve livability. With the appropriate polices and institutions, many countries with low per capita incomes can enjoy considerably better service levels (figures 7.1 and 7.2). In developing countries with a relatively high per capita GDP, the percentage of urban households with access to water and sanitation services (two important indices of the quality of urban life) is already relatively high. Among countries with low income levels, access to these services—as well to affordable housing—varies widely. Clearly, some low-income countries have provided much better access to essential services than others.

Since the 1950s the dominant model for providing basic infrastructure and services in developing countries has assigned primary responsibility to the public sector. But this arrangement has left much to be desired in most low-income developing countries.[1] The service gaps left by the public sector have been filled largely by the unregulated

private sector and by community initiatives—a remarkable response that has provided affordable housing and services to millions of urban households. But unregulated and isolated community initiatives cannot serve as the building blocks for sustained citywide improvements. Cities need to turn away from an unsuccessful model that leaves the most dynamic providers of essential services outside the planning and implementation framework to one that associates them in productive partnerships. This step clearly requires changing the rules so that partnerships are facilitated and services provided in ways that are guided by and respond to public demand.

This chapter seeks to describe how an appropriate blend of policies and institutions can improve urban living conditions at various levels of economic development. The chapter begins by reviewing the principal issues of urban livability, then briefly examines the history of service provision (both public and private). The aim of this review is to identify the factors responsible for the public sector's poor performance in providing essential services in developing

Figure 7.1
Even low-income countries can achieve high levels of basic water and sanitation services

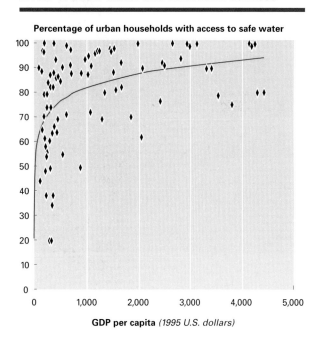

Percentage of urban households with access to safe water

GDP per capita *(1995 U.S. dollars)*

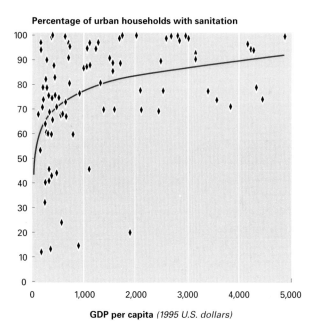

Percentage of urban households with sanitation

GDP per capita *(1995 U.S. dollars)*

Note: Safe water includes public taps within 200 meters that offer adequate supplies for daily needs. *Urban sanitation* is the percentage of urban households with a connection to public sewers or with a household system such as a pit privy, septic tank, or communal toilet.
Source: World Bank, *World Development Indicators,* 1999.

countries. The discussion then turns to the roles of the public and private sectors and community initiatives in service provision. This analysis draws on recent experience in a number of areas: housing, water supply, sanitation, transportation, and social protection. The chapter does not try to provide technical solutions for sectoral problems. Instead it shows how an institutional framework built on partnerships, inclusiveness, and information sharing and responsive to demand holds genuine promise for improving urban living conditions.

In meeting the urban challenges of the 21st century, the most effective institutions and policy initiatives will exploit the opportunities globalization and localization present. Globalization can provide the impetus for economic growth, while successful localization can empower communities to act as agents of change and give rise to mechanisms that promote transparency and accountability in public sector decisionmaking. For developing countries ready to exploit them, these opportunities can have a lasting impact on the daily lives of millions of urban households.

The unfinished urban agenda

Cities provide their residents with chances for upward mobility that are often absent in rural areas, and for that reason urban areas act as magnets for rural migrants.[2] But living conditions for many of the most recent arrivals (as well as for other disenfranchised social groups) have remained below acceptable thresholds, even though urban living conditions have improved since World War II. Thus the urban agenda for improved livability begins with reducing poverty and inequality. But it also includes creating a healthful urban environment, minimizing crime and violence, establishing a civil protection system, and making services more accessible.[3]

Cities have often been overwhelmed by population growth, leaving them unable to provide sufficient basic services. In 1994 at least 220 million urban dwellers (13 percent of the developing world's urban population) lacked access to clean drinking water, and almost twice as many had no access even to the simplest latrines. Roughly half of all solid waste went uncollected, piling up on streets and in drains and contributing to flooding and the spread of disease. Domestic and industrial effluents were being released into waterways with little or no treatment, often affecting the quality of water far beyond the city. The La Paz River flowing through Bolivia's capital is still so polluted that down-

Figure 7.2
Housing affordability varies significantly at low levels of income

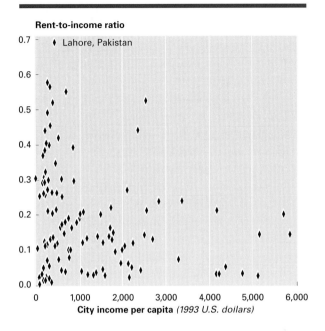

Rent-to-income ratio

◆ Lahore, Pakistan

City income per capita *(1993 U.S. dollars)*

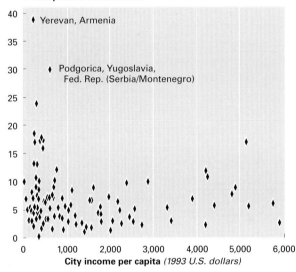

House price-to-income ratio

◆ Yerevan, Armenia

◆ Podgorica, Yugoslavia,
   Fed. Rep. (Serbia/Montenegro)

City income per capita *(1993 U.S. dollars)*

Source: UNCHS 1995.

stream horticultural production has been curtailed.[4] And the Pasig River that created the lush vegetation of Manila is now biologically dead.[5]

The lack of basic services continues to exact a high toll on human health. Epidemiological studies show that improving access to water, drainage, and sanitation facilities can reduce the incidence of diarrheal disease

by more than 20 percent.[6] When these facilities break down or do not keep up with a city's expanding population, the health hazards increase for a range of waterborne diseases and diseases spread by water-related vectors (malaria and dengue fever being the most threatening). At any given time, close to half the urban population in developing countries is suffering from one or more of these diseases.[7] Airborne illnesses such as acute respiratory infections and tuberculosis also spread faster in overcrowded urban residential quarters with inadequate ventilation (see box 7).

Air pollution, which is closely associated with urbanization and industrialization in developing countries, seriously impinges on the health of children and adults alike. Pollution particularly affects those already suffering from malnutrition and infectious disease, which lower their ability to resist chemical pollutants. For most children in the large cities of developing countries, breathing the air may be as harmful as smoking two packs of cigarettes a day.

- In Delhi the incidence of bronchial asthma in the 5–16 age group is 10–12 percent, and air pollution is one of the major causes.[8]
- A 1990 study of atmospheric lead pollution in Bangkok estimated that 30,000 to 70,000 children risked losing 4 or more IQ points because of high lead levels, and many more risked smaller reductions in intelligence.[9]
- China has 9 of the 10 cities with the highest counts of total suspended particulates (TSPs). Industrial and industrializing cities such as Jiaozou, Lanzhou, Taiyuan, Urumqi, Wanxian, and Yichang all have mean annual concentrations of TSPs exceeding 500 micrograms per cubic meter. The World Health Organization (WHO) puts acceptable levels at less than 100 micrograms per cubic meter.[10]

Problems of inadequate infrastructure have economic as well as human costs. In Jakarta a poor resident typically pays 10 times more than a rich resident does for a liter of clean water and suffers 2 to 4 times more gastroenteritis, typhoid, and malaria.[11] As traffic continues to clog the streets of most large cities in developing countries, the costs of traffic congestion grow. Estimated losses from traffic jams in Bangkok range from $272 million to $1 billion a year, depending on how the value of time lost in traffic jams is computed.[12] In Seoul time losses from traffic congestion are estimated at $154 million.[13] If China maintains its business-as-usual response to air pollution, the health costs of urban residents' exposure to TSPs will rise from $32 billion in 1995 to nearly $98 billion in 2020.[14]

The poor suffer most from these problems. The locus of poverty is shifting to urban areas, yet cities can go only so far in addressing issues of income redistribution, which often require central government action. On average, health indicators show that people are better off in cities than in rural areas, but the statistics mask inequalities within the urban population. Recent evidence suggests that health conditions for the poor in many developing cities are worse than in rural areas. In Bangladesh, for example, reported infant mortality rates in urban slums exceed rural rates (table 7.1).[15] More than 1.1 billion people—poor and rich alike—live in cities with levels of air pollution in excess of WHO standards. But poor urban dwellers are likely to be exposed to additional indoor air pollution from inadequate, badly ventilated cooking facilities and to further outdoor pollution from industrial sites. The poorer areas of cities are often adjacent to such sites, either because no one else will live there or because the poor have no voice in deciding where industries are located.[16]

Urban dwellers in poor districts of metropolitan areas suffer disproportionately because of crime and violence, which increase alongside poverty and inequality.[17] According to WHO, the global cost of injuries from violence is almost $500 billion a year in medical care and lost productivity.[18] Estimates of the social costs of crime and violence range from about 2 percent of GDP in Asia to 7.5 percent of GDP in Latin America.[19]

Learning from the past

Since the 1950s the common model of urban management in developing countries has charged the public sector with planning and delivering basic services. But this model has failed to yield satisfactory outcomes in low-income countries. One argument holds that governments should withdraw as primary service providers and assume the role of enabler, relying increasingly on the private sector to deliver basic services.[20] But the public sector has successfully provided such services in industrial countries since the late 1800s. Why have publicly provided essential services been satisfactory in the one case and not in the other?

Urban reform

Around 1850 European cities faced many of the same problems cities in developing countries face today. Rural migrants were arriving in urban areas daily, increasing populations so precipitously that the supply of basic services could not keep up with demand. Urban mortality rates were often far higher than those in the surrounding rural areas, in part because of epidemics of diseases such as cholera. Public officials investigating the frequent epidemics associated the problems with the lack of decent sanitary conditions in the parts of the city where the new arrivals settled. A revolution in public sanitation ensued, with cities investing heavily in housing and in water, sewerage, and drainage facilities. North American cities shared the experience of their European counterparts.[21]

These reforms succeeded for one important reason. Wealthy residents of cities could not escape the effects of unhealthy living conditions. Thus, although the risks were far worse in poor areas where structures such as tenements abounded, wealthier urban residents could not ignore the threat to their own well-being.[22] Their support, often in the form of influential political coalitions, affected the allocation of resources at both the national and subnational levels and helped direct public funds to urban areas in need of appropriate sanitary facilities.

By the time rapid urbanization began to affect developing countries, however, technological advances had altered the situation and weakened the impetus for public action, much to the disadvantage of the urban poor. Advances in medicine, in particular, were making it possible for individuals to protect themselves against disease. Portable electricity generators and pumps had been developed that gave individual households access to light and water. More recently, filters and bottled water have become available, mitigating (for those who can afford them) the shortcomings of the public system. Vacuum trucks and septic tanks permit households to develop their own solutions to sanitation problems. Air-conditioned residences, automobiles, and

Table 7.1
Infant mortality rate, Bangladesh, 1990
(per 1,000 live births)

	National	Rural	Urban	Urban slums (1991)
Total	94	97	71	134
Male	98	101	73	123
Female	91	93	68	146

Source: Harpham and Tanner 1995.

offices block out the worst effects of air pollution. Urban enclaves or suburbs and private security arrangements partially insulate the wealthy from crime and violence. And with time, the medical community has learned how to prevent the diseases of poverty from engulfing entire urban populations. The ability to provide for and protect oneself and one's immediate family has become a given in modern urban life, undermining the impetus to lobby for changes that will benefit society as a whole. Individual action produces faster and more reliable results and is more readily available to members of politically influential groups—precisely those groups that once lobbied for action on a grander scale.[23]

As a result of these changes, cities around the world have been divided into those who can afford to supply their own needs and those who cannot. Municipal governments and public agencies often cater to one part of a city and, at best, adopt a posture of benign neglect toward the other, making the division even deeper. This interpretation of urban history is supported by several recent episodes in which concerted public action has occurred only when negative externalities spilled beyond poor neighborhoods. Major initiatives in Calcutta were spurred by cholera outbreaks in the 1950s and 1960s, and more recent reforms in Surat and Ahmadabad, India, date from an outbreak of the plague in 1994. The economic impact of the plague spread beyond the cities to threaten India's national tourism industry. Those same public sector agencies that were responsible for neglecting their municipalities quickly began to focus on solid waste collection and disposal. Their actions transformed Surat into India's second-cleanest city.[24] Such examples support the conclusion that the absence of influential political lobbies for urban reform in developing countries is at least partly responsible for the lack of progress in providing decent services.[25]

Providing essential services privately

In the late 19th and early 20th centuries in England and the United States, gas, water, canals, trolleys, highways, and electricity were mostly provided privately. By 1890 private companies owned 57 percent of the waterworks in the United States. Municipalities often arranged long-term contracts with these firms, primarily for financial reasons: cities lacked capital, and national subsidies were quite limited. At this early stage of urban development, demand patterns varied widely (especially among low-income homeowners, tenants, and home-based producers), and metering technology

was not yet available. Given the situation, private "niche" providers with an intimate knowledge of neighborhoods and customers were better able to match supply and demand. By the early 19th century, private water companies had been serving London for over 200 years. Eight companies were operating in the city at the end of the century.[26]

Over time, however, people became dissatisfied with private providers.[27] Complaints centered on the lack of services in outlying areas, high prices, poor quality, and political corruption. The introduction of flush toilets increased the amount of wastewater, polluting the local water supply, and private companies proved reluctant to invest in more distant water sources. As fire-fighting technology changed, requiring more water at greater pressures, disagreements arose about how to supply water to fight fires and who should pay for it.[28] Courts of law found it difficult to cope with the complex regulatory problems that cropped up in these disputes.[29]

At the same time, rising incomes led to much greater homogeneity in the demand for services such as gas, water, sanitation, and electricity, eroding one advantage of having small niche providers. These providers also could not exploit the scale economies of networked services offered by regionally managed water resources, reservoirs, and centralized facilities for treating wastewater. All these considerations led to a major shift in the way essential services were provided in the 20th century. Public or semiregulated, autonomous entities assumed responsibility for delivering basic services in industrial countries such as the United Kingdom and, to a lesser extent, the United States.

Private provision is now making a significant comeback in industrial countries. The United Kingdom undertook major reforms in the 1980s, and a profound change appears to be under way in Europe as the private and public sectors develop partnerships to fund and operate infrastructure projects.[30] These partnerships are in part the result of public expenditure constraints imposed during the process leading up to the birth of the euro, the single European currency. But Europe's shift to private infrastructure also reflects advances in regulatory capabilities, which were seriously limited in the late 19th century.

France's experience illustrates the importance and difficulty of regulating providers of basic services. France has a long history of private provision of public services. Its decentralized public-private system of municipal concessions developed during the 20th century has proved very successful. But the French experience also shows that such a system is not always easy to implement—and that it requires strong monitoring mechanisms. In the mid-1990s municipal water concessions were hit with allegations of corruption.[31] Disputes arose between municipalities and water concessionaires, in part because of the uncertainty introduced by repeated legislative changes in the early 1990s and in part because of the number of unfavorable contracts inexperienced municipalities had negotiated. As a result, private-public partnerships fell out of favor with elected officials. The situation is changing, with two associations of local governments joining forces to create a consulting agency, Service Public 2000, that will help municipalities negotiate contracts and design regulations. Several laws have also been passed since 1995 that require greater transparency and public disclosure from concessionaires. These developments have substantially improved the situation and restored confidence in water concessions.[32]

The history of urban services management in Buenos Aires is in some ways similar to France's experience.[33] In the late 19th century private companies operating in a competitive market provided most infrastructure and essential services, which compared well with what European cities enjoyed. Over time, however, politicians began to interfere in the regulatory process, causing service to suffer and, in the mid-20th century, providing a justification for introducing centralized public management. But the public sector was not up to the task. Increasingly the demands of local users and the priorities of the federally controlled utilities came into conflict, and once again the quality of service declined. At the same time, the number of residents with no access to services increased. Around 1990 the government began to replace public sector monopolies with private monopoly providers. It is too early to evaluate the results of this latest phase, but in order for private provision to succeed, it will have to be effectively regulated. Regulation is a particularly important issue in low-income developing countries, where regulatory mechanisms are still weak.

Service provision in developing countries

The public sector in developing countries has enjoyed a broad mandate when it comes to urban areas. In many cities the public sector owns most of the land. It is often the monopoly provider of many services, especially those based on physical networks: water supply,

sewerage, electricity, gas, and telecommunications. In these cases its franchise is exclusive, and private provision is illegal. In other areas, such as housing, the public sector establishes standards and regulations.

When this broad mandate is executed well, the combination of exclusive control and centralized management can theoretically yield economies of scale for networked services. However, when it is not properly carried out, it can generate severe problems. When the public sector falls short, private companies and individuals begin offering water, transportation, accommodation, and other services on an ad hoc basis, outside the reach of formal rules—a situation that creates many dilemmas and inefficiencies.

For many services, such as housing and water supply, the private sector is more than ready to respond to demand, since providing these services can be profitable. But in many developing countries private firms cannot offer affordable housing without violating the building codes. More often than not, these codes are based on sophisticated engineering standards that are inappropriate in a low-income country. Furthermore, the private sector is unwilling to make long-term investments when it is operating outside the law and is at the mercy of the public authorities. This scenario causes serious problems. Pushing basic services into an informal area of shadowy legality prevents investments large enough to benefit from economies of scale. It also gives rise to an underground economy in which the acquisition of state land, its subdivision, development, and settlement, and the provision of public services are all opaque and somewhat mysterious.

One of India's best-known corruption fighters, K. J. Alphons, described the agency he worked for, the Delhi Development Authority (DDA), as "the most corrupt institution in the country." Those who corrupt it, he added, help illegal builders grab DDA land and then build houses and shops that are sold to unwitting buyers. Unauthorized buildings range from shanties for the poor to shopping centers for the middle class to mansions for the rich, all established on government land under false pretenses, with political complicity. Moreover, Alphons reported, nothing gets built, legal or illegal, without a bribe.[34] Many developing cities are serviced in this fashion, with essential services available only at a very heavy social cost. Karachi, Pakistan needs an estimated 80,000 housing units each year, but between 1987 and 1992 the authorities issued an average of only 26,700 building permits annually. The gap, of course, is being filled in much the same way as it is in Delhi.[35] Without reforms, the urban future of developing countries will probably continue along these lines, with overcrowded squatter settlements, illegal subdivisions, deteriorating environmental conditions, and costly service provision.[36]

When confronted with a public provider that is unresponsive to demand but holds a franchise shutting out private providers, households and businesses often resort to providing basic services like water and electricity themselves. This "self-provision" is a very inefficient form of privatization. Typically, the small producer or consumer cannot fully utilize the equipment that has been installed, cannot take advantage of economies of scale, and is unable to sell any surplus capacity in a market that is, in any case, prevented from forming. Where technological advances have broken the link to physical networks, as in telecommunications, private providers have been able to establish markets that greatly benefit consumers. But physical networks remain necessary in areas like water, sewerage, and electricity.

In other situations when the private sector does not respond to demand for essential services, communities have often organized themselves as providers. Such arrangements are most common in the area of wastewater and solid waste disposal. Nongovernmental organizations (NGOs) often play a key role in these initiatives, providing technical input during the design and implementation phases. This type of decentralized service provision has been successful in meeting the needs of many households. But municipal authorities often do not integrate it into trunk infrastructure, either because the settlements are considered "irregular" or because the community-provided infrastructure does not conform to existing codes. Public sector proposals for future citywide development often ignore the existence of functional community infrastructure that is already meeting the demands of households and represents millions of dollars worth of private, unsubsidized investment.

These responses to inadequate public sector services suggest a new partnership-based model for service provision that incorporates the dynamism of the private sector and community groups into public planning. Models of this type are already being used in countries around the world, and because of their success they have been described as the "quiet revolution" in local governance.[37] Latin American cities have been in the vanguard, and the process is under way elsewhere. But the pace of this revolution has been uneven. Communities are often unable to agree on a course of action because of ethnic fragmentation or other divisions. Even in India—which has been a democracy for more than half a century, has undergone constitutional decentralization, and has strong NGOs—progress has been hindered by the lack of sufficient political pressure from below and the absence of support from above.[38] In addition, local governments often lack the technical and institutional capacity to form partnerships with community-based organizations.

This embryonic approach to urban management requires strategic partnerships and reformed institutions that are approved by both the public and private sectors. These partnerships also need to address citizens' rights, security, participation, transparency, and accountability. Fully utilizing them may require redesigning national constitutions, as it did in Brazil and South Africa.[39] Despite these issues, and even without wide-ranging reform, a growing number of examples are proving the effectiveness of the approach. In Karachi partnerships are providing sanitation services for informal settlements. In Cali, Colombia, they are being used to combat crime and violence. Such partnerships, which incorporate municipal governments and community-based organizations, with NGOs as intermediaries, can form the basis for new institutions. The following sections review experiences in a number of specific sectors that demonstrate the potential of these partnerships.

Urban housing

Public sector attempts to provide new housing for low-income groups in developing countries have not met with much success. Sometimes the locations chosen have been inappropriate, but more often building regulations have priced the target populations out of the market. In most developing economies formal building regulations are largely unrealistic, mandating oversized plots and rights-of-way and setting standards for infrastructure and building materials that result in structures low-income households cannot afford. Not surprisingly, the stock of housing complying with these regulations has not been able to satisfy demand.[40] The result of this shortage is a proliferation of privately developed and quite illegal settlements in many cities throughout the developing world. Over half the urban population in Turkey resides in such settlements, which are known there as *gecekondus*. An equal number in Karachi live in *katchi abadis* (see chapter 8). And in São Paulo, Brazil, the proportion of the urban population living in *favelas* is reported to have increased from 9 percent in 1987 to 19 percent in 1993.[41]

The public sector has had much greater success when it has entered into partnerships with communities—for instance, in order to upgrade slums. Some large upgrading programs, such as Indonesia's Kampung Improvement Programs (KIPs), have had national impact. KIPs have been implemented in more than 500 urban areas since 1968 and have benefited almost 15 million people. Other successful upgrading programs—including those in the Aguablanca district of Cali and the El Mezquital settlement in Guatemala City, the Million Houses Program in Sri Lanka, and others in Fortaleza, Brazil; Sambizanga, Angola; and Amman and Aqaba, Jordan—show that such efforts reduce costs and subsidies significantly, improve targeting, and provide security of tenure.[42] In order to succeed, however, these programs require community and individual participation and initiative. In Indonesia's KIPs, for instance, residents generate requests for building materials based on need and take responsibility for installing and constructing paths and drains.

Housing is a private good, unlike infrastructure for services like water or sewerage, and is best provided through market mechanisms except when social safety measures justify public sector regulation. The enabling approach endorsed by the United Nations Global Shelter Strategy for the Year 2000, which is likely to continue into the 21st century, calls for private developers and voluntary agencies, community organizations, and NGOs to provide a bigger share of housing.[43] To reduce costs and respond faster to changing demands, the UN strategy relies on market forces for many aspects of housing provision, including markets for land, building materials, financing, and construction. Community organizations, assisted by NGOs and public sector agencies, have a strong role to play in providing technical advice and additional financing. The Community Mortgage Program in the Philippines is an example of a relatively successful housing program. Since 1988 it has made loans in 33 cities through more than 300 projects to allow communities to purchase the land they live on. In the past five years the program has served an average of 10,000 families annually.

With this approach the government's role in housing markets is to address areas in which private unregulated markets do not work well. The public sector needs to focus on property rights, housing finance and subsidies, building regulations, and trunk infrastructure.[44] The experience of the Russian Federation and the East European countries suggests that infrastructure investment alone will not suffice to stimulate housing construction in the absence of an institutional framework for mortgage financing and land property rights.[45] The transition in the former socialist economies has been disastrous for new housing construction, leading to significant reductions in production and mismatches between supply and demand.

Only well-functioning land markets can provide an adequate supply of housing, and maintaining these markets is another task that deserves the attention of the public sector. Providing universal registration and establishing clear property rights to all urban land will require strengthening existing institutions. Ill-defined land rights render land useless and discourage the redevelopment of entire portions of a city. But simply providing security of tenure creates incentives to improve housing and infrastructure dramatically.[46] To avoid adding to the backlog of problem housing and neighborhoods, new developments must meet basic—but not excessive—compliance standards. For the sake of the poor, developments must seek to overcome the "spatial mismatch" that occurs when informal neighborhoods are situated far from centers of economic activity and thus from jobs. However, the task of formulating appropriate regulations without also creating opportunities for rent-seeking by regulators remains a challenge if there is no pressure for accountability (box 7.1).

Water

Inefficient and inadequate public provision of water has been a glaring problem in many developing cities. Public utilities often do not know where half or more of their water goes. Many years of international assistance aimed at upgrading networks and building capacity in cities like Manila have not improved the situation. While 80 percent of high-income urban residents in the developing world have a water supply connection, only 18 percent of low-income residents do, though some share water taps with neighbors. Those without access to safe water (like the low-income residents of Lima) must buy from vendors at costs that are many times those for piped city water.[47] Studies of water vending report similar cost differentials for small towns in many parts of the world.[48] The results of this failure are everywhere evident in the developing world. Publicly provided water is often of such poor quality that residents

Box 7.1
A spatial mismatch: Jakarta's kampung residents

Land rights in Indonesia are complex, combining informal traditional rural processes with a modern registry system. Large tracts of land in the Jakarta Utara harbor area, particularly in the low-income kampungs, have often been held by families for some generations in traditional housing developments. Typically, residents do not have a registered claim of ownership— they owned the land before titles were registered. They have possessory rights, so generally they cannot be displaced without some compensation. They can strengthen their claims to ownership by paying property taxes and having their claims recognized by kampung officials. But paying taxes can be difficult, since some tax officials refuse to accept payments precisely to avoid strengthening residents' ownership claims. Land without a secure title changes hands among local residents at prices that are estimated to be 45 percent below the costs of securely titled land of the same quality.

In a dynamic developing city, informal property rights foster spatial mismatches and hinder urban redevelopment. In Jakarta the pattern of industrial growth under globalization is moving low-skill manufacturing jobs to distant suburban locations. Jakarta has also made street vending illegal, severely restricting the informal food-processing and -service industry. Many low-income residents would be financially better off selling their land and moving to the suburbs where jobs and business opportunities are located. The city would also be better

off, because Jakarta needs upscale, mixed-use land development in the harbor area. But the system of land rights prevents this natural market exchange.

Since kampung residents typically lack secure titles to the lands their families have lived on for generations, they cannot sell their land to developers for new uses. They are literally trapped in the kampung areas. The result is a spatial mismatch between business and employment opportunities in the suburbs and residents stuck in the inner city. Many workers must make a long commute to the suburbs each day, and many others remain under- or unemployed. The result is a is no-win situation for both workers and the city.

To deal with the situation, the city government has proposed the Jakarta Water Development Program. To find space for the needed mixed-use developments, the city will build out into the existing harbor, a process requiring expensive and environmentally risky land reclamation. Kampung residents would be asked to yield their lands voluntarily in return for new public housing accommodation in the harbor area. But this plan would only make the spatial mismatch worse. A more plausible solution is to give traditional kampung residents full title to their land, allowing them to sell it and move to the suburbs to seek employment. With the money they receive for their land, the residents would have the capital they need not ony to relocate but also to seek new business opportunities.

must treat it before using it. Service is often intermittent and water pressure low. And many households must spend money they can ill afford on bottled water just to meet their daily needs.[49]

As incomes rise, households in many cities are responding to poor water service by investing in private systems that provide a continuous supply with adequate pressure to support modern showers, flush toilets, and washing machines. Gujranwala, a dynamic secondary city in Pakistan with a population of more than 1 million, exemplifies the response to inadequate water service. Just over half the city's households have access to the piped public water supply. Of this half, two-thirds have made additional investments in storage tanks and pumps to upgrade the level of service. Households without access to the public supply, many of them low income, have installed manual or electric pumps to draw water from the shallow aquifer.[50] These investments reveal a great deal of willingness to pay for reliable water service. They also suggest that much of the water supply has been informally privatized.

But having each household provide or upgrade its own supply of water is not an efficient form of priva

tization. Aggregate private investments often exceed the full cost of an equivalent supply of public water, even at the high construction rates public contractors charge.[51] This kind of privatization is also environmentally problematic because of the risk of contaminating the shallow aquifers from which well water is drawn. Finally, informal privatization makes proper management of regional water resources impossible.

In urban neighborhoods a collective water supply system is much more cost-effective than a widespread system of wells and pumps, even when high-quality groundwater is easily accessible. Quite minimal scale economies for a collective system ensure such an advantage. Yet private piped supplies are often not allowed to compete with the public water monopoly.

Two approaches to resolving the water supply problem are available, both involving partnerships with the private sector. One involves replacing public service providers with centralized private concessions, and some large cities (Buenos Aires, Manila, and Jakarta) are doing just that by signing contracts with international firms. This approach raises two questions, however: whether a private monopoly provider will be more successful than the public sector at assessing and responding to the demands of low-income communities, and whether the state can provide appropriate regulation. Côte d'Ivoire, where a private company operates the water utilities, provides a positive example. In Abidjan and other, smaller cities, SODECI—a private joint venture between domestic and French firms—has assumed responsibility for attracting investments and has maintained full cost recovery with its private contracts. Under a policy designed to provide low-income households with direct access to water, 75 percent of SODECI's domestic connections have been provided without a connection charge.[52]

Smaller cities may find that having private firms provide water in a decentralized, competitive system offers many advantages. In Paraguay the water market was opened to private entrepreneurs, allowing them to legally drill wells and lay pipes in public streets. Business flourished, and an estimated 500 vendors (*aguateros*) now compete to supply households with water, with negligible water losses and full cost recovery.[53] In cities that rely on regional water resources, this system generally succeeds only if the private providers purchase water from a regional agency that carefully manages prices. In low-income areas with heterogeneous demand patterns, this type of competitive privatization may be preferable to replacing the public monopoly with a private monopoly, since small niche providers interact much more closely with their customers.[54] Competitive markets also considerably reduce regulatory problems. A natural process of consolidation and scale exploitation may ensue as the market matures and sorts out providers according to their efficiency and performance. In both the privatization alternatives, public-private partnerships point the way forward.

Partnerships with community organizations can also improve the performance of public water utilities. Community participation has dramatically improved the performance of the Haiphong Water Supply Company in Vietnam (box 7.2).

Sewerage

Piped sewerage is necessary in high-density urban areas, but the costs of providing access based on the standard engineering designs public agencies commonly adopt are high. The high-cost, centralized sewerage systems used throughout industrial countries are not feasible in developing cities that have no sewerage service at all. The very high up-front costs of collecting and treating wastewater at the city level, combined with the reluc-

Box 7.2
Haiphong: partnering with consumers

A partnership with consumers helped Vietnam's state-owned Haiphong Water Supply Company (HWSC) transform itself into a profit-making utility. The utility improved the system one ward at a time (a ward is the smallest unit of government administration). Within four years of entering into the partnership, the HWSC was serving 68 percent of the urban population with metered, reliable, high-pressure water. In the wards it served, it increased the hours when water is available from 8 to 24 hours a day and tripled its rate of bill collection.

In each ward the HWSC opened suboffices that provide a direct link to customers for meter reading, billing, collection, and troubleshooting. By metering consumers and fining them for lack of payment, the company has created incentives for consumers to conserve water. It has also improved service in some outlying wards where the service was poorest, signaling its intentions to make future improvements throughout the city.

The suboffices are staffed by people from the community and enjoy a close association with the neighborhood. A set of publicly displayed objectives and a "water contract" between HWSC and the consumers help to clarify the responsibilities of the offices. The HWSC is fostering a sense of partnership between consumers and the service provider, heightening mutual responsibility and providing the community with a convenient venue for communicating its needs. The HWSC gives bonuses to employees for achieving clear targets, such as reducing the quantity of unbilled water or increasing the percentage of bills collected. These targets serve as indicators of corporate performance and provide the staff with incentives. They also help discourage the rent-seeking that often characterizes close relationships between consumers and local employees.

Ward water supply employees are monitored by their community, but they are also motivated to do well by the inherent opportunity and challenge of their discretionary, broadly defined, situation-responsive tasks. An employee contract and the temporal framework provided by meter reading, billing, and collection give structure to their varied tasks. Monthly meetings with the ward People's Committee and with HWSC headquarters reaffirm the ward office's responsibility to the HWSC and provide an opportunity to exchange ideas and suggestions with other wards. The Haiphong model is being evaluated for replication by other city utilities.

Source: Coffee 1999.

tance of many households to pay for a system beyond their homes, make these designs unworkable from the start.[55] For example, the immense up-front costs of sewer systems led the World Bank to conclude that in Jakarta, waterborne sewerage systems are unlikely to be economically justifiable for any but the most wealthy residential areas for the foreseeable future.[56] The logic of this conclusion, which confuses economic justification with the ability to cover costs, has been challenged.[57] However, the practical impact of aiming for an expensive, modern, centralized sewerage system has been that monopoly public providers have failed to increase access at a satisfactory rate.

Full cost recovery, particularly from user fees, remains virtually impossible with sewerage services. Under the "polluter pays" principle, all households should contribute to collection and treatment costs, but in practice it is difficult to collect such fees. If high fees are imposed, people seek informal solutions, and cheap and easy methods of improper disposal and treatment abound—all of them difficult to monitor and regulate. As a result the private sector, which would need to build in accordance with existing engineering standards, has not entered this market in developing countries in the same way that it has entered the market for water supply.

Yet certain communities wanting improved sanitation have still managed to initiate affordable alternatives. Lesotho's urban areas have had success with ventilated improved pit latrines. Brazil's northeastern cities have used shallow small-bore sewer schemes, in which condominial sewers run through all the households in a block. Wastewater is discharged from a single point into the main trunk line—an effective alternative to connecting each household to the trunk.[58] Applied in a number of Brazilian cities—including Brasilia and Recife—this design has lowered costs to affordable levels. The experience highlights the importance of community involvement and especially of intensive consultation between public agency staff and residents when projects are being designed and implemented.[59]

Community organizations, often with NGOs providing technical assistance, have also gone beyond the household and lane levels to address neighborhood sewerage problems. An unplanned low-income settlement in Karachi known as Orangi offers an example of successful community cooperation. In 1980 this community of almost 1 million had only bucket latrines or soak pits in which to dispose of human excreta, and only open drains to dispose of wastewater. The incidence of disease was high, as were expenditures on medical care (which could have been avoided). Poor drainage was waterlogging the land, reducing property values. The Orangi Pilot Project motivated, trained, and guided the community to build an underground sewer system at its own cost. More than 88,000 households in 5,856 lanes have built sanitary pour-flush latrines, lane sewers, and more than 400 secondary sewers to carry wastewater out of the neighborhood. The costs were much lower than the costs of an equivalent public sector project, and the system has been well maintained for over 15 years.

Through this work the Orangi Research and Training Institute has developed a concept for providing sewerage systems in which communities and the city or state are partners. Communities finance and build household latrines, lane sewers, and secondary sewers. These three components are termed "internal development," and evidence shows that communities can finance and manage them with appropriate technical support and managerial guidance. But municipal or state governments or semiautonomous regional agencies must help with long collector sewers, trunks, and treatment plants—the "external development" component. The cost ratio of internal to external development is typically about three to one. By adopting the partnership model, the government can use its limited funds to increase coverage and save on maintenance costs as well. Since 1987 the Orangi institute has worked with communities in more than 45 other settlements in Karachi and in 7 other cities, and the model has proved to be relatively simple to replicate.[60]

Decentralized neighborhood and community-based systems with shallow sewers and basic community treatment facilities lower unit costs significantly. The Orangi model would never have worked if the capital costs per household were not low. This example has great relevance for other services. If incentives are created that control costs, services become more affordable, especially when they are combined with innovative repayment procedures. Repayments for water and sewer connections can be integrated into monthly bills, so that users repay capital costs over months or even a few years. The willingness of households to pay for sewerage increases when the sanitation system is technically adequate and thus acceptable to the users, as the success of Lesotho's low-cost solution demonstrates.

Urban transportation

Automobile use increases as incomes rise and employment is decentralized to outlying areas of a metropolis, weakening mass transit systems.[61] The major problems of urban transportation relate to traffic congestion, pollution from emissions, and the limited mobility of the poor. The appropriate policies for addressing these issues require urban governments to optimize land use, manage traffic and demand for transportation, formulate environmental policies and measures to mitigate congestion, improve fuel efficiency, and set up vehicle emissions control and inspection systems.[62]

While public-private partnerships have proved helpful, the public sector plays a major role in the overall planning of the transportation sector. Perhaps the greatest payoff is from integrated land use and transportation planning. New roads open the doors to land development, and compact urban centers increase the possibilities for mass transit. Curitiba, Brazil, is a convincing example of how integrated public planning can improve accessibility at relatively low cost. By channeling urban growth along mass transit routes, the city has reduced the use of private cars—despite having the second-highest rate of per capita car ownership in Brazil. On a typical workday, more than 70 percent of commuters travel by bus in the city. As a result, Curitiba's gasoline use per capita is 25 percent lower than that of eight comparable Brazilian cities, and the city has one of Brazil's lowest rates of ambient air pollution.[63]

Coordinating transportation and land use policies remains politically difficult in many developing countries, although sooner or later such coordination may become unavoidable. A start could be made in urban areas (such as Ho Chi Minh City, Vietnam) where motor vehicle ownership is still low, land remains available, and land use patterns are still evolving.

Even cities with high rates of automobile ownership can develop efficient transportation alternatives that accommodate the needs of all social groups. Many cities have combined innovations in mass transit with effective planning and controls for automobile use: Copenhagen; Curitiba; Freiburg, Germany; Hong Kong, China; Perth, Australia; Portland (Oregon), United States; Singapore; Surabaya, Indonesia; Toronto, Canada; and Zurich, Switzerland.[64] Space for walking and cycling is also consciously integrated into transportation planning in some of these cities, such as Surabaya. In addition to improving housing and infrastructure, Surabaya's Kampung Improvement Program has revamped alleyways and made them attractive with plantings and pedestrian zones. Privatizing and deregulating bus services have improved the quality of service and reduced costs in Colombo, Sri Lanka, and in New Zealand. Informal transit services that cater to low- and middle-income groups—such as jeepneys in Manila and kabu-kabus in Lagos—can also be integrated into formal transportation networks, improving safety and efficiency.

Reducing air pollution is an important factor in making cities more livable. Inspecting all vehicles to ensure that they comply with emissions standards is not feasible for most cities in developing countries because of the expense involved and problems of enforcement. A more flexible institutional approach is needed. One possibility shifts the focus of such regulations to large fleets of vehicles such as buses, which are easier to regulate (and which frequently emit large quantities of pollutants). Cities can make compliance with vehicle efficiency standards part of a contract with private bus companies trying to establish routes. Random emissions testing is another approach. Quezon City, Philippines, began such an inspection campaign in 1993 after a six-month education period. The owners of vehicles that failed the test (about 65 percent) were fined, had their licenses taken away, and were given 24 hours to have their vehicles fixed. More than 95 percent of vehicles passed the second test.[65]

A creative and low-cost solution that relies on partnerships with large trucking firms has used the lure of a positive corporate image as an incentive to stop polluting. This approach has yielded dividends in Manila (box 7.3).

Social protection

Households need protection against crime and violence, but they also need protection against income shocks that impair their ability to sustain themselves. Cities acting on their own cannot provide this type of long-term security. If a city enjoying economic growth offers a strong safety net, it will attract low-income households and individuals from nearby areas, swelling the ranks of those receiving benefits and straining the local treasury. Conversely, if a city receives a severe economic shock that creates massive local unemployment, its ability to help its unemployed is severely limited (box 7.4).

Poverty must be addressed as a national issue, and most redistribution programs need to be financed through national transfers, as chapter 5 suggests. But policies and institutions operating (and typically designed) at the local level by individual cities influence the quality of life and the health of the urban poor. In particular, community-driven public work schemes—often nationally funded and locally designed—have emerged as an effective means of enabling the poor to expand their income-earning potential. When designed as a public guarantee of work with below-market wages, such

Box 7.3
Manila: a positive corporate image as an incentive to reduce pollution

San Miguel Corporation, one of the largest business conglomerates in the Philippines, took the lead in banning high-polluting vehicles from its premises. A pollution control officer at one of the company's breweries, the San Miguel Polo Brewery, began requiring suppliers and haulers to have their trucks' emissions tested. Only those whose trucks passed the test were allowed to enter the plant premises and do business with the company. The approved vehicles were given stickers and retested every six months. The San Miguel Corporation received much positive publicity for this initiative and may actually have increased its sales as a result. Good environmental practices, it found, can be good marketing.

When the program started in April 1993, nearly a third of the vehicles tested failed to meet emissions standards. Today, only 3 percent fail. The company has expanded the program to all its plants and vehicles across the country, including vehicles belonging to employees.

Many other firms have followed San Miguel's example. Corporate members of Philippine Business for Social Progress, the Management Association of the Philippines, and the Philippine Chamber of Commerce and Industry have banded together to establish the Center for Corporate Citizenship, which is actively promoting the emissions program. More than 100 companies have adopted it. These companies have erected billboards at the entrances to their plants and compounds proudly declaring that the areas are "No Smoke-Belching Compounds." Some companies (Pilipinas Shell, Far East Bank and Trust Company, and Isuzu Zexel Corporation) have gone a step further, donating emissions-testing equipment to local government teams.

The approach has caught on with operators of public utility vehicles, who have signed agreements with the Department of Environmental and Natural Resources to field only vehicles that meet emissions standards. For operators and drivers, knowledge of the health effects of air pollution is key in convincing them to participate. Schools and residential subdivisions have also decided to implement the program, not only to manage their own microenvironments but also to help everyone breathe clean air.

schemes can screen out the nonneedy and increase equality across households. They can also build infrastructure of value to communities, especially when communities identify and determine what is needed. Targeted grant programs and the involvement of NGOs and community-based organizations are also important to the success of such programs. Some successful examples include Bolivia's Emergency Social Fund, Chile's Minimum Employment Program, and Senegal's AGETIP.[66]

Nongovernmental safety nets can also be useful tools, even though their effectiveness in addressing urban poverty is limited. Such informal mechanisms can take the form of food sharing, microfinancing, and the sharing of housing.[67] Variants of microcredit programs can increase employment opportunities through both self-employment and wage employment. The Full Circle Fund in Chicago, United States, and the emergency loan system (Mahila Milan) in Mumbai, India, have helped poor women generate incomes of their own. During a crisis, microcredit programs can also mitigate the risk of permanent income losses by allowing people to keep their productive assets. Such programs require careful targeting, and clients must have a full understanding of the nature of the assistance.[68] Successful programs can also strengthen social connections in urban communities, since microcredit often relies on social collateral in the form of peer pressure and support.

Poverty reduction programs are more likely to succeed when low-income groups successfully negotiate for resources and room for autonomous action.[69] Naga City, south of metropolitan Manila, has developed an urban poverty program targeting those in informal settlements. It relies on a partnership among communities, an NGO, the local government, and the national housing authority. Among other things, the program has helped create land-swapping and land-sharing schemes that provide land and security of tenure for squatters. This unique local resource mobilization scheme contributes to equity and helps with the provision of basic services.[70] Collective action enables the poor to lobby with municipal agencies for rights and services—and to help each other in times of temporary difficulties. When collective efforts occur, investments that improve the delivery of services rise substantially, as they did in the Wat Chonglom neighborhood in Bangkok.[71] These examples confirm the willingness and ability of the poor to invest in welfare-improving measures—and the potential of partnership arrangements.

Reducing the incidence of crime and violence lessens another burden on the urban poor. Here again, the trend is toward community-based actions that involve community policing and citizen-police liaison committees.[72] One such initiative, Programa de Desarrollo, Seguridad, y Paz (DESEPAZ) in Cali, has received worldwide attention. DESEPAZ has established municipal security councils that bring together government officials and community leaders in public meetings in each of Cali's 20 districts. This process has generated programs in law enforcement and public education. DESEPAZ is too recent for a rigorous evaluation, but the

Box 7.4
Shenyang: social welfare in a struggling industrial city

Shenyang is the central node of the industrial complex that covers China's three northeastern provinces. The northeast area is the most urbanized of China's seven regions, an agglomeration of cities and towns with tightly linked economies, all heavily dependent on state enterprises. When economic reforms began in 1979, the northeast was a showplace, with its many heavy industries, model state enterprises, skilled, well-educated labor force, and a per capita income second only to that of Beijing, Tianjin, and Shanghai. But as the reforms enter their third decade, the state enterprises have become better known for their losses than for their products. The region's high per capita income is steadily slipping, and unemployment is spreading.

The losses many of Shenyang's state enterprises have sustained in the past few years have debilitated the city's social welfare system. State enterprises in Shenyang, as elsewhere, have always been responsible for the social welfare of their employees and often of their families. The companies finance and administer old-age pensions, health care, and housing and in many cases provide ancillary services such as water systems for both current and retired employees. They also run schools and hospitals. Except when they are in dire straits, enterprises are expected to keep their surplus employees on the books, provide them with a living allowance, help them find new jobs, and retrain them. In Liaoning Province—Shenyang is its capital city—unemployment in disguise, known as *xiagang*, was estimated at 15 percent in 1997, or more than 1.8 million persons—more than four times the 440,000 workers who are formally unemployed.

The enterprise-based social welfare system has been under stress for some time. It is now beginning to collapse under multiple pressures: a sharp deterioration in the financial position of state enterprises, new competition from other regions and imports, and the rising number of pensioners and surplus employees. Many enterprises are defaulting on old-age pensions, living allowances to *xiagang* employees, reimbursements of health care expenses, and sometimes also wages and salaries. Such defaults were the exception a few years ago, but they are now widespread in Shenyang and even more so in small and medium-size cities in Liaoning.

The northeast has remained on the sidelines of two developments spearheading the growth of the nonstate sector in China: the dramatic increase in village and household enterprises, and the proliferation of foreign-funded businesses. As a result, the area has missed out on product and organizational diversification and still has an economic structure very similar to that of the prereform period. An alternative to enterprise-based social welfare is taking shape but is years away from being fully operational. The system emerging in Shenyang and in other cities is founded on a number of changes:

- Transferring social welfare administration to the municipal social security bureau
- Implementing joint financing of social insurance by employees, employers, and the municipal government, and eventually pooling risks at the provincial level
- Revising the benefits schedule
- Gradually transferring social facilities such as schools and utilities to the municipal government
- Privatizing the housing market.

The administration of old-age pensions is moving to recently established social security bureaus, and joint financing for pensions has been introduced. Responsibility for the xiagang employees is now divided among enterprises, the municipal government, and the unemployment insurance fund, with each paying a third. A system for pooling large medical expenses across enterprises is in place, and municipal-level health insurance along the lines of trial schemes in Jiujiang and Zhenjiang in the east is being introduced. Nondeductibles, copayments, and tight regulation of the cost of drugs and medical intervention have been adopted. The central government is soon to unveil a national framework for municipal health insurance schemes.

The immediate problem is that many enterprises cannot afford to pay their social insurance contribution. Moreover, many of the municipal governments that depend heavily on taxes from local state enterprises face a fiscal squeeze because of the eroding tax base. Safety net programs at the national level are urgently needed. Shenyang has succeeded so far in preventing destitution, but it has not been able to avoid economic distress. The city is struggling to find a way to maintain a robust social safety net while negotiating the path to a more diversified economic structure.

---

measures are reported to have produced results in Cali, as well as in Medellín and Bogotá, where the initiative has been extended.[73]

Looking ahead

The improvements in essential urban services discussed throughout this chapter offer hope and direction for the future. Land use and transportation planning in Curitiba, slum upgrades in Jakarta, community sanita-

tion in Karachi, water partnerships in Haiphong, environmental improvements in Surat, community policing in Cali—all represent remarkable achievements. The challenge now (and it is by no means out of reach) is to bring similar achievements to every city.

The success stories also reaffirm the importance for cities of developing appropriate institutions that get the most from the private sector, community-based organizations, and NGOs. A number of communities, like

Wat Chonglom in Thailand and Orangi in Karachi, Pakistan, are fortunate to have solved some of their problems through self-help (with guidance from NGOs) and to have developed the confidence and cohesion to interact with the municipality. The internal-external approach to infrastructure provision demonstrated in Orangi is now a model for future partnerships. Such partnerships point to some of the most valuable assets for cities: the capacity of civil and community organizations to identify local problems and their causes, to organize and manage community initiatives, and to monitor the effectiveness of public or external inputs.

This self-generated community development process is a very slow one, however. The Orangi experience identified four barriers that must be overcome: a psychological barrier created by the expectation that the municipal government should provide all services; an economic barrier created by the high costs of conventional infrastructure provision; a technical barrier that hampers the initiation of self-help activities; and a sociological barrier stemming from a lack of trust that militates against collective action.[74]

For every Wat Chonglom and Orangi, there are thousands of communities, especially in smaller urban centers, where community development processes have not even been initiated. Cities need to be proactive in establishing formal but friendly institutional mechanisms to encourage partnerships that will bring dynamism to development. The much-appraised experience of Porto Alegre, Brazil, offers an example of how such a process can be initiated.[75] In Porto Alegre, a city of 9.6 million, the mayor organized the division of the city into 16 districts, each of which set up a popular council made up of representatives of community associations. Two elected representatives from each district council sit on the citywide council of representatives, and city hall officials are assigned to act as permanent liaisons with the district representatives.

The key institutional innovation in Porto Alegre is the municipal budget forum, where the council of representatives sets the agenda for municipal spending based on district priorities. The final decisions on public spending are made in a three-way meeting of city hall officials, the council of representatives, and the chamber of councillors (who are elected on a citywide basis). Once projects are selected, community representatives supervise their progress and monitor expenditures. The opportunity to articulate community demands and vote on project selection creates an incentive for neighbor-hoods to organize themselves. Participatory budgeting is now in place in some 50 other Brazilian cities, and the system is scheduled to be implemented in Buenos Aires and Rosario, Argentina, and in Montevideo, Uruguay.[76]

Involving the private sector in partnerships requires, as a starting point, modifying rules that inhibit the private provision of services. Private water providers in Paraguay provide a good example of the kind of action that is needed. These vendors compete legally with the public water companies and with each other. They pay commercial, corporate, and income taxes to the government and operate within a clear set of rules. Many governments are now putting legislation in place to allow the private sector to invest in infrastructure, typically using a build-operate-transfer (that is, transfer to the public sector) framework. The accumulating experiences with such systems are generating model concession agreements that combine transparency, flexibility, and provisions for fair arbitration. Results have been forthcoming in the form of major international private investments in water, electricity, and telecommunication infrastructure. Regulatory uncertainties still need to be reduced, but training programs for regulators have begun to address this need.

To improve the accountability of service providers, citizens and community representatives are becoming involved in performance monitoring through "voice mechanisms."[77] Even approaches as straightforward as a poll or survey of users' views on services or the gathering of data from both users and service providers can sometimes offer an effective alternative to elaborate participatory arrangements. The public transparency that hard data generate can in turn encourage and mobilize citizen groups, creating pressure for reform. Citizens' report cards on the performance of municipal agencies are beginning to show results in India (box 7.5). They are now spreading to other cities, including Washington, D.C.

Successful urban development also requires strategic citywide or regional planning to guide trunk investments and identify the most appropriate locations for jobs, residences, and transportation. The process can help cities avoid the worst outcomes of unplanned growth. An overall strategic plan needs to be followed by coherent decentralized implementation that creates a substantial role for the private sector. This type of careful planning and implementation is particularly important in developing megacities, some of which are larger than many countries. It is not an argument for the type of central

Box 7.5
Bangalore: citizens' report cards

A "report card" on urban public services is an innovative way to gather systematic feedback from citizens on the performance of a city's service providers. In 1993 in Bangalore, India, local civic groups used a report card on services to nudge their monopolistic service providers into responding more effectively to their customers.

A small group of people concerned about deteriorating public services enlisted a market research agency to survey citizens on the city's services. The findings were used to create a report card that rated the performance of all the major public agencies. The report card was sent to the heads of all agencies, and its findings were widely disseminated through the media. What started as an informal endeavor soon led to the creation of a new nonprofit body, the Public Affairs Center, which has continued the work in different parts of India.

The Bangalore experiment used separate surveys for middle-class and slum households. Both surveys confirmed that public dissatisfaction with the city's services ran high. Even the better-rated service providers received no more than a 25 percent satisfaction rating. The worst, the Bangalore Development Authority, received a mere 1 percent satisfaction rating—but it won the highest rating for corruption. The ratings received much media and public attention and were also discussed in public forums.

The objective was to create public interest and awareness and to pressure service providers to respond positively to the citizen feedback. Not surprisingly, given their large bureaucracies, these public agencies took some time to respond. The first to respond was the Bangalore Development Authority, which reviewed its internal systems for service delivery, introduced training for lower-level staff, and strengthened its ser-vice function. It also joined with the Bangalore Municipal Corporation, which initiated experiments in such areas as waste management, and created a forum of NGOs and public agencies to deal with key concerns. More recently the Karnataka Electricity Board has formalized periodic dialogues with residents' associations to improve its services in the city. Several agencies have strengthened their systems for redressing consumer grievances.

Of the eight agencies covered by the report card, four remained indifferent. But the service providers that mattered most to the people did respond. The experiment has given the public a greater appreciation of the value of citizen feedback and of how civil society can improve local governance.

Whether the quality of services has improved, however, is a difficult question. A small survey conducted a year ago showed that a majority of people perceived modest improvements in some services and in the responsiveness of agency staff to their problems. But fewer than a third of respondents believed that corruption had declined. The problems are deeply rooted, and there are no quick fixes. Some 90 percent of respondents felt that citizens' groups were more active than before, a sure sign that public pressure on service providers will continue.

The Public Affairs Center has since prepared report cards on services in six other large cities of India, mostly in partnership with NGOs and local civic groups. Report cards have also been issued for specialized services such as hospitals and public transport. In all cases, citizens have used the report cards as a trigger for collective action to increase the responsiveness of public agencies.

Source: Paul 1998.

---

planning that led to the misallocation of public investments in Eastern Europe.[78] Rather, it is based on the type of strategic planning that directed urban expansion along transportation corridors and made Curitiba a model to emulate. The contribution of the Orangi Pilot Project sewerage investment in Karachi could have been considerably enhanced if it had been part of an overall city sewerage plan. To encourage public participation, the planning process needs to guarantee that all plans will be disclosed before they are implemented and that affected parties will have the right to lodge objections. Many local governments in Japan have recently done just that, enacting ordinances on information disclosure that make information on the environment easily available.[79]

As the private sector and community organizations provide more services, the public sector needs to assume a revised regulatory role. The traditional approach to regulation suffered from industry influence, political in-terference, and a lack of transparency in dealings between regulators and the firms they regulated. Here again partnerships offer a promising institutional innovation. The monitoring and verification of information can be contracted out to professional private sector firms, educational institutes, think tanks, or NGOs, all of which have reputations for independence to defend. Citizen involvement based on the public disclosure of information can then provide a stimulus for providers to improve. This model of public performance audits—in which the regulatory task is contracted out to reputable agencies and the public uses information to motivate good behavior—holds great promise in developing countries. It has been successfully implemented for industrial regulation in Indonesia and is to be used to regulate the recently privatized water supply in Manila.[80]

The policies and institutional approaches described in this chapter are intended to further the "quiet revolution" in local governance that is already leading cities and parts of cities to improve their livability. Many of the innovative and successful programs suggest models of partnerships that can be institutionalized and promoted. Such partnerships allow synergy and the combining of resources among the public sector, international organizations, the voluntary and community sector, individuals, and households. The next step is to initiate an empowerment process that enables community-based groups to define their own goals and options—and to assume responsibility for actions to achieve these goals. The growing movement toward democratization and the decentralization of power and decisionmaking that are expected to characterize the 21st century will help make this possibility a reality.

8

Case Studies and Recommendations

Countries around the world have been initiating reforms aimed at integrating their economies into the global marketplace and devolving central power to local governments. This report has presented a series of policy prescriptions for globalizing and localizing economies, and the five case studies included in this chapter describe how some of those recommendations can be put into practice. The examples differ, both because the type and extent of the reforms each country needs vary widely and because each set of reforms has been implemented in a vastly different economic and policy environment. Context is particularly important here, since the feasibility of reform depends on the political conditions in a country. Successful reform requires careful sequencing and the willingness to exploit sometimes fleeting opportunities.

The five cases discussed here—in the Arab Republic of Egypt, Hungary, Brazil, Pakistan, and Tanzania—represent a regional sampling of fairly typical policy situations (box 8.1). Each case study describes the policy setting, the recommended reform strategy, and the success of new policies thus far. In Brazil, Egypt,

and Hungary, some of the reforms are already under way though more remains to be done. Pakistan and Tanzania are at an earlier stage in the reform process.

Making the most of trade liberalization: Egypt

The number of regional trading arrangements has surged since 1990, and many countries are now members of large free trade areas or customs unions such as the European Union (EU) and Mercado Común del Sur (MERCOSUR). Should countries that are not members of a regional trading arrangement seek preferential access to their neighbors' markets? How does this option compare with unilateral or multilateral liberalization? This examination of Egypt's trade policy options illustrates the trade-offs many developing countries face in choosing whether to join a regional trade group (box 8.2). And it demonstrates the importance of some of the recommendations in chapters 2 and 3.

Since the mid-1970s, Egypt has been steadily liberalizing its trade policies, which has contributed to economic growth. But the benefits from liberalized trade have been stymied by domestic

Box 8.1
Five case studies

Making the most of trade liberalization: Egypt. This case applies chapter 2's proposals for trade reform, showing how international trade agreements can be used to demonstrate commitment to freer trade. It also illustrates some of the disadvantages of regional (as opposed to global) trade agreements and the kinds of domestic reforms the Egyptian government will have to implement to take advantage of the opportunities offered by global trade.

Reforming weak banking systems: Hungary. This case study deals with the financial sector reforms discussed in chapter 3. It demonstrates clearly that regulators need to take prompt action when a bank violates specific guidelines or procedures, as the report has argued. Taking steps to reduce this so-called "regulatory forbearance" is the next major challenge facing Hungarian policymakers.

Macromanaging under fiscal decentralization: Brazil. Building on the themes of decentralization and democratic subnational governance discussed in chapter 5, this case study illustrates the need for carefully sequenced decentralization. It also identifies the changes Brazil will need to make in order for its newly centralized structure to function effectively, including establishing electoral rules, creating regulations to manage relations between national and subnational governments, and drafting rules for subnational borrowing.

Improving urban living conditions: Karachi. The Karachi case study draws on chapter 7 to show how community groups and informal developers can complement the efforts of the public sector to provide essential services.

Cultivating rural-urban synergies: Tanzania. The final case study focuses on reforming foreign trade (chapter 2) and establishing policies that deal with urbanization and growth (chapter 6). It demonstrates how one country can use international trade and urban-rural economic linkages to stimulate growth in both the urban and rural sectors.

constraints, including an inefficient service sector, a slow-moving government bureaucracy, and overcrowded ports and transportation facilities. For some time, Egyptian industrial goods have had duty-free access to European markets, but Egypt is now considering signing an expanded preferential trading arrangement with the EU.[1] Such an agreement may reassure investors of Egypt's commitment to liberal trade policies, but—as explained in box 2.1—it would also mean that the pattern of Egypt's imports and exports will be shaped less by market forces and more by the differences in tariff treatment between Europe and Egypt's other trading partners.

Initial reforms

Economic growth in Egypt accelerated between 1975 and 1985 following the adoption of open-door policies.

It was fueled by sizable increases in foreign assistance, remittances from Egyptians working abroad, and foreign direct investment.[2] This growth spurt ended in 1986, largely because of a regional economic slowdown caused by declining oil prices. The level of aggregate demand in the economy then fell further in the early 1990s because of government spending cuts, an increase in real interest rates, and a drop in exports to the former Soviet Union and Eastern Europe. Per capita growth of real national output slowed from an average of 2.5–3.0 percent a year in 1989–91 to 0.4 percent in 1992 and 1993.

The Egyptian government responded with an impressive program of economic reform. Fiscal tightening reduced marginal tax rates and the government's budget deficit.[3] Monetary reforms included decontrolling interest rates, devaluing and unifying exchange rates, reducing the growth of the money supply, and liberalizing the capital account. A 1991 law established a legal basis for privatization, and by September 1998, 113 of the initial 314 public enterprises originally targeted had been at least partially privatized. In the same year, the Parliament ratified a law authorizing the privatization of banks.

Foreign investors were quick to react. In 1995 they put $400 million in foreign direct investment into Egypt, followed by $800 million in 1996 and around $1.2 billion in 1997. Half the foreign direct investment is in manufacturing and 30 percent in banking. Tariff revenues as a share of total imports fell from 25 percent in 1985 to 17 percent by 1997, reflecting the country's increased openness to trade. As a result of these flows and trade reforms, real gross domestic product (GDP) grew by 5.1 percent in 1996 and by 5.9 percent in 1997.

Red tape and inefficient services constrain exports

Despite its reforms, Egypt has yet to take full advantage of the potential of trade liberalization. The country has many advantages to exploit in producing manufactured exports, including a convenient location and wages that are one-tenth those in Israel or Tunisia. Given these positive factors and its duty-free access to European markets, the country was expected to increase its manufactured exports rapidly.[4] Manufactured exports (in 1992 prices) did increase, but slowly, rising from $1.4 billion in 1988 to an estimated $2.4 billion in 1996—still only about 17 percent of total goods and services export revenues.

Box 8.2
The Arab Republic of Egypt at a glance

Poverty and social indicators [a]	Egypt, Arab Rep.	Middle East and North Africa	Lower-middle-income countries	
GNP per capita (U.S. dollars) [b]	1,180	2,060	1,230	
Poverty (percentage of population below $1 per day)	7.6	. .	. .	
Urban population (percentage of total population)	45	57	42	
Life expectancy at birth (years)	66	67	69	

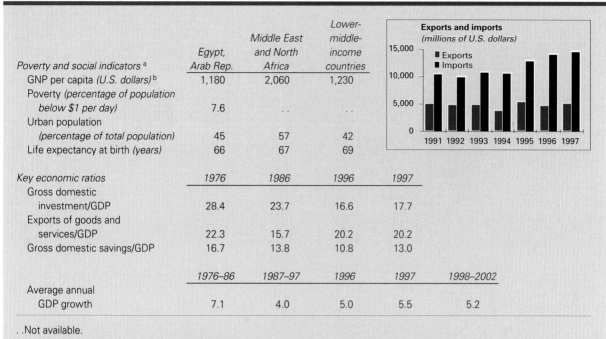

Exports and imports (millions of U.S. dollars)

Key economic ratios	1976	1986	1996	1997	
Gross domestic investment/GDP	28.4	23.7	16.6	17.7	
Exports of goods and services/GDP	22.3	15.7	20.2	20.2	
Gross domestic savings/GDP	16.7	13.8	10.8	13.0	

	1976–86	1987–97	1996	1997	1998–2002
Average annual GDP growth	7.1	4.0	5.0	5.5	5.2

. .Not available.
a. Data shown are from the latest available year within the range 1991–97. *GNP per capita* figures are from 1997.
b. Calculated using World Bank *Atlas* method.
Source: World Bank, *World Development Indicators,* 1999.

One reason for this sluggish growth is the inefficiency of services, which raises the price of inputs and transactions costs to exporting firms and undermines their competitiveness.[5] For example, the four main Egyptian ports (Damietta, Port Said, Dekheila, and Alexandria) are essentially state monopolies, and their service charges are three times those of their closest competitors. Container freight rates to Egyptian ports are generally 15 to 20 percent higher than rates to other Mediterranean ports, and air freight rates to and from northern Egyptian cities are twice those to cities in Israel.

In addition, all trade transactions are subject to an onerous bureaucratic burden. A 10 percent sales tax is applied to all commodities, including inputs to goods produced for export, making it harder for firms to sell abroad at competitive prices. A process does exist for refunding import tariffs on inputs to goods for export, but it involves four forms, a letter, a permit, and two separate committee reviews. Imports also face delays, as all goods must go through multiple clearance, licensing, and inspection procedures that impose a cost estimated as equal to an extra 15 percent tariff. Each Egyptian customs official clears an average of $600,000

worth of imports a year; in Singapore the average is $666 million a year.[6]

The government has begun to reduce bureaucratic delays and charges and lower transportation costs.[7] But further reform remains essential. For example, the customs system could be improved in a number of ways, including the following: bringing in international inspection firms; accepting valuations of imports based on invoices, rather than having the customs service value items; focusing tests of imported goods on safety, which is a legitimate concern, not on quality, which can be better judged by the ultimate buyer; and accepting international standards of certification.

Local transportation networks also have to be strengthened. Private competition should be introduced in port handling, a move that has reduced shipping charges by as much as 50 percent in Mexico and Chile. The build-operate-transfer contract offered to the private sector for the expansion of the Cairo inland port of Athr al-Nabi and the construction of two new specialized ports are encouraging steps in this direction. New projects are on the drawing board to improve road transportation, including an upgrade of the Mediterranean coastal road as part of the North African coastal road (which will eventually link with Europe's road network via the Gibraltar crossing). A 113-kilometer Greater Cairo Ring Road is also under construction, but there is still much room for improvement, as the high incidence of traffic fatalities indicates—44 deaths per 100,000 kilometers driven.

Nontrade constraints on foreign direct investment will also have to be eased. At the moment, entry into a market requires government approval. Moreover, restrictive labor laws make exit expensive, which discourages firms from entering markets in the first place. Surveys of firms suggest that about 30 percent of managers' time is devoted to coping with regulatory demands. Removing these regulatory impediments, especially those that discriminate against foreign investors, is crucial if a country is to increase investment rates, as chapters 3 and 6 emphasize.

Further trade reform

In Egypt dissatisfaction with export performance has led to renewed interest in trade reform. But entry into some form of preferential agreement with the EU requires careful assessment. As noted earlier, Egyptian exporters have had duty-free access to EU markets for industrial goods since the 1970s. Egypt is currently negotiating a European-Mediterranean Agreement with the EU that would seek to liberalize trade in other ways. However, there are different types of preferential agreements with the EU, not all of which would benefit Egypt.

A first option is for Egypt and the EU to eliminate their tariffs on imports of goods from one another. Such an agreement could lead Egyptian importers to shift their purchases away from the most efficient foreign supplier to EU firms whose cost of supplying the Egyptian market is artificially lowered because they pay no tariffs. Indeed, one analysis suggests that such an agreement could actually reduce Egyptian welfare by the equivalent of 0.2 percent of GDP. In contrast, full unilateral elimination by Egypt of such tariff barriers would benefit Egypt.[8] A preferential liberalization that is confined to tariffs on goods offers little to developing countries, especially when compared with unilateral elimination of tariffs on goods trade.

However, a preferential trade agreement that includes liberalization in goods, harmonization of standards, and greater access to service markets can offer substantial benefits to developing countries such as Egypt. As services are used extensively as inputs in the export sector, measures taken to enhance competition in the service sector, such as permitting foreign direct investment, can improve the productivity of many industries further down the stream of production. Furthermore, to the extent that such an agreement reduces regulatory barriers to Egyptian exports (because those exports now comply with EU health, safety, and product standards), the benefits could be as much as 1.8 percent of Egyptian GDP.[9] Even further gains will accrue to Egypt if enhanced foreign investment enables its firms to fuse into the global production networks of European firms.

Only a comprehensive trade reform agenda that tackles red tape and brings down barriers to trade and investments in goods and services will benefit Egypt. A broad preferential trade agreement with the EU would enable Egypt to harmonize its domestic regulations with those of its major trading partner. But such an agreement is no substitute for Egypt's full participation in the forthcoming Millennium Round of World Trade Organization (WTO) negotiations, which holds out the promise of multilateral reform in services and agriculture.

Reforming weak banking systems: Hungary

The many banking crises in developing countries over the last several decades—with their deleterious consequences for poverty reduction, social stability, and growth—illustrate the importance of a sound regulatory framework for banks. The need becomes all the greater as capital flows move freely across national borders and as the number and complexity of financial instruments available to banks expand. Making progress toward a strong independent bank regulatory regime, as described in chapter 3, should be a primary concern for policymakers in developing countries. Hungary's progress points to several lessons of wider applicability—and to the challenges facing countries that have inherited state-run banking systems with substantial bad debts (box 8.3).

In the last 10 years Hungary has dramatically transformed its banking sector. Once dominated by insolvent government-owned institutions, the sector now has many privately owned banks and is oriented toward serving a market economy. Hungary made this transformation as part of a radical restructuring of the economy aimed at replacing socialist principles with a private market system.

Hungary's experience illustrates three recommendations from chapter 3. First, it demonstrates the need to strengthen bank supervision and to insulate it from gov-

Box 8.3
Hungary at a glance

Poverty and social indicators[a]	Hungary	Europe and Central Asia	Upper-middle-income countries
GNP per capita (U.S. dollars)[b]	4,430	2,320	4,520
Poverty (percentage of population below $1 per day)	25	..	..
Urban population (percentage of total population)	66	67	73
Life expectancy at birth (years)	70	69	70

Exports and imports
(millions of U.S. dollars)

Key economic ratios	1976	1986	1996	1997
Gross domestic investment/GDP	35.9	26.9	26.8	..
Exports of goods and services/GDP	38.8	39.6	38.9	..
Gross domestic savings/GDP	31.8	25.5	25.7	..

	1976–86	1987–97	1996	1997	1998–2002
Average annual GDP growth	2.4	–0.8	1.3	4.4	5.2

. .Not available.
a. Data shown are from the latest available year within the range 1991–97. *GNP per capita* figures are from 1997.
b. Calculated using World Bank *Atlas* method.
Source: World Bank, *World Development Indicators,* 1999.

ernment interference. The inability of Hungarian banking supervisors to take early action against banks with deteriorating loan portfolios worsened the country's banking difficulties. Second, Hungary's experience supports the case for complementing regulatory reforms with private sector monitoring of banks. Hungary strengthened its monitoring capabilities by reforming the public deposit insurance scheme, improving corporate governance of banks, and mandating the issue of subordinated debt. Third, Hungary's experience demonstrates that foreign participation in national banking systems need not wait until domestic banks have been strengthened. A recent analysis has suggested that foreign participation in transition economies' banking systems has tended to improve their performance.[10]

Initial reforms

When the Berlin Wall fell in 1989, Hungary was slightly more advanced in banking reform than its East European neighbors. But the government still faced many of the same problems as they did. Most of the banking sector was in public hands, and its assets were dominated by directed loans to state enterprises.[11] As a

result of the breakup of the Council of Mutual Economic Assistance (COMECON) and the collapse of the Soviet Union, Hungarian firms lost 60 percent of their export market. Many enterprises were unable to adjust to the competitive pressure of a liberalized import regime, which pitted them against both domestic and foreign firms. As a result, enterprise arrears to banks skyrocketed, endangering the banking system.

Hungary's early attempts at bank reform were tentative.[12] The government began by creating a two-tier structure in 1987, shifting the corporate banking business of the National Bank of Hungary to three newly formed commercial banks. The number of banks (excluding deposit associations and innovation funds) expanded from 8 in 1986 to 30 in 1990 as a result of new entry and the conversion of small, specialized financial institutions into commercial banks. The market share of the four largest commercial banks fell from 58 to 48 percent between 1987 and 1990. But large institutions continued to dominate the banking sector. Together with the government-owned national savings bank, the five largest banks accounted for 82 percent of total assets in 1990.

In 1991 the government introduced a new regulatory framework based on market-oriented principles.[13] The 1991 banking act introduced prudential concepts, Bank for International Settlements (BIS) regulations on provisioning, and limits on exposure. The accounting act introduced international accounting standards. The new bankruptcy code prohibited banks from simply rolling over unpaid loans at maturity and forced them to provision fully for their losses.

While these reforms were enacted, they were not always enforced. Nor did they address the immediate problem of bank insolvency. Government-owned banks were burdened by nonperforming loans, including many inherited from the former regime and some more recent loans to state-owned enterprises. Under the terms of two workout programs in 1991–92, the government took over about $1 billion, or 90 percent, of the banks' nonperforming debt.

Unfortunately, this debt relief was provided unconditionally. Banks receiving funds were not forced to modernize, the same managers remained in place, and regulations were not enforced. As a result, bank managers continued to believe that the government was ready to provide unconditional relief to any bank in trouble. Not surprisingly, poor lending practices continued.

In 1994 the government decided to go one step further and privatize the banks. To make the banks salable, it had to inject about 9 percent of GDP into the banking system. Banks were recapitalized to meet BIS standards by the end of 1995. In each troubled bank, loans were separated so that a core bank with a solid portfolio could be readied for privatization. Unlike the bailouts of 1991 and 1992, this plan stipulated that banks receiving state funds modernize their systems of control and operation, replenish the funds they held in liquid form against the risk of loan defaults, and adopt best practices in loan appraisal, risk assessment, and asset clarification. In some cases senior bank managers were replaced.

When privatization started in 1994, foreign banks purchased many Hungarian banks. Between 1994 and 1998 foreign ownership in Hungary's banking sector increased from 15 to 60 percent, while direct state ownership of the sector fell from 67 to 20 percent. Privatization appeared to have the desired effect on bank performance. MKB, the first large bank to be privatized, saw its income triple, the number of branches double, and its staff shrink from 1,800 to 1,240. Returns on bank assets increased from 0.5 to 1.0 percent in 1994–98, and doubtful loans as a proportion of assets dropped from 20 to 3 percent in 1993–97. Margins on loans also began to fall with increased competition—from 7 to 5 percent in 1998.

But Hungary's banking system faces continuing challenges. For example, problems remain in enforcing regulations on domestically owned banks. Two such banks failed in 1998. One was the second biggest in Hungary; it appears that its management was largely unconstrained by a dispersed local ownership, believed that it was too big for government to allow it to fail, and so lent recklessly. Regulators were slow to act, despite a bank run in February 1997. Rather than force prompt corrective action, the government provided cash infusions and suspended capital requirements. Only in June 1998 was the management replaced and in-depth restructuring begun.

Future reforms

This episode, in which it took more than a year after a bank run to restructure a bank, originated in part in legal impediments on the power of the supervisory authorities. The Basle Accords core principles suggest that banking supervisors should have the legal authority to issue and enforce the regulations necessary to maintain the soundness of the banking system. But in Hungary the Ministry of Finance—rather than banking supervisors—had exclusive power to issue regulations. Moreover, the supervisory authority appeared constrained in its ability to take appropriate disciplinary actions. Because under current law disciplinary measures can only be taken on the basis of audited accounts, Hungary's bank supervisors could not respond quickly to regulatory infractions.

Strengthening the hand of banking supervisors will help the stability of the banking system, but traditional bank regulation may be insufficient by itself to forestall excessive risk-taking by banks. As discussed in chapter 3, countries should consider how to complement government regulation by stimulating private sector monitoring of banks, through such steps as improving the corporate governance of banks and mandating the issue of subordinated debt.[14]

If Hungary can take further steps to reduce regulatory forbearance and build a greater role for private sector monitoring of banks, then the country will be well on its way to cultivating a first-class banking system. At a fundamental level, Hungary has looked outward to find solutions to its banking problems. It has recognized the value of adopting and enforcing international banking standards, while increasingly resisting bank bailouts to politically connected insiders.

The Hungarian experience offers pointers for other transition countries, especially in Eastern Europe. Given the central role that banks play in transforming both domestic and international flows of savings into growth-enhancing investments, the payoff to a sound banking system will reach far beyond minimizing the risk and costs of banking crises.

Macromanagement under fiscal decentralization: Brazil

In the early decades of the 21st century, demands for greater local political autonomy will mold the political structures of developing countries. Policymakers will have to manage the process of reallocating rights and obligations to different tiers of government. Brazil's experience with decentralization, which resulted in a series of intergovernmental fiscal crises, highlights the difficulty of managing the politics of fiscal decentralization in a period of democratic and economic transition. It also confirms three of chapter 5's policy recommenda-

tions: first, that the decentralization of revenues match the decentralization of expenditures; second, that central governments maintain a hard budget constraint in their dealings with subnational governments; and third, that constitutional mandates, particularly electoral rules, be in place so that the first two measures can be enforced (box 8.4).

Formal decentralization

In 1988 Brazil's first postmilitary constitution sought to decentralize political power. Power at the federal level is now divided among the executive, legislative, and judicial branches. The president, who heads the executive branch, is elected by direct popular vote for a four-year term. Congress has two houses—the Chamber of Deputies, in which each state receives a certain number of seats according to its population, and the Senate, in which each state has three senators.

In principle, the constitution gives the president considerable powers over the legislature. The president has the exclusive right to initiate legislation in some policy areas, including those that create jobs or increase salaries in many parts of the public sector. The presi-

Box 8.4
Brazil at a glance

Poverty and social indicators[a]	Brazil	Latin America and the Caribbean	Upper-middle-income countries	
GNP per capita (U.S. dollars)[b]	4,720	3,880	4,520	
Poverty (percentage of population below $1 per day)	17	. .	. .	
Urban population (percentage of total population)	80	74	73	
Life expectancy at birth (years)	67	70	70	

Key economic ratios	1976	1986	1996	1997
Gross domestic investment/GDP	23.1	19.1	20.7	22.8
Exports of goods and services/GDP	7.0	8.8	7.1	6.2
Gross domestic savings/GDP	20.7	21.6	18.6	20.6

	1976–86	1987–97	1996	1997	1998–2002
Average annual GDP growth	2.9	1.9	2.8	3.2	3.5

Exports and imports
(millions of U.S. dollars)

. .Not available.
a. Data shown are from the latest available year within the range 1991–97. *GNP per capita* figures are from 1997.
b. Calculated using World Bank *Atlas* method.
Source: World Bank, *World Development Indicators,* 1999.

dent alone prepares the annual budget and must seek congressional approval for it. The Congress is restricted in the kinds of amendments it can propose to the budget, and it cannot initiate programs or projects not included in the president's budget.[15]

In practice the president's power is circumscribed by the difficulty of marshaling support in a political system with so many parties (15 are represented in the Congress) and weak party discipline at the national level. The electoral system, and particularly proportional representation, are partly responsible for this multiplicity of parties. Candidates for the Chamber of Deputies run at large in each state rather than facing off in single-seat districts, so small parties must scour an entire state to obtain enough votes to win a seat or two. Strong state loyalties lead politicians to form alliances in support of projects that will benefit their own state, regardless of their party. Sitting state governors command the loyalty of federal deputies, since the governor's support is more useful in their campaigns than the president's. Because of their influence over deputies and senators in their party, state governors can thwart or propel presidential designs.[16]

The constitution sets up a three-tier governmental structure consisting of the federal government, 26 states (plus a federal district with the status of a state), and about 5,500 municipalities. States elect their governors directly and have unicameral legislatures, with the members elected at large by proportional representation. This structure is repeated at the municipal level, with mayors elected directly and municipal councillors elected at large. The constitution gives subnational governments broad but vaguely defined powers and creates no real boundary between them. It grants states "all powers not otherwise prohibited to them by the constitution" and municipalities "the power to provide services of local interest." Since the constitution makes the municipal authorities the third tier of government, states have no power over the actions of the municipalities within their jurisdictions.

Although the constitution is vague about the division of responsibilities among levels of government, it divides up revenues very explicitly. It assigns specific tax bases to each level of government and creates a system of tax sharing that substantially redistributes revenue among both the levels of government and the regions.[17] The tax-sharing system has two major components. The first consists of fixed shares of the federal government's two principal taxes—the income tax and the industrial products tax—which are distributed according to a set formula to states and municipal governments. The second involves the state value added tax (VAT), which state governments must share with the municipalities in their jurisdictions. Consequently, the municipal share of net tax revenues after transfers increased by roughly 40 percent in six years, rising from 12 percent in 1987 to 17 percent in 1992.[18]

Although the 1988 constitution emphasizes decentralization, it does strengthen the central government's control in one essential area: personnel. It defines the rights of public sector employees at all three levels of government and provides employees with job and salary security. Governments cannot dismiss redundant civil servants or reduce nominal salaries. The constitution also gives public employees generous pension rights, which have been a factor in subsequent fiscal crises, since labor costs are a significant share of subnational expenditures.[19] These controls exemplify the problem of overregulating subnational governments described in chapter 5.

State borrowing and the debt crisis

Decentralization in Brazil has resulted in a prolonged macroeconomic crisis sparked by the growing indebtedness of the states.[20] While the new constitution gives the national Senate the power to deny all subnational proposals for borrowing, the Senate has rarely done so. As a result, states and municipalities continue to borrow from a wide variety of sources. They have issued bonds on the domestic market and have borrowed from domestic private commercial banks and various federal intermediaries, including the federal housing and savings bank and the federal development bank. All but two of the 26 states own commercial banks from which they have occasionally borrowed. More frequently, they have forced these banks to lend to favored clients. States have also borrowed abroad, both from multilateral agencies (which demand federal guarantees) and from private lenders (which do not).

The debt crisis unfolded in three acts. The opening act was a legacy of the international debt crisis of the 1980s, when states—along with the federal government—ceased servicing their debt to foreign creditors. Once the government and creditors at the national level had reached an agreement, the federal government tried to induce the states to resume servicing their debt. In 1989 the federal government agreed to transform the accumulated arrears and remaining principal into a single debt to the federal treasury, rescheduling $19 billion on these terms.[21]

The second act, which began in the late 1980s, involved the states' debts to federal financial institutions. It was resolved by rescheduling roughly $28 billion in loans and transferring them to the federal treasury. But the federal government wrote an escape clause into the agreement. If the ratio of states' debt-servicing costs to their revenues rises above a threshold fixed by the Senate, the excess can be deferred and capitalized into the outstanding stock of debt. By rescheduling the principal and placing a ceiling on debt-servicing costs, these agreements considerably reduced the states' immediate burden. But the escape clause also made it seem that the federal government was prepared to provide debt relief to any state that required it.

The third act began in the early 1990s and revolved around defaults on state domestic bonds. Four large states do the most financing through bonds: São Paulo, Rio de Janeiro, Minas Gerais, and Rio Grande do Sul. Traditionally, the states' commercial banks underwrite these bonds, which are ultimately sold to private banks and investors. They generally have a five-year maturity date, with interest due then. Ironically, the bond crisis was precipitated by the considerable success of the government's stabilization plan, the Plano Real. The plan dramatically reduced inflation, so states could no longer count on inflation to reduce real salaries and pensions over time.[22] As a result, state governments soon found themselves with payrolls equal to 80 or 90 percent of their revenues.

As state finances became more precarious, private banks began increasing their interest rates and shortening the length of time they would hold bonds. Ultimately, private banks declined to hold state debt at any price. The states found themselves unable either to pay or to reschedule their debts and sought relief from the federal government, which authorized them to exchange their bonds for more readily marketable federal bonds. But with the interest rate on federal bonds hovering at 25–30 percent in real terms, the stock of bond debt exploded by $12 billion in 1995 and by another $10.7 billion in 1996. At the end of 1996 the stock of state (and municipal) bond debt stood at $52 billion. The heavy interest obligations on this growing stock of debt, combined with the states' inability to reduce personnel costs or raise revenues, has resulted in growing state and municipal deficits. From a surplus of 0.7 percent of GDP in 1992, the operational balance of state and municipal governments fell to a deficit of 2.3 percent of GDP in 1997—52 percent higher than the federal government deficit.

Negotiations to resolve the debt situation began in mid-1995 with three parties: the federal Congress, the president and his economic team, and the states. But not until December 1997 did the first major debtor state, São Paulo, sign a binding agreement with the federal government. The other major debtor states followed over the next nine months. In general, the agreements followed the pattern of the two previous debt agreements. Debt was rescheduled rather than written off, and a debt service ceiling was imposed above which costs could be capitalized into the stock of debt. The main innovation of the new debt agreements is a large interest rate subsidy. Rather than requiring subnational governments to pay the existing interest rate on federal bonds, the federal government agreed to impose a fixed real interest rate of 6 percent.

With each debt workout, the federal government has tried to tighten the regulations on state borrowing. States benefiting from debt rescheduling are required to permit the federal government to deduct debt service from intergovernmental transfers. New federal lending to states currently in default is prohibited. The constitution has been amended to prohibit the issue of new state bonds until 2000, and the central bank does not allow private banks to increase their holdings of state debt. These federal regulations have not been enough to forestall the most recent act of the debt crisis that started in 1999, since most of the recent growth in debt stems not from new borrowing but from the capitalization of interest on existing debt.

The macroeconomic effects of the rescheduling agreements have been limited. Although the agreements lowered the interest rates the states pay, the federal government continued to be the states' creditor and to pay the actual cost of borrowing funds. The interest rate paid by the public sector as a whole has not declined. The terms of the agreements, moreover, have not been enough to forestall the capitalization of interest on debt owed to the federal government. State debt has continued to grow, so the agreements have not reduced the aggregate interest costs paid by the public sector. They have merely shifted more of the interest costs to the federal treasury.

What can be done?

Some aspects of the solution to this financial and intergovernmental crisis are not hard to identify. Initially, the federal government must address the underlying source of the debt crisis by finding a way to control personnel costs, which consume 80–90 percent of current revenues. Reducing these costs will require eliminating the controls on state personnel policies mandated in the 1988 constitution, so that states can dismiss redundant staff, negotiate salary reductions, adopt stricter criteria for retirement, and reduce pension benefits.

The government must also act to eliminate the expectation of federal bailouts. The first bailout signaled states and their lenders that the federal government was ready to step in to rescue debt-ridden local governments. While some lenders may actually have believed their borrowers were creditworthy, they also believed that the federal government would make good on state obligations if the stability of the financial system were threatened or a breakdown of services in a major state loomed. This implicit federal guarantee permitted states to continue to borrow well past the point at which they had the means to service their debts.

The current federal regulations to limit subnational borrowing are clearly not sufficient to counteract this expectation. But the states cannot borrow unless someone is willing to lend to them. If private lenders are convinced that the federal government will not bail out defaulting states, the lenders themselves will act as a source of restraint.[23] Convincing lenders that no federal bailout will be forthcoming requires more than a statement of intent, particularly given Brazil's recent history of bailouts. The federal government needs to demonstrate its commitment by allowing a state government to default and leaving the lender and the state to work out a settlement. Once private lenders are persuaded that financing subnational governments carries real risks, they are likely to restrain their lending despite the supplications of state governors. Establishing a constitutional restraint on the federal government's ability to lend to the states will enhance the credibility of this policy.[24]

Softening federal mandates on subnational personnel policies and hardening the budget constraint on subnational borrowing will help to forestall future debt crises. But ultimately, sustainable reform requires changing the political circumstances that gave rise to these policies. The distribution of power between the president and the legislature needs to be reexamined, along with the electoral rules that result in such a high degree of party fragmentation and lack of discipline. Several measures discussed in chapter 5 are especially relevant to the Brazilian case. To make it harder for interest groups from the states to conspire against the whole, the office of the president must be strengthened, perhaps by requiring a supermajority to override a presidential veto.

Since the height of the debt crisis, Brazil has taken several positive steps. In 1998 the Congress approved a constitutional amendment that would allow states to dismiss staff (provided their personnel spending exceeded a certain percentage of state revenues). In 1999 the government responded to one state's much-publicized default on rescheduled debt by exercising its new authority to deduct the overdue debt service from federal-to-state transfers. Later in the year the Congress opened debate on a proposal to change the electoral rules for the lower house, replacing the current system of proportional representation with one in which half the seats would be filled from single-seat electoral districts. The first two of these actions will go a long way toward providing states with the means and incentive to respond to fiscal pressures without resorting to default. The third, if it functions as its advocates anticipate, may reduce party fragmentation and strengthen the government's ability to resist appeals for bailouts.

Improving urban living conditions: Karachi

The explosive growth of urban populations in developing countries will challenge the capacity of society to improve urban living conditions. This case study suggests how the recommendations of chapter 7 concerning the provision of municipal services can be translated into action in Karachi, Pakistan's major metropolis.[25] Karachi is representative of many large cities in developing countries where the public sector has had difficulty coping with rapid urban growth. It shares many characteristics with Bombay, Istanbul, Jakarta, and Lagos, though the reasons for the difficulties in providing services differ from city to city. As chapter 7 recommends, in Karachi the public sector needs to tap the knowledge and dynamism of the rest of society through partnerships with private enterprise, community groups, and nongovernmental organizations (NGOs). With their support, the public sector can focus on those services only it can provide, including land titling, appropriate building and development regulation, and trunk infrastructure for water, sewerage, and roads.

Karachi today

Karachi's 11 million people account for around 8 percent of Pakistan's total population and a quarter of its urban population (box 8.5). The city grew rapidly after the massive migration that followed the partition of British India in 1947, putting severe stress on the housing market.[26] The public sector, which owned most of

Box 8.5
Pakistan at a glance

Poverty and social indicators[a]	Pakistan	South Asia	Low-income countries
GNP per capita (U.S. dollars)[b]	490	390	350
Poverty (percentage of population below $1 per day)	34	..	..
Urban population (percentage of total population)	35	27	28
Life expectancy at birth (years)	64	62	59

Exports and imports (millions of U.S. dollars)
■ Exports ■ Imports
(bar chart for years 1991–1997)

Key economic ratios	1976	1986	1996	1997
Gross domestic investment/GDP	17.2	18.8	18.7	17.4
Exports of goods and services/GDP	10.7	12.3	16.5	16.2
Gross domestic savings/GDP	7.9	10.9	14.2	12.4

	1976–86	1987–97	1996	1997	1998–2002
Average annual GDP growth	6.8	4.7	4.7	–0.4	5.8

. .Not available.
a. Data shown are from the latest available year within the range 1991–97. GNP per capita figures are from 1997.
b. Calculated using World Bank Atlas method.
Source: World Bank, World Development Indicators, 1999.

the land in and around Karachi, reserved for itself the dominant role in land development. Regulations on land development drove up the cost of new housing by mandating large plot sizes, making generous allocations for rights-of-way, setting high on-site infrastructure standards, and mandating costly building materials. This excessive regulation priced most households out of the market. Delays in extending trunk infrastructure—roads, piped water, and sewerage—limited the supply of land with access to those services and raised still further the prices of plots that already had them. These constraints on the supply of housing interacted with constraints on demand, especially the inability of low- and middle-income households to obtain mortgage financing. The result has been an informal, unplanned, and unregulated system of housing development.

From 1970 to 1985 the informal sector managed an estimated 33 percent of all residential land conversion and development in the metropolitan region and met more than 50 percent of the city's housing needs. Although Karachi needs an estimated 80,000 housing units each year, between 1987 and 1992 an average of only 26,700 building permits were issued yearly. The informal sector created about 28,000 units each year in

unplanned settlements termed *katchi abadis,* in which half the city's people now live. The population of katchi abadis has grown at an annual rate of 9 percent, nearly twice the city's overall population growth rate of 4.8 percent. Densification of existing housing in inner-city areas and illegal construction in the suburbs have met the rest of the housing gap.

A supporting industry has emerged in connection with katchi abadis. Unregulated land developers obtain land—often in collusion with government development authorities—and divide it into plots that are sold to individual households. Such middlemen illegally acquire at least 1,000 acres of state land every year in Karachi and use it for informal housing. Water distribution is controlled by the so-called "water mafia," which takes water from various water hydrants and distributes it by truck. Even high-income areas regularly have water delivered by tankers. A 1,200-gallon tank sells for Rs. 200 ($3.40), and the price per unit increases for water sold in smaller quantities to households unable to afford the money or storage space for larger amounts. Over time, low-income neighborhoods acquire trunk water connections by lobbying their representatives on the municipal council or by collecting money and bribing public officials. Alternatively, the supply can be arranged by the land developers, who create illegal connections to the public piped network. Communities often collect money and lay internal water supply networks at their own cost.

Katchi abadis also arrange their own wastewater disposal. A survey of 136 katchi abadis in Karachi comprising 79,426 houses and 8,479 lanes shows that these communities have laid sewer lines in 82 percent of the lanes at an estimated investment of Rs. 200 million ($3.4 million). In Orangi township, 88,211 houses in 5,856 lanes have built their latrines, lane sewers, and over 400 collector sewers with an investment of Rs. 74 million ($1.5 million). At public sector rates, this construction might well have cost nearly 10 times as much.

A massive informal sector is far from the optimal approach to housing shortages. Because households obtain their land through irregular channels, they do not own their primary asset and cannot use it as collateral to finance housing construction. The insecurity of their property rights undermines what should be a natural incentive to invest in property and infrastructure. Economies of scale do not exist for the delivery of essential services because services are provided piecemeal (and sometimes illegally). Facilities are often of questionable quality because the informal sector does not have the necessary technical capacity. And the illegal dumping of wastes and inadequate treatment of sewage lead to increasingly dangerous health conditions. Sewage remains a particular problem in the informal settlements, which often discharge it into open natural drains. Community-built sewerage systems are seldom integrated into official sewerage system plans. If they were, the costs would be dramatically reduced, the projects would be completed in a fraction of the time it takes to complete them now, and the poor, not the contractors, would be the beneficiaries.

Governments have so far been indifferent, if not hostile, to the katchi abadis even though they house half the city's population. The rationale is that katchi abadis are a transitory phenomenon. Formal plans and projects ignore the existing investment in these communities on the assumption that the government will ultimately provide high-quality standard solutions. Community-based organizations and NGOs have pressed for a change in policy, but official responsibility for housing is fragmented among overlapping city, provincial, and federal agencies, making concrete action difficult.[27]

The path to reform

What institutional changes and arrangements would yield the most favorable outcomes, given Karachi's condition today? As a key first step, the government needs to recognize that what exists on the ground is not a temporary situation, but a reality. The katchi abadis represent the starting point for thinking about Karachi's future. These vast community investments in housing and infrastructure are part of the city's future, and wiping them out in order to start again from scratch is simply not feasible. Thus, any housing plan the government puts forward must take the informal communities into account.

The government must also nurture—and ultimately institutionalize—positive interactions among government agencies, interest groups (formal and informal), and communities. Currently, there is little trust among the various actors in the housing drama, especially between the government and organizations representing low-income households. These groups have the most accurate knowledge of housing conditions and are well positioned to articulate residents' needs. Working with them will help ensure that housing priorities are met, but the groups need access to good information if they are to function effectively. An additional method of reestablishing trust is to rationalize the overlapping responsibilities of municipal, provincial, and federal agencies in order to strengthen accountability at each level.

Overregulation of the housing market has resulted in Karachi's current unworkable system of housing provision. This system needs to be replaced by one that incorporates legitimate private construction firms into the market for low-income residents. Standards for subdividing and building, for example, should be made more realistic. While housing must meet public health and safety requirements, it need not be so elaborate that it unnecessarily raises the price of housing out of the reach of low-income people.

The public sector, for its part, should confine its role in the formal system of housing production to areas in which it has a comparative advantage. The first of these areas is property rights. The government should pursue title adjudication and improve the administration of property registration systems. The second area is trunk infrastructure. Karachi needs new water and sewer lines and trunk roads that will connect the tertiary networks already existing in the katchi abadis to existing public infrastructure. The third area is housing credit. The government can improve housing prospects for low-income residents by allowing them to apply for credit collectively. Community groups able to make an acceptable down payment on land can be an important source of infrastructure development. Once they have acquired title to the land, they can use this asset as collateral for infrastructure loans.

These three measures can reduce the cost of new and tenured housing with access to essential services. But the government must also address the current problems of the katchi abadis, possibly by adopting the model of development offered by the Orangi Pilot Project described in chapter 7.[28] This model reduces the cost of internal development to about 10 percent of conventional planning costs and makes maintenance and operation feasible. It is socially acceptable and can be upgraded over time. The city can design future infrastructure that incorporates community-built facilities into the overall network. It can also provide technical advice to the informal contractors, perhaps through certification processes to upgrade their skills.

For water supply, the government could consider formalizing the de facto privatization that has already occurred. Rather than attempting to extend its water networks into informal settlements, the Karachi water authority might be better off considering competitive wholesale water concessions. Paraguay's experience shows that when small private providers are allowed to operate competitively in a stable environment, truckers will eventually find it in their economic interest to progress to piped distribution (chapter 7). In the meantime, however, private providers can better tailor their services to the socioeconomic and physical characteristics of the neighborhoods they serve.

Over time, these measures can transform Karachi's housing market. As the cost of formal housing declines, the proportion of households relying on the informal system of housing production will fall. And as governments take a more supportive approach to katchi abadis, the number of households lacking secure tenure and trunk infrastructure will decline as well.

Cultivating rural-urban synergies: Tanzania

Of all the developing regions, Sub-Saharan Africa has registered the weakest overall growth in the last 15 years. The area has become increasingly marginalized in the global economy, and its debt burden as a share of GDP is now the heaviest of any region. Sub-Saharan Africa is also experiencing the fastest increase in its urban population. The prognosis for the continent, having brightened briefly in 1995–97, once again looks uncertain, however. For the typical, predominantly rural African economy such as Tanzania, globalization and urbanization open a small window of hope (box 8.6). How can Tanzania exploit these forces to galvanize its rural economy and make it an engine of growth for a country whose GDP is currently rising at 3–4 percent per year?

Initial conditions

Three-quarters of all Tanzanians live in rural areas, and agriculture accounts for over 50 percent of the country's GDP. Most farming is traditional land-extensive, low-input, subsistence agriculture. Agricultural production has increased in recent years, largely because farmers are cultivating more land (yields are low and have stagnated for almost three decades). Manufacturing contributes a bare 7 percent of GDP, a share that has declined over the past two decades as tariff barriers have been removed and the public sector has withdrawn from some loss-making production activities. The main activities are food processing, and manufacture of building materials and paper and packaging, largely for the domestic market. Tanzania's exports consist of unprocessed agricultural products and minerals and have diversified little since the mid-1980s. Export crops, which are produced mostly by smallholders, account for only around 8 percent of agricultural production, although sales of cut flowers are rising. Apart from these items and commodities like coffee, tea, cashews, maize, cotton, and fish, the main foreign exchange earner is tourism, a significant source of income for the country. Over the medium term, exports of gold could overshadow income from cash crops.

In 1998 Tanzania attracted $140 million a year in foreign direct investment, as against $70 million in the mid-1990s, most of it going into mining and the balance into infrastructure for tourism. The privatization of banks and utilities is beginning to draw funds into some other sectors, such as telecommunications. Domestic savings and public sector resource mobilization are modest, as they are in most African countries. But investment, financed in part by international aid, is fairly high relative to GDP.

Tanzania's urban population is growing at about 5 percent annually—a rapid but not unusual rate, given the country's relatively low level of urbanization (figure 8.1). The six largest cities generate over one-third of

Box 8.6
Tanzania at a glance

Poverty and social indicators[a]	Tanzania	Sub-Saharan Africa	Low-income countries
GNP per capita *(U.S. dollars)*[b]	210	500	350
Poverty *(percentage of population below $1 per day)*	51	..	..
Urban population *(percentage of total population)*	24	32	28
Life expectancy at birth *(years)*	51	52	59

Exports and imports (millions of U.S. dollars)

Key economic ratios	1976	1986	1996	1997
Gross domestic investment/GDP	..	22.0	18.0	19.5
Exports of goods and services/GDP	..	7.8	21.5	23.2
Gross domestic savings/GDP	..	9.9	3.4	12.6

	1976–86	1987–97	1996	1997	1998–2002
Average annual GDP growth	..	2.9	4.1	3.9	5.5

. .Not available.
a. Data shown are from the latest available year within the range 1991–97. *GNP per capita* figures are from 1997.
b. Calculated using World Bank *Atlas* method.
c. Import data for 1997 are not available.
Source: World Bank, *World Development Indicators,* 1999.

GDP, with Dar es Salaam accounting for 17 percent. If Tanzania is to achieve and maintain growth rates of 7–8 percent over the next two decades (as it must to make substantial progress against poverty), more growth must come from its cities. However, given the preponderance of the rural sector, overall economic performance will depend upon the multiplying of rural-urban linkages, the commercialization of agriculture, and the spread of nonfarm activities. Currently, agricultural diversification and productivity are at low levels, and nonfarm incomes are below the average for the Sub-Saharan Africa region. But such development is most likely to flourish in the periurban areas and then spread to the hinterland, deriving impetus from markets and agglomeration economies in cities.[29]

Urban-rural partnerships

How would an urban-rural partnership work? The experience of other low-income agricultural economies, such as China, Indonesia, and Vietnam, suggests four ways of improving the links between rural and urban areas that can help raise rural productivity. These include employing new technical and organizational

knowledge, expanding access to markets for agricultural produce, and harnessing new biological, chemical, and mechanical inputs. Tanzania can adapt these approaches by taking the following steps:

Step 1. Establish support networks that create trusting relationships between urban businesses and periurban and rural producers. With over 70 percent of its rural income dependent on agriculture, Tanzania has great scope for developing rural industry.[30] Furthermore, with only one-third of agricultural output currently marketed at all, rural-urban linkages have much to contribute to agricultural development. Tanzanian farmers lack information, infrastructure, transportation, and credit because of the small size and subsistence orientation of farming activities.[31] In rural areas that are relatively close to cities, however, proximity to markets and information can help overcome these problems. Market transactions must operate against a backdrop of assurances that most of the time, obligations will be met, bills will be paid, goods will be delivered, and transactions costs will be manageable. Formal legal and insurance contracts are one mechanism for providing these assurances. But ties of ethnicity, religion, and kin-

Figure 8.1
The population in Tanzania is increasingly urbanized

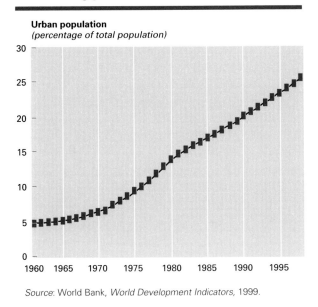

Urban population
(percentage of total population)

Source: World Bank, *World Development Indicators*, 1999.

ship are a source of social capital and support flexible production arrangements, subcontracting, and outsourcing schemes (see box 2). Such social networks flourish in eastern Nigeria along an axis that includes Aba, Nnewi, and Onitsha. In Nnewi, for example, members of the Igbo community have established a motor parts industry that relies on ethnic ties to reduce transactions costs.[32]

Intermediaries with strong rural connections, play a large part in building such networks. Much depends on periurban-urban social relationships and on the willingness of urban business groups to reach out to the surrounding rural areas.[33] In such cities as Arusha and Moshi, an entrenched business elite—the Chaggas—may already possess a local network, along with adequate financing, that could serve as a basis for expansion. Likewise, Asian communities in Dar es Salaam, Lindi, and elsewhere could enlarge their marketing networks among the periurban villages. But a deepening of formal institutions that safeguard rights would supplement informal arrangements.

Step 2. Build infrastructure. A modern economy depends on efficient surface transportation and telecommunications, which link rural producers, service providers such as freight transporters and marketing firms, and urban businesses. In transportation, the government's imperative is to appreciably strengthen the road

system. Good roads are particularly needed in the immediate vicinity of the major urban areas in order to facilitate the integration of cities and the surrounding countryside. Only 12 percent of Tanzania's roads are in good condition, with the rest imposing excess vehicle operating costs equivalent to a third of export earnings in 1990.[34] The implications for the development of marketed crops are severe: in the past, when rising prices have resulted in a spurt in production, crops could not be moved because of inadequate transportation. As a result, farmers had difficulties selling their produce, and production quickly fell back again.[35]

Improved transportation and communications are important not only because they will strengthen ties within Tanzania but also because they will link the country more closely with the global economy. To maintain close contact with foreign markets—and to ship and receive goods on exacting schedules—Tanzania's businesses need a well-managed infrastructure that keeps handling and user charges at seaports and airports to a minimum.[36] The same is true for international telecommunications rates. For Tanzanian exporters to compete effectively against suppliers in South Africa and South Asia, the country's infrastructure must deliver comparable services and charge similar rates. This requires the private sector to play a large role in building and operating the transportation, communication, and electricity infrastructure.

Step 3. Improve channels for agricultural and industrial research and extension services to bring new technology to the rural economy. The diffusion of technology, by private businesses, government research institutes, and the media, is vital to raising Tanzania's agricultural productivity, incomes, and demand for nonfarm products. It can also nurture processing and industrial activities in the belts around cities, where the potential returns from these activities are highest and most visible.[37]

Specialized agricultural extension services managed from the top down have not worked well in East Africa.[38] But experience in other countries suggests that extension services can be made more effective. They must be client driven, customized to the needs of particular groups, and capable of delivering the newest technologies.[39] They must operate in areas with sound infrastructure, especially roads and electricity, ready access to modern agricultural inputs, and good market access, for example, in the vicinity of cities. These efforts must also be directed to those groups that are most likely to be innovative—that is, to groups that have the educational level to exploit the opportunities new technologies present.

Providing effective research and extension services requires an understanding of the rural economy around cities, where the incentive to innovate is greatest. The services can then be oriented to the emerging periurban commercial agriculture with industrial linkages and can evolve with the changing economic environment. Trying to provide such services everywhere in the country will probably have a negligible payoff. But concentrating what capacity there is in areas where the scope for rural-urban synergy is greatest might create the dynamic clusters of growth that Tanzania so badly needs.

Step 4. Exploit the advantages of global business and intellectual linkages. Tanzania does have an indigenous business community connected to the Middle East, Europe, and South Asia (see chapter 1). But a history of government constraints on private sector activity has channeled much of the energies of this community into trade, wholesaling, and retailing activities.[40] Whether the objective is to encourage local businesses to expand and diversify or to make Tanzania more attractive to foreign investors, effective constitutional and legal rules are needed to safeguard property rights, enforce contracts, and reduce state interference.[41] A free press can support these legal measures by acting as an agent of restraint and by helping enforce accountability of public as well as private bodies. The basic framework exists in Tanzania but lacks credibility in the eyes of investors, who recently ranked Tanzania as one of the world's most corrupt countries.[42]

The progressive lowering of trade barriers will improve urban entrepreneurs' access to the equipment, inputs, and technology they need to build competitive business operations. But openness embraces more than free trade. It also involves subscribing to rules governing commercial codes, contracts, and individual rights. In this deeper sense, openness can reinforce the government's assurances to the business community on property rights and contractual agreements. It can also stimulate private domestic investment and increase the flow of foreign direct investment in industry.[43]

A secure and open business environment is likely to lead to a reflux of skills from abroad and to generate the incentives that encourage individuals to acquire technical expertise. Several East Asian economies, after experiencing a brain drain from the 1960s through the early 1980s, established open and flexible business environments that drew back many of those who had left.

The entrepreneurship, knowledge, and capital from this reverse migration have helped these countries find new overseas markets. But reverse migration is at best a partial solution. Tanzania must expand its secondary education facilities and rebuild its tertiary education and research facilities. Tanzanian universities have been drained of talent and barely partake in the international commerce in ideas and research.[44] Strengthening the scientific culture and the competitiveness of universities are necessary steps to rapid and sustainable development in a globalizing environment where technology is one of the principal drivers.[45] For example, the promise of transgenic technology to enhance the yield and disease resistance of staple crops, such as maize, will only be realized by building the research base and biosafety regulatory capacity and by enforcing rules to protect breeders' rights. Without these, there is limited prospect that the country will participate as an informed stakeholder in the biotechnology business.[46]

Laying the foundation for this new strategy requires political initiative. Tanzania's leaders must change the climate of opinion in the country, building a consensus among local and foreign businesses and following up their views with credible institutions. The government can signal its commitment to change by more actively pursuing privatization and transparent reforms in the banking industry.

Policies that support macroeconomic stability, liberalize the market, and build human capital should provide some of the conditions for future development in Tanzania. But Tanzania must do more in order to experience the kind of development that will substantially reduce poverty. The government needs to establish strong political and legal institutions that reduce the risk to local and foreign investors of doing business in the country. It must also invest in urban and periurban infrastructure, especially transportation and communication. Finally, by fostering openness the government can help create competitive markets, spread knowledge, and build human capital.

The shifting development landscape at the dawn of the 21st century

In 1990 many in the development community and elsewhere expected the raw vitality of market capitalism to lift billions of people out of poverty into a new era of sustainable development. These expectations have not been borne out. Some nations have achieved remarkable progress. But with nearly 1.5 billion people living on less than $1 a day and more than 2 billion on less than $2 a day, the task is very far from completed.

Development policy is being rethought. The World Bank's Comprehensive Development Framework (CDF), this report, and the 2000/2001 report on poverty alleviation strive for better understanding of all aspects of development—drawing from experience and the forces that will shape the development landscape to provide pointers for the future course of development policy. This reexamination has been wide ranging. It suggests that no one element of development is above all others; no one future trend is all-encompassing; no one institutional or policy initiative is likely to be a panacea.

This report argues that two forces will significantly alter the development landscape in the early decades of the 21st century, with implications for how the development agenda can be tackled, who the relevant actors will be, and what forms their interactions are likely to take:

- *Globalization*—the continued integration of the world's economies through expanding flows of goods, services, capital, labor, and ideas and through collective action by countries to address global environmental problems
- *Localization*—the increasing demands of local communities for greater autonomy, which will be bolstered by the growing concentration of developing countries' populations in urban centers.

These forces interact in many ways. The urban centers discussed in chapters 6 and 7 have much to gain from the open world trading system of chapter 2 and the global capital flows of chapter 3. Foreign direct investment (chapter 3) will play a significant role in providing the needed urban services (chapter 7). Many more such connections have been drawn throughout the report. These disparate yet interrelated forces pose many challenges for the development process, each requiring a different type of institutional and policy response.

Three central implications for development policy

First, these forces underscore the *growing global interdependence across space, time, and issues.* The rapid spread of financial contagion from East Asia to the Russian Federation and Latin America in 1997–98 stands as a compelling testimonial to the growing interdependencies that can undermine economic growth and increase poverty.

The recognition that the health of a country's banking system can alter investor perceptions of the health of neighboring countries' banks has transformed the calculus of international cooperation. Yet, as chapter 3 pointed out, merely adopting common banking standards without adequately enforcing them is unlikely to restrain excessive risk-taking. Countries must not only adopt sound banking standards but must also devise institutional structures to ensure that these standards are enforced by insulating bank regulators from external pressures. They also need to consider establishing a system of regional surveillance of banking practices, as is taking place in the Manila Framework.

Some of the starkest examples of growing interdependencies appear in the discussion of the global commons in chapter 4. Although slow progress has been achieved in negotiating an agreement to substantially reduce greenhouse gas emissions, the growing recognition of the linkages among international environmental problems suggests that better policies and new institutions will be needed.

A second outcome of the forces of globalization and localization is a *more crowded development scene.* Nation-states will less and less be the sole agents for development. Instead, countries will increasingly act through multinational agreements, and through their interactions with multinational corporations, nongovernmental actors, and subnational entities, especially cities. Institutions and norms will have to evolve to define relations between these new actors and nation-states. This will have implications for the way global accords are negotiated, for how governments within a country manage central-local relations, and for how enduring partnerships are established within cities.

In describing the challenge of localization, chapter 5 offers suggestions for avoiding the pitfalls highlighted in the case study of Brazil. Chapter 7 points to the important role partnerships play in revitalizing cities and improving the quality of life for urban residents. Each of these developments requires new institutions that will accommodate the growing number of development actors.

Despite the new supranational and subnational challenges, governments will remain central players in the development process. National governments may well undertake fewer functions, ceding responsibility to other entities. But they remain the linchpin that holds the institutions of governance together. They alone can define the constitutional rules within their borders and shape their relations with each other.

The greater mobility of capital and labor between and within countries—and the potential competition among national, subnational, and urban governments for scarce resources—underlies the third implication of these forces: *the rewards for successful development strategies, and the punishments for failure, are likely to be greater and experienced more quickly than in the past.* For example, urban centers that provide stable property rights and an environment conducive to the accumulation of social and human capital can attract more foreign investment and more skilled migrants. The consequences of delays and partial, half-hearted attempts at reform, giving little thought to building long-term credibility, will become apparent much more immediately than in the past, as discussed in chapters 2, 3, and 6.

The central role of institutions

This report's focus on the institutions of governance does not diminish the key role government policymaking plays in development. Fostering the administrative and analytical capacity to formulate, innovate, and implement policies will remain essential to promoting development in the future.

However, government policies alone will not suffice. Responding to these new forces of globalization and localization requires robust mediating institutions, especially when countries commit to take actions in a crisis, separately or collectively. Institutions serve to balance the diverse interests of society and to determine how the forces of development distribute their benefits and advantages, and their costs and risks. Fortunately, developing countries do not need to create all of these institutional structures from scratch; in many cases, they can build upon existing international agreements and internationally recognized standards. Countries can use the procedures of the WTO to enhance the credibility of their unilateral trade reforms by binding reforms into their multilateral commitments, as discussed in chapter 2. By moving toward international banking standards, as discussed in chapter 3 and in the case study of Hun-

gary in this chapter, developing countries can use preexisting and accepted global standards to guide and support the credibility of their reforms.

These institutions do not arise in a vacuum, and due regard must be given to how rules are negotiated and enforced. Whether the concern is global or local, farsighted policymakers have to induce the participation of every actor with the capacity to enhance or reduce the collective welfare. No doubt some government entities will be tempted to "hold up" negotiations to press for greater benefits from such agreements. However, such tactics are likely to prove less and less successful: growing interdependencies will create linkages across issues, and pariahs will be shut out of the benefits of cooperation on many fronts.

These institutions, once established, will evolve in response to numerous factors: the changing needs of members, technological advances, growing or receding consensus among experts, and pressures from nonmembers. Such institutions will also have to be robust enough to handle rapid changes in sentiment—abetted by improvements in communications, disseminating new information faster to greater numbers of concerned parties.

The last 10 years have been a mixed blessing for developing countries. East Asian nations surrendered some previous gains in a crisis with substantial human and economic costs. Large parts of Africa have had yet another lost decade. No one wants to see these experiences repeated. We have learned from the past, and we have a better sense of the forces that will mold the development landscape over the coming decades. Globalization and localization are transforming many aspects of the human experience—so many that only a comprehensive, multilayered response of policy and institutional reform will be adequate. If we fail to meet this challenge, we will condemn the world's poor to a cycle of instability, hunger, and despair. By seizing the opportunities presented at the dawn of the 21st century, together we can turn our dream into a reality—a world free of poverty.

Bibliographical Note

This report has drawn on a wide range of World Bank documents and on numerous outside sources. World Bank sources include ongoing research as well as country economic, sector, and project work. These and other sources are listed alphabetically by author and organization in two groups: background papers and references. The background papers were commissioned for this report and are available on the *World Development Report 1999/2000* World Wide Web page *(http://www.worldbank. org/wdr/)*. In addition, some background papers will be made available through the Policy Research Working Paper series or as other World Bank publications, and the rest will be available through the World Development Report office. The views they express are not necessarily those of the World Bank or of this report.

In addition to the principal sources listed, many persons, both inside and outside the World Bank, provided advice and guidance. Valuable comments and contributions were provided by Richard Ackermann, James Adams, Ehtisham Ahmad, Junaid Ahmad, Tauheed Ahmed, Jock Anderson, Lance Anelay, Preeti Arora, Jehan Arulpragasam, Roy Bahl, J. Michael Bamberger, Suman Bery, Sofia Bettencourt, Amar Bhattacharya, Richard Bird, Ilona Blue, Clemens Boonekamp, François Bourguignon, Nicolette L. Bowyer, John Briscoe, Lynn R. Brown, Robin Burgess, Shahid Javed Burki, William Byrd, Jerry Caprio, Richard Carey, Gonzalo Castro, Herman Cesar, Ajay Chhibber, Kenneth Chomitz, Paul Collier, Maureen Cropper, Angus Deaton, Julia Devlin, Samir El Daher, A. Charlotte de Fontaubert, Dipak Dasgupta, Alan Deardorff, Shantayanan Devarajan, Hinh Truong Dinh, Simeon Djankov, Gunnar Eskeland, François Falloux, Caroline Farah, Charles Feinstein, J. Michael Finger, Louis Forget, Per Fredriksson, David Freestone, Lev Freinkman, Caroline Freund, Christopher Gibbs, Marcelo Giugale, Steve Gorman, Vincent Gouarne, Elisea G. Gozun, Emma Grant, Angela Griffin, Jeffrey Gutman, Kirk Hamilton, Sonia Hammam, Trudy Harpham, Nigel Harris, Arif Hasan, Ian Graeme Heggie, Jesko S. Hentschel, Bernard Hoekman, Gordon Hughes, David Hummels, Athar Hussain, Zahid Hussain, Roumeen Islam, Emmanuel Jimenez, Ian Johnson, Barbara Kafka, Ravi Kanbur, Kamran Khan,

Anupam Khanna, Homi Kharas, Bona Kim, Daniela Klingebiel, Tufan Kolan, Mihaly Kopanyi, Nicholas Kraft, Kathie Krumm, Donald Larson, Kyu Sik Lee, Danny Leipziger, Robert Litan, Peter Lloyd, Millard Long, Susan Loughhead, Patrick Low, Michael Lyons, Dorsati Madani, Antonio Magalhaes, Catherine Mann, Manuel Marino, Keith Maskus, Douglas Massey, Subodh Mathur, Alexander F. McCalla, Kathleen B. McCollom, Dominique van der Mensbrugghe, Patrick Messerlin, Jonathan Michie, Steven Miller, Pradeep Mitra, Gobind Nankani, Benno Ndulu, Vikram Nehru, Eric Neumayer, Kenneth Newcombe, Ian Newport, Francis Ng, Judy O'Connor, W. Paatii Ofosu-Amaah, Alexandra Ortiz, Tracey Osborne, Kyran O'Sullivan, Samuel K. E. Otoo, Berk Ozler, John Page, Stefano Pagiola, Eul Yong Park, Antonio Parra, Odil Tunali Payton, Guy Pfeffermann, Rachel Phillipson, Robert Picciotto, Gunars Platais, Lant Pritchett, Tom Prusa, Rudolf V. Van Puymbroeck, Regine Qualmann, Navaid Qureshi, S. K. Rao, Martin Ravallion, Gordon Redding, Don Reisman, J. David Richardson, Gabriel Roth, Arun Sanghvi, Barbara Santos, Karl Sauvant, Norbert Schady, Sergio Schmulker, Jitendra J. Shah, Zmarak Shalizi, Howard Shatz, Martin Slough, Stephen Smith, Richard Stren, Maria Stuttaford, Hiroaki Suzuki, Hans Helmut Taake, Vito Tanzi, Stanley Taylor, Brigida Tuason, P. Zafiris Tzannatos, Anthony Venables, David Vines, Michael Walton, Robert Watson, Dana Weist, George T. West, Matthew Westfall, Debbie Wetzel, John Whalley, David Wheeler, Alex Wilks, Fahrettin Yagci, Kei-Mu Yi, Roberto Zagha, Akbar Zaidi, Anders Zeijlon, and Heng-Fu Zou.

Other valuable assistance was provided by Nobuko Aoki, Pansy Chintha, Meta de Coquereaumont, Kate Hull, Keiko Itoh, Mika Iwasaki, Mani Jandu, Polly Means, Boris Pleskovic, Jean Gray Ponchamni, F. Halsey Rogers, Bruce Ross-Larson, and Tomoko Hagimoto.

A wide range of consultations was undertaken for this report. We wish to thank Scott Barrett, Chia Siow Yue, David Currie, Patrice Dufour, Riccardo Faini, Carlos Fortin, Norman Gall, Morris Goldstein, E. Monty Graham, Katherine Hagen, Andrew Hughes Hallett, Gudrun Kochendorfer, Patrick Low, Martin Mayer, Andrew Rogerson, Jagdish Saigal, Robert Skidelsky, and Alfredo Sfeir-Younis; *in Dar es Salaam:* James Adams, Haidiri Amani, Patrick Asea, Melvin Ayogu, Enos Bukuku, Sumana Dhar, Augustin F. Fosu, T. Ayme Gogue, Mats Harsmar, Satu Kahkonen, Brian Kahn, Louis Kasekende, Frederick Kilby, A. K. Maziku,

Theresa Moyo, Fidelis Mtatifikolo, Charles Mutalemwa, Crispin Mwanyika, Mthuli Ncube, Dominique Njinkeu, Temitope Oshikoya, T. Ademole Oyejide, Hajji Semboja, Joseph Semboja, and Moshe Syrquin; *in London (NGOs):* T. Allen, Tamsyn Barton, Teddy Brett, Ashvin Dayal, Nicholas Fenton, Alistair Fraser, Caroline Harper, A. Hussain, Duncan McLaren, Richard McNally, Claire Melamet, Brian O'Riordan, and David Woodward; *in Paris:* Scott Barrett, Jean Claude Berthélemy, François Bourguignon, Richard Carey, Won Hho Cho, Daniel Cohen, Jean-Marie Cour, A. De Palma, Zdenek Drabek, Patrice J. Dufour, Richard Eglin, John Hawkins, Pierre Jacquet, Ad Koekkoek, Patrick Messerlin, Robert F. Owen, Pier Carlo Padoan, Hubert Prevot, Rémy Prud'homme, Thérèse Pujolle, Regine Qualman, Helmut Reisen, Karl Sauvant, Paul Spray, Rolph Van Der Hoeven, Daniel Voizot, and Soogil Young; *in São Paulo:* Suman Bery, Shahid Javed Burki, Claudia Dutra, Javier Fraga, Carlos Langoni, Marcos Mendes, Gobind Nankani, Fernando Rezende, Richard Webb, Jorge Wilheim, and Juan Zapata; *in Singapore:* Shankar Acharya, Kym Anderson, Masahisa Fujita, Utis Kaothien, Ya-Yeow Kueh, Rajiv Lall, Rakesh Mohan, Romeo Ocampo, Phang Sock Yong, Mohd. Haflah Piei, Peter J. Rimmer, David Satterthwaite, Guo Shuqing, Victor Sit, Lyn Squire, Augustine Tan, Douglas Webster, John Wong, and Chia Siow Yue; *in Tokyo:* Kengo Akizuki, Masahiko Aoki, Judith Banister, Sang-Chuel Choe, Ryo Fujikura, Yukiko Fukagawa, Shun'Ichi Furukawa, Fan Gang, Kazumi Goto, Naomi Hara, Yujiro Hayami, Akiyoshi Horiuchi, Shigeru Ishikawa, Yoshitsugu Kanemoto, Hisakazu Kato, Tetsuo Kidokoro, Fukunari Kimura, Naohiro Kitano, Fu-Chen Lo, Katsuji Nakagane, Shuzo Nakamura, Katsutoshi Ohta, Takashi Onishi, M. G. Quibria, John M. Quigley, Kunio Saito, Yuji Suzuki, Kazuo Takahashi, Junichi Yamada, Toru Yanagihara, and Yue-Man Yeung; *NGOs in Tokyo:* Takeo Asakura, Kazuko Aso, Ienari Dan, Francisco P. Flores, Yoko Kitazawa, Satoru Matsumoto, Setsuko Matsumoto, Sakoe Saito, Kiyotake Takahashi, Michiko Takahashi, Kunio Takaso, and Yoshiko Wakayamwa.

The team consulted with the Asian Development Bank (ADB), the Bank for International Settlements (BIS), the European Bank for Reconstruction and Development (EBRD), the Organisation for Economic Co-operation and Development (OECD), the International Labour Organization (ILO), the United Nations Conference on Trade and Development (UNCTAD), the World Trade Organization (WTO), the United Nations Development Programme (UNDP), the International Monetary Fund (IMF), the German Development Forum, the Commonwealth Secretariat, the U.K. Department for International Development (DFID), the Overseas Economic Cooperation Fund (Japan), the Foundation for Advanced Studies on International Development (Japan), and the Institute of Southeast Asian Studies (Singapore).

Endnotes

Introduction

1. Pritchett 1997.

2. Among some of the more widely cited papers on why and how convergence is not happening are Bernard and Durlauf 1996; Easterly and Levine 1997; Pritchett 1997, 1998; Quah 1993; and Sachs and Warner 1997b.

3. Some papers that find strong evidence of conditional convergence are: Barro 1991; Mankiw, Romer, and Weil 1992; Sachs 1996; and Sala-i-Martin 1997. Caselli, Esquivel and Lefort (1996) suggest the convergence rate to country-specific steady states could be even faster than the cross-country rate of two percent per year.

4. See Aziz and Wescott (1997) on the need for macro policy complimentarity and Stiglitz (1998a) on the need for a broader approach involving a range of elements.

5. Lewis 1955.

6. Stiglitz 1998b.

7. Devarajan, Easterly, and Pack 1999.

8. Levine and Renelt 1992.

9. Easterly and Fischer 1995.

10. Psacharopoulos 1994.

11. World Bank 1991.

12. Buckley 1999.

13. Stiglitz 1999b.

14. Stiglitz 1996.

15. Stiglitz and Uy 1996.

16. Evans and Bataille 1997; Isham, Narayan, and Pritchett 1994; World Bank 1991, 1997d.

17. Buckley 1999.

18. Evans and Battaile 1997.

19. This box is drawn largely from the World Bank's Social Capital Web Page *(http://www.worldbank.org/poverty/scapital/index.htm)*.

20. Coleman and Hoffer 1987; Francis and others 1998.

21. Drèze and Sen 1995.

22. Narayan and Pritchett 1997.

23. Portes and Landolt 1996.

24. Evans and Bataille 1997.

25. Buckley 1999.

26. WHO 1999.

27. UNDP 1998.

28. WHO 1999.

29. World Bank 1999k.

30. WHO 1999.

31. Easterly 1999.

32. Thomas 1999.

33. World Bank 1999a; Dollar 1999.

34. North 1997.

35. A complete political economy model needs to include an agent with the authority to establish or alter the rules under which any game is played. In the national context the government is such an agent. It is neither a benevolent despot maximizing a societal welfare function nor a neutral umpire, but a privileged, self-interested agent in the game. Moreover, government consists of layers of agents who are responsible to each other and to outside constituencies in differing ways. For a general treatment of rule makers, see Altaf (1983).

36. The examples in this and the following four paragraphs are drawn from the last two *World Development Reports* (World Bank 1998m; World Bank 1997d), unless otherwise noted.

37. Burki and Perry 1998.

38. Burki and Perry 1998.

39. Ravallion and Chen 1998.

40. UNDP 1998.

41. Ravallion and Chen 1998.

42. World Bank 1998.

43. WHO 1999.

44. Jamison 1993.

45. See Ridley (1997) on future disease threats in an urban environment.

46. Walt 1998.

47. Fredland (1998) explores the wider political and psychological consequences of AIDS for the course of development in Sub-Saharan Africa.

48. WHO 1999; Marsh 1998.

49. WHO 1999.

50. There are now between 50–100 million cases of dengue fever worldwide (Rigau-Perez and others 1998). See Howson, Fineberg, and Bloom (1998).

51. Mortality tends to be higher in HIV-positive patients infected by the tuberculin bacillus (Del Ano and others 1999). On South Africa see Millard (1998).

52. Although some 70 percent of the nearly 47 million cases of HIV are in Africa, the disease is also spreading rapidly in South and Southeast Asia with the poor being most affected. See Tibaijuka 1997; *Lancet* 1996; *New England Journal of Medicine* 1996; *Financial Times,* "Toll from AIDS Heaviest Among the World's Poor." June 24, 1998; Caron 1999; *Financial Times,* "AIDS May Kill Half South African Youth." October 10/11 1998. The intergenerational effects of AIDS are described starkly in UNESCO (1999), which notes that by 2000, 13 million children in Sub-Saharan Africa will have lost one or both parents to the disease.

53. See *The Economist* (1999f) and AIDS Analysis (1998) on loss of life expectancy in several African countries.

54. This is proving to be an exceedingly by complex task with many leads being pursued. See *The Economist* 1998b; *Financial Times,* "Simple to Identify, Difficult to Destroy." July 16, 1998.

55. Good 1999; *Business Week* 1998.

56. *New England Journal of Medicine* 1997.

57. Nearly two thirds of all infections caused by staphyloccocus aureus in Europe are methicillin-resistant and also resistant

to most other antibiotics. Howson, Fineberg, and Bloom (1998); *Lancet* 1998; *New England Journal of Medicine* 1998; Cohen 1992. Walsh (1999) describes the attempt to modify vancomycin to cope with new superbugs. See also *Business Week* (1999).

58. *Oxford Analytica,* "Africa: HIV/AIDS Concentration." December 1, 1998. TB is not just a serious problem for low-income countries and is also spreading in middle-income countries such as Russia, see Feschbach (1999); Farmer (1999).

59. In Southeast Asia alone, 10–15 million people cross borders each year. *Oxford Analytica,* "Southeast Asia: Spreading Diseases." July 15, 1998; Guerrant 1998.

60. *The Economist* 1998a.

61. Curtis and Kanki 1998.

62. Ambio 1995; The *New York Times,* "Malaria, A Swamp Dweller Finds a Hillier Home." July 21, 1999.

63. See John and others (1998) on surveillance procedures; WHO 1999.

64. Harvard Working Group 1994; Ewald and Cochran 1999. On the infectious causes of many malignancies, including cancers, see Parsonnet (1999).

65. Jamison, Frank, and Kaul 1998; Walt 1998; Howson, Fineberg, and Bloom 1998; *The Economist* 1998c.

66. Watson and others 1998.

67. This box is based on Gardner-Outlaw and Engelman (1997); Rogers and Lydon (1994); Seckler and others (1998); and "World Day for Water, 22 March 1999," a news release issued jointly by UNEP and United Nations University.

68. Peterson 1999.

69. Commentators sometimes downplay the role of technology in globalization, pointing out the limited extent of global communications just a hundred years ago. In fact, U.S. exports in the late 1900s are only 1 percent higher as a percentage of GDP than they were in the late 1800s, and international capital movements are a smaller percentage of output than they were in the 1880s (*International Herald Tribune,* May 23, 1999). But the absolute levels are clearly much larger. Trade has a much broader base that involves a far larger percentage of manufactures and services, and finance includes more short-term investment that relies on highly sophisticated information technology.

Chapter 1

1. Analyses of the recent growth in trade flows (Baldwin and Martin 1999) and capital flows (Bordo, Eichengreen, and Kim 1998; Obstfeld and Taylor 1999) have identified factors that were also present during the period of globalization before World War I and, more important, factors that are unique to the end of the 20th century.

2. Recent work by Frankel and Romer (1999) brings out strongly the relationship between trade and income growth. In fact, their results suggest that a 1 percentage point increase in the trade-to-GDP ratio raises income per capita by between 0.5 and 2 percent.

3. Anderson 1999.

4. *The Economist* 1999d; *Oxford Analytica,* "East Asia, Electronic Commerce." June 1, 1999.

5. Kleinknecht and der Wengel 1998.

6. Bank lending to developing countries dropped by $75 billion in 1998, but official development assistance increased by

$3.2 billion to $51.5 billion (*Financial Times,* "Bank Loans Cut to Emerging Economies." May 31, 1999; *The Economist* 1999e).

7. The cost of a three-minute transatlantic call dropped from $31.58 in 1970 to less than $1 in 1998. Computer use is increasing at a dramatic pace as more and more people gain access to the Internet. Access speeds themselves have risen from 14.4 kilobytes to 10 megabytes per second. *Financial Times,* "Banker's Black Hole." July 21, 1999.

8. Feldstein 1998.

9. Eberstadt 1998.

10. Higgins and Williamson 1997; Horioka 1990; Kosai, Saito, and Yashiro 1998.

11. Average fertility rate in Mexico has fallen from 7.0 in the mid-1960s to 2.5 in the late 1990s (*The New York Times,* "Smaller Families to Bring Big Change in Mexico." June 8, 1999).

12. Attanasio and Banks 1998.

13. Giddens 1998.

14. Costa 1998.

15. Peterson 1999.

16. Deaton 1998.

17. Vamvakidis and Wacziarg 1998.

18. UNCTAD 1998.

19. OECD 1998. Much of the foreign direct investment in developing countries goes to fewer than 20 East Asian and Latin American economies (Fry 1995).

20. Until the early 1990s, reducing financial repression was viewed as a way to support growth but was not considered as important as other factors. New research is changing that perception. Financial deepening, including the development of well-functioning stock markets, is now seen as contributing substantially to future growth, principally by improving the allocation of resources. The relationship to growth is stronger in some regions than in others, and the evidence quite plausibly suggests that well-regulated banking systems facilitate growth. The availability of equity financing and venture capital closely parallels industrial progress and is especially important to small and medium-size enterprises seeking to exploit new technologies and to industries that depend heavily on external funding. Of course the causation could run both ways (Fry 1995). Data for five industrial countries between 1870 and 1929 show that financial intermediation spurs output. These results buttress the findings for more recent periods, as well as Gerschenkron's, which were based on his historical studies of European countries (Gerschenkron 1962; Gregorio and Guidotti 1995; Levine 1997, 707; Levine and Zervos 1998c; Rajan and Zingales 1998; Rousseau and Wachtel 1998).

21. Fry 1995.

22. Levine 1997.

23. Flannery 1998; Knight 1998.

24. Dobson and Jacquet 1998.

25. Eichengreen and others 1999; McKinnon 1991.

26. Goldstein 1998.

27. UNDP 1999.

28. Bennell 1997.

29. *Far Eastern Economic Review* 1998; Urata 1996.

30. Foreign direct investment accounted for 14 percent of financing for fixed assets in China between 1979 and 1997, out of a total of $220 billion (Guo 1998).

31. Prahalad and Liebenthal 1998.

32. The number of interfirm technology arrangements recorded by UNCTAD rose from an annual average of 300 in the mid-1980s to 600 in the mid-1990s. Those involving firms from developing countries have quadrupled from 10 per year to 40 (UNCTAD 1998; Kobrin 1997).

33. McKinnon 1998.

34. In its attempt to upgrade the 1988 accord, the Basle Committee has proposed a number of changes, including the use of both ratings by external agencies to determine banks' capital ratios and internally defined credit ratings of certain banks (*Financial Times*, "Radical Banking Reforms Announced." June 4, 1999).

35. Between 1990 and 1997 the United States alone admitted close to a million immigrants each year. See Population Reference Bureau (1999).

36. Oceania encompasses Australia, New Zealand, and the South Pacific islands.

37. Zlotnik 1998.

38. Kane 1995.

39. U.S. Committee for Refugees 1996.

40. Cohen and Deng 1998.

41. For a recent examination of European migration policies see Faini (1998). His analysis of wage differences and demographic pressures suggests that West European countries are more likely to see migration from North Africa than from Eastern Europe. See also Dervis and Shafiq (1998). For a recent exploration of the impact of demographic changes on migration, see Teitelbaum and Winter (1998).

42. Borjas 1998.

43. Bohning and de Beiji (1995) examine the effects of policies that attempt to facilitate the entry of migrant workers into labor markets. Faini (1998) assesses the difficulties faced by migrants as they assimilate into European countries. As they do, intense ethnic rivalries can develop that have little to do with the level of unemployment or the degree to which migrants displace existing workers in service or low-skilled jobs.

44. Carrington and Detragiache 1998.

45. From IMF, *International Financial Statistics*, cited in Russell and Teitelbaum (1992) and Taylor and others (1996).

46. See the evidence assembled on this point in Taylor and others (1996). In addition, see the evidence on remittances from Asian migrants to the Gulf States in Amjad (1989).

47. Castles 1998.

48. The influx of immigrants from Russia to Israel in the first half of the 1990s encouraged the growth of moderately skill-intensive sectors. See Gandal, Hanson, and Slaughter (1999).

49. Greif 1998.

50. Redding 1998; Skeldon 1998.

51. Redding 1998.

52. Meyer and others 1997.

53. *The New York Times*, "Human Influences on Climate Are Becoming Clearer." June 29, 1999.

54. *Nature* 1998.

55. *Science* 1999.

56. Around this long-run average there is likely to be a lot of variation. Already over the past 30 years the average wintertime temperature in northern latitudes is 4–5°C higher, up to

10 times the global average (*Financial Times*, "Stormy Forecast." June 3, 1999).

57. Apart from methyl chloride and methyl bromide, whose concentrations have remained roughly constant, the rising burden of chlorofluorocarbons is entirely traceable to human activity and began rising in the early 20th century (Butler 1999). The relationship between atmospheric gases and warming was first discerned by the great French mathematician Jean-Baptiste Fourier in an article published in 1824 (Christianson 1999).

58. While higher carbon dioxide concentrations could enhance plant growth and increase efficiency of water use, changes in tissue chemistry will render some plants less palatable. Heat and water stress on vegetation will offset some of the gains from an increase in the concentration of carbon dioxide (*Science* 1997, 496).

59. One alarming possibility is the melting and eventual disappearance of Himalayan glaciers in about 40 years, leading initially to flooding and then to the drying up of the rivers feeding the Indian plains (*New Scientist* 1999). Although current research suggests that climate change should not significantly disrupt the U.S. economy or agriculture, the impact on some regions of the country could be quite severe (Lewandrowski and Schimmelpfennig 1999).

60. The flooding in Bangladesh, Central America, and China in 1998 prompted Argentina and Kazakhstan to call for a cap on developing countries' greenhouse gas emissions that would be incorporated into the Kyoto Agreement at the Buenos Aires meetings in November 1998.

61. Sims (1999) describes the regulatory problems confronting China.

62. Flavin 1997.

63. Prescott-Allen 1995.

64. Madeley 1995a.

65. Speech at the World Economic Forum 1999, quoted in the *New York Times*, February 7, 1999.

66. Hay and Shleifer 1998.

67. Root 1998.

68. Garrett 1998; Rodrik 1998b.

69. Alesina 1998.

70. Boniface 1998. However, Pegg (1999) argues that the likelihood of new states appearing is low. Regions within countries prefer autonomy to secession, and, as in the case of Somaliland, external recognition of sovereignty is granted reluctantly.

71. Panizza (1999) finds that fiscal decentralization is positively correlated with ethnic fractionalization and level of democracy (as well as with country size and per capita income).

72. IMF 1997, 1998c.

73. Wetzel and Dunn 1998.

74. Gavin and Perotti 1997.

75. Alesina and Spolaore 1997. The end of the Cold War and the social history of these countries largely explain the appearance of 22 new countries between 1991 and 1998.

76. Wiseman 1997.

77. Research suggests that the absence of any significant devolution of authority is related in part to the quality of governance at different levels (Huther and Shah 1998).

78. Shah 1997.

79. The future course of decentralization will depend upon the experiences with ongoing experimentation in countries with

both centralized and more diffuse political regimes (Willis, Garman, and Hoggard, 1999).

80. Tyler 1997.

81. A fairly typical study of a sample of municipalities in Latin America indicates that building the capacity of local organizations is a function of leadership and community participation (Fiszbein 1997).

82. Verdier 1998.

83. Brockerhoff and Brennan 1998.

84. Khilnani 1997.

85. Lloyd-Sherlock 1997. Although a current and reliable global headcount of the urban poor is unavailable for developing countries, scattered evidence suggests that the number is significantly higher than the estimated 300 million for 1988 (Haddad, Ruel, and Garrett 1998).

86. Bourguignon 1998; Fajnzylber, Lederman, and Louyza 1998.

87. Tonry 1997.

88. Caldeira 1996.

89. Szreter 1997.

90. World Bank 1979.

91. Begg 1999. Globalization and the advances in information technology sharpen the competition between cities.

92. Krugman (1998a) notes the neglect of spatial issues in economics texts. However, geographers have not neglected spatial issues and locational decisions. And during the 1960s and 1990s, economists made notable contributions to the field of urban development. But recent advances in economic modelling have raised the profile of urban economics and its importance to economists more generally (Boddy 1999; Martin 1999).

93. Scott 1976. Elster (1989) strikes a similar note when he discusses how social norms might be weakened in modern society because of mobility, the ephemeral nature of interaction, and the pace of change. Although the public provision of safety nets for the poor to replace informal kinship- or patron-based insurance schemes has been widely discussed, creating viable schemes is and will remain a considerable challenge.

94. Crystal 1997.

95. Satterthwaite 1996. Curitiba, Brazil, is a famous example of efficient transport planning and land use. But the virtual absence of other success stories is testimony to the difficulties confronting municipal regulatory agencies. Prudhomme and Lee (1998), show that urban sprawl and the speed with which trips can be made strongly affect the nature of the labor market.

96. An analysis of urban economic growth in Australia, measured by the increase in the price of labor, finds that growth is dependent on the quality of life, as reflected by the availability of community services, local administration, public amenities, the degree of congestion, and the initial level of human capital (Bradley and Gans 1998).

97. ILO 1998. See also Porter (1998).

98. Mani 1996.

99. Despite two decades of decentralization, urban authorities have only a meager amount to invest. Most are still largely dependent on national (or higher levels of subnational) governments and international agencies (Satterthwaite 1996).

100. Cohen 1998; Kremer 1993; ILO 1998.

101. Fujikura 1998. In order to act on environmental concerns, the community needs the support of laws and government regulations that provide access to information on pollution. Without such access, individuals, groups, and NGOs are handicapped. Even in the European Union and Japan, obtaining such information is often difficult, and the situation is much worse in developing countries (*New Scientist* 1998).

Chapter 2

1. Drabek and Laird 1998.

2. This is not to suggest that the WTO is the only international institution committed to facilitating the expansion of international trade. The International Monetary Fund and the World Bank share these goals and have designed programs to achieve them. These institutions are also taking steps to promote interagency coordination, including the formulation of a "coherence" approach to policymaking. The foundations of this approach are laid out in the "Report of the Managing Director of the International Monetary Fund, the President of the World Bank, and the Director General of the World Trade Organization on Coherence," October 2, 1998.

3. Srinivasan 1998. François, McDonald, and Nordström (1996) found that the static impact of the Uruguay Round on developing countries raised national incomes by 0.3 percent. Harrison, Rutherford, and Tarr (1996) found gains of 0.38 percent.

4. Foroutan 1996; Harrison 1994; Krishna and Mitra 1998; Levinsohn 1993. In contrast to evidence cited here, the impact of trade on firms' performance through economies of scale, external economies of scale, and learning by doing is relatively weak (see Tybout 1998).

5. Feenstra and others 1997.

6. Aw and Batra 1998; Clerides, Lach, and Tybout 1998.

7. See chapter 6; Fujita, Krugman, and Venables 1999; Glaeser 1998; Puga 1998; Venables 1998.

8. Quigley 1998.

9. Bolbol (1999), among others, points to the benefits for Arab countries of joining the rule-based WTO.

10. As of February 10, 1999. See the World Trade Organization's internet site *(www.wto.org)* for the latest information on membership.

11. Kleinknecht and der Wengel 1998.

12. See Frankel (1997). This result must be interpreted carefully, as increased interregional trade flows may have encouraged policymakers to sign the RTA, in turn generating more intraregional trade. The very fact that establishing causality is difficult gives some credence to the notion that RTAs are associated with greater interregional trade flows.

13. Rodrik 1994.

14. The nation named in the complaint can appeal the panel's decision, and the case moves to an appellate body for review.

15. Baldwin and Venables 1995.

16. See Finger and Schuknecht (1999) for evidence on the minuscule amount of textile liberalization that has occurred since the end of the Uruguay Round.

17. As could happen with measures justified on phytosanitary grounds. See Hertel, Bach, Dimaranan, and Martin (1996);

Hertel, Martin, Yanagishima, and Dimaranan (1996); Krueger (1998); Srinivasan (1998); Thomas and Whalley (1998); and Trela (1998).

18. Rodrik 1994.

19. Usually this compensation is in the form of enhanced access to other markets in the same economy, a practice that is likely to have detrimental effects on import-competing firms in those markets. Anticipating such compensation, these firms are likely to oppose businesses that favor reversing the reforms in the first place. And if a country reverses its reforms without offering compensation, it may well find itself a defendant in a complaint brought under the WTO's dispute settlement mechanism. Such a flagrant breach of WTO obligations is likely to result in sanctions against the offender, often in the form of reduced market access. Again, foreseeing this chain of events, the exporters will apply pressure not to reverse the reforms in the first place. In both cases, binding lower trade barriers into the country's WTO obligations sharpens the incentives of domestic parties who have an interest in preserving the improved access to domestic markets and signals to the private sector that the trade reforms are there to stay.

20. Finger and Winters 1998.

21. Fung and Ng 1998.

22. Keesing 1998.

23. Michalopoulos 1999; Short 1999.

24. For a careful study of the differential effects of trade flows on the concentrations of a number of pollutants, see Antweiler, Copeland, and Taylor (1998). See also box 4.7.

25. Feenstra 1998.

26. EBRD 1998.

27. These laws are sanctioned by a WTO agreement (Jackson 1997, 1998; Financial Times, "Developing World Leads in Anti-dumping." October 29, 1998).

28. For a series of case studies of the detrimental effects of antidumping actions see Finger (1993) and Lawrence (1998). The recent surge in antidumping cases in Europe and the United States against Asian steel producers highlights the effect antidumping laws can have on market access. As Asian countries try to stabilize their output levels, they find themselves faced with export restrictions that hinder their efforts. Tharakan (1999) presents proposals for the reform of antidumping laws, while Horlick and Sugarman (1999) offer proposals to reform the application of these laws to "nonmarket" economies.

29. Burtless and others 1998; Cohen, D. 1998; The Economist, 1999b; Hufbauer and Kotschwar 1998; Rodrik 1997, 1998a; Williamson 1998.

30. For a careful survey of this debate see Cline (1997). Anderson and Brenton (1998) offer a more recent analysis of the effect of trade and technology on income inequality in the United States.

31. Aghion and Williamson (1998) provide a conceptual and empirical analysis of the effect of globalization on income inequality and growth.

32. Prusa 1997.

33. For a recent survey of the costs of adjusting to trade reform see Matusz and Tarr (1998) and UNDP (1999).

34. Lawrence 1996.

35. Burtless and others 1998.

36. Graham 1996; Rodrik 1997.

37. Maskus 1997.

38. Countries are attaching increasing importance to the dispute settlement mechanisms. The substantial attention given to international trade disputes over imports of genetically modified foods, bananas, and beef into the European Union and magazine imports into Canada highlights this attention.

39. Ostry 1997, 1998.

40. Anderson (1999) provides a succinct account of these and other issues for trade reform.

41. Ryan (1998) provides an in-depth analysis of the intellectual property rights issue too.

42. Hoekman and Anderson 1999.

43. Josling 1998a, 1998b.

44. Laird 1997.

45. Josling 1998a.

46. Hoekman and Anderson 1999; Ingco and Ng 1998.

47. World Bank 1998o.

48. James and Anderson 1998; Roberts and DeRemer 1997.

49. However, this agreement has already come under pressure with disagreements between the European Union and the United States over genetically modified crops and food, in particular beef. Some have gone so far as to advocate banning international trade in genetically modified crops, in direct contravention of WTO rules. See Financial Times, "Genetically Modified Trade Wars." February 18, 1999, and The Economist (1999a).

50. Kerr (1999) assesses the prospects for future agricultural trade disputes, pointing to the increased burdens that they will place on the WTO's Dispute Settlement Mechanism.

51. For a recent analysis of the effects of introducing more competition into the maritime sector, see François and Wooton (1999).

52. Deardorff and others 1998. This potential development reinforces the argument that Western firms can expect to face growing competition from developing countries in most areas of international trade.

53. Cairncross 1997.

54. Hoekman and Djankov 1997b.

55. In addition to the traditional disciplines of most favored nation treatment and national treatment, there were disciplines on market access that in effect prohibited nations from using six particular restrictions on service suppliers. See Hoekman and Primo Braga (1997) for details.

56. Hoekman 1996.

57. Krueger 1998.

58. Negotiations in the telecommunications and financial service sectors have been completed since the signing of the Uruguay Round. While useful, sector-specific negotiations only permit countries to make trade-offs of commitments within each sector rather than across sectors, where the differences in national cost levels and the gains from liberalization are likely to be greater. See WTO (1998a) for an account of the financial services agreement concluded in December 1997.

59. For a qualitative discussion of the importance of these networks for trade see Krugman (1995), and Feenstra (1998). Hummels, Ishii, and Yi (1999) carefully document the rise of trade in vertically differentiated products. Deardorff (1998) pro-

vides a novel theoretical treatment of production fragmentation across borders.

60. Cairncross 1997.

61. Graham 1996.

62. UNCTAD 1997.

63. Yeats 1998.

64. For recent estimates of the effects of infrastructure and transportation on trade flows, see Bougheas, Demetriades, and Morgenroth (1999).

65. Graham 1996; Vernon 1998.

66. For an analysis of how corporate tax rates and rules on the repatriation of profits affect firms' location decisions, see Mutti and Grubert (1998).

67. Vernon 1998.

68. See chapters 6 and 7 for a more extensive discussion of urban issues.

Chapter 3

1. Bordo, Eichengreen, and Irwin 1999.

2. Recent evidence suggests that investors' appetite for high-risk investment vehicles remains strong. Despite the 1998 collapse of Long-Term Capital Management, which was at the heart of the hedge fund crisis, estimates show that the total amount invested in risky hedge funds in early 1999 was less than 2 percent lower than it was a year earlier. See *The Economist* (1999c).

3. This section draws on various editions of the IMF's *International Capital Markets*. Mussa and Richards (1999) present a detailed overview of the magnitude and composition of capital flows in the 1990s.

4. Foreign direct investment (FDI) involves investments in companies that account for more than 10 percent of the recipient company's assets. In contrast, foreign portfolio investment (FPI) refers to purchases of foreign liquid financial assets. In practice, the distinction is not clear cut, since financial transactions may involve elements of both. However, portfolio investment is presumed to have higher liquidity and to be more "footloose" than FDI. For a further discussion of the definition and measurement of foreign investment, see Lipsey (1999). FDI and FPI should not be confused with short-term borrowing from abroad.

5. See Eichengreen and Mussa (1998).

6. For a detailed account of the pace of capital account liberalization, see Quirk and Evans (1995) and recent editions of the IMF's *Annual Report on Exchange Rate Arrangements and Exchange Restrictions*.

7. This discussion of foreign direct investment draws on IFC (1998), Knight (1998), Mallampally and Sauvant (1999), and UNCTAD (1998).

8. The canonical survey on these issues is found in Caves (1996), chapter 7. See also Oxley and Yeung (1998).

9. UNCTAD 1998.

10. UNCTAD 1998.

11. Mallampally and Sauvant (1999) report that by 1997 there were 1,794 double-taxation treaties in effect.

12. UNCTAD 1996, 1998.

13. For a detailed analysis of the geographic distribution of foreign investment, see Lipsey (1999).

14. The case for liberalizing international capital flows was laid out succinctly by the IMF's Deputy Managing Director Stanley Fischer in a speech in September 1997. See "Financial Instability," *Oxford Analytica*, November 4, 1998. For a careful discussion of the effects of international capital mobility on the efficiency of the worldwide allocation of resources, see Cooper (1999).

15. World Bank 1998b.

16. This discussion draws on Caprio and Klingebiel (1996), Demirgüç-Kunt and Detragiache (1998), Eichengreen and Rose (1998), Goldstein (1998), Goldstein and Turner (1996), and World Bank (1998h).

17. Eichengreen 1999.

18. "Financial Instability," *Oxford Analytica*, November 4, 1998.

19. Eichengreen and Rose 1998.

20. Widespread borrowing is more likely when inadequate corporate governance systems undermine monitoring and other measures to restrict risk-taking.

21. Kaminsky and Reinhart 1998; Calvo 1999.

22. Goldstein and Hawkins 1998.

23. Radelet and Sachs 1998.

24. Leipziger 1998.

25. By extension, global contagion provides a rationale for global banking standards (Goldstein 1997).

26. Rodrik 1998c. However, the evidence presented in Quinn (1997) points to the positive effect of capital account liberalization on growth.

27. For a detailed analysis of the nature, causes, and consequences of financial contagion, see IMF (1999b). Evidence of the correlation between key financial variables, thought to be a central feature of contagion, is marshaled in Wolf (1999).

28. For a comprehensive list of all of the measures promoted to enhance the stability of the international financial system, see IMF (1999a).

29. The relative importance of capital markets and bank intermediation is determined in part by national policies. See Berthélemy and Varoudakis (1996).

30. Levine 1997, 1998.

31. Stiglitz 1999a.

32. Levine (1998) presents cross-country evidence of the importance of creditors' rights and other legal institutions in facilitating banking sector development. Demirgüç-Kunt and Detragiache (1998) find that the impact of domestic financial liberalization on the probability of a banking crisis is greater in nations with widespread corruption, inefficient bureaucracies, and little respect for the rule of law. See also G-22 Committee (1998b).

33. "Financial Infrastructure," *Oxford Analytica*, November 9, 1998.

34. Dewatripont and Tirole 1994.

35. Garcia 1996, 1998; Lindgren and Garcia 1996.

36. Kane 1998.

37. Litan 1998.

38. Calomiris 1997.

39. See G-22 Committee (1998a).

40. Krugman 1998b.

41. For an account of the difficulties caused by provincial banks in Argentina's bank crisis in 1995, see Leipziger (1998).

42. It has recently been argued that banking activities have become so complex that senior bank executives are unlikely to know (and in some cases to understand) the consequences of their employees' actions (*Financial Times*, "Too Much on Their Plate." February 4, 1999). Holders of subordinated debt may be similarly disadvantaged.

43. Evanoff 1998; Calomiris 1997, 1999.

44. Calomiris 1997.

45. *Financial Times*, "G7 Offers Shelter from Storm." February 22, 1999. The Group of Seven industrial nations set up a "financial stability forum" in February 1999 designed to strengthen surveillance and supervision of the international financial system. Central bankers, finance ministry officials, and supervisory officials will serve on this committee. Initially, members will come from Group of Seven countries.

46. Goldstein 1997, 1998. High capital requirements come at a cost—the opportunity cost of forgone lending that lower capital requirements could sustain.

47. For an extensive discussion of the pros and cons of the admission of foreign banks, see Caprio (1998). See also Calomiris 1999 and EBRD 1998.

48. Claessens, Demirgüç-Kunt, and Huizinga 1998.

49. Hellman, Murdock, and Stiglitz 1998; Stiglitz 1999a.

50. Peek and Rosengren 1997.

51. World Bank 1998h; Eichengreen 1998, 1999; Eichengreen and Mussa 1998; Johnston, Darbar, and Echeverria 1997; McKinnon 1991.

52. Harwood 1997; Johnston 1997.

53. A theoretical and emprical analysis by Rodrik and Velasco (1999) concludes that measures to restrict short-term borrowing are desirable.

54. Feldstein 1999; Eichengreen and Mussa 1998; McKinnon and Pill 1998.

55. Two recent studies of the East Asian and Latin American experience with capital controls are broadly supportive of their use (Le Fort and Budnevich 1998; Park and Song 1998). Dornbusch (1998) explores the pros and cons of various restrictions on capital inflows, pointing out situations in which such controls improve economic performance.

56. Caprio 1998; Eichengreen 1998. In 1997 Malaysia introduced controls on both short-term capital inflows and certain capital outflows. Although it is too soon to determine the overall impact of these measures, since 1997 foreign direct investment in Malaysia has not been affected any more adversely than in neighboring countries that did not impose controls.

57. Johnston, Darbar, and Echeverria 1997; Reinhart and Reinhart 1998; Velasco and Cabezas 1998; United Kingdom 1998; *Oxford Analytica*, "Financial Regulation." December 29, 1998.

58. An alternative is to permanently raise reserve requirements on foreign deposits or capital adequacy requirements on foreign borrowings.

59. The evidence in Edwards (1998a) suggests that these controls had a temporary effect on interest rate differentials between Chile and overseas markets. For information on Chilean capital controls, see Chumacero, Laban, and Larrain (1996); Cooper (1999); Eichengreen and Fishlow (1998); Hernández and Schmidt-Hebbel (1999); and Valdes-Prieto and Soto (1996). For a critical survey of the effects of capital controls, see Dooley (1996).

60. Baliño, Bennett, and Borensztein (1999).

61. For a lengthy discussion of the effects of dollarization on developing countries, see Baliño, Bennett, and Borensztein (1999).

62. Such a run might be caused by an increase in foreign interest rates.

63. Calomiris (1999) has proposed changing the IMF's role to include a discount window lending facility that would provide liquidity to qualified countries. See also Feldstein (1999).

64. The need for interventions can be seen in another way. Recent studies have suggested that the best predictor of a crisis is the ratio of short-term foreign indebtedness to reserves. Thus, if a firm borrows more short-term money abroad, its government—if it wishes to maintain a prudential stance—must set aside more funds in reserves, typically holding these reserves as U.S. Treasury bills or similar instruments from other industrial economies.

65. Eichengreen 1998.

66. Borensztein, De Gregorio, and Lee 1998; UNCTAD 1998. Of course, foreign direct investment is not the only source of technology transfer—patent licensing schemes were used in Korea and Japan in the early stages of the countries' development. See Kim and Ma (1997).

67. Wacziarg 1998.

68. Borensztein, De Gregorio, and Lee 1998.

69. Berthélemy, Dessus, and Varoudakis 1997.

70. De Mello 1997.

71. This evidence is taken from Kozul-Wright and Rowthorn (1998).

72. Kinoshita and Mody 1997.

73. De Mello 1997.

74. Kozul-Wright and Rowthorn 1998.

75. See Moran (1999) for detailed case studies of each of these policy instruments. Moran did find that information dissemination and purely promotional initiatives by developing countries are effective tools for boosting foreign direct investment.

76. Gastanaga, Nugent, and Pashamova 1998.

77. World Bank 1997d.

78. Vernon 1998.

79. *Oxford Analytica*, "Energy Investment." February 1, 1996.

80. Blomström and Kokko 1997.

81. Claessens and Rhee 1994; Demirgüç-Kunt and Levine 1995; Levine and Zervos 1998a.

82. Levine 1997; Levine and Zervos 1998a, 1998b.

83. Saudagaran and Diga 1997.

84. Levine 1997, 1999. Strong shareholder rights may also play a role in reducing excess short-term foreign borrowing by company managers.

85. Bryant 1995; Eichengreen and Kenen 1994; Sachs and McKibbin 1991.

86. Rajan 1998.

87. ADBI 1998.

88. Rajan 1998.

89. Bergsten 1998.

Chapter 4

1. World Bank 1992b.
2. Pearce and others 1996.
3. World Bank 1998g.
4. Antarctica Project 1999.
5. Watson and others 1998.
6. Imber 1996; Porter and others 1998.
7. Grossman and Krueger 1995.
8. For information on Kazakhstan and Uzbekistan, see World Bank (1998l). For China, see Chinese State Council (1994). Since 1994 senior Chinese officials have reiterated their concerns about environmental issues, and the government has invested considerable resources in protecting air and water. But much remains to be done (see World Bank 1997a). Agenda 21, the principal agreement to emerge from the Rio Earth Summit, committed national leaders to action programs organized under the following six themes: quality of life, efficient use of natural resources, protection of the global commons, management of human settlements, waste management, and sustainable economic growth. See Flavin (1997) and World Bank (1997b).
9. Wapner 1995; Zurn 1998.
10. Cesar 1998.
11. Below-market sales of timber concessions constitute another subsidy that affects the rate of deforestation. In 1990 the Indonesian government sold timber concessions at prices far below prevailing market prices, capturing only 17 percent of the value of the trees and costing the treasury more than $2.1 billion in forgone revenue. By contrast, the Brazilian government's decision in 1988 to cancel tax credits for ranchers who cleared land slowed deforestation in the Amazon significantly—and saved the government money. Subsidies for building roads affect deforestation because access roads markedly increase the probability that a forest will be converted to agricultural use. Chapter 5 discusses the complexities of government support for infrastructure investments, but one thing that is clearly important is to take the environmental impact of such decisions into account (Roodman 1997).
12. Eskeland and Feyzioglu 1994.
13. Anderson and McKibbin 1997.
14. The transition economies of Eastern Europe and Asia have shown that it is politically possible to phase out these subsidies fairly rapidly. China's subsidies for coal, which is the source of 70 percent of the country's energy, fell from 61 to 11 percent over 1984–95, cutting government costs from $25 billion in 1990–91 to $10 billion in 1995–96 (Watson and others 1998).
15. World Bank 1998f. More recent estimates from Malawi suggest that middle-income customers may receive as much as $180 in annual subsidies.
16. Roodman 1997.
17. World Bank 1996a.
18. It should be noted that poorly maintained diesel buses can be a serious source of pollutants. Even so, making the switch from private cars to buses nearly always reduces urban air pollution dramatically. In Mexico City, for example, taking a bus instead of driving a car equipped with a catalytic converter reduces nitrogen oxide emissions by 40 percent per passenger-mile, hydrocarbon emissions by 95 percent, and carbon monoxide emissions by 98 percent. If the car does not have a converter, the reductions are even greater (Ornusal and Gautam 1997).
19. See Goulder (1994), however, who suggests that carbon taxes would not be efficient in the United States because they would be likely to replace income taxes—which are even more broadly based.
20. World Bank 1999d.
21. Elster 1988; Schlicht 1985.
22. Madeley 1995b.
23. de Fontaubert 1996.
24. Peterson 1993.
25. Rose and Crane 1995.
26. French 1997; Ornusal and Gautam 1997.
27. Chomitz and Kumari 1998.
28. Lampietti and Dixon 1995. Clearly, these numbers are very rough estimates that will vary dramatically from forest to forest.
29. Perrings 1995.
30. Lampietti and Dixon 1995. It should be noted that these species were all "prominent"—grizzly bears, whooping cranes, and bald eagles—rather than different types of beetle.
31. World Bank 1998g; Porter and others 1998. GEF funding for ozone projects amounted to nearly $126 million by mid-1999, according to World Bank sources.
32. The Kyoto meeting is officially termed the Third Conference of the Parties to the United Nations Framework Convention on Climate Change.
33. No limits on emissions in developing countries (other than the economies in transition) were set at the Kyoto meeting.
34. However, the ozone hole over Antarctica continues to grow (*The Sciences* 1997).
35. WRI 1998.
36. French 1997; Miller 1995.
37. Seaver 1997.
38. Barrett 1998a, 1998b.
39. French 1997.
40. UNEP 1999.
41. Barrett 1998a, 1998b.
42. Sell 1996; Seaver 1997.
43. Sell 1996.
44. Sell 1996.
45. Seaver 1997.
46. World Bank 1998m.
47. Barkin and Shambaugh 1996.
48. Miller 1995.
49. Barrett 1998a, 1998b.
50. Barrett 1998a, 1998b.
51. Seaver 1997.
52. Pearce and others 1996.
53. Hourcade 1996.
54. Sell 1996.
55. Roodman 1997.
56. The United States is only indicative of a wider trend; public sector energy R&D expenditure fell sixfold in the United Kingdom and fourfold in Germany and Italy between 1984 and 1994 (President's Committee of Advisors on Science and Technology Panel on Energy Research and Development 1997).

57. To enforce an agreement, whether based on taxes or on quotas, it might be necessary to charge offsetting, or even punitive, charges on imports from countries that have failed to make or live up to commitments for greenhouse gas reductions. This suggests the possible use of fines (such as those contemplated in the European Union for violations of the fiscal stabilization pact) or economic sanctions. But it would be difficult to deny imports related to greenhouse gas emissions without, in effect, prohibiting trade with the offending country, since carbon dioxide–producing energy is required for virtually all production. Calculating the optimal punitive tariff also turns out to be very complex, and present multilateral trade rules do not allow trade restrictions based on how a product was made. As mentioned earlier, the credibility of trade sanctions is strongly linked with the costs and benefits of treaty compliance, and in this case many countries might find their costs of imposing sanctions to be larger than the benefits of enforcing treaty compliance (Stiglitz 1997; Barrett 1998c; World Bank 1998d).

58. Sell 1996.

59. Stiglitz 1997.

60. World Bank 1998d.

61. Cooper 1998.

62. Stiglitz 1997.

63. World Bank 1998k.

64. Trading mechanisms are not free from controversy. At Kyoto some developing countries opposed trading, seeing it as a mechanism for wealthy countries to buy their way out of emissions restrictions and transfer those limits to poor countries, where such limits would interfere with development (Anderson 1998).

65. World Bank 1998d.

66. Watson and others 1998.

67. Calculated from World Bank (1999i). This is clearly a poor way to measure stocks of biodiversity. Many of these plants and animals will be present in more than one country, and many of the animals are not threatened with extinction. The point remains, however, that the majority of species left on the planet resides in developing countries.

68. Heywood 1995.

69. Madeley 1995a.

70. Miller 1995.

71. Simpson, Sedjo, and Reid 1996.

72. The convention contains only vague language on payment for genetic resources. Article 15 states that contracting parties will share in "a fair and equitable way the results of research and development and the benefits arising from commercial and other utilization of genetic resources . . . [on] mutually agreed terms," without defining a framework for the terms or the words "fair and equitable." Industrial countries have encouraged the notion that biodiversity is a global good that should not be assigned to nations as property, while at the same time arguing that companies should be able to patent products they develop from plants and animals. Without some kind of reform, resource transfers for such drugs will continue to run from developing to industrial countries rather than the other way. Despite the value of the drugs developed from the rosy periwinkle, for instance, Madagascar still receives nothing in royalty pay-

ments—although it should be noted that this situation developed before the Rio Convention (Munson 1995; Miller 1995).

73. Sell 1996.

74. Miller 1995.

75. Simpson, Sedjo, and Reid 1996. This figure is low. While many thousands, if not millions, of species are represented in each hectare, dividing the total number of endemic species types by the total number of hectares in western Ecuador produces a small number of endemic species per hectare.

76. Regional agreements (such as the Joint Comprehensive Environmental Action Program for the Baltic, which supports information flows, technical assistance, and environmental funding) can also play an important role in preserving genetic biodiversity and habitats (Freestone 1999).

77. Charnovitz 1996.

78. Freestone and Makuch 1998.

79. Charnovitz 1996.

80. Charnovitz 1996.

81. *The Economist* 1998d; Howse and Trebilcock 1996.

82. Howse and Trebilcock 1996.

83. In Costa Rica there is evidence that species in high-altitude forests are dying out because climate change is lifting cloud cover above the forests (see, for example, Holmes 1999).

84. Watson and others 1998.

85. Watson and others 1998.

86. WRI 1998.

87. World Bank 1998e.

88. This program falls under the auspices of the Kyoto Protocol's Clean Development Mechanism.

89. Goodman 1998.

Chapter 5

1. Subnational elections are held in 71 out of 75 multiparty democracies for which data were available. The total number of multiparty democracies in the world, as classified by Freedom House, is 117. See appendix table A.1 for details on decentralization and Freedom House (1998) for multiparty democracy classification.

2. Decentralization and devolution are used synonymously throughout the chapter.

3. Smith 1996. See also Dahl (1986) and Stepan (1999) on the relation between democracy and decentralization. In a strict sense, only a constitutional democracy can credibly guarantee that the prerogatives of subunits will be respected.

4. Treisman 1998.

5. Hommes 1996.

6. Litvack 1994.

7. Musgrave and Musgrave 1973; Oates 1972; Tiebout 1956.

8. Ostrom, Schroeder, and Wynne 1993.

9. Junaid Ahmad contributed to the writing of this box, which is also based on Ablo and Reinikka (1998) and a note by Paul Smoke.

10. Breton 1996.

11. A number of studies are available, though they tend to focus on a particular sector within a country (King and Ozler 1998; Ablo and Reinikka 1998) or a particular tier of government within a country (Faguet 1998; World Bank 1995b).

They all support the notion that the consequences of decentralization depend on the way it is designed and implemented.

12. King and Ozler 1998.

13. Burki, Perry, and Dillinger 1999.

14. Litvack, Ahmad, and Bird 1998.

15. Ahmad and Craig 1997.

16. Local governments generally have access to a more complete set of information about both the population's preferences and their own resources and performance. This information gives local authorities an advantage in delivering the appropriate mix of services. But the fact that the central government may not share this information complicates the task of monitoring the local government's performance and establishing the true need for financial assistance. For a discussion of these issues and the means of overcoming them, see Ravallion (1999a, 1999b) and Burgess (1998).

17. Bird and Rodriguez 1999.

18. Ahmad and Craig 1997.

19. For means of resolving this issue, see Ravallion (1999b).

20. Ravallion 1999a.

21. Ravallion 1999b.

22. Alderman 1998.

23. World Bank 1999h.

24. Ravallion 1999b.

25. Faguet 1998.

26. Tanzi 1996.

27. China, which is neither wealthy nor a federation, is a notable exception. Subnational entities are responsible for a large share of the tax collection and for expenditures (box 5.5). Comparable data from China were not available for figures 5.1 and 5.2.

28. Gavin and Perotti 1997 (Latin America); McKinnon 1997 (United States); Spahn 1998 (Western Europe). For further discussions of macroeconomic stability and decentralization, see Fornasari, Webb, and Zou (1999); McLure (1999); Prud'homme (1995); Sewell (1996); Shah (1998); Tanzi (1996); and Wildasin (1997). For a discussion on decentralization and growth, see Davoodi and Zou (1998); Xie, Zou, and Davoodi (1999). For the relation between decentralization and the size of government see Jin and Zou (1998); Persson and Tabellini (1994); Quigley and Rubinfeld (1997). For an overall review of decentralization and growth see Martinez-Vasquez and McNab (1997).

29. de Figueiredo and Weingast 1998.

30. Linz and Stepan 1997; Elster and Slagsrad 1993.

31. Weingast 1995.

32. In "bottom-up federations" like the European Union and the United States, the constituent members decide upon the initial set of rules. Such federations tend to generate a much weaker center than top-down ones. See de Figueiredo and Weingast (1998).

33. Ordeshook and Shvetsova 1997.

34. This box is based on Bahl (1999b); Lall and Hofman (1994); Qian and Weingast (1997); Wong (1998); World Bank (1995a). *The Washington Post*, February 27, 1999, reported in "China Praises Sichuan Election" on the local election that took place in Buyun (Sichuan Province) after the people there had forced the township's leader out of office for governing badly.

The article also reported that similar protests against corrupt or abusive officials were occurring around the country. Information on corruption is from the *Financial Times*, March 5, 1999, "Officials Arrested over Chinese Fraud Scandal" and "Tentacles of Corruption May Threaten the State."

35. Public spending has been found to be biased in favor of the least populous regions in Brazil and Argentina, which have territorial representation in both houses. In contrast, public spending per capita does not vary significantly across Mexican and U.S. states, where territorial representation is applied only to the Senate (Gibson, Calvo, and Falleti 1999).

36. This was also the practice in the United States until 1913 and in Argentina until 1994.

37. In Brazil, for example, it is estimated that roughly 40 percent of senators have been governors and that many senators aspire to be governors. Further, in the 1991–94 legislature, approximately 35 percent of the sitting deputies exhibited a preference or actually gave up their seat for a state-level post. In this context, national parliamentarians are more likely to care about pleasing their constituents and the governor of their state than about the national good (Stepan 1999).

38. Ordeshook and Shvetsova 1997.

39. In contrast, plurality or first-past-the-post systems virtually guarantee parliamentary majorities (Lijphart 1994).

40. Carey 1997. Even when coalition partners have enough power to block change, they may not have enough leverage to effect positive change on their own (Alesina and Perotti 1997; Roubini and Sachs 1989). Evidence for both Latin America and Europe shows that the central government's ability to respond decisively to shocks, restrain expenditures, and contain the size of government is lower in countries with proportional representation. In Europe, however, budgetary rules seem to help overcome these problems (Hallerberg and von Hagen 1997; Stein, Talvi, and Grisanti 1998).

41. Gamble and others 1992. See Lijphart (1994) for a full discussion.

42. Lijphart 1994.

43. This section is based on Ordeshook and Shvetsova (1997).

44. For a discussion of this point in the Latin American context, see Willis, Garman, and Haggard (1999).

45. In Yugoslavia, the first competitive elections were held at the subnational level and were won by regional and ethnic nationalist parties. The civil wars occurred before there was a nationwide election. In the founding election in Nigeria in 1959, there were virtually no elected representatives of nationwide parties, a situation that directly contributed to the escalation of ethnic tensions and the civil war over the Biafran secessionist attempt (Stepan 1999).

46. The integration of party structures can be built into the political system in a variety of ways. In Germany, for example, the upper house, which represents subnational interests, has very limited powers. But half of the lower house is elected with the use of regional lists that are controlled by the same parties that elect candidates to Länder (state) positions (Ordeshook and Shvetsova 1997).

47. Oates 1972; Tiebout 1956; Musgrave and Musgrave 1973.

48. Donahue 1997.

49. Musgrave 1997.

50. Hemming and Spahn 1998.

51. This model is the traditional Tiebout (1956) one of "voice" and "exit."

52. For a discussion of these assumptions and their relevance to the fiscal federalist model, see Oates (1998).

53. Manning 1998; Fay and others 1998.

54. Wetzel and Dunn 1998.

55. The number of school districts in the United States decreased markedly in the 1950s as jurisdictions tried to put together groups of students large enough to run grade-differentiated primary schools. Germany has reduced the number of municipalities (Gemeinden) by half. The United Kingdom has eliminated a tier of subnational government in Scotland, Wales, and the metropolitan areas of England. With the exception of France, the lowest tier of subnational government in large OECD countries has an average population of about 5,000–7,000. In Japan, however, this figure can run as high as 39,000, and in the United Kingdom, it can reach 109,000.

56. Vaillancourt 1998.

57. The number of municipios in Brazil increased from 3,000 to nearly 5,000 in the 15 years following the return of democracy. The new constitution of the Philippines recognizes not only 1,605 cities and municipalities but also nearly 42,000 neighborhood organizations (barangays) as units of local government.

58. For a discussion of these trade-offs in the context of the European Union, see Alesina and Wacziarg (1998).

59. Diamond 1999.

60. See Wildasin (1997) for a further discussion on the topic.

61. The property tax is potentially one of the best sources of revenues for local governments. For a discussion of problems and possible reforms of the property tax, see Dillinger (1992).

62. For further discussion of subnational tax reform see Bahl and Linn (1992), Bird (1999), McLure (1999), Norregaard (1997), and Vehorn and Ahmad (1997). See also Bird, Ebel, and Wallich (1995) and Bird and Vaillancourt (1999) for country-specific examples and Inman and Rubinfeld (1996) for a more theoretical treatment.

63. The Scandinavian countries, which have allocated substantial taxing powers to their local governments, are a rare exception. See Litvack, Ahmad, and Bird (1998).

64. Diamond 1999.

65. This section is largely based on Bahl and Linn (1992).

66. This box is based on McLure (1999); Bird and Gendron (1997); and Inman and Rubinfeld (1996). For a discussion of subnational VATs see Bird and Gendron (1997).

67. Bahl and Linn 1992; Bahl 1999a.

68. See Ter-Minassian and Craig (1997) for a more detailed discussion.

69. Ter-Minassian and Craig 1997.

70. In the United States, states that have formal controls on borrowing have lower debt levels on average (Poterba 1994) but they are equally prone to serious fiscal crisis (Von Hagen 1991). In addition, these controls are self-imposed and not the result of federal government mandates—that is, they have been voluntarily written by state assemblies into state constitutions rather than imposed by the central government.

71. Stotsky and Sunley 1997.

72. In the United Kingdom each municipal council has the authority to set its salary scales, but 90 percent of them participate in collective bargaining with the national public employees' union. In Germany subnational governments are required by statute to adhere to agreements negotiated jointly with the federal government and public employees unions.

73. Smith 1996. More generally, the expected payoffs affect participation. Individuals must believe that the benefits they will receive will exceed the costs of their time, labor, and money (Hirschman 1970; North 1990; Ostrom, Schroeder, and Wynne 1993).

74. Galeotti 1992.

75. Bridges 1997; Hawley 1970.

76. Poterba 1994.

77. Dahl 1971.

78. Stren 1998.

79. The 1994 Popular Participation Law formalized the role of community organizations as watchdogs at the municipal level, granting them the right to report suspected wrongdoing to the Senate (Campbell 1998).

80. Tendler 1997; Vivian 1994; Zaidi 1999.

81. World Bank 1992a.

82. O'Donnell, Schmitter, and Whitehead 1986.

83. Wiseman 1997.

84. Boeninger 1992; Przeworski and Limongi 1997.

85. Diamond 1996.

86. Bird and Vaillancourt 1999.

87. Dillinger and Webb 1999a.

88. Under the revised local government code effective in 1992, central government agencies were required to transfer to subnational units specific activities (including agricultural extension, forest management, local hospital operations, primary health care programs, local roads, water supply, and communal irrigation infrastructure). To finance these costs local governments received a larger share of national tax revenues. In the first year of implementation, the code required the central government to provide funds to cover the cost of personnel devolved to the local governments in addition to the increase in revenue sharing.

89. A number of countries seem to be faring reasonably well, but none has emerged as an unmitigated success.

Chapter 6

1. Hohenberg 1998.

2. Glaeser and Rappaport 1998.

3. Richardson (1987) provides evidence from Brazil, France, Peru, and the United States on the high cost of city living.

4. Shukla 1996.

5. Mazumdar 1986; Mills and Becker 1986.

6. Krugman 1993; Quigley 1998.

7. Dumais, Ellison, and Glaeser 1997; Glaeser 1997; Jaffe, Trajtenberg, and Henderson 1993.

8. Henderson 1998; Henderson, Lee, and Lee 1998.

9. Lucas 1998.

10. Brown and McCalla 1998.

11. Rousseau 1995; Thomas 1980.

12. Ades and Glaeser 1995.

13. Gertler 1997.

14. Yeates 1997.

15. Black and Henderson 1998.

16. Gaspar and Glaeser 1998.

17. Choe and Kim 1999.

18. UNCHS 1996.

19. Tarver 1995.

20. Lucas 1998; Mills 1998; Tacoli 1998.

21. Henderson 1998.

22. Head and Ries 1995.

23. Ades and Glaeser 1995.

24. Henderson and Kuncoro 1996.

25. Gertler 1997.

26. This calculation assumes per capita costs of $150 for water, $300 for sewers. It also assumes that 30 percent of the urban population has no access to potable water and that 40 percent lack access to sewers. GDP figure from World Bank (1998l).

27. Mayo and Angel 1993.

28. Mohan 1999.

29. The subject of local tax revenue sources is beyond the scope of the WDR. A key reference is Bahl and Linn (1992). Property taxes remain the key revenue source for many cities because they are relatively easy to collect, although collections are often incomplete and discriminatory. In theory land taxation is a nondistortionary source of funding, but in practice assessing pure land values is difficult. All land has been improved to some degree, tempting governments to overassess.

30. Dailami and Leipziger 1998.

31. AB Assesores 1998; Freire, Huertas, and Darche 1998.

32. Peterson and Hammam 1997.

33. Peterson and Hammam 1997; Dailami and Leipziger 1998.

34. Private communication with S. Mayo (Lincoln Institute), 1998.

35. Colgan 1995.

36. Colgan 1995.

37. Markusen 1998.

38. Miranda and Rosdil 1995; Bradbury, Kodrzycki, and Tannenwald 1997.

39. ILO 1998.

40. Markusen 1998.

41. Bertaud and others 1997.

42. Cour 1998a.

43. Cour 1998b.

Chapter 7

1. World Bank 1994.

2. Upward mobility in Karachi, Pakistan, is discussed in Altaf and others (1993). A case study of Karachi is presented in chapter 8.

3. Kessides 1998; Evans 1998.

4. Brown and McCalla 1998.

5. Douglass 1992.

6. WRI 1996. An earlier WHO study (1986) estimated the reduction at 40–50 percent.

7. WHO 1995.

8. Chhabra and others 1998.

9. WRI 1996.

10. WRI-WHO 1999.

11. World Bank 1994.

12. WRI 1996.

13. UNDP 1998.

14. World Bank 1997a.

15. WRI 1996; Harpham and Tanner 1995. For recent evidence on urban differentials in the United States, see Claudio and others (1999).

16. WRI 1996; Haddad, Ruel, and Garrett 1999.

17. Other determinants are important as well, including cultural and political alienation, ethnic conflicts, and media violence. See also Bourguignon (1998).

18. Zaidi 1998.

19. Bourguignon 1998. A recent estimate for South Africa places the costs of crime and violence at 6 percent (at least) of the country's GDP (*Business Times*, February 14, 1999).

20. World Bank 1994.

21. Rosen 1993.

22. Rosen 1993.

23. In many cities (Bogotá, Karachi, Manila, and Taipei, for instance) the rich remain vulnerable to crime and kidnappings. Even the most stringent security measures are unable to guarantee personal safety. See Simon Romero, "Cashing in on Security Worries," *The New York Times,* July 24, 1999.

24. G. Shah 1997.

25. Chaplin 1999.

26. Tynan and Cowen 1998.

27. Foreman-Peck and Millward 1994.

28. Anderson 1988.

29. Shugart 1997.

30. *Financial Times*, April 29, 1999.

31. A report issued by the French Auditor's Office (Cour des Comptes) for the water and wastewater sector in January 1997 reported a lack of transparency in a number of instances and found that in some cases private participants appeared to be preventing good information from reaching elected officials. The report did conclude that water services overall were delivered satisfactorily. See Shugart (1997) for a discussion.

32. "Gestion de l'eau: renégociations en chaîne des contrats avec les groupes privés," *Les Echos*, March 25, 1999.

33. Pirez 1998.

34. Quoted in Root (1998).

35. See chapter 8 for a case study of Karachi.

36. Hardoy and Satterthwaite 1990.

37. Campbell 1998; Stren 1998.

38. Root 1998.

39. Harpham and Stuttaford 1999.

40. Mayo and Angel 1993.

41. Hasan 1997a; Leitman and Baharoglu 1998; Lloyd-Sherlock 1997.

42. Espinosa and López Rivera 1994; UNCHS 1996; World Bank 1996b.

43. Buckley and Mayo 1989; UNCHS 1996. Although the UN strategy formally endorsed the enabling approach, strong advocates appeared much earlier. The 1979 *World Development Report* proposed an urban housing strategy for developing countries that would focus on encouraging the private sector to improve the housing supply (World Bank 1979).

44. Reforms should include the following: developing property rights and expanding land registration, streamlining the regulatory process and regulations to reduce housing costs, encouraging greater competition in housing construction, providing trunk infrastructure at full cost recovery, fostering the development of mortgage financing systems, and, particularly, improving access to credit and targeting subsidies (Mayo and Angel 1993; UNCHS 1996).

45. Strong, Reiner, and Szyrmer 1996; Struyk 1997.

46. Gilbert and Gugler 1992; Hasan 1997a.

47. WRI 1996.

48. Whittington, Lauria, and Mu 1991.

49. *The Wall Street Journal,* "Populist Perrier? Nestle Pitches Bottled Water to World's Poor." June 18, 1999.

50. Atlaf 1994a.

51. Altaf 1994b.

52. World Bank 1994.

53. Solo 1999.

54. Porter 1996; Cowen and Tynan 1999.

55. Porter 1996.

56. World Bank 1993a.

57. Porter 1996.

58. Blackett 1994; World Bank 1994; WRI 1996.

59. On condominial sewers, see Watson (1995) and World Bank (1992b). But because households often convert from dry latrines to pour-flush systems without connecting to proper drain fields, these systems may discharge into open street drains. Such patterns have been documented in Gujranwala, Pakistan; Kumasi, Ghana; and Ouagadougou, Burkina Faso. See Altaf (1994a); Altaf and Hughes (1994); Whittington and others (1993).

60. Hasan 1998.

61. Ingram 1998.

62. Kitano 1998.

63. Rabinovitch 1992; WRI 1996.

64. Copenhagen is an example of a city that has reduced automobile dependency by revitalizing downtown housing and street life and restricting parking in the city center. Freiburg's improvements to public transport have focused on extending and upgrading its light rail system, which uses buses as feeders. Perth has had limited success trying to discourage automobile use by integrating bus services with the newly constructed electric rail system. See UNCHS (1996).

65. WRI 1996.

66. Burgess 1999; Frigenti and Harth 1998; Graham 1994.

67. Haddad, Ruel, and Garrett 1999.

68. World Bank 1999e.

69. Mitlin and Satterthwaite 1998.

70. UNCHS 1996.

71. Douglass 1992; Evans 1998.

72. Japan's neighborhood police stations, or *kobans*, provide a model of effective community policing. A vast network of community-based crime control organizations operating in neighborhoods, schools, and workplaces is credited with reducing crime rates in Japan, which are very low and falling. The Crime Prevention Associations have 540,000 local liaison units. Officers are required to visit every family and business in their neighborhoods at least twice a year and to provide many community services, such as helping to organize newsletters, meetings, and sports events. The koban system is highly effective in crime control: in 1989 koban officers were responsible for 73 percent of all arrests and 76 percent of all the theft cases that were solved. See Zaidi (1998).

73. Ayres 1997.

74. Hasan 1998.

75. Conger 1999.

76. Participatory budgeting has also been introduced in cities in Mexico and Venezuela. See Campbell (1998) and Coelho (1996).

77. World Bank 1992a.

78. Anderson 1998.

79. Fujikura 1999.

80. Afsah, Laplante, and Wheeler 1997.

Chapter 8

1. Hoekman and Djankov 1996.

2. World Bank 1998c.

3. Egypt benefited significantly from its participation in the Gulf War (1990–91) and subsequently received substantial debt relief from the United States and others.

4. World Bank 1998c.

5. Hoekman and Djankov 1997a; World Bank 1998c.

6. Kenny 1999.

7. Hoekman, Konan, and Maskus 1998.

8. Konan and Maskus 1997.

9. Hoekman and Konan 1999.

10. EBRD 1998.

11. Long and Kopanyi 1998; Vittas and Neal 1992.

12. Abel and Szakadat 1997–98.

13. Long and Kopanyi 1998.

14. Calomiris 1997.

15. Souza 1996.

16. Mendes 1999.

17. The state governments are assigned a value-added tax (VAT), which they assess and collect directly. As the highest-yielding revenue source in Brazil, the VAT gives the states an independent power base, particularly in the wealthy southeast, where it is the principal source of state revenues.

18. Afonso 1992; Rezende 1995.

19. Mainwaring 1997.

20. Two of the 26 states, Bahia and Ceará, have since undertaken substantial adjustment and reform. See Dillinger and Webb (1999).

21. Dillinger 1997.

22. After the plan was introduced in mid-1994, annual inflation (as measured by the INPC index) fell from 929 percent in 1994 to 22 percent in 1995, 9 percent in 1996, 4.3 percent in 1997, and 2.5 percent in 1998.

23. Ter-Minassian and Craig 1997.

24. An option worth exploring is prohibiting all government lending to subnational governments. Argentina and Colombia, for example, leave subnational financing entirely to the private sector; a practice that so far has forestalled any claims for federal debt relief.

25. The case study is based on Hasan, Zaidi, and Younus 1998.

26. Mahmood 1999.

27. Zaidi 1997.

28. Hasan 1997b.

29. World Bank 1999j. Food processing, beverage preparation, and trading activities have begun to multiply in the periurban villages, helping to supplement household incomes (Baker 1999).

30. Brautigam 1997.

31. World Bank 1999j.

32. Lele and Christiansen 1989. Only 20 percent of farmland in Tanzania is in farm blocks of more than 10 hectares. In Kenya 43 percent of farmland is in units of over 200 hectares (Tomich, Kilby, and Johnston 1995).

33. Buckley 1997.

34. EIU 1998.

35. Carr 1993. More generally in Tanzania, food crops are still given priority over cash crops because of the fear that it will be impossible to sell cash crops and buy food at the end of the growing season.

36. On average, Sub-Saharan African countries pay freight charges on their exports that are 20 percent higher than those paid by exporters in East Asia. Additional costs abound in Tanzania because of delays in customs clearance, inefficient cargo handling facilities, and high forwarding charges (Hertel, Masters, and Elbehri 1998). The building of a cargo center with refrigeration facilities at Nairobi's Jomo Kenyatta Airport will provide the capacity for handling 160,000 tons per year of horticultural and other produce. This will be helpful for Tanzanian producers, but more capacity at Arusha's airport or at Dar es Salaam might be more advantageous (*Financial Times*, "Kenyan Air Cargo Capacity Boosted." June 2, 1999).

37. Islam 1997.

38. Gautam and Anderson 1998.

39. Tendler 1997.

40. The contrast with East Asia is instructive. In China's Fujian and Guandong provinces as well as in Taiwan (China), the "relational networks" created in the hinterland of towns have served as the basis of highly successful industrial clusters that make effective use of subcontracting arrangements and reach out to international markets. See Hayami (1998) and the discussion in chapter 1.

41. After reviewing constraints on growth in the manufacturing sector, Tybout (1998) concludes that the primary problems revolve around uncertainty about policies and demand, weak laws, and corruption.

42. Transparency International 1998.

43. Bennell 1997.

44. Yudkin 1999; *Nature* 1999.

45. Cole and Phelan (1999) associate the research output of a country with its wealth and with the number of research scientists, but also with a culture that attaches a high value to scientific achievement and with competition among universities to attract talent of the highest caliber.

46. See Wambugu (1999) and Lipton (1999). Between 1994 and 1998, the acreage devoted to transgenic crops worldwide rose from 4 million acres to 70 million acres. But little of this was in Africa, where the yields of staples such as potatoes and maize are the lowest for any region. Cramer (1999) draws attention to the importance of research on cashew nut tree varieties, grafting techniques, and processing methods so as to enable African countries to raise yields as well as enlarge their export market share of processed nuts.

Background papers

Barrett, Scott. "Facilitating International Cooperation."

Bourguignon, Francois. "Crime as a Social Cost of Poverty and Inequality: A Review Focusing on Developing Countries."

Burgess, Robin. "Social Protection, Globalization, and Decentralization."

Castles, Stephen. "Impacts of Emigration on Countries of Origin."

Choe, Sang-Chuel, and Won Bae Kim. "Globalization and Urbanization in Korea."

Cooper, Richard N. "International Approaches to Global Climate Change."

Deaton, Angus. "Global and Regional Effects of Aging and of Demographic Change."

Fay, Marianne. "How Many Tiers? How Many Jurisdictions? A Review of Decentralization Structures across Countries."

Glaeser, Edward L., and Jordan Rappaport. "Cities and Governments."

Henderson, Vernon. "Urbanization In Developing Countries."

Hohenberg, Paul M. "Urban Systems and Economic Development in Historical Perspective: The European Long Term and Its Implications."

Hufbauer, Gary, and Barbara Kotschwar. "The Future Course of Trade Liberalization."

Hughes Hallett, A. J. "Policy Co-ordination: Globalization or Localization in International Monetary Arrangements?"

Litan, Robert. "Toward a Global Financial Architecture for the 21st Century."

Lucas, Robert E. B. "Internal Migration and Urbanization: Recent Contributions and New Evidence."

Malpezzi, Stephen. "The Regulation of Urban Development: Lessons from International Experience."

Mohan, Rakesh. "Financing of Sub-National Public Investment in India."

Satterthwaite, David, and Diana Mitlin. "Urban Poverty: Some Thoughts about Its Scale and Nature and about Responses to It by Community Organizations, NGOs, Local Governments and National Agencies."

Smoke, Paul. "Strategic Fiscal Decentralization in Developing Countries: Issues and Cases."

Srinivasan, T. N. "Think Globally, Act Locally! Development Policy at the Turn of the Century."

Stren, Richard. "Urban Governance and Politics in a Global Context: The Growing Importance of the Local."

References

The word *processed* describes informally reproduced works that may not be commonly available through libraries.

AB Assesores. 1998. "Sub-Sovereign Capital Market Transactions in Latin America: Six Case Studies." World Bank Joint Program on Sub-Sovereign Capital Markets. World Bank, Washington, D.C. Processed.

Abel, I., and L. Szakadat. 1997–98. "Bank Restructuring in Hungary." *Acta Oeconomica* 49(1–2): 157–90.

Ablo, Emmanuel, and Ritva Reinikka. 1998. "Do Budgets Really Matter? Evidence from Public Spending on Education and Health in Uganda." Policy Research Working Paper 1926. World Bank, Africa Region, Washington, D.C.

ADBI (Asian Development Bank Institute). 1998. "Executive Summary of Workshop on Economic Monitoring of Financial Systems in East and Southeast Asia." Tokyo. Processed.

Ades, Alberto, and E. Glaeser. 1995. "Trade and Circuses: Explaining Urban Giants." *Quarterly Journal of Economics* 110(1): 195–258.

Afonso, José Roberto Rodrigues. 1992. "Federalismo Fiscal e Reforma Institucional: Falácias, Conquistas e Descentralização." Discussion Paper 3. Centro de Estudos de Politicas Publicas, Rio de Janeiro.

Afsah, Shakeb, Benoit Laplante, and David Wheeler. 1997. "Regulation in the Information Age: Indonesian Public Information Program for Environmental Management." World Bank, Development Research Group, Washington, D.C. Processed.

Aghion, Philippe, and Jeffrey G. Williamson.1998. *Growth, Inequality and Globalization.* Cambridge: Cambridge University Press.

Ahmad, Ehtisham, and Jon Craig. 1997. "Intergovernmental Transfers." In *Fiscal Federalism in Theory and Practice,* edited by Teresa Ter-Minassian. Washington, D.C.: International Monetary Fund.

Ahmad, Junaid K. 1999. "Decentralizing Borrowing Powers." Poverty Reduction and Economic Management Network (PREM) Notes 15. World Bank, Washington, D.C.

Ahmad, Junaid K., and Charles E. McLure, Jr. 1994. "Intergovernmental Fiscal Relations in South Africa: A Case Study of Policy-Induced Dysfunction." World Bank, Washington, D.C. Processed.

AIDS Analysis. 1998. "World Population Profile Reveals Bleak Data." 8(3/June): 1–2.

Alderman, Harold. 1998. "Do Local Officials Know Something We Don't? Decentralization of Targeted Transfers in Albania." World Bank, Washington, D.C. Processed.

Alesina, Alberto. 1998. "Too Large and Too Small Governments." Conference on Economic Policy and Equity. International Monetary Fund, Washington, D.C.

Alesina, Alberto, and Robert Perotti. 1997. "Fiscal Adjustments in OECD Countries: Composition and Macroeconomic Effects." *IMF Staff Papers* 44(2): 210–48. Washington, D.C.

———. 1998. "Economic Risk and Political Risk in Fiscal Unions." *The Economic Journal* 108: 989–1008.

Alesina, Alberto, and E. Spolaore. 1997. "On the Number and Size of Nations." *Quarterly Journal of Economics* 112: 1027–56.

Alesina, Alberto, and Romain Wacziarg. 1998. "Is Europe Going Too Far?" Massachusetts Institute of Technology. Processed.

Altaf, Mir A. 1983. "The Strategic Implications of Varying Environments, Aspects of Decisionmaking under Instability." Ph.D. diss., Stanford University. Processed.

———. 1994a. "Household Demand for Improved Water and Sanitation in a Large Secondary City: Findings from a Study in Gujranwala, Pakistan." *Habitat International* 18(1).

———. 1994b. "The Economics of Household Response to Inadequate Water Supplies: Evidence from Pakistan." *Third World Planning Review* 16(1).

Altaf, Mir A., and Jeffrey A. Hughes. 1994. "Measuring the Demand for Improved Urban Sanitation Services: Results of a Contingent Valuation Study in Ouagadougou, Burkina Faso." *Urban Studies* 31(10).

Altaf, Mir A., A. Ercelawn, K. Bengali, and A. Rahim. 1993. "Poverty in Karachi: Incidence, Location, Characteristics, and Upward Mobility." *Pakistan Development Review* 32(2).

Ambio. 1995. "Malaria and Malaria Potential Transmission to Climate." 24(6): 200–07.

Amjad, Rashid. 1989. "To the Gulf and Back: Studies on the Economic Impact of Asian Labour Migration." International Labour Organisation, Geneva.

Anderson, Bob, and Paul Brenton. 1998. "The Dollar, Trade, Technology, and Inequality in the USA." *National Institute Economic Review* 166 (October): 78–86.

Anderson, J. 1998. "The Kyoto Protocol on Climate Change: Background, Unresolved Issues and Next Steps." Resources for the Future, Washington, D.C. Processed.

Anderson, Kym. 1999. "The WTO Agenda for the New Millennium." *The Economic Record* 75(228).

Anderson, Kym, and Warwick McKibbin. 1997. "Reducing Coal Subsidies and Trade Barriers: Their Contribution to Greenhouse Gas Abatement." World Bank, Washington, D.C. Processed.

Anderson, Letty. 1988. "Fire and Disease: The Development of Water Supply Systems in New England, 1879–1900." In *Technology and the Rise of the Networked City in Europe and America,* edited by Joel A. Tarr and Gabriel Dupuy. Philadelphia: Temple University Press.

Anderson, Mats. 1998. "Improving Urban Quality of Life in Europe and Central Asia." World Bank, Europe and Central Asia Region (ECA) Urban Sector, Washington, D.C. Processed.

Antarctica Project. 1999. "The Antarctic Treaty System." Washington, D.C. Available online at *http:// www.asoc.org/.*

Antweiler, Werner, Brian R. Copeland, and M. Scott Taylor. 1998. "Is Free Trade Good for the Environment?" Working Paper 6707. National Bureau of Economic Research, Cambridge, Mass.

Attanasio, Orazio, and James Banks. 1998. "Trends in Household Saving Don't Justify Tax Incentives to Book Saving." *Economic Policy* 27(October).

Aw, Bee-Yan, and Geetra Batra. 1998. "Technological Capability and Firm Efficiency in Taiwan (China)." *World Bank Economic Review* 12(1): 59–80.

Ayres, Robert L. 1997. *Crime and Violence as Development Issues in Latin America and the Caribbean.* World Bank, Latin America and the Caribbean Studies, Washington, D.C. Processed.

Aziz, Jahangir, and Robert F. Wescott. 1997. "Policy Complementarities and the Washington Consensus." Working Paper 97/118. International Monetary Fund, Washington, D.C.

Bahl, Roy W. 1999a. "Intergovernmental Transfers in Developing and Transition Countries: Principles and Practice." School of Political Studies, Georgia State University, Atlanta. Processed.

———. 1999b. *Fiscal Policy in China: Taxation and Intergovernmental Fiscal Relations.* San Francisco: The 1990 Institute.

Bahl, Roy W., and Johannes F. Linn. 1992. *Urban Public Finance in Developing Countries.* New York: Oxford University Press.

Baker, Jonathan. 1999. "Rural-Urban Links and Economic Differentiation in Northwest Tanzania." *African Rural and Urban Studies* 3(1): 25–48.

Baldwin, Richard E., and Philippe Martin. 1999. "Two Waves of Globalization: Superficial Similarities, Fundamental Differences." Working Paper 6904. National Bureau of Economic Research, Cambridge, Mass.

Baldwin, Richard E., and Anthony J. Venables. 1995. "Regional Economic Integration." In *Handbook of International Economics,* edited by Gene Grossman and Kenneth Rogoff, 3: 1597–1643. Amsterdam: Elsevier Science B.V.

Baliño, Tomás J. T., Adam Bennett, and Eduardo Borensztein. 1999. "Monetary Policy in Dollarized Economies." Occasional Paper 171. International Monetary Fund, Washington, D.C.

Barkin, Samuel, and George Shambaugh. 1996. "Common-Pool Resources and International Environmental Politics." *Environmental Politics* 5(3): 429–47.

Baron, James. N., and Michael T. Hannan. 1994. "The Impact of Economics on Contemporary Sociology." *Journal of Economic Literature* 32: 1111–46.

Barrett, Scott. 1998a. "Facilitating International Cooperation." Background Paper for *World Development Report 1999/2000.* World Bank, Washington, D.C.

———. 1998b. "Montreal v. Kyoto: International Cooperation and the Global Environment." Prepared for the Office of Development Studies, UNDP (United Nations Development Programme) Project on Global Public Goods. Processed.

———. 1998c. "The Credibility of Trade Sanctions in International Environmental Agreements." London Business School, London. Processed.

Barro, Robert. 1991. "Economic Growth in a Cross Section of Countries." *Quarterly Journal of Economics* 106: 407–43.

Barth, James R., Gerard C. Caprio, and Ross Levine. 1999. "Financial Regulation and Performance: Cross-Country Evidence." Policy Research Working Paper 2037. World Bank, Washington, D.C.

Begg, Iain. 1999. "Cities and Competitiveness." *Urban Studies* 36(5–6).

Begum, Shamshad, and A. F. M. Shamsuddin. 1998. "Exports and Economic Growth in Bangladesh." *Journal of Development Studies* 35(1/October): 89–114.

Bennell, Paul. 1997. "Foreign Direct Investment in Africa: Rhetoric and Reality." *SAIS Review* (Summer/Fall): 127–40.

Bergsten, C. Fred. 1998. "A New Strategy for the Global Crisis." International Economics Policy Brief. Institute for International Economics, Washington, D.C.

Bernard, Andrew, and Steven Durlauf. 1996. "Interpreting Tests of the Convergence Hypothesis." *Journal of Econometrics* 71: 161–73.

Bertaud, Alain, and Bertrand Renaud. 1997. "Socialist Cities without Land Markets." *Journal of Urban Economics* 41: 137–51.

Bertaud, Alain, Robert Buckley, Margret Thalwitz, and Cracow Real Estate Institute. 1997. "Cracow in the Twenty-first Century: Princes or Merchants?" Paper presented to Lincoln Institute Conference on Land Prices, Land Information Systems, and the Market for Land Information. Cambridge. World Bank, Washington, D.C. Processed.

Berthélemy, Jean-Claude, and Aristomène Varoudakis. 1996. "Policies for Economic Take-off." Policy Brief 12: 1–32. Organisation for Economic Co-operation and Development, Paris.

Berthélemy, Jean-Claude, Sébastien Dessus, and Aristomène Varoudakis. 1997. "Capital humain, ouverture extérieure et croissance: estimation sur données de panel d'un modèle a coefficients variables." Policy Brief 121: 1–32. Organisation for Economic Co-operation and Development, Paris.

Bhagwati, Jagdish. 1991. *The World Trading System at Risk.* Princeton: Princeton University Press.

Bird, Richard M. 1999. "Rethinking Tax Assignment: The Need for Better Subnational Taxes." International Monetary Fund, Washington, D.C. Processed.

Bird, Richard M., and Pierre-Pascal Gendron. 1997. "Dual VATs and Cross-Border Trade: Two Problems, One Solution?" *International Tax and Public Finance* 5: 429–42.

Bird, Richard M., and Edgard R. Rodriguez. 1999. "Decentralization and Poverty Alleviation: International Experience and the Case of the Philippines." Department of Economics, University of Toronto. Processed.

Bird, Richard M., and François Vaillancourt, eds. 1999. *Fiscal Decentralization in Developing Countries.* Cambridge: Cambridge University Press.

Bird, Richard M., Robert D. Ebel, and Christine I. Wallich, eds. 1995. *Decentralization of the Socialist State.* Washington, D.C.: World Bank.

Black, D., and J. V. Henderson. 1998. "Urban Evolution in the USA." Department of Economics, Brown University, Providence R.I. Processed.

Blackett, Isabel C. 1994. "Low-Cost Urban Sanitation in Lesotho." Water and Sanitation Discussion Paper Series 10. UNDP–World Bank Water and Sanitation Program. World Bank, Washington, D.C.

Blomström, Magnus, and Ari Kokko. 1997. "Regional Integration and Foreign Direct Investment: A Conceptual Framework and Three Cases." Policy Research Working Paper 1750. World Bank, Washington, D.C.

Boddy, Martin. 1999. "Geographical Competitiveness: A Critique." *Urban Studies* 36(5–6).

Boeninger, Edgardo. 1992. "Governance and Development: Issues and Constraints." In *Proceedings of the World Bank Annual Conference on Development Economics,* edited by Lawrence Summers and Shekhar Shah. Washington, D.C.: World Bank.

Bohning W. R., and R. Zegers de Beiji. 1995. "The Integration of Migrant Workers in the Labour Market: Policies and Their Impact." International Migration Papers 8: 1–59. International Labour Office, Geneva.

Bolbol, Ali A. 1999. "Arab Trade and Free Trade: A Preliminary Analysis." *International Journal of Middle Eastern Studies* 31: 3–17.

Boniface, Pascal. 1998. "The Proliferation of States." *The Washington Quarterly* 21(3).

Bordo, Michael D., Barry Eichengreen, and Douglas A. Irwin. 1999. "Is Globalization Today Really Different Than Globalization a Hundred Years Ago?" Paper for the Brookings Institution Trade Policy Forum on Governing in a Global Economy. Washington D.C., April 15–16.

Bordo, Michael D., Barry Eichengreen, and Jongwoo Kim. 1998. "Was There Really an Earlier Period of International Financial Integration Comparable to Today?" Working Paper 6738. National Bureau of Economic Research, Cambridge, Mass.

Borensztein, Eduardo, José De Gregorio, and Johng-wha Lee. 1998. "How Does Foreign Direct Investment Affect Economic Growth?" *Journal of International Economics* 45(1): 115–35.

Borjas, George J. 1998. "Economic Research on the Determinants of Immigration: Lessons for the European Union." Department of Economics, Harvard University, Cambridge, Mass. Processed.

Bougheas, Spiros, Panicos O. Demetriades, and Edgar L. W. Morgenroth. 1999. "Infrastructure, Transport Costs and Trade." *Journal of International Economics* 47: 169–89.

Bourguignon, François. 1998. "Crime as a Social Cost of Poverty and Inequality: A Review Focusing on Developing Countries." Background Paper for *World Development Report 1999/2000*. World Bank, Washington, D.C.

Bradbury, L. Katherine, Yolanda K. Kodrzycki, and Robert Tannenwald. 1997. "The Effects of State and Local Public Policies on Economic Development: An Overview." *New England Economic Review* March/April: 1–12.

Bradley, Rebecca, and Joshua S. Gans. 1998. "Growth in Australian Cities." *Economic Record* 74: 266–78.

Brautigam, Deborah. 1997. "Substituting for the State: Institutions and Industrial Development in Eastern Nigeria." *World Development* 25(7): 1081–93.

Breton, Albert. 1996. *Competitive Governments.* Cambridge: Cambridge University Press.

Bridges, Amy. 1997. *Morning Glories: Municipal Reform in the Southwest.* Princeton: Princeton University Press.

Brockerhoff, Martin, and E. Brennan. 1998. "The Poverty of Cities in Developing Regions." *Population and Development Review* 24(1/March).

Brown, Lynn, and Alex F. McCalla. 1998. "Global Urbanization Trends: Implications for Food Systems and Food Services." World Bank, Washington, D.C. Processed.

Brunetti, Aymo. 1997. *Politics and Economic Growth: A Cross-Country Data Perspective.* Development Centre Studies. Paris: Organisation for Economic Co-operation and Development.

Bryant, Ralph. 1995. *International Coordination of National Stabilization Policies.* Washington, D.C.: The Brookings Institution Press.

Buckley, Graeme. 1997. "Microfinance in Africa: Is It Either the Problem or the Solution?" *World Development* 25(7): 1063–80.

Buckley, Robert. 1999. *1998 Annual Review of Development Effectiveness.* Washington, D.C.: World Bank.

Buckley, Robert, and Stephen Mayo. 1989. "Housing Policy in Developing Economies: Evaluating the Macroeconomic Impacts." *Review of Urban and Regional Development Studies* 2(27).

Burgess, Robin. 1998. "Social Protection, Globalization, and Decentralisation." Department of Economics, London School of Economics. Processed.

———. 1999. "Social Protection, Globalization and Decentralisation." Background Paper for *World Development Report 1999/2000*. World Bank, Washington, D.C.

Burki, Shahid Javed, and Guillermo E. Perry. 1998. *Beyond the Washington Consensus: Institutions Matter.* World Bank Latin American and Caribbean Studies: Viewpoints. Washington, D.C.: World Bank.

Burki, Shahid Javed, Guillermo E. Perry, and William Dillinger. 1999. *Beyond the Center: Decentralizing the State.* World Bank Latin American and Caribbean Studies: Viewpoints. Washington, D.C.: World Bank.

Burtless, Gary, Robert Z. Lawrence, Robert E. Litan, and Robert J. Shapiro. 1998. *Globaphobia.* Washington, D.C.: The Brookings Institution Press.

Business Week. 1998. "A Fresh Shot at Malaria." September 21.

———. 1999. "Fresh Strains of Unzappable Germs." August 2.

Butler, James H. 1999. "A Record of Atmospheric Halocarbons during the Twentieth Century from Polar Air." *Nature* 339(June 24): 749–55.

Cairncross, Frances. 1997. *The Death of Distance: How the Communications Revolution Will Change Our Lives.* Cambridge: Harvard Business School Press.

Caldeira, Teresa P. R. 1996. "Building up Walls: The New Pattern of Spatial Segregation in São Paulo." *International Social Science Journal* (147/March).

Calomiris, Charles. 1997. *The Postmodern Bank Safety Net: Lessons from Developed and Developing Countries.* Washington, D.C.: American Enterprise Institute.

———. 1999. "How to Invent a New IMF." *The International Economy* (January/February): 32ff.

Calvo, Sarah. 1999. "Reducing Vulnerability to Speculative Attacks." Poverty Reduction and Economic Management Network (PREM) Economic Policy Notes 16. World Bank, Washington, D.C.

Campbell, Tim E. 1998. "The Quiet Revolution: The Rise of Political Participation and Local Government with Decentralization in Latin America and the Caribbean." World Bank, Washington, D.C. Processed.

Caprio, Gerard C. 1998. "International Financial Integration: Pitfalls and Possibilities." World Bank, Washington, D.C. Processed.

Caprio, Gerard C., and Daniela Klingebiel. 1996. "Bank Insolvencies: Cross-Country Experience." Policy Research Working Paper 1620. World Bank, Washington, D.C.

———. 1999. "Table of Episodes of Major Bank Insolvencies." World Bank, Washington, D.C. Processed.

Carey, John M. 1997. "Institutional Designs and Party Systems." In *Consolidating the Third Wave Democracies.* Baltimore: The Johns Hopkins University Press.

Caron, Mary. 1999. "The Politics of Life and Death." *World Watch* (May/June): 30–38.

Carr, Stephen. 1993. *Improving Cash Crops in Africa: Factors Influencing the Productivity of Cotton, Coffee, and Tea Grown by Smallholders.* Technical Paper 216. Washington, D.C.: World Bank.

Carrington, William J., and Enrica Detragiache. 1998. "How Big Is the Brain Drain?" Working Paper 98/102. International Monetary Fund, Washington, D.C.

Caselli, Francesco, G. Esquivel, and F. Lefort. 1996. "Reopening the Convergence Debate: A New Look at Cross-Country Growth Empirics." *Journal of Economic Growth* 1 (September): 363–89.

Castles, Stephen. 1998. "Impacts of Emigration on Countries of Origin." Background Paper for *World Development Report 1999/2000.* World Bank, Washington, D.C.

Caves, Richard E. 1996. *Multinational Enterprise and Economic Analysis,* 2nd ed. Cambridge: Cambridge University Press.

Cesar, Herman. 1998. "Indonesian Coral Reefs: A Precious but Threatened Resource." In *Coral Reefs: Challenges and Opportunities for Sustainable Management,* edited by Maria Hatziolos, Anthony Hooten, and Martin Fodor. Washington, D.C.: World Bank.

Chaplin, Susan E. 1999. "Cities, Sewers, and Poverty: India's Politics of Sanitation." *Environment and Urbanization* 11(1): 145–58.

Charnovitz, Steve. 1996. "Trade Measures and the Design of International Regimes." *Journal of Environment and Development* 5(2): 168–96.

Chhabra, S. K., C. K. Gupta, P. Chhabra, and S. Rajpal. 1998. "Prevalence of Bronchial Asthma in Schoolchildren of Delhi." *Journal of Asthma* 35(3).

Chinese State Council. 1994. "A White Paper on Chinese Population, Environment and Development in the Twenty-first Century, Adopted at the Sixteenth Regular Meeting of the State Council." March 25. Translated excerpts reprinted in *Chinese Environment and Development,* 7(4): 74–95.

Choe, Sang-Chuel, and Won Bae Kim. 1999. "Globalization and Urbanization in Korea." Background Paper for *World Development Report 1999/2000.* World Bank, Washington, D.C.

Chomitz, K., and K. Kumari. 1998. "The Domestic Benefits of Tropical Forests: A Critical Review." *World Bank Research Observer* 13(1): 13–35.

Christianson, Gale E. 1999. *Greenhouse.* New York: Walker and Company.

Chumacero, Romulo, Raul Laban, and Felipe Larrain. 1996. "What Determines Capital Inflows: An Empirical Analysis for Chile." Universidad Católica de Chile, Santiago. Unpublished manuscript.

Claessens, Stijn, and Moon-Whoan Rhee. 1994. "The Effects of Barriers on Equity Investments in Developing Countries." Policy Research Working Paper 1263. World Bank, Washington, D.C.

Claessens, Stijn, Asli Demirgüç-Kunt, and Harry Huizinga. 1998. "How Does Foreign Entry Affect the Domestic Banking Market?" World Bank, Washington, D.C. Processed.

Claudio, L., L. Tulton, J. Doucette, P. J. Landrigan. 1999. "Socioeconomic Factors and Asthma Hospitalization Rates in New York City." *Asthma* 36(4): 343–50.

Clerides, Sofronis, Saul Lach, and James Tybout. 1998. "Is Learning-by-Exporting Important? Micro-Dynamic Evidence from Colombia, Mexico and Morocco." *Quarterly Journal of Economics* 113: 903–47.

Cline, William R. 1997. *Trade and Income Distribution.* Washington, D.C.: Institute for International Economics.

Coelho, Magda Prates. 1996. "Urban Governance in Brazil." In *Cities and Governance: New Directions in Latin America, Asia and Africa,* edited by Patricia L. McCarney. Toronto: University of Toronto Press.

Coffee, Joyce Elena. 1999. "Innovations in Municipal Service Delivery: The Case of Vietnam's Haiphong Water Supply Company." Master's diss. Massachusetts Institute of Technology, Cambridge, Mass. Processed.

Cohen, Barney. 1998. "The Emerging Fertility Transition in Sub-Saharan Africa." *World Development* 26.

Cohen, Daniel. 1998. *The Wealth of the World and the Poverty of Nations.* Cambridge, Mass.: MIT Press.

Cohen, Mitchell L. 1992. "Epidemiology of Drug Resistance: Implications for a Post Microbial Era." *Science.* August.

Cohen, Roberta, and Francis M. Deng. 1998. *Masses in Flight: The Global Crisis of Internal Displacement.* Washington, D.C.: The Brookings Institution Press.

Cole, Stephen, and Thomas J. Phelan. 1999. "The Scientific Productivity of Nations." *Minerva* 37(1): 1–23.

Coleman, James, and Thomas Hoffer. 1987. *Public and Private High Schools: The Impact of Communities.* New York: Basic Books.

Colgan, Charles S. 1995. "International Regulation of State and Local Subsidies." *Economic Development Quarterly* 9(2).

Collier, Paul, and David Dollar. 1998. "Aid Allocation and Poverty Reduction." World Bank, Washington, D.C. Processed.

Conger, Lucy. 1999. "Porto Alegre: Where the Public Controls the Purse Strings." *Urban Age* 6(4): 4–5.

Connelly, James. 1996. "Review of Making Nature, Shaping Culture: Plant Biodiversity in Global Context." *Environmental Politics* 5(4): 770–1.

Cooke, Philip, and Kevin Morgan. 1998. *The Associational Economy. Firms, Regions, and Innovation.* Oxford: Oxford University Press.

Cooper, Richard N. 1998. "International Approaches to Global Climate Change." Background Paper for *World Development Report 1999/2000.* World Bank, Washington, D.C.

———. 1999. "Should Capital Controls Be Banished?" Department of Economics, Harvard University. Processed.

Costa, L. Dora. 1998. *The Evolution of Retirement.* Chicago: University of Chicago Press.

Cour, Jean-Marie. 1998a. "Draft Proposal for a Data System for the Durban Metropolitan Area." Club du Sahel. OECD (Organisation for Economic Co-operation and Development), Paris. Processed.

———. 1998b. "First Lessons from the Ecolog Program." Note from the Club du Sahel Secretariat. OECD (Organisation for Economic Co-operation and Development), Paris.

Covarrubias, Alvaro. 1999. "Lending for Electric Power in Sub-Saharan Africa." World Bank, Washington, D.C. Processed.

Cowen, Penelope Brook, and Nicola Tynan. 1999. "Reaching the Urban Poor with Private Infrastructure." Finance, Private Sector, and Infrastructure Network Viewpoint 188. World Bank, Washington, D.C.

Coyle, Diane. 1998. *The Weightless World.* Cambridge, Mass.: MIT Press.

Cramer, Christopher. 1999. "Can Africa Industrialize by Processing Primary Commodities? The Case of Mozambican Cashew Nuts." *World Development* 27(7): 1247–66.

Crystal, David. 1997. *English as a Global Language.* Cambridge: Cambridge University Press.

Curtis, Valerie, and Bernadette Kanki. 1998. "Bednets and Malaria." *Africa Health.* May.

Dahl, Robert A. 1971. *Polyarchy: Participation and Opposition.* New Haven: Yale University Press.

———. 1986. "Federalism and the Democratic Process." In *Democracy, Identity and Equality.* Oslo: Norwegian University Press.

Dailami, Mansoor, and Danny Leipziger. 1998. "Infrastructure Project Finance and Capital Flows: A New Perspective." World Bank, Washington D.C.

Davoodi, Hamid, and Heng-fu Zou. 1998. "Fiscal Decentralization and Economic Growth: A Cross-Country Study." World Bank, Policy Research Department, Washington, D.C. Processed.

de Figueiredo, Rui J. P. Jr., and Barry R. Weingast. 1998. "Self-Enforcing Federalism: Solving the Two Fundamental Dilemmas." Department of Political Science, Stanford University, Stanford, Calif. Processed.

de Fontaubert, A. Charlotte. 1996. "The United Nations Conference on Straddling Fish Stocks and Highly Migratory Fish Stocks: Another Step in the Implementation of the Law of the Sea Convention." *Living Resources.*

De Mello, Luiz R. 1997. "Foreign Direct Investment in Developing Countries and Growth: A Selective Survey." *Journal of Development Studies* 34: 1–34.

Deardorff, Alan V. 1998. "Fragmentation in Simple Trade Models." Department of Economics, University of Michigan, Ann Arbor. Processed.

Deardorff, Alan V., Saul H. Hymans, Robert M. Stern, and Chong Xiang. 1998. "The Economic Outlook for U.S. Trade in Services, 1999–2001." Department of Economics, University of Michigan, Ann Arbor. Processed.

Deaton, Angus. 1998. "Global and Regional Effects of Aging and of Demographic Change." Background Paper for *World Development Report 1999/2000.* Princeton University. Processed.

Deininger, Klaus, and Lyn Squire. 1996. "A New Data Set Measuring Income Inequality." *World Bank Economic Review* 10(September): 565–91.

Del Amo, Julia, and others. 1999. "Does Tuberculosis Accelerate the Progression of HIV Disease? Evidence from Basic Science and Epidemiology." *AIDS* 13(10).

Demirgüç-Kunt, Asli, and Enrica Detragiache. 1998. "Financial Liberalization and Financial Fragility." Working Paper 98/83. International Monetary Fund, Washington, D.C.

Demirgüç-Kunt, Asli, and Ross Levine. 1995. "Stock Market Development and Financial Intermediaries: Stylized Facts." World Bank, Washington, D.C. Processed.

Dervis, Kemal, and Nemat Shafiq. 1998. "The Middle East and North Africa: A Tale of Two Futures." *Middle East Journal* 52(4): 505–16.

Devarajan, Shantayanan, William Easterly, and Howard Pack. 1999. "Is Investment in Africa Too Low or Too High?" World Bank, Washington, D.C. Processed.

Dewatripont, Mathias, and Jean Tirole. 1994. *The Prudential Regulation of Banks.* Cambridge: MIT Press.

Diamond, Larry. 1996. "Is the Third Wave Over?" *Journal of Democracy* 7(3).

———. 1999. *Developing Democracy: Toward Consolidation.* Baltimore: Johns Hopkins University Press.

Dillinger, William. 1992. "Urban Property Tax Reform". Urban Management Program Working Paper 1. World Bank, Washington, D.C.

———. 1997. "Brazil's State Debt Crisis: Lessons Learned." Latin America and the Caribbean Region Economic Notes. World Bank, Washington, D.C.

Dillinger, William, and Steven B. Webb. 1999a. "Decentralization and Fiscal Management in Colombia." Policy Research Working Paper 2122. World Bank, Washington, D.C.

———. 1999b. "Fiscal Management in Federal Democracies: Argentina and Brazil." Policy Research Working Paper 2121. World Bank, Washington, D.C.

Dobson, Wendy, and Pierre Jacquet. 1998. *Financial Services Liberalization in the WTO.* Washington, D.C.: Institute for International Economics.

Dollar, David. 1999. "The Comprehensive Development Framework and Recent Development Research." World Bank, Washington, D.C. Processed.

Donahue, John D. 1997. "Tiebout? Or Not Tiebout? The Market Metaphor and America's Devolution Debate." *Journal of Public Economics* 11: 73–82.

Dooley, Michael P. 1996. "A Survey of Literature on Controls over International Capital Transactions." *IMF Staff Papers* 43: 639–87. International Monetary Fund, Washington, D.C.

Dornbusch, Rudi. 1998. "Cross-Border Payments Taxes and Alternative Capital Account Regimes." In *Capital Account Regimes and the Developing Countries*, edited by G. K. Helleiner. New York: St. Martin's Press.

Douglass, Mike. 1992. "The Political Economy of Urban Poverty and Environmental Management in Asia: Access, Empowerment and Community-Based Alternatives." *Environment and Urbanization* 4(2).

Drabek, Zdenek, and Sam Laird. 1998. "The New Liberalism: Trade Policy Developments in Emerging Markets." *Journal of World Trade* 32(5): 241–69.

Drèze, Jean, and Amartya Sen. 1995. *India: Economic Development and Social Opportunity.* New York: Oxford University Press.

Dumais, Guy, Glenn Ellison, and Edward L Glaeser. 1997. "Geographic Concentration as a Dynamic Process." National Bureau of Economic Research, Cambridge, Mass.

Easterly, William. 1999. "Life during Growth." World Bank, Washington, D.C. Processed.

Easterly, William, and Stanley Fischer. 1995. "The Soviet Economic Decline." *World Bank Economic Review* 9(September): 341–71.

Easterly, William, and Ross Levine. 1997. "Africa's Growth Tragedy: Policies and Ethnic Divisions." *Quarterly Journal of Economics* 112(November): 1203–50.

Eberstadt, Nicholas. 1998. "Asia Tomorrow, Gray and Male." *National Interest* 53(Fall).

EBRD (European Bank for Reconstruction and Development). 1997. *Transition Report 1997: Economic Performance and Growth*. London.

———. 1998. *Transition Report 1998: Economic Performance and Growth*. London.

The Economist. 1998a. "Lost without a Trace." August 1.

———. 1998b. "Recipes for an AIDS vaccine." July 14.

———. 1998c. "Repositioning the WHO." May 9.

———. 1998d. "Turtle Soup." October 17.

———. 1999a. "Seeds of Discontent." February 20.

———. 1999b. "Throwing Sand in the Gears." January 30.

———. 1999c. "Trimmed, Not Axed." February 27.

———. 1999d. "A Survey of Business and the Internet." June 26.

———. 1999e. "International Aid." July 3.

———. 1999f. "Global Disaster." January 2.

Edwards, Sebastian. 1998a. "Capital Flows, Real Exchange Rates, and Capital Controls: Some Latin American Experiences." University of California, Los Angeles. Unpublished manuscript.

———. 1998b. "Openness, Productivity, and Growth: What Do We Really Know?" *The Economic Journal* 108(March): 383–98.

Eichengreen, Barry. 1998. "International Economic Policy in the Wake of the Asian Crisis." Working Paper C98-102. University of California, Berkeley.

———. 1999. *Toward a New International Financial Architecture*. Washington, D.C.: Institute for International Economics.

Eichengreen, Barry, and Albert Fishlow. 1998. "Contending with Capital Flows: What Is Different about the 1990s?" In *Capital Flows and Financial Crises*, edited by Miles Kahler. Ithaca: Cornell University Press.

Eichengreen, Barry, and Peter B. Kenen. 1994. "Managing the World Economy under the Bretton Woods System: An Overview." In *Managing the World Economy*, edited by Peter B. Kenen. Washington, D.C.: Institute for International Economics.

Eichengreen, Barry, and Michael Mussa. 1998. "Capital Account Liberalization: Theoretical and Practical Aspects." Occasional Paper 172. International Monetary Fund, Washington, D.C.

Eichengreen, Barry, and Andrew K. Rose. 1998. "Staying Afloat When the Wind Shifts: External Factors and Emerging-Market Banking Crises." Working Paper 6370. National Bureau of Economic Research, Cambridge, Mass.

Eichengreen, Barry, and others. 1999. "Liberalizing Capital Movements: Some Analytical Issues." *Economic Issues* (February), International Monetary Fund, Washington, D.C.

EIU (Economist Intelligence Unit). 1998. "Country Profile: Tanzania." London.

Ekpo, Akpan H. and John E. U. Ndebbio. 1998. "Local Government Fiscal Operations in Nigeria." Research Paper 73. African Economic Research Consortium, Nairobi.

Elkins, James. 1999. "Chlorofluorocarbons (CFCs)." In *The Chapman and Hall Encyclopedia of Environmental Science*, edited by David Alexander and Rhodes Fairbridge. New York: Chapman and Hall.

Elster, Jon. 1988. "Is There (or Should There Be) a Right to Work?" In *Democracy and the Welfare State*, edited by A. Guttman. Princeton: Princeton University Press.

———. 1989. *The Cement of Society*. Cambridge: Cambridge University Press.

Elster, Jon, and Rune Slagsrad. 1993. *Constitutionalism and Democracy*. Cambridge: Cambridge University Press.

Eskeland, Gunnar, and Tarhan Feyzioglu. 1994. "Is Demand for Polluting Goods Manageable? An Econometric Study of Car Ownership and Use in Mexico." Policy Research Working Paper 1309. World Bank, Washington, D.C.

Espinosa, Lair, and Oscar A. López Rivera. 1994. "UNICEF's Urban Basic Services Program in Illegal Settlements in Guatemala City." *Environment and Urbanization* 6 (2).

Evanoff, Douglas D. 1998. "Global Banking Crises: Commonalities, Mistakes, and Lessons." In *Preventing Bank Crises: Lessons from Recent Global Bank Failures*, edited by Gerard C. Caprio. Washington, D.C.: Federal Reserve Bank of Chicago and the World Bank Economic Development Institute.

Evans, Peter. 1998. "Looking for Agents of Urban Livability in a Globalized Political Economy." University of California, Berkeley. Draft.

Evans, Alison, and William Bataille. 1997. *Annual Review of Development Effectiveness*. Washington, D.C.: World Bank.

Faguet, Jean-Paul. 1998. "Decentralization and Local Government Performance: Improving Public Service in Bolivia." Discussion Paper 999. Centre for Economic Performance, London.

Faini, Riccardo. 1998. "European Migration Policies in American Perspective." In *Transatlantic Economic Relations in the Post–Cold War Era*, edited by Barry Eichengreen. New York: Council on Foreign Relations Press.

Fajnzylber, Pablo, Daniel Lederman, and Norman Louyza. 1998. *Determinants of Crime Rates in Latin America and the World: An Empirical Assessment*. World Bank Latin America and the Caribbean Studies. Washington, D.C.: World Bank.

Fallon, Peter, and Zafiris Tzannatos. 1998. "Child Labor: Issues and Directions for the World Bank." World Bank, Washington, D.C. Processed.

FAO (Food and Agriculture Organization of the United Nations). 1990. *Fishery Statistics Catch and Landing 1988*. Rome.

———. 1998a. *Aquacultural Production Statistics 1987–96*. Rome.

———. 1998b. *Fishery Statistics Catch and Landing 1996*. Rome.

———. 1999a. *Aquacultural Production Statistics*. Rome.

———. 1999b. *Fishery Statistics Catch and Landing 1997*. Rome.

Far Eastern Economic Review. 1998. December 24.

Farmer, Paul. 1999. "TB Superbugs: The Coming Plague on All Our Houses." *Natural History* No. 4.

Fay, Marianne, Darfy Chaponda, Helen Mbao, and Winnie Mulongo. 1998. "A Review of Local Institutions in Zambia." World Bank, Washington, D.C. Processed.

Feenstra, Robert C. 1998. "Integration of Trade and Disintegration of Production in the Global Economy." *Journal of Economic Perspectives* 12(4): 31–50.

Feenstra, Robert C., Dorsati Madani, Tzu-Han Yang, and Chi-Yuan Liang. 1997. "Testing Endogenous Growth in South Korea and Taiwan." Working Paper 6028. National Bureau of Economic Research, Cambridge, Mass.

Feldstein, Martin. 1998. "International Capital Flows: Introduction." Remarks at the National Bureau of Economic Research Conference on International Capital Flows. Woodstock, Vermont, October 17–18.

———. 1999. "A Self-Help Guide for Emerging Markets." *Foreign Affairs* 78(2): 93–109.

Fernandez, Raquel, and Jonathan Portes. 1998. "Returns to Regionalism: An Analysis of Nontraditional Gains from Regional Trade Agreements." *World Bank Economic Review* 12(2): 197–220.

Feshback, Murray. 1999. "Dead Souls." *Atlantic* (January): 26–27.

Finger, J. Michael, ed. 1993. *Antidumping: How It Works and Who Gets Hurt.* Ann Arbor: University of Michigan Press.

Finger, J. Michael, and Ludger Schuknecht. 1999. "Implementing the Uruguay Round Market Access Agreements." World Bank, Washington, D.C.

Finger, J. Michael, and L. Alan Winters. 1998. "What Can the WTO Do for Developing Countries?" In *The WTO as an International Organization*, edited by Anne O. Krueger. Chicago: University of Chicago Press.

Fischer, Stanley. 1999. "On the Need for an International Lender of Last Resort." Speech delivered to a joint luncheon of the American Economic Association and the American Finance Association. New York, January 3.

Fiszbein, Ariel. 1997. "The Emergence of Local Capacity: Lessons from Colombia." *World Development* 25: 1029–43.

Flannery, Mark J. 1998. "Using Market Information in Prudential Bank Supervision: A Review of the U.S. Empirical Evidence." *Journal of Money, Credit, and Banking* 30(3): 273–305.

Flavin, C. 1997. "The Legacy of Rio." In *State of the World*, edited by Lester Brown. New York: W. W. Norton.

Foreman-Peck, James, and Robert Millward. 1994. *Public and Private Ownership of British Industry 1829–1990.* Oxford: Clarendon Press.

Fornasari, Francesca, Steven B. Webb, and Heng-Fu Zou. 1999. "Decentralized Spending and Central Government Deficits: International Evidence." World Bank, Washington, D.C. Processed.

Foroutan, Faezeh. 1996. "Turkey, 1976–85: Foreign Trade, Industrial Productivity, and Competition." In *Industrial Evolution in Developing Countries*, edited by Mark J. Roberts and James Tybout. New York: Oxford University Press.

Fox, William, and Christine Wallich. 1997. "Fiscal Federalism in Bosnia-Herzegovina." Policy Research Working Paper 1714. World Bank, Washington, D.C.

Francis, Paul A., and others. 1998. *Hard Lessons: Primary Schools, Community, and Social Capital in Nigeria.* Technical Paper 420. Washington, D.C.: World Bank.

François, Joseph F., Bradley McDonald, and Håkan Nordström. 1996. "The Uruguay Round: A Numerically Based Qualitative Assessment." In *The Uruguay Round and the Developing Countries*, edited by Alan Winters and William Martin. Cambridge: Cambridge University Press.

François, Joseph F., and Ian Wooton. 1999. "Trade in International Transport Services: The Role of Competition." Center for Economic Policy Research. European Research Workshop in International Trade. Bergen, Norway, June 24–27.

Frankel, Jeffrey. 1997. *Regional Trading Blocs in the World Economic System.* Washington, D.C.: Institute for International Economics.

Frankel, Jeffrey A., and David Romer. 1999. "Does Trade Cause Growth?" *American Economic Review* 89(3): 379–98.

Fredland, Richard A. 1998. "Aids and Development: An Inverse Correlation?" *The Journal of Modern African Studies* 36(4): 547–68.

Freedom House. 1990. *Freedom in the World: The Annual Survey of Political Rights and Civil Liberties.* New York.

———. 1991. *Freedom in the World: The Annual Survey of Political Rights and Civil Liberties.* New York.

———. 1992. *Freedom in the World: The Annual Survey of Political Rights and Civil Liberties.* New York.

———. 1993. *Freedom in the World: The Annual Survey of Political Rights and Civil Liberties.* New York.

———. 1994. *Freedom in the World: The Annual Survey of Political Rights and Civil Liberties.* New York.

———. 1995. *Freedom in the World: The Annual Survey of Political Rights and Civil Liberties.* New York.

———. 1996a. *Freedom in the World: The Annual Survey of Political Rights and Civil Liberties.* New York.

———. 1996b. *Freedom Review* 27 (January–February). New York.

———. 1998. *Freedom in the World: The Annual Survey of Political Rights and Civil Liberties.* New York.

Freeman, R., and D. Lindauer. 1998. "Why Not Africa?" World Bank, Washington, D.C. Processed.

Freestone, D. 1999. Review of *The Implementation and Effectiveness of International Environmental Commitments*, edited by D. Victor, K. Raustiala, and E. Skolnikoff. World Bank, Washington, D.C. Processed.

Freestone, D., and Z. Makuch. 1998. "The New International Environmental Law of Fisheries: The 1995 United Nations Straddling Stocks Agreement." *Yearbook of International Environmental Law* 7. New York.

Freinkman, Lev. 1998. "Russian Federation: Subnational Budgeting in Russia: Preempting a Potential Crisis." World Bank, Washington, D.C. Processed.

Freire, Maria E., Marcela Huertas, and Benjamin Darche. 1998. "Subnational Access to the Capital Markets: The Latin

American Experience." World Bank, Washington, D.C. Processed.

French, Hilary. 1997. "Learning from the Ozone Experience." In *State of the World*, edited by Lester Brown. New York: W. W. Norton.

Frigenti, Laura, and Alberto Harth. 1998. "Local Solutions to Regional Problems: The Growth of Social Funds and Public Works and Employment Projects in Sub-Saharan Africa." World Bank, Washington, D.C. Processed.

Fry, Maxwell J. 1995. *Money, Interest and Banking in Economic Development,* 2nd ed. Baltimore: The Johns Hopkins University Press.

Fuente, A. 1995. "The Empirics of Growth and Convergence: A Selective Review." Discussion Paper 1275. Center for Economic Policy Research, London.

Fujikura, Ryo. 1998. "Public Participation in Urban Environmental Management in Japan." Paper for *World Development Report 1999/2000*, Tokyo Workshop. Processed.

———. 1999. "Public Participation in Urban Environmental Management in Japan." Background Paper for *World Development Report 1999/2000*. World Bank, Washington, D.C.

Fujita, Masahisa, P. R. Krugman, and A. J. Venables. 1999. *The Spatial Economy: Cities, Regions and International Trade.* Cambridge, Mass.: MIT Press.

Fung, K. C., and Francis Ng. 1998. "What Do Trade Negotiators Negotiate About? Some Evidence from the Uruguay Round." Working Paper 412. Department of Economics, University of California, Santa Cruz.

Galeotti, Gianluigi. 1992. "Decentralization and Political Rents." In *Local Government Economics in Theory and Practice*, edited by David King. London: Routledge.

Gamble, John King, Zachary T. Irwin, Charles M. Redenius, and James W. Weber. 1992. *Introduction to Political Science.* Englewood Cliffs, N.J.: Prentice Hall.

Gandal, Neil, Gordon H. Hanson, and Matthew J. Slaughter. 1999. "Rybczynski Effects and Adjustment to Immigration in Israel." CEPR (Centre for Economic Policy Research) Workshop in International Trade. June 24–27.

Gang, Fan. 1999. "Impacts of Globalization on the Developing Countries: The Case of China." Background Paper for *World Development Report 1999/2000*, Tokyo Workshop.

Garcia, Gillian G. 1996. "Deposit Insurance: Obtaining the Benefits and Avoiding the Pitfalls." Working Paper 96/83. International Monetary Fund, Washington, D.C.

———. 1998. "Deposit Insurance." In *Preventing Bank Crises: Lessons from Recent Global Bank Failures*, edited by Gerard C. Caprio. Washington, D.C.: Federal Reserve Bank of Chicago and the World Bank Economic Development Institute.

Gardner-Outlaw, Tom, and Robert Engelman. 1997. "Easing Scarcity: A Second Update." Population Action International, Washington, D.C.

Garrett, Geoffrey. 1998. *Partisan Politics in the Global Economy.* Cambridge: Cambridge University Press.

Gaspar, Jess, and Edward L. Glaeser. 1998. "Information Technology and the Future of Cities." *Journal of Urban Economics* 43(136).

Gastanaga, Victor M., Jeffrey B. Nugent, and Bistra Pashamova. 1998. "Host Country Reforms and FDI Inflows: How Much Difference Do They Make?" *World Development* 26: 1299–1314.

Gautam, Madhur, and Jock R. Anderson. 1998. "Returns to T&V Extension in Kenya: Some Alternative Findings." World Bank, Operations Evaluations Department. Washington, D.C. Processed.

Gavin, Michael, and Roberto Perotti. 1997. "Fiscal Policy in Latin America." *National Bureau of Economic Research (NBER) Macroeconomics Annual.* Cambridge, Mass.

Gerschenkron, Alexander. 1962. *Economic Backwardness in Historical Perspective.* Cambridge, Mass.: Belknap Press.

Gertler, Meric S. 1997. "Globality and Locality: The Future of 'Geography' and the Nation-State." In *Pacific Rim Development: Integration and Globalisation in the Asia-Pacific Economy*, edited by Peter Rimmer. Canberra City, Australia: Aussie Print.

Gibson, Edward L., Ernesto F. Calvo, and Tulia G. Falleti. 1999. "Reallocative Federalism: Overrepresentation and Public Spending in the Western Hemisphere." Department of Political Science, Northwestern University. Processed.

Giddens, Anthony. 1998. *Conversations by Anthony Giddens.* Cambridge, United Kingdom: Polity Press.

Gilbert, Alan, and Josef Gugler. 1992. *Cities, Poverty and Development.* New York: Oxford University Press.

Glaeser, Edward L. 1997. "Learning in Cities." Discussion Paper 1814: 1–23. Harvard Institute of Economic Research, Cambridge, Mass.

———. 1998. "Are Cities Dying?" *Journal of Economic Perspectives* 12(2): 139–60.

Glaeser, Edward L., and Jordan Rappaport. 1998. "Cities and Governments." Background Paper for *World Development Report 1999/2000*. World Bank, Washington, D.C.

Glaeser, Edward L., Hedi D. Kallal, José A. Scheinkman, and Andrei Shleifer. 1992. "Growth in Cities." *Journal of Economic Perspectives* 12(2): 1126–53.

Goldstein, Morris. 1997. *The Case for an International Banking Standard.* Washington, D.C.: Institute for International Economics.

———. 1998. "The Case for International Banking Standards." In *Preventing Bank Crises: Lessons from Recent Global Bank Failures*, edited by Gerard C. Caprio. Washington, D.C.: Federal Reserve Bank of Chicago and the World Bank Economic Development Institute.

Goldstein, Morris, and John Hawkins. 1998. "The Origins of the Asian Financial Turmoil." Discussion Paper 9805. Reserve Bank of Australia, Canberra.

Goldstein, Morris, and Philip Turner. 1996. "Banking Crises in Emerging Economies: Origins and Policy Options." Economic Papers 46. Bank for International Settlements, Geneva.

Good, Michael F. 1999. "Tying the Conductor's Arms." *Nature.* July 15.

Goodhart, Charles, Philipp Hartmann, David Llewellyn, Liliana Rojas-Suarez, and Steven Weisbrod. 1998. *Financial Regulation.* London: Routledge.

Goodman, A. 1998. "Carbon Trading Up and Running." *Tomorrow Magazine* (May/June).

Goulder, Lawrence H. 1994. "Energy Taxes: Traditional Efficiency Effects and Environmental Implications." *Tax Policy and the Economy* 8:105–58.

Graham, Carol. 1994. "Safety Nets, Politics and the Poor: Transition to Market Economies." The Brookings Institution, Washington, D.C.

Graham, Edward. 1996. *Global Corporations and National Governments.* Washington, D.C.: Institute for International Economics.

Gregorio, José De, and P. E. Guidotti. 1995. "Financial Development and Economic Growth." *World Development* 23(3): 443–48.

Greif, Avner. 1998. "Historical and Comparative Institutional Analysis." *American Economic Review, Papers and Proceedings* 88: 80–84.

Grootaert, Christiaan, and Ravi Kanbur. 1995. "Child Labor: A Review." Policy Research Working Paper 1454. World Bank, Washington, D.C.

Grossman, Gene M., and Alan B. Krueger. 1995. "Economic Growth and the Environment." *Quarterly Journal of Economics* 110: 353–77.

G-22 (Group of Twenty-two) Committee. 1998a. "Report of the Working Group on Strengthening Financial Systems." Washington, D.C. Informal publication.

———. 1998b. "Report of the Working Group on Transparency and Accountability." Washington, D.C. Informal publication.

Guerrant, Richard L. 1998. "Why America Must Care about Tropical Medicine: Threats to Global Health and Security from Tropical Infectious Diseases." *American Journal of Tropical Medicine and Hygiene* 59(1): 3–16.

Guo, Shuqing. 1998. "Globalization and China's Economy." Background Paper for *World Development Report 1999/2000.* World Bank, Washington, D.C. Processed.

Haddad, Lawrence, Marie T. Ruel, and James L. Garrett. 1999. "Are Urban Poverty and Undernutrition Growing? Some Newly Assembled Evidence." Discussion Paper 63, Food Consumption and Nutrition Division, International Food Policy Research Institute.

Hallerberg, Mark, and Jürgen von Hagen. 1997. "Electoral Institutions, Cabinet Negotiations, and Budget Deficits in the European Union." Georgia Institute of Technology, Atlanta. Processed.

Hardoy, Jorge, and David Satterthwaite. 1990. "The Future City." In *The Poor Die Young,* edited by J. E. Hardoy, S. Cairncross, and D. Satterthwaite. London: Earthscan.

Harpham, Trudy, and M. Stuttaford. 1999. "Health, Governance and the Environment." In *Sustainability in Cities in Developing Countries: Theory and Practice at the Millennium,* edited by Cedric Pugh. London: Earthscan.

Harpham, Trudy, and M. Tanner, eds. 1995. *Urban Health in Developing Countries: Progress and Prospects.* London: Earthscan.

Harrison, Ann. 1994. "Productivity, Imperfect Competition, and Trade Reform: Theory and Evidence." *Journal of International Economics* (36): 53–73.

Harrison, Glenn W., Thomas F. Rutherford, and David G. Tarr. 1996. "Quantifying the Uruguay Round." In *The Uruguay Round and the Developing Countries,* edited by Alan Winters and William Martin. Cambridge: Cambridge University Press.

Harvard Working Group. 1994. "The Emergence of New Diseases." *American Scientist* 82(1): 52–60.

Harwood, Alison. 1997. "Financial Reform in Developing Countries." In *Sequencing? Financial Strategies for Developing Countries,* edited by Alison Harwood and Bruce L. R. Smith. Washington, D.C.: The Brookings Institution Press.

Hasan, Arif. 1997a. *Urban Housing Policies and Approaches in a Changing Asian Context.* Karachi: City Press.

———. 1997b. *Working with Government.* Karachi: City Press.

———. 1998. *Community Initiatives: Four Case Studies from Karachi.* Karachi: City Press.

Hasan, Arif, Akbar Zaidi, and Muhammad Younis. 1998. Background Note on Karachi Prepared for *World Development Report 1999/2000.* Washington, D.C.

Hathaway, Dale E., and Merlinda D. Ingco. 1996. "Agricultural Liberalization and the Uruguay Round." In *The Uruguay Round and the Developing Countries,* edited by Alan Winters and William Martin. Cambridge: Cambridge University Press.

Hawley, Willis D. 1970. *Nonpartisan Elections and the Case of Party Politics.* New York: Wiley Press.

Hay, Jonathan R., and Andrei Shleifer. 1998. "Private Enforcement of Public Laws: A Theory of Legal Reform." *American Economic Review, Papers and Proceedings,* 88: 398–407.

Hayami, Yujiro. 1998. "Toward a New Model of Rural-Urban Linkages under Globalization." Background Paper for *World Development Report 1999/2000,* Tokyo Workshop.

Head, Keith, and John Ries. 1995. "Inter-City Competition for Foreign Investment: Static and Dynamic Effects of China's Incentive Areas." *Journal of Urban Economics* 40(July 1996): 38–60.

Hellman, Thomas, Kevin Murdock, and Joseph E. Stiglitz. 1998. "Liberalization, Moral Hazard in Banking, and Prudential Regulaton: Are Capital Requirements Enough?" Graduate School of Business, Stanford University, Calif.

Hemming, Richard, and Paul Bernard Spahn. 1998. "European Integration and the Theory of Fiscal Federalism." In *Macroeconomic Dimensions of Public Finance: Essays in Honour of Vito Tanzi,* edited by Bario Blejer and Teresa Ter-Minassian. Washington, D.C.: International Monetary Fund.

Hemming, Richard, Neven Mates, and Barry Potter. 1997. "India." In *Fiscal Federalism in Theory and Practice,* edited by Teresa Ter-Minassian. Washington, D.C.: International Monetary Fund.

Henderson, J. Vernon. 1998. *Urban Development: Theory, Fact and Illusion.* New York: Oxford University Press.

Henderson, J. Vernon, and Ari Kuncoro. 1996. "Industrial Centralization in Indonesia." *World Bank Economic Review* 10: 513–40.

Henderson, J. Vernon, T. Lee, and J-Y Lee. 1998. "Externalities, Location, and Industrial Deconcentration in a Tiger Economy." Department of Economics, Brown University. Processed.

Hernández, Leonardo, and Klaus Schmidt-Hebbel. 1999. "Capital Controls in Chile: Effective? Efficient? Endurable?" Paper presented at World Bank/International Monetary Fund/ World Trade Organization Conference on Capital Flows, Financial Crises, and Policies. Washington, D.C., April 15–16.

Hertel, Thomas W., William A. Masters, and Aziz Elbehri. 1998. "The Uruguay Round and Africa: A Global General Equilibrium Analysis." *Journal of African Economies* 7(2): 208–34.

Hertel, Thomas W., Christian F. Bach, Betina Dimaranan, and Will Martin. 1996. "Growth, Globalization, and Gains from the Uruguay Round." Policy Research Working Paper 1614. World Bank, Washington, D.C.

Hertel, Thomas W., Will Martin, Koji Yanagishima, and Betina Dimaranan. 1996. "Liberalizing Manufactures Trade in a Changing World Economy." *The Uruguay Round and the Developing Countries*, edited by Alan Winters and William Martin. Cambridge: Cambridge University Press.

Heywood, V. H., ed. 1995. *Global Biodiversity Assessment.* Cambridge: Cambridge University Press.

Higgins, Matthew, and Jeffrey G. Williamson. 1997. "Age Structure Dynamics in Asia and Dependence on Foreign Capital." *Population and Development Review* 23(2): 261–93.

Hirschman, Alberto. 1970. *Exit, Voice and Loyalty.* Cambridge, Mass.: Harvard University Press.

Hoekman, Bernard. 1996. "Assessing the General Agreement on Trade in Services." In *The Uruguay Round and the Developing Countries*, edited by Alan Winters and William Martin. Cambridge: Cambridge University Press.

Hoekman, Bernard, and Kym Anderson. 1999. "Developing Country Agriculture and the New Trade Agenda." World Bank, Washington, D.C. Processed.

Hoekman, Bernard, and Simeon Djankov. 1996. "The European Union's Mediterranean Free Trade Initiative." *The World Economy* 19(4): 387–406.

———. 1997a. "Effective Protection and Investment Incentives in Egypt and Jordan during the Transition to Free Trade with Europe." *World Development* 25(2): 281–91.

———. 1997b. "Towards a Free Trade Agreement with the European Union: Issues and Policy Options for Egypt." In *Regional Partners in Global Markets: Limits and Possibilities of the Euro-Med Agreements*, edited by Ahmed Galal and Bernard Hoekman. Centre for Egyptian Policy Research/ Egyptian Centre for Economic Studies, London.

Hoekman, Bernard, and Denise Konan. 1999. "Deep Integration, Nondiscrimination, and Euro-Mediterranean Free Trade." World Bank, Washington, D.C.

Hoekman, Bernard, and Carlos A. Primo Braga. 1997. "Protection and Trade in Services: A Survey." *Open Economies Review* 8: 285–308.

Hoekman, Bernard, Denise Konan, and Keith Maskus. 1998. "An Egypt–United States Free Trade Agreement: Economic Incentives and Effects." Discussion Paper 1882. Centre for Economic Policy Research, London.

Hohenberg, Paul M. 1998. "Urban Systems and Economic Development: The European Long Term and Its Implications." Background Paper for *World Development Report 1999/2000.* World Bank, Washington, D.C.

Holmes, Robert. 1999. "Head in the Clouds." *New Scientist* 162(2185).

Hommes, Rudolf. 1996. "Conflicts and Dilemmas of Decentralization." In *Annual World Bank Conference on Development Economics 1995*, edited by Michael Bruno and Boris Pleskovic. Washington, D.C.: World Bank.

Horioka, C. Y. 1990. "Why Is Japan's Household Saving So High? A Literature Survey." *Journal of Japanese and International Economics* 4(1): 49–92.

Horlick, Gary N., and Steven A. Sugarman. 1999. "Antidumping Policy as a System of Law." In *Trade Rules in the Making*, edited by Miguel Rodriguez Mendoza, Patrick Low, and Barbara Kotschwar. Washington, D.C.: The Brookings Institution Press.

Hourcade, J. 1996. "A Review of Mitigation Cost Studies." In *Climate Change 1995, Economic and Social Dimensions of Climate Change: Contribution of Working Group III to the Second Assessment Report of the Intergovernmental Panel on Climate Change*, edited by James Bruce, Hoesung Lee, and Erik Haites. Cambridge: Cambridge University Press.

Howse, Robert, and Michael Trebilcock. 1996. "The Fair Trade–Free Trade Debate: Trade, Labour and the Environment." *International Review of Law and Economics* 16: 61–79.

Howson, Christopher P., Harvey V. Fineberg, and Barry R. Bloom. 1998. "The Pursuit of Global Health: The Relevance of Engagement for Developed Countries." *Lancet* 351(21/February).

Hufbauer, Gary, and Barbara Kotschwar. 1998. "The Future Course of Trade Liberalization." Background Paper for *World Development Report 1999/2000.* World Bank, Washington, D.C.

Hughes Hallett, A. J. 1998. "Policy Coordination: Globalization or Localization in International Monetary Arrangements?" Background Paper for *World Development Report 1999/2000.* World Bank, Washington, D.C.

Hummels, David. 1998. "Data on International Transportation Costs: A Report Prepared for the World Bank." Background Paper for *World Development Report 1999/2000.* World Bank, Washington, D.C.

Hummels, David, Jun Ishii, and Kei-Mu Yi. 1999. "The Nature and Growth of Vertical Specialization in World Trade." University of Chicago Graduate School of Business and the Federal Reserve Bank of New York. Processed.

Hunter, Brian, ed. 1998. *Statesman's Yearbook: A Statistical, Political and Economic Account of the States of the World for the Year 1998–99.* London: Macmillan.

Huther, Jeff, and Anwar Shah. 1998. "Applying a Simple Measure of Good Governance to the Debate on Fiscal Decentralization." Policy Reaearch Working Paper 1894. World Bank, Washington, D.C.

IFC (International Finance Corporation). 1998. *Foreign Direct Investment.* Lessons of Experience 5. Washington, D.C.

ILO (International Labour Office). 1993. *World Labour Report.* Geneva.

ILO (International Labour Organisation). 1998. "Employability in the Global Economy: How Training Matters." *World Employment Report 1998–99.* Geneva.

Imber, Mark. 1996. "The Environment and the United Nations." In *The Environment and International Relations*, edited by John Vogler and Mark Imber. London: Routledge.

IMF (International Monetary Fund). Various years. *Annual Report on Exchange Arrangements and Exchange Restrictions.* Washington, D.C.

———. 1997. *Government Finance Statistics.* Washington, D.C.

———. 1998a. *Balance of Payments Statistics Yearbook.* Washington, D.C.

———. 1998b. *Government Finance Statistics.* Washington, D.C.

———. 1998c. *International Capital Markets.* Washington, D.C.

———. 1999a. "A Guide to Progress in Strengthening the Architecture of the International Financial System" (*http://www.imf.org/external/np/exr/facts/arch.htm*).

———. 1999b. *World Economic Outlook Database.* Washington, D.C.

Ingco, Merlinda, and Francis Ng. 1998. "Distortionary Effects of State Trading in Agriculture: Issues for the Next Round of Multilateral Trade Negotiations." Policy Research Working Paper 1915. World Bank, Washington, D.C.

Ingram, Gregory K. 1998. "Patterns of Metropolitan Development: What Have We Learned?" *Urban Studies* 35(7).

Inman, Robert P., and Daniel L. Rubinfeld. 1996. "Designing Tax Policy in Federalist Economies: An Overview." *Journal of Public Economics* 60: 307–34.

Intergovernmental Panel on Climate Change (IPCC). 1995. *Climate Change 1995: Economic and Social Dimensions. Working Group I, Contribution to the Second Assessment Report of the Intergovernmental Panel on Climate Change.* Cambridge: Cambridge University Press.

Isham, Jonathan, Deepa Narayan, and Lant Pritchett. 1994. "Does Participation Improve Performance? Empirical Evidence from Project Data." Policy Research Working Paper 1357. World Bank, Washington, D.C.

Islam, Nurul. 1997. "The Nonfarm Sector and Rural Development: Review of Issues and Evidence." Food, Agriculture, and the Environment Discussion Paper 22. International Food Policy Research Institute, Washington D.C.

Jackson, John. 1997. *The World Trading System,* 2nd edition. Cambridge, Mass.: MIT Press.

———. 1998. *The World Trade Organization: Constitution and Jurisprudence.* The Royal Institute of International Affairs, London.

Jaffe, Adam B., Manuel Trajtenberg, and Rebecca Henderson. 1993. "Geographic Localization of Knowledge Spillovers as Evidenced by Patent Citation." *Quarterly Journal of Economics* 108: 577–98.

James, S., and Kym Anderson. 1998. "On the Need for More Economic Assessment of Quarantine Policies." *Australian Journal of Agricultural and Resource Economics* 41(4/December): 525–44.

Jamison, Dean T. 1993. "Investing in Health." *Finance and Development* (September): 2–5.

Jamison, Dean T., Julio Frenk, and Felicia Kaul. 1998. "International Collective Action in Health Objectives, Functions and Rationale." *Lancet* 351(14/February).

Jin, Jing, and Heng-fu Zou. 1998. "The Effects of Fiscal Decentralization on the Sizes of Governments: A Cross-Country Study." Development Research Group, World Bank, Washington, D.C. Processed.

John, T. Jacob, Reuben Samuel, Vinohar Balraj, and Rohan John. 1998. "Disease Surveillance at the District Level: A Model for Developing Countries." *Lancet* 352:(4/July).

Johnston, R. Barry. 1997. "The Speed of Financial Sector Reforms: Risks and Strategies." In *Sequencing? Financial Strategies for Developing Countries,* edited by Alison Harwood and Bruce L. R. Smith. Washington, D.C.: The Brookings Institution Press.

Johnston, R. Barry, Salim M. Darbar, and Claudia Echeverria. 1997. "Sequencing Capital Account Liberalization: Lessons from the Experiences in Chile, Indonesia, Korea, and Thailand." Working Paper 97/157. International Monetary Fund, Washington, D.C.

Josling, Timothy. 1998a. "Agricultural Trade Policy: Completing the Reform." In *Launching New Global Trade Talks: An Action Agenda,* Special Report 12, edited by Jeffrey J. Schott. Washington, D.C.: Institute for International Economics.

———. 1998b. "Agricultural Trade Policy: Completing the Reform." Institute for International Economics. Washington, D.C.

Kaminsky, Graciela L., and Carmen M. Reinhart. 1998. "Financial Crises in Asia and Latin America: Then and Now." *American Economic Review Papers and Proceedings* 88(2): 444–48.

Kane, Edward J. 1998. "Understanding and Preventing Bank Crises." In *Preventing Bank Crises: Lessons from Recent Global Bank Failures,* edited by Gerard C. Caprio. Washington, D.C.: Federal Reserve Bank of Chicago and the World Bank Economic Development Institute.

Kane, Hal. 1995. "What's Driving Migration?" *Worldwatch* (January/February).

Keesing, Donald B. 1998. *Improving Trade Policy Reviews in the World Trade Organization.* Washington, D.C.: Institute for International Economics.

Kenny, Charles. 1999. "Telecommunications and Competitive Cities." In *World Urban Economic Development,* edited by Elizabeth Cooper. London: World Markets Research Center.

Kenny, Charles J., and David Williams. 1999. "What Do We Know about Economic Growth? or Why Don't We Know Very Much?" Lady Margaret Hall, Oxford University. Processed.

Kerr, William A. 1999. "International Trade in Transgenic Food Products: A New Focus for Agricultural Trade Disputes." *The World Economy* 22(2): 245–59.

Kessides, Christine. 1998. "A Strategic View of Urban and Local Government Issues: Implications for the Bank." World Bank, Washington, D.C. Processed.

Khilnani, Sunil. 1997. *The Idea of India.* New York: Farrar, Straus, and Giroux.

Kilgour, D. Marc, and Ariel Dinar. 1995. "Are Stable Agreements for Sharing International River Waters Now Possible?" Policy Research Working Paper 1474. World Bank, Washington, D.C.

Kim, Hyung-Ki, and Jun Ma. 1997. "The Role of Government in Acquiring Technological Capability: The Case of the Petrochemical Industry in East Asia." In *The Role of Govern-*

ment in East Asian Economic Development, edited by Masahiko Aoki, Hyung-ki Kim, and Mashiro Okuno-Funiwara. New York: Oxford University Press.

King, Elizabeth M., and Berk Ozler. 1998. "What's Decentralization Got to Do with Learning? The Case of Nicaragua's School Autonomy Reform." Impact Evaluation of Education Working Paper Series 9. World Bank, Washington, D.C.

Kinoshita, Yuko, and Ashoka Mody. 1997. "The Usefulness of Private and Public Information for Foreign Investment Decisions." Policy Research Working Paper 1733. World Bank, Washington, D.C.

Kitano, Naohiro. 1998. "Analysis of Spatial Organization and Transportation Demand in an Expanding Urban Area Using Centrographic Methods: Sendai 1972–1992." Paper for *World Development Report 1999/2000*, Tokyo Workshop. World Bank, Washington, D.C.

Kleinknecht, Alfred, and Jan der Wengel. 1998. "The Myth of Economic Globalization." *Cambridge Journal of Economics* 22: 637–47.

Knight, Malcolm. 1998. "Developing Countries and the Globalization of Financial Markets." Working Paper 98/105. International Monetary Fund, Washington, D.C.

Kobrin, Stephen J. 1997. "The Architecture of Globalization: State Sovereignty in a Networked Global Economy." In *Governments, Globalization and International Business*, edited by John H. Dunning. New York: Oxford University Press.

Konan, Denise, and Keith E. Maskus. 1997. "A Computable General Equilibrium Analysis of Egyptian Trade Liberalization Scenarios." In *Regional Partners in Global Markets: Limits and Possibilities of the Euro-Med Agreements*, edited by Ahmed Galal and Bernard Hoekman. Centre for Egyptian Policy Research/Egyptian Centre for Economic Studies, London.

Kono, Masamichi, and Ludger Schuknecht. 1999. "Financial Services Trade, Capital Flows, and Financial Stability." Paper presented at the World Bank/International Monetary Fund/World Trade Organization Conference on Capital Flows, Financial Crises, and Policies. Washington, D.C., April 15–16.

Kosai, Yutaka, Jun Saito, and Nashiro Yashiro. 1998. "Declining Population and Sustained Economic Growth: Can They Coexist?" *American Economic Review.* 88(2): 412–16.

Kozul-Wright, Richard, and Robert Rowthorn. 1998. "Spoilt for Choice? Multinational Corporations and the Geography of International Production." *Oxford Review of Economic Policy* 14(2): 74–92.

Kremer, Michael. 1993. "O-Ring Theory of Economic Development." *Quarterly Journal of Economics* (108): 551–75.

Krishna, Pravin, and Devahish Mitra. 1998. "Trade Liberalization, Market Discipline, and Productivity Growth: New Evidence from India." *Journal of Development Economics* 56: 447–62.

Krueger, Anne O. 1998. "The Developing Countries and the Next Round of Multilateral Trade Negotiations." Stanford University, Calif. Processed.

Krugman, Paul. 1993. "On the Number and Location of Cities." *European Economic Review* 37: 293–28.

———. 1995. "Growing World Trade: Causes and Consequences." *Brookings Papers on Economic Activity* 1: 327–77.

———. 1998a. "Space: The Final Frontier." *Journal of Economic Perspectives* 12(2): 161–74.

———. 1998b. "What Happened to Asia?" On Paul Krugman's web page (*http:/web.mit.edu/people/krugman/index.html*).

Laird, Sam. 1997. "Issues for the Forthcoming Multilateral Negotiations in Agriculture." WTO (World Trade Organization), Geneva.

Lall, Rajiv, and Bert Hofman. 1994. "Decentralization and Government Deficit in Chile." World Bank, Washington, D.C. Processed.

Lall, Sanjaya. 1998. "Exports of Manufactures by Developing Countries: Emerging Patterns of Trade and Location." *Oxford Review of Economic Policy* 14: 54–73.

Lampietti, Julian, and John Dixon. 1995. "To See the Forest for the Trees: A Guide to Non-Timber Forest Benefits." Paper No. 13. Environment Department, World Bank, Washington, D.C.

Lancet. 1996. "HIV Epidemic in India. Opportunity to Learn from the Past." 347 (18/May): 1349–50.

———. 1998. "Action Against Antibiotic Resistance." 351 (2/May).

Law, Lisa. 1997. "Cebu and Ceboom: The Political Place of Globalisation in a Philippine City." In *Pacific Rim Development: Integration and Globalisation in the Asia-Pacific Economy*, edited by Peter Rimmer. Canberra City, Australia: Aussie Print.

Lawrence, Robert Z. 1996. "Current Economic Policies: Social Implications over the Longer Term." In *Social Cohesion and the Globalising Economy: What Does the Future Hold*? Paris: Organisation for Economic Co-operation and Development.

———, ed. 1998. *Brookings Trade Forum 1998*. Washington, D.C.: The Brookings Institution Press.

Le Fort, V. Guillermo, and Carlos Budnevich. 1998. "Capital Account Relations and Macroeconomic Policy: Two Latin American Experiences." In *Capital Account Regimes and the Developing Countries*, edited by G. K. Helleiner. New York: St. Martin's Press.

Le Houerou, Philippe. 1996. "Fiscal Management in Russia." World Bank, Washington, D.C. Processed.

Leipziger, Danny M. 1998. "The Argentine Banking Crisis: Observations and Lessons." In *Preventing Bank Crises: Lessons from Recent Global Bank Failures*, edited by Gerard C. Caprio. Washington, D.C.: Federal Reserve Bank of Chicago and the World Bank Economic Development Institute.

Leitmann, Josef, and Deniz Baharoglu. 1998. "Informal Rules! Using Institutional Economics to Understand Service Provision in Turkey's Spontaneous Settlements." *Journal of Development Studies* 34(5).

Lele, Uma J., and Robert E. Christiansen. 1989. "Markets, Marketing Boards, and Cooperatives in Africa: Issues in Adjustment Policy." World Bank, Washington, D.C. Processed.

Levine, Ross. 1997. "Financial Development and Economic Growth: Views and Agenda." *Journal of Economic Literature* 35: 688–726.

———. 1998. "The Legal Environment, Banks, and Long-Run Economic Growth." *Journal of Money, Credit, and Banking* 30(3): 596–613.

———. 1999. "Napoleon, Bourses and Growth: With a Focus on Latin America." Paper delivered at the IRIS Market Augmenting Government Conference. Washington, D.C., March 26–27.

Levine, Ross, and David Renelt. 1992. "Sensitivity Analysis of Cross-Country Growth Regressions." *American Economic Review* 82(September): 942–63.

Levine, Ross, and Sara Zervos. 1998a. "Capital Control Liberalization and Stock Market Development." *World Development* 26(7): 1169–83.

———, ed. 1998b. *Brookings Trade Forum 1998.* Washington, D.C.: The Brookings Institution Press.

———. 1998c. "Stock Markets, Banks and Economic Growth." *American Economic Review* 88(3): 537–54.

Levinsohn, James. 1993. "Testing the Imports-as-Market-Discipline Hypothesis." *Journal of International Economics* 35: 1–22.

Lewandrowski, Jan, and David Schimmelpfennig. 1999. "Economic Implications of Climate Change for U.S. Agriculture: Assessing Recent Evidence." *Land Economics* 75(1): 39–57.

Lewis, W. Arthur. 1955. *The Theory of Economic Growth.* Reprint, New York: Harper Torchbooks, 1970.

Lijphart, Arend. 1994. *Electoral Systems and Party Systems: A Study of Twenty-Seven Democracies 1945–1990.* New York: Oxford University Press.

Lindgren, Carl-Johan, and Gillian Garcia. 1996. "Deposit Insurance and Crisis Management." Monetary and Exchange Affairs Department Operation Paper 96/3. International Monetary Fund, Washington, D.C.

Linz, Juan J., and Alfred Stepan. 1997. "Toward Consolidated Democracies." In *Consolidating the Third Wave Democracies*, edited by Larry Diamond, Marc F. Plattner, Yun-han Chu, and Hung-mao Tien. Baltimore: The Johns Hopkins University Press.

Lipsey, Robert E. 1999. "The Role of Foreign Direct Investment in International Capital Flows." Working Paper Series 7094. National Bureau of Economic Research, Cambridge, Mass.

Lipton, Michael. 1999. "Saving Undernourished Lives." *Financial Times,* Letters to the Editor. June 2.

Litan, Robert E. 1998. "Toward a Global Financial Architecture for the 21st Century." Background Paper for *World Development Report 1999/2000.* World Bank, Washington, D.C.

Litvack, Jennie. 1994. "Regional Demands and Fiscal Federalism." In *Russia and the Challenge of Fiscal Federalism,* edited by Christine Wallich. World Bank, Washington, D.C.

Litvack, Jennie, Junaid Ahmad, and Richard Bird. 1998. "Rethinking Decentralization in Developing Countries." World Bank, Washington, D.C

Lloyd-Sherlock, Peter. 1997. "The Recent Appearance of Favelas in São Paulo City: An Old Problem in a New Setting." *Latin American Studies* 16(3).

Long, Millard, and Mihaly Kopanyi. 1998. "Hungary: Financial Sector Development." World Bank, Washington, D.C. Processed.

Lucas, Robert. 1998. "Internal Migration and Urbanization: Recent Contributions and New Evidence." Background Paper for *World Development Report 1999/2000.* World Bank, Washington, D.C.

Madeley, John. 1995a. "Biodiversity: A Matter of Extinction." Panos Media Briefing 17. Panos Institute, London. Processed.

———. 1995b. "Fish: A Net Loss for the Poor." Panos Media Briefing 15. Panos Institute, London. Processed.

Mahmood, Saman. 1999. "Shelter within My Reach: Medium-Rise Apartment Housing for the Middle Income Group in Karachi, Pakistan." Master's diss., Massachusetts Institute of Technology, Cambridge, Mass. Processed.

Mainwaring, Scott. 1997. "Multipartism, Robust Federalism, and Presidentialism in Brazil." In *Presidentialism and Democracy*, edited by Scott Mainwaring and Matthew Soburt Shogart. New York: Cambridge University Press.

Mallampally, Padma, and Karl P. Sauvant. 1999. "Foreign Direct Investment in Developing Countries." *Finance and Development* 36(1): 34–37.

Mani, Sunil. 1996. "Economic Liberalization and Kerala's Industrial Sector." *Economic and Political Weekly* (August 24–31).

Mankiw, N. Gregory, David Romer, and David Weil. 1992. "Contribution to the Empirics of Economic Growth." *Quarterly Journal of Economics* 107: 407–37.

Manning, Nick. 1998. "Unbundling the State: Autonomous Agencies and Service Delivery." World Bank, Washington, D.C. Processed.

Markusen, Ann. 1998. "What Distinguishes Success Among Second Tier Cities?" Presentation at *World Development Report 1999/2000*, July Workshop. World Bank, Washington, D.C.

Marsh, Kevin. 1998. Malaria Disaster in Africa. *Lancet* 352 (19/September): 924.

Martin, Ron. 1999. "The New Geographical Turn in Economics." *Cambridge Journal of Economics* (January).

Martinez-Vasquez, Jorge. 1998. "Fiscal Decentralization in the Russian Federation: Major Trends and Issues." School of Political Studies, Georgia State University, Atlanta. Processed.

Martinez-Vasquez, Jorge, and Robert M. McNab. 1997. "Fiscal Decentralization, Economic Growth and Democratic Governance." School of Political Studies, Georgia State University, Atlanta. Processed.

Maskus, Keith E. 1997. "Should Core Labor Standards Be Imposed through International Trade Policy?" Policy Research Working Paper 1817. World Bank, Washington, D.C.

Mathur, Om Prakash. 1999. "Decentralization in India: A Report Card." National Institute of Public Finance and Policy, New Delhi.

Matusz, Steven, and David Tarr. 1998. "Adjusting to Trade Policy Reform." World Bank, Washington, D.C. Processed.

Mayo, Stephen K., and Shlomo Angel. 1993. *Housing: Enabling Markets To Work.* World Bank Policy Paper. Washington, D.C.

Mazumdar, Dipak. 1986. "Rural-Urban Migration in Developing Countries." In *Handbook of Regional and Urban Economics,* edited by Peter Nijkamp. New York: North-Holland.

McKinnon, Ronald I. 1991. *The Order of Economic Liberalization: Financial Control in the Transition to a Market Economy.* Baltimore: The Johns Hopkins University Press.

———. 1997. "Monetary Regimes, Government Borrowing Constraints and Market Preserving Federalism: Implications for EMU." Stanford University, Calif. Processed.

———. 1998. "The IMF. The East Asian Currency Crisis and the World Dollar Standard." Paper presented at the American Economics Association meetings. Chicago, January 3–5.

McKinnon, Ronald I., and Huw Pill. 1998. "International Overborrowing: A Decomposition of Credit and Currency Risks." *World Development* 26(7): 1267–82.

McLure, Charles E., Jr. 1999. "Intergovernmental Fiscal Relations and Local Financial Management." World Bank, Washington, D.C. Processed.

Mendes, Marcos Jose. 1999. *Incentivos Eleitorais e Desequilibrio Fiscal de Estados e Municipios.* São Paulo: Instituto Fernand Braudel de Economia Mundial.

Meyer, John W., David J. Frank, Ann Hironaka, Evan Schofer, and Nancy B. Tuma. 1997. "The Structuring of a World Environmental Regime, 1870–1990." *International Organization* 51(4): 623–51.

Michalopoulos, Constantine. 1999. "Developing Countries' Participation in the World Trade Organization." *The World Economy* 22(1): 117–44.

Millard, F. J. C. 1998. South Africa: A Physician's View. *Lancet* 351(7/March): 748–49.

Miller, Marian. 1995. *The Third World in Global Environmental Politics.* Boulder, Colo.: Lynne Reinner.

Mills, Edwin S. 1998. "Internal Functioning of Urban Areas." Kellogg Graduate School of Management, Northwestern University. Processed.

Mills, Edwin S., and Charles Becker. 1986. *Studies in Indian Urban Development.* New York: Oxford University Press.

Miranda, Jorge, Raul A. Torres, and Mario Ruiz. 1998. "The International Use of Anti-Dumping: 1987–1997." World Trade Organization, Geneva. Processed.

Miranda, Rowan, and Donald Rosdil. 1995. "From Boosterism to Qualitative Growth." *Urban Affairs Review* 30(6).

Mitlin, Diana, and David Satterthwaite. 1998. "Urban Poverty: Some Thoughts about Its Scale and Nature and about Responses to It by Community Organizations, NGOs, Local Governments and National Agencies." Paper for *World Development Report 1999/2000*, Singapore Workshop. World Bank, Washington, D.C.

Mohan, Rakesh. 1999. "Financing of Sub-National Public Investment in India." Paper for *World Development Report 1999/2000*, Singapore Workshop. World Bank, Washington, D.C.

Moran, Theodore, H. 1999. *Foreign Direct Investment and Development: The New Policy Agenda for Developing Countries and Economies in Transition.* Washington, D.C.: Institute for International Economics.

Munson, Abby. 1995. "The United Nations Convention on Biological Diversity." In *The Earthscan Reader in Sustainable Development,* edited by John Kirby, Phil O'Keefe, and Lloyd Timberlake. London: Earthscan.

Musgrave, Richard A. 1997. "Devolution, Grants, and Fiscal Competition." *Journal of Public Economics* 11: 65–72.

Musgrave, Richard A., and Peggy Musgrave. 1973. *Public Finance in Theory and Practice.* New York: McGraw Hill.

Mussa, Michael, and Anthony Richards. 1999. "Capital Flows in the 1990s before and after the Asian Crisis." Paper presented at the World Bank/International Monetary Fund/World Trade Organization Conference on Capital Flows, Financial Crises, and Policies. Washington, D.C., April 15–16.

Mutti, John, and Harry Grubert. 1998. "The Significance of International Tax Rules for Sourcing Income: The Relationship between Income Taxes and Trade Taxes." In *Geography and Ownership as Bases for Economic Accounting,* edited by Robert E. Baldwin, Robert E. Lipsey, and J. David Richardson. National Bureau of Economic Research (NBER) Studies in Income and Wealth, vol. 59.

Narayan, Deepa, and Lant Pritchett. 1997. "Cents and Sociability: Household Income and Social Capital in Rural Tanzania." Policy Research Working Paper 1796. World Bank, Washington, D.C.

Nature. 1998. "Falling Satellites, Rising Temperatures." August.

———. 1999. "Scientific Societies Build Better Nations." June 17.

New England Journal of Medicine. 1996. "The March of AIDS through Asia." 335(5).

———. 1997. "Multi-drug Resistance in Plague." 337(10).

———. 1998. "The Global Threat of Multi Drug Resistant Tuberculosis" 338(23).

New Scientist. 1998. "Dirty Secrets." August 29.

Ng, Francis, and Alexander Yeats. 1997. "Open Economies Work Better! Did Africa's Protectionist Policies Cause Its Marginalization in World Trade?" *World Development* 25: 889–975.

Norregaard, John. 1997. "Tax Assignment." In *Fiscal Federalism in Theory and Practice,* edited by Teresa Ter-Minassian. Washington, D.C.: International Monetary Fund.

North, Douglass C. 1990. *Institutions, Institutional Change and Economic Performance.* Cambridge: Cambridge University Press.

———. 1997. "Prologue." In *The Frontiers of the New Institutional Economics,* edited by John N. Drobak and J. V. C. Nye. San Diego: Academic Press.

Oates, Wallace. 1972. *Fiscal Federalism.* New York: Harcourt Brace Jovanovich.

———. 1998. "An Essay on Fiscal Federalism." *Journal of Economic Literature.* Forthcoming.

Obstfeld, Maurice, and Alan M. Taylor. 1999. *Global Capital Markets: Integration, Crisis, and Growth.* Cambridge: Cambridge University Press.

O'Donnell, Guillermo, Philippe C. Schmitter, and Laurence Whitehead. 1986. *Transitions from Authoritarian Rule.* Baltimore: The Johns Hopkins University Press.

OECD (Organisation for Economic Co-operation and Development). 1997. "Managing across Levels of Government." Paris.

———. 1998. *Open Markets Matter: The Benefits of Trade and Investment Liberalisation.* Paris.

Ordeshook, Peter C., and Olga Shvetsova. 1997. "Federalism and Constitutional Design." *Journal of Democracy* 8(1): 28–42.

Ornusal, B., and S. Gautam. 1997. *Vehicular Air Pollution: Experience from Seven Latin American Urban Centers.* Technical Paper 373. Washington, D.C.: World Bank.

Ostrom, Elinor, Larry D. Schroeder, and Susan G. Wynne. 1993. *Institutional Incentives and Sustainable Development.* Boulder, Colo.: Westview Press.

Ostry, Sylvia. 1997. *The Post–Cold War Trading System: Who's on First?* Chicago: University of Chicago Press.

———. 1998. "Reinforcing the WTO." Occasional Paper 56. Group of Thirty, Washington, D.C.

Oxley, Joanne, and Bernard Yeung. 1998. "Industrial Location Growth and Government Activism: The Changing Economic Landscape." School of Business Administration, University of Michigan, Ann Arbor. Processed.

Panagariya, Arvind. 1998. "The Regionalism Debate: An Overview." Department of Economics, University of Maryland, College Park. Processed.

———. 1999. "The Regionalism Debate: An Overview." *The World Economy* 22(4): 477–512.

Panagariya, Arvind, and T. N. Srinivasan. 1997. "The New Regionalism: A Benign or Malign Growth?" Department of Economics, University of Maryland, College Park. Processed.

Panizza, Ugo. 1999. "On the Determinants of Fiscal Decentralization: Theory and Evidence." *Journal of Public Economics.* Forthcoming.

Park, Yung Chul, and Chi-Young Song. 1998. "Capital Inflows and Macroeconomic Policy in Sub-Saharan Africa." In *Capital Account Regimes and the Developing Countries*, edited by G. K. Helleiner. New York: St. Martin's Press.

Parry, M., and M. Livermore. 1997. *Climate Change and Its Impacts.* London: Crown Publishers.

Parsonnet, Julie, ed. 1999. *Microbes and Malignancy.* New York: Oxford University Press.

Paul, Samuel. 1998. "Making Voice Work: The Report Card on Bangalore's Public Service." Policy Research Working Paper 1921. World Bank, Washington, D.C.

Pearce, D., and others. 1996. "The Social Costs of Climate Change." In *Climate Change 1995, Economic and Social Dimensions of Climate Change: Contribution of Working Group III to the Second Assessment Report of the Intergovernmental Panel on Climate Change*, edited by James Bruce, Hoesung Lee, and Erik Haites. Cambridge: Cambridge University Press.

Pearce, David W., and Jeremy J. Warford. 1993. *World Without End: Economics, Environment and Sustainable Development.* New York: Oxford University Press.

Peek, Joe, and Eric S. Rosengren. 1997. "The International Transmission of Financial Shocks: The Case of Japan." *American Economic Review* (87): 495–505.

Pegg, Scott. 1999. "The Nonproliferation of States: A Reply to Pascal Boniface." *Washington Quarterly* 22(2): 139–47.

Perrings, Charles. 1995. "The Economic Value of Diversity." In *Global Biodiversity Assessment,* edited by V. H. Heywood. Cambridge: Cambridge University Press.

Persson, Torsten, and Guido Tabellini. 1994. "Does Decentralization Increase the Size of Government?" *European Economic Review* 38: 765–73.

Peterson, George E., and Sonia Hammam. 1997. "Building Local Credit Systems." World Bank, Washington D.C. Processed.

Peterson, M. J. 1993. "International Fisheries Management." In *Institutions for the Earth: Sources of Effective International Environmental Protection*, edited by Peter Haas, Robert Keohane, and Marc Levy. Cambridge, Mass.: MIT Press.

Peterson, Peter G. 1999. *Gray Dawn: How the Coming Age Wave Will Transform America—and the World.* New York: Times Books.

Pirez, Pedro. 1998. "The Management of Urban Services in the City of Buenos Aires." *Environment and Urbanization* 10(2).

Population Reference Bureau. 1999. "Immigration to the United States." *Population Bulletin* 54(2).

Porter, G., R. Clemencon, W. Ofusu-Amaah, and M. Phillips. 1998. "Study of GEF's Overall Performance." Global Environment Facility, Washington, D.C.

Porter, Michael E. 1998. "Location, Clusters, and the 'New' Microeconomics of Competition." *Business Economics* 33 (January): 7–13.

Porter, Richard C. 1996. *The Economics of Water and Waste: A Case Study of Jakarta, Indonesia.* Aldershot, U.K.: Avebury.

Portes, Alejandro, and Patricia Landolt. 1996. "The Downside of Social Capital." *The American Prospect* 26(May/June): 18–21.

Poterba, James M. 1994. "State Responses to Fiscal Crises: The Effects of Budgetary Institutions and Politics." *Journal of Political Economy* 102(4): 799–821.

Prahalad, C. K., and Kenneth Liebenthal. 1998. "The End of Corporate Imperialism." *Harvard Business Review* (July/August).

Prescott-Allen, Robert. 1995. "Conservation of Wild Genetic Resources." In *The Earthscan Reader in Sustainable Development*, edited by John Kirby, Phil O'Keefe, and Lloyd Timberlake. London: Earthscan.

President's Committee of Advisors on Science and Technology Panel on Energy Research and Development. 1997. "Report to the President on Federal Energy Research and Development for the Challenges of the Twenty-first Century." Washington, D.C.

Primo Braga, Carlos A., Raed Safadi, and Alexander Yeats. 1994. "NAFTA's Implications for East Asian Exports." Policy Research Working Paper 1351. World Bank, Washington, D.C.

Pritchett, Lant. 1997. "Divergence, Big Time." *Journal of Economic Perspectives* 11(3/Summer).

———. 1998. "Patterns of Economic Growth: Hills, Plateaus, Mountains and Plains." Policy Research Working Paper 1947. World Bank, Washington, D.C.

Prud'homme, Rémy. 1995. "The Dangers of Decentralization." *World Bank Research Observer* 10(2): 201–20.

Prusa, Thomas J. 1997. "The Trade Effects of U.S. Antidumping Actions." Working Paper 5440. National Bureau of Economic Research, Cambridge, Mass.

Przeworski, Adam, and Fernando Limongi. 1993. "Political Regimes and Economic Growth." *Journal of Economic Perspectives* 7: 51–69.

———. 1997. "Modernization: Theories and Facts." *World Politics* 49 (January):155–83.

Psacharopoulos, George. 1994. "Returns to Investment in Education: A Global Update," *World Development* 22(9): 1325–43.

Puga, Diego. 1998. "Urbanization Patterns: European vs. Less-Developed Countries." *Journal of Regional Science* 38: 231–52.

Putnam, Robert D. 1993. *Making Democracy Work.* Princeton: Princeton University Press.

Qian, Yingyi, and Barry R. Weingast. 1997. "China's Transition to Markets: Market-Preserving Federalism, Chinese Style." *Policy Reform* 1: 149–85.

Quah, Danny. 1993. "Empirical Cross-Section Dynamics in Economic Growth." *European Economic Review* 37: 426–34.

Quigley, John M. 1998. "Urban Diversity and Economic Growth." *Journal of Economic Perspectives* 12: 127–38.

Quigley, John M., and Daniel L. Rubinfeld. 1997. "Federalism as a Device for Reducing the Budget of the Central Government." Burch Working Paper B96-11. Burch Center for Tax Policy and Public Finance, University of California, Berkeley.

Quinn, Dennis. 1997. "The Correlation of Change in International Financial Regulation." *American Political Science Review* 91: 700–36.

Quirk, Peter J., and Owen Evans. 1995. "Capital Account Convertibility: Review of Experience and Implications for IMF Policies." Occasional Paper 131. International Monetary Fund, Washington, D.C.

Rabinovitch, Jonas. 1992. "Curitiba: Towards Sustainable Urban Development." *Environment and Urbanization* 4(2).

Rabinovitch, Jonas, and Josef Leitman 1996. "Urban Planning in Curitiba." *Scientific American* (March).

Radelet, Steven, and Jeffrey D. Sachs. 1998. "The Onset of the East Asian Financial Crisis." Harvard Institute for International Development, Cambridge, Mass.

Rajan, Raghuram G., and Luigi Zingales. 1998. "Financial Dependence and Growth." *American Economic Review* 88(3): 559–85.

Rajan, Ramkishen. 1998. "Regional Initiatives in Response to the East Asian Crisis." Institute of Policy Studies, Singapore.

Rao, M. Govinda. 1999. "India: Intergovernmental Fiscal Relations in a Planned Economy." In *Fiscal Decentralization in Developing Countries,* edited by Richard M. Bird and François Vaillancourt. Cambridge: Cambridge University Press.

Ravallion, Martin. 1998. "Reaching Poor Areas in a Federal System." Development Research Group, World Bank, Washington, D.C. Processed.

———. 1999a. "Are Poorer States Worse at Targeting Their Poor?" World Bank, Washington, D.C. Processed.

———. 1999b. "Monitoring Targeting Performance When Decentralized Allocations to the Poor are Unobserved." Development Research Group. Policy Research Working Paper 2080. World Bank, Washington, D.C.

Ravallion, Martin, and Shaohua Chen. 1998. "Poverty Reduction and the World Bank Progress in Fiscal 1998." Harvard Institute for International Development, Cambridge, Mass. Forthcoming.

Redding, S. Gordon. 1998. "International Network Capitalism Chinese Style." Background Paper for *World Development Report 1999/2000.* World Bank, Washington, D.C.

Reinhart, Carmen M., and Vincent Raymond Reinhart. 1998. "Some Lessons for Policy Makers Who Deal With the Mixed Blessing of Capital Inflows." In *Capital Flows and Financial Crises,* edited by Miles Kahler. Ithaca: Cornell University Press.

Rezende, Fernando. 1995. "Descentralização e Desenvolvimento: Problemas Atuais do Financiamento das Politicas Publicas." Ministry of Development, Industry, and Commerce, Government of Brazil. Processed.

Richardson, Harry W. 1987. "The Costs of Urbanization: A Four-Country Comparison." *Economic Development and Cultural Change* 35: 561–80.

Ridley, Matt. 1997. *The Future of Disease.* London: Phoenix.

Rigau-Perez, Jose and others. 1998. "Dengue and Dengue Haemorrhagic Fever." *Lancet.* 352 (19/September).

Roberts D., and K. DeRemer. 1997. "Overview of Foreign Technical Barriers to U.S. Agricultural Exports." Staff Paper 9705. ERS, U.S. Department of Agriculture, Washington, D.C.

Rodrik, Dani. 1994. "Developing Countries after the Uruguay Round." Discussion Paper Series 1084. Centre for Economic Policy Research, London.

———. 1997. *Has Globalization Gone Too Far?* Washington, D.C.: Institute for International Economics.

———. 1998a. "Symposium on Globalization in Perspective: An Introduction." *Journal of Economic Perspectives* 12(4). 3–8.

———. 1998b. "Where Did All the Growth Go? External Shocks, Social Conflict and Growth Collapses." Discussion Paper 1789. CEPR (Centre for Economic Policy Research), London.

———. 1998c. "Who Needs Capital-Account Convertibility?" Symposium Paper to appear in Princeton Essays in International Finance. Princeton University.

Rodrik, Dani, and Andrés Velasco. 1999. "Short-Term Capital Flows." Paper prepared for the 1999 Annual World Bank Conference on Development Economics. World Bank, Washington, D.C. Processed.

Rogers, Peter, and Peter Lydon, eds. 1994. *Water in the Arab World: Perspectives and Progress.* Cambridge: Harvard University Press.

Roodman, David. 1997. "Reforming Subsidies." In *State of the World 1997,* edited by Lester Brown. New York: W. W. Norton.

Root, Hilton L. 1998. "A Liberal India: The Triumph of Hope over Experience." *Asian Survey* (38)5: 510–33.

Rose, Greg, and Sandra Crane. 1995. "The Evolution of International Whaling Law." In *The Earthscan Reader in Sustainable Development,* edited by John Kirby, Phil O'Keefe, and Lloyd Timberlake. London: Earthscan.

Rosegrant, Mark. 1997. *Water Resources in the Twenty-first Century: Challenges and Implications for Action.* Washington, D.C.: International Food Policy Research Institute.

Rosen, George. 1993. *A History of Public Health.* Baltimore: The Johns Hopkins University Press.

Roubini, Nouriel, and Jeffrey D. Sachs. 1989. "Political and Economic Determinants of Budget Deficits in the Industrial Democracies." *European Economic Review* 33: 903–38.

Rousseau, Marie-Paule. 1995. "Les Parisiens sont surproductifs." *Etudes foncières* (68): 13–18.

Rousseau, Peter L., and Paul Wachtel. 1998. "Financial Intermediation and Economic Performance: Historical Evidence from Five Industrialized Countries." *Journal of Money, Credit, and Banking* 30(4): 657–78.

Russell, Sharon Stanton, and Michael S. Teitelbaum. 1992. *International Migration and International Trade.* Discussion Paper 160. Washington, D.C.: World Bank.

Ryan, Michael P. 1998. *Knowledge Diplomacy: Global Competition and the Politics of Intellectual Property.* Washington, D.C.: The Brookings Institution Press.

Sabel, Charles. 1989. "Flexible Specialization and the Re-emergence of Regional Economics." In *Reversing Industrial Decline*, edited by Paul Hirst and Jonthan Zeitlan. Oxford: Oxford University Press.

———. 1998. "Local Development in Ireland; Partnership, Innovation, and Social Justice." Organisation for Economic Co-operation and Development, Paris.

Sachs, Jeffrey D. 1996. "Growth in Africa: It Can Be Done." *The Economist.* June 29.

Sachs, Jeffrey D., and Andrew Warner. 1997a. "Fundamental Sources of Long-run Growth." *American Economic Review* 87(2): 184–88.

———. 1997b. "Sources of Slow Growth in African Economies." *Journal of African Economies* 6 (October): 335–76.

Sachs, Jeffrey D., and Warwick J. McKibbin. 1991. *Global Linkages.* Washington, D.C.: The Brookings Institution Press.

Sala-i-Martin, Xavier. 1997. "I Just Ran Four Million Regressions." Working Paper Series 6252. National Bureau of Economic Research, Cambridge, Mass.

Samuels, David J. 1998. "Institutions of Their Own Design? Democratization and Fiscal Decentralization in Brazil, 1975–95." Paper presented at the American Political Science Association. Boston. Processed.

Satterthwaite, David. 1996. "Sustainable Cities or Cities that Contribute to Sustainable Development." *Urban Studies* 39(4).

Saudagaran, Shahrokh, and Joselita G. Diga. 1997. "Financial Reporting in Emerging Capital Markets: Characteristics and Policy Issues." *Accounting Horizons* 11(2): 41–64.

Schiff, Maurice, and L. Alan Winters. 1998. "Dynamics and Politics in Regional Integration Arrangements: An Introduction." *World Bank Economic Review* 12(2): 177–96.

Schlicht, E. 1985. "The Emotive and Cognitive View of Justice." Institute for Advanced Studies, Princeton University. Processed.

Science. 1997. "Human Domination of Earth's Ecosystems." July 25.

———. 1999. "Lack of Icebergs Another Sign of Global Warming." July 2.

Scott, James C. 1976. *The Moral Economy of the Peasant.* New Haven: Yale University Press.

Seaver, Brenda. 1997. "Stratospheric Ozone Protection: IR Theory and the Montreal Protocol on Substances that Deplete the Ozone Layer." *Environmental Politics* 6(3): 31–67.

Seckler, David, Upali Amarasinghe, David Molden, Radhika de Silva, and Randolph Barker. 1998. "World Water Demand and Supply, 1990 to 2025: Scenarios and Issues." Research Report 19. International Water Management Institute, Colombo, Sri Lanka.

Sell, Susan. 1996. "North-South Environmental Bargaining: Ozone, Climate Change and Biodiversity." *Global Governance* 2: 97–118.

Serra, Jaime, Guillermo Aguilar, José Cordoba, Gene Grossman, Carla Hills, John Jackson, Julius Katz, Pedro Noyola, and Michael Wilson. 1998. *Reflections on Regionalism: Report of the Study Group on International Trade.* Washington, D.C.: The Brookings Institution Press.

Sewell, David. 1996. "The Dangers of Decentralization According to Prud'homme: Some Further Aspects." *World Bank Research Observer* 11(1).

Shah, Anwar. 1997. "Federalism Reform Imperatives, Restructuring Principles and Lessons for Pakistan." *Pakistan Development Review* 36(4 Part II Winter): 499–536.

———. 1998. "Fiscal Federalism and Macroeconomic Governance." Policy Research Working Paper 2005. World Bank, Washington, D.C.

Shah, Ghanshyam. 1997. *Public Health and Urban Development: The Plague in Surat.* New Delhi: Sage Publications.

Sharma, Narenda, and others. 1996. *African Water Resources: Challenges and Opportunities for Sustainable Development.* Technical Paper 331. Washington, D.C.: World Bank.

Short, Clare. 1999. "Future Multilateral Trade Negotiations: A 'Development Round'?" Speech presented at United Nations Conference on Trade and Development, Geneva.

Shugart, Chris. 1997. "Decentralization and the Challenges of Regulation for Local-Level Public Services in Central and Eastern Europe." Extended version of a commentary given at an EBRD seminar on Commercial Infrastructure Challenges in Transition Economies. April 12.

Shukla, Vibhotti. 1996. *Urbanization and Economic Growth.* Delhi: Himalaya Publishing House.

Simpson, R., R. Sedjo, and J. Reid. 1996. "Valuing Biodiversity for Use in Pharmaceutical Research." *Journal of Political Economy* 104: 163–85.

Sims, Holly. 1999. "One Fifth of the Sky: China's Environmental Stewardship." *World Development* 27(7): 1227–45.

Skeldon, R. 1998. *Migration and Development: A Global Perspective.* Harlow, U.K.: Addison Wesley Longman.

Smith, B. C., 1996. "Sustainable Local Democracy." *Public Administration and Development* 16: 164–78.

Solo, Tova Maria. 1999. "Small-Scale Entrepreneurs in the Urban Water and Sanitation Market." *Environment and Urbanization* 11(1): 117.

Solo, Tova, and Suzanne Snell. 1998. "Water and Sanitation Services for the Urban Poor: Small-Scale Providers—Profiles and Typology." UNDP–World Bank Water and Sanitation Program, Washington, D.C. Draft.

Souza, Celina. 1996. "Redemocratization and Decentralization in Brazil: The Strength of the Member States." *Development and Change* 27: 529–55.

Spahn, Paul Bernd. 1998. "Decentralized Government and Macroeconomic Control." University of Frankfurt am Main, Frankfurt. Processed.

Srinivasan, T. N. 1998. *Developing Countries and the Multilateral Trading System.* Boulder, Colo.: Westview Press.

Stein, Ernesto, Ernesto Talvi, and Alejandro Grisanti. 1998. "Institutional Arrangements and Fiscal Performance: The Latin American Experience." Working Paper 6358. National Bureau of Economic Research, Cambridge, Mass.

Stepan, Alfred. 1999. "Toward a New Comparative Analysis of Democracy and Federalism: Demos Constraining and Demos Enabling Federations." In *Arguing Comparative Politics,* by Alfred Stephan. Oxford: Oxford University Press. Forthcoming.

Stiglitz, Joseph E. 1996. "Some Lessons from the East Asian Miracle." *World Bank Research Observer* 11(2).

———. 1997. "Stepping Towards Balance: Addressing Global Climate Change." Speech delivered at the Conference on Environmentally and Socially Sustainable Development. Washington D.C., October 6.

———. 1998a. "More Instruments and Broader Goals: Moving toward the Post-Washington Consensus." The 1998 WIDER Annual Lecture. Helsinki, January 7.

———. 1998b. "Towards a New Paradigm for Development: Strategies, Policies, and Processes." Prebisch Lecture. United Nations Conference on Trade and Development, Geneva.

———. 1999a. "Principles of Financial Regulation: A Dynamic, Portfolio Approach." World Bank, Washington, D.C. Processed.

———. 1999b. "Two Principles for the Next Round: Or, How to Bring Developing Countries in from the Cold." Speech delivered in Stockholm, Sweden, April 12.

Stiglitz, Joseph E., and Marilou Uy. 1996. "Financial Markets, Public Policy, and the East Asian Miracle." The *World Bank Research Observer* 11(2).

Stotsky, Janet G., and Emil M. Sunley. 1997. "United States." In *Fiscal Federalism in Theory and Practice*, edited by Teresa Ter-Minassian. Washington, D.C.: International Monetary Fund.

Stren, Richard. 1998. "Urban Governance and Politics in a Global Context: The Growing Importance of the Local." Background Paper for *World Development Report 1999/2000*. World Bank, Washington, D.C.

Strong, Ann L., Thomas A. Reiner, and Janusz Szyrmer. 1996. *Transitions in Land and Housing: Bulgaria, the Czech Republic, and Poland.* New York: St. Martin's Press.

Struyk, Raymond J., ed. 1997. *Restructuring Russia's Housing Sector: 1991–1997.* Washington, D.C.: The Urban Institute.

Summers, Robert, and Alan W. Heston. 1988. "A New Set of International Comparisons of Real Product and Prices: Estimates for 130 Countries: 1950–1985." International Association for Research in Income and Wealth, Philadelphia.

Szreter, Simon. 1997. "The Politics of Public Health in Nineteenth Century Britain." *Population and Development Review* 3(4/December).

Tacoli, Cecilia. 1998. "Rural-Urban Interactions: A Guide to the Literature." *Environment and Urbanization* 10(1/April).

Tanzi, Vito. 1995. *Taxation in an Integrating World.* Washington, D.C.: The Brookings Institution Press.

———. 1996. "Fiscal Federalism and Decentralization: A Review of Some Efficiency and Macroeconomic Aspects." *Proceedings of the Annual World Bank Conference on Development Economics 1995.* World Bank, Washington, D.C.

Tarver, James D. 1995. *Urbanization in Africa: A Handbook.* London: Greenwood Press.

Taylor J. Edward, Joaquin Arango, Graeme Hugo, Aki Kouaouci, Douglas S. Massey, and Adela Pellegrino. 1996. "International Migration and National Development." *Population Index* 62(2/Summer): 181–212.

Teitelbaum, Michael S., and Jay Winter. 1998. *A Question of Numbers.* New York: Hill and Wang.

Tendler, Judith. 1997. *Good Government in the Tropics.* Baltimore: The John Hopkins University Press.

Ter-Minassian, Teresa. 1997. "Intergovernmental Fiscal Relations in a Macroeconomic Perspective: An Overview." In *Fiscal Federalism in Theory and Practice*, edited by Teresa Ter-Minassian. Washington, D.C.: International Monetary Fund.

Ter-Minassian, Teresa, and Jon Craig. 1997. "Control of Subnational Government Borrowing." In *Fiscal Federalism in Theory and Practice*, edited by Teresa Ter-Minassian. Washington, D.C.: International Monetary Fund.

Tharakan, P. K. M. 1999. "Is Anti-Dumping Here to Stay?" *The World Economy* 22(2): 179–206.

The Sciences. 1997. "The Hole the World Is Watching." July 25.

Thomas, Harmon, and John Whalley, eds. 1998. *Uruguay Round Results and the Emerging Trade Agenda: Quantitative-Based Analyses from the Development Perspective.* Geneva: United Nations Conference on Trade and Development.

Thomas, Vinod. 1980. "Spatial Differences in the Cost of Living." *Journal of Urban Economics* 8: 108–22.

———. 1999. "Revisiting the Challenge of Development." World Bank, Washington, D.C. Processed.

Tibaijuka, Anna Kajumulo. 1997. "AIDS and Economic Welfare in Peasant Agriculture. Case Studies from Kagabiro Village, Kagera Region, Tanzania." *World Development* 25(6): 963–75.

Tiebout, Charles. 1956. "A Pure Theory of Local Expenditures." *Journal of Political Economy* 64(5): 416–24.

Tomich, Thomas P., Peter Kilby, and Bruce F. Johnston. 1995. *Transforming Agrarian Economies: Opportunities Seized, Opportunities Missed.* Ithaca: Cornell University Press.

Tonry, Michael. 1997. *Ethnicity, Crime and Immigration.* Chicago: University of Chicago Press.

Transparency International. 1998. "1998 Corruption Perception Index." Berlin.

Treisman, Daniel. 1998. *After the Deluge: Regional Crisis and Political Consolidation in Russia.* Ann Arbor: University of Michigan Press.

Trela, Irene. 1998. "Phasing Out the MFA in the Uruguay Round: Implications for Developing Countries." In *Uruguay Round Results and the Emerging Trade Agenda*, edited by Harmon Thomas and John Whalley. New York: United Nations.

Tsur, Yacov, and Ariel Dinar. 1995. "Efficiency and Equity Considerations in Pricing and Allocating Irrigation Water." Policy Research Working Paper 1460. World Bank, Washington, D.C.

Tybout, James. 1998. "Manufacturing Firms in Developing Countries: How Well They Do and Why?" Policy Research Working Paper 1965. World Bank, Washington, D.C.

Tyler, Tom. 1997. "Citizen Discontent with Legal Procedures: A Social Science Perspective on Civil Procedure Reform." *American Journal of Comparative Law* 45(4).

Tynan, Nicola, and Tyler Cowen. 1998. "The Private Provision of Water in 18th and 19th Century London." Department of Economics, George Mason University. Draft. Processed.

U.S. Central Intelligence Agency. 1998. *The World Factbook.* Washington, D.C.

U.S. Committee for Refugees. 1996. *World Refugee Survey.* Washington, D.C.

UNCHS (United Nations Center for Human Settlements). 1995. *Global Urban Indicators Database.* Nairobi.

———. 1996. *An Urbanizing World: Global Report on Human Settlements 1996.* Oxford: Oxford University Press.

UNCTAD (United Nations Conference on Trade and Development). 1996. *World Investment Report 1996.* New York and Geneva.

———. 1997. *World Investment Report 1997: Transnational Corporations, Market Structure and Competition Policy.* New York and Geneva.

———. 1998. *World Investment Report 1998.* New York and Geneva.

UNDIESA (United Nations Department of International Economic and Social Affairs). 1996. *World Urbanization Prospects.* New York.

———. 1998. *World Urbanization Prospects.* New York.

UNDP (United Nations Development Programme). 1998. *Human Development Report.* New York: Oxford University Press.

———. 1999. *Human Development Report.* New York: Oxford University Press.

UNEP (United Nations Environment Programme). 1999. *Synthesis of the Reports of the Scientific, Environmental Effects, and Technological and Economic Assessment Panels of the Montreal Protocol.* Nairobi.

UNESCO (United Nations Education, Scientific, and Cultural Organization). 1999. *Progress of Nations.* New York.

United Kingdom, Commonwealth Secretariat. 1998. "Report of the Expert Group on Protecting Countries against Destabilizing Effects of Volatile Capital Controls." London.

Urata, Shujiro. 1996. "Trade Liberalization and Productivity Growth in Asia: Introduction and Major Findings." *Developing Economies* 32(4).

Vaillancourt, François. 1998. "Morocco and Tunisia: Financing Local Governments—The Impact of Infrastructure Finance." In *Fiscal Decentralization in Developing Countries,* edited by Richard Bird and François Vaillancourt. Cambridge: Cambridge University Press.

Valdes-Prieto, Salvador, and Marcelo Soto. 1996. "New Selective Capital Controls in Chile: Are They Effective?" Universidad Católica de Chile, Santiago. Unpublished manuscript.

Vamvakidis, Athanasios, and Roman Wacziarg. 1998. "Developing Countries and the Feldstein-Horioka Puzzle." Working Paper 98/2. International Monetary Fund, Washington, D.C.

Vehorn, Charles L., and Ehtisham Ahmad. 1997. "Tax Administration." In *Fiscal Federalism in Theory and Practice,* edited by Teresa Ter-Minassian. Washington, D.C.: International Monetary Fund.

Velasco, Andres, and Pablo Cabezas. 1998. "Alternative Responses to Capital Inflows: A Tale of Two Countries." In *Capital Flows and Financial Crises,* edited by Miles Kahler. Ithaca: Cornell University Press.

Venables, Anthony. 1998. "Cities and Trade: External Trade and Internal Geography in Developing Economies." World Bank, Washington, D.C. Processed.

Verdier, David. 1998. "Domestic Responses to Capital Market Internationalization under the Gold Standard 1870–1914." *International Organization* 52(1).

Vernon, Raymond. 1998. *In the Hurricane's Eye: The Troubled Prospects of Multinational Enterprises.* Cambridge, Mass.: Harvard University Press.

Vittas, Dimitri, and Craig Neal. 1992. "Competition and Efficiency in Hungarian Banking." Policy Research Working Paper 1010, World Bank, Washington, D.C.

Vivian, Jessica. 1994. "NGOs and Sustainable Development in Zimbabwe: No Magic Bullets." *Development and Change* 25(1): 167–93.

von Hagen, Jürgen. 1991. "A Note on the Empirical Effectiveness of Formal Fiscal Restraints." *Journal of Public Economics* 44: 199–210.

Wacziarg, Romain. 1998. "Measuring the Dynamic Gains from Trade." Policy Research Working Paper 2001. World Bank, Washington, D.C.

Wallensteen, P., and A. Swain. 1997. "Comprehensive Assessment of the Water Resources of the World." Stockholm Environment Institute, Stockholm.

Wallerstein, Immanuel. 1974. *The Modern World System.* New York: Academic Press.

Walsh, Christopher. 1999. "Deconstructing Vancomycin." *Science.* April 16.

Walt, Gill. 1998. "Globalization of International Health." *Lancet* 351(7/February).

Wambugu, Florence. 1999. "Why Africa Needs Agricultural Biotech." *Nature.* July 1.

Wapner, Paul. 1995. "The State and Environmental Challenges: A Critical Exploration of Alternatives to the State System." *Environmental Politics* 4(1): 44–69.

Watson, Gabrielle. 1995. "Good Sewers Cheap? Agency-Customer Interactions in Low-Cost Urban Sanitation in Brazil." World Bank, Washington, D.C. Processed.

Watson, Robert Tony, John Dixon, Stephen Hamburg, Anthony Janetos, and Richard Moss. 1998. "Protecting Our Planet, Securing Our Future: Linkages among Global Environmental Issues and Human Needs." United Nations Environment Programme, Nairobi; U.S. National Aeronautics and Space Administration, Washington, D.C.; World Bank, Washington, D.C.

Wei, Shang-Jin, and Jeffrey Frankel. 1996. "Can Regional Blocs Be Stepping Stones to Global Free Trade?" *Review of International Economics and Finance* 5(4).

Weingast, Barry R. 1995. "The Economic Role of Political Institutions: Market-Preserving Federalism and Economic Development." *Journal of Law, Economics, and Organization* 11(1).

Wetzel, Deborah, and Jonathan Dunn. 1998. "Decentralization in the ECA Region: Progress and Prospects." World Bank, Washington, D.C. Processed.

Whittington, Dale, D. T. Lauria, and X. Mu. 1991. "A Study of Water Vending and Willingness to Pay for Water in Onitsha, Nigeria." *World Development* 19(2/3).

Whittington, Dale, D. T. Lauria, A. M. Wright, K. Choe, J. Hughes, and V. Swarna. 1993. "Household Demand for Improved Sanitation Services in Kumasi, Ghana: A Contingent Valuation Study." *Water Resources Research* 29(6).

WHO (World Health Organization). 1986. "Intersectoral Action for Health." Geneva.

———. 1995. *World Health Report 1995: Bridging the Gaps.* Geneva.

———. 1999. *World Health Report 1999.* Geneva.

Wildasin, David E. 1997. "Externalities and Bailouts." Policy Research Working Paper 1843. World Bank, Washington, D.C.

Wildavsky, A. 1995. *But Is It True?* Cambridge, Mass.: Harvard University Press.

Williamson, Jeffrey G. 1998. "Globalization, Labor Markets and Policy Backlash in the Past." *Journal of Economic Perspectives* 12(4): 51–72.

Willis, Eliza, Christopher da C. B. Garman, and Stephan Haggard. 1999. "The Politics of Decentralization in Latin America." *Latin American Research Review* 34(1): 7–56.

Wiseman, John H. 1997. "The Rise and Fall and Rise (and Fall?) of Democracy in Sub-Saharan Africa." In *Democratization*, edited by David Potter, David Goldblatt, Margaret Kiloh, and Paul Lewis. Cambridge: Polity Press.

Wolf, Holger. 1999. "International Asset Price and Capital Flow Comovements during Crisis: The Role of Contagion, Demonstration Effects and Fundamentals." Paper presented at the World Bank/International Monetary Fund/World Trade Organization Conference on Capital Flows, Financial Crises, and Policies. World Bank, Washington, D.C. Processed.

Wolfensohn, James D. 1998. "The Other Crisis." Address to the Board of Governors of the World Bank. Washington, D.C., October 6.

Wong, Christine P. 1998. "A Note on the Outcomes of the 1994 Fiscal Reforms." World Bank Resident Mission in China, Note 3. January 23. World Bank.

Woolcock, Michael. 1998. "Social Capital and Economic Development: Toward a Theoretical Synthesis and Policy Framework." *Theory and Society* (27)2.

World Bank. 1979. *World Development Report 1979.* New York: Oxford University Press.

———. 1990. *World Development Report 1990: Poverty.* New York: Oxford University Press.

———. 1991. *World Development Report 1991: The Challenge of Development.* New York: Oxford University Press.

———. 1992a. *Governance and Development.* World Bank, Washington, D.C.

———. 1992b. *World Development Report 1992: Development and the Environment.* New York: Oxford University Press.

———. 1993a. "Indonesia: Environment and Development: Challenges for the Future." Washington, D.C. Processed.

———. 1993b. *World Development Report 1993: Investing in Health.* New York: Oxford University Press.

———. 1994. *World Development Report 1994: Infrastructure for Development.* New York: Oxford University Press.

———. 1995a. *China: Macroeconomic Stability in a Decentralized Economy. A World Bank Country Study.* Washington, D.C.

———. 1995b. *Local Government Capacity in Colombia: Beyond Technical Assistance. A World Bank Country Study.* Washington, D.C.

———. 1995c. *World Development Report 1995: Workers in an Integrating World.* New York: Oxford University Press.

———. 1996a. *Sustainable Transport: Priorities for Policy Reform.* Washington, D.C.: World Bank.

———. 1996b. "The Hashemite Kingdom of Jordan: Housing Finance and Urban Sector Reform Project." Staff Appraisal Report. Washington, D.C.

———. 1996c. *World Development Report 1996: From Plan to Market.* New York: Oxford University Press.

———. 1997a. *Clear Water, Blue Skies: China's Environment in the New Century.* Washington, D.C.

———. 1997b. *Five Years after Rio: Innovations in Environmental Policy.* Environmentally Sustainable Development Studies and Monographs Series 18. Washington, D.C.

———. 1997c. *Private Capital Flows to Developing Countries.* New York: Oxford University Press.

———. 1997d. *World Development Report 1997: The State in a Changing World.* New York: Oxford University Press.

———. 1998a. *Assessing Aid: What Works, What Doesn't, and Why.* New York: Oxford University Press.

———. 1998b. *East Asia: The Road to Recovery.* Washington, D.C.

———. 1998c. *Egypt in the Global Economy: Strategic Choices for Savings, Investments, and Long-Term Growth.* MENA Economic Studies. Washington, D.C.

———. 1998d. *Environmental and Socially Sustainable Development Website* (*http://www-esd.worldbank.org*).

———. 1998e. "Forest Carbon Action Plan: World Bank's Program to Improve the Understanding of the Climate Benefits of Forestry and Land Management." Washington, D.C. Processed.

———. 1998f. "Fuel for Thought. A New Environmental Strategy for the Energy Sector." Washington, D.C.

———. 1998g. GEF Programs at (*http://www.gefweb.org/OPERPORT/PROGLIST.PDF*).

———. 1998h. *Global Economic Prospects 1998/99.* Washington, D.C.

———. 1998i. "India: Urban Infrastructure Services Report. Draft Country Study." Washington, D.C.

———. 1998j. "Meeting the Challenge for Rural Energy and Development." Washington, D.C.

———. 1998k. "Questions and Answers on the World Bank and Climate Change." Washington, D.C. Processed.

———. 1998l. *World Development Indicators 1998.* Washington, D.C.

———. 1998m. *World Development Report 1998: Knowledge for Development.* New York: Oxford University Press.

———. 1998n. *New Opportunities for Development: The Desertification Convention.* Washington, D.C.

———. 1998o. "Agricultural Policy Reform and the Least Developed and Net Importing Countries." Washington, D.C. Processed.

———. 1999a. "A Proposal for a Comprehensive Development Framework." Processed.

———. 1999b. "Ethiopia Regionalization Study." Report 188898-ET. Washington, D.C.

———. 1999c. *Global Development Finance 1999.* Washington, D.C.

———. 1999d. "Greening Industry: New Roles for Communities, Markets and Governments." Washington, D.C.

———. 1999e. "Poverty Reduction and the World Bank Progress in Fiscal 1998." Washington, D.C. Processed.

———. 1999f. "The Child Labor Program." Human Development Network. Washington, D.C.

———. 1999g. "Trade Blocs and Beyond." Policy Research Report. Washington, D.C. Draft.

———. 1999h. "Uzbekistan Structural Policy Review: An Economic Report." Washington, D.C.

———. 1999i. *World Development Indicators 1999.* Washington, D.C.

———. 1999j. "Tanzania: Peri-Urban Development in the African Mirror." Report No. 19526-TA. Washington, D.C.

———. 1999k. "Africa Regional Gender Action Plan." Washington, D.C. Processed.

WRI (World Resources Institute). 1996. *The Urban Environment 1996–97.* A joint publication by WRI, UNEP, UNDP, and IBRD. New York: Oxford University Press.

———. 1998. *World Resources 1998–99: Environmental Change and Human Health.* A joint publication by WRI, UNEP, UNDP, and IBRD. New York: Oxford University Press.

WRI (World Resources Institute) and WHO (World Health Organization). 1999. "An International Comparative Study of Air Pollution Health Risks in Major Urban Areas in Developed and Developing Countries." Washington, D.C. Processed.

WTO (World Trade Organization). 1995. *Annual Report.* Geneva.

———. 1996. *Annual Report.* Geneva.

———. 1997. *Annual Report.* Geneva.

———. 1998a. *Annual Report.* Geneva.

———. 1998b. "Financial Services." Background Note by the Secretariat. Geneva.

Xie, Danyang, Heng-fu Zou, and Hamid Davoodi. 1999. "Fiscal Decentralization and Economic Growth in the United States." *Journal of Urban Economics* 45: 1–12.

Yanagihara, Toru. 1998. "Regional Policy Coordination in Asia." Background Paper for *World Development Report 1999/2000.* Processed.

Yeates, Noel R. 1997. "Creating a Global City: Recent Changes to Sydney's Economic Structure." In *Pacific Rim Development: Integration & Globalization in the Asia-Pacific Economy*, edited by Peter Rimmer. Canberra City, Australia: Aussie Print.

Yeats, Alexander J. 1996. "Does Mercosur's Trade Performance Raise Concerns about the Effects of Regional Trade Arrangements?" Policy Research Working Paper 1729. World Bank, Washington, D.C.

Yeats, Alexander J. 1998. "Just How Big is Global Production Sharing?" Policy Research Working Paper 1871. World Bank, Washington, D.C.

Yudkin, John S. 1999. "Tanzania: Still Optimistic after All These Years?" *Lancet* 353(May): 1519–21.

Zaidi, S. Akbar. 1997. "Politics, Institutions, and Poverty: The Case of Karachi." *Economic and Political Weekly* 32(5).

———. 1998. "Urban Safety and Crime Prevention." UNCHS Regional Symposium on Urban Poverty. Fukuoka, Japan, October 27–29.

———. 1999. "NGO Failure and the Need to Bring Back the State." *Journal of International Development.* Forthcoming.

Zlotnik, Hania. 1998. "International Migration 1965–96. An Overview." *Population and Development Review* 24(3): 429–68.

Zurn, Michael. 1998. "The Rise of International Environmental Politics: A Review of Current Research." *World Politics* 50: 617–49.

Selected Indicators on Decentralization, Urbanization, and the Environment

he following data presentation conventions are used in this section.

Italics indicate data for years or periods other than those specified. The closest available year is shown instead.

Aggregates of ratios are generally calculated as weighted averages of the ratios (indicated by the letter *w*), using the value of the denominator as a weight.

The letter *t* denotes totals where missing values are imputed.

The letter *s* denotes totals where missing values are not imputed.

The symbol – means not applicable.

The symbol . . means not available.

Table A.1. Decentralization

Data on national and subnational government revenue and expenditure are from the electronic edition of the *Government Finance Statistics Yearbook* (GFS) of the International Monetary Fund. Data on subnational elections, on tiers of elected subnational governments, and on the number of jurisdictions are from "How Many Tiers? How Many Jurisdictions? A Review of Decentralization

Structures across Countries," by Marianne Fay, a *World Development Report 1999/2000* background paper. The data were compiled from a variety of sources, including the Area Handbook Series published by the Federal Research Division of the Library of Congress; the CIA *World Factbook 1998*; *The Statesman's Yearbook 1998–99*; *Local Finance in the Fifteen Countries of the European Union,* published by DEXIA in 1997; *The Directory of Local Government Systems in Africa,* published in 1998 by the Municipal Development Program; "Decentralization in the ECA Region: Progress and Prospects," by Deborah Wetzel and Jonathan Dunn, a World Bank paper (1998); and various World Bank country reports. This information was crosschecked with World Bank country teams and country diplomatic representatives in Washington.

Share of subnational government in total public expenditure is calculated from information in the GFS. It is the ratio of expenditure by subnational (intermediate and local) governments to total expenditure by all levels of government. Both current and capital transfers among levels of government are excluded to prevent double counting. Using the IMF's GFS codes, the formula is [CII local + (CIII – C3.2 – C7.1.1) intermediate]/[CII local + (CIII – C3.2 – C7.1.1) intermediate + (CIII – C3.2 – C7.1.1) consolidated central government]. **Share of subnational government in total tax revenue** is calculated from information in the GFS. It is the ratio of tax revenue (GFS code AIV) collected by subnational governments to total tax revenue collected by all levels of government. The 1990 figure is in italics if the data were not available for 1990 and were replaced by data from the year, in the period 1988–92, closest to 1990 for which data were available. The 1997 figure is in italics if the data were not available for 1997 and were replaced by data for the most recent year for which data were available in the period 1993–97. The entry for either column under **subnational elections** is "Yes" if the most recent data indicate that elections are held at that level and that an elected government is currently in place. "No+" indicates that, although the legislature is elected, a nominated executive head (for example, a mayor or governor) holds significant powers. **Number of elected subnational tiers** indicates the number of tiers of currently sitting elected government below the central or federal government. It excludes subnational governments headed by an appointed executive who holds significant powers. **Number of jurisdictions** indicates, for each tier of subnational elected government, the number of separate jurisdictions at that tier. At the intermediate level, it indicates the number of states (in federations), provinces, or province equivalents; at the local level, it indicates the number of municipalities or equivalent local governments. Comparisons should be made with care, as the size and functions of subnational governments vary from country to country, and even within countries.

Table A.2. Urbanization

Data on urban population are from the United Nations' *World Urban Prospects: The 1996 Revision*. Total population figures are World Bank estimates. Data on access to sanitation in urban areas are from the World Health Organization. The table includes those economies with populations exceeding 1 million for which data are available for at least 5 of the 11 indicators, including the most recent data on access to sanitation.

Estimates of the population of a city or metropolitan area depend on the boundaries chosen. For exam-

ple, Tehran, Islamic Republic of Iran, contains 6.8 million people in the 700-square-kilometer core of the city, but the greater metropolitan area covers 2,100 square kilometers and is home to more than 10 million. Thus, depending on which boundaries are used, Tehran's population can vary from 11 percent to 18.5 percent of the total population of Iran.

When urban boundaries are redefined in the world's more populous countries, such as China or India, it can significantly alter the estimate of the world's urban population. In the mid-1990s, for example, when China's State Statistical Bureau reclassified many of the country's hundreds of towns as cities, it more than doubled the measured share of China's urban population. At the end of 1996 about 43 percent of the country's population was considered urban, compared with only 20 percent in 1994. Estimates by international organizations such as the United Nations and the World Bank indicate that 47 percent of the world's population is urban, but using the new figures for China would suddenly increase that share to more than half. Because the estimates in the table are based on national definitions of what constitutes an urban area, cross-country comparisons should be made with caution.

Aggregate measures for regions and income groups include all 210 economies for which data are available.

Urban population is the combined midyear population of all areas defined as urban in each country, as reported to the United Nations. **Urban population by size of city** shows a breakdown of the urban population according to city size. **Population share of largest city** is the percentage share of the urban population living in the country's largest metropolitan area. This is a measure of concentration of the urban population. **Access to sanitation in urban areas** is the share of the urban population served by connections to public sewers or other systems such as pit privies, pour-flush latrines, septic tanks, communal toilets, and similar facilities.

Table A.3. Urban living conditions

Data are from the Global Urban Indicators database of the Urban Indicators Programme of the United Nations Centre for Human Settlements (UNCHS). The table shows selected indicators and cities from the UNCHS data set, which covers 46 key urban indicators and 237 cities. Cities are included in the table if data for at least 6 indicators were available out of the 11 shown.

The data should be used with care. Countries may use different data collection methods and definitions, making comparisons misleading. Also, the sample is biased toward smaller cities. Data are available only for 1993, so no inferences can be made about conditions improving or worsening.

Urban area refers to the city proper, the suburban fringe, and any other built-up, thickly settled areas lying outside but adjacent to the city boundaries. **Urban population** refers to the population of the urban agglomeration, a contiguous inhabited territory defined without regard to administrative boundaries. **Average household income** is the average of household incomes by quintile. Household income is income of all household members from all sources, including wages, pensions or benefits, business earnings, rents, and the value of any business or subsistence products consumed (for example, foodstuffs). **Income differential** is the ratio of the average household income in the top quintile to that in the bottom quintile. **House price–income ratio** is the average house price divided by the average household income. **Crowding** is measured as the median floor area of usable living space per person. **Work trips by public transportation** is the percentage of trips to work made by bus or minibus, tram, or train. Other means of transport commonly used in developing countries, such as taxis, ferries, rickshaws, or animals, are not included. **Travel time to work** is the average time in minutes, for all modes, for a one-way trip to work. **Households with sewerage connection** is the percentage of households with a connection to sewerage. **Households with regular waste collection** is the percentage of households served by regular waste collection, whether household-by-household collection or regular "dumpster" group collection. It does not include households that transport their own garbage to a local dump. **Households with access to potable water** is the percentage of households with access to potable water within 200 meters of the dwelling, where potable water is water that is free from contamination and safe to drink without further treatment.

Table A.4. Environment

Data on carbon dioxide emissions are from the Carbon Dioxide Information Analysis Center, which is sponsored by the U.S. Department of Energy. Data on electricity and fossil fuel production are from the International Energy Agency. Data on biodiversity are from the World Conservation Monitoring Center's *Biodiversity Data Sourcebook 1994* and the World Conservation Union's (IUCN) *1997 IUCN Red List of Threatened Animals* and *1997 IUCN Red List of Threatened Plants*. Data on fisheries are from the *Yearbook of Fishery Statistics,* volume 82, published by the Food and Agriculture Organization (FAO), supplemented by data that the FAO makes available electronically to the World Bank. Data selection is based on availability and on the global significance of each economy on these measures. Economies are included if their carbon dioxide emissions exceed 2 percent of the world total, fossil fuel production is over 50 million metric tons, the number of threatened bird and mammal species exceeds 100, or the marine fish catch is over 10 million metric tons. The aggregate measures by income level and region include all economies (out of a maximum of 210) for which data are available and aggregation is possible.

Carbon dioxide emissions refers to emissions stemming from the burning of fossil fuels and the manufacture of cement. It includes carbon dioxide produced during consumption of solid, liquid, and gas fuels and gas flaring. **Electricity production** is measured at the terminals of all alternator sets at the power station. The percentage from fossil fuel is the share produced by oil, petroleum products, coal, and natural gas. **Fossil fuel production** is total production of all types of fossil fuels, converted to metric tons of crude oil of equivalent energy content. **Mammal and bird species** excludes whales and includes birds within wintering ranges of countries. **Higher plant species** refers to native vascular plant species. The number of species threatened is the number classified by the IUCN as endangered, vulnerable, rare, indeterminate, previously endangered but now stabilized, or insufficiently known. **Annual marine catch** is the total catch of fish taken for all purposes (commercial, industrial, recreation, and subsistence) by all types and classes of fishing units (individual fishermen, fishing vessels, etc.) from the waters of the Atlantic, Indian, and Pacific Oceans and their adjacent seas.

Table A.1.   Decentralization

Economy	Fiscal decentralization				Electoral decentralization				
	Share of subnational government (%)				Subnational elections[a]		No. of elected subnational tiers 1999	No. of jurisdictions	
	In total public expenditure		In total tax revenue		Intermediate[b] 1999	Local[c] 1999		Intermediate[b] 1999	Local[c] 1999
	1990	1997	1990	1997					
Albania	..	24.9	..	0.9	No	Yes	1	..	374
Algeria	..	..	..	..	No+	No+	0	48	1,552
Angola	..	..			No	No	0	..	..
Argentina	46.3	43.9	38.2	41.1	Yes	Yes	2	24	1,617
Armenia	..	5.1[d]	..	3.3[d]	No	Yes	1	..	931
Australia	50.9	47.9	20.0	22.7	Yes	Yes	2	8	900
Austria	31.9	32.2	21.7	20.7	Yes	Yes	2	9	2,353
Azerbaijan	..	..	..	..	No	No	0	..	..
Bangladesh	..	..	..	..	No	Yes	1[e]	..	4,642
Belarus	30.6	32.5	29.4	23.7	No	No+	0	..	179
Belgium	11.9	11.8	4.5	5.4	Yes	Yes	2	10	589
Benin	..	..	..	..	No	No	0[f]	..	77
Bolivia	17.7	36.3	15.1	19.1	No+	Yes	1	9	312
Bosnia and Herzegovina	..	..	..	..	Yes	Yes	3[g]	2	137
Botswana	7.9	3.8	0.1	0.6	No	Yes	1	..	17
Brazil	35.3	36.5	30.9	31.3	Yes	Yes	2	28	5,581
Bulgaria	18.9	15.7	22.4	11.8	No	Yes	1	..	294
Burkina Faso	..	..	..	..	Yes	Yes	2	45	250
Burundi	..	..	..	..	No	No	0	..	..
Cambodia	..	..	..	..	No	No	0[h]	..	..
Cameroon	..	..	..	..	No	Yes	1	..	336
Canada	58.7	49.4	49.5	43.5	Yes	Yes	2	12	4,507
Central African Republic	..	..	..	..	No	Yes	1	..	174
Chad	..	..	..	..	No	No	0	..	..
Chile	7.2	8.5	6.4	7.0	No	Yes	1	..	340
China	..	55.6	..	51.4	No	No	0	..	..
Colombia	..	..	..	..	Yes	Yes	2	33	1,068
Congo, Dem. Rep.	..	..	..	..	No	No	0	..	..
Costa Rica	3.0	2.8	2.3	2.3	No	No+	0[i]	..	496
Côte d'Ivoire	..	..	..	..	No+	Yes	1	50	196
Croatia	..	12.1	..	7.5	Yes	Yes	2	21	543
Cuba	..	..	..	..	Yes	Yes	2	15	169
Czech Republic	..	21.3	..	12.3	No	Yes	1	..	5,768
Denmark	54.8	54.5	31.1	31.5	Yes	Yes	2	16	275
Dominican Republic	1.6	2.6	0.5	0.2	No	Yes	1	..	90
Ecuador	..	..	..	..	Yes	Yes	2	21	1,079
Egypt, Arab Rep.	..	..	..	..	No	No+	0	..	199
El Salvador	..	..	..	..	No	Yes	1	..	262
Eritrea	..	..	..	..	No+	Yes	1[j]	6	..
Estonia	34.8	22.4	26.5	14.2	No	Yes	1	..	254
Ethiopia	1.5	..	1.6	..	Yes	Yes	2	11	910
Finland	46.5	41.2	25.9	27.6	No	Yes	1	..	455
France	18.7	18.6	9.7	10.8	Yes	Yes	3	22	36,559
Georgia	..	..	..	..	No	Yes	1 or 2	..	4,000
Germany	40.2	37.8	28.9	28.8	Yes	Yes	3	16	16,121
Ghana	..	..	..	..	No	Yes	1	..	110
Greece	..	..	..	..	Yes	Yes	2	13	5,922
Guatemala	10.1	10.3	1.3	1.7	No	Yes	1	..	324
Guinea	..	..	..	..	No	Yes	1	..	33
Haiti	..	..	..	..	No	Yes	1	..	133
Honduras	..	..	..	..	No	Yes	1	..	293
Hungary	20.6	23.7	7.6	8.9	Yes	Yes	2	20	3,153
India	51.1	53.3	33.8	36.1	Yes	Yes	2	32	237,687[k]
Indonesia	13.1	14.8	2.9	2.9	No	No	0	..	..
Iran, Islamic Rep.	4.9	..	8.4	..	No	Yes	1	..	720
Iraq	..	..	..	..	No	No	0	..	..
Ireland	27.9	30.7	2.5	2.4	Yes	Yes	3	8	80
Israel	12.7	15.1	6.9	6.2	No	Yes	1	..	273
Italy	22.8	25.4	3.6	6.5	Yes	Yes	3	20	8,104
Japan	..	..	37.8	..	Yes	Yes	2	47	3,233
Jordan	..	..	..	..	No	Yes	1	..	669
Kazakhstan	..	..	..	..	No+	No+	0	16	303
Kenya	4.4	3.5	2.2	1.9	No	Yes	1	..	168
Korea, Dem. Rep.	..	..	..	..	No	No	0	..	..
Korea, Rep.	..	..	..	..	Yes	Yes	2	15	204
Kyrgyz Republic	..	..	..	..	No+	Yes	1	7	61
Lao PDR	..	..	..	..	No	No	0	..	..
Latvia	..	25.8	..	15.8	No+	Yes	1	33	566
Lebanon	..	..	..	..	No	No	0	..	..
Libya	..	..	..	..	No	Yes	1	..	1,500
Lithuania	30.4	22.6	14.4	16.2	No+	Yes	1	10	56
Madagascar	..	..	..	..	No	Yes	1[l]	..	1,391
Malawi	..	..	..	..	No	No	0[m]	..	..
Malaysia	20.2	19.1	3.7	2.4	No+	No	0	13	143
Mali	..	..	..	..	No	Yes	1	..	279

Economy	Fiscal decentralization				Electoral decentralization				
	Share of subnational government (%)				Subnational elections[a]		No. of elected subnational tiers	No. of jurisdictions	
	In total public expenditure		In total tax revenue		Intermediate[b]	Local[c]		Intermediate[b]	Local[c]
	1990	1997	1990	1997	1999	1999	1999	1999	1999
Mexico	17.8	*26.1*	19.0	*20.6*	Yes	Yes	2	32	2,418
Moldova	..	..	..	..	No+	Yes	1	3	35
Morocco	..	..	..	..	No+	Yes	1	65	1,547
Mozambique	..	..	..	..	Yes	Yes	2	10	33
Myanmar	..	..	..	..	No	No	0	..	..
Nepal	..	..	..	..	Yes	Yes	2	75	4,053
Netherlands	29.0	26.1	3.4	4.1	Yes	Yes	2	12	572
New Zealand	*9.3*	10.8	6.9	6.3	Yes	Yes	3	12	155
Nicaragua	3.5	*9.6*	2.5	*8.3*	No	Yes	1	..	143
Niger	..	..	..	..	No+	No+	0	32	150
Nigeria	..	..	..	..	Yes	Yes	2	31	589
Norway	36.7	*37.4*	20.9	*19.6*	No	Yes	1	..	435
Pakistan	..	..	..	..	No+	No+	0[n]	4	5,195
Papua New Guinea	..	..	..	..	No	Yes	1	..	284
Paraguay	1.9	*2.6*	0.8	*2.0*	Yes	Yes	2	17	212
Peru	9.8	24.4	1.2	2.1	No	Yes	1	..	1,808
Philippines	6.5	..	4.0	..	Yes	Yes	2	76	1,541
Poland	..	22.0	*21.3*	9.6	Yes	Yes	3[o]	16	2,489
Portugal	8.7	*11.6*	3.6	5.9	No	Yes	2[p]	..	275
Romania	15.4	13.3	12.8	9.2	No+	Yes	1	41	2,948
Russian Federation	..	*37.6*	..	*40.0*	Yes	Yes	3	90	2,000
Rwanda	..	..	..	..	No	No+	0	..	143
Saudi Arabia	..	..	..	..	No	..	0	..	..
Senegal	..	..	..	..	No+	No+	0	10	99
Sierra Leone	..	..	..	..	No	Yes	1	..	204
Slovak Republic	..	..	..	..	No	Yes	1	..	2,834
Slovenia	..	..	..	..	No	Yes	1	..	192
South Africa	20.7	49.8	5.5	5.3	Yes	Yes	2	9	840
Spain	34.3	*35.0*	13.3	*13.8*	Yes	Yes	3	17	8,082
Sri Lanka	..	..	..	..	No+	Yes	1	9	238
Sudan	..	..	..	..	No[q]	Yes	1	..	615
Sweden	39.8	36.2	28.2	31.4	Yes	Yes	2	24	286
Switzerland	*51.2*	49.3	37.0	35.5	Yes	Yes	2	26	3,000
Syrian Arab Republic	..	..	..	..	No	Yes	1	..	300
Tajikistan	..	..	..	..	No+	No+	0[r]	3	41
Tanzania	..	..	..	..	No	Yes	1	..	101
Thailand	7.5	*9.6*	4.4	*5.5*	No	Yes[t]	1	..	149[s]
Togo	..	..	..	..	No	Yes	1	..	30
Tunisia	..	..	..	..	No	Yes	1	..	257
Turkey	..	..	..	..	No+	Yes	1	80	2,801
Turkmenistan	..	..	..	..	No	No	0	..	..
Uganda	..	..	..	..	Yes	Yes	2	58	1,040
Ukraine	..	..	..	..	No+	Yes	1	27	619
United Kingdom	29.0	*27.0*	5.9	*3.6*	Yes	Yes	1 or 2	135	319
United States	42.0	*46.4*	33.8	*32.9*	Yes	Yes	3	51	70,500
Uruguay	..	..	..	..	No	Yes	1	..	19
Uzbekistan	..	..	..	..	No+[u]	No+[u]	0	14	281
Venezuela	..	..	..	..	Yes	Yes	2	24	330
Vietnam	..	..	..	..	No	No	0	..	..
Yemen, Rep.	..	..	..	..	No	..	0	..	..
Zambia	..	..	..	..	No	Yes	1	..	72
Zimbabwe	13.5	..	3.4	..	No	Yes	1	..	80

a. "No+" indicates that, although the legislature is elected, a nominated executive head (for example, a mayor or governor) holds significant powers. b. State, province, region, department, or other elected entity between the local and the national government. c. Municipality or equivalent. d. Subnational fiscal data come from World Bank country data and staff calculations. e. The 1996 Local Government Commission recommended a four-tier subnational government system composed (from the bottom up) of approximately 85,000 villages; 4,633 unions, and municipalities; 460 *thanas* and *upazilas;* and 64 *zilas*. Parliament has passed the upazila council bill, and elections are scheduled for 1999; the zila council bill had not been passed as of June 1999. Elected local government currently exists only at the municipal level, composed of 4,500 union *parishads* in rural areas, 129 *pourashavas,* or smaller municipalities, and 4 city corporations. f. A law passed in 1998 allows for elections at the commune level, but elections have not yet taken place. g. Bosnia and Herzegovina is divided into a federation and the Republika Srpska, with two substate levels within the federation (10 cantons and 73 municipalities), but only one in the Republika Srpska (64 municipalities). h. Local elections are planned for late 1999 or early 2000. A law is being drafted to define the powers and responsibilities of elected commune councils. i. Heads of local government are currently appointed, although this is slated to change in 1999. j. Villages elect representatives, who represent them at the district level and in turn elect a provincial parliament. The provincial governor is appointed by the head of state. Eritrea is in the process of changing its constitution, which could modify this system. k. Local government consists of 3,609 urban local bodies and, in rural areas, 474 *zila parishads,* which wield some authority over the 5,906 *panchayats samithis,* which in turn have some authority over the 227,698 *gram panchayats.* It is therefore not strictly correct to aggregate these into one level of local authority. l. A 1998 revision of the constitution allows for six provinces and an unspecified number of regions, in addition to the existing municipalities. Only the municipalities currently have sitting elected governments. m. Malawi has a local government administration, but no elected local government has been in place for several years. Local elections are expected in October 1999. n. Local elections have been held infrequently, and local governments are established by provincial governments. o. The three tiers are the 16 *gminas,* 368 *powiats,* and 2,365 municipalities. p. Portugal also has 4,207 submunicipalities as a second tier of elected local government. q. At the intermediate level the country is divided into 26 states, some of which have elected governors, whereas others have nominated governors. r. The assemblies of the *oblasts* (provinces) and *rains* (districts) are elected, but their heads are nominated by the president. At the *jamoat,* or community, level, the local governing authority is elected at a general meeting of the residents. s. Thailand currently has elected municipal governments governing 149 cities. In addition there are 1,050 sanitary districts, which provide services in densely populated areas outside cities. Each is governed by a board composed of appointed and elected members; 983 of these districts will soon be upgraded to municipality status. There are up to 7,823 *tambon* administrative organizations, which provide basic services in rural areas and are governed by elected assemblies and appointed executives. The 1997 constitution mandates that executives and councils of local authorities be largely elected. These changes are expected to be completed by October 1999, in which case the country would still have only one tier of elected local government but close to 8,955 fully elected local governments. t. Not all mayors are elected; about 10 are appointed. u. Appointed *khokims* (governors or mayors) exercise almost unlimited power in *oblasts* and *rayons,* with quasi-elected councils having very limited authority.

Table A.2. Urbanization

Economy	Urban population Millions 1980	Urban population Millions 1997	Urban population % of total population 1980	Urban population % of total population 1997	Urban population by size of city % of total urban population <750,000 1995	Urban population by size of city % of total urban population 750,000—3 million 1995	Urban population by size of city % of total urban population >3 million 1995	Population share of largest city % of urban population 1980	Population share of largest city % of urban population 1995	Access to sanitation in urban areas % of urban population 1982	Access to sanitation in urban areas % of urban population 1995
Albania	0.9	1.3	34	38	..	..	..	..	..	..	97
Algeria	8.1	16.8	43	57	76	0	24	25	24	95	..
Angola	1.5	3.8	21	32	39	61	0	63	61	27	71
Argentina	23.3	31.6	83	89	51	11	39	43	39	76	80
Armenia	2.0	2.6	66	69	50	50	0	51	50	..	..
Australia	12.6	15.7	86	85	32	24	44	26	23	..	..
Austria	4.9	5.2	65	64	60	40	0	42	40	..	..
Azerbaijan	3.3	4.3	53	56	56	44	0	48	44	..	67
Bangladesh	9.8	24.1	11	19	45	16	39	33	39	20	41
Belarus	5.4	7.4	56	72	76	24	0	24	24	..	..
Belgium	9.4	9.9	95	97	89	11	0	13	11	..	..
Benin	0.9	2.3	27	40	..	..	..	..	..	45	60
Bolivia	2.4	4.8	46	62	53	47	0	30	28	51	77
Bosnia and Herzegovina	1.5	1.0	36	42	..	..	..	..	..	..	71
Botswana	0.1	1.0	15	65	..	..	..	..	..	79	91
Brazil	80.5	130.1	66	80	56	14	30	16	13	33	74
Bulgaria	5.4	5.7	61	69	79	21	0	20	21	..	..
Burkina Faso	0.6	1.8	9	17	48	52	0	44	52	38	..
Burundi	0.2	0.5	4	8	..	..	..	..	..	90	71
Cameroon	2.7	6.5	31	46	59	41	0	19	22	..	73
Canada	18.6	23.3	76	77	46	20	34	16	19	..	..
Chad	0.8	1.6	19	23	45	55	0	40	55	..	74
Chile	9.0	12.3	81	84	59	0	41	41	41	79	95
China	192.3	390.7	20	32	60	19	21	6	4	..	68
Hong Kong, China	4.6	6.2	91	95	1	0	99	100	99	..	..
Colombia	18.2	29.4	64	74	53	14	33	20	22	96	70
Congo, Dem. Rep.	7.8	13.7	29	29	60	6	34	28	34	8	53
Congo, Rep.	0.7	1.6	41	60	33	67	0	67	67	17	15
Costa Rica	1.0	1.7	43	50	45	55	0	61	55	100	100
Côte d'Ivoire	2.9	6.3	35	45	52	48	0	44	48	13	..
Croatia	2.3	2.7	50	57	63	37	0	28	37	72	71
Cuba	6.6	8.5	68	77	73	27	0	29	27	..	92
Czech Republic	6.5	6.8	64	66	82	18	0	18	18	..	..
Denmark	4.3	4.5	84	85	70	30	0	32	30	..	..
Dominican Republic	2.9	5.1	51	63	8	27	65	50	65	72	89
Ecuador	3.7	7.2	47	60	54	46	0	30	27	79	70
Egypt, Arab Rep.	17.9	27.2	44	45	44	5	51	38	37	95	..
El Salvador	1.9	2.7	42	46	52	48	0	39	48	89	89
Ethiopia	4.0	9.7	11	16	72	28	0	30	28	..	..
Finland	2.9	3.3	60	64	67	33	0	22	33	100	100
France	39.5	44.0	73	75	70	8	22	23	22	..	..
Gabon	0.2	0.6	34	52	..	..	..	..	..	..	79
Georgia	2.6	3.2	52	59	58	42	0	42	42	..	..
Germany	64.7	71.3	83	87	49	28	23	10	9	..	..
Ghana	3.4	6.6	31	37	73	27	0	30	27	47	61
Greece	5.6	6.3	58	60	34	16	50	54	50	..	..
Guatemala	2.6	4.2	37	40	43	57	0	29	57	73	91
Guinea	0.9	2.1	19	31	19	81	0	65	81	54	24
Guinea-Bissau	0.1	0.3	17	23	..	..	..	..	..	21	32
Haiti	1.3	2.5	24	33	36	64	0	55	64	42	43
Honduras	1.2	2.7	35	45	60	40	0	33	40	22	91
Hungary	6.1	6.7	57	66	69	31	0	34	31	..	..
India	158.8	264.1	23	27	59	18	23	5	6	25	46
Indonesia	32.9	74.8	22	37	73	14	13	18	13	30	88
Iran, Islamic Rep.	19.4	36.6	50	60	57	23	20	26	20	90	86
Iraq	8.5	16.5	66	75	55	17	28	39	28	30	85
Ireland	1.9	2.1	55	58	56	44	0	48	44	..	..
Israel	3.4	5.3	89	91	61	39	0	41	39	..	100
Italy	37.6	38.4	67	67	66	15	19	14	11	..	..
Jamaica	1.0	1.4	47	55	..	..	..	..	..	92	99
Japan	89.0	98.9	76	78	50	8	42	25	28	..	..
Jordan	1.3	3.2	60	73	61	39	0	49	39	91	91
Kazakhstan	..	9.6	54	60	87	13	0	..	13	..	..
Kenya	2.7	8.7	16	30	77	23	0	32	23	75	69
Korea, Dem. Rep.	10.1	14.2	57	62	82	18	0	18	18	100	100
Korea, Rep.	21.7	38.3	57	83	29	28	43	2	2	100	100
Kuwait	1.2	1.8	90	97	29	71	0	67	71	100	100
Kyrgyz Republic	1.4	1.8	38	39	..	..	..	..	..	78	87
Lao PDR	0.4	1.1	13	22	..	..	..	..	..	..	13
Latvia	1.7	1.8	68	73	50	50	0	49	50	..	90
Lebanon	2.2	3.7	74	88	48	52	0	55	52	94	..
Lesotho	0.2	0.5	13	26	..	..	..	..	..	22	76
Libya	2.1	4.5	69	86	41	59	0	38	40	100	90
Madagascar	1.6	3.9	18	28	75	25	0	29	25	8	64
Malawi	0.6	1.5	9	14	..	..	..	..	..	88	82

Economy	Urban population				Urban population by size of city % of total urban population			Population share of largest city % of urban population		Access to sanitation in urban areas % of urban population	
	Millions		% of total population		<750,000	750,000–3 million	>3 million				
	1980	1997	1980	1997	1995	1995	1995	1980	1995	1982	1995
Malaysia	5.8	11.9	42	55	89	11	0	16	11	..	94
Mali	1.2	2.9	19	28	65	35	0	40	35	90	..
Mexico	44.8	69.6	66	74	55	15	30	31	25	77	93
Moldova	1.6	2.3	40	53	66	34	0	..	..	..	96
Morocco	8.0	14.5	41	53	68	9	23	26	23	85	97
Mozambique	1.6	6.0	13	36	59	41	0	47	41	51	68
Myanmar	8.1	11.7	24	27	65	0	35	27	35	34	44
Namibia	0.2	0.6	23	38	..	..	..	..	..		78
Nepal	0.9	2.4	7	11	..	..	..	..	..	5	34
Netherlands	12.5	13.9	88	89	84	16	0	8	8	..	100
New Zealand	2.6	3.2	83	86	69	31	0	30	31	..	..
Nicaragua	1.6	3.0	53	63	59	41	0	41	41	35	88
Nigeria	19.1	48.7	27	41	73	3	23	23	23	30	82
Norway	2.9	3.2	71	74	..	..	..	..	..	..	100
Oman	0.3	1.8	32	79	..	..	..	..	..	60	98
Pakistan	23.2	45.4	28	35	42	23	35	22	23	48	60
Panama	1.0	1.5	50	56	34	66	0	62	66	99	99
Papua New Guinea	0.4	0.7	13	17	..	..	..	..	..	51	95
Paraguay	1.3	2.7	42	54	57	43	0	52	43	66	20
Peru	11.2	17.5	65	72	60	0	40	39	40	67	78
Philippines	18.1	41.1	37	56	73	3	24	33	24	..	..
Poland	20.7	24.9	58	64	66	20	14	16	14	..	..
Portugal	2.9	3.6	29	37	47	53	0	46	53	..	..
Puerto Rico	2.1	2.8	67	74	52	48	0	51	48	..	..
Romania	10.9	12.8	49	57	83	17	0	18	17	..	81
Russian Federation	97.0	112.9	70	77	73	14	13	8	8	..	..
Saudi Arabia	6.2	16.8	66	84	69	31	0	16	17	100	..
Senegal	2.0	4.0	36	45	53	47	0	47	47	87	..
Singapore	2.3	3.1	100	100	0	0	100	100	100	85	100
Slovenia	0.9	1.0	48	52	..	..	..	..	..	90	100
South Africa	13.3	20.2	48	50	36	64	0	12	11	..	78
Spain	27.2	30.2	73	77	75	12	14	16	14	..	..
Sri Lanka	3.2	4.2	22	23	..	..	..	..	..	..	81
Sudan	3.7	9.2	20	33	73	27	0	31	27	70	79
Sweden	6.9	7.4	83	83	69	31	0	20	21	..	..
Switzerland	3.6	4.4	57	62	79	21	0	20	21	..	..
Syrian Arab Republic	4.1	7.9	47	53	47	53	0	34	28	58	97
Tajikistan	1.4	2.0	34	32	..	..	..	..	..	..	83
Tanzania	2.7	8.0	15	26	62	38	0	30	24	93	97
Thailand	7.9	12.5	17	21	45	0	55	59	55	50	98
Togo	0.6	1.4	23	32	..	..	..	..	..	34	76
Trinidad and Tobago	0.7	0.9	63	73	..	..	..	..	..	100	97
Tunisia	3.3	5.8	52	63	69	31	0	35	31	64	100
Turkey	19.5	45.7	44	72	63	18	19	23	19	..	..
Turkmenistan	1.3	2.1	47	45	..	..	..	..	..	..	70
Uganda	1.1	2.7	9	13	60	40	0	42	40	40	60
Ukraine	30.9	36.1	62	71	73	27	0	7	8	..	70
United Arab Emirates	0.7	2.2	71	85	59	41	0	31	41	93	..
United Kingdom	50.0	52.7	89	89	71	15	15	15	15	..	..
United States	167.6	204.8	74	77	44	27	29	9	8	..	..
Uruguay	2.5	3.0	85	91	54	46	0	49	46	59	56
Uzbekistan	6.5	9.9	41	42	76	24	0	28	24	..	46
Venezuela	12.0	19.7	79	86	58	26	16	21	16	57	74
Vietnam	10.3	15.0	19	20	67	9	25	27	25	..	..
Yemen, Rep.	1.7	5.7	20	35	..	..	..	..	..	..	40
Yugoslavia, FR (Serb./Mont.)	4.5	6.1	46	58	80	20	0	24	20	..	..
Zambia	2.3	4.1	40	44	66	34	0	23	34	56	66
Zimbabwe	1.6	3.8	22	33	60	40	0	39	40	100	99
World	1,748.2 s	2,676.0 s	39 w	46 w	59 w	19 w	22 w	18 w	17 w	..	..
Low income	307.7	577.7	22	28	59	21	20	16	19	29	56
Middle income	824.3	1,389.9	37	49	62	18	19	19	16	..	77
Lower middle income	559.0	966.2	31	42	64	18	18	16	14	..	75
Upper middle income	265.4	423.7	62	74	58	20	22	24	20	..	..
Low and middle income	1,132.1	1,967.7	31	40	61	19	20	18	17	..	..
East Asia & Pacific	288.4	578.0	21	33	64	16	20	13	9	..	74
Europe & Central Asia	240.1	317.7	56	67	71	20	9	15	15	..	..
Latin America & Carib.	233.8	366.5	65	74	55	17	28	31	25	60	80
Middle East & N. Africa	83.7	161.9	48	58	58	20	22	31	27	81	..
South Asia	198.5	345.5	22	27	56	19	25	9	11	27	48
Sub-Saharan Africa	87.6	198.0	23	32	62	30	9	28	30	..	..
High income	616.1	708.4	75	76	53	20	27	17	16	..	..

Table A.3.   Urban living conditions

Economy	City	Urban area km² 1993	Urban population Thousands 1993	Average household income Dollars 1993	Income differential Ratio of top to bottom quintile 1993	House price–income ratio 1993	Crowding m² of floor space per person 1993	Work trips by public transportation % 1993	Travel time to work Minutes 1993	Sewerage connection % 1993	Regular waste collection % 1993	Access to potable water % 1993
Armenia	Yerevan	215	1,223	1,407	28.4	39.0	13.0	98	52	93	81	98
Australia	Melbourne	1,148	3,023	30,216	12.0	3.6	55.0	16	25	99	100	100
Azerbaijan	Baku	2,300	..	977	8.7	13.0	12.9	80	57	79	..	100
Bangladesh	Dhaka	1,194	7,500	478	6.9	5.0	2.7	..	..	44	50	..
	Tangail	32	155	228	6.9	8.0	1.2	..	15	..	..	51
Benin	Cotonou	88	559	2,745	6.0	1.6	5.9	..	60	1	25	60
	Porto Novo	50	183	1,479	6.1	3.4	5.5	..	40	1	25	76
Bolivia	Santa Cruz de la Sierra	165	742	3,786	7.6	2.6	..	60	25	22	100	87
	La Paz	51	726	3,787	11.7	1.2	..	51	35	58	92	90
	El Alto	58	442	1,786	7.2	1.4	..	..	25	20	95	86
	Cochabamba	68	425	4,035	8.3	2.6	..	46	17	47	95	71
Botswana	Gaborone	..	473	..	..	7.2	12.5	42	20	33	98	100
Brazil	Rio de Janeiro	1,255	5,554	12,087	20.3	2.5	18.9	67	51	87	88	98
	Recife	..	1,503	815	28.7	2.2	15.5	70	40	38	95	95
	Curitiba	..	1,352	1,091	16.1	5.7	21.0	72	30	75	95	97
	Brasilia	..	..	12,087	20.3	3.0	17.3	..	49	74	95	89
Bulgaria	Sofia	..	1,294	..	..	5.8	16.7	75	35	98	95	100
Burkina Faso	Ouagadougou	170	716	2,622	3.3	8.5	12.2	..	22	..	40	75
	Bobo-Dioulasso	67	284	2,379	9.1	10.2	12.0	..	15	..	30	81
Burundi	Bujumbura	100	278	1,823	17.0	1.9	5.8	..	30	29	41	93
Cameroon	Douala	144	1,094	..	..	4.6	10.0	11	45	3	60	83
	Yaounde	..	923	677	..	3.9	12.6	6	50	3	44	85
Canada	Toronto	..	4,236	49,791	9.5	3.9	41.1	30	23	100	100	100
Central African Republic	Bangui	163	471	..	..	6.2	11.2	..	45	1	25	45
Chile	Santiago	..	4,820	8,043	16.6	2.4	14.4	54	36	92	95	98
China	Hefei	..	3,809	2,080	13.8	..	11.0	0	..	57	..	100
	Qingdao	..	2,121	1,165	1.8	..	11.1	..	..	11	..	100
	Foshan	32	385	3,354	3.2	..	16.3	0	..	100	..	100
Colombia	Bogotá	482	5,314	7,120	14.7	3.1	8.8	75	39	99	94	97
Congo, Dem. Rep.	Kinshasa	591	4,566	2,241	6.7	..	..	61	120	3	0	70
Côte d'Ivoire	Abidjan	369	2,462	2,827	7.9	7.2	7.2	49	90	45	70	62
	Bouake	..	439	1,820	9.5	5.6	7.4	10	35	..	35	28
Croatia	Zagreb	..	868	4,354	5.9	11.0	22.1	52	26	80	100	90
Cuba	Havana	..	2,176	..	..	2.1	16.0	58	42	85	100	85
	Camaguey	155	296	..	..	..	18.7	6	30	46	93	71
	Cienfuegos	44	131	..	..	1.5	19.2	0	30	70	97	100
	Pinar del Rio	28	129	..	..	3.7	21.0	0	80	48	100	93
Czech Republic	Prague	496	1,214	..	..	11.9	26.0	67	57	94	100	100
Denmark	Copenhagen	2,863	..	29,320	14.0	3.1	44.0	27	22	100	100	100
Djibouti	Djibouti	..	..	6,856	12.0	3.7	13.1	19	22	15	65	69
Ecuador	Guayaquil	178	1,773	5,406	12.1	2.0	15.6	50	45	55	70	85
	Quito	178	1,615	..	..	2.4	8.6	0	..	93	89	..
Egypt, Arab Rep.	Cairo	420	14,524	1,658	6.1	4.9	13.0	58	60	91	65	98
	Gharbeya	..	383	1,656	6.1	3.9	13.3	32	30	91	45	99
	Assiout	10	322	1,721	6.7	3.1	14.0	29	25	30	25	93
El Salvador	San Salvador	163	1,343	4,320	12.7	2.7	6.6	0	..	80	46	91
	Santa Ana	18	142	2,998	10.6	3.2	8.1	0	..	57	90	82
	San Miguel	..	132	3,420	13.2	4.3	9.7	0	..	46	99	56
Estonia	Tallinn	185	468	..	..	3.6	21.3	0	27	95	99	100
France	Paris	2,586	9,319	20,899	14.7	4.3	30.0	40	35	98	100	100
	Marseille	351	800	14,640	5.2	..	..	0	25	99	99	100
	Strasbourg	78	388	15,942	9.7	..	..	0	15	98	100	100
Gambia, The	Banjul	..	479	230	8.1	4.8	11.5	60	40	13	35	74
Georgia	Tbilisi	204	1,295	..	..	..	16.2	98	70	100	52	100
Germany	Cologne	405	1,006	..	..	..	34.0	17	..	99	100	100
	Duisburg	233	536	..	..	7.9	32.1	21	..	100	100	100
	Leipzig	151	481	..	..	..	33.0	33	..	95	100	100
	Wiesbaden	204	266	..	..	..	37.0	23	..	100	100	100
	Erfurt	268	213	..	..	5.1	29.1	32	..	95	100	100
Ghana	Accra	411	1,718	403	..	8.0	6.2	47	45	12	60	86
	Kumasi	..	758	822	2.9	17.8	5.8	55	20	12	11	57
	Tamale	22	193	682	1.9	17.4	5.2	45	18	6	5	38
Greece	Athens	..	1,464	..	..	3.1	29.0	34	53	95	90	100
Guatemala	Guatemala City	..	1,327	2,760	76.7	9.0	8.0	53	40	..	53	64
Guinea	Conakry	..	1,308	..	..	6.4	6.5	26	55	17	50	75
Hungary	Budapest	..	320	5,621	9.2	7.7	29.4	66	40	90	100	100
India	Mumbai	..	12,810	1,504	6.7	3.5	3.5	79	33	51	90	96
	Delhi	624	8,957	1,196	11.4	7.0	6.9	53	44	40	77	92
	Chennai	612	5,651	1,184	8.0	7.0	6.2	42	22	37	90	60
	Bangalore	..	4,472	1,224	6.5	10.8	9.5	46	18	35	96	81
	Lucknow	..	1,804	992	7.5	4.6	5.5	1	23	30	74	88
	Varanasi	104	1,078	928	7.8	5.1	4.5	21	22	41	88	85
	Mysore	..	701	1,236	6.4	7.5	11.8	13	20	60	60	90
	Bhiwandi	26	572	..	..	0.3	2.4	8	15	15	40	86
	Gulbarga	..	330	1,028	7.6	3.5	6.1	8	11	14	74	90
	Tumkur	..	194	809	6.1	4.9	7.4	21	8	..	50	86
	Hubli-Dharbad	..	..	1,114	7.1	3.6	6.2	37	22	37	89	89

Economy	City	Urban area km² 1993	Urban population Thousands 1993	Average household income Dollars 1993	Income differential Ratio of top to bottom quintile 1993	House price–income ratio 1993	Crowding m² of floor space per person 1993	Work trips by public transportation % 1993	Travel time to work Minutes 1993	Households with Sewerage connection % 1993	Households with Regular waste collection % 1993	Households with Access to potable water % 1993
Indonesia	Jakarta	..	13,048	2,460	6.6	9.9	15.0	38	82	..	84	93
	Bandung	..	1,819	1,625	5.8	12.0	13.1	0	29	27	97	86
	Medan	..	1,810	1,674	4.5	5.5	13.9	44	30	19	19	94
	Semarang	..	1,076	1,351	6.0	5.4	12.0	14	25	..	69	88
	Banjarmasin	..	..	1,474	4.4	4.0	6.4	12	37	..	70	94
	Surabaya	..	..	1,970	8.1	8.6	11.5	23	23	..	87	99
Jordan	Amman	..		12,813	13.9	6.5	15.4	14	31	79	100	100
Kazakhstan	Almaty	..	1,173	..	..	7.2	14.5	43	35	88	83	100
Kenya	Mombasa	234	382	..	..	1.9	5.9	31	27	2	40	95
	Nairobi	64	333	..	..	1.8	15.6	0	64	..	63	45
Latvia	Riga	..	1,026	..	..	..	19.4	57	27	97	85	100
Liberia	Monrovia	..	697	..	..	24.0	14.0	75	60	1	0	20
Lithuania	Vilnius	..	670	..	..	5.4	16.2	49	25	94	95	100
Malawi	Blantyre	..	403	..	..	8.3	8.3	39	44	8	20	80
	Lilongwe	..	220	..	..	4.2	6.6	5	31	12	..	80
Mali	Bamako	267	..	..	..	3.7	3.2	12	40	2	95	53
Mauritania	Nouakchott	72	576	1,481	8.9	6.4	10.0	45	50	4	15	68
Moldova	Chisinau	131	662	1,055	9.7	13.0	15.0	48	25	86	83	100
Mongolia	Ulaanbaatar	3,542	..	317	3.2	37.7	9.2	85	29	51	..	49
Morocco	Rabat	..	1,345	7,514	8.1	6.8	10.0	0	..	95	90	100
Mozambique	Maputo	..	..	414	4.9	..	12.0	13	..	23	37	73
Namibia	Windhoek	69	142	11,618	15.2	6.0	43.0	0	20	75	93	98
Netherlands	Amsterdam	202	724	21,687	5.2	3.5	38.3	0	22	100	100	100
New Zealand	Auckland	..	942	25,900	8.1	4.4	40.0	6	..	98	..	..
Niger	Niamey	224	505	1,369	13.2	7.3	7.7	17	27	..	25	77
Nigeria	Lagos	959	5,968	492	18.2	10.0	5.5	54	85	2	8	75
	Ibadan	2,937	1,941	415	50.0	6.8	9.0	40	40	..	40	70
	Kano	123	1,510	340	6.9	3.2	2.8	56	..	25	38	16
	Onitsha	9	..	623	18.5	..	12.0	53	33	..	38	95
Pakistan	Lahore	..	5,150	3,298	7.7	16.0	1.2	16	25	74	50	90
Paraguay	Asunción	67	949	5,496	8.8	5.3	4.7	31	60	10	79	58
Peru	Lima	..	6,232	1,109	..	9.2	25.7	65	35	69	57	87
	Trujillo	45	509	..	..	3.8	15.2	74	30	71	48	98
Philippines	Manila	..	..	5,318	8.4	..	34.1	40	120	80	85	94
Poland	Warsaw	..	..	3,021	3.1	5.4	18.2	0	34	91	97	100
Romania	Bucharest	..	2,350	..	..	6.8	12.9	65	78	90	86	98
Russian Federation	Kostroma	..	..	2,357	5.1	5.1	17.8	65	21	91	90	100
	Moscow	..	..	4,040	7.6	17.0	19.7	85	62	100	100	100
	Nizhny Novgorod	..	..	2,459	4.6	6.4	17.1	78	35	95	100	100
	Novgorod	..	..	2,865	5.9	7.3	16.3	44	30	96	99	100
	Ryazan	..	..	2,348	6.9	8.9	16.2	88	25	92	99	100
Senegal	Dakar	..	1,801	3,008	17.0	3.0	8.1	53	45	25	75	92
	Kaolack	..	187	1,488	20.9	..	..	13	27	3	..	56
	Ziguinchor	..	155	1,150	22.0	..	..	27	20	2	..	30
	Mbour	..	101	2,192	15.9	..	..	20	31	2	..	79
Sierra Leone	Freetown	82	395	370	11.4	..	10.0	0	..	1	..	53
Slovak Republic	Bratislava	2,144	651	3,984	5.1	5.6	22.3	72	34	96	100	100
Slovenia	Ljubljana	275	316	11,729	6.1	..	..	1	22	99	99	100
	Maribor	738	185	9,314	6.2	..	..	41	28	58	90	100
Sri Lanka	Colombo	..	2,190	436	3.4	..	18.7	74	35	60	94	98
Sudan	Khartoum	249	826	..	..	..	21.9	63	42	3	12	55
Sweden	Stockholm	309	..	30,840	4.5	4.6	40.0	37	35	100	100	100
Tanzania	Arusha	..	..	564	4.1	5.0	5.0	61	30	16	..	60
	Dar es Salaam	..	..	564	4.1	5.0	4.5	48	30	6	25	60
	Mwanza	94	..	..	..	5.0	4.0	24	30	8	15	74
Togo	Lome	288	802	..	..	3.5	12.0	30	30	..	37	..
Tunisia	Tunis	..	1,684	4,032	6.0	5.2	12.0	0	45	73	61	96
Uganda	Kampala	202	840	..	..	2.3	4.0	45	23	9	20	87
United Arab Emirates	Dubai	604	594	26,564	22.8	..	..	0	18	60	100	100
United Kingdom	Hertfordshire	1,604	1,000	28,270	10.9	6.0	34.8	7	27	100	100	100
	Glasgow	..	618	7,329	1.8	4.5	..	39	..	99	..	99
	Bedfordshire	..	539	32,080	10.9	3.0	34.6	10	..	93	98	98
	Cardiff	137	306	..	..	2.9	17.5	13	..	100	100	100
United States	New York	..	..	39,256	14.8	6.3	..	51	37	99	..	100
Vietnam	Hanoi	47	..	32,966	3.4	10.4	5.8	0	..	40	45	100
Yemen, Rep.	Sana'a	..	..	183	..	17.0	4.0	0	15	12	51	60
Yugoslavia FR (Serb./Mont.)	Belgrade	765	1,318	..	..	16.0	19.4	0	35	71	86	99
	Novi Sad	290	232	..	..	30.0	21.8	60	21	93	95	100
	Nis	150	214	..	..	17.4	19.7	61	25	84	87	92
Zambia	Lusaka	..	..	867	14.0	6.5	6.9	65	20	36	..	60
Zimbabwe	Harare	..	..	754	5.0	9.8	8.0	48	56	93	100	97

Table A.4. Environment

	Climate change				Biodiversity				Fisheries	
	Carbon dioxide emissions		Electricity production		Fossil fuel production	Mammal and bird species		Higher plant species		Annual marine catch	
Economy	Million metric tons 1996	% of world 1996	Billion kWh 1996	% from fossil fuel 1996	Thousand metric tons 1996	Number 1997	Number threatened 1997	Number 1997	Number threatened 1997	Thousand metric tons 1970	1996
Algeria	94.3	0.4	21	99	115,700	284	23	3,164	141	25	103
Argentina	129.9	0.6	70	56	68,249	1,217	68	9,372	247	163	925
Australia	306.6	1.4	177	90	182,819	901	103	15,638	2,245	54	128
Bolivia	10.1	0.0	3	36	4,290	1,590	51	17,367	227	0	1
Brazil	273.4	1.2	290	5	49,577	1,886	174	56,215	1,358	407	545
Canada	409.4	1.8	571	21	293,525	619	12	3,270	278	1,127	443
Chile	48.8	0.2	31	45	2,684	387	34	5,284	329	1,101	7,270
China	3,363.5	14.9	1,080	81	874,408	1,494	165	32,200	312	2,076	10,087
Colombia	65.3	0.3	45	20	56,817	2,054	99	51,220	712	16	103
Costa Rica	4.7	0.0	5	14	..	805	27	12,119	527	5	16
Cuba	31.2	0.1	13	92	1,221	168	22	6,522	888	86	57
Denmark	56.6	0.3	54	95	16,005	239	5	1,450	2	1,184	1,578
Ecuador	24.5	0.1	9	32	20,100	1,690	81	19,362	824	81	484
Egypt, Arab Rep.	97.9	0.4	58	81	57,621	251	26	2,076	82	25	105
Germany	861.2	3.8	551	65	93,004	315	13	2,682	14	851	198
Greece	80.6	0.4	42	90	7,765	346	23	4,992	571	84	138
Guatemala	6.8	0.0	4	21	740	708	12	8,681	355	1	1
India	997.4	4.4	435	82	193,816	1,239	148	16,000	1,236	941	2,420
Indonesia	245.1	1.1	67	83	172,364	1,955	232	29,375	264	732	2,868
Iran, Islamic Rep.	266.7	1.2	91	92	219,538	463	34	8,000	2	16	237
Italy	403.2	1.8	239	80	22,129	324	17	5,599	311	295	261
Jamaica	10.1	0.0	6	93	..	137	11	3,308	744	9	9
Japan	1,167.7	5.2	1,003	59	6,327	382	62	5,565	707	7,229	4,587
Kazakhstan	173.8	0.8	59	88	61,923	..	30	..	71	..	0
Kenya	6.8	0.0	4	9	..	1,203	67	6,506	240	8	4
Korea, Dem. Rep.	254.3	1.1	35	36	18,107	..	26	2,898	4	445	1,599
Korea, Rep.	408.1	1.8	223	66	2,228	161	25	2,898	66	521	1,729
Kuwait	..	..	25	100	112,600	41	4	234	0	3	6
Libya	40.6	0.2	18	100	77,617	167	13	1,825	57	6	34
Madagascar	1.2	0.0	..	..	..	307	74	9,505	306	11	71
Malaysia	119.1	0.5	51	90	66,757	787	76	15,500	490	243	921
Mauritius	1.7	0.0	..	..	..	31	14	750	294	5	17
Mexico	348.1	1.5	163	72	195,899	1,219	100	26,071	1,593	212	981
Netherlands	155.2	0.7	85	92	71,543	246	9	1,221	1	200	380
New Zealand	29.8	0.1	36	21	8,965	160	47	2,382	211	40	453
Nigeria	83.3	0.4	15	63	105,266	955	35	4,715	37	78	212
Norway	67.0	0.3	104	0	198,023	297	7	1,715	12	2,896	2,475
Panama	6.7	0.0	4	37	..	950	27	9,915	1,302	46	162
Peru	26.2	0.1	17	22	6,972	1,882	110	18,245	906	12,468	9,441
Philippines	63.2	0.3	37	63	523	548	135	8,931	360	784	1,561
Poland	356.8	1.6	141	98	97,962	311	16	2,450	27	447	388
Portugal	47.9	0.2	34	54	60	270	20	5,050	269	453	237
Puerto Rico	15.8	0.1	..	..	..	121	14	2,493	223	2	2
Russian Federation	1,579.5	7.0	846	68	889,367	897	69	..	214	..	3,787
Saudi Arabia	267.8	1.2	98	100	474,997	232	20	2,028	7	17	39
South Africa	292.7	1.3	198	93	113,023	843	49	23,420	2,215	1,205	560
Spain	232.5	1.0	173	43	10,981	360	29	5,050	985	1,235	967
Sri Lanka	7.1	0.0	5	28	..	338	25	3,314	455	86	204
Tanzania	2.4	0.0	2	12	3	1,138	63	10,008	436	20	39
Thailand	205.4	0.9	87	91	21,951	881	79	11,625	385	946	2,462
Turkey	178.3	0.8	95	57	16,018	418	29	8,650	1,876	168	578
Ukraine	397.3	1.8	182	51	57,293	..	25	..	52	..	381
United Arab Emirates	81.8	0.4	20	100	148,818	92	7	..	0	40	105
United Kingdom	557.0	2.5	346	70	242,852	280	6	1,623	18	1,028	781
United States	5,301.0	23.4	3,652	69	1,386,112	1,078	85	19,473	4,669	1,575	3,580
Venezuela	144.5	0.6	75	29	188,822	1,486	46	21,073	426	98	367
Vietnam	37.6	0.2	17	100	17,470	748	85	10,500	341	407	412
World	22,653.9 t	100.0 w	13,621 t	62 w	..	..	..	..	..	46,462 t	75,144 t
Low income	1,448.1	6.4	672	72	..	..	..	..	..	..	..
Middle income	10,068.9	44.4	4,447	69	..	..	..	..	..	22,657	48,358
Lower middle income	7,512.7	33.2	3,041	72	..	..	..	..	..	18,360	35,282
Upper middle income	2,556.2	11.3	1,407	61	..	..	..	..	..	4,297	13,075
Low and middle income	11,517.0	50.8	5,119	69	..	..	..	..	..	25,531	53,749
East Asia & Pacific	4,309.5	19.0	1,379	81	..	..	..	..	..	6,003	20,646
Europe & Central Asia	3,412.7	15.1	1,780	68	1,308,476	..	..	..	..	..	..
Latin America & Carib.	1,209.1	5.3	810	32	..	..	..	..	..	14,752	20,592
Middle East & N. Africa	988.6	4.4	380	93	1,089,769	..	..	..	..	567	1,567
South Asia	1,125.1	5.0	509	79	..	..	..	..	..	..	..
Sub-Saharan Africa	472.1	2.1	261	79	..	..	..	..	..	..	2,266
High income	11,136.9	49.2	8,503	58	..	..	..	..	..	20,931	21,396

Selected
World
Development
Indicators

Contents

Introduction to Selected World Development Indicators 226

Tables

World View
    Table 1   Size of the economy 230
    Table 2   Quality of life 232

People
    Table 3   Population and labor force 234
    Table 4   Poverty 236
    Table 5   Distribution of income or consumption 238
    Table 6   Education 240
    Table 7   Health 242

Environment
    Table 8   Land use and agricultural productivity 244
    Table 9   Water use, deforestation, and protected areas 246
    Table 10   Energy use and emissions 248

Economy
    Table 11   Growth of the economy 250
    Table 12   Structure of output 252
    Table 13   Structure of demand 254
    Table 14   Central government finances 256
    Table 15   Balance of payments, current account, and international reserves 258

States and Markets
    Table 16   Private sector finance 260
    Table 17   Role of government in the economy 262
    Table 18   Power and transportation 264
    Table 19   Communications, information, and science and technology 266

Global Links
    Table 20   Global trade 268
    Table 21   Aid and financial flows 270

    Table 1a   Key indicators for other economies 272

Technical Notes 273

Data Sources 289

Classification of Economies by Income and Region, 1999 290

Introduction to Selected World Development Indicators

elected World Development Indicators provides a core set of standard indicators drawn from the World Bank's development databases. The layout of the 21 tables retains the tradition of presenting comparative socioeconomic data for more than 130 economies for the most recent year for which data are available and for an earlier year. An additional table presents basic indicators for 78 economies with sparse data or with populations of less than 1.5 million.

The indicators presented here are a selection from more than 500 included in *World Development Indicators 1999*. Published annually, *World Development Indicators* reflects a comprehensive view of the development process. Its opening chapter reports on the record of and the prospects for social and economic progress in developing countries, measured against six international goals. Its five main sections recognize the contribution of a wide range of factors: human capital development, environmental sustainability, macroeconomic performance, private sector development, and the global links that influence the external environment for development. *World De-velopment Indicators* is complemented by a separately published CD-ROM database that gives access to over 1,000 data tables and 500 time-series indicators for 227 countries and regions.

Organization of Selected World Development Indicators

Tables 1 and 2, *World View,* offer an overview of key development issues: How rich or poor are the people in each economy? What is their real level of welfare as reflected in child malnutrition and mortality rates? What is the life expectancy of newborns? What percentage of adults is illiterate?

Tables 3 to 7, *People,* show the rate of progress in social development during the past decade. Data on population growth, labor force participation, and income distribution are included. Measures of well-being such as expenditure on health care, school enrollment ratios, and gender differences in access to educational attainment are also provided.

Tables 8 to 10, *Environment,* bring together key indicators on land use and agricultural output, water resources, energy consumption, and carbon dioxide emissions.

Tables 11 to 15, *Economy*, present information on the structure and growth of the world's economies, including government finance statistics and a summary of the balance of payments.

Tables 16 to 19, *States and Markets*, look at the roles of the public and the private sector in creating the necessary infrastructure for economic growth. These tables present information on private investment, stock markets, and the economic activities of the state (including military expenditure), as well as a full table of indicators on information technology and research and development.

Tables 20 and 21, *Global Links*, contain information on trade and financial flows, including aid and lending to developing countries.

Because the World Bank's primary business is providing lending and policy advice to its low- and middle-income members, the issues covered in these tables focus mainly on these economies. Where available, information on the high-income economies is also provided for comparison. Readers may wish to refer to national statistical publications and publications of the Organisation for Economic Co-operation and Development and the European Union for more information on the high-income economies.

Classification of economies

As in the rest of the report, the main criterion used in the Selected World Development Indicators to classify economies and broadly distinguish stages of economic development is GNP per capita. Economies are classified into three categories according to income. The classification used in this edition has been updated to reflect the World Bank's current operational guidelines. The GNP per capita cutoff levels are as follows: low-income, $760 or less in 1998; middle-income, $761 to $9,360; and high-income, $9,361 and above. A further division at GNP per capita $3,030 is made between lower-middle-income and upper-middle-income economies. Economies are further classified by region. See the table on Classification of Economies at the end of this volume for a list of economies in each group (including those with populations of less than 1.5 million).

From time to time an economy's classification is revised because of changes in the above cutoff values or in the economy's measured level of GNP per capita. When such changes occur, aggregates based on those classifications are recalculated for the past period so that a consistent time series is maintained. Between 1998 and 1999 several large countries changed classification, resulting in significant changes in the income and regional aggregates. For example, the Republic of Korea, previously classified as a high-income economy, now falls in the upper-middle-income group; therefore data for Korea are also included in the aggregates for developing countries in East Asia and Pacific. Revisions to estimates of China's GNP per capita have caused that economy to be reclassified as low-income. The following changes are also reflected: South Africa moved from upper-middle- to lower-middle-income; Indonesia and the Solomon Islands from lower-middle- to low-income; Grenada and Panama from lower-middle- to upper-middle-income; and Albania and Bosnia and Herzegovina from low-income to lower-middle-income.

Data sources and methodology

Socioeconomic and environmental data presented here are drawn from several sources: primary data collection by the World Bank, member country statistical publications, research institutes such as the World Resources Institute, and international organizations such as the United Nations and its specialized agencies, the International Monetary Fund, and the Organisation for Economic Co-operation and Development (see the Data Sources following the Technical Notes for a complete listing). Although international standards of coverage, definition, and classification apply to most statistics reported by countries and international agencies, there are inevitably differences in coverage, currentness, and the capabilities and resources devoted to basic data collection and compilation. For some topics, competing sources of data require review by World Bank staff to ensure that the most reliable data available are presented. In some instances, where available data are deemed too weak to provide reliable measures of levels and trends or do not adequately adhere to international standards, the data are not shown.

The data presented are generally consistent with those in *World Development Indicators 1999*. However, data have been revised and updated wherever new information has become available. Differences may also reflect revisions to historical series and changes in methodology. Thus data of different vintages may be published in different editions of World Bank publications. Readers are advised not to compile data series from different publications or different editions of the same publication. Consistent time-series data are available on *World Development Indicators 1999 CD-ROM*.

All dollar figures are in current U.S. dollars unless otherwise stated. The various methods used to convert from national currency figures are described in the Technical Notes.

Summary measures

The summary measures at the bottom of each table are either totals (indicated by **t** if the aggregates include estimates for missing data and nonreporting countries, or by an *s* for simple sums of the data available), weighted averages (**w**), or median values (**m**) calculated for groups of economies. Data for the countries excluded from the main tables (those presented in table 1a) have been included in the summary measures, where data are available, or by assuming that they follow the trend of reporting countries. This gives a more consistent aggregated measure by standardizing country coverage for each period shown. Where missing information accounts for a third or more of the overall estimate, however, the group measure is reported as not available. The section on "Statistical methods" in the Technical Notes provides further information on aggregation methods. Weights used to construct the aggregates are listed in the technical notes for each table.

Terminology and country coverage

The term *country* does not imply political independence but may refer to any territory for which authorities report separate social or economic statistics. Data are shown for economies as they were constituted in 1998, and historical data are revised to reflect current political arrangements. Throughout the tables, exceptions are noted.

As of July 1, 1997, China resumed its exercise of sovereignty over the Special Administrative Region of Hong Kong. Data for Hong Kong, China, are shown on a separate line following the entry for China and are included in the aggregates for high-income economies. Data for China do not include data for Taiwan, China, unless otherwise noted.

Data are shown separately whenever possible for the countries formed from the former Czechoslovakia: the Czech Republic and the Slovak Republic.

Data are shown separately for Eritrea whenever possible; in most cases prior to 1992, however, they are included in the data for Ethiopia.

Data for Germany refer to the unified Germany, unless otherwise noted.

Data for Jordan refer to the East Bank only, unless otherwise noted.

In 1991 the Union of Soviet Socialist Republics was formally dissolved into 15 countries: Armenia, Azerbaijan, Belarus, Estonia, Georgia, Kazakhstan, the Kyrgyz Republic, Latvia, Lithuania, Moldova, the Russian Federation, Tajikistan, Turkmenistan, Ukraine, and Uzbekistan. Whenever possible, data are shown for the individual countries.

Data for the Republic of Yemen refer to that country as constituted from 1990 onward; data for previous years refer to the former People's Democratic Republic of Yemen and the former Yemen Arab Republic, unless otherwise noted.

Whenever possible, data are shown for the individual countries formed from the former Yugoslavia: Bosnia and Herzegovina, Croatia, the Former Yugoslav Republic of Macedonia, Slovenia, and the Federal Republic of Yugoslavia (Serbia and Montenegro).

Technical notes

Because data quality and intercountry comparisons are often problematic, readers are encouraged to consult the Technical Notes, the table on Classification of Economies by Income and Region, and the footnotes to the tables. For more extensive documentation see *World Development Indicators 1999*. The Data Sources section at the end of the Technical Notes lists sources that contain more comprehensive definitions and descriptions of the concepts used.

For more information about the Selected World Development Indicators and the World Bank's other statistical publications, please contact:

Information Center, Development Data Group
The World Bank
1818 H Street, N.W.
Washington, D.C. 20433
Hotline: (800) 590-1906 or (202) 473-7824
Fax: (202) 522-1498
E-mail: info@worldbank.org
World Wide Web: http://www.worldbank.org/wdi

To order World Bank publications, e-mail your request to books@worldbank.org, or write to World Bank Publications at the address above, or call (202) 473-1155.

The World by Income

This map presents economies classified according to World Bank estimates of 1998 GNP per capita.
Not shown on the map due to space constraints are: American Samoa (upper middle income); Fiji, Kiribati, Samoa, Tonga (lower middle income); French Polynesia (high income); Tuvalu (no data).

Low $760 or less
Lower middle $761 to $3,030
Upper middle $3,031 to $9,360
High $9,361 or more

No data

IBRD 30358
AUGUST 1999

Table 1. Size of the economy

Economy	Population Millions 1998	Surface area Thousands of sq. km 1996	Population density People per sq. km 1998	Gross national product (GNP) Billions of dollars 1998[b]	Rank 1998	Avg. annual growth rate (%) 1997–98	GNP per capita Dollars 1998[b]	Rank 1998	Avg. annual growth rate (%) 1997–98	GNP measured at PPP[a] Billions of dollars 1998	Per capita Dollars 1998	Rank 1998
Albania	3	29	123	2.7	137	..	810	144	..	..	..	..
Algeria	30	2,382	13	46.5	50	7.3	1,550	116	5.0	131.4[c]	4,380[c]	104
Angola	12	1,247	10	4.1	121	7.9	340	178	4.8	10.1[c]	840[c]	197
Argentina	36	2,780	13	324.1	17	4.0	8,970	55	2.7	368.5	10,200	64
Armenia	4	30	135	1.8	156	..	480	162	..	..	..	..
Australia	19	7,741	2	380.6	14	3.8	20,300	24	2.6	377.5	20,130	25
Austria	8	84	98	217.2	21	3.4	26,850	12	3.2	183.9	22,740	16
Azerbaijan	8	87	91	3.9	125	9.4	490	161	8.1	14.3	1,820	157
Bangladesh	126	144	965	44.0	52	5.0	350	175	3.4	137.7	1,100	188
Belarus	10	208	49	22.5	61	..	2,200	102	..	..	..	..
Belgium	10	33	311	259.0	19	2.9	25,380	15	2.7	239.7	23,480	12
Benin	6	113	54	2.3	142	4.5	380	173	1.5	7.5	1,250	182
Bolivia	8	1,099	7	7.9	94	4.7	1,000	138	2.3	22.4	2,820	140
Botswana	2	582	3	5.6	107	5.5	3,600	82	3.5	13.0	8,310	70
Brazil	166	8,547	20	758.0	8	0.0	4,570	72	–1.4	1,021.4	6,160	88
Bulgaria	8	111	75	10.1	84	..	1,230	131	..	..	..	..
Burkina Faso	11	274	39	2.6	140	6.3	240	196	3.8	11.0[c]	1,020[c]	191
Burundi	7	28	256	0.9	173	4.6	140	206	2.2	4.1[c]	620[c]	207
Cambodia	11	181	61	3.0	135	–0.1	280	191	–2.3	13.3	1,240	184
Cameroon	14	475	31	8.7	89	6.7	610	156	3.8	25.9	1,810	158
Canada	31	9,971	3	612.2	9	6.1	20,020	26	5.1	735.6	24,050	9
Central African Republic	3	623	6	1.0	170	4.5	300	186	2.6	4.5[c]	1,290[c]	181
Chad	7	1,284	6	1.7	160	..	230	197	..	..	..	..
Chile	15	757	20	71.3	42	8.0	4,810	71	6.5	191.1	12,890	53
China	1,239	9,597[d]	133	928.9	7	7.4	750	149	6.5	3,983.6	3,220	129
Hong Kong, China	7	1	6,755	158.3[c]	24	–5.1	23,670[c]	21	–7.8	147.1	22,000	18
Colombia	41	1,139	39	106.1	35	5.6	2,600	95	3.7	306.0	7,500	76
Congo, Dem. Rep.	48	2,345	21	5.3	108	4.0	110	209	0.7	36.4[c]	750[c]	200
Congo, Rep.	3	342	8	1.9	151	11.9	690	153	8.9	4.0	1,430	174
Costa Rica	4	51	69	9.8	85	4.7	2,780	93	3.1	23.3	6,620	86
Côte d'Ivoire	14	322	46	10.1	83	5.7	700	152	3.6	25.0	1,730	161
Croatia	5	57	82	20.7	63	..	4,520	73	..	..	..	..
Czech Republic	10	79	133	51.8	48	..	5,040	69	..	..	..	..
Denmark	5	43	125	176.4	23	3.0	33,260	6	2.6	126.4	23,830	11
Dominican Republic	8	49	171	14.6	78	6.5	1,770	109	4.6	38.8	4,700	99
Ecuador	12	284	44	18.6	70	2.1	1,530	119	0.2	56.3	4,630	100
Egypt, Arab Rep.	61	1,001	62	79.2	40	5.1	1,290	127	3.3	192.5	3,130	132
El Salvador	6	21	292	11.2	81	3.6	1,850	107	1.4	17.3	2,850	139
Eritrea	4	118	38	0.8	176	–4.0	200	202	–6.7	3.7	950	193
Estonia	1	45	34	4.9	112	..	3,390	87	..	..	..	..
Ethiopia	61	1,104	61	6.1	104	–0.8	100	210	–3.2	30.8	500	208
Finland	5	338	17	124.3	30	5.2	24,110	19	4.8	104.5	20,270	23
France	59	552	107	1,466.2	4	3.2	24,940	17	2.9	1,312.0	22,320	17
Georgia	5	70	78	5.1	109	..	930	139	..	..	..	..
Germany	82	357	235	2,122.7	3	–0.4	25,850	13	–0.4	1,708.5	20,810	20
Ghana	18	239	81	7.2	98	4.6	390	171	1.9	29.8[c]	1,610[c]	168
Greece	11	132	82	122.9	31	3.7	11,650	47	3.4	137.2	13,010	52
Guatemala	11	109	100	17.7	72	4.8	1,640	115	2.1	44.0	4,070	107
Guinea	7	246	29	3.8	127	4.3	540	159	1.9	12.5	1,760	160
Haiti	8	28	277	3.1	134	3.0	410	167	1.1	9.6[c]	1,250[c]	182
Honduras	6	112	55	4.5	117	3.9	730	151	1.0	13.2	2,140	154
Hungary	10	93	110	45.6	51	..	4,510	74	..	..	..	..
India	980	3,288	330	421.3	11	6.1	430	165	4.2	1,660.9	1,700	163
Indonesia	204	1,905	112	138.5	28	–14.8	680	154	–16.2	568.9	2,790	141
Iran, Islamic Rep.	62	1,633	38	109.6	33	..	1,770	109	..	..	..	..
Ireland	4	70	53	67.5	43	9.0	18,340	27	8.5	67.5	18,340	30
Israel	6	21	290	95.2	36	1.9	15,940	32	–0.4	103.4	17,310	33
Italy	58	301	196	1,166.2	6	2.3	20,250	25	2.2	1,163.4	20,200	24
Jamaica	3	11	238	4.3	118	–1.1	1,680	113	–1.9	8.3	3,210	130
Japan	126	378	335	4,089.9	2	–2.6	32,380	7	–2.8	2,928.4	23,180	14
Jordan	5	89	51	6.9	100	0.3	1,520	120	–2.5	14.8	3,230	128
Kazakhstan	16	2,717	6	20.6	64	–2.6	1,310	126	–2.0	53.4	3,400	126
Kenya	29	580	51	9.7	86	1.5	330	180	–0.9	33.1	1,130	187
Korea, Rep.	46	99	470	369.9	15	–6.3	7,970	59	–7.1	569.3	12,270	55
Kuwait	2	18	105	..	..	..	[f]	..	..	..	..	..
Kyrgyz Republic	5	199	24	1.6	162	4.2	350	175	2.8	10.3	2,200	152
Lao PDR	5	237	22	1.6	163	4.0	330	180	1.4	6.5[c]	1,300[c]	180
Latvia	2	65	39	5.9	105	..	2,430	98	..	..	..	..
Lebanon	4	10	412	15.0	77	4.3	3,560	84	2.7	25.9	6,150	89
Lesotho	2	30	68	1.2	168	–3.1	570	158	–5.4	4.8[c]	2,320[c]	147
Lithuania	4	65	57	9.0	88	5.6	2,440	97	5.9	15.9	4,310	105
Macedonia, FYR	2	26	79	2.6	139	2.9	1,290	127	2.2	7.4	3,660	116
Madagascar	15	587	25	3.8	128	4.8	260	193	1.6	13.1	900	194
Malawi	11	118	112	2.1	144	1.8	200	202	–0.7	7.7	730	203
Malaysia	22	330	68	79.8	39	–6.3	3,600	82	–8.4	155.1[c]	6,990[c]	79

Note: For data comparability and coverage, see the Technical Notes. Figures in italics are for years other than those specified. Rankings are based on 210 economies, including the 78 listed in Table 1a. See Technical Notes.

Economy	Population Millions 1998	Surface area Thousands of sq. km 1996	Population density People per sq. km 1998	GNP Billions of dollars 1998[b]	GNP Rank 1998	GNP Avg. annual growth rate (%) 1997–98	GNP per capita Dollars 1998[b]	GNP per capita Rank 1998	GNP per capita Avg. annual growth rate (%) 1997–98	PPP Billions of dollars 1998	PPP Per capita Dollars 1998	PPP Rank 1998
Mali	11	1,240	9	2.6	138	5.3	250	194	2.2	7.7	720	204
Mauritania	3	1,026	2	1.0	171	5.2	410	167	2.4	4.2[c]	1,660[c]	165
Mexico	96	1,958	50	380.9	13	4.8	3,970	76	3.0	785.8[c]	8,190[c]	71
Moldova	4	34	130	1.8	158	..	410	167	..	..	..	..
Mongolia	3	1,567	2	1.0	172	4.9	400	170	3.2	3.9	1,520	170
Morocco	28	447	62	34.8	56	0.8	1,250	130	−1.0	86.8	3,120	133
Mozambique	17	802	22	3.6	130	11.3	210	199	9.2	14.5[c]	850[c]	196
Myanmar	44	677	68	..	..	..	..[g]	..	..	..	..	..
Namibia	2	824	2	3.2	131	1.2	1,940	106	−1.2	8.2[c]	4,950[c]	94
Nepal	23	147	160	4.8	114	2.2	210	199	−0.1	24.9	1,090	189
Netherlands	16	41	463	388.7	12	3.3	24,760	18	2.7	339.3	21,620	19
New Zealand	4	271	14	55.8	46	1.4	14,700	36	0.5	60.1	15,840	40
Nicaragua	5	130	40	..	..	..	..[g]	..	..	8.6[c]	1,790[c]	159
Niger	10	1,267	8	1.9	150	4.3	190	204	0.8	8.4	830	198
Nigeria	121	924	133	36.4	55	1.1	300	186	−1.7	99.7	820	199
Norway	4	324	14	152.1	25	2.4	34,330	4	1.8	107.6	24,290	8
Pakistan	132	796	171	63.2	44	5.0	480	162	2.5	204.9	1,560	169
Panama	3	76	37	8.5	91	3.8	3,080	90	2.0	19.2	6,940	81
Papua New Guinea	5	463	10	4.1	120	2.3	890	140	0.0	12.4[c]	2,700[c]	142
Paraguay	5	407	13	9.2	87	0.2	1,760	111	−2.1	19.0	3,650	117
Peru	25	1,285	19	61.1	45	..	2,460	96	..	..	..	..
Philippines	75	300	252	78.9	41	0.1	1,050	135	−2.1	265.6	3,540	122
Poland	39	323	127	150.8	26	5.4	3,900	79	5.4	260.7	6,740	83
Portugal	10	92	109	106.4	34	3.9	10,690	51	3.8	143.1	14,380	45
Romania	22	238	98	31.3	58	−5.6	1,390	125	−5.3	89.3	3,970	109
Russian Federation	147	17,075	9	337.9	16	−6.6	2,300	101	−6.3	579.8	3,950	110
Rwanda	8	26	329	1.9	155	9.9	230	197	7.1	5.6	690	206
Saudi Arabia	21	2,150	10	..	..	..	..[h]	..	..	..	..	..
Senegal	9	197	47	4.8	115	6.0	530	160	3.1	15.4	1,710	162
Sierra Leone	5	72	68	0.7	181	−0.7	140	206	−2.9	1.9	390	210
Singapore	3	1	5,186	95.1	37	1.5	30,060	9	−0.4	90.5	28,620	5
Slovak Republic	5	49	112	20.0	66	..	3,700	80	..	..	..	..
Slovenia	2	20	99	19.4	67	..	9,760	52	..	..	..	..
South Africa	41	1,221	34	119.0	32	0.6	2,880	92	−1.2	288.7[c]	6,990[c]	79
Spain	39	506	79	553.7	10	3.7	14,080	39	3.7	631.5	16,060	38
Sri Lanka	19	66	290	15.2	76	..	810	144	..	..	..	..
Sweden	9	450	22	226.9	20	3.5	25,620	14	3.5	172.5	19,480	27
Switzerland	7	41	180	284.8	18	2.1	40,080	3	1.8	189.1	26,620	7
Syrian Arab Republic	15	185	83	15.6	75	4.4	1,020	136	1.8	45.8	3,000	136
Tajikistan	6	143	43	2.1	143	..	350	175	..	..	..	..
Tanzania	32	945	36	6.7[i]	101	3.2	210[i]	199	0.6	15.9	490	209
Thailand	61	513	120	134.4	29	−7.7	2,200	102	−8.5	357.1	5,840	91
Togo	4	57	82	1.5	164	−1.0	330	180	−3.5	6.2	1,390	176
Tunisia	9	164	60	19.2	69	5.5	2,050	105	3.9	48.3	5,160	93
Turkey	63	775	82	200.5	22	..	3,160	89	..	..	..	..
Turkmenistan	5	488	10	..	136	..	..[g]	..	..	24.5[c]	1,170[c]	185
Uganda	21	241	105	6.7	102	5.8	320	185	2.9	..	..	..
Ukraine	50	604	87	42.7	53	..	850	142	..	..	..	..
United Kingdom	59	245	244	1,263.8	5	2.0	21,400	22	1.9	1,218.6	20,640	22
United States	270	9,364	29	7,921.3	1	3.7	29,340	10	2.8	7,922.6	29,340	3
Uruguay	3	177	19	20.3	65	6.6	6,180	67	5.8	31.2	9,480	67
Uzbekistan	24	447	58	20.9	62	3.0	870	141	1.2	69.8	2,900	138
Venezuela	23	912	26	81.3	38	−0.4	3,500	85	−2.4	190.4	8,190	71
Vietnam	78	332	238	25.6	60	4.0	330	180	2.8	131.0	1,690	164
Yemen, Rep.	16	528	31	4.9	110	7.3	300	186	4.6	12.1	740	202
Zambia	10	753	13	3.2	132	−1.8	330	180	−4.0	8.3	860	195
Zimbabwe	12	391	30	7.1	99	−0.4	610	156	−2.2	25.2	2,150	153
World	**5,897 s**	**133,567 s**	**45 w**	**28,862.2 t**		**1.5 w**	**4,890 t**		**0.1 w**	**36,556.8 t**	**6,200 w**	
Low income	3,515	42,695	85	1,843.7		3.8	520		2.1	7,475.1	2,130	
Excl. China & India	1,296	29,810	45	493.5		−3.9	380		−5.9	1,821.3	1,400	
Middle income	1,496	58,789	26	4,419.6		−0.4	2,950		−1.5	8,315.8	5,560	
Lower middle income	908	36,729	25	1,557.4		−1.5	1,710		−2.6	3,709.4	4,080	
Upper middle income	588	22,060	27	2,862.1		0.2	4,860		−1.1	4,606.3	7,830	
Low and middle income	5,011	101,484	50	6,263.3		1.0	1,250		−0.5	15,790.8	3,150	
East Asia & Pacific	1,817	16,384	114	1,801.6		−1.1	990		−2.2	6,179.5	3,400	
Europe & Central Asia	473	24,208	20	1,038.8		..	2,190		..	2,005.5	4,240	
Latin America & Carib.	502	20,462	25	1,977.6		2.5	3,940		0.8	3,401.5	6,780	
Middle East & N. Africa	285	11,000	26	585.6		..	2,050		..	1,203.3	4,220	
South Asia	1,305	5,140	273	555.5		5.9	430		3.9	2,100.4	1,610	
Sub-Saharan Africa	628	24,290	27	304.2		2.2	480		−0.4	900.6	1,430	
High income	885	32,082	29	22,599.0		1.6	25,510		1.1	20,766.0	23,440	

a. Purchasing power parity; see the Technical Notes. b. Preliminary World Bank estimates calculated using the World Bank *Atlas* method. c. Estimate based on regression; others are extrapolated from the latest International Comparison Programme benchmark estimates. d. Includes Taiwan, China. e. GNP data refer to GDP. f. Estimated to be high income ($9,361 or more). g. Estimated to be low income ($760 or less). h. Estimated to be upper middle income ($3,031 to $9,360). i. Data refer to mainland Tanzania only.

Table 2. Quality of life

Economy	Growth of private consumption per capita Avg. annual growth rate (%) 1980–97		Prevalence of child malnutrition % of children under age 5 1992–97[a]	Under-5 mortality rate Per 1,000		Life expectancy at birth Years 1997		Adult illiteracy rate % of people 15 and above 1997		Urban population % of total		Access to sanitation in urban areas % of urban pop. with access 1995
	Uncorrected	Distribution-corrected		1980	1997	Males	Females	Males	Females	1980	1998	
Albania	..	..	..	57	40	69	75	..	..	34	38	97
Algeria	−1.8	−1.2	13	139	39	69	72	27	52	43	58	..
Angola	−7.8	..	35	261	209	45	48	..	..	21	33	71
Argentina	..	..	2	38	24	70	77	3	4	83	89	80
Armenia	..	..	..	..	..	70	77	..	..	66	69	..
Australia	1.7	1.1	0	13	7	76	81	..	..	86	85	..
Austria	2.0	1.6	..	17	7	74	81	..	..	65	65	..
Azerbaijan	..	..	10	..	23	67	75	..	..	53	57	..
Bangladesh	2.1	1.5	56	211	104	58	58	50	73	11	20	41
Belarus	−3.5	−2.7	..	..	..	63	74	0	2	56	73	..
Belgium	1.6	1.2	..	15	7	73	80	..	..	95	97	..
Benin	−0.7	..	29	214	149	52	55	52	79	27	41	60
Bolivia	0.1	0.0	8	170	96	60	63	9	23	46	63	77
Botswana	2.3	..	27	94	88	46	48	28	23	15	68	91
Brazil	0.5	0.2	6	..	44	63	71	16	16	66	80	74
Bulgaria	−0.6	−0.4	..	25	24	67	74	1	2	61	69	..
Burkina Faso	0.3	..	33	..	169	44	45	70	89	9	17	..
Burundi	−0.8	..	38	193	200	41	44	46	64	4	8	..
Cambodia	..	..	38	330	147	53	55	..	..	12	22	..
Cameroon	−1.5	..	..	173	78	55	58	21	35	31	47	..
Canada	1.3	0.9	..	13	8	76	82	..	..	76	77	..
Central African Republic	−1.5	..	23	..	160	43	47	44	70	35	40	..
Chad	0.0	..	39	235	182	47	50	..	..	19	23	74
Chile	3.8	1.7	1	35	13	72	78	5	5	81	84	95
China	7.7	4.5	16	65	39	68	71	9	25	20	33	68
Hong Kong, China	5.2	..	..	..	..	76	82	4	12	91	95	..
Colombia	1.2	0.5	8	58	30	67	73	9	9	64	74	70
Congo, Dem. Rep.	−4.5	..	34	210	148	49	52	..	..	29	30	53
Congo, Rep.	0.2	..	24	125	145	46	51	15	30	41	61	..
Costa Rica	0.8	0.4	5	29	15	74	79	5	5	43	51	100
Côte d'Ivoire	−2.3	−1.5	24	170	140	46	47	49	66	35	45	..
Croatia	..	..	1	23	10	68	77	1	4	50	57	71
Czech Republic	..	..	1	19	8	71	78	..	..	64	66	..
Denmark	1.7	1.3	..	10	6	73	78	..	..	84	86	..
Dominican Republic	−0.2	−0.1	6	92	47	69	73	17	18	51	64	89
Ecuador	−0.2	−0.1	17	101	39	68	73	7	11	47	61	70
Egypt, Arab Rep.	2.0	1.3	15	175	66	65	68	35	60	44	45	95
El Salvador	2.9	1.5	11	120	39	67	73	20	26	42	46	89
Eritrea	..	..	44	..	95	49	52	..	..	14	18	12
Estonia	−2.2	−1.3	..	25	13	64	76	..	..	70	74	..
Ethiopia	−0.4	..	48	213	175	42	44	59	71	11	17	..
Finland	1.4	1.1	..	9	5	73	81	..	..	60	64	100
France	1.7	1.1	..	13	6	74	82	..	..	73	75	..
Georgia	..	..	..	..	21	69	77	..	..	52	60	..
Germany	..	..	..	16	6	74	80	..	..	83	87	..
Ghana	0.2	0.1	27	157	102	58	62	23	43	31	37	75
Greece	1.8	..	..	23	9	75	81	2	5	58	60	..
Guatemala	0.1	0.0	27	..	55	61	67	26	41	37	40	91
Guinea	1.0	0.5	24	299	182	46	47	..	..	19	31	24
Haiti	..	..	28	200	125	51	56	52	57	24	34	43
Honduras	−0.2	−0.1	18	103	48	67	72	29	30	35	46	91
Hungary	−0.1	−0.1	..	26	12	66	75	1	1	57	66	..
India	2.7	1.9	53	177	88	62	64	33	61	23	28	..
Indonesia	4.5	3.0	34	125	60	63	67	9	20	22	38	88
Iran, Islamic Rep.	0.2	..	16	126	35	69	70	19	34	50	61	86
Ireland	2.7	1.8	..	14	7	73	79	..	..	55	58	..
Israel	3.3	2.1	..	19	8	76	79	2	7	89	91	100
Italy	2.2	1.5	..	17	7	75	82	1	2	67	67	..
Jamaica	2.2	1.3	10	39	14	72	77	19	10	47	55	99
Japan	2.9	..	..	11	6	77	83	..	..	76	79	..
Jordan	−1.2	−0.7	10	48	35	69	73	8	18	60	73	..
Kazakhstan	..	..	8	..	29	60	70	..	..	54	61	..
Kenya	0.9	0.4	23	115	112	51	53	13	28	16	31	..
Korea, Rep.	7.0	..	..	18	11	69	76	1	4	57	84	100
Kuwait	..	..	11	35	13	74	80	17	23	90	97	100
Kyrgyz Republic	..	..	11	..	..	63	71	..	..	38	40	..
Lao PDR	..	..	40	200	..	52	55	..	..	13	22	..
Latvia	..	..	..	26	19	64	75	0	1	68	74	90
Lebanon	..	..	3	..	32	68	72	9	22	74	89	..
Lesotho	−2.8	−1.2	16	168	137	55	57	29	7	13	26	76
Lithuania	..	..	..	24	13	66	77	0	1	61	74	..
Macedonia, FYR	..	..	..	69	17	70	75	..	..	53	61	..
Madagascar	−2.4	−0.2	34	216	158	56	59	..	..	18	28	..
Malawi	0.6	..	30	265	224	43	43	27	57	9	15	94
Malaysia	3.1	1.6	20	42	14	70	75	10	19	42	56	94

Note: For data comparability and coverage, see the Technical Notes. Figures in italics are for years other than those specified.

WORLD VIEW

Economy	Growth of private consumption per capita Avg. annual growth rate (%) 1980–97		Prevalence of child malnutrition % of children under age 5 1992–97[a]	Under-5 mortality rate Per 1,000		Life expectancy at birth Years 1997		Adult illiteracy rate % of people 15 and above 1997		Urban population % of total		Access to sanitation in urban areas % of urban pop. with access 1995
	Uncorrected	Distribution-corrected		1980	1997	Males	Females	Males	Females	1980	1998	
Mali	−0.4	. .	40	. .	235	49	52	57	72	19	29	61
Mauritania	0.1	0.1	23	175	149	52	55	51	72	27	55	44
Mexico	0.1	0.0	14	74	38	69	75	8	12	66	74	93
Moldova	. .	. .	. .	. .	24	63	70	1	3	40	54	96
Mongolia	. .	. .	12	. .	68	64	67	. .	. .	52	62	100
Morocco	1.6	1.0	10	152	67	65	69	41	67	41	54	97
Mozambique	−2.3	. .	26	223	201	44	47	43	75	13	38	68
Myanmar	. .	. .	43	134	131	59	62	11	21	24	27	56
Namibia	−3.0	. .	26	114	101	55	57	19	22	23	39	. .
Nepal	2.1	1.3	47	180	117	58	57	44	79	7	11	74
Netherlands	1.6	1.1	. .	11	7	75	81	. .	. .	88	89	. .
New Zealand	0.9	. .	. .	16	7	75	80	. .	. .	83	87	. .
Nicaragua	−2.6	−1.3	12	143	57	66	71	37	37	53	64	88
Niger	−2.6	−1.7	43	320	. .	45	50	78	93	13	20	. .
Nigeria	−4.7	−2.6	39	196	122	52	55	31	49	27	42	82
Norway	1.5	1.2	. .	11	6	76	81	. .	. .	71	74	100
Pakistan	2.0	1.4	38	161	136	61	63	45	75	28	36	75
Panama	1.6	0.7	6	36	26	72	76	8	10	50	57	99
Papua New Guinea	−1.1	−0.5	30	100	82	57	59	. .	. .	13	17	. .
Paraguay	1.8	0.7	. .	61	28	68	72	6	9	42	55	20
Peru	−0.5	−0.3	8	126	52	66	71	6	16	65	72	78
Philippines	0.7	0.4	30	81	41	67	70	5	6	37	57	88
Poland	0.9	0.6	. .	. .	12	69	77	0	0	58	65	. .
Portugal	3.1	. .	. .	31	8	71	79	6	12	29	37	. .
Romania	0.3	0.2	6	36	26	65	73	1	3	49	57	. .
Russian Federation	. .	. .	3	. .	25	61	73	0	1	70	77	. .
Rwanda	−1.1	−0.8	29	. .	209	39	42	29	44	5	6	. .
Saudi Arabia	. .	. .	. .	85	28	69	72	19	38	66	85	. .
Senegal	−0.7	−0.3	22	190	110	51	54	55	75	36	46	68
Sierra Leone	−3.2	−1.2	. .	336	286	36	39	. .	. .	24	35	. .
Singapore	4.9	. .	. .	13	6	73	79	4	13	100	100	. .
Slovak Republic	. .	. .	. .	23	. .	69	77	. .	. .	52	60	. .
Slovenia	. .	. .	. .	18	6	71	79	0	0	48	52	100
South Africa	−0.3	−0.1	9	91	65	62	68	15	17	48	50	78
Spain	2.2	1.5	. .	16	7	75	82	2	4	73	77	. .
Sri Lanka	2.8	1.9	38	48	19	71	75	6	12	22	23	81
Sweden	0.7	0.5	. .	9	5	77	82	. .	. .	83	83	. .
Switzerland	0.6	0.4	. .	11	6	76	82	. .	. .	57	62	. .
Syrian Arab Republic	1.0	. .	13	73	38	67	71	13	43	47	54	. .
Tajikistan	. .	. .	. .	. .	36	66	71	1	2	34	33	. .
Tanzania	0.0	0.0	31	176	136	47	49	18	38	15	26	. .
Thailand	5.5	2.9	. .	58	38	66	72	3	7	17	21	98
Togo	−0.5	. .	19	175	138	48	50	31	62	23	32	76
Tunisia	1.0	0.6	9	100	33	68	71	22	44	52	64	100
Turkey	2.5	. .	10	133	50	67	72	8	26	44	73	. .
Turkmenistan	. .	. .	. .	. .	50	62	69	. .	. .	47	45	. .
Uganda	1.7	1.0	26	180	162	43	42	25	47	9	14	60
Ukraine	. .	. .	. .	. .	17	62	73	. .	. .	62	72	. .
United Kingdom	2.6	1.8	. .	14	7	75	80	. .	. .	89	89	. .
United States	1.9	1.1	1	15	. .	73	79	. .	. .	74	77	. .
Uruguay	2.4	. .	4	42	20	70	78	3	2	85	91	56
Uzbekistan	. .	. .	19	. .	31	66	72	. .	. .	41	42	. .
Venezuela	−0.8	−0.4	5	42	25	70	76	7	8	79	87	74
Vietnam	. .	. .	45	105	40	66	71	5	11	19	20	. .
Yemen, Rep.	. .	. .	29	198	137	54	55	36	79	20	36	40
Zambia	−3.7	−2.0	24	149	189	43	43	17	33	40	44	66
Zimbabwe	0.3	. .	16	108	108	51	54	6	12	22	34	. .
World	**3.1 w**	**2.1 w**		**125 w**	**79 w**	**65 w**	**69 w**	**18 w**	**33 w**	**39 w**	**46 w**	**. . w**
Low income	3.9	2.7		151	97	62	64	22	42	21	31	. .
Excl. China & India	0.4	. .		178	130	55	58	30	47	21	31	. .
Middle income	1.2	. .		. .	42	66	72	10	16	55	66	. .
Lower middle income	. .	. .		. .	47	65	71	11	18	50	58	. .
Upper middle income	1.5	. .		. .	34	67	74	9	13	63	77	83
Low and middle income	3.3	2.2		137	83	63	67	19	34	32	41	. .
East Asia & Pacific	6.8	4.0		81	46	67	70	9	22	22	35	75
Europe & Central Asia	. .	. .		. .	30	64	73	2	6	56	68	. .
Latin America & Carib.	0.5	0.2		. .	41	66	73	12	14	65	75	80
Middle East & N. Africa	0.7	. .		137	62	66	68	27	50	48	58	. .
South Asia	2.5	1.8		180	100	62	63	36	63	22	27	. .
Sub-Saharan Africa	−2.1	. .		189	147	49	52	34	50	23	33	. .
High income	2.1	1.2		15	7	74	81	. .	. .	75	76	. .

a. Data are for the most recent year available within the period.

Table 3. Population and labor force

	Population						Labor force								
	Total Millions		Avg. annual growth rate (%)		Aged 15–64 Millions		Total Millions		Avg. annual growth rate (%)		Female % of labor force		Children aged 10–14 % of age group	
Economy	1980	1998	1980–90	1990–98	1980	1998	1980	1998	1980–90	1990–98	1980	1998	1980	1998
Albania	2.7	3.4	2.3	0.3	2	2	1	2	3.1	0.6	39	41	4	1
Algeria	18.7	30.0	4.7	2.6	9	18	5	10	7.1	4.9	21	26	7	1
Angola	7.0	12.0	5.4	3.8	4	6	3	6	4.7	3.4	47	46	30	27
Argentina	28.1	36.1	2.5	1.5	17	22	11	14	3.0	2.2	28	32	8	4
Armenia	3.1	3.8	2.0	1.0	2	2	1	2	2.5	1.3	48	48	0	0
Australia	14.7	18.8	2.4	1.3	10	13	7	10	3.5	1.6	37	43	0	0
Austria	7.6	8.1	0.7	0.7	5	6	3	4	1.1	1.0	41	40	0	0
Azerbaijan	6.2	7.9	2.5	1.4	4	5	3	3	2.2	1.6	48	44	0	0
Bangladesh	86.7	125.6	3.7	1.9	44	71	41	64	4.5	3.3	42	42	35	29
Belarus	9.6	10.2	0.6	0.0	6	7	5	5	0.4	0.0	50	49	0	0
Belgium	9.8	10.2	0.4	0.3	6	7	4	4	0.6	0.7	34	41	0	0
Benin	3.5	6.0	5.4	3.3	2	3	2	3	4.8	3.3	47	48	30	27
Bolivia	5.4	7.9	3.9	2.7	3	4	2	3	4.5	2.7	33	38	19	13
Botswana	0.9	1.6	5.4	2.9	0	1	0	1	5.4	2.9	50	46	26	16
Brazil	121.7	165.9	3.1	1.6	70	108	47	76	4.7	2.3	28	35	19	15
Bulgaria	8.9	8.2	−0.7	−0.8	6	6	5	4	−0.9	−0.8	45	48	0	0
Burkina Faso	7.0	10.7	4.3	2.7	3	5	4	5	3.4	2.1	48	47	71	48
Burundi	4.1	6.6	4.7	2.7	2	3	2	4	4.5	2.7	50	49	50	49
Cambodia	6.5	10.7	5.0	3.1	4	6	4	6	4.6	3.1	55	52	27	24
Cameroon	8.7	14.3	5.0	3.2	5	8	4	6	4.8	3.5	37	38	34	24
Canada	24.6	30.6	2.2	1.4	17	21	12	17	3.0	1.6	40	45	0	0
Central African Republic	2.3	3.5	4.1	2.4	1	2	..	..	..	..	..	..	39	30
Chad	4.5	7.4	5.0	3.5	2	3	2	4	4.6	3.5	43	45	42	38
Chile	11.1	14.8	2.8	1.8	7	10	4	6	4.5	2.5	26	33	0	0
China	981.2	1,238.6	2.3	1.2	586	836	540	743	3.2	1.5	43	45	30	10
Hong Kong, China	5.0	6.7	2.8	2.3	3	5	2	3	3.4	2.5	34	37	6	0
Colombia	28.4	40.8	3.6	2.2	16	25	9	18	6.3	3.2	26	38	12	6
Congo, Dem. Rep.	27.0	48.2	5.8	3.6	14	24	12	20	5.3	3.6	45	43	33	29
Congo, Rep.	1.7	2.8	5.1	3.2	1	1	1	1	4.9	2.9	42	43	27	26
Costa Rica	2.3	3.5	4.3	2.1	1	2	1	1	5.7	2.8	21	31	10	5
Côte d'Ivoire	8.2	14.5	5.7	3.1	4	8	3	6	5.7	3.9	32	33	28	20
Croatia	4.6	4.6	0.0	−0.6	3	3	2	2	0.4	0.0	40	44	0	0
Czech Republic	10.2	10.3	0.1	−0.1	6	7	5	6	0.8	0.7	47	47	0	0
Denmark	5.1	5.3	0.3	0.4	3	4	3	3	0.9	0.2	44	46	0	0
Dominican Republic	5.7	8.3	3.7	2.1	3	5	2	4	5.2	3.2	25	30	25	15
Ecuador	8.0	12.2	4.2	2.4	4	7	3	5	6.0	3.6	20	27	9	5
Egypt, Arab Rep.	40.9	61.4	4.1	2.3	23	37	14	23	4.6	3.0	27	30	18	10
El Salvador	4.6	6.1	2.8	2.4	2	4	2	3	4.9	3.9	27	36	17	15
Eritrea	2.4	3.9	4.9	3.0	..	2	1	2	4.7	3.0	47	47	44	39
Estonia	1.5	1.4	−0.3	−1.2	1	1	1	1	−0.3	−0.9	51	49	0	0
Ethiopia	37.7	61.3	4.9	2.6	20	31	17	26	4.4	1.9	42	41	46	42
Finland	4.8	5.2	0.8	0.5	3	3	2	3	1.0	0.2	47	48	0	0
France	53.9	58.8	0.9	0.5	34	38	24	26	1.1	0.8	40	45	0	0
Georgia	5.1	5.4	0.7	−0.1	3	4	3	3	0.5	−0.1	49	47	0	0
Germany	78.3	82.1	0.5	0.5	52	56	38	41	0.9	0.5	40	42	0	0
Ghana	10.7	18.5	5.4	3.1	6	10	5	9	5.4	3.1	51	51	16	13
Greece	9.6	10.5	0.9	0.5	6	7	4	5	1.9	1.2	28	37	5	0
Guatemala	6.8	10.8	4.6	3.0	3	6	2	4	5.2	3.4	22	28	19	15
Guinea	4.5	7.1	4.6	3.0	2	4	2	3	4.0	2.7	47	47	41	33
Haiti	5.4	7.6	3.6	2.4	3	4	3	3	2.9	2.0	45	43	33	24
Honduras	3.6	6.2	5.5	3.3	2	3	1	2	6.3	4.5	25	31	14	8
Hungary	10.7	10.1	−0.6	−0.3	7	7	5	5	−0.6	0.3	43	45	0	0
India	687.3	979.7	3.5	2.0	394	596	302	431	3.5	2.7	34	32	21	13
Indonesia	148.3	203.7	3.2	1.9	83	130	58	98	5.2	3.1	35	40	13	9
Iran, Islamic Rep.	39.1	61.9	4.6	1.9	20	36	12	19	4.6	2.3	20	26	14	4
Ireland	3.4	3.7	0.8	0.7	2	2	1	2	1.8	2.2	28	34	1	0
Israel	3.9	6.0	4.3	3.5	2	4	1	3	5.8	4.9	34	41	0	0
Italy	56.4	57.6	0.2	0.2	36	39	23	25	1.2	0.5	33	38	2	0
Jamaica	2.1	2.6	1.9	1.0	1	2	1	1	3.3	1.8	46	46	0	0
Japan	116.8	126.3	0.8	0.3	79	87	57	68	1.8	0.9	38	41	0	0
Jordan	2.2	4.6	7.4	5.2	1	3	1	1	9.3	6.2	15	23	4	0
Kazakhstan	14.9	15.7	0.5	−0.6	..	10	..	8	..	−0.3	48	47	0	0
Kenya	16.6	29.3	5.7	3.1	8	15	8	15	6.5	4.0	46	46	45	40
Korea, Rep.	38.1	46.4	2.0	1.1	24	33	16	23	4.0	2.3	39	41	0	0
Kuwait	1.4	1.9	3.1	−1.8	1	1	0	1	3.9	−2.9	13	31	0	0
Kyrgyz Republic	3.6	4.7	2.6	1.0	2	3	2	2	2.6	1.6	48	47	0	0
Lao PDR	3.2	5.0	4.4	3.0	2	3	..	..	..	..	..	..	31	26
Latvia	2.5	2.4	−0.4	−1.3	2	2	1	1	−0.8	−1.6	51	50	0	0
Lebanon	3.0	4.2	3.4	2.1	2	3	1	1	5.3	3.4	23	29	5	0
Lesotho	1.3	2.1	4.3	2.6	1	1	1	1	4.0	2.9	38	37	28	22
Lithuania	3.4	3.7	0.8	−0.1	2	2	2	2	0.6	−0.1	50	48	0	0
Macedonia, FYR	1.9	2.0	0.6	0.8	1	1	1	1	1.3	1.1	36	41	1	0
Madagascar	8.9	14.6	5.0	3.2	5	8	4	7	4.6	3.2	45	45	40	35
Malawi	6.2	10.5	5.3	3.1	3	5	3	5	4.9	2.8	51	49	45	34
Malaysia	13.8	22.2	4.8	2.8	8	13	5	9	5.5	3.5	34	37	8	3

Note: For data comparability and coverage, see the Technical Notes. Figures in italics are for years other than those specified.

PEOPLE

	Population						Labor force								
	Total Millions		Avg. annual growth rate (%)		Aged 15–64 Millions		Total Millions		Avg. annual growth rate (%)		Female % of labor force		Children aged 10–14 % of age group	
Economy	1980	1998	1980–90	1990–98	1980	1998	1980	1998	1980–90	1990–98	1980	1998	1980	1998
Mali	6.6	10.6	4.7	3.2	3	5	3	5	4.3	2.9	47	46	61	53
Mauritania	1.6	2.5	4.9	3.2	1	1	1	1	4.5	3.5	45	44	30	23
Mexico	67.6	95.9	3.5	2.0	35	59	22	38	5.4	3.1	27	33	9	6
Moldova	4.0	4.3	0.7	–0.2	3	3	2	2	0.3	0.1	50	49	3	0
Mongolia	1.7	2.6	4.4	2.2	1	2	1	1	5.0	3.1	46	47	4	2
Morocco	19.4	27.8	3.6	2.1	10	17	7	11	4.4	2.8	34	35	21	4
Mozambique	12.1	16.9	3.4	2.6	6	9	7	9	2.8	2.3	49	48	39	33
Myanmar	33.8	44.4	2.7	1.3	19	29	17	24	3.1	1.9	44	43	28	24
Namibia	1.0	1.7	4.8	3.0	1	1	0	1	4.3	2.6	40	41	34	20
Nepal	14.5	22.9	4.5	2.8	8	13	7	11	4.1	2.8	39	40	56	44
Netherlands	14.2	15.7	1.0	0.7	9	11	6	7	2.7	1.0	32	40	0	0
New Zealand	3.1	3.8	2.0	1.7	2	2	1	2	3.7	2.3	34	45	0	0
Nicaragua	2.9	4.8	5.0	3.2	1	3	1	2	6.6	4.8	28	35	19	13
Niger	5.6	10.1	6.0	3.9	3	5	3	5	5.3	3.3	45	44	48	45
Nigeria	71.1	121.3	5.3	3.3	36	64	29	49	5.1	3.3	36	36	29	25
Norway	4.1	4.4	0.8	0.6	3	3	2	2	1.6	1.2	41	46	0	0
Pakistan	82.7	131.6	4.6	2.8	44	71	29	49	5.2	3.2	23	28	23	17
Panama	2.0	2.8	3.5	2.0	1	2	1	1	5.3	3.1	30	35	6	3
Papua New Guinea	3.1	4.6	4.0	2.6	2	3	2	2	4.0	2.6	42	42	28	18
Paraguay	3.1	5.2	5.1	3.0	2	3	1	2	5.1	3.4	27	30	15	7
Peru	17.3	24.8	3.6	2.0	9	15	5	9	5.4	3.2	24	31	4	2
Philippines	48.3	75.1	4.4	2.6	27	44	19	32	5.2	3.3	35	38	14	7
Poland	35.6	38.7	0.8	0.2	23	26	19	20	0.6	0.8	45	46	0	0
Portugal	9.8	10.0	0.2	0.1	6	7	5	5	0.8	0.4	39	44	8	2
Romania	22.2	22.5	0.1	–0.5	14	15	11	11	–0.3	–0.1	46	44	0	0
Russian Federation	139.0	146.9	0.6	–0.1	95	101	76	78	0.2	0.1	49	49	0	0
Rwanda	5.2	8.1	4.5	2.2	3	4	3	4	5.1	2.7	49	49	43	42
Saudi Arabia	9.4	20.7	7.9	3.9	5	12	3	7	8.9	3.5	8	15	5	0
Senegal	5.5	9.0	4.9	3.0	3	5	3	4	4.7	3.0	42	43	43	30
Sierra Leone	3.2	4.9	4.1	2.8	2	2	1	2	3.5	2.8	36	37	19	15
Singapore	2.3	3.2	3.3	2.2	2	2	1	2	4.1	2.0	35	39	2	0
Slovak Republic	5.0	5.4	0.8	0.3	3	4	2	3	1.6	1.1	45	48	0	0
Slovenia	1.9	2.0	0.4	–0.1	1	1	1	1	0.4	0.2	46	46	0	0
South Africa	27.6	41.3	4.0	2.3	16	25	10	16	4.3	2.3	35	38	1	0
Spain	37.4	39.3	0.5	0.2	23	27	14	17	2.2	1.2	28	37	0	0
Sri Lanka	14.7	18.8	2.4	1.4	9	12	5	8	3.9	2.4	27	36	4	2
Sweden	8.3	8.9	0.6	0.5	5	6	4	5	1.2	0.5	44	48	0	0
Switzerland	6.3	7.1	1.2	0.8	4	5	3	4	2.4	1.1	37	40	0	0
Syrian Arab Republic	8.7	15.3	5.6	3.3	4	8	2	5	6.6	4.8	24	26	14	4
Tajikistan	4.0	6.1	4.3	2.0	2	3	2	2	4.1	2.8	47	44	0	0
Tanzania	18.6	32.1	5.5	3.3	9	17	9	16	5.5	3.0	50	49	43	38
Thailand	46.7	61.1	2.7	1.4	26	42	24	37	4.1	2.1	47	46	25	15
Togo	2.6	4.5	5.3	3.4	1	2	1	2	4.6	3.1	39	40	36	28
Tunisia	6.4	9.4	3.8	2.0	3	6	2	4	5.2	3.5	29	31	6	0
Turkey	44.5	63.5	3.6	1.8	25	42	19	30	4.9	3.3	36	37	21	22
Turkmenistan	2.9	4.7	5.0	3.6	2	3	1	2	5.5	4.3	47	46	0	0
Uganda	12.8	20.9	4.9	3.5	6	10	7	10	4.3	3.0	48	48	49	45
Ukraine	50.0	50.3	0.4	–0.5	33	34	27	25	–0.5	–0.5	50	49	0	0
United Kingdom	56.3	59.1	0.5	0.4	36	38	27	30	0.9	0.4	39	44	0	0
United States	227.2	270.0	1.7	1.1	151	177	109	138	2.3	1.4	41	46	0	0
Uruguay	2.9	3.3	1.2	0.8	2	2	1	1	2.4	1.1	31	41	4	2
Uzbekistan	16.0	24.1	4.1	2.3	9	14	6	10	4.6	3.3	48	47	0	0
Venezuela	15.1	23.2	4.3	2.5	8	14	5	9	5.9	3.6	27	34	4	1
Vietnam	53.7	77.6	3.7	2.3	28	47	26	40	4.3	2.3	48	49	22	8
Yemen, Rep.	8.5	16.5	6.6	4.7	4	8	2	5	7.6	5.6	33	28	26	20
Zambia	5.7	9.7	5.2	3.1	3	5	2	4	5.2	3.4	45	45	19	16
Zimbabwe	7.0	11.7	5.2	2.6	3	6	3	5	5.3	2.6	44	44	37	28
World	**4,429.9 s**	**5,896.5 s**	**2.9 w**	**1.6 w**	**2,586 s**	**3,697 s**	**2,028 s**	**2,847 s**	**3.4 w**	**2.0 w**	**39 t**	**41 t**	**20 w**	**13 w**
Low income	2,508.6	3,514.7	3.4	2.0	1,423	2,155	1,206	1,759	3.8	2.3	40	41	28	17
Excl. China & India	840.0	1,296.4	4.3	2.6	442	723	364	585	4.7	3.0	40	41	29	24
Middle income	1,132.1	1,496.4	2.8	1.5	658	950	465	658	3.5	2.0	37	39	10	6
Lower middle income	695.0	908.3	2.7	1.4	404	572	292	397	3.1	1.7	40	40	9	4
Upper middle income	437.1	588.1	3.0	1.6	254	379	173	261	4.1	2.4	33	36	11	9
Low and middle income	3,640.7	5,011.1	3.2	1.8	2,080	3,105	1,672	2,417	3.7	2.2	39	40	23	14
East Asia & Pacific	1,397.5	1,817.1	2.6	1.5	820	1,204	718	1,026	3.6	1.8	43	44	26	10
Europe & Central Asia	425.8	473.4	1.1	0.2	265	315	207	236	1.3	0.6	47	46	3	4
Latin America & Carib.	360.3	501.9	3.3	1.9	201	313	130	212	4.9	2.7	28	34	13	9
Middle East & N. Africa	173.7	285.1	5.0	2.6	91	165	54	94	5.5	3.4	24	27	14	5
South Asia	902.6	1,305.3	3.7	2.1	508	778	392	574	3.8	2.8	34	33	23	16
Sub-Saharan Africa	380.7	628.3	5.0	3.0	195	330	170	275	4.8	3.0	42	42	35	30
High income	789.2	885.5	1.2	0.7	505	592	357	430	1.9	1.1	38	43	0	0

Table 4.   Poverty

Economy	National poverty lines								International poverty lines				
	Survey year	Population below the poverty line (%)			Survey year	Population below the poverty line (%)			Survey year	Population below $1 PPP a day[a] %	Poverty gap at $1 PPP a day[a] %	Population below $2 PPP a day[a] %	Poverty gap at $2 PPP a day[a] %
		Rural	Urban	Total		Rural	Urban	Total					
Albania	1994	28.9	..	..	1996	..	19.6	..		..	..	..	..
Algeria	1988	16.6	7.3	12.2	1995	30.3	14.7	22.6	1995	<2	..	17.6	4.4
Angola		..	..	..		..	..	..		..	..	..	..
Argentina	1991	..	..	25.5		..	..	..		..	..	..	..
Armenia		..	..	..		..	..	..		..	..	..	..
Australia		..	..	..		..	..	..		..	..	..	..
Austria		..	..	..		..	..	..		..	..	..	..
Azerbaijan	1995	..	..	68.1		..	..	..		..	..	..	..
Bangladesh	1991–92	46.0	23.3	42.7	1995–96	39.8	14.3	35.6		..	..	..	..
Belarus	1995	..	..	22.5		..	..	..	1993	<2	..	6.4	0.8
Belgium		..	..	..		..	..	..		..	..	..	..
Benin	1995	..	..	33.0		..	..	..		..	..	..	..
Bolivia		..	..	..		..	..	..		..	..	..	..
Botswana		..	..	..		..	..	..	1985–86	33.0	12.4	61.0	30.4
Brazil	1990	32.6	13.1	17.4		..	..	..	1995	23.6	10.7	43.5	22.4
Bulgaria		..	..	..		..	..	..	1992	2.6	0.8	23.5	6.0
Burkina Faso		..	..	..		..	..	..		..	..	..	..
Burundi	1990	..	..	36.2		..	..	..		..	..	..	..
Cambodia	1993–94	43.1	24.8	39.0	1997	40.1	21.1	36.1		..	..	..	..
Cameroon	1984	32.4	44.4	40.0		..	..	..		..	..	..	..
Canada		..	..	..		..	..	..		..	..	..	..
Central African Republic		..	..	..		..	..	..		..	..	..	..
Chad	1995–96	67.0	63.0	64.0		..	..	..		..	..	..	..
Chile	1992	..	..	21.6	1994	..	..	20.5	1992	15.0	4.9	38.5	16.0
China	1994	11.8	<2	8.4	1996	7.9	<2	6.0	1995	22.2	6.9	57.8	24.1
Hong Kong, China		..	..	..		..	..	..		..	..	..	..
Colombia	1991	29.0	7.8	16.9	1992	31.2	8.0	17.7	1991	7.4	2.3	21.7	8.4
Congo, Dem. Rep.		..	..	..		..	..	..		..	..	..	..
Congo, Rep.		..	..	..		..	..	..		..	..	..	..
Costa Rica		..	..	..		..	..	..	1989	18.9	7.2	43.8	19.4
Côte d'Ivoire		..	..	..		..	..	..	1988	17.7	4.3	54.8	20.4
Croatia		..	..	..		..	..	..		..	..	..	..
Czech Republic		..	..	..		..	..	..	1993	3.1	0.4	55.1	14.0
Denmark		..	..	..		..	..	..		..	..	..	..
Dominican Republic	1989	27.4	23.3	24.5	1992	29.8	10.9	20.6	1989	19.9	6.0	47.7	20.2
Ecuador	1994	47.0	25.0	35.0		..	..	..	1994	30.4	9.1	65.8	29.6
Egypt, Arab Rep.		..	..	..		..	..	..	1990–91	7.6	1.1	51.9	15.3
El Salvador	1992	55.7	43.1	48.3		..	..	..		..	..	..	..
Eritrea		..	..	..		..	..	..		..	..	..	..
Estonia	1994	14.7	6.8	8.9		..	..	..	1993	6.0	1.6	32.5	10.0
Ethiopia		..	..	..		..	..	..	1981–82	46.0	12.4	89.0	42.7
Finland		..	..	..		..	..	..		..	..	..	..
France		..	..	..		..	..	..		..	..	..	..
Georgia		..	..	..		..	..	..		..	..	..	..
Germany		..	..	..		..	..	..		..	..	..	..
Ghana	1992	34.3	26.7	31.4		..	..	..		..	..	..	..
Greece		..	..	..		..	..	..		..	..	..	..
Guatemala		..	..	..		..	..	..	1989	53.3	28.5	76.8	47.6
Guinea		..	..	..		..	..	..	1991	26.3	12.4	50.2	25.6
Haiti	1987	..	..	65.0	1995	81.0	..	..		..	..	..	..
Honduras	1992	46.0	56.0	50.0		..	..	..	1992	46.9	20.4	75.7	41.9
Hungary	1993	..	..	25.3		..	..	..	1993	<2	..	10.7	2.1
India	1992	43.5	33.7	40.9	1994	36.7	30.5	35.0	1994	47.0	12.9	87.5	42.9
Indonesia	1987	16.4	20.1	17.4	1990	14.3	16.8	15.1	1996	7.7	0.9	50.4	15.3
Iran, Islamic Rep.		..	..	..		..	..	..		..	..	..	..
Ireland		..	..	..		..	..	..		..	..	..	..
Israel		..	..	..		..	..	..		..	..	..	..
Italy		..	..	..		..	..	..		..	..	..	..
Jamaica	1992	..	..	34.2		..	..	..	1993	4.3	0.5	24.9	7.5
Japan		..	..	..		..	..	..		..	..	..	..
Jordan	1991	..	..	15.0		..	..	..	1992	2.5	0.5	23.5	6.3
Kazakhstan	1996	39.0	30.0	34.6		..	..	..	1993	<2	..	12.1	2.5
Kenya	1992	46.4	29.3	42.0		..	..	..	1992	50.2	22.2	78.1	44.4
Korea, Rep.		..	..	..		..	..	..		..	..	..	..
Kuwait		..	..	..		..	..	..		..	..	..	..
Kyrgyz Republic	1993	48.1	28.7	40.0		..	..	..	1993	18.9	5.0	55.3	21.4
Lao PDR	1993	53.0	24.0	46.1		..	..	..		..	..	..	..
Latvia		..	..	..		..	..	..	1993	<2	..	<2	..
Lebanon		..	..	..		..	..	..		..	..	..	..
Lesotho	1993	53.9	27.8	49.2		..	..	..	1986–87	48.8	23.8	74.1	43.5
Lithuania		..	..	..		..	..	..	1993	<2	..	18.9	4.1
Macedonia, FYR		..	..	..		..	..	..		..	..	..	..
Madagascar		..	..	..		..	..	..	1993	72.3	33.2	93.2	59.6
Malawi	1990–91	..	..	54.0		..	..	..		..	..	..	..
Malaysia	1989	..	..	15.5		..	..	..	1995	4.3	0.7	22.4	6.8

Note: For data comparability and coverage, see the Technical Notes. Figures in italics are for years other than those specified.

PEOPLE

Economy	National poverty lines								International poverty lines				
	Survey year	Population below the poverty line (%)			Survey year	Population below the poverty line (%)			Survey year	Population below $1 PPP a day[a] %	Poverty gap at $1 PPP a day[a] %	Population below $2 PPP a day[a] %	Poverty gap at $2 PPP a day[a] %
		Rural	Urban	Total		Rural	Urban	Total					
Mali		..	..	..		..	..	..		..	..	..	..
Mauritania	1990	..	..	57.0		..	..	..	1988	31.4	15.2	68.4	33.0
Mexico	1988	..	..	10.1		..	..	..	1992	14.9	3.8	40.0	15.9
Moldova		..	..	..		..	..	..	1992	6.8	1.2	30.6	9.7
Mongolia	1995	33.1	38.5	36.3		..	..	..		..	..	..	..
Morocco	1984–85	32.6	17.3	26.0	1990–91	18.0	7.6	13.1	1990–91	<2	..	19.6	4.6
Mozambique		..	..	..		..	..	..		..	..	..	..
Myanmar		..	..	..		..	..	..		..	..	..	..
Namibia		..	..	..		..	..	..		..	..	..	..
Nepal	1995–96	44.0	23.0	42.0		..	..	..	1995	50.3	16.2	86.7	44.6
Netherlands		..	..	..		..	..	..		..	..	..	..
New Zealand		..	..	..		..	..	..		..	..	..	..
Nicaragua	1993	76.1	31.9	50.3		..	..	..	1993	43.8	18.0	74.5	39.7
Niger	1989–93	66.0	52.0	63.0		..	..	..	1992	61.5	22.2	92.0	51.8
Nigeria	1985	49.5	31.7	43.0	1992–93	36.4	30.4	34.1	1992–93	31.1	12.9	59.9	29.8
Norway		..	..	..		..	..	..		..	..	..	..
Pakistan	1991	36.9	28.0	34.0		..	..	..	1991	11.6	2.6	57.0	18.6
Panama		..	..	..		..	..	..	1989	25.6	12.6	46.2	24.5
Papua New Guinea		..	..	..		..	..	..		..	..	..	..
Paraguay	1991	28.5	19.7	21.8		..	..	..		..	..	..	..
Peru	1994	67.0	46.1	53.5	1997	64.7	40.4	49.0		..	..	..	..
Philippines	1994	53.1	28.0	40.6	1997	51.2	22.5	37.5	1994	26.9	7.1	62.8	27.0
Poland	1993	..	..	23.8		..	..	..	1993	6.8	4.7	15.1	7.7
Portugal		..	..	..		..	..	..		..	..	..	..
Romania	1994	27.9	20.4	21.5		..	..	..	1992	17.7	4.2	70.9	24.7
Russian Federation	1994	..	..	30.9		..	..	..	1993	<2	<2	10.9	2.3
Rwanda	1993	..	..	51.2		..	..	..	1983–85	45.7	11.3	88.7	42.3
Saudi Arabia		..	..	..		..	..	..		..	..	..	..
Senegal	1991	40.4	16.4	33.4		..	..	..	1991–92	54.0	25.5	79.6	47.2
Sierra Leone	1989	76.0	53.0	68.0		..	..	..		..	..	..	..
Singapore		..	..	..		..	..	..		..	..	..	..
Slovak Republic		..	..	..		..	..	..	1992	12.8	2.2	85.1	27.5
Slovenia		..	..	..		..	..	..	1993	<2	..	<2	..
South Africa		..	..	..		..	..	..	1993	23.7	6.6	50.2	22.5
Spain		..	..	..		..	..	..		..	..	..	..
Sri Lanka	1985–86	45.5	26.8	40.6	1990–91	38.1	28.4	35.3	1990	4.0	0.7	41.2	11.0
Sweden		..	..	..		..	..	..		..	..	..	..
Switzerland		..	..	..		..	..	..		..	..	..	..
Syrian Arab Republic		..	..	..		..	..	..		..	..	..	..
Tajikistan		..	..	..		..	..	..		..	..	..	..
Tanzania	1991	..	..	51.1		..	..	..		..	..	..	..
Thailand	1990	..	..	18.0	1992	15.5	10.2	13.1	1992	<2	..	23.5	5.4
Togo	1987–89	..	..	32.3		..	..	..		..	..	..	..
Tunisia	1985	29.2	12.0	19.9	1990	21.6	8.9	14.1	1990	3.9	0.9	22.7	6.8
Turkey		..	..	..		..	..	..		..	..	..	..
Turkmenistan		..	..	..		..	..	..	1993	4.9	0.5	25.8	7.6
Uganda	1993	..	..	55.0		..	..	..	1989–90	69.3	29.1	92.2	56.6
Ukraine	1995	..	..	31.7		..	..	..	1992	<2	..	<2	..
United Kingdom		..	..	..		..	..	..		..	..	..	..
United States		..	..	..		..	..	..		..	..	..	..
Uruguay		..	..	..		..	..	..		..	..	..	..
Uzbekistan		..	..	..		..	..	..		..	..	..	..
Venezuela	1989	..	..	31.3		..	..	..	1991	11.8	3.1	32.2	12.2
Vietnam	1993	57.2	25.9	50.9		..	..	..		..	..	..	..
Yemen, Rep.	1992	19.2	18.6	19.1		..	..	..		..	..	..	..
Zambia	1991	88.0	46.0	68.0	1993	..	..	86.0	1993	84.6	53.8	98.1	73.4
Zimbabwe	1990–91	..	..	25.5		..	..	..	1990–91	41.0	14.3	68.2	35.5

a. 1985 prices.

Table 5. Distribution of income or consumption

Economy	Survey year	Gini index	Percentage share of income or consumption						
			Lowest 10%	Lowest 20%	Second 20%	Third 20%	Fourth 20%	Highest 20%	Highest 10%
Albania	..	..	..	..	..	..	..	..	..
Algeria	1995[a,b]	35.3	2.8	7.0	11.6	16.1	22.7	42.6	26.8
Angola	..	..	..	..	..	..	..	..	..
Argentina	..	..	..	..	..	..	..	..	..
Armenia	..	..	..	..	..	..	..	..	..
Australia	1989[c,d]	33.7	2.5	7.0	12.2	16.6	23.3	40.9	24.8
Austria	1987[c,d]	23.1	4.4	10.4	14.8	18.5	22.9	33.3	19.3
Azerbaijan	..	..	..	..	..	..	..	..	..
Bangladesh	1992[a,b]	28.3	4.1	9.4	13.5	17.2	22.0	37.9	23.7
Belarus	1995[c,d]	28.8	3.4	8.5	13.5	17.7	23.1	37.2	22.6
Belgium	1992[c,d]	25.0	3.7	9.5	14.6	18.4	23.0	34.5	20.2
Benin	..	..	..	..	..	..	..	..	..
Bolivia	1990[c,d]	42.0	2.3	5.6	9.7	14.5	22.0	48.2	31.7
Botswana	..	..	..	..	..	..	..	..	..
Brazil	1995[c,d]	60.1	0.8	2.5	5.7	9.9	17.7	64.2	47.9
Bulgaria	1992[c,d]	30.8	3.3	8.3	13.0	17.0	22.3	39.3	24.7
Burkina Faso	1994[a,b]	48.2	2.2	5.5	8.7	12.0	18.7	55.0	39.5
Burundi	..	..	..	..	..	..	..	..	..
Cambodia	..	..	..	..	..	..	..	..	..
Cameroon	..	..	..	..	..	..	..	..	..
Canada	1994[c,d]	31.5	2.8	7.5	12.9	17.2	23.0	39.3	23.8
Central African Republic	..	..	..	..	..	..	..	..	..
Chad	..	..	..	..	..	..	..	..	..
Chile	1994[c,d]	56.5	1.4	3.5	6.6	10.9	18.1	61.0	46.1
China	1995[c,d]	41.5	2.2	5.5	9.8	14.9	22.3	47.5	30.9
Hong Kong, China	..	..	..	..	..	..	..	..	..
Colombia	1995[c,d]	57.2	1.0	3.1	6.8	10.9	17.6	61.5	46.9
Congo, Dem. Rep.	..	..	..	..	..	..	..	..	..
Congo, Rep.	..	..	..	..	..	..	..	..	..
Costa Rica	1996[c,d]	47.0	1.3	4.0	8.8	13.7	21.7	51.8	34.7
Côte d'Ivoire	1988[a,b]	36.9	2.8	6.8	11.2	15.8	22.2	44.1	28.5
Croatia	..	..	..	..	..	..	..	..	..
Czech Republic	1993[c,d]	26.6	4.6	10.5	13.9	16.9	21.3	37.4	23.5
Denmark	1992[c,d]	24.7	3.6	9.6	14.9	18.3	22.7	34.5	20.5
Dominican Republic	1989[c,d]	50.5	1.6	4.2	7.9	12.5	19.7	55.7	39.6
Ecuador	1994[a,b]	46.6	2.3	5.4	8.9	13.2	19.9	52.6	37.6
Egypt, Arab Rep.	1991[a,b]	32.0	3.9	8.7	12.5	16.3	21.4	41.1	26.7
El Salvador	1995[c,d]	49.9	1.2	3.7	8.3	13.1	20.5	54.4	38.3
Eritrea	..	..	..	..	..	..	..	..	..
Estonia	1995[c,d]	35.4	2.2	6.2	12.0	17.0	23.1	41.8	26.2
Ethiopia	1995[a,b]	40.0	3.0	7.1	10.9	14.5	19.8	47.7	33.7
Finland	1991[c,d]	25.6	4.2	10.0	14.2	17.6	22.3	35.8	21.6
France	1989[c,d]	32.7	2.5	7.2	12.7	17.1	22.8	40.1	24.9
Georgia	..	..	..	..	..	..	..	..	..
Germany	1989[c,d]	28.1	3.7	9.0	13.5	17.5	22.9	37.1	22.6
Ghana	1997[a,b]	32.7	3.6	8.4	12.2	15.8	21.9	41.7	26.1
Greece	..	..	..	..	..	..	..	..	..
Guatemala	1989[c,d]	59.6	0.6	2.1	5.8	10.5	18.6	63.0	46.6
Guinea	1994[a,b]	40.3	2.6	6.4	10.4	14.8	21.2	47.2	32.0
Haiti	..	..	..	..	..	..	..	..	..
Honduras	1996[c,d]	53.7	1.2	3.4	7.1	11.7	19.7	58.0	42.1
Hungary	1993[c,d]	27.9	4.1	9.7	13.9	16.9	21.4	38.1	24.0
India	1994[a,b]	29.7	4.1	9.2	13.0	16.8	21.7	39.3	25.0
Indonesia	1996[c,d]	36.5	3.6	8.0	11.3	15.1	20.8	44.9	30.3
Iran, Islamic Rep.	..	..	..	..	..	..	..	..	..
Ireland	1987[c,d]	35.9	2.5	6.7	11.6	16.4	22.4	42.9	27.4
Israel	1992[c,d]	35.5	2.8	6.9	11.4	16.3	22.9	42.5	26.9
Italy	1991[c,d]	31.2	2.9	7.6	12.9	17.3	23.2	38.9	23.7
Jamaica	1991[a,b]	41.1	2.4	5.8	10.2	14.9	21.6	47.5	31.9
Japan	..	..	..	..	..	..	..	..	..
Jordan	1991[a,b]	43.4	2.4	5.9	9.8	13.9	20.3	50.1	34.7
Kazakhstan	1993[c,d]	32.7	3.1	7.5	12.3	16.9	22.9	40.4	24.9
Kenya	1994[a,b]	44.5	1.8	5.0	9.7	14.2	20.9	50.2	34.9
Korea, Rep.	..	..	..	..	..	..	..	..	..
Kuwait	..	..	..	..	..	..	..	..	..
Kyrgyz Republic	1993[c,d]	35.3	2.7	6.7	11.5	16.4	23.1	42.3	26.2
Lao PDR	1992[a,b]	30.4	4.2	9.6	12.9	16.3	21.0	40.2	26.4
Latvia	1995[c,d]	28.5	3.3	8.3	13.8	18.0	22.9	37.0	22.4
Lebanon	..	..	..	..	..	..	..	..	..
Lesotho	1986–87[a,b]	56.0	0.9	2.8	6.5	11.2	19.4	60.1	43.4
Lithuania	1993[c,d]	33.6	3.4	8.1	12.3	16.2	21.3	42.1	28.0
Macedonia, FYR	..	..	..	..	..	..	..	..	..
Madagascar	1993[a,b]	46.0	1.9	5.1	9.4	13.3	20.1	52.1	36.7
Malawi	..	..	..	..	..	..	..	..	..
Malaysia	1989[c,d]	48.4	1.9	4.6	8.3	13.0	20.4	53.7	37.9

Note: For data comparability and coverage, see the Technical Notes. Figures in italics are for years other than those specified.

PEOPLE

Economy	Survey year	Gini index	Percentage share of income or consumption						
			Lowest 10%	Lowest 20%	Second 20%	Third 20%	Fourth 20%	Highest 20%	Highest 10%
Mali	1994[a,b]	50.5	1.8	4.6	8.0	11.9	19.3	56.2	40.4
Mauritania	1995[a,b]	38.9	2.3	6.2	10.8	15.4	22.0	45.6	29.9
Mexico	1995[c,d]	53.7	1.4	3.6	7.2	11.8	19.2	58.2	42.8
Moldova	1992[c,d]	34.4	2.7	6.9	11.9	16.7	23.1	41.5	25.8
Mongolia	1995[a,b]	33.2	2.9	7.3	12.2	16.6	23.0	40.9	24.5
Morocco	1990–91[a,b]	39.2	2.8	6.6	10.5	15.0	21.7	46.3	30.5
Mozambique		..	..	..	..	..	..	..	..
Myanmar		..	..	..	..	..	..	..	..
Namibia		..	..	..	..	..	..	..	..
Nepal	1995–96[a,b]	36.7	3.2	7.6	11.5	15.1	21.0	44.8	29.8
Netherlands	1991[c,d]	31.5	2.9	8.0	13.0	16.7	22.5	39.9	24.7
New Zealand		..	..	..	..	..	..	..	..
Nicaragua	1993[a,b]	50.3	1.6	4.2	8.0	12.6	20.0	55.2	39.8
Niger	1995[a,b]	50.5	0.8	2.6	7.1	13.9	23.1	53.3	35.4
Nigeria	1992–93[a,b]	45.0	1.3	4.0	8.9	14.4	23.4	49.3	31.4
Norway	1991[c,d]	25.2	4.1	10.0	14.3	17.9	22.4	35.3	21.2
Pakistan	1996[a,b]	31.2	4.1	9.4	13.0	16.0	20.3	41.2	27.7
Panama	1995[c,d]	57.1	0.7	2.3	6.2	11.3	19.8	60.4	43.8
Papua New Guinea	1996[a,b]	50.9	1.7	4.5	7.9	11.9	19.2	56.5	40.5
Paraguay	1995[c,d]	59.1	0.7	2.3	5.9	10.7	18.7	62.4	46.6
Peru	1996[c,d]	46.2	1.6	4.4	9.1	14.1	21.3	51.2	35.4
Philippines	1994[a,b]	42.9	2.4	5.9	9.6	13.9	21.1	49.6	33.5
Poland	1992[a,b]	27.2	4.0	9.3	13.8	17.7	22.6	36.6	22.1
Portugal		..	..	..	..	..	..	..	..
Romania	1994[c,d]	28.2	3.7	8.9	13.6	17.6	22.6	37.3	22.7
Russian Federation	1996[a,b]	48.0	1.4	4.2	8.8	13.6	20.7	52.8	37.4
Rwanda	1983–85[a,b]	28.9	4.2	9.7	13.2	16.5	21.6	39.1	24.2
Saudi Arabia		..	..	..	..	..	..	..	..
Senegal	1991[a,b]	53.8	1.0	3.1	7.4	12.1	19.5	57.9	42.3
Sierra Leone	1989[a,b]	62.9	0.5	1.1	2.0	9.8	23.7	63.4	43.6
Singapore		..	..	..	..	..	..	..	..
Slovak Republic	1992[c,d]	19.5	5.1	11.9	15.8	18.8	22.2	31.4	18.2
Slovenia	1993[c,d]	29.2	4.0	9.3	13.3	16.9	21.9	38.6	24.5
South Africa	1993–94[a,b]	59.3	1.1	2.9	5.5	9.2	17.7	64.8	45.9
Spain	1990[c,d]	32.5	2.8	7.5	12.6	17.0	22.6	40.3	25.2
Sri Lanka	1990[a,b]	30.1	3.8	8.9	13.1	16.9	21.7	39.3	25.2
Sweden	1992[c,d]	25.0	3.7	9.6	14.5	18.1	23.2	34.5	20.1
Switzerland	1982[c,d]	36.1	2.9	7.4	11.6	15.6	21.9	43.5	28.6
Syrian Arab Republic		..	..	..	..	..	..	..	..
Tajikistan		..	..	..	..	..	..	..	..
Tanzania	1993[a,b]	38.2	2.8	6.8	11.0	15.1	21.6	45.5	30.1
Thailand	1992[a,b]	46.2	2.5	5.6	8.7	13.0	20.0	52.7	37.1
Togo		..	..	..	..	..	..	..	..
Tunisia	1990[a,b]	40.2	2.3	5.9	10.4	15.3	22.1	46.3	30.7
Turkey		..	..	..	..	..	..	..	..
Turkmenistan	1993[c,d]	35.8	2.7	6.7	11.4	16.3	22.8	42.8	26.9
Uganda	1992–93[a,b]	39.2	2.6	6.6	10.9	15.2	21.3	46.1	31.2
Ukraine	1995[c,d]	47.3	1.4	4.3	9.0	13.8	20.8	52.2	36.8
United Kingdom	1986[c,d]	32.6	2.4	7.1	12.8	17.2	23.1	39.8	24.7
United States	1994[c,d]	40.1	1.5	4.8	10.5	16.0	23.5	45.2	28.5
Uruguay		..	..	..	..	..	..	..	..
Uzbekistan		..	..	..	..	..	..	..	..
Venezuela	1995[c,d]	46.8	1.5	4.3	8.8	13.8	21.3	51.8	35.6
Vietnam	1993[a,b]	35.7	3.5	7.8	11.4	15.4	21.4	44.0	29.0
Yemen, Rep.	1992[a,b]	39.5	2.3	6.1	10.9	15.3	21.6	46.1	30.8
Zambia	1996[a,b]	49.8	1.6	4.2	8.2	12.8	20.1	54.8	39.2
Zimbabwe	1990[a,b]	56.8	1.8	4.0	6.3	10.0	17.4	62.3	46.9

a. Refers to expenditure shares by percentiles of population. b. Ranked by per capita expenditure. c. Refers to income shares by percentiles of population. d. Ranked by per capita income.

Table 6. Education

Economy	Public expenditure on education % of GNP		Net enrollment ratio[a] % of relevant age group				Percentage of cohort reaching grade 5				Expected years of schooling			
			Primary		Secondary		Males		Females		Males		Females	
	1980	1996	1980	1996	1980	1996	1980	1996	1980	1996	1980	1995	1980	1995
Albania	..	3.1	..	102	..	..	..	81	..	83	..	..	..	..
Algeria	7.8	5.1	81	94	31	56	90	94	85	95	9	11	6	10
Angola	..	..	..	..	..	..	..	..	..	..	8	..	7	..
Argentina	2.7	3.5	..	..	..	..	..	..	..	..	..	..	..	..
Armenia	..	2.0	..	..	..	..	..	..	..	..	..	..	..	..
Australia	5.5	5.6	102	95	70	92	..	..	..	..	12	16	12	16
Austria	5.4	5.6	87	100	..	88	..	..	..	..	11	14	11	14
Azerbaijan	..	3.3	..	..	..	..	..	..	..	..	..	..	..	..
Bangladesh	1.5	2.9	..	..	..	..	18	..	26	..	..	..	..	..
Belarus	..	6.1	..	85	..	..	..	..	..	..	..	..	..	..
Belgium	6.0	3.2	97	98	..	99	..	..	..	..	14	16	13	15
Benin	..	3.2	..	63	..	..	59	64	62	57	..	..	..	..
Bolivia	4.4	5.6	79	..	16	..	..	..	..	..	9	..	8	..
Botswana	6.0	10.4	76	81	14	45	85	87	88	93	7	11	8	11
Brazil	3.6	5.5	80	90	14	20	..	..	..	..	9	..	9	..
Bulgaria	4.5	3.3	96	92	73	74	..	..	..	..	11	12	11	13
Burkina Faso	2.2	1.5	15	31	..	..	77	74	74	77	2	3	1	2
Burundi	3.4	3.1	20	..	..	..	100	..	96	..	3	5	2	4
Cambodia	..	2.9	..	98	..	..	..	..	..	..	..	..	..	..
Cameroon	3.6	2.9	..	..	15	..	70	..	70	..	8	..	6	..
Canada	6.9	7.0	..	95	..	93	..	..	..	..	15	17	15	18
Central African Republic	..	..	56	..	..	..	63	..	50	..	..	..	..	..
Chad	..	2.4	..	46	..	6	..	62	..	53	..	..	..	..
Chile	4.6	3.1	..	88	..	58	94	100	97	100	..	12	..	12
China	2.5	2.3	..	102	..	..	..	93	..	94	..	..	..	..
Hong Kong, China	2.4	2.9	95	90	61	71	98	..	99	..	12	13	12	13
Colombia	2.4	4.4	..	85	..	50	36	70	39	76	..	..	..	..
Congo, Dem. Rep.	2.6	..	..	54	..	17	..	..	..	..	..	7	..	4
Congo, Rep.	7.0	6.2	96	..	..	..	81	40	83	78	..	..	..	..
Costa Rica	7.8	5.3	89	91	39	43	77	86	82	89	10	..	10	..
Côte d'Ivoire	7.2	5.0	..	55	..	..	86	77	79	71	..	..	..	..
Croatia	..	5.3	..	82	..	66	..	..	..	..	..	12	..	12
Czech Republic	..	5.4	..	91	..	87	..	..	..	..	..	13	..	13
Denmark	6.8	8.2	96	99	88	87	99	100	99	99	14	15	14	15
Dominican Republic	2.2	2.0	..	81	..	22	..	..	..	..	..	11	..	11
Ecuador	5.6	3.5	..	97	..	..	..	84	..	86	..	..	..	..
Egypt, Arab Rep.	5.7	4.8	..	93	..	68	92	..	88	..	..	11	..	9
El Salvador	3.9	2.2	..	78	..	21	46	76	48	77	..	10	..	10
Eritrea	..	1.8	..	30	..	16	..	73	..	67	..	5	..	4
Estonia	..	7.3	..	87	..	83	..	96	..	97	..	12	..	13
Ethiopia	3.1	4.0	..	28	..	..	..	57	..	53	..	..	..	..
Finland	5.3	7.6	..	99	..	93	..	100	..	100	..	15	..	16
France	5.0	6.1	100	100	79	94	..	..	..	..	13	15	13	16
Georgia	..	5.2	..	87	..	71	..	..	..	..	..	10	..	10
Germany	..	4.8	..	100	..	87	..	..	..	..	..	15	..	15
Ghana	3.1	..	..	..	..	..	..	..	..	..	..	..	..	..
Greece	2.0	3.0	96	90	..	87	99	..	98	..	12	14	12	14
Guatemala	1.8	1.7	59	..	13	..	..	52	..	47	..	..	..	..
Guinea	..	..	..	37	..	..	59	..	41	..	..	..	..	..
Haiti	1.5	..	..	..	..	..	33	..	34	..	..	..	..	..
Honduras	3.2	3.6	78	90	..	..	..	..	..	..	..	..	..	..
Hungary	4.7	4.7	95	97	..	87	96	..	97	..	9	12	10	13
India	3.0	3.4	..	..	..	..	..	..	..	..	..	..	..	..
Indonesia	1.7	1.4	88	97	..	42	..	..	..	..	..	10	..	10
Iran, Islamic Rep.	7.5	4.0	..	90	..	69	..	..	..	..	..	..	..	..
Ireland	6.3	5.8	100	100	78	86	..	..	..	..	11	14	11	14
Israel	7.9	7.2	..	..	..	..	..	..	..	..	..	..	..	..
Italy	..	4.7	..	100	..	..	99	100	99	100	..	..	..	..
Jamaica	7.0	7.4	96	..	64	..	91	..	91	..	..	11	..	11
Japan	5.8	3.6	101	103	93	98	100	..	100	..	13	14	12	14
Jordan	6.6	7.3	..	..	..	..	92	..	94	..	12	..	12	..
Kazakhstan	..	4.7	..	..	..	..	..	..	..	..	..	..	..	..
Kenya	6.8	6.6	91	..	..	..	60	..	62	..	..	..	..	..
Korea, Rep.	3.7	3.7	104	92	70	97	94	100	94	100	12	15	11	14
Kuwait	2.4	5.7	85	54	..	54	..	..	..	..	..	9	..	9
Kyrgyz Republic	..	5.7	..	95	..	..	..	..	..	..	..	..	..	..
Lao PDR	..	2.5	..	72	..	18	..	..	..	..	..	8	..	6
Latvia	3.3	6.5	..	90	..	79	..	..	..	..	..	11	..	12
Lebanon	..	2.5	..	76	..	..	..	..	..	..	..	..	..	..
Lesotho	5.1	7.0	67	70	13	17	50	..	68	..	..	8	..	9
Lithuania	..	5.6	..	..	..	80	..	..	..	..	..	..	..	..
Macedonia, FYR	..	5.6	..	95	..	51	..	95	..	95	..	10	..	10
Madagascar	4.4	1.9	..	61	..	..	..	49	..	33	..	..	..	..
Malawi	3.4	5.5	43	68	..	..	48	..	40	..	..	..	..	..
Malaysia	6.0	5.2	..	102	..	..	97	..	97	..	..	..	..	..

Note: For data comparability and coverage, see the Technical Notes. Figures in italics are for years other than those specified.

PEOPLE

Economy	Public expenditure on education % of GNP 1980	1996	Net enrollment ratio[a] % of relevant age group — Primary 1980	1996	Secondary 1980	1996	Percentage of cohort reaching grade 5 — Males 1980	1996	Females 1980	1996	Expected years of schooling — Males 1980	1995	Females 1980	1995
Mali	3.7	2.2	20	28	..	..	48	87	42	82	..	..	..	..
Mauritania	..	5.1	..	57	..	..	..	61	..	68	..	..	..	..
Mexico	4.7	4.9	..	101	..	51	..	85	..	86	..	..	..	..
Moldova	..	9.7	..	..	..	..	..	..	..	..	..	..	..	..
Mongolia	..	6.4	..	81	..	53	..	..	..	..	..	6	..	8
Morocco	6.1	5.3	62	74	20	..	79	79	78	77	..	..	..	..
Mozambique	4.4	..	..	40	..	6	..	52	..	39	5	4	4	3
Myanmar	1.7	1.2	..	..	..	..	..	..	..	..	..	..	..	..
Namibia	1.3	9.1	..	91	..	36	..	..	..	..	..	..	..	..
Nepal	1.8	2.8	..	..	..	..	..	..	..	..	..	..	..	..
Netherlands	7.6	5.2	93	99	81	91	94	..	98	..	14	16	13	15
New Zealand	5.8	7.3	..	100	81	97	94	..	94	..	14	16	13	17
Nicaragua	3.4	3.7	70	78	23	27	40	..	47	..	8	9	9	9
Niger	3.1	..	21	25	4	6	74	72	72	74	..	..	..	..
Nigeria	6.4	0.9	..	..	..	..	..	..	..	..	..	..	..	..
Norway	6.5	7.5	98	99	84	96	100	100	100	100	13	15	13	15
Pakistan	2.0	3.0	..	..	..	..	..	..	..	..	..	..	..	..
Panama	4.9	4.6	89	..	46	..	74	..	79	..	11	..	11	..
Papua New Guinea	..	..	..	..	..	..	..	..	..	..	..	..	..	..
Paraguay	1.5	3.9	89	91	..	38	59	..	58	..	..	9	..	9
Peru	3.1	2.9	86	91	..	53	78	..	74	..	11	13	10	12
Philippines	1.7	2.2	94	101	45	60	68	..	73	..	10	11	11	11
Poland	..	5.2	98	95	71	85	..	..	..	..	12	13	12	13
Portugal	3.8	5.5	99	104	..	78	..	..	..	..	..	14	..	15
Romania	3.3	3.6	..	95	..	73	..	..	..	..	..	12	..	11
Russian Federation	3.5	4.1	..	93	..	..	..	..	..	..	..	..	..	..
Rwanda	2.7	..	59	..	..	..	55	..	59	..	..	..	..	..
Saudi Arabia	4.1	5.5	49	61	21	42	82	87	86	92	7	9	5	8
Senegal	..	3.5	37	58	..	..	89	89	82	81	..	..	..	..
Sierra Leone	3.5	..	..	..	..	..	..	..	..	..	..	..	..	..
Singapore	2.8	3.0	99	..	..	..	100	..	100	..	11	..	11	..
Slovak Republic	..	4.9	..	..	..	..	..	..	..	..	..	..	..	..
Slovenia	..	5.8	..	95	..	..	..	..	..	..	..	..	..	..
South Africa	..	7.9	..	..	..	51	..	72	..	79	..	13	..	13
Spain	2.3	4.9	102	105	74	..	95	..	94	..	13	15	12	16
Sri Lanka	2.7	3.4	..	..	..	..	92	83	91	84	..	..	..	..
Sweden	9.0	8.3	..	102	..	98	98	98	99	97	12	14	13	15
Switzerland	4.8	5.3	..	..	..	..	..	..	..	..	14	15	13	14
Syrian Arab Republic	4.6	4.2	90	91	39	38	93	93	88	94	11	10	8	9
Tajikistan	..	2.2	..	..	..	..	..	..	..	..	..	..	..	..
Tanzania	..	..	68	48	..	..	89	..	90	..	..	..	..	..
Thailand	3.4	4.1	..	..	..	..	..	..	..	..	..	..	..	..
Togo	5.6	4.7	..	85	..	..	59	..	45	..	..	..	..	..
Tunisia	5.4	6.7	82	98	23	..	89	90	84	92	10	..	7	..
Turkey	2.2	2.2	..	96	..	50	..	..	..	..	..	11	..	9
Turkmenistan	..	..	..	..	..	..	..	..	..	..	..	..	..	..
Uganda	1.2	2.6	..	..	..	..	82	..	73	..	..	..	..	..
Ukraine	5.6	7.2	..	..	..	..	..	..	..	..	..	..	..	..
United Kingdom	5.6	5.4	100	100	79	92	..	..	..	..	13	16	13	17
United States	6.7	5.4	..	95	..	90	..	..	..	..	14	15	15	16
Uruguay	2.3	3.3	..	93	..	..	..	97	..	99	..	..	..	..
Uzbekistan	..	8.1	..	..	..	..	..	..	..	..	..	..	..	..
Venezuela	4.4	5.2	82	84	14	22	..	86	..	92	..	10	..	11
Vietnam	..	2.6	95	..	..	..	..	..	..	..	..	..	..	..
Yemen, Rep.	..	6.5	..	52	..	..	..	..	..	..	..	..	..	..
Zambia	4.5	2.2	77	75	..	17	88	..	82	..	..	8	..	7
Zimbabwe	6.6	8.3	..	..	..	..	82	78	76	79	..	..	..	..
World	**4.0 m**	**4.8 m**	..	..w	..	..w	..w	..w	..w	..w				
Low income	3.2	3.9	..	..	..	..	..	..	..	..				
Excl. China & India	3.4	..	..	..	..	..	..	..	..	..				
Middle income	4.0	5.1	..	..	..	..	..	..	..	..				
Lower middle income	4.2	5.3	..	..	..	..	..	..	..	..				
Upper middle income	4.0	5.0	..	94	..	43	..	..	..	..				
Low and middle income	3.5	4.1	..	..	..	..	..	..	..	..				
East Asia & Pacific	2.5	2.3	..	101	..	..	..	93	..	94				
Europe & Central Asia	..	5.4	..	92	..	..	..	..	..	..				
Latin America & Carib.	3.8	3.7	..	91	..	33	..	..	..	..				
Middle East & N. Africa	5.0	5.3	..	85	..	61	88	..	84	..				
South Asia	2.0	3.0	..	..	..	..	..	..	..	..				
Sub-Saharan Africa	4.1	4.3	..	..	..	..	..	..	..	..				
High income	5.6	5.4	..	97	..	90	..	..	..	..				

a. Net enrollment ratios exceeding 100 indicate discrepancies between estimates of the school-age population and reported enrollment data.

Table 7.   Health

Economy	Public expenditure on health % of GDP 1990–97[a]	Access to safe water % of population with access		Access to sanitation % of population with access		Infant mortality rate Per 1,000 live births		Contraceptive prevalence rate % of women aged 15–49 1990–98[a]	Total fertility rate Births per woman		Maternal mortality rate Per 100,000 live births 1990–97[a]
		1982	1995	1982	1995	1980	1997		1980	1997	
Albania	2.5	92	76	..	58	47	26	..	3.6	2.5	28[b]
Algeria	3.3	77	..	..	..	98	32	51	6.7	3.6	140[b]
Angola	3.9	28	32	18	15	154	125	..	6.9	6.8	1,500[c]
Argentina	4.3	55	65	69	75	35	22	..	3.3	2.6	100[c]
Armenia	3.1	..	..	..	..	26	15	..	2.3	1.5	21[b]
Australia	5.8	99	99	99	..	11	5	..	1.9	1.8	9[c]
Austria	5.7	99	..	..	..	14	5	..	1.6	1.4	10[c]
Azerbaijan	1.1	..	..	..	36	30	20	..	3.2	2.1	44[b]
Bangladesh	1.2	40	84	4	35	132	75	49	6.1	3.2	850[c]
Belarus	5.2	100	..	..	..	16	12	..	2.0	1.2	22[b]
Belgium	6.7	98	..	..	..	12	6	..	1.7	1.6	10[c]
Benin	1.7	14	72	10	24	116	88	16	7.0	5.8	500[d]
Bolivia	3.8	53	70	36	41	118	66	45	5.5	4.4	370[d]
Botswana	1.8	77	70	36	55	71	58	..	6.1	4.3	250[c]
Brazil	1.9	75	69	24	67	70	34	77	3.9	2.3	160[d]
Bulgaria	3.5	85	..	..	..	20	18	..	2.0	1.1	20[b]
Burkina Faso	4.7	35	..	5	..	121	99	8	7.5	6.6	930[c]
Burundi	1.0	23	58	52	48	122	119	..	6.8	6.3	1,300[c]
Cambodia	0.7	..	13	..	..	201	103	..	4.7	4.6	900[c]
Cameroon	1.0	36	41	36	40	94	52	16	6.4	5.3	550[c]
Canada	6.3	97	99	60	95	10	6	..	1.7	1.6	6[c]
Central African Republic	2.0	16	23	19	45	117	98	14	5.8	4.9	700[d]
Chad	1.6	31	24	14	21	123	100	4	6.9	6.5	840[d]
Chile	2.3	86	91	67	81	32	11	..	2.8	2.4	65[b]
China	2.1	..	83	..	..	42	32	85	2.5	1.9	95[c]
Hong Kong, China	2.3	..	..	..	..	11	5	..	2.0	1.3	7[c]
Colombia	2.9	91	75	68	59	41	24	72	3.9	2.8	100[c]
Congo, Dem. Rep.	0.2	..	..	..	..	112	92	..	6.6	6.4	870[c]
Congo, Rep.	1.8	..	..	40	9	89	90	..	6.3	6.1	890[c]
Costa Rica	6.0	93	100	95	97	20	12	..	3.7	2.8	55[c]
Côte d'Ivoire	1.4	20	72	17	51	108	87	11	7.4	5.1	810[d]
Croatia	8.4	70	63	67	61	21	9	..	..	1.6	12[b]
Czech Republic	6.4	100	..	..	..	16	6	69	2.1	1.2	2[b]
Denmark	5.1	..	..	..	100	8	6	..	1.5	1.8	9[c]
Dominican Republic	1.8	49	73	66	80	76	40	64	4.2	3.0	110[c]
Ecuador	2.0	58	55	57	53	74	33	57	5.0	3.0	150[c]
Egypt, Arab Rep.	1.7	90	84	70	70	120	51	48	5.1	3.2	170[c]
El Salvador	2.4	51	53	62	77	84	32	53	4.9	3.2	300[c]
Eritrea	1.1	..	7	..	..	91	62	8	..	5.8	1,000[c]
Estonia	5.8	..	..	..	..	17	10	..	2.0	1.2	52[b]
Ethiopia	1.6	4	26	..	8	155	107	4	6.6	6.5	1,400[c]
Finland	5.7	95	98	100	100	8	4	..	1.6	1.9	11[c]
France	7.7	98	100	..	..	10	5	..	1.9	1.7	15[c]
Georgia	0.6	..	..	..	..	25	17	..	2.3	1.5	19[b]
Germany	8.1	90	..	..	..	12	5	..	1.4	1.4	22[c]
Ghana	2.9	..	65	26	32	94	66	20	6.5	4.9	740[c]
Greece	5.3	85	..	..	..	18	7	..	2.2	1.3	10[c]
Guatemala	1.7	58	67	54	67	84	43	32	6.3	4.5	190[d]
Guinea	1.2	20	55	12	14	185	120	2	6.1	5.5	880[d]
Haiti	1.2	38	39	19	26	123	71	18	5.9	4.4	600[d]
Honduras	2.8	50	77	32	82	70	36	50	6.5	4.3	220[c]
Hungary	4.5	87	..	..	..	23	10	..	1.9	1.4	14[b]
India	0.7	54	85	8	16	115	71	41	5.0	3.3	440[d]
Indonesia	0.7	39	65	30	55	90	47	57	4.3	2.8	390[d]
Iran, Islamic Rep.	1.7	50	90	60	81	87	32	73	6.7	2.8	120[c]
Ireland	5.1	97	..	..	..	11	5	60	3.2	1.9	10[c]
Israel	0.3	100	99	..	100	15	7	..	3.2	2.7	7[c]
Italy	5.3	99	..	..	..	15	5	..	1.6	1.2	12[c]
Jamaica	2.5	96	93	91	74	21	12	65	3.7	2.7	120[c]
Japan	5.7	99	96	99	100	8	4	..	1.8	1.4	18[b]
Jordan	3.7	89	98	76	98	41	29	53	6.8	4.2	150[c]
Kazakhstan	2.5	..	..	..	..	33	24	59	2.9	2.0	53[b]
Kenya	1.9	27	45	44	45	75	74	38	7.8	4.7	650[c]
Korea, Rep.	2.3	83	83	100	100	26	9	..	2.6	1.7	30[b]
Kuwait	3.5	100	100	100	100	27	12	..	5.3	2.9	20[b]
Kyrgyz Republic	2.9	..	81	..	..	43	28	60	4.1	2.8	32[b]
Lao PDR	1.3	..	51	..	32	127	98	..	6.7	5.6	660[c]
Latvia	3.5	..	..	..	..	20	15	..	2.0	1.1	15[b]
Lebanon	3.0	92	94	59	97	48	28	..	4.0	2.5	300[c]
Lesotho	3.7	18	62	12	..	119	93	23	5.5	4.8	610[c]
Lithuania	5.0	..	..	..	..	20	10	..	2.0	1.4	13[b]
Macedonia, FYR	6.2	..	..	..	..	54	16	..	2.5	1.9	22[b]
Madagascar	1.4	31	16	..	34	119	94	19	6.6	5.8	500[d]
Malawi	2.3	32	60	60	64	169	133	22	7.6	6.4	620[d]
Malaysia	1.4	71	89	75	94	30	11	..	4.2	3.2	34[b]

Note: For data comparability and coverage, see the Technical Notes. Figures in italics are for years other than those specified.

PEOPLE

Economy	Public expenditure on health % of GDP 1990–97[a]	Access to safe water % of population with access 1982	Access to safe water % of population with access 1995	Access to sanitation % of population with access 1982	Access to sanitation % of population with access 1995	Infant mortality rate Per 1,000 live births 1980	Infant mortality rate Per 1,000 live births 1997	Contraceptive prevalence rate % of women aged 15–49 1990–98[a]	Total fertility rate Births per woman 1980	Total fertility rate Births per woman 1997	Maternal mortality rate Per 100,000 live births 1990–97[a]
Mali	2.0	..	48	21	37	184	118	7	7.1	6.6	580[d]
Mauritania	1.8	37	64	..	32	120	92	..	6.3	5.5	800[c]
Mexico	2.8	82	95	57	76	51	31	..	4.7	2.8	110[c]
Moldova	6.2	..	56	..	50	35	20	74	2.4	1.6	23[b]
Mongolia	4.3	100	54	50	..	82	52	..	5.3	2.6	65[c]
Morocco	1.2	32	57	50	68	99	51	50	5.4	3.1	370[f]
Mozambique	4.6	9	24	10	23	145	135	6	6.5	5.3	1,100[c]
Myanmar	0.4	20	60	20	43	109	79	..	4.9	2.4	580[c]
Namibia	4.1	..	60	..	42	90	65	29	5.9	4.9	220[d]
Nepal	1.2	11	59	0	23	132	83	..	6.1	4.4	1,500[c]
Netherlands	6.2	100	99	..	100	9	5	..	1.6	1.5	12[c]
New Zealand	5.9	87	90	88	..	13	7	..	2.0	1.9	25[c]
Nicaragua	5.3	50	62	27	59	84	43	44	6.3	3.9	160[c]
Niger	1.6	37	48	9	17	150	118	8	7.4	7.4	590[d]
Nigeria	0.2	36	50	..	57	99	77	6	6.9	5.3	1,000[c]
Norway	6.2	99	100	..	100	8	4	..	1.7	1.9	6[c]
Pakistan	0.8	38	62	16	39	127	95	24	7.0	5.0	340[c]
Panama	4.7	82	84	81	90	32	21	..	3.7	2.6	55[c]
Papua New Guinea	2.8	..	31	..	25	78	61	26	5.8	4.3	370[c]
Paraguay	1.8	23	39	49	32	50	23	51	5.2	3.8	190[d]
Peru	2.2	53	66	48	61	81	40	64	4.5	3.2	280[c]
Philippines	1.3	65	83	57	77	52	35	48	4.8	3.6	210[d]
Poland	4.8	82	..	..	..	26	10	..	2.3	1.5	5[b]
Portugal	4.9	66	82	..	..	24	6	..	2.2	1.4	15[c]
Romania	2.9	77	62	..	44	29	22	57	2.4	1.3	41[b]
Russian Federation	4.1	..	..	..	..	22	17	34	1.9	1.3	53[b]
Rwanda	1.9	..	..	..	94	128	124	21	8.3	6.2	1,300[c]
Saudi Arabia	6.4	91	93	76	86	65	21	..	7.3	5.9	18[b]
Senegal	1.2	44	50	..	..	117	70	13	6.8	5.6	510[d]
Sierra Leone	1.6	24	34	13	..	190	170	..	6.5	6.1	..
Singapore	1.5	100	100	85	100	12	4	..	1.7	1.7	10[c]
Slovak Republic	6.1	..	..	43	51	21	9	..	2.3	1.4	8[b]
Slovenia	7.1	..	98	80	98	15	5	..	2.1	1.3	5[b]
South Africa	3.6	..	59	..	53	67	48	69	4.6	2.8	230[c]
Spain	5.8	99	..	..	97	12	5	..	2.2	1.1	7[c]
Sri Lanka	1.4	37	70	66	75	34	14	..	3.5	2.2	30[b]
Sweden	7.2	100	..	..	..	7	4	..	1.7	1.7	7[c]
Switzerland	7.1	100	100	..	..	9	5	..	1.5	1.5	6[c]
Syrian Arab Republic	..	71	88	45	71	56	31	40	7.4	4.0	180[b]
Tajikistan	2.4	..	69	..	62	58	30	..	5.6	3.5	58[b]
Tanzania	1.1	52	49	..	86	108	85	18	6.7	5.5	530[d]
Thailand	2.0	66	89	47	96	49	33	..	3.5	1.7	200[c]
Togo	1.6	35	55	14	41	110	86	..	6.6	6.1	640[c]
Tunisia	3.0	72	90	46	80	69	30	60	5.2	2.8	170[c]
Turkey	2.7	69	..	..	..	109	40	..	4.3	2.5	180[c]
Turkmenistan	1.2	..	60	..	60	54	40	..	4.9	3.0	44[b]
Uganda	1.9	16	42	13	67	116	99	15	7.2	6.6	550[f]
Ukraine	3.9	..	55	..	49	17	14	..	2.0	1.3	30[b]
United Kingdom	5.7	100	100	..	96	12	6	..	1.9	1.7	9[b]
United States	6.6	100	73	98	..	13	7	76	1.8	2.0	12[c]
Uruguay	1.9	83	89	59	61	37	16	..	2.7	2.4	85[c]
Uzbekistan	3.3	..	57	..	18	47	..	..	4.8	3.3	24[b]
Venezuela	1.0	84	79	45	72	36	21	..	4.2	3.0	120[b]
Vietnam	1.1	..	47	30	60	57	29	75	5.0	2.4	105[b]
Yemen, Rep.	1.3	..	39	..	19	141	96	21	7.9	6.4	1,400[c]
Zambia	2.9	48	53	47	51	90	113	26	7.0	5.6	650[d]
Zimbabwe	1.7	10	77	5	66	80	69	48	6.4	3.8	280[d]
World	**2.5 w**	**.. w**	**75 w**	**.. w**	**.. w**	**80 w**	**56 w**		**3.7 w**	**2.8 w**	
Low income	1.0	..	74	..	..	98	69		4.3	3.2	
Excl. China & India	..	37	55	21	45	114	84		6.0	4.4	
Middle income	2.4	74	..	..	..	59	33		3.7	2.5	
Lower middle income	2.2	..	..	..	..	61	38		3.6	2.5	
Upper middle income	3.0	78	79	52	75	57	27		3.7	2.4	
Low and middle income	1.8	..	75	..	..	87	60		4.1	2.9	
East Asia & Pacific	1.8	..	77	..	..	55	37		3.0	2.1	
Europe & Central Asia	3.9	..	..	..	..	41	23		2.5	1.7	
Latin America & Carib.	2.6	73	75	46	68	60	32		4.1	2.7	
Middle East & N. Africa	2.3	69	..	62	..	95	49		6.2	3.7	
South Asia	0.8	50	81	9	20	119	77		5.3	3.5	
Sub-Saharan Africa	1.7	..	47	..	47	115	91		6.6	5.5	
High income	6.0	98	..	..	..	12	6		1.8	1.7	

a. Data are for the most recent year available within the period. b. Official estimate. c. UNICEF-WHO estimate based on statistical modeling. d. Indirect estimate based on a sample survey. e. Based on a survey covering 30 provinces. f. Based on a sample survey.

Table 8.   Land use and agricultural productivity

Economy	Land under permanent crops % of land area		Irrigated land % of cropland		Arable land Hectares per capita		Agricultural machinery Tractors per thousand agricultural workers		Agricultural productivity Agr. value added per agricultural worker 1995 dollars		Food production index 1989–91 = 100	
	1980	1996	1979–81	1994–96	1979–81	1994–96	1979–81	1994–96	1979–81	1995–97	1979–81	1995–97
Albania	4.3	4.6	53.0	48.4	0.22	0.18	15	10	1,193	1,717	..	..
Algeria	0.3	0.2	3.4	6.9	0.37	0.27	27	43	1,411	1,903	69.7	118.2
Angola	0.4	0.4	2.2	2.1	0.41	0.27	4	3	..	..	91.9	130.1
Argentina	0.8	0.8	5.8	6.3	0.89	0.72	132	190	12,195	13,833	94.9	121.9
Armenia	..	3.5	..	43.7	..	0.15	..	64	..	4,477	..	82.3
Australia	0.0	0.0	3.5	4.8	2.97	2.68	751	698	20,880	29,044	91.5	126.9
Austria	1.2	1.1	0.2	0.3	0.20	0.18	945	1,492	9,761	15,474	92.3	100.0
Azerbaijan	..	4.6	..	50.0	..	0.21	..	31	..	847	..	55.6
Bangladesh	2.0	2.5	17.1	39.1	0.10	0.07	0	0	181	221	79.2	106.0
Belarus	..	0.7	..	1.9	..	0.60	..	131	..	3,461	..	58.9
Belgium	0.4	0.5	0.1	0.1	..	..	917	1,130	..	..	88.4	114.4
Benin	4.0	4.1	0.3	0.5	0.39	0.26	0	0	302	504	63.4	129.5
Bolivia	0.2	0.2	6.6	3.7	0.35	0.27	4	4	..	..	71.0	126.7
Botswana	0.0	0.0	0.5	0.3	0.44	0.25	9	21	619	647	87.6	104.2
Brazil	1.2	1.4	3.3	4.9	0.32	0.32	31	51	2,047	3,931	69.5	122.2
Bulgaria	3.2	1.8	28.3	18.7	0.43	0.48	66	61	2,754	4,351	105.3	68.3
Burkina Faso	0.1	0.1	0.4	0.7	0.39	0.34	0	0	134	159	62.6	122.4
Burundi	10.1	12.9	0.7	1.3	0.22	0.13	0	0	177	139	80.5	96.4
Cambodia	0.4	0.6	4.9	4.5	0.30	0.37	0	0	..	407	51.1	124.8
Cameroon	2.2	2.3	0.2	0.3	0.68	0.45	0	0	834	958	83.2	118.7
Canada	0.0	0.0	1.3	1.6	1.86	1.53	824	1,683	..	..	79.9	112.7
Central African Republic	0.1	0.1	..	..	0.81	0.59	0	0	396	439	79.9	122.7
Chad	0.0	0.0	0.2	0.4	0.70	0.48	0	0	155	212	90.6	117.5
Chile	0.3	0.4	29.6	32.6	0.36	0.25	43	44	2,612	5,211	71.5	128.7
China	0.4	1.2	45.1	37.0	0.10	0.10	2	1	162	296	61.0	155.8
Hong Kong, China	1.0	1.0	43.8	28.6	0.00	0.00	0	0	..	..	97.4	56.7
Colombia	1.4	2.4	7.7	23.4	0.13	0.05	8	7	1,926	2,890	76.0	110.8
Congo, Dem. Rep.	0.3	0.4	0.1	0.1	0.25	0.16	0	0	270	285	71.9	104.9
Congo, Rep.	0.1	0.1	0.7	0.6	0.07	0.05	2	1	391	470	80.3	114.5
Costa Rica	4.4	4.8	12.1	23.8	0.12	0.08	22	23	3,159	4,627	73.0	128.4
Côte d'Ivoire	7.2	13.5	1.0	1.0	0.24	0.21	1	1	1,074	1,005	70.9	119.2
Croatia	..	2.2	..	0.2	..	0.24	..	14	..	7,144	..	57.7
Czech Republic	..	3.1	..	0.7	..	0.30	..	148	..	..	..	81.9
Denmark	0.3	0.2	14.5	20.3	0.52	0.45	973	1,088	21,321	46,621	83.2	102.5
Dominican Republic	7.2	11.4	11.7	13.7	0.19	0.17	3	3	1,839	2,454	85.1	109.1
Ecuador	3.3	5.2	19.4	8.1	0.20	0.14	6	7	1,206	1,764	76.6	136.9
Egypt, Arab Rep.	0.2	0.5	100.0	100.0	0.06	0.05	4	10	721	1,163	68.4	129.8
El Salvador	8.0	10.5	14.8	14.2	0.12	0.11	5	5	2,013	1,705	90.8	109.5
Eritrea	..	0.8	..	5.4	..	0.12	..	1	..	..	..	102.3
Estonia	..	0.4	..	..	..	0.76	..	475	..	3,342	..	49.3
Ethiopia	..	0.6	..	1.6	..	0.20	..	0	..	..	90.2	..
Finland	..	..	..	..	0.54	0.49	721	1,301	16,995	28,296	92.8	92.4
France	2.5	2.1	4.6	8.2	0.32	0.31	737	1,189	14,956	34,760	93.7	103.6
Georgia	..	4.7	..	42.2	..	0.14	..	28	..	1,838	..	74.6
Germany	1.4	0.7	3.7	3.9	0.15	0.14	624	954	..	19,930	91.0	90.9
Ghana	7.5	7.5	0.2	0.1	0.18	0.16	1	1	663	533	73.5	147.7
Greece	7.9	8.4	24.2	33.8	0.30	0.28	120	267	8,804	12,611	91.2	98.4
Guatemala	4.4	5.1	5.0	6.5	0.19	0.14	3	2	2,110	1,902	69.9	114.0
Guinea	0.9	1.2	12.8	10.9	0.11	0.09	0	0	..	262	96.5	129.2
Haiti	12.5	12.7	7.9	9.7	0.10	0.08	0	0	578	407	105.5	90.5
Honduras	1.8	3.1	4.1	3.6	0.44	0.30	5	7	697	1,018	88.2	104.7
Hungary	3.3	2.4	3.6	4.2	0.47	0.47	59	54	3,389	4,655	91.0	76.8
India	1.8	2.4	22.8	32.0	0.24	0.17	2	5	253	343	68.4	117.1
Indonesia	4.4	7.2	16.2	15.0	0.12	0.09	0	1	610	745	63.5	122.4
Iran, Islamic Rep.	0.5	1.0	35.5	38.0	0.36	0.30	17	39	2,533	3,831	60.9	136.8
Ireland	0.0	0.0	..	..	0.33	0.37	606	978	..	..	83.3	106.2
Israel	4.3	4.2	49.3	45.3	0.08	0.06	294	336	..	..	85.7	114.1
Italy	10.0	9.1	19.3	24.9	0.17	0.14	370	867	9,994	19,001	101.5	99.7
Jamaica	5.5	6.1	13.6	14.0	0.08	0.07	9	11	892	1,294	86.0	117.9
Japan	1.6	1.0	62.6	62.7	0.04	0.03	209	593	15,698	28,665	94.2	96.9
Jordan	0.4	1.0	11.0	18.2	0.14	0.08	48	42	1,447	1,634	55.3	157.3
Kazakhstan	..	0.1	..	6.9	..	2.04	..	106	..	1,477	..	68.5
Kenya	0.8	0.9	0.9	1.5	0.23	0.15	1	1	262	230	67.7	102.9
Korea, Rep.	1.4	2.0	59.6	60.7	0.05	0.04	1	34	3,957	10,962	77.9	119.1
Kuwait	..	..	..	..	0.00	0.00	3	14	..	..	98.9	139.3
Kyrgyz Republic	..	2.7	..	76.8	..	0.23	..	44	..	2,917	..	123.8
Lao PDR	0.1	0.2	15.4	20.3	0.21	0.17	0	0	..	526	71.2	112.4
Latvia	..	0.5	..	..	..	0.68	..	284	..	3,125	..	49.8
Lebanon	8.9	12.5	28.3	28.4	0.07	0.05	28	77	..	..	57.8	117.6
Lesotho	..	..	..	..	0.22	0.17	6	6	498	319	89.4	104.4
Lithuania	..	0.9	..	..	..	0.79	..	239	..	2,907	..	69.8
Macedonia, FYR	..	1.9	..	9.4	..	0.31	..	323	..	1,528	..	95.9
Madagascar	0.9	0.9	21.5	35.0	0.28	0.19	1	1	198	180	82.1	105.3
Malawi	0.9	1.1	1.3	1.6	0.20	0.16	0	0	100	122	91.2	105.3
Malaysia	11.6	17.6	6.7	4.5	0.07	0.09	4	23	3,279	6,267	55.4	124.0

Note: For data comparability and coverage, see the Technical Notes. Figures in italics are for years other than those specified.

ENVIRONMENT

Economy	Land under permanent crops % of land area 1980	1996	Irrigated land % of cropland 1979–81	1994–96	Arable land Hectares per capita 1979–81	1994–96	Agricultural machinery Tractors per thousand agricultural workers 1979–81	1994–96	Agricultural productivity Agr. value added per agricultural worker 1995 dollars 1979–81	1995–97	Food production index 1989–91 = 100 1979–81	1995–97
Mali	0.0	0.0	2.9	2.3	0.31	0.37	0	1	225	241	79.7	118.7
Mauritania	0.0	0.0	22.8	10.3	0.14	0.20	1	1	301	439	86.1	103.2
Mexico	0.8	1.1	20.3	23.1	0.34	0.27	16	20	1,482	1,690	84.9	120.6
Moldova	. .	12.5	. .	14.1	. .	0.41	. .	82	. .	1,473	. .	58.3
Mongolia	0.0	0.0	3.0	6.1	0.71	0.54	32	22	727	1,085	88.2	81.6
Morocco	1.1	1.9	15.2	13.0	0.38	0.33	7	10	1,117	1,593	55.9	94.9
Mozambique	0.3	0.3	2.1	3.4	0.24	0.19	1	1	. .	76	99.2	119.5
Myanmar	0.7	0.9	10.4	15.9	0.28	0.22	1	1	. .	. .	87.8	133.5
Namibia	0.0	0.0	0.6	0.8	0.64	0.51	10	11	876	1,235	107.4	118.8
Nepal	0.2	0.4	22.5	30.6	0.16	0.13	0	0	162	187	65.1	113.5
Netherlands	0.9	1.0	58.5	61.5	0.06	0.06	561	646	21,663	43,836	87.0	106.1
New Zealand	3.7	6.4	5.2	8.9	0.80	0.43	619	451	. .	. .	90.8	120.3
Nicaragua	1.5	2.4	6.0	3.3	0.39	0.54	6	7	1,334	1,407	117.9	123.7
Niger	0.0	0.0	0.7	1.4	0.62	0.53	0	0	222	190	101.4	118.4
Nigeria	2.8	2.8	0.7	0.7	0.39	0.27	1	1	370	541	57.7	134.2
Norway	. .	. .	. .	. .	0.20	0.22	824	1,251	17,044	31,577	91.8	99.7
Pakistan	0.4	0.7	72.7	80.2	0.24	0.17	5	12	392	585	66.4	130.5
Panama	1.6	2.1	5.0	4.9	0.22	0.19	27	20	2,122	2,463	85.6	102.5
Papua New Guinea	0.9	1.1	. .	. .	0.01	0.01	1	1	717	827	86.1	106.8
Paraguay	0.3	0.2	3.4	3.0	0.52	0.45	14	25	2,506	3,295	60.6	116.7
Peru	0.3	0.4	32.8	41.8	0.19	0.16	5	3	1,349	1,619	78.4	131.5
Philippines	14.8	14.4	14.0	16.7	0.09	0.07	1	1	1,348	1,379	86.4	120.6
Poland	1.1	1.2	0.7	0.7	0.41	0.37	112	277	. .	1,647	87.9	84.8
Portugal	7.8	8.2	20.1	21.7	0.25	0.22	72	203	. .	5,574	71.9	99.8
Romania	2.9	2.4	21.9	31.4	0.44	0.41	39	80	. .	3,170	112.7	100.5
Russian Federation	. .	0.1	. .	4.0	. .	0.88	. .	122	. .	2,540	. .	69.5
Rwanda	10.3	12.2	0.4	0.3	0.15	0.13	0	0	307	201	89.7	76.9
Saudi Arabia	0.0	0.1	28.9	38.7	0.20	0.20	2	11	2,167	10,507	31.0	90.8
Senegal	0.0	0.1	2.6	3.1	0.42	0.27	0	0	341	321	74.5	109.1
Sierra Leone	0.7	0.8	4.1	5.4	0.14	0.11	0	1	368	404	84.5	94.7
Singapore	9.8	0.0	. .	. .	0.00	0.00	3	16	13,937	39,851	154.3	37.9
Slovak Republic	. .	2.7	. .	13.4	. .	0.28	. .	100	. .	3,347	. .	74.4
Slovenia	. .	2.7	. .	0.7	. .	0.12	. .	2,762	. .	26,006	. .	100.9
South Africa	0.7	0.7	8.4	8.1	0.45	0.38	90	69	2,465	3,355	92.8	97.5
Spain	9.9	9.8	14.8	17.7	0.42	0.39	200	513	. .	12,022	82.1	99.4
Sri Lanka	15.9	15.5	28.3	29.2	0.06	0.05	8	9	648	732	98.4	113.0
Sweden	. .	. .	. .	. .	0.36	0.32	715	931	. .	. .	100.2	95.1
Switzerland	0.5	0.6	6.2	5.9	0.06	0.06	494	616	. .	. .	95.8	96.2
Syrian Arab Republic	2.5	3.9	9.6	20.4	0.60	0.33	29	65	. .	. .	94.5	136.7
Tajikistan	. .	0.5	. .	80.6	. .	0.14	. .	37	. .	. .	. .	67.9
Tanzania	1.0	1.0	3.8	4.6	0.12	0.10	1	1	. .	159	76.8	97.2
Thailand	3.5	6.6	16.4	23.2	0.35	0.29	1	7	630	928	79.9	107.2
Togo	6.6	6.6	0.3	0.3	0.76	0.50	0	0	345	510	77.0	129.9
Tunisia	9.7	13.1	4.9	7.5	0.51	0.32	30	39	1,743	2,750	67.6	108.3
Turkey	4.1	3.2	9.6	15.4	0.57	0.40	38	57	1,852	1,835	75.8	106.3
Turkmenistan	. .	0.1	. .	87.8	. .	0.32	. .	83	. .	. .	. .	108.7
Uganda	8.0	8.8	0.1	0.1	0.32	0.26	0	1	. .	326	70.5	107.7
Ukraine	. .	1.8	. .	7.5	. .	0.65	. .	92	. .	2,259	. .	69.9
United Kingdom	0.3	0.2	2.0	1.8	0.12	0.10	726	871	. .	. .	91.6	100.5
United States	0.2	0.2	10.8	12.0	0.83	0.67	1,230	1,452	. .	34,727	94.7	113.7
Uruguay	0.3	0.3	5.4	10.7	0.48	0.39	171	172	6,822	9,384	86.8	128.8
Uzbekistan	. .	0.9	. .	81.6	. .	0.20	. .	59	. .	2,085	. .	100.7
Venezuela	0.9	1.0	3.6	5.2	0.19	0.12	50	58	4,041	4,931	79.6	114.0
Vietnam	1.9	3.8	24.1	29.6	0.11	0.07	1	4	. .	226	64.0	132.7
Yemen, Rep.	0.2	0.2	19.9	31.3	0.16	0.09	3	2	. .	305	75.0	115.5
Zambia	0.0	0.0	0.4	0.9	0.89	0.59	3	2	331	226	74.2	95.6
Zimbabwe	0.3	0.3	3.1	4.6	0.36	0.27	7	7	307	316	82.1	94.8
World	**0.9 w**	**1.0 w**	**17.8 w**	**18.8 w**	**0.24 w**	**0.24 w**	**19 w**	**20 w**	**. . w**	**. . w**	**76.0 w**	**128.2 w**
Low income	0.9	1.3	25.5	28.9	0.18	0.15	2	3	. .	339	69.3	137.5
Excl. China & India	1.0	1.3	16.2	19.4	0.23	0.18	. .	. .	. .	. .	74.9	123.1
Middle income	1.2	1.0	15.8	14.1	0.23	0.36	25	46	. .	. .	80.1	118.4
Lower middle income	1.3	0.8	22.9	14.9	0.16	0.39	17	34	. .	. .	. .	. .
Upper middle income	1.1	1.3	10.3	12.4	0.34	0.30	37	71	. .	. .	78.6	116.7
Low and middle income	1.0	1.1	21.9	21.5	0.20	0.21	5	8	. .	601	72.0	132.6
East Asia & Pacific	1.5	2.6	37.0	35.5	0.11	0.11	2	2	. .	. .	67.1	152.9
Europe & Central Asia	3.2	0.4	11.6	9.9	0.14	0.61	. .	102	. .	2,272	. .	. .
Latin America & Carib.	1.1	1.3	11.6	13.3	0.33	0.28	25	34	. .	. .	80.7	121.0
Middle East & N. Africa	0.4	0.7	25.8	35.0	0.29	0.21	12	24	. .	. .	70.5	128.5
South Asia	1.5	1.9	28.7	38.9	0.23	0.16	2	5	189	380	70.8	119.1
Sub-Saharan Africa	0.7	0.8	4.0	4.3	0.32	0.26	3	2	269	355	80.2	119.6
High income	0.5	0.5	9.8	11.1	0.46	0.41	520	877	. .	. .	93.1	105.2

Table 9.   Water use, deforestation, and protected areas

Economy	Freshwater resources Cu. meters per capita 1996	Annual freshwater withdrawals Billion cu. m^a	% of total resources^a	% for agriculture^b	% for industry^b	% for domestic use^b	Access to safe water % of population with access 1995 Urban	Rural	Annual deforestation 1990–95 Square kilometers	Avg. annual % change	Nationally protected areas 1996 Thousand square km	% of total land area
Albania	16,785c	0.2d	0.4c	76	18	6	*97*	*70*	0	0.0	0.8	2.9
Algeria	463c	4.5	33.2c	60e	15e	25e	..	..	234	1.2	58.9	2.5
Angola	15,782	0.5	0.3	76e	10e	14e	69	15	2,370	1.0	81.8	6.6
Argentina	27,861c	27.6d	2.8c	73	18	9	71	24	894	0.3	46.6	1.7
Armenia	2,136c	3.8	47.0c	72	15	13	..	..	−84	−2.7	2.1	7.4
Australia	18,508	14.6d	4.3	33	2	65	..	..	−170	0.0	563.9	7.3
Austria	11,187c	2.4	2.6c	9	58	33	..	..	0	0.0	23.4	28.3
Azerbaijan	4,339c	15.8	47.9c	74	22	4	..	..	0	0.0	4.8	5.5
Bangladesh	19,065c	22.5	1.0c	96	1	3	49	..	88	0.8	1.0	0.8
Belarus	1,841c	3.0	15.9c	19	49	32	..	..	−688	−1.0	8.6	4.1
Belgium	1,227c	9.0	72.2c	4	85	11	..	..	0	0.0	0.8	..
Benin	4,451c	0.2	0.6c	67e	10e	23e	82	69	596	1.2	7.8	7.1
Bolivia	38,625	1.2	0.4	85	5	10	88	43	5,814	1.2	156.0	14.4
Botswana	9,589c	0.1	0.7c	48e	20e	32e	100	77	708	0.5	105.0	18.5
Brazil	42,459c	36.5	0.5c	59	19	22	80	28	25,544	0.5	355.5	4.2
Bulgaria	24,663c	13.9	6.8c	22	76	3	..	..	−6	0.0	4.9	4.4
Burkina Faso	1,671	0.4	2.2	81e	0e	19e	..	..	320	0.7	28.6	10.5
Burundi	559	0.1	2.8	64e	0e	36e	..	..	14	0.4	1.4	5.5
Cambodia	47,530c	0.5	0.1c	94	1	5	20	12	1,638	1.6	28.6	16.2
Cameroon	19,231	0.4	0.1	35e	19e	46e	..	*30*	1,292	0.6	21.0	4.5
Canada	95,785c	45.1	1.6c	12	70	18	..	..	−1,764	−0.1	921.0	10.0
Central African Republic	41,250	0.1	0.0	74e	5e	21e	*20*	*25*	1,282	0.4	51.1	8.2
Chad	6,011c	0.2	0.4c	82e	2e	16e	*48*	*17*	942	0.8	114.9	9.1
Chile	32,007	16.8d	3.6	89	5	6	99	47	292	0.4	141.3	18.9
China	2,282	460.0	16.4	87	7	6	..	..	866	0.1	598.1	6.4
Hong Kong, China	..	..	..	..	..	..	..	..	..	..	0.4	40.4
Colombia	26,722	5.3	0.5	43	16	41	90	32	2,622	0.5	93.6	9.0
Congo, Dem. Rep.	21,816c	0.4	0.0c	23e	16e	61e	89	26			101.9	4.5
Congo, Rep.	307,283c	0.0	0.0c	11e	27e	62e	..	11	416	0.2	15.4	4.5
Costa Rica	27,425	1.4d	1.4	89	7	4	100	99	414	3.0	7.0	13.7
Côte d'Ivoire	5,468	0.7	0.9	67e	11e	22e	..	..	308	0.6	19.9	6.3
Croatia	12,879	..	..	..	..	..	75	41	0	0.0	3.7	6.6
Czech Republic	5,649	2.7	4.7	2	57	41	..	..	−2	0.0	12.2	15.8
Denmark	2,460c	1.2	9.2c	43	27	30	..	..	0	0.0	13.7	32.3
Dominican Republic	2,467	3.0	14.9	89	6	5	88	55	264	1.6	12.2	25.2
Ecuador	26,305	5.6	1.8	90	3	7	81	10	1,890	1.6	119.3	43.1
Egypt, Arab Rep.	966c	55.1	94.5c	86e	8e	6e	95	*74*	0	0.0	7.9	0.8
El Salvador	3,197	1.0d	5.3	89	4	7	82	24	38	3.3	0.1	0.5
Eritrea	2,332c	..	..c	..	..	..	..	..	0	0.0	5.0	5.0
Estonia	12,071c	3.3	18.8c	3	92	5	..	..	−196	−1.0	5.1	12.1
Ethiopia	1,841	2.2	2.0	86e	3e	11e	..	..	624	0.5	55.2	5.5
Finland	21,985c	2.2	1.9c	3	85	12	..	..	166	0.1	18.2	6.0
France	3,029c	37.7	21.3c	15	69	16	100	100	−1,608	−1.1	58.8	10.7
Georgia	8,291c	4.0	8.9c	42	37	21	..	..	0	0.0	1.9	2.7
Germany	2,084c	46.3	27.1c	20	70	11	..	..	0	0.0	94.2	27.0
Ghana	2,958c	0.3d	0.6c	52e	13e	35e	*88*	*52*	1,172	1.3	11.0	4.8
Greece	5,289c	5.0	9.1c	63	29	8	..	..	−1,408	−2.3	3.1	2.4
Guatemala	11,028	0.7d	0.6	74	17	9	97	48	824	2.0	18.2	16.8
Guinea	32,661	0.7	0.3	87e	3e	10e	55	44	748	1.1	1.6	0.7
Haiti	1,468	0.0	0.4	68	8	24	38	39	8	3.4	0.1	0.4
Honduras	9,259c	1.5	2.7c	91	5	4	91	66	1,022	2.3	11.1	9.9
Hungary	11,817c	6.8	5.7c	36	55	9	..	..	−88	−0.5	6.3	6.8
India	2,167c	380.0d	18.2c	93	4	3	..	82	−72	0.0	142.9	4.8
Indonesia	12,625	16.6	0.7	76	11	13	87	57	10,844	1.0	192.3	10.6
Iran, Islamic Rep.	1,339c	70.0d	85.8c	92	2	6	98	82	284	1.7	83.0	5.1
Ireland	13,657c	0.8d	1.6c	10	74	16	..	..	−140	−2.7	0.6	0.9
Israel	377c	1.9	84.1c	79e	5e	16e	100	95	0	0.0	3.1	15.0
Italy	2,903c	56.2	33.7c	59	27	14	..	..	−58	−0.1	21.5	7.3
Jamaica	3,250	0.3d	3.9	86	7	7	..	..	158	7.2	0.0	0.0
Japan	4,338	90.8	16.6	50	33	17	..	..	132	0.1	25.5	6.8
Jordan	198c	0.5d	51.1c	75	3	22	..	..	12	2.5	3.0	3.4
Kazakhstan	8,696c	37.9	27.6c	79	17	4	..	..	−1,928	−1.9	73.4	2.7
Kenya	1,056c	2.1	6.8c	76e	4e	20e	..	..	34	0.3	35.0	6.1
Korea, Rep.	1,438	27.6	41.7	46	35	19	93	77	130	0.2	6.8	6.9
Kuwait	11	0.5	2,700.0	60	2	37	100	100	0	0.0	0.3	1.7
Kyrgyz Republic	2,509	11.0	94.9	95	3	2	..	..	0	0.0	6.9	3.6
Lao PDR	55,679	1.0	0.4	82	10	8	..	..	..	..	0.0	0.0
Latvia	13,793c	0.7	2.1c	14	44	42	*92*	..	−250	−0.9	7.8	12.6
Lebanon	941c	1.3e,d	33.1c	68	4	28	..	..	52	7.8	0.0	0.0
Lesotho	2,597	0.1	1.0	56e	22e	22e	64	60	0	0.0	0.1	0.3
Lithuania	6,531c	4.4	18.2c	3	90	7	..	..	−112	−0.6	6.5	10.0
Macedonia, FYR	..	..	..	..	..	..	..	..	2	0.0	1.8	7.1
Madagascar	23,819	16.3	4.8	99e	0e	1e	..	..	1,300	0.8	11.2	1.9
Malawi	1,814c	0.9	4.8c	86e	3e	10e	*97*	*52*	546	1.6	10.6	11.3
Malaysia	21,046	9.4d	2.1	47	30	23	100	86	4,002	2.4	14.8	4.5

Note: For data comparability and coverage, see the Technical Notes. Figures in italics are for years other than those specified.

ENVIRONMENT

Economy	Freshwater resources Cu. meters per capita 1996	Annual freshwater withdrawals Billion cu. m[a]	% of total resources[a]	% for agriculture[b]	% for industry[b]	% for domestic use[b]	Access to safe water % of population with access 1995 Urban	Rural	Annual deforestation 1990–95 Square kilometers	Avg. annual % change	Nationally protected areas 1996 Thousand square km	% of total land area
Mali	9,718[c]	1.4	1.4[c]	97[c]	1[e]	2[e]	56	20	1,138	1.0	45.3	3.7
Mauritania	4,632[c]	1.6[d]	14.3[c]	92	2	6	87	41	0	0.0	17.5	1.7
Mexico	3,788	77.6[d]	21.7	86	8	6	..	..	5,080	0.9	71.0	3.7
Moldova	397[c]	3.7	216.4[c]	23	70	7	98	18	0	0.0	0.4	1.2
Mongolia	9,677	0.6	2.2	62	27	11	100	68	0	0.0	161.3	10.3
Morocco	1,088	10.9	36.5	92[c]	3[c]	5[c]	97	20	118	0.3	3.2	0.7
Mozambique	12,989[c]	0.6	0.3[c]	89	2[c]	9[c]	..	40	1,162	0.7	47.8	6.1
Myanmar	24,651	4.0	0.4	90	3	7	78	50	3,874	1.4	1.7	0.3
Namibia	28,042[c]	0.3	0.5[c]	68[e]	3[e]	29[e]	..	..	420	0.3	106.2	12.9
Nepal	7,616	2.7	1.6	95	1	4	61	59	548	1.1	11.1	7.8
Netherlands	5,767[c]	7.8	8.7[c]	34	61	5	..	..	0	0.0	2.4	7.1
New Zealand	532	2.0	100.0	44	10	46	..	..	−434	−0.6	63.3	23.6
Nicaragua	37,420	0.9[d]	0.5	54	21	25	93	28	1,508	2.5	9.0	7.4
Niger	3,317[c]	0.5	1.5[c]	82[e]	2[e]	16[e]	70	44	0	0.0	96.9	7.6
Nigeria	2,375[c]	3.6	1.3[c]	54[e]	15[e]	31[e]	80	39	1,214	0.9	30.2	3.3
Norway	89,008[c]	2.0	0.5[c]	8	72	20	100	100	−180	−0.2	93.7	30.5
Pakistan	3,256[c]	155.6[d]	37.2[c]	97	2	2	85	56	550	2.9	37.2	4.8
Panama	52,961	1.3	0.9	77	11	12	99	73	636	2.1	14.2	19.1
Papua New Guinea	177,963	0.1	0.0	49	22	29	..	..	1,332	0.4	0.1	0.0
Paraguay	61,750[c]	0.4	0.1[c]	78	7	15	70	6	3,266	2.6	14.0	3.5
Peru	1,641	6.1	15.3	72	9	19	91	31	2,168	0.3	34.6	2.7
Philippines	4,393	29.5[d]	9.1	61	21	18	91	81	2,624	3.5	14.5	4.9
Poland	1,454[c]	12.3	21.9[c]	11	76	13	..	..	−120	−0.1	29.1	9.6
Portugal	6,998[c]	7.3	10.5[c]	48	37	15	..	..	−240	−0.9	5.9	6.4
Romania	9,222[c]	26.0	12.5[c]	59	33	8	..	..	12	0.0	10.7	4.6
Russian Federation	30,168[c]	117.0	2.6[c]	23	60	17	..	..	0	0.0	516.7	3.1
Rwanda	798	0.8	12.2	94[e]	2[e]	5[e]	79	44	4	0.2	3.6	14.6
Saudi Arabia	120	17.0[d]	709.2	90	1	9	..	..	18	0.8	49.6	2.3
Senegal	4,482[c]	1.4	3.5[c]	92[e]	3[e]	5[e]	90	44	496	0.7	21.8	11.3
Sierra Leone	33,698	0.4	0.2	89[e]	4[e]	7[e]	58	21	426	3.0	0.8	1.1
Singapore	193	0.2[d]	31.7	4	51	45	..	..	0	0.0	0.0	0.0
Slovak Republic	5,720	1.8	5.8	..	..	..	..	..	−24	−0.1	10.5	21.8
Slovenia	..	..	..	..	..	..	..	..	0	0.0	1.1	5.5
South Africa	1,231[c]	13.3	26.6[c]	72[e]	11[e]	17[e]	90	33	150	0.2	65.8	5.4
Spain	2,398[c]	30.8	32.6[c]	62	26	12	..	..	0	0.0	42.2	8.4
Sri Lanka	2,329	6.3[d]	14.6	96	2	2	88	65	202	1.1	8.6	13.3
Sweden	20,340[c]	2.9	1.6[c]	9	55	36	..	..	24	0.0	36.2	8.8
Switzerland	7,054[c]	1.2	2.4[c]	4	73	23	100	100	0	0.0	7.1	18.0
Syrian Arab Republic	859[c]	14.4	112.6[c]	94	2	4	96	79	52	2.2	0.0	0.0
Tajikistan	..	12.6	..	88	7	5	..	..	0	0.0	5.9	4.2
Tanzania	2,842[c]	1.2	1.3[c]	89[e]	2[e]	9[e]	..	..	3,226	1.0	138.2	15.6
Thailand	2,954[c]	31.9	17.8[c]	90	6	4	94	88	3,294	2.6	70.7	13.8
Togo	2,762[c]	0.1	0.8[c]	25[e]	13[e]	62[e]	82	41	186	1.4	4.3	7.9
Tunisia	447[c]	3.1	74.5[c]	89[e]	3[e]	9[e]	100	76	30	0.5	0.4	0.3
Turkey	2,246[c]	31.6	22.1[c]	72[e]	11[e]	16[e]	..	..	0	0.0	10.7	1.4
Turkmenistan	3,950[c]	22.8	123.9[c]	91	8	1	..	..	0	0.0	19.8	4.2
Uganda	3,248[c]	0.2	0.3[c]	60	8	32	60	36	592	0.9	19.1	9.6
Ukraine	4,556[c]	34.7	15.0[c]	30	54	16	..	..	−54	−0.1	9.0	1.6
United Kingdom	1,203	11.8	16.6	3	77	20	100	100	−128	−0.5	50.6	20.9
United States	9,259[c]	467.3	18.9[c]	42[e]	45[e]	13[e]	..	..	−5,886	−0.3	1,226.7	13.4
Uruguay	37,966[c]	0.7[d]	0.5[c]	91	3	6	99	..	4	0.0	0.5	0.3
Uzbekistan	5,476[c]	82.2	63.4[c]	84	12	4	..	..	−2,260	−2.7	8.2	2.0
Venezuela	57,821[c]	4.1[d]	0.3[c]	46	11	43	79	79	5,034	1.1	319.8	36.3
Vietnam	4,902	28.9	7.7	78	9	13	..	..	1,352	1.4	9.9	3.0
Yemen, Rep.	255	2.9	71.5	92	..	..	74	14	0	0.0	0.0	0.0
Zambia	12,284[c]	1.7	1.5[c]	77[e]	7[e]	16[e]	66	37	2,644	0.8	63.6	8.6
Zimbabwe	1,744[c]	1.2	6.1[c]	79[e]	7[e]	14[e]	..	..	500	0.6	30.7	7.9
World	**8,338 w**			**69 w**	**22 w**	**9 w**	**.. w**	**.. w**	**101,724 s**	**0.3 w**	**8,542.7 s**	**6.6 w**
Low income	5,214			90	5	5	..	..	49,332	0.7	2,439.4	5.9
Excl. China & India	..			..	..	..	..	..	..	..	..	..
Middle income	14,950			67	22	11	..	..	64,086	0.3	2,809.9	4.8
Lower middle income	11,573			67	24	9	..	..	21,162	0.2	1,563.6	4.3
Upper middle income	..			68	19	13	..	..	42,924	0.5	1,246.3	5.7
Low and middle income	8,095			80	13	7	..	..	113,418	0.4	5,249.3	5.3
East Asia & Pacific	..			82	10	8	..	..	29,956	0.8	1,102.2	6.9
Europe & Central Asia	13,255			54	36	10	..	..	−5,798	−0.1	768.0	3.2
Latin America & Carib.	27,386			77	11	12	83	36	57,766	0.6	1,456.3	7.3
Middle East & N. Africa	1,045			90	4	6	..	..	800	0.9	242.0	2.2
South Asia	4,085			94	3	3	84	84	1,316	0.2	213.0	4.5
Sub-Saharan Africa	8,565			85	4	10	74	32	29,378	0.7	1,467.8	6.2
High income	..			39	46	15	..	..	−11,694	−0.2	3,293.4	10.8

a. Refers to any year from 1980 to 1997, unless otherwise noted. b. Unless otherwise noted, percentages are estimated for 1987. c. Includes river flows from other countries. d. Data refer to estimates for years before 1980 (see *World Development Indicators*, 1999). e. Data refer to years other than 1987 (see *World Development Indicators*, 1999).

Table 10. Energy use and emissions

Economy	Commercial energy use — Thousand metric tons of oil equivalent 1980	1996	Per capita Kg of oil equivalent 1980	1996	Avg. annual % growth 1980–96	GDP per unit of energy use 1995 $ per kg 1980	1996	Net energy imports % of commercial energy use 1980	1996	Carbon dioxide emissions Total Million metric tons 1980	1996	Per capita Metric tons 1980	1996
Albania	3,049	1,188	1,142	362	–7.8	0.8	2.2	–12	9	4.8	1.9	1.8	0.6
Algeria	12,410	24,150	665	842	1.0	2.5	1.8	–440	–381	66.2	94.3	3.5	3.3
Angola	4,538	6,017	647	532	–1.2	..	0.9	–149	–573	5.3	5.1	0.8	0.5
Argentina	41,868	58,921	1,490	1,673	0.7	5.7	5.0	7	–27	107.5	129.9	3.8	3.7
Armenia	1,070	1,790	346	474	–4.9	5.2	1.7	–18	59	..	3.7	..	1.0
Australia	70,372	100,612	4,790	5,494	0.9	3.3	3.7	–22	–88	202.8	306.6	13.8	16.7
Austria	23,450	27,187	3,105	3,373	0.9	7.1	8.7	67	71	52.2	59.3	6.9	7.4
Azerbaijan	15,002	11,862	2,433	1,570	–5.6	..	0.3	1	–21	..	30.0	..	4.0
Bangladesh	14,920	23,928	172	197	0.9	1.3	1.7	11	10	7.6	23.0	0.1	0.2
Belarus	2,385	24,566	247	2,386	7.5	..	0.8	–8	87	..	61.7	..	6.0
Belgium	46,100	56,399	4,682	5,552	1.4	4.6	4.9	84	79	127.2	106.0	12.9	10.4
Benin	1,363	1,920	394	341	–1.0	0.9	1.1	11	–2	0.5	0.7	0.1	0.1
Bolivia	2,335	3,633	436	479	0.0	2.3	1.9	–84	–44	4.5	10.1	0.8	1.3
Botswana	..	..	..	..	..	..	..	..	..	1.0	2.1	1.1	1.4
Brazil	108,997	163,374	896	1,012	1.0	4.7	4.4	43	31	183.4	273.4	1.5	1.7
Bulgaria	28,673	22,605	3,235	2,705	–2.0	0.4	0.5	73	54	75.3	55.3	8.5	6.6
Burkina Faso	..	..	..	..	..	..	..	..	..	0.4	1.0	0.1	0.1
Burundi	..	..	..	..	..	..	..	..	..	0.1	0.2	0.0	0.0
Cambodia	..	..	..	..	..	..	..	..	..	0.3	0.5	0.0	0.0
Cameroon	3,687	5,000	426	369	–1.1	1.7	1.7	–58	–100	3.9	3.5	0.4	0.3
Canada	193,000	236,170	7,848	7,880	0.3	2.1	2.5	–7	–51	420.9	409.4	17.1	13.7
Central African Republic	..	..	..	..	..	..	..	..	..	0.1	0.2	0.0	0.1
Chad	..	..	..	..	..	..	..	..	..	0.2	0.1	0.0	0.0
Chile	9,525	20,456	855	1,419	3.7	2.8	3.1	41	62	27.9	48.8	2.5	3.4
China	593,109	1,096,800	604	902	2.6	0.3	0.7	–3	0	1,476.8	3,363.5	1.5	2.8
Hong Kong, China	5,681	12,190	1,127	1,931	4.4	10.0	12.0	99	100	16.3	23.1	3.2	3.7
Colombia	19,127	31,393	672	799	1.0	2.4	2.6	5	–113	39.8	65.3	1.4	1.7
Congo, Dem. Rep.	8,706	13,799	322	305	–0.2	1.0	0.5	0	1	3.5	2.3	0.1	0.1
Congo, Rep.	845	1,205	506	457	–0.6	1.5	1.9	–370	–854	0.4	5.0	0.2	1.9
Costa Rica	1,527	2,248	669	657	0.7	3.7	4.0	50	67	2.5	4.7	1.1	1.4
Côte d'Ivoire	3,662	5,301	447	382	–0.6	2.3	2.0	34	10	4.6	13.1	0.6	0.9
Croatia	..	6,765	..	1,418	..	..	2.8	..	42	..	17.5	..	3.7
Czech Republic	46,910	40,404	4,585	3,917	–1.7	..	1.3	9	22	..	126.7	..	12.3
Denmark	19,734	22,870	3,852	4,346	0.8	6.8	8.2	95	23	62.9	56.6	12.3	10.7
Dominican Republic	3,464	5,191	608	652	0.1	2.2	2.5	62	72	6.4	12.9	1.1	1.6
Ecuador	5,191	8,548	652	731	0.2	2.4	2.1	–126	–156	13.4	24.5	1.7	2.1
Egypt, Arab Rep.	15,970	37,790	391	638	2.6	1.8	1.6	–114	–58	45.2	97.9	1.1	1.7
El Salvador	2,540	4,058	554	700	1.0	2.9	2.4	25	36	2.1	4.0	0.5	0.7
Eritrea	..	..	..	..	..	..	..	..	..	..	..	..	..
Estonia	..	5,621	..	3,834	..	..	0.9	..	31	..	16.4	..	11.2
Ethiopia	11,157	16,566	296	284	–0.1	*0.4*	0.4	5	6	1.8	3.4	0.0	0.1
Finland	25,413	31,482	5,316	6,143	1.1	3.7	4.1	73	57	54.9	59.2	11.5	11.5
France	190,111	254,196	3,528	4,355	1.6	6.1	6.1	76	49	482.7	361.8	9.0	6.2
Georgia	4,474	1,576	882	291	–5.8	2.7	2.1	–5	55	..	3.0	..	0.5
Germany	360,441	349,552	4,603	4,267	–0.5	..	7.0	48	60	..	861.2	..	10.5
Ghana	4,071	6,657	379	380	0.4	1.0	1.0	19	16	2.4	4.0	0.2	0.2
Greece	15,960	24,389	1,655	2,328	2.5	5.7	4.8	77	64	51.7	80.6	5.4	7.7
Guatemala	3,754	5,224	550	510	0.0	2.9	2.9	33	23	4.5	6.8	0.7	0.7
Guinea	..	..	..	..	..	..	..	..	..	0.9	1.1	0.2	0.2
Haiti	2,099	1,968	392	268	–2.8	1.5	1.4	11	19	0.8	1.1	0.1	0.1
Honduras	1,877	2,925	526	503	–0.2	1.4	1.4	30	40	2.1	4.0	0.6	0.7
Hungary	28,895	25,470	2,699	2,499	–0.8	1.6	1.8	48	50	82.5	59.5	7.7	5.8
India	242,024	450,287	352	476	1.9	0.6	0.8	8	13	347.3	997.4	0.5	1.1
Indonesia	59,561	132,419	402	672	3.5	1.3	1.6	–116	–66	94.6	245.1	0.6	1.2
Iran, Islamic Rep.	38,918	89,340	995	1,491	3.2	1.4	*1.1*	–116	–147	116.1	266.7	3.0	4.4
Ireland	8,484	11,961	2,495	3,293	2.0	4.0	5.9	78	71	25.2	34.9	7.4	9.6
Israel	8,609	16,185	2,220	2,843	2.6	5.1	5.6	98	96	21.1	52.3	5.4	9.2
Italy	138,629	161,140	2,456	2,808	1.3	6.0	6.8	86	82	371.9	403.2	6.6	7.0
Jamaica	2,378	3,718	1,115	1,465	2.3	1.3	1.1	91	85	8.4	10.1	4.0	4.0
Japan	346,491	510,359	2,967	4,058	2.4	9.3	10.5	88	80	920.4	1,167.7	7.9	9.3
Jordan	1,714	4,487	786	1,040	0.6	2.2	1.5	100	96	..	..	..	..
Kazakhstan	76,799	43,376	5,163	2,724	–4.9	..	0.5	0	–44	..	173.8	..	10.9
Kenya	9,791	13,279	589	476	–1.1	0.6	0.7	19	15	6.2	6.8	0.4	0.2
Korea, Rep.	43,756	162,874	1,148	3,576	8.1	3.1	3.0	72	86	125.2	408.1	3.3	9.0
Kuwait	9,564	13,859	6,956	8,167	0.7	2.4	*1.7*	–884	–712	..	..	..	..
Kyrgyz Republic	1,717	2,952	473	645	4.1	..	1.2	–27	51	..	6.1	..	1.3
Lao PDR	..	..	..	..	..	..	..	..	..	0.2	0.3	0.1	0.1
Latvia	..	4,171	..	1,674	..	16.0	1.5	54	76	..	9.3	..	3.7
Lebanon	2,483	4,747	827	1,164	1.7	..	..	93	96	6.2	14.2	2.1	3.5
Lesotho	..	..	..	..	..	..	..	..	..	..	..	..	..
Lithuania	11,701	8,953	3,428	2,414	–4.0	..	0.8	95	53	..	13.8	..	3.7
Macedonia, FYR	..	..	..	..	..	..	..	..	..	..	12.7	..	6.4
Madagascar	..	..	..	..	..	..	..	..	..	1.6	1.2	0.2	0.1
Malawi	..	..	..	..	..	..	..	..	..	0.7	0.7	0.1	0.1
Malaysia	11,128	41,209	809	1,950	6.0	2.9	2.3	–50	–69	28.0	119.1	2.0	5.6

Note: For data comparability and coverage, see the Technical Notes. Figures in italics are for years other than those specified.

ENVIRONMENT

Economy	Commercial energy use — Thousand metric tons of oil equivalent 1980	1996	Per capita — Kg of oil equivalent 1980	1996	Avg. annual % growth 1980–96	GDP per unit of energy use 1995 $ per kg 1980	1996	Net energy imports % of commercial energy use 1980	1996	Carbon dioxide emissions — Total Million metric tons 1980	1996	Per capita Metric tons 1980	1996
Mali	..	..	..	..	..	..	..	..	..	0.4	0.5	0.1	0.0
Mauritania	..	..	..	..	..	..	..	..	..	0.6	2.9	0.4	1.2
Mexico	98,904	141,384	1,464	1,525	0.2	2.3	2.1	−51	−51	251.6	348.1	3.7	3.8
Moldova	..	4,601	..	1,064	..	..	0.6	106	99	..	12.1	..	2.8
Mongolia	..	..	..	..	..	..	..	..	..	6.8	8.9	4.1	3.6
Morocco	4,778	8,822	247	329	2.1	4.5	4.2	82	90	15.9	27.9	0.8	1.0
Mozambique	8,386	7,813	693	481	−2.0	0.2	0.3	−2	7	3.2	1.0	0.3	0.1
Myanmar	9,430	12,767	279	294	0.3	..	..	−1	7	4.8	7.3	0.1	0.2
Namibia	..	..	..	..	..	..	..	..	..	..	..	..	..
Nepal	4,663	6,974	322	320	0.1	0.5	0.7	3	9	0.5	1.6	0.0	0.1
Netherlands	65,000	75,797	4,594	4,885	0.9	4.4	5.4	−11	3	152.6	155.2	10.8	10.0
New Zealand	9,251	16,295	2,972	4,388	2.9	4.7	3.8	41	17	17.6	29.8	5.6	8.0
Nicaragua	1,562	2,391	535	525	−0.1	1.3	1.0	42	37	2.0	2.9	0.7	0.6
Niger	..	..	..	..	..	..	..	..	..	0.6	1.1	0.1	0.1
Nigeria	52,846	82,669	743	722	−0.1	0.4	0.4	−181	−106	68.1	83.3	1.0	0.7
Norway	18,819	23,150	4,600	5,284	1.2	5.1	6.7	−196	−799	90.4	67.0	22.1	15.3
Pakistan	25,479	55,903	308	446	2.3	1.0	1.1	18	26	31.6	94.3	0.4	0.8
Panama	1,865	2,280	957	853	−0.3	2.8	3.6	72	67	3.5	6.7	1.8	2.5
Papua New Guinea	..	..	..	..	..	..	..	..	..	1.8	2.4	0.6	0.5
Paraguay	2,094	4,285	672	865	1.5	2.8	2.1	23	−56	1.5	3.7	0.5	0.7
Peru	11,700	13,933	675	582	−1.2	4.1	4.3	−25	11	23.6	26.2	1.4	1.1
Philippines	21,212	37,992	439	528	1.1	2.7	2.1	50	55	36.5	63.2	0.8	0.9
Poland	124,806	108,411	3,508	2,807	−2.0	0.9	1.2	2	6	456.2	356.8	12.8	9.2
Portugal	10,291	19,148	1,054	1,928	4.5	6.8	5.6	86	87	27.1	47.9	2.8	4.8
Romania	64,694	45,824	2,914	2,027	−2.9	0.6	0.7	19	32	191.8	119.3	8.6	5.3
Russian Federation	764,349	615,899	5,499	4,169	−3.6	0.5	0.5	2	−54	..	1,579.5	..	10.7
Rwanda	..	..	..	..	..	..	..	..	..	0.3	0.5	0.1	0.1
Saudi Arabia	35,357	92,243	3,773	4,753	0.4	3.0	1.4	−1,408	−415	130.7	267.8	14.0	13.8
Senegal	1,921	2,588	347	302	−0.7	1.6	1.8	46	39	2.8	3.1	0.5	0.4
Sierra Leone	..	..	..	..	..	..	..	..	..	0.6	0.4	0.2	0.1
Singapore	6,054	23,851	2,653	7,835	8.1	4.6	3.8	*100*	100	30.1	65.8	13.2	21.6
Slovak Republic	20,810	17,449	4,175	3,266	−1.8	..	1.1	84	72	..	39.6	..	7.4
Slovenia	4,313	6,167	2,269	3,098	1.0	..	3.1	62	55	..	13.0	..	6.5
South Africa	65,355	99,079	2,370	2,482	−0.4	1.7	1.4	−12	−29	211.3	292.7	7.7	7.3
Spain	68,583	101,411	1,834	2,583	2.8	5.7	5.6	77	68	200.0	232.5	5.3	5.9
Sri Lanka	4,493	6,792	305	371	0.7	1.5	2.0	29	38	3.4	7.1	0.2	0.4
Sweden	40,984	52,567	4,932	5,944	0.9	4.5	4.5	61	39	71.4	54.1	8.6	6.1
Switzerland	20,861	25,622	3,301	3,622	0.8	12.1	12.0	66	59	40.9	44.2	6.5	6.3
Syrian Arab Republic	5,348	14,541	614	1,002	2.4	1.7	1.2	−78	−132	19.3	44.3	2.2	3.1
Tajikistan	1,650	3,513	416	594	5.1	..	0.5	−20	62	..	5.8	..	1.0
Tanzania	10,280	13,798	553	453	−1.1	..	0.3	8	5	1.9	2.4	0.1	0.1
Thailand	22,740	79,987	487	1,333	7.3	2.3	2.2	51	45	40.0	205.4	0.9	3.4
Togo	..	..	..	..	..	..	..	..	..	0.6	0.8	0.2	0.2
Tunisia	3,900	6,676	611	735	1.4	2.7	2.9	−79	6	9.4	16.2	1.5	1.8
Turkey	31,314	65,520	704	1,045	2.6	2.8	2.8	45	59	76.3	178.3	1.7	2.8
Turkmenistan	7,948	12,164	2,778	2,646	−10.5	..	0.3	−1	−168	..	34.2	..	7.4
Uganda	..	..	..	..	..	..	..	..	..	0.6	1.0	0.1	0.1
Ukraine	97,893	153,937	1,956	3,012	1.0	..	0.5	−12	49	..	397.3	..	7.8
United Kingdom	201,299	234,719	3,574	3,992	0.8	4.0	4.8	2	−14	583.8	557.0	10.4	9.5
United States	1,811,650	2,134,960	7,973	8,051	0.4	2.7	3.4	14	21	4,575.4	5,301.0	20.1	20.0
Uruguay	2,637	2,955	905	912	0.2	5.8	6.4	75	65	5.8	5.6	2.0	1.7
Uzbekistan	4,821	42,406	302	1,826	7.0	..	0.5	4	−12	..	95.0	..	4.1
Venezuela	35,026	54,962	2,321	2,463	−0.4	1.7	1.4	−280	−253	89.6	144.5	5.9	6.5
Vietnam	19,348	33,750	360	448	0.7	..	0.7	7	−14	16.8	37.6	0.3	0.5
Yemen, Rep.	1,424	2,936	167	187	0.6	..	1.3	96	−519	..	..	..	..
Zambia	4,551	5,790	793	628	−1.7	0.7	0.6	8	7	3.5	2.4	0.6	0.3
Zimbabwe	6,511	10,442	929	929	0.3	0.7	0.7	13	16	9.6	18.4	1.4	1.6
World	**6,954,847 t**	**9,317,404 t**	**1,622 w**	**1,684 w**	**2.9 w**	**3.1 w**	**3.2 w**	**.. w**	**.. w**	**13,640.7 t**	**22,653.9 t**	**3.4 w**	**4.0 w**
Low income	1,153,366	2,063,558	480	640	3.9	..	..	−14	−9	2,126.1	5,051.8	0.9	1.5
Excl. China & India	318,233	516,471	433	486	3.7	..	0.8	..	..	302.0	690.9	0.4	0.6
Middle income	2,030,275	2,588,365	1,852	1,801	5.0	2.4	1.7	−35	−33	2,804.5	6,871.5	3.3	4.8
Lower middle income	1,368,743	1,537,541	2,040	1,763	7.4	1.7	1.0	−13	−20	1,150.1	4,194.9	2.6	4.8
Upper middle income	661,532	1,050,824	1,557	1,861	2.8	2.8	2.6	−98	−65	1,654.4	2,676.6	4.0	4.7
Low and middle income	3,183,641	4,651,923	910	998	4.5	1.4	1.3	−32	−28	4,930.6	11,923.3	1.5	2.5
East Asia & Pacific	812,075	1,621,801	588	925	4.6	..	..	..	..	1,958.5	4,717.5	1.4	2.7
Europe & Central Asia	1,339,527	1,287,193	3,349	2,739	7.6	..	0.8	7	−13	886.9	3,412.7	..	7.4
Latin America & Carib.	376,913	557,686	1,062	1,163	2.4	3.5	3.2	−24	−35	848.5	1,209.1	2.4	2.5
Middle East & N. Africa	146,215	337,073	842	1,244	5.1	2.2	1.6	−577	−225	493.6	986.9	3.0	3.9
South Asia	301,578	543,884	334	441	3.9	0.7	0.9	10	15	392.4	1,125.1	0.4	0.9
Sub-Saharan Africa	207,332	304,286	720	670	2.3	..	..	..	..	350.7	472.1	0.9	0.8
High income	3,771,206	4,665,482	4,792	5,346	1.6	4.1	5.0	27	24	8,710.2	10,730.6	12.3	12.3

Table 11. Growth of the economy

	Average annual % growth												
	Gross domestic product		GDP implicit deflator		Agriculture value added		Industry value added		Services value added		Exports of goods and services		Gross domestic investment
Economy	1980–90	1990–98	1980–90	1990–98	1980–90	1990–98	1980–90	1990–98	1980–90	1990–98	1980–90	1990–98	1990–98
Albania	1.5	1.8	–0.4	58.1	1.9	8.1	2.1	–9.7	–0.4	4.7	..	18.3	26.9
Algeria	2.7	1.2	8.1	21.4	4.6	2.6	2.3	–2.0	3.6	4.8	4.1	3.0	–0.8
Angola	3.7	–0.4	5.9	921.1	0.5	–4.3	6.4	3.6	1.8	–5.7	3.7	5.9	12.6
Argentina	–0.4	5.3	389.8	10.0	0.7	2.1	–1.3	4.6	0.0	3.9	3.8	9.3	12.5
Armenia	..	–10.3	..	482.8	..	0.2	..	–18.1	..	–10.8	..	2.3	–10.9
Australia	3.4	3.6	7.3	1.8	3.3	1.1	2.9	2.5	3.7	4.4	6.9	8.1	5.4
Austria	2.2	2.0	3.3	2.5	1.1	–0.7	1.9	1.3	2.5	2.2	4.9	4.0	2.6
Azerbaijan	..	–10.5	..	316.5	..	–2.7	..	4.2	..	9.9	..	19.5	108.8
Bangladesh	4.3	4.8	9.5	3.6	2.7	1.5	4.9	7.0	5.0	5.2	7.7	13.7	7.0
Belarus	..	–6.1	..	561.4	..	–5.9	..	–7.8	..	–3.8	..	–23.3	–12.2
Belgium	2.0	1.6	4.4	2.3	2.0	1.6	2.2	0.7	1.8	1.3	4.3	4.4	–0.3
Benin	2.9	4.6	1.3	10.1	5.5	5.2	3.0	4.0	1.4	4.3	–2.4	3.3	4.6
Bolivia	–0.2	4.2	327.9	10.0	..	..	..	..	..	..	1.0	6.7	6.9
Botswana	10.3	4.8	13.6	10.3	3.3	0.1	10.2	3.1	11.7	7.1	10.6	4.9	2.0
Brazil	2.7	3.3	284.0	347.3	2.8	3.1	2.0	3.2	3.3	3.4	7.5	5.6	3.9
Bulgaria	3.4	–3.3	1.8	109.5	–2.1	–3.1	5.2	–5.5	4.5	–0.6	–3.5	2.3	–12.8
Burkina Faso	3.6	3.5	3.3	6.6	3.1	3.4	3.8	3.1	4.6	3.2	–0.4	–0.8	4.1
Burundi	4.4	–3.2	4.4	12.2	3.1	–2.4	4.5	–7.8	5.6	–2.9	3.4	0.1	–16.1
Cambodia	..	5.5	..	37.8	..	2.2	..	10.7	..	7.6	..	..	..
Cameroon	3.4	0.6	5.6	6.1	2.1	5.0	5.9	–3.3	2.1	0.0	5.9	–1.5	–1.6
Canada	3.3	2.2	4.5	1.6	1.2	1.2	3.1	1.8	3.6	1.8	6.3	9.0	1.5
Central African Republic	1.4	1.5	7.9	5.4	1.6	3.5	1.4	0.2	1.0	–1.3	–1.2	14.3	–5.4
Chad	3.7	4.6	2.9	7.3	2.3	5.4	8.1	0.0	7.7	–0.5	6.5	3.7	18.6
Chile	4.2	7.9	20.7	9.4	5.9	5.2	3.5	6.8	2.9	7.7	6.9	9.8	13.9
China	10.2	11.1	5.9	9.8	5.9	4.3	11.1	15.4	13.7	9.3	11.5	14.9	13.4
Hong Kong, China	6.9	4.4	7.7	6.4	..	..	..	..	..	..	14.4	9.5	8.9
Colombia	3.6	4.2	24.8	21.7	2.9	1.6	5.0	2.9	2.8	4.9	7.5	6.8	13.6
Congo, Dem. Rep.	1.6	–5.1	62.9	1,423.1	2.5	2.9	0.9	–11.7	1.3	–15.2	9.6	–5.5	–3.5
Congo, Rep.	3.3	1.0	0.5	7.1	3.4	1.6	5.2	0.2	2.1	1.4	5.1	4.9	4.1
Costa Rica	3.0	3.7	23.6	17.4	3.1	2.8	2.8	3.3	3.1	4.3	6.1	8.7	2.8
Côte d'Ivoire	0.7	3.5	2.8	8.7	0.3	2.4	4.4	5.1	–0.3	3.5	1.9	4.5	18.0
Croatia	..	–1.0	..	218.1	..	–4.4	..	–8.2	..	–3.9	..	0.9	1.2
Czech Republic	1.7	–0.2	1.5	17.1	..	..	..	..	..	..	..	7.0	5.0
Denmark	2.3	2.8	5.6	1.7	3.1	1.7	2.9	1.9	2.6	1.4	4.3	3.7	0.1
Dominican Republic	3.1	5.5	21.6	10.6	0.4	3.6	3.6	6.1	3.5	5.6	4.5	20.4	11.8
Ecuador	2.0	2.9	36.4	32.7	4.4	2.7	1.2	3.7	1.7	2.5	5.4	4.4	4.2
Egypt, Arab Rep.	5.4	4.2	13.7	9.7	2.7	2.9	5.2	4.2	6.6	4.1	5.2	4.3	4.2
El Salvador	0.2	5.3	16.3	9.1	–1.1	1.3	0.1	5.4	0.7	6.3	–3.4	13.2	7.7
Eritrea	..	5.2	..	10.1	..	..	..	..	..	..	..	4.7	..
Estonia	2.2	–2.1	2.3	75.5	..	–4.3	..	–5.9	..	0.5	..	..	–3.6
Ethiopia[a]	1.1	4.9	4.6	7.9	0.2	2.8	0.4	6.5	3.1	6.4	2.4	9.0	15.4
Finland	3.3	2.0	6.8	1.8	–0.2	0.2	3.3	2.1	4.1	–0.1	2.2	9.2	–5.5
France	2.3	1.5	6.0	1.7	2.0	0.4	1.1	0.1	3.0	1.6	3.7	4.1	–2.0
Georgia	0.4	–16.3	1.9	1,033.2	..	..	..	..	..	..	..	..	..
Germany[b]	2.2	1.6	..	2.2	1.7	0.8	1.2	..	2.9	2.5	..	2.8	0.8
Ghana	3.0	4.2	42.1	28.6	1.0	2.8	3.3	4.4	5.7	5.6	2.5	10.2	2.8
Greece	1.8	2.0	18.0	10.6	–0.1	2.0	1.3	–0.5	2.7	1.8	7.2	4.0	3.4
Guatemala	0.8	4.2	14.6	11.5	1.2	2.2	–0.2	4.3	0.9	5.0	–1.8	7.2	3.7
Guinea	..	5.0	..	5.9	..	4.4	..	1.6	..	7.8	..	2.6	5.7
Haiti	–0.2	–2.5	7.5	25.3	–0.1	–4.9	–1.7	–2.7	0.9	–0.7	1.2	–4.4	1.8
Honduras	2.7	3.6	5.7	20.8	2.7	3.2	3.3	3.8	2.5	3.8	1.1	2.2	9.1
Hungary	1.3	–0.2	8.9	22.8	1.7	–3.8	0.2	1.1	2.1	0.3	3.6	4.9	7.3
India	5.8	6.1	8.0	7.5	3.1	3.4	7.0	6.7	6.9	7.9	5.9	12.4	5.9
Indonesia	6.1	5.8	8.5	12.5	3.4	2.8	6.9	9.9	7.0	7.2	2.9	8.6	4.4
Iran, Islamic Rep.	1.7	4.0	14.4	32.5	4.5	4.8	3.3	3.8	–1.0	6.0	6.9	2.4	–0.8
Ireland	3.2	7.5	6.6	1.9	..	..	..	..	..	..	9.0	12.6	1.9
Israel	3.5	5.4	101.1	10.9	..	..	..	..	..	..	5.5	8.6	8.9
Italy	2.4	1.2	10.0	4.4	0.1	1.3	2.0	0.8	2.8	1.1	4.1	7.5	–1.9
Jamaica	2.0	0.1	18.6	29.5	0.6	2.3	2.4	–0.4	1.8	0.2	5.4	0.0	6.0
Japan	4.0	1.3	1.7	0.4	1.3	–2.0	4.2	0.2	3.9	2.0	4.5	3.9	0.2
Jordan	2.5	5.4	4.3	3.3	6.8	–3.1	1.7	6.8	2.0	5.3	5.9	7.8	4.4
Kazakhstan	..	–6.9	..	329.9	..	–12.7	..	–10.2	..	2.1	..	–0.3	–15.3
Kenya	4.2	2.2	9.1	15.0	3.3	1.2	3.9	2.0	4.9	3.5	4.3	2.7	4.3
Korea, Rep.	9.4	6.2	6.1	5.1	2.8	2.1	12.1	7.5	9.0	7.8	12.0	15.7	6.3
Kuwait	1.3	..	–2.8	..	14.7	..	1.0	..	2.1	..	–2.3	..	..
Kyrgyz Republic	..	–7.3	..	157.8	..	–1.2	..	–12.0	..	–7.2	..	–1.8	8.6
Lao PDR	..	6.7	..	12.2	3.4	4.5	6.1	11.9	3.4	6.7	..	..	..
Latvia	3.5	–8.5	0.0	87.7	2.3	–10.8	4.3	–15.9	3.2	–0.2	..	–0.6	–25.1
Lebanon	..	7.7	..	24.0	..	3.2	..	2.1	..	2.6	..	15.6	18.4
Lesotho	4.4	7.2	13.8	7.7	2.2	6.0	7.1	9.2	4.6	6.2	4.1	11.1	11.1
Lithuania	..	–5.2	..	111.5	..	–1.4	..	–10.1	..	–0.4	..	..	..
Macedonia, FYR	..	–0.1	..	44.8	..	1.9	..	–4.6	..	–0.6	..	0.6	2.1
Madagascar	1.1	1.3	17.1	22.1	2.5	1.5	0.9	1.5	0.3	1.5	–1.7	1.3	0.4
Malawi	2.5	3.9	14.6	32.8	2.0	8.9	2.9	1.3	3.6	0.1	2.5	4.7	–8.0
Malaysia	5.3	7.7	1.7	4.5	3.8	2.0	7.2	10.8	4.2	8.8	10.9	13.2	10.8

Note: For data comparability and coverage, see the Technical Notes. Figures in italics are for years other than those specified.

ECONOMY

	Average annual % growth												
	Gross domestic product		GDP implicit deflator		Agriculture value added		Industry value added		Services value added		Exports of goods and services		Gross domestic investment
Economy	1980–90	1990–98	1980–90	1990–98	1980–90	1990–98	1980–90	1990–98	1980–90	1990–98	1980–90	1990–98	1990–98
Mali	0.9	3.7	4.5	9.2	3.3	3.3	4.3	7.6	1.9	2.2	4.8	9.2	1.5
Mauritania	1.8	4.2	8.4	5.9	1.7	5.0	4.9	3.4	0.4	4.6	3.6	–2.3	4.0
Mexico	0.7	2.5	72.1	19.8	0.8	1.4	1.1	3.2	0.6	2.4	7.0	14.7	2.4
Moldova	3.0	–14.1	..	222.5	..	–7.1	..	–13.0	..	–19.9	..	6.4	–21.9
Mongolia	5.4	0.1	–1.6	78.4	1.4	1.9	6.7	–2.0	5.8	1.2	..	..	..
Morocco	4.2	2.1	7.1	3.8	6.7	0.3	3.0	3.2	4.2	2.1	6.8	6.6	1.3
Mozambique	–0.1	5.7	38.3	41.3	6.6	4.8	–4.5	8.5	8.1	5.3	–6.8	14.8	8.9
Myanmar	0.6	6.3	12.2	24.2	0.5	5.0	0.5	10.1	0.8	6.4	1.9	8.8	13.0
Namibia	0.9	3.5	13.9	9.5	1.8	2.9	–1.2	3.3	1.5	3.6	–0.1	5.4	4.1
Nepal	4.6	4.8	11.1	9.0	4.0	2.3	8.7	7.3	3.9	9.6	3.9	16.8	6.0
Netherlands	2.3	2.6	1.6	2.1	3.4	3.7	1.6	1.2	2.6	2.3	4.5	4.5	0.6
New Zealand	1.8	3.2	10.8	1.7	3.8	2.2	1.1	3.7	1.9	3.5	4.0	5.8	8.8
Nicaragua	–2.0	4.1	422.6	67.7	–5.8	8.7	2.1	–4.8	–2.8	2.0	–7.8	10.6	9.8
Niger	–0.1	1.9	1.9	6.8	1.7	2.2	–1.7	1.7	–0.7	1.6	–2.9	–0.2	4.4
Nigeria	1.6	2.6	16.7	38.6	3.3	2.9	–1.1	1.2	3.7	3.6	–0.3	5.2	8.0
Norway	2.8	3.9	5.6	1.8	–0.2	4.5	3.3	5.6	2.7	3.1	5.2	5.9	4.1
Pakistan	6.3	4.1	6.7	11.2	4.3	3.8	7.3	5.0	6.8	4.6	8.4	3.2	2.7
Panama	0.5	4.3	1.9	2.4	2.5	1.7	–1.3	6.3	0.7	4.1	–0.6	0.7	12.9
Papua New Guinea	1.9	5.7	5.3	6.7	1.8	4.1	1.9	8.9	2.0	4.3	3.3	10.6	8.2
Paraguay	2.5	2.8	24.4	14.5	3.6	2.9	0.3	3.1	3.1	2.6	12.2	7.3	3.6
Peru	–0.3	5.9	231.3	33.7	2.7	5.5	–0.9	7.1	–0.7	4.9	–1.6	8.2	11.3
Philippines	1.0	3.3	14.9	8.5	1.0	1.5	–0.9	3.6	2.8	3.8	3.5	11.0	4.4
Poland	1.8	4.5	53.8	27.0	–0.7	–1.6	–1.3	4.7	2.8	3.0	4.5	12.3	10.6
Portugal	3.1	2.3	18.0	5.8	..	–0.4	..	0.5	..	2.3	8.7	4.8	2.2
Romania	0.5	–0.6	2.5	113.3	..	–0.2	..	–0.8	..	–0.2	..	6.1	–8.3
Russian Federation	..	–7.0	..	235.3	..	–6.9	..	–8.1	..	–4.7	..	2.0	–14.8
Rwanda	2.2	–3.3	4.0	18.4	0.5	–5.2	2.5	–0.6	5.5	–2.9	3.4	–9.8	–3.9
Saudi Arabia	0.0	1.6	–4.9	1.0	13.4	0.7	–2.3	1.5	1.3	2.0	..	..	..
Senegal	3.1	3.0	6.5	6.1	2.8	1.4	4.3	4.0	2.8	3.1	3.7	2.3	2.2
Sierra Leone	0.3	–4.7	64.0	32.5	3.1	1.5	1.7	–7.8	–2.8	–3.1	2.1	–9.4	–13.3
Singapore	6.6	8.0	2.2	2.5	–6.2	2.1	5.4	8.8	7.5	8.4	10.8	13.3	9.8
Slovak Republic	2.0	0.6	1.8	12.6	1.6	–0.4	2.0	–6.5	0.8	8.1	..	12.1	2.1
Slovenia	..	1.4	..	32.3	..	0.2	..	0.8	..	3.8	..	–2.3	9.0
South Africa	1.2	1.6	14.9	9.8	2.9	2.7	0.0	0.9	2.4	1.8	1.9	5.1	3.4
Spain	3.0	1.9	9.3	4.2	..	–2.5	..	–0.4	..	–13.1	5.7	10.4	–1.5
Sri Lanka	4.0	5.3	11.0	9.8	2.2	1.5	4.6	6.5	4.7	6.3	4.9	9.0	5.8
Sweden	2.3	1.2	7.4	2.3	1.5	–1.9	2.8	–0.7	2.6	–0.1	4.3	7.6	–3.2
Switzerland	2.0	0.4	3.4	1.7	..	..	..	..	..	..	3.5	1.6	–0.9
Syrian Arab Republic	1.5	5.9	15.3	8.9	–0.6	..	6.6	..	0.1	..	7.3	5.4	8.3
Tajikistan	..	–16.4	..	394.3	..	..	..	..	..	..	..	..	..
Tanzania[c]	..	2.9	..	24.3	..	3.7	..	1.8	..	2.3	..	10.9	–2.3
Thailand	7.6	7.4	3.9	4.8	3.9	3.1	9.8	9.0	7.3	7.1	14.1	11.1	6.5
Togo	1.7	2.3	4.8	8.8	5.6	4.5	1.1	2.6	–0.3	0.2	0.1	0.8	12.6
Tunisia	3.3	4.4	7.4	4.8	2.8	1.7	3.1	4.5	3.5	5.2	5.6	5.1	3.1
Turkey	5.4	4.1	45.2	79.3	1.3	1.1	7.8	5.0	4.4	4.1	..	12.1	4.2
Turkmenistan	..	–9.6	..	1,074.2	..	..	..	..	..	..	..	..	..
Uganda	3.2	7.4	104.0	15.3	2.1	3.6	5.0	13.3	2.8	8.3	1.8	16.1	10.0
Ukraine	..	–13.1	..	591.0	..	–21.4	..	–16.4	..	–8.6	..	–3.2	–15.4
United Kingdom	3.2	2.2	5.7	3.0	..	..	..	..	..	..	3.9	5.5	1.4
United States	3.0	2.9	4.2	2.2	..	2.0	..	4.3	..	1.9	4.7	8.1	5.8
Uruguay	0.4	3.9	61.3	40.4	0.0	4.2	–0.2	1.2	0.8	5.1	4.3	8.0	8.3
Uzbekistan	..	–1.9	..	355.1	..	–1.6	..	–5.0	..	–0.9	..	..	..
Venezuela	1.1	2.0	19.3	49.7	3.0	1.1	1.6	3.5	0.4	0.5	2.8	5.4	3.9
Vietnam	4.6	8.6	210.8	19.7	4.3	5.1	..	13.3	..	8.8	..	27.7	28.4
Yemen, Rep.	..	3.8	..	24.2	..	4.3	..	6.4	..	1.0	..	6.9	8.8
Zambia	1.0	1.0	42.2	63.5	3.6	–4.9	0.8	–4.7	–0.4	8.9	–3.4	2.0	12.1
Zimbabwe	3.6	2.0	11.6	22.4	3.1	3.4	3.2	–1.0	3.1	3.1	4.3	8.9	4.5
World	**3.2 w**	**2.4 w**			**2.7 w**	**1.2 w**	**.. w**	**2.1 w**	**.. w**	**2.0 w**	**5.2 w**	**6.4 w**	**2.3 w**
Low income	6.6	7.3			4.1	3.5	7.8	11.0	8.0	7.3	5.9	11.1	9.9
Excl. China & India	4.1	3.6			3.0	2.5	4.6	5.9	5.0	4.7	2.7	7.0	5.2
Middle income	2.6	1.9			2.6	–0.2	2.5	1.6	2.7	2.7	6.1	7.5	1.9
Lower middle income	..	–1.3			..	–2.2	..	–2.8	..	0.4	..	2.8	–4.0
Upper middle income	2.7	3.9			2.5	1.9	2.5	4.4	2.7	4.0	7.6	11.5	5.9
Low and middle income	3.5	3.3			3.4	1.7	3.7	4.2	3.7	3.7	6.1	8.4	4.2
East Asia & Pacific	8.0	8.1			4.4	3.5	9.5	11.5	8.8	7.9	9.6	14.0	10.6
Europe & Central Asia	..	–4.3			..	–6.3	..	–5.5	..	–1.4	..	3.9	–7.5
Latin America & Carib.	1.6	3.7			2.1	2.6	1.2	3.7	1.6	3.4	5.4	9.3	5.7
Middle East & N. Africa	2.0	3.0			5.5	1.7	0.6	2.2	2.1	3.6	..	..	..
South Asia	5.7	5.7			3.2	3.2	6.8	6.5	6.5	7.1	6.6	10.5	5.7
Sub-Saharan Africa	1.8	2.2			2.5	2.6	0.9	1.2	2.4	2.1	2.4	4.6	4.2
High income	3.1	2.1			..	0.3	..	1.5	..	1.8	5.1	6.1	1.7

a. Data prior to 1992 include Eritrea. b. Data prior to 1990 refer to the Federal Republic of Germany before unification. c. Data cover mainland Tanzania only.

Table 12. Structure of output

| Economy | Gross domestic product Millions of dollars | | Value added as a % of GDP | | | | | | | |
| | | | Agriculture | | Industry | | Manufacturing | | Services | |
	1980	1998	1980	1998	1980	1998	1980	1998	1980	1998
Albania	..	2,460	34	63	45	18	..	..	21	19
Algeria	42,345	49,585	10	12	54	47	9	9	36	41
Angola	..	6,648	..	14	..	54	..	5	..	32
Argentina	76,962	344,360	6	7	41	37	29	25	52	56
Armenia	..	1,628	..	41	..	36	..	25	..	23
Australia	160,110	364,247	5	3	36	26	19	14	58	71
Austria	78,539	212,069	4	1	36	30	25	20	60	68
Azerbaijan	..	4,127	..	19	..	44	..	9	..	36
Bangladesh	17,430	42,775	34	23	24	28	18	18	42	49
Belarus	..	22,629	..	14	..	44	..	37	..	42
Belgium	119,938	247,076	2	1	34	27	21	18	64	72
Benin	1,405	2,322	35	39	12	14	8	8	52	47
Bolivia	2,750	8,558	..	16	..	33	..	4	..	52
Botswana	1,105	5,690	11	4	45	46	5	5	44	51
Brazil	234,873	778,292	11	8	44	36	33	23	45	56
Bulgaria	20,040	10,085	14	23	54	26	..	18	32	50
Burkina Faso	1,709	2,581	33	32	22	28	16	21	45	40
Burundi	920	949	62	49	13	19	7	11	25	32
Cambodia	..	3,089	..	51	..	15	..	6	..	34
Cameroon	6,741	8,736	31	42	26	22	10	11	43	36
Canada	266,002	598,847	4	..	38	..	19	..	58	..
Central African Republic	797	1,057	40	55	20	18	7	9	40	27
Chad	1,033	1,603	45	39	9	15	..	12	46	46
Chile	27,572	78,025	7	8	37	35	22	17	55	57
China	201,687	960,924	30	18	49	49	41	37	21	33
Hong Kong, China	28,495	166,554	1	0	32	15	24	7	67	85
Colombia	33,399	91,108	22	13	35	38	26	19	43	49
Congo, Dem. Rep.	14,922	6,964	25	58	33	17	14	..	42	25
Congo, Rep.	1,706	1,961	12	12	47	50	7	8	42	39
Costa Rica	4,815	10,252	18	14	27	22	19	16	55	64
Côte d'Ivoire	10,175	11,041	26	25	20	23	13	19	54	52
Croatia	..	19,081	..	..	..	..	..	..	..	..
Czech Republic	29,042	52,035	7	..	63	..	..	..	30	..
Denmark	67,791	174,272	5	..	29	..	20	..	66	..
Dominican Republic	6,631	15,489	20	12	28	33	15	17	52	56
Ecuador	11,733	19,766	12	12	38	34	18	22	50	54
Egypt, Arab Rep.	22,912	78,097	18	17	37	33	12	26	45	50
El Salvador	3,574	12,148	38	13	22	28	16	22	40	59
Eritrea	..	650	..	9	..	30	..	16	..	61
Estonia	..	5,462	..	5	..	27	..	17	..	67
Ethiopia[a]	5,179	6,568	56	..	12	..	8	..	32	..
Finland	51,306	125,673	10	4	40	34	28	25	51	62
France	664,596	1,432,902	4	2	34	26	24	19	62	72
Georgia	..	5,244	24	32	36	23	28	18	40	45
Germany	..	2,142,018	..	1	..	..	..	24	..	44
Ghana	4,445	7,501	58	37	12	25	8	8	30	38
Greece	48,613	120,304	14	..	25	..	16	..	61	..
Guatemala	7,879	19,281	25	21	22	19	17	13	53	60
Guinea	..	3,615	..	22	..	35	..	4	..	42
Haiti	1,462	2,815	..	31	..	20	..	..	..	48
Honduras	2,566	4,722	24	23	24	30	15	18	52	47
Hungary	22,186	45,725	19	6	47	34	..	25	34	60
India	186,439	383,429	38	25	24	30	16	19	39	45
Indonesia	78,013	96,265	24	16	42	43	13	26	34	41
Iran, Islamic Rep.	92,664	..	18	..	32	..	9	..	50	..
Ireland	20,080	80,880	..	..	..	..	..	..	..	..
Israel	21,885	100,031	..	..	..	..	..	..	..	..
Italy	449,913	1,171,044	6	3	39	31	28	20	55	66
Jamaica	2,652	6,607	8	7	38	35	17	16	54	58
Japan	1,059,254	3,783,140	4	..	42	..	29	..	54	..
Jordan	3,962	7,015	8	3	28	25	13	13	64	72
Kazakhstan	..	21,029	..	10	..	27	..	12	..	63
Kenya	7,265	11,083	33	29	21	16	13	10	47	55
Korea, Rep.	62,803	297,900	15	6	40	43	28	26	45	51
Kuwait	28,639	30,373	0	..	75	..	6	..	25	..
Kyrgyz Republic	..	1,704	..	46	..	24	..	18	..	30
Lao PDR	..	1,753	..	52	..	21	..	16	..	27
Latvia	..	5,527	12	7	51	31	46	21	37	62
Lebanon	..	17,073	..	12	..	27	..	17	..	61
Lesotho	369	792	24	11	29	42	7	17	47	47
Lithuania	..	10,517	..	14	..	40	..	26	..	46
Macedonia, FYR	..	2,201	..	12	..	27	..	0	..	61
Madagascar	4,042	3,749	30	31	16	14	..	11	54	56
Malawi	1,238	1,643	44	39	23	19	14	15	34	41
Malaysia	24,488	71,302	22	12	38	48	21	34	40	40

Note: For data comparability and coverage, see the Technical Notes. Figures in italics are for years other than those specified.

ECONOMY

| | Gross domestic product Millions of dollars | | Value added as a % of GDP | | | | | | | |
| | | | Agriculture | | Industry | | Manufacturing | | Services | |
Economy	1980	1998	1980	1998	1980	1998	1980	1998	1980	1998
Mali	1,787	2,695	48	45	13	21	7	6	38	34
Mauritania	709	971	30	24	26	30	..	9	44	45
Mexico	223,505	393,224	8	5	33	27	22	20	59	68
Moldova	..	1,872	..	31	..	35	..	28	..	34
Mongolia	..	1,043	15	33	33	28	..	..	52	40
Morocco	18,821	33,514	18	16	31	30	17	17	51	54
Mozambique	3,526	3,959	48	34	30	18	..	10	22	48
Myanmar	..	..	47	59	13	10	10	7	41	31
Namibia	2,262	3,108	11	10	55	34	9	14	34	56
Nepal	1,946	4,479	62	40	12	22	4	10	26	38
Netherlands	171,861	382,487	3	..	32	..	18	..	64	..
New Zealand	22,395	54,093	11	..	31	..	22	..	58	..
Nicaragua	2,144	1,971	23	34	31	22	26	16	45	44
Niger	2,509	2,048	43	41	23	17	4	6	34	42
Nigeria	64,202	41,353	21	32	46	41	8	5	34	27
Norway	63,419	145,896	4	2	35	32	15	11	61	66
Pakistan	23,690	63,895	30	25	25	25	16	17	46	50
Panama	3,810	9,218	9	7	19	17	11	9	72	76
Papua New Guinea	2,548	4,639	33	28	27	36	10	9	40	36
Paraguay	4,579	8,571	29	25	27	22	16	15	44	53
Peru	20,658	64,122	10	7	42	38	20	22	48	55
Philippines	32,500	65,096	25	17	39	32	26	22	36	52
Poland	57,068	148,863	..	4	..	26	..	17	..	70
Portugal	28,729	106,650	..	..	..	..	..	..	..	..
Romania	..	34,843	..	15	..	36	..	25	..	48
Russian Federation	..	446,982	..	9	..	42	..	..	..	49
Rwanda	1,163	2,082	50	34	23	23	17	16	27	43
Saudi Arabia	156,487	125,840	1	6	81	45	5	10	18	49
Senegal	2,986	4,836	19	17	15	23	11	15	66	59
Sierra Leone	1,199	647	33	44	21	24	5	6	47	32
Singapore	11,718	85,425	1	0	38	35	29	24	61	65
Slovak Republic	..	19,461	..	5	..	33	..	..	..	62
Slovenia	..	18,201	..	5	..	39	..	29	..	57
South Africa	78,744	116,730	7	4	50	38	23	24	43	57
Spain	213,308	551,923	..	3	..	..	..	18	..	..
Sri Lanka	4,032	15,093	28	22	30	26	18	17	43	52
Sweden	125,557	224,953	4	..	34	..	23	..	63	..
Switzerland	107,474	264,352	..	..	..	..	..	..	..	..
Syrian Arab Republic	13,062	17,899	20	..	23	..	..	..	56	..
Tajikistan	..	1,990	..	..	..	..	..	..	..	..
Tanzania[b]	..	7,917	..	46	..	14	..	7	..	40
Thailand	32,354	153,909	23	11	29	40	22	29	48	49
Togo	1,136	1,510	27	42	25	21	8	9	48	37
Tunisia	8,742	22,041	14	14	31	28	12	18	55	58
Turkey	68,824	189,878	26	15	22	28	14	18	51	57
Turkmenistan	..	4,397	..	..	..	..	..	..	..	..
Uganda	1,244	6,653	72	43	4	18	4	9	23	39
Ukraine	..	49,677	..	12	..	40	..	6	..	48
United Kingdom	537,389	1,357,429	2	2	43	31	27	21	55	67
United States	2,709,000	8,210,600	3	2	33	27	22	18	64	71
Uruguay	10,132	20,155	14	8	34	27	26	18	53	64
Uzbekistan	..	14,194	..	28	..	30	..	13	..	42
Venezuela	69,417	105,756	5	4	46	43	16	17	49	52
Vietnam	..	24,848	..	26	..	31	..	..	..	43
Yemen, Rep.	..	4,318	..	18	..	49	..	11	..	34
Zambia	3,884	3,352	14	16	41	30	18	12	44	55
Zimbabwe	6,679	5,908	16	18	29	24	22	17	55	58
World	10,939,459 t	28,854,043 t	7 w	5 w	38 w	.. w	25 w	20 w	56 w	61 w
Low income	801,498	1,811,106	31	21	38	41	27	29	30	38
Excl. China & India	451,756	451,051	29	25	32	33	13	18	39	42
Middle income	2,303,442	4,420,845	13	9	41	36	25	21	46	56
Lower middle income	..	1,704,528	..	12	..	36	..	..	..	52
Upper middle income	1,165,003	2,816,378	11	7	42	35	26	22	47	57
Low and middle income	3,106,342	6,251,315	18	12	40	37	25	23	42	51
East Asia & Pacific	503,834	1,688,394	24	15	42	45	31	31	33	41
Europe & Central Asia	..	1,137,953	..	11	..	34	..	..	..	55
Latin America & Carib.	782,173	2,076,540	10	8	40	34	29	22	50	58
Middle East & N. Africa	..	..	10	..	53	..	9	..	37	..
South Asia	237,343	517,654	36	25	24	29	16	19	40	46
Sub-Saharan Africa	270,391	316,517	18	17	39	34	16	19	43	50
High income	7,936,460	22,560,624	3	2	37	..	25	19	59	65

a. Data prior to 1992 include Eritrea.   b. Data cover mainland Tanzania only.

Table 13.   Structure of demand

	Percentage of GDP											
	Private consumption		General government consumption		Gross domestic investment		Gross domestic saving		Exports of goods and services		Resource balance	
Economy	1980	1998	1980	1998	1980	1998	1980	1998	1980	1998	1980	1998
Albania	56	*103*	9	*11*	35	*12*	35	*–13*	23	*12*	0	*–25*
Algeria	43	56	14	11	39	27	43	33	34	29	4	6
Angola	..	48	..	39	..	25	..	13	..	57	..	–12
Argentina	76	78	..ᵃ	3	25	22	24	19	5	9	–1	–2
Armenia	..	116	..	13	..	9	..	–29	..	20	..	–38
Australia	59	*63*	18	*17*	25	*20*	24	*21*	16	*21*	–2	*–1*
Austria	55	*57*	18	*20*	29	*24*	27	*23*	36	*42*	–2	*–1*
Azerbaijan	..	90	..	11	..	34	..	–1	..	25	..	–35
Bangladesh	86	80	2	4	22	21	13	15	4	14	–9	–6
Belarus	..	59	..	19	..	26	..	22	..	60	..	–4
Belgium	64	*63*	18	*15*	22	*18*	19	*22*	57	*73*	–3	*5*
Benin	96	81	9	10	15	16	–5	9	23	24	–20	–8
Bolivia	67	75	14	15	17	19	19	9	25	15	2	–9
Botswana	46	40	20	25	37	25	34	35	50	45	–2	10
Brazil	70	67	9	14	23	21	21	19	9	7	–2	–2
Bulgaria	55	*70*	6	*12*	34	*12*	39	*17*	36	*61*	5	*6*
Burkina Faso	95	*77*	10	12	17	26	–6	11	10	14	–23	–14
Burundi	91	90	9	11	14	8	–1	–1	9	6	–14	–9
Cambodia	..	87	..	9	..	16	..	4	..	30	..	–12
Cameroon	69	71	10	9	21	18	22	20	28	27	1	2
Canada	53	*58*	22	*21*	23	*18*	25	*21*	28	*41*	2	*2*
Central African Republic	94	84	15	12	7	14	–9	4	25	16	–16	–9
Chad	*100*	*92*	*4*	*7*	*3*	*19*	*–9*	*1*	*17*	*17*	*–12*	*–18*
Chile	71	72	12	6	21	27	17	22	23	25	–4	–5
China	51	44	15	13	35	39	35	43	6	22	0	5
Hong Kong, China	60	60	6	9	35	30	34	30	90	125	–1	0
Colombia	70	77	10	9	19	18	20	14	16	17	1	–4
Congo, Dem. Rep.	82	*83*	8	*8*	10	8	10	9	16	*24*	0	*2*
Congo, Rep.	47	59	18	14	36	35	36	26	60	63	0	–9
Costa Rica	66	63	18	13	27	27	16	24	26	43	–10	–3
Côte d'Ivoire	63	65	17	11	27	18	20	24	35	43	–6	6
Croatia	..	66	..	30	..	15	..	3	..	42	..	*–11*
Czech Republic	..	51	..	20	31	34	..	28	..	58	..	–5
Denmark	56	..	27	..	18	..	16	..	33	..	–2	..
Dominican Republic	77	72	8	10	25	26	15	19	19	32	–10	–7
Ecuador	60	68	15	15	26	21	26	17	25	25	0	–4
Egypt, Arab Rep.	69	80	16	10	28	19	15	10	31	17	–12	–9
El Salvador	72	86	14	10	13	17	14	5	34	24	1	–12
Eritrea	..	81	..	48	..	41	..	–29	..	20	..	–70
Estonia	..	62	..	21	..	26	..	17	..	76	..	–9
Ethiopiaᵇ	79	*77*	*14*	*14*	*13*	20	7	9	*11*	16	–6	*–11*
Finland	54	*53*	18	*22*	29	*17*	28	*25*	33	*40*	–1	*9*
France	59	*61*	18	*19*	24	*17*	23	*20*	22	*24*	–1	*3*
Georgia	56	*95*	13	*9*	29	*7*	31	*–4*	..	*12*	2	*–11*
Germany	..	58	..	20	..	21	..	22	..	27	..	2
Ghana	84	77	11	10	6	23	5	13	8	27	–1	–10
Greece	62	*75*	12	*14*	33	*19*	27	*11*	16	*15*	–6	*–9*
Guatemala	79	88	8	5	16	14	13	7	22	17	–3	–7
Guinea	..	74	..	7	..	22	..	19	..	22	..	–3
Haiti	82	97	10	7	17	10	8	–4	22	8	–9	–15
Honduras	70	*62*	13	*13*	25	*30*	17	*25*	36	*42*	–8	*–5*
Hungary	61	*63*	10	*10*	31	*27*	29	*27*	39	*45*	–2	*0*
India	73	71	10	11	20	23	17	18	6	12	–3	–5
Indonesia	51	*63*	11	*7*	24	*31*	38	*31*	34	*28*	14	*0*
Iran, Islamic Rep.	53	..	21	..	30	..	26	..	13	..	–3	..
Ireland	67	*53*	19	*14*	27	*18*	14	*33*	48	*76*	–13	*15*
Israel	53	62	40	29	22	22	7	9	44	32	–16	–13
Italy	61	*61*	15	*16*	27	*17*	24	*22*	22	*27*	–3	*4*
Jamaica	64	54	20	21	16	34	16	24	51	49	0	–9
Japan	59	..	10	..	32	..	31	..	14	..	–1	..
Jordan	79	68	29	25	37	27	–8	6	40	50	–44	–21
Kazakhstan	..	75	..	12	..	16	..	13	..	34	..	–3
Kenya	62	72	20	15	29	18	18	13	28	26	–11	–5
Korea, Rep.	64	55	12	*11*	32	35	24	34	34	*38*	–7	*–1*
Kuwait	31	47	11	28	14	13	58	25	78	53	44	12
Kyrgyz Republic	..	82	..	16	..	18	..	2	..	35	..	–16
Lao PDR	..	81	..	7	..	29	..	11	..	24	..	–17
Latvia	59	67	8	23	26	20	33	10	..	50	7	–10
Lebanon	..	98	..	15	..	28	..	–13	..	11	..	–40
Lesotho	133	121	26	22	43	49	–59	–43	20	33	–102	–91
Lithuania	..	67	..	20	..	28	..	14	..	50	..	–14
Macedonia, FYR	..	83	..	12	..	20	..	4	..	45	..	–15
Madagascar	89	89	12	6	15	13	–1	5	13	21	–16	–8
Malawi	70	80	19	14	25	18	11	5	25	33	–14	–13
Malaysia	51	42	17	11	30	32	33	47	58	118	3	15

Note: For data comparability and coverage, see the Technical Notes. Figures in italics are for years other than those specified.

ECONOMY

	Percentage of GDP											
	Private consumption		General government consumption		Gross domestic investment		Gross domestic saving		Exports of goods and services		Resource balance	
Economy	1980	1998	1980	1998	1980	1998	1980	1998	1980	1998	1980	1998
Mali	87	77	12	13	15	21	0	10	15	24	–14	–11
Mauritania	68	80	25	13	36	22	7	7	37	40	–29	–15
Mexico	65	68	10	8	27	26	25	24	11	31	–2	–2
Moldova	..	74	..	26	..	24	..	0	..	53	..	–24
Mongolia	44	60	29	16	63	23	27	24	21	68	–36	1
Morocco	68	65	18	16	24	22	14	18	17	28	–10	–3
Mozambique	98	90	12	9	6	21	–11	1	11	12	–16	–20
Myanmar	82	88	..[a]	..[a]	21	13	18	12	9	1	–4	–1
Namibia	47	56	17	26	29	19	37	19	76	63	8	0
Nepal	82	82	7	9	18	21	11	9	12	23	–7	–11
Netherlands	61	60	17	14	22	20	22	26	51	56	0	7
New Zealand	62	63	18	14	21	22	20	22	30	29	–1	1
Nicaragua	82	84	20	13	17	28	–2	3	24	41	–19	–25
Niger	75	84	10	13	28	10	15	3	25	16	–14	–7
Nigeria	56	77	12	11	21	20	31	12	29	23	10	–8
Norway	47	48	19	20	28	23	34	32	43	41	6	7
Pakistan	83	77	10	10	18	17	7	13	12	16	–12	–4
Panama	52	57	18	18	28	27	31	25	51	36	2	–2
Papua New Guinea	61	44	24	23	25	37	15	33	43	56	–10	–4
Paraguay	76	73	6	10	32	21	18	17	15	45	–13	–4
Peru	57	68	11	12	29	25	32	20	22	12	3	–5
Philippines	67	73	9	13	29	25	24	15	24	56	–5	–11
Poland	67	65	9	16	26	24	23	20	28	25	–3	–4
Portugal	65	65	13	18	34	24	21	17	25	31	–13	–9
Romania	60	77	5	10	40	20	35	13	35	24	–5	–7
Russian Federation	..	67	..	10	..	20	..	24	..	27	..	3
Rwanda	83	96	12	11	16	10	4	–7	14	5	–12	–17
Saudi Arabia	22	35	16	30	22	20	62	35	71	45	41	14
Senegal	85	75	20	10	12	20	–5	15	27	32	–17	–5
Sierra Leone	..	93	21	8	..	8	..	–1	18	22	–10	–9
Singapore	53	39	10	10	46	37	38	51	215	..	–9	14
Slovak Republic	..	49	..	22	..	35	..	28	..	56	..	–7
Slovenia	..	57	..	20	..	24	..	23	..	57	..	–1
South Africa	50	61	13	22	28	16	36	17	36	29	8	1
Spain	66	62	13	16	23	21	21	21	16	26	–2	1
Sri Lanka	80	72	9	10	34	24	11	17	32	36	–23	–7
Sweden	51	52	29	26	21	15	19	21	29	44	–2	7
Switzerland	62	61	12	14	29	20	25	24	35	40	–3	4
Syrian Arab Republic	67	70	23	11	28	29	10	18	18	29	–17	–11
Tajikistan	..	..	..	..	..	..	..	..	..	..	..	..
Tanzania[c]	..	85	..	9	..	16	..	6	..	16	..	–10
Thailand	65	54	12	10	29	35	23	36	24	47	–6	1
Togo	54	81	22	11	28	14	23	7	51	34	–5	–7
Tunisia	62	61	14	15	29	25	24	24	40	42	–5	–2
Turkey	77	68	12	12	18	25	11	19	5	25	–7	–6
Turkmenistan	..	..	..	..	..	..	..	..	..	..	..	..
Uganda	89	84	11	10	6	15	0	6	19	10	–7	–10
Ukraine	..	62	..	22	..	20	..	16	..	41	..	–4
United Kingdom	59	64	22	21	17	16	19	15	27	29	2	0
United States	64	68	17	16	20	18	19	16	10	12	–1	–1
Uruguay	76	81	12	7	17	13	12	12	15	22	–6	–1
Uzbekistan	..	57	..	22	..	23	..	22	..	22	..	–1
Venezuela	55	78	12	6	26	16	33	16	29	17	7	–1
Vietnam	..	70	..	9	..	29	..	21	..	46	..	–8
Yemen, Rep.	..	76	..	22	..	22	..	2	..	34	..	–19
Zambia	55	84	26	11	23	14	19	5	41	29	–4	–9
Zimbabwe	68	63	19	17	17	21	14	20	23	45	–3	–2
World	61 w	63 w	15 w	16 w	25 w	20 w	24 w	21 w	20 w	25 w	–1 w	0 w
Low income	60	57	12	12	28	30	28	32	12	19	0	0
Excl. China & India	65	70	11	9	22	24	24	20	25	27	2	–3
Middle income	63	63	12	14	26	24	25	23	22	22	–1	–2
Lower middle income	..	65	..	14	..	23	..	22	..	28	..	–2
Upper middle income	64	68	11	11	25	23	25	21	20	19	–1	–2
Low and middle income	62	65	12	12	27	25	26	24	19	21	–1	–1
East Asia & Pacific	56	52	13	11	32	36	31	37	21	34	–1	1
Europe & Central Asia	..	65	..	14	..	23	..	21	..	31	..	–2
Latin America & Carib.	68	70	10	10	24	22	22	20	12	14	–2	–2
Middle East & N. Africa	45	..	18	..	27	..	38	..	42	..	11	..
South Asia	76	73	9	10	21	22	15	17	8	13	–5	–5
Sub-Saharan Africa	59	67	14	17	24	18	26	15	33	30	2	–3
High income	60	63	16	17	25	19	24	19	20	24	–1	0

a. General government consumption figures are not available separately; they are included in private consumption. b. Data prior to 1992 include Eritrea. c. Data cover mainland Tanzania only.

Table 14. Central government finances

| | Percentage of GDP | | | | | | | | | | Percentage of total expenditure[b] | | | |
| | Current tax revenue | | Current nontax revenue | | Current expenditure | | Capital expenditure | | Overall deficit/surplus[a] | | Goods and services | | Social services[c] | |
Economy	1980	1997	1980	1997	1980	1997	1980	1997	1980	1997	1980	1997	1980	1997
Albania	..	16.6	..	4.6	..	25.5	..	5.5	..	−9.0	..	26.2	..	33.0
Algeria	..	..	..	..	..	..	..	..	..	..	..	..	..	..
Angola	..	..	..	..	..	..	..	..	..	..	..	..	..	..
Argentina	10.4	11.2	5.2	1.1	18.2	12.7	0.0	1.1	−2.6	−1.3	57.1	21.4	28.6	63.6
Armenia	..	..	..	..	..	..	..	..	..	..	..	..	..	..
Australia	19.5	23.2	2.2	1.9	21.1	25.3	1.5	0.9	−1.5	0.4	21.1	21.9	45.5	60.7
Austria	31.2	34.4	2.6	2.8	33.3	38.6	3.3	3.1	−3.3	−4.1	25.6	24.2	70.0	65.7
Azerbaijan	..	..	..	..	..	..	..	..	..	..	..	..	..	..
Bangladesh	5.7	..	2.7	..	..	..	..	..	1.8	..	..	..	20.1	..
Belarus	..	29.4	..	2.4	..	28.9	..	5.1	..	−1.9	..	29.0	..	45.7
Belgium	41.2	43.0	1.8	1.1	45.9	45.9	4.2	2.4	−8.0	−3.2	22.2	18.6	60.2	..
Benin	..	..	..	..	..	..	..	..	..	..	..	..	..	..
Bolivia	..	15.0	..	1.9	..	18.4	..	3.5	..	−2.3	..	37.7	..	53.6
Botswana	21.9	14.7	8.0	29.5	20.3	28.5	9.5	6.8	−0.1	8.4	40.5	46.8	30.6	42.7
Brazil	17.8	..	4.8	..	18.6	..	1.6	..	−2.4	..	16.1	..	32.3	..
Bulgaria	..	25.2	..	6.8	..	30.9	..	2.6	..	2.1	..	32.9	..	42.0
Burkina Faso	10.4	..	1.2	..	9.8	..	2.3	..	0.2	..	69.4	..	30.1	‡..
Burundi	13.2	12.7	0.8	1.0	11.5	17.3	10.9	3.7	−3.9	−5.5	39.2	55.2	..	23.0
Cambodia	..	..	..	..	..	..	..	..	..	..	..	..	..	..
Cameroon	14.9	9.4	1.3	3.6	10.5	11.4	5.2	1.1	0.5	0.2	54.7	52.6	25.4	21.0
Canada	16.0	..	2.5	..	20.8	..	0.2	..	−3.5	..	20.9	..	43.8	..
Central African Republic	15.0	..	1.5	..	18.5	..	1.3	..	−3.5	..	66.0	..	28.6	..
Chad	..	..	..	..	..	..	..	..	..	..	..	..	..	..
Chile	25.6	18.9	6.4	3.8	25.3	17.3	2.7	3.5	5.4	1.9	40.2	28.8	57.6	66.2
China	..	4.9	..	0.6	..	..	..	..	..	−1.6	..	..	..	2.6
Hong Kong, China	..	..	..	..	..	..	..	..	..	..	..	..	..	..
Colombia	10.3	..	1.7	..	10.4	..	4.1	..	−1.8	..	35.2	..	44.1	..
Congo, Dem. Rep.	8.3	4.9	1.1	0.4	9.9	8.0	2.4	0.3	−0.8	0.0	65.2	94.5	22.1	1.6
Congo, Rep.	27.0	..	8.3	..	21.8	..	17.7	..	−5.2	..	..	23.0	..	..
Costa Rica	16.8	23.5	1.0	3.2	21.3	27.6	5.2	2.9	−7.4	−3.9	52.2	47.1	62.4	59.6
Côte d'Ivoire	21.1	..	1.7	..	19.1	..	9.0	..	−10.8	..	..	..	..	..
Croatia	..	42.8	..	2.6	..	41.2	..	5.5	..	−0.5	..	47.9	..	62.6
Czech Republic	..	32.7	..	1.2	..	32.6	..	3.3	..	−1.1	..	14.3	..	71.3
Denmark	30.7	33.7	4.0	5.1	35.9	40.0	2.7	1.5	−2.6	−1.9	21.3	18.9	56.3	54.5
Dominican Republic	11.1	13.9	3.2	1.2	11.4	9.0	5.2	6.3	−2.6	−0.3	49.5	36.5	35.4	41.5
Ecuador	12.3	..	0.5	..	11.9	..	2.3	..	−1.4	..	28.2	..	43.9	..
Egypt, Arab Rep.	28.8	21.5	15.2	13.9	39.5	27.7	10.8	6.6	−11.7	0.9	34.1	31.2	20.9	31.6
El Salvador	11.1	10.4	0.5	0.8	11.7	10.5	2.8	2.3	−5.7	−0.6	49.8	55.0	34.3	37.7
Eritrea	..	..	..	..	..	..	..	..	..	..	..	..	..	..
Estonia	..	30.1	..	3.4	..	28.7	..	2.9	..	2.4	..	42.0	..	57.5
Ethiopia[d]	12.8	11.9	3.5	5.2	18.0	18.1	3.3	7.1	−3.1	−4.5	85.9	52.4	19.6	30.8
Finland	25.1	28.4	2.1	5.1	25.2	38.5	3.0	1.6	−2.2	−6.3	20.4	17.6	50.3	53.6
France	36.7	39.2	2.9	2.6	37.4	44.6	2.1	2.0	−0.1	−3.5	30.1	23.6	69.4	..
Georgia	..	..	..	..	..	..	..	..	..	..	..	..	..	..
Germany	..	26.7	..	5.0	..	32.1	..	1.3	..	−1.4	33.9	31.6	68.8	..
Ghana	6.4	..	0.5	..	9.8	..	1.1	..	−4.2	..	47.3	..	35.1	..
Greece	22.6	20.6	2.7	2.4	25.7	28.5	4.6	4.3	−4.1	−8.5	44.3	29.3	51.2	36.8
Guatemala	8.7	8.7	0.7	0.7	7.3	6.8	5.1	2.3	−3.4	−1.0	46.6	53.1	29.8	..
Guinea	..	..	..	..	..	..	..	..	..	..	..	..	..	..
Haiti	9.3	..	1.3	..	13.9	..	3.5	..	−4.7	..	81.6	..	..	..
Honduras	13.6	..	0.9	..	..	..	..	..	..	..	..	..	..	..
Hungary	44.8	32.5	8.6	4.7	48.7	38.5	7.5	4.1	−2.8	−2.6	19.4	18.6	26.7	43.2
India	9.0	10.8	1.8	3.3	10.8	14.7	1.4	1.7	−6.0	−4.9	20.4	20.5	5.5	8.7
Indonesia	20.2	14.7	1.0	2.3	11.7	8.7	10.4	6.0	−2.3	1.2	23.7	27.9	11.8	36.2
Iran, Islamic Rep.	6.9	6.7	14.7	17.8	27.7	15.7	8.0	7.6	−13.8	1.4	57.3	55.8	36.7	41.1
Ireland	30.9	32.4	3.9	1.6	40.4	34.4	4.6	3.7	−12.5	−1.4	17.3	18.1	49.3	60.3
Israel	44.9	36.8	7.3	5.8	69.7	45.1	2.9	3.4	−16.2	0.4	46.2	35.0	25.7	59.9
Italy	29.3	42.2	2.5	2.5	37.8	45.4	2.2	2.5	−10.8	−3.1	17.1	18.5	48.8	..
Jamaica	27.8	..	1.2	..	..	..	..	..	−15.5	..	..	..	..	..
Japan	11.0	..	0.6	..	14.8	..	3.6	..	−7.0	..	12.6	..	..	..
Jordan	14.0	22.4	4.0	6.3	25.9	28.0	12.1	7.0	−9.3	−1.4	39.5	60.0	23.0	44.7
Kazakhstan	..	..	..	..	..	..	..	..	..	..	..	..	..	..
Kenya	19.2	23.4	2.8	3.7	19.4	25.6	5.9	3.4	−4.5	−0.9	52.9	44.5	30.3	29.6
Korea, Rep.	15.5	18.6	2.2	2.9	14.8	14.7	2.4	4.1	−2.2	−1.4	38.6	21.6	22.0	27.8
Kuwait	2.7	1.2	86.6	..	18.9	35.8	8.9	5.8	58.7	..	40.5	..	24.0	..
Kyrgyz Republic	..	..	..	..	..	..	..	..	..	..	..	..	..	..
Lao PDR	..	..	..	..	..	..	..	..	..	..	..	..	..	..
Latvia	..	29.2	..	3.3	..	30.6	..	1.5	..	0.9	..	30.6	..	58.3
Lebanon	..	14.1	..	3.3	..	29.4	..	8.5	..	−20.6	..	30.8	..	17.2
Lesotho	29.4	30.7	4.8	7.0	32.9	26.5	12.4	13.3	−7.4	1.0	50.0	54.3	22.8	..
Lithuania	..	25.4	..	1.0	..	25.0	..	2.4	..	−1.9	..	44.9	..	50.2
Macedonia, FYR	..	..	..	..	..	..	..	..	..	..	..	..	..	..
Madagascar	12.9	8.5	0.3	0.2	..	10.5	..	6.8	..	−1.3	..	24.6	..	16.5
Malawi	16.6	..	2.5	..	18.0	..	16.6	..	−15.9	..	32.4	..	14.2	..
Malaysia	23.5	19.4	2.8	4.2	19.2	15.5	9.9	4.6	−6.0	3.0	33.5	40.5	26.8	42.5

Note: For data comparability and coverage, see the Technical Notes. Figures in italics are for years other than those specified.

ECONOMY

| Economy | Percentage of GDP | | | | | | | | | | Percentage of total expenditure[b] | | | |
| | Current tax revenue | | Current nontax revenue | | Current expenditure | | Capital expenditure | | Overall deficit/surplus[a] | | Goods and services | | Social services[c] | |
	1980	1997	1980	1997	1980	1997	1980	1997	1980	1997	1980	1997	1980	1997
Mali	8.7	..	0.8	..	11.2	..	1.7	..	-4.2	..	43.8	..	20.7	..
Mauritania	..	..	..	..	..	..	..	..	..	..	..	..	..	..
Mexico	13.9	12.8	1.1	2.5	11.7	13.7	5.0	1.9	-3.0	-0.2	30.2	25.9	42.0	50.1
Moldova	..	..	..	..	..	..	..	..	..	..	..	..	..	..
Mongolia	..	17.0	..	4.8	..	16.0	..	3.7	..	-6.0	..	24.1	..	..
Morocco	20.4	23.8	2.9	4.7	22.8	26.1	10.3	7.2	-9.7	-4.4	46.6	48.5	27.0	26.9
Mozambique	..	..	..	..	..	..	..	..	..	..	..	..	..	..
Myanmar	9.6	4.0	6.4	2.9	12.1	4.7	3.8	5.4	1.2	-3.2	..	..	26.5	18.9
Namibia	..	..	..	..	..	..	..	..	..	..	..	..	..	..
Nepal	6.6	8.9	1.3	1.8	..	..	..	..	-3.0	-4.1	..	..	15.6	25.9
Netherlands	44.1	42.7	5.3	3.0	48.2	46.0	4.6	1.7	-4.6	-1.7	15.3	15.4	62.9	63.9
New Zealand	30.7	31.2	3.5	2.7	35.9	31.4	2.4	0.9	-6.7	4.0	27.1	52.7	57.0	76.5
Nicaragua	20.3	23.9	2.4	1.5	24.8	22.3	5.7	10.9	-6.8	-0.6	59.6	28.8	33.2	..
Niger	12.3	..	2.2	..	9.5	..	9.1	..	-4.8	..	29.1	..	24.8	..
Nigeria	..	..	..	..	..	..	..	..	..	..	..	..	..	..
Norway	33.7	32.5	3.5	9.2	32.5	35.1	2.0	1.7	-1.7	5.1	17.9	20.3	36.8	50.2
Pakistan	13.3	12.9	2.9	3.1	14.5	19.9	3.1	2.8	-5.7	-7.9	36.6	50.0	..	..
Panama	18.6	15.9	6.8	10.1	25.0	23.9	5.5	3.5	-5.2	-0.7	49.7	49.2	39.6	64.0
Papua New Guinea	20.6	..	2.4	..	29.2	..	5.2	..	-1.9	..	56.4	..	27.2	..
Paraguay	9.8	..	0.9	..	7.5	..	2.4	..	0.3	..	57.2	..	33.6	..
Peru	15.8	14.0	1.3	1.7	15.0	13.1	4.4	2.4	-2.4	0.3	44.7	38.0	..	..
Philippines	12.5	17.0	1.5	2.0	9.9	16.3	3.4	2.2	-1.4	0.1	52.2	51.1	20.8	26.5
Poland	..	35.2	..	3.4	..	39.3	..	1.9	..	-1.4	..	25.3	..	71.4
Portugal	24.1	31.1	1.9	3.1	28.7	36.2	4.4	5.3	-8.4	-2.3	32.0	40.8	46.0	..
Romania	10.1	24.4	35.2	2.1	29.8	29.1	15.0	2.9	0.5	-3.9	11.3	30.1	18.8	49.0
Russian Federation	..	17.9	..	1.1	..	..	..	..	..	-4.5	..	..	..	31.1
Rwanda	11.0	..	1.8	..	9.3	..	5.0	..	-1.7	..	56.8	..	..	..
Saudi Arabia	..	..	..	..	..	..	..	..	..	..	..	..	..	..
Senegal	21.0	..	1.5	..	22.5	..	1.9	..	0.9	..	71.6	..	36.8	..
Sierra Leone	13.6	10.2	1.5	0.3	19.6	13.4	5.0	4.3	-11.8	-6.0	..	39.0	..	..
Singapore	17.5	15.9	7.8	8.3	15.6	11.6	4.5	5.0	2.1	11.6	47.6	36.7	24.1	23.2
Slovak Republic	..	..	..	..	..	..	..	..	..	..	..	..	..	..
Slovenia	..	..	..	..	..	..	..	..	..	..	..	..	..	..
South Africa	20.5	27.5	3.0	2.0	19.1	32.5	3.0	1.3	-2.3	-3.8	39.9	29.2	..	..
Spain	22.1	28.3	1.9	2.0	23.6	34.9	2.9	1.9	-4.2	-6.0	37.6	16.4	64.8	49.2
Sri Lanka	19.1	16.2	1.1	2.3	24.7	20.7	16.6	5.0	-18.3	-4.5	30.4	39.5	23.6	33.6
Sweden	30.1	36.9	4.9	5.1	37.5	43.2	1.8	1.1	-8.1	-1.3	15.8	14.0	58.2	58.1
Switzerland	17.2	21.1	1.4	1.6	17.9	25.3	1.3	1.0	-0.2	-1.2	27.1	26.5	63.6	70.6
Syrian Arab Republic	10.5	16.5	16.3	6.7	30.3	14.3	17.9	9.4	-9.7	-0.2	..	..	17.6	18.2
Tajikistan	..	..	..	..	..	..	..	..	..	..	..	..	..	..
Tanzania	..	..	..	..	..	..	..	..	..	..	51.8	..	21.9	..
Thailand	13.2	16.1	1.2	1.9	14.4	11.0	4.4	7.7	-4.9	-0.9	53.3	49.8	28.0	39.1
Togo	27.0	..	4.3	..	23.7	..	8.9	..	-2.0	..	51.9	..	39.9	..
Tunisia	23.9	24.8	6.9	4.8	22.1	25.9	9.4	6.7	-2.8	-3.1	38.3	37.9	34.2	46.6
Turkey	14.3	15.2	3.7	3.1	15.5	24.7	5.9	2.2	-3.1	-8.4	46.6	32.7	23.8	19.0
Turkmenistan	..	..	..	..	..	..	..	..	..	..	..	..	..	..
Uganda	3.1	..	0.1	..	5.4	..	0.8	..	-3.1	..	..	..	23.5	..
Ukraine	..	..	..	..	..	..	..	..	..	..	..	..	..	..
United Kingdom	30.6	33.4	4.6	2.8	36.4	39.6	1.8	2.1	-4.6	-5.3	30.2	29.6	43.7	51.7
United States	18.5	19.8	1.7	1.5	20.7	21.0	1.3	0.7	-2.8	-0.3	28.3	22.2	48.8	53.5
Uruguay	21.0	27.9	1.2	2.3	20.1	30.0	1.7	1.7	0.0	-1.3	46.7	28.8	61.1	74.6
Uzbekistan	..	..	..	..	..	..	..	..	..	..	..	..	..	..
Venezuela	18.9	17.5	3.4	6.4	14.9	17.4	4.0	3.4	0.0	2.2	41.9	22.8	..	..
Vietnam	..	..	..	..	..	..	..	..	..	..	..	..	..	..
Yemen, Rep.	..	13.3	..	24.5	..	33.6	..	5.6	..	-2.6	..	39.0	..	19.4
Zambia	23.1	17.1	1.8	1.5	33.0	14.3	4.0	7.1	-18.5	0.7	45.8	39.0	17.4	29.8
Zimbabwe	15.4	..	3.9	..	26.5	..	1.4	..	-8.8	..	55.3	..	28.5	..

a. Includes grants. b. Total expenditure includes lending minus repayments. c. Refers to education, health, social security, welfare, housing, and community amenities.
d. Data prior to 1992 include Eritrea.

Table 15. Balance of payments, current account, and international reserves

	Goods and services				Net income		Net current transfers		Current account balance		Gross international reserves	
	Exports		Imports									
Economy	1980	1997	1980	1997	1980	1997	1980	1997	1980	1997	1980	1998
Albania	378	222	371	809	4	50	6	265	16	−272	..	382
Algeria	14,128	14,779	12,311	8,568	−1,869	−2,523	301	..	249	..	7,064	8,452
Angola	..	5,223	..	5,389	..	−826	..	3,841	..	3,266	..	206
Argentina	9,897	29,382	13,182	34,968	−1,512	−4,190	23	347	−4,774	−9,429	9,297	24,856
Armenia	..	330	..	952	..	102	..	217	..	−303	..	328
Australia	25,755	83,703	27,089	81,891	−2,688	−14,132	−425	−270	−4,447	−12,591	6,366	16,144
Austria	26,650	88,266	29,921	91,446	−528	−122	−66	−1,695	−3,865	−4,996	17,725	25,208
Azerbaijan	..	1,150	..	2,101	..	−33	..	45	..	−939	..	447
Bangladesh	885	5,096	2,545	7,677	14	−91	802	1,770	−844	−902	331	1,936
Belarus	..	8,306	..	9,103	..	−79	..	78	..	−798	..	339
Belgium[a]	70,498	185,415	74,259	173,865	61	6,287	−1,231	−3,898	−4,931	13,939	27,974	21,013
Benin	226	524	421	673	8	−38	151	..	−36	..	15	261
Bolivia	1,030	1,362	833	2,049	−263	−266	60	248	−6	−705	553	1,130
Botswana	645	3,030	818	2,365	−33	−145	55	201	−151	721	344	6,025
Brazil	21,869	60,256	27,826	79,817	−7,018	−16,091	144	1,812	−12,831	−33,840	6,875	43,902
Bulgaria	9,302	6,277	7,994	5,730	−412	−357	58	237	954	427	..	3,127
Burkina Faso	210	298	577	654	−3	−33	322	..	−49	..	75	373
Burundi	..	96	..	139	..	−12	..	60	..	4	105	70
Cambodia	..	896	..	1,252	..	−43	..	188	..	−210	..	324
Cameroon	1,880	2,443	1,829	2,041	−628	−609	83	87	−495	−121	206	1
Canada	74,977	247,438	70,259	236,225	−10,764	−20,913	−42	439	−6,088	−9,261	15,462	24,023
Central African Republic	201	171	327	241	3	−17	81	..	−43	..	62	146
Chad	71	271	79	563	−4	−2	24	..	12	..	12	120
Chile	5,968	20,608	7,052	22,218	−1,000	−2,975	113	528	−1,971	−4,057	4,128	16,014
China	23,637	207,251	18,900	166,754	451	−15,923	486	5,144	5,674	29,718	10,091	152,843
Hong Kong, China	25,585	228,877	27,017	231,485	..	..	..	..	−1,432	−2,608	..	89,620
Colombia	5,328	15,861	5,454	18,784	−245	−3,371	165	612	−206	−5,682	6,474	8,397
Congo, Dem. Rep.	..	..	..	..	..	..	..	..	..	..	380	83
Congo, Rep.	1,021	1,800	1,025	1,368	−162	−664	−1	−20	−167	−252	93	1
Costa Rica	1,195	4,478	1,661	4,666	−212	−202	15	136	−664	−254	197	1,064
Côte d'Ivoire	3,577	4,927	4,145	3,693	−553	−849	−706	−350	−1,826	35	46	855
Croatia	..	8,199	..	11,402	..	−83	..	852	..	−2,434	..	2,816
Czech Republic	..	29,868	..	32,713	..	−791	..	365	..	−3,271	..	12,625
Denmark	21,989	63,680	21,727	57,971	−1,977	−3,635	−161	−1,190	−1,875	883	4,347	15,881
Dominican Republic	1,271	7,060	1,919	7,780	−277	−795	205	1,352	−720	−163	279	507
Ecuador	2,887	6,000	2,946	5,787	−613	−1,347	30	391	−642	−743	1,257	1,739
Egypt, Arab Rep.	6,246	16,171	9,157	18,296	−318	884	2,791	4,146	−438	2,905	2,480	18,824
El Salvador	1,214	2,706	1,170	3,885	−62	−87	52	1,363	34	96	382	1,748
Eritrea	..	201	..	583	..	−3	..	364	..	−21	..	..
Estonia	..	3,609	..	4,142	..	−146	..	117	..	−562	..	813
Ethiopia[b]	569	1,017	782	1,683	7	−43	80	259	−126	−450	262	520
Finland	16,802	48,228	17,307	37,976	−783	−2,736	−114	−852	−1,403	6,664	2,451	10,271
France	153,197	365,342	155,915	319,781	2,680	2,693	−4,170	−8,780	−4,208	39,474	75,592	73,773
Georgia	..	622	..	1,192	..	35	..	196	..	−339	..	192
Germany[c]	224,224	590,984	225,599	558,835	914	−2,436	−12,858	−32,487	−13,319	−2,774	104,702	108,265
Ghana	1,210	1,655	1,178	2,640	−83	−131	81	576	30	−541	330	457
Greece	8,122	14,863	11,145	25,601	−273	−1,632	1,087	7,510	−2,209	−4,860	3,607	18,501
Guatemala	1,731	3,187	1,960	4,193	−44	−224	110	607	−163	−624	753	1,397
Guinea	..	741	..	834	..	−114	..	116	..	−91	..	122
Haiti	306	218	481	810	−14	−14	89	463	−101	−138	27	83
Honduras	942	2,191	1,128	2,511	−152	−212	22	260	−317	−272	159	824
Hungary	9,671	24,514	9,152	25,067	−1,113	−1,426	63	997	−531	−982	..	9,348
India	11,265	44,102	17,378	59,236	356	−2,507	2,860	11,830	−2,897	−5,811	12,010	30,647
Indonesia	23,797	63,238	21,540	62,830	−3,073	−6,332	250	1,034	−566	−4,890	6,803	23,606
Iran, Islamic Rep.	13,069	23,251	16,111	18,072	606	−410	−2	463	−2,438	5,232	12,783	..
Ireland	9,610	61,447	12,044	51,711	−902	−9,708	1,204	1,956	−2,132	1,984	3,071	9,527
Israel	8,668	30,320	11,511	38,810	−757	−2,791	2,729	6,266	−871	−5,014	4,055	22,674
Italy	97,298	310,550	110,265	261,884	1,278	−11,202	1,101	−4,040	−10,587	33,424	62,428	53,880
Jamaica	1,363	3,192	1,408	4,005	−212	−193	121	624	−163	−382	105	682
Japan	146,980	478,542	156,970	431,094	770	55,739	−1,530	−8,834	−10,750	94,354	38,919	222,443
Jordan	1,181	3,572	2,417	5,186	36	−209	1,481	1,852	281	29	1,745	1,988
Kazakhstan	..	7,611	..	8,279	..	−315	..	75	..	−909	..	1,965
Kenya	2,007	2,994	2,846	3,771	−194	−232	157	632	−876	−377	539	783
Korea, Rep.	19,815	164,920	25,152	171,300	−512	−2,455	536	667	−5,312	−8,167	3,101	52,100
Kuwait	21,857	16,041	9,823	12,876	4,847	6,277	−1,580	−1,507	15,302	7,935	5,425	4,678
Kyrgyz Republic	..	676	..	817	..	−65	..	68	..	−139	..	188
Lao PDR	..	417	..	715	..	−19	..	91	..	−225	..	117
Latvia	..	2,871	..	3,348	..	55	..	77	..	−345	..	800
Lebanon	..	1,557	..	8,053	..	380	..	2,635	..	−3,481	7,025	9,210
Lesotho	90	267	475	1,080	266	318	175	..	56	..	50	575
Lithuania	..	5,224	..	6,237	..	−198	..	230	..	−981	..	1,463
Macedonia, FYR	..	1,330	..	1,862	..	−34	..	290	..	−275	..	335
Madagascar	516	755	1,075	1,032	−44	−109	47	210	−556	−153	9	171
Malawi	313	672	487	1,269	−149	−96	63	..	−260	..	76	273
Malaysia	14,098	92,897	13,526	91,521	−836	−5,074	−2	−1,094	−266	−4,792	5,755	26,236
* Taiwan, China	21,495	139,396	22,361	132,739	48	2,391	−95	−1,327	−913	7,721	4,055	94,246

Note: For data comparability and coverage, see the Technical Notes. Figures in italics are for years other than those specified.

ECONOMY

Millions of dollars

Economy	Goods and services Exports 1980	Goods and services Exports 1997	Goods and services Imports 1980	Goods and services Imports 1997	Net income 1980	Net income 1997	Net current transfers 1980	Net current transfers 1997	Current account balance 1980	Current account balance 1997	Gross international reserves 1980	Gross international reserves 1998
Mali	262	642	519	896	−17	−51	150	126	−124	−178	26	403
Mauritania	253	407	449	414	−27	−46	90	76	−133	22	146	206
Mexico	22,622	121,831	27,601	122,424	−6,277	−12,108	834	5,247	−10,422	−7,454	4,175	31,863
Moldova	..	1,024	..	1,431	..	63	..	76	..	−267	..	144
Mongolia	475	624	1,272	588	−11	−5	0	77	−808	39	..	103
Morocco	3,233	9,510	5,207	10,627	−562	−1,175	1,130	2,205	−1,407	−87	814	4,638
Mozambique	399	500	844	1,005	22	−113	56	283	−367	−359	..	608
Myanmar	539	1,439	806	2,415	−48	−64	7	430	−307	−610	409	382
Namibia	..	1,726	..	1,908	..	54	..	322	..	193	..	260
Nepal	224	1,295	365	1,855	13	5	36	95	−93	−460	272	800
Netherlands	90,380	216,530	91,622	193,107	1,535	4,686	−1,148	−6,123	−855	21,985	37,549	31,155
New Zealand	6,403	18,224	6,934	18,269	−538	−5,444	96	336	−973	−5,153	365	4,204
Nicaragua	495	863	907	1,609	−124	−222	124	367	−411	−601	75	355
Niger	617	300	956	441	−33	−21	97	31	−276	−152	132	53
Nigeria	27,071	15,994	20,014	14,213	−1,304	−3,145	−576	1,916	5,178	552	10,640	4,329
Norway	27,264	63,213	23,749	52,286	−1,922	−1,391	−515	−1,424	1,079	8,112	6,746	18,947
Pakistan	2,958	9,956	5,709	14,677	−281	−2,167	2,163	3,213	−868	−3,675	1,568	1,626
Panama	3,422	8,316	3,394	8,649	−397	−419	40	160	−329	−592	117	954
Papua New Guinea	1,029	2,557	1,322	2,407	−179	−310	184	61	−289	−99	458	211
Paraguay	701	4,343	1,314	4,960	−4	87	0	47	−618	−483	783	784
Peru	4,631	8,356	3,970	10,842	−909	−1,602	147	681	−101	−3,407	2,804	9,882
Philippines	7,235	40,365	9,166	50,477	−420	4,681	447	1,080	−1,904	−4,351	3,978	10,789
Poland	16,061	39,717	17,842	46,367	−2,357	−1,129	721	2,035	−3,417	−5,744	574	27,383
Portugal	6,674	32,339	10,136	40,684	−608	−245	3,006	6,713	−1,064	−1,877	13,863	21,606
Romania	12,087	9,853	13,730	12,448	−777	−322	..	579	−2,420	−2,338	2,511	3,793
Russian Federation	..	102,196	..	90,065	..	−9,200	..	−362	..	2,569	..	12,043
Rwanda	165	152	319	488	2	−16	104	260	−48	−93	187	169
Saudi Arabia	106,765	64,939	55,793	52,399	526	3,156	−9,995	−15,439	41,503	257	26,129	8,843
Senegal	807	1,281	1,215	1,557	−98	−62	120	166	−386	−200	25	431
Sierra Leone	275	91	471	160	−22	11	53	26	−165	−127	31	44
Singapore	24,285	156,252	25,312	144,168	−429	3,906	−106	−1,187	−1,563	14,803	6,567	74,928
Slovak Republic	..	10,959	..	12,367	..	−124	..	173	..	−1,359	..	3,240
Slovenia	..	10,450	..	10,631	..	131	..	88	..	37	..	3,639
South Africa	28,627	35,440	22,073	34,626	−3,285	−2,602	239	−143	3,508	−1,931	7,888	5,508
Spain	32,140	148,357	38,004	142,478	−1,362	−6,396	1,646	3,003	−5,580	2,486	20,473	60,881
Sri Lanka	1,293	5,514	2,197	6,569	−26	−165	274	832	−655	−388	283	1,998
Sweden	38,151	100,989	39,878	84,779	−1,380	−6,174	−1,224	−2,736	−4,331	7,301	6,996	15,457
Switzerland	48,595	120,696	51,843	107,187	4,186	13,566	−1,140	−3,360	−201	23,714	64,748	65,158
Syrian Arab Republic	2,477	5,661	4,531	5,092	785	−504	1,520	499	251	564	828	..
Tajikistan	..	772	..	808	..	−68	..	20	..	−84	..	..
Tanzania	748	1,200	1,384	1,961	−14	−124	129	341	−521	−544	20	599
Thailand	7,939	72,415	9,996	72,437	−229	−3,480	210	479	−2,076	−3,024	3,026	29,537
Togo	550	709	691	836	−40	7	86	..	−95	..	85	118
Tunisia	3,262	8,081	3,766	8,644	−259	−863	410	785	−353	−640	700	1,856
Turkey	3,621	52,004	8,082	56,536	−1,118	−3,013	2,171	4,866	−3,408	−2,679	3,298	20,568
Turkmenistan	..	1,691	..	1,532	..	..	..	..	..	43	..	..
Uganda	329	825	441	1,651	−7	−17	−2	322	−121	−521	3	725
Ukraine	..	20,355	..	21,891	..	−644	..	845	..	−1,335	..	793
United Kingdom	146,072	375,033	134,200	375,128	−418	18,171	−4,592	−7,773	6,862	10,304	31,755	38,830
United States	271,800	937,434	290,730	1,043,473	29,580	−9,487	−8,500	−39,849	2,150	−155,375	171,413	146,006
Uruguay	1,526	4,256	2,144	4,450	−100	−208	9	81	−709	−321	2,401	2,587
Uzbekistan	..	3,980	..	4,417	..	−175	..	29	..	−583	..	..
Venezuela	19,968	25,120	15,130	18,282	329	−2,031	−439	−123	4,728	4,684	13,360	14,729
Vietnam	..	11,485	..	13,465	−72	−602	17	713	−775	−1,870	..	1,986
Yemen, Rep.	..	2,522	..	3,005	..	−636	..	1,254	..	135	..	1,010
Zambia	1,609	1,321	1,765	1,270	−205	−543	−155	..	−516	..	206	69
Zimbabwe	1,610	3,059	1,730	3,692	−61	−405	31	..	−149	..	419	310
World	2,291,841 t	6,886,726 t	2,323,396 t	6,763,911 t								
Low income	100,391	410,532	125,802	407,224								
Excl. China & India	79,559	159,077	101,300	181,262								
Middle income	509,704	1,282,683	470,588	1,335,448								
Lower middle income	197,222	476,598	208,570	496,002								
Upper middle income	312,785	805,648	267,306	838,247								
Low and middle income	632,929	1,693,448	596,880	1,742,630								
East Asia & Pacific	105,229	661,970	110,191	640,933								
Europe & Central Asia	..	347,889	..	371,154								
Latin America & Carib.	114,161	337,037	129,051	377,410								
Middle East & N. Africa	180,284	177,797	130,208	155,923								
South Asia	17,314	66,540	28,820	90,646								
Sub-Saharan Africa	87,905	100,807	81,894	106,398								
High income	1,680,398	5,195,331	1,732,925	5,022,907								

a. Includes Luxembourg. b. Data prior to 1992 include Eritrea. c. Data prior to 1990 refer to the Federal Republic of Germany before unification.

Table 16.   Private sector finance

Economy	Private investment % of gross domestic fixed investment		Stock market capitalization Millions of dollars		No. of listed domestic companies		Interest rate spread (lending minus deposit rate) Percentage points		Domestic credit provided by the banking sector % of GDP	
	1980	1997	1990	1998	1990	1997	1990	1998	1990	1998
Albania	..	..	..	..	..	..	2.1	7.2	..	53.2
Algeria	67.4	72.5	..	..	..	..	..	..	74.7	42.9
Angola	..	88.0	..	..	..	..	..	8.1		14.3
Argentina	..	94.2	3,268	45,332	179	136	..	3.1	32.4	28.3
Armenia	..	53.7	..	16	..	59	..	23.5	62.3	8.2
Australia	73.5	81.8	107,611	696,656	1,089	1,219	4.5	3.4	103.5	89.4
Austria	..	..	11,476	35,724	97	101	..	3.8	123.0	131.9
Azerbaijan	..	96.5	..	..	..	..	..	..	57.2	13.5
Bangladesh	57.7	67.8	321	1,034	134	202	4.0	5.6	24.1	32.8
Belarus	..	..	..	..	..	..	..	12.7	..	17.7
Belgium	..	..	65,449	136,965	182	138	6.9	4.2	70.9	147.9
Benin	..	59.5	..	..	..	..	9.0	..	22.4	7.0
Bolivia	..	58.1	..	344	..	11	18.0	26.6	30.7	67.1
Botswana	60.4	44.6	261	724	9	12	1.8	4.8	−46.4	−74.5
Brazil	89.8	88.7	16,354	160,887	581	536	..	..	89.8	53.3
Bulgaria	85.9	..	..	992	..	15	8.9	10.3	118.5	30.0
Burkina Faso	..	52.4	..	..	..	..	9.0	..	13.7	13.4
Burundi	8.1	30.9	..	..	..	..	..	..	24.5	25.4
Cambodia	..	68.9	..	..	..	..	..	10.5	..	7.7
Cameroon	77.8	93.7	..	..	..	..	11.0	17.0	31.2	16.8
Canada	87.4	86.3	241,920	567,635	1,144	1,362	1.3	1.6	85.8	99.0
Central African Republic	46.5	42.2	..	..	..	..	11.0	17.0	12.9	10.6
Chad	..	..	..	..	..	..	11.0	17.0	10.9	9.8
Chile	..	80.9	13,645	51,866	215	295	8.6	5.3	73.0	65.6
China	43.4	49.1	2,028	231,322	14	764	0.7	2.6	90.0	120.0
Hong Kong, China	85.1	..	83,397	413,323	284	658	3.3	2.4	156.3	146.8
Colombia	58.2	59.1	1,416	13,357	80	189	8.8	9.7	35.9	45.7
Congo, Dem. Rep.	42.4	64.4	..	..	..	..	..	..	25.3	..
Congo, Rep.	..	66.5	..	..	..	..	11.0	17.0	29.1	21.8
Costa Rica	61.3	80.0	475	820	82	114	11.4	9.7	29.9	46.1
Côte d'Ivoire	53.2	70.2	549	1,818	23	35	9.0	..	44.5	28.1
Croatia	..	59.6	..	3,190	1	77	499.3	11.1	..	46.4
Czech Republic	..	..	..	12,045	..	276	..	4.7	..	74.2
Denmark	..	..	39,063	93,766	258	237	6.2	4.8	63.0	61.2
Dominican Republic	68.4	83.0	..	140	..	6	15.2	8.0	31.5	33.1
Ecuador	59.7	82.9	69	1,527	65	41	−6.0	10.4	17.2	45.9
Egypt, Arab Rep.	30.1	68.4	1,765	24,381	573	650	7.0	3.7	106.8	95.5
El Salvador	44.8	77.0	..	499	..	59	3.2	4.7	32.0	40.8
Eritrea	..	53.8	..	..	..	..	..	..	..	..
Estonia	..	74.4	..	519	..	22	..	8.6	65.0	31.6
Ethiopia	..	56.6	..	..	..	..	3.6	4.5	50.4	44.1
Finland	..	..	22,721	73,322	73	124	4.1	3.3	84.3	57.4
France	..	..	314,384	674,368	578	683	6.0	3.3	106.1	103.3
Georgia	..	84.0	..	..	..	..	..	..	..	..
Germany	..	..	355,073	825,233	413	700	4.5	6.1	108.5	145.8
Ghana	..	46.4	76	1,384	13	21	..	..	13.2	27.7
Greece	51.5	..	15,228	79,992	145	230	8.1	7.9	73.3	56.3
Guatemala	63.8	80.4	..	139	..	7	5.1	11.1	17.4	16.1
Guinea	..	68.5	..	..	..	..	0.2	..	5.4	6.8
Haiti	..	51.0	..	..	..	..	..	10.6	32.9	25.8
Honduras	62.1	72.2	40	..	26	119	8.3	12.1	40.9	28.5
Hungary	..	..	505	14,028	21	49	4.1	3.2	82.6	..
India	55.1	68.7	38,567	105,188	6,200	5,843	..	..	50.6	48.2
Indonesia	..	60.5	8,081	21,224	125	282	3.3	−6.9	45.5	57.9
Iran, Islamic Rep.	..	..	34,282	15,123	97	263	..	..	62.1	..
Ireland	..	..	..	24,135	..	83	5.0	5.8	57.3	100.2
Israel	..	..	3,324	39,628	216	640	12.0	5.2	106.2	82.3
Italy	..	..	148,766	344,665	220	235	7.3	4.7	90.1	93.6
Jamaica	..	..	911	2,139	44	49	6.6	19.1	34.8	42.7
Japan	..	..	2,917,679	2,216,699	2,071	2,387	3.4	2.1	266.8	137.4
Jordan	51.3	84.0	2,001	5,838	105	139	2.2	3.2	110.0	93.2
Kazakhstan	..	..	..	..	..	..	..	..	..	9.1
Kenya	54.7	61.8	453	2,024	54	58	5.1	11.1	52.9	51.7
Korea, Rep.	86.0	..	110,594	114,593	669	776	0.0	2.0	56.9	84.1
Kuwait	..	..	..	25,880	..	74	0.4	2.6	217.6	92.3
Kyrgyz Republic	..	94.9	..	5	..	27	..	37.7	..	19.1
Lao PDR	..	..	..	..	..	..	2.5	11.5	5.1	16.4
Latvia	..	89.2	..	382	..	50	..	9.0	..	15.2
Lebanon	..	79.3	..	2,904	..	9	23.1	6.9	132.6	134.9
Lesotho	..	81.8	..	..	..	..	7.4	9.3	27.4	−27.2
Lithuania	..	88.2	..	1,074	..	607	..	6.2	..	11.7
Macedonia, FYR	..	91.2	..	..	..	..	..	9.4	..	20.7
Madagascar	..	46.9	..	..	..	..	5.3	15.6	26.2	13.9
Malawi	21.4	27.7	..	..	..	..	8.9	18.6	17.8	6.5
Malaysia	62.6	73.0	48,611	107,104	282	708	1.3	2.1	77.9	162.4

Note: For data comparability and coverage, see the Technical Notes. Figures in italics are for years other than those specified.

STATES AND MARKETS

Economy	Private investment % of gross domestic fixed investment		Stock market capitalization Millions of dollars		No. of listed domestic companies		Interest rate spread (lending minus deposit rate) Percentage points		Domestic credit provided by the banking sector % of GDP	
	1980	1997	1990	1998	1990	1997	1990	1998	1990	1998
Mali	..	60.8	..	..	..	..	9.0	..	13.7	14.4
Mauritania	..	78.3	..	..	..	..	5.0	..	54.7	2.4
Mexico	57.0	81.5	32,725	91,746	199	198	..	14.9	36.6	34.8
Moldova	..	86.2	..	..	..	..	..	9.1	62.8	26.7
Mongolia	..	..	..	54	..	434	..	15.7	68.5	13.3
Morocco	..	70.4	966	15,676	71	49	0.5	..	42.9	81.7
Mozambique	..	43.7	..	..	..	..	..	..	15.6	2.4
Myanmar	20.6	55.0	..	..	..	..	2.1	4.0	44.7	34.4
Namibia	42.0	62.2	21	689	3	13	10.6	7.8	19.5	53.9
Nepal	60.2	65.8	..	200	..	98	2.5	5.1	33.4	35.9
Netherlands	85.1	86.3	119,825	468,736	260	201	8.4	3.4	107.4	131.5
New Zealand	69.2	87.2	8,835	90,483	171	190	4.4	4.4	74.3	104.5
Nicaragua	..	38.6	..	..	..	..	12.5	10.9	206.6	141.0
Niger	20.1	45.3	..	..	..	..	9.0	..	16.2	9.3
Nigeria	..	44.0	1,372	2,887	131	182	5.5	13.1	23.7	14.2
Norway	70.3	..	26,130	66,503	112	196	4.6	0.7	67.4	62.4
Pakistan	36.1	65.4	2,850	5,418	487	781	..	..	50.9	50.9
Panama	..	83.3	226	2,175	13	21	3.6	4.1	52.7	92.9
Papua New Guinea	58.6	84.9	..	..	..	..	6.9	4.0	35.8	35.7
Paraguay	85.1	67.5	..	389	..	60	8.1	14.0	14.9	33.4
Peru	75.6	84.7	812	11,645	294	248	2,335.0	15.7	16.2	22.0
Philippines	69.0	..	5,927	35,314	153	221	4.6	4.7	23.2	69.8
Poland	..	86.6	144	20,461	9	143	462.5	6.3	19.5	38.6
Portugal	..	..	9,201	62,954	181	148	7.8	3.9	71.8	108.0
Romania	..	..	..	1,016	..	76	..	..	79.7	24.2
Russian Federation	..	76.6	244	20,598	13	208	..	24.7	..	35.6
Rwanda	..	18.0	..	..	..	..	6.3	..	17.1	12.1
Saudi Arabia	..	..	48,213	42,563	59	70	..	..	14.4	..
Senegal	58.1	70.1	..	..	..	..	9.0	..	33.8	21.8
Sierra Leone	..	..	..	..	..	..	12.0	16.7	26.3	52.1
Singapore	75.6	..	34,308	106,317	150	303	2.7	2.8	60.9	85.4
Slovak Republic	..	..	..	965	..	872	..	4.9	..	71.8
Slovenia	..	90.4	..	2,450	24	26	142.0	5.5	36.8	35.8
South Africa	50.8	72.9	137,540	170,252	732	642	2.1	5.3	102.7	83.4
Spain	..	..	111,404	290,383	427	384	5.4	2.1	110.9	114.9
Sri Lanka	77.4	77.6	917	1,705	175	239	−6.4	−7.0	43.1	32.2
Sweden	..	79.7	97,929	272,730	258	245	6.8	4.0	145.5	80.9
Switzerland	..	..	160,044	575,338	182	216	−0.9	3.4	179.0	177.2
Syrian Arab Republic	36.1	..	..	..	..	..	..	..	56.6	38.5
Tajikistan	..	..	..	..	..	..	..	..	..	..
Tanzania	..	83.8	..	..	..	..	..	18.9	39.2	13.5
Thailand	68.1	67.7	23,896	34,903	214	431	2.2	3.8	91.1	159.5
Togo	28.3	85.0	..	..	..	..	9.0	..	21.3	24.9
Tunisia	46.9	49.3	533	2,268	13	34	..	..	62.5	53.3
Turkey	..	78.5	19,065	33,646	110	257	..	..	25.9	34.1
Turkmenistan	..	..	..	..	..	..	..	..	..	..
Uganda	..	63.6	..	..	..	..	7.4	9.5	17.7	7.0
Ukraine	..	0.0	..	570	..	..	..	32.2	83.2	24.7
United Kingdom	70.0	87.0	848,866	1,996,225	1,701	2,046	2.2	2.7	123.0	129.3
United States	86.5	85.9	3,059,434	11,308,779	6,599	8,851	..	..	114.6	162.8
Uruguay	..	72.1	..	212	36	16	76.6	42.8	60.1	41.3
Uzbekistan	..	..	..	465	..	4	..	..	..	..
Venezuela	51.4	43.6	8,361	7,587	76	91	0.5	11.3	37.4	17.5
Vietnam	..	79.7	..	..	..	..	..	5.3	15.9	22.6
Yemen, Rep.	..	63.2	..	..	..	..	..	..	62.0	35.7
Zambia	..	60.1	..	705	..	6	9.4	18.7	67.8	63.5
Zimbabwe	87.3	88.7	2,395	1,310	57	64	2.9	13.0	41.7	62.7
World	.. w	.. w	9,398,391 s	23,540,720 s	29,189 s	40,394 s			125.2 w	126.2 w
Low income	47.7	55.2	54,588	387,184	7,211	8,948			60.0	86.0
Excl. China & India	..	63.0	16,021	52,352	1,011	2,341			38.1	37.4
Middle income	..	82.4	430,570	1,404,501	4,914	9,193			57.9	52.9
Lower middle income	..	70.5	176,701	524,675	2,455	4,433			..	57.5
Upper middle income	69.1	87.6	253,869	879,826	2,459	4,760			54.1	51.8
Low and middle income	..	73.3	485,158	1,791,685	12,125	18,141			58.5	65.3
East Asia & Pacific	57.3	66.9	197,109	426,006	1,443	3,624			70.9	108.6
Europe & Central Asia	..	75.3	19,065	243,096	110	2,711			..	32.9
Latin America & Carib.	70.0	84.0	78,470	608,395	1,748	2,238			59.1	41.9
Middle East & N. Africa	..	..	5,265	125,286	817	1,328			54.3	..
South Asia	53.8	68.6	42,655	143,250	6,996	7,163			48.3	47.2
Sub-Saharan Africa	52.0	67.3	142,594	245,652	1,011	1,077			57.5	45.5
High income	..	..	8,913,233	21,749,035	17,064	22,253			140.0	140.4

Table 17.   Role of government in the economy

Economy	Subsidies and other current transfers % of total expenditure		Value added by state-owned enterprises % of GDP		Military expenditure % of GNP		Composite ICRG risk rating[a]	Institutional Investor credit rating[a]	Highest marginal tax rate[a] Individual			Corporate %
									%	On income over (dollars)		
	1985	1997	1985–90	1990–96	1985	1995	February 1999	March 1999	1998	1998	1998
Albania	..	48	..	..	5.3	1.1	60.5	10.7	..	..	..
Algeria	..	..	..	..	2.5	3.2	52.8	25.2	..	..	..
Angola	..	..	..	..	19.9	3.0	46.5	11.5	..	..	..
Argentina	59	58	2.7	1.3	3.8	1.7	76.3	42.7	33	120,000	33
Armenia	..	..	..	..	..	0.9	61.0	..	..	..	..
Australia	63	69	..	..	2.7	2.5	80.0	74.3	47	32,404	36
Austria	58	59	..	..	1.3	0.9	84.8	88.7	50	55,564	34
Azerbaijan	..	..	..	..	..	2.8	56.0	..	40	1,850	32
Bangladesh	..	..	3.1	3.4	1.7	1.7	66.0	25.0	..	..	..
Belarus	..	54	..	..	..	0.8	59.8	11.9	..	..	..
Belgium	56	59	2.8	..	3.1	1.7	80.5	83.5	55	65,547	39
Benin	..	..	..	..	2.2	1.2	..	16.3	..	..	..
Bolivia	27	40	13.9	13.8	3.3	2.3	67.5	28.0	..	..	25
Botswana	29	31	5.6	5.6	2.5	5.3	82.0	53.5	30	21,008	15
Brazil	42	..	7.6	8.0	0.8	1.7	61.5	37.4	25	19,459	15
Bulgaria	..	37	..	..	14.1	2.8	75.5	28.6	40	7,232	30
Burkina Faso	9	..	..	..	1.9	2.9	65.5	18.8	..	..	..
Burundi	..	11	7.3	..	3.0	4.4	..	..	..	..	..
Cambodia	..	..	..	..	..	3.1	..	..	..	..	..
Cameroon	14	13	18.0	8.5	1.9	..	63.5	18.1	60	12,345	39
Canada	60	..	..	..	2.2	1.7	82.8	83.0	29	41,370	38
Central African Republic	..	..	4.1	..	1.8	..	..	..	..	..	..
Chad	2	..	..	..	2.0	3.1	..	..	..	..	..
Chile	51	52	14.4	8.1	4.0	3.8	74.0	61.8	45	6,748	15
China	..	..	..	..	4.9	2.3	75.5	57.2	45	12,077	30
Hong Kong, China	..	..	..	..	..	..	76.3	61.8	20	11,688	17
Colombia	48	..	7.0	..	1.6	2.6	57.3	44.5	35	38,764	35
Congo, Dem. Rep.	7	2	..	..	1.2	0.3	39.5	11.1	50	13,167	..
Congo, Rep.	..	..	15.1	..	4.0	2.9	50.0	9.7	..	..	..
Costa Rica	33	23	8.1	..	0.7	0.6	76.3	38.4	25	15,746	30
Côte d'Ivoire	..	..	..	..	..	..	67.3	24.3	10	3,950	35
Croatia	..	38	..	..	..	10.5	70.8	39.0	..	..	..
Czech Republic	..	74	..	..	..	2.3	76.5	..	40	23,750	35
Denmark	57	64	..	..	2.3	1.8	86.0	84.7	58	..	34
Dominican Republic	17	17	..	..	1.2	1.4	72.0	28.1	25	16,176	25
Ecuador	..	..	10.2	..	2.8	3.7	61.5	25.5	25	66,226	25
Egypt, Arab Rep.	31	25	..	..	12.8	5.7	69.0	44.4	32	13,749	40
El Salvador	11	20	1.8	..	5.7	1.1	76.8	31.2	30	22,857	25
Eritrea	..	..	..	..	..	..	..	..	..	..	..
Estonia	..	47	..	..	..	1.1	73.0	42.8	26	..	26
Ethiopia	7	13	..	..	6.7	2.2	57.8	16.2	..	..	..
Finland	67	65	..	..	1.7	2.0	86.5	82.2	38	56,450	28
France	64	65	11.2	..	4.0	3.1	81.8	90.8	..	..	33
Georgia	..	..	..	..	..	2.4	..	10.9	..	..	..
Germany	55	58	..	..	..	..	82.8	92.5	53	66,988	30
Ghana	10	..	8.5	..	1.0	1.4	62.8	29.5	35	7,269	35
Greece	35	22	11.5	..	7.0	5.5	76.3	56.1	45	55,923	35
Guatemala	14	8	1.9	2.1	1.6	1.3	68.3	27.2	25	29,221	30
Guinea	..	..	..	..	..	1.5	60.5	15.4	..	..	..
Haiti	43	..	..	..	1.5	2.9	55.0	11.2	..	..	..
Honduras	..	..	5.5	..	3.5	1.4	58.8	19.8	30	75,758	15
Hungary	69	55	..	..	7.2	1.5	77.8	55.9	42	5,394	18
India	44	38	13.4	13.4	3.5	2.4	63.3	44.5	40	5,059	40
Indonesia	24	21	14.5	..	2.4	1.8	48.5	27.9	30	8,938	30
Iran, Islamic Rep.	13	15	..	..	7.7	2.6	66.3	27.7	54	173,227	12
Ireland	57	60	..	..	1.7	1.3	87.5	81.8	46	14,493	32
Israel	33	48	..	..	20.3	9.6	64.8	54.3	50	57,387	36
Italy	57	57	..	..	2.2	1.8	80.8	79.1	46	181,801	37
Jamaica	1	..	..	..	0.9	0.8	71.3	28.0	25	2,215	33
Japan	52	..	..	..	1.0	1.0	83.3	86.5	50	230,592	38
Jordan	14	11	..	..	15.5	7.7	73.8	37.3	..	..	..
Kazakhstan	..	..	..	..	..	0.9	69.0	27.9	40	..	30
Kenya	18	18	11.6	..	2.3	2.3	63.8	24.1	33	384	35
Korea, Rep.	38	49	10.3	..	5.0	3.4	74.5	52.7	40	56,529	28
Kuwait	26	20	..	..	5.7	11.6	73.5	56.5	0	..	6
Kyrgyz Republic	..	..	..	..	..	..	..	..	40	250	30
Lao PDR	..	..	..	..	7.4	4.2	..	..	..	..	..
Latvia	..	61	..	..	..	0.9	71.0	38.0	25	..	25
Lebanon	..	13	..	..	..	3.7	55.3	31.9	..	..	..
Lesotho	5	9	..	..	5.3	1.9	..	..	..	..	..
Lithuania	..	41	..	..	..	0.5	73.5	..	33	..	29
Macedonia, FYR	..	..	..	..	..	3.3	..	..	..	..	..
Madagascar	..	8	..	..	1.9	0.9	66.0	..	..	..	..
Malawi	7	..	4.3	..	2.0	1.6	61.8	20.4	38	1,969	38
Malaysia	13	24	..	..	3.8	3.0	70.8	51.0	30	38,961	28

Note: For data comparability and coverage, see the Technical Notes. Figures in italics are for years other than those specified.

STATES AND MARKETS

Economy	Subsidies and other current transfers % of total expenditure		Value added by state-owned enterprises % of GDP		Military expenditure % of GNP		Composite ICRG risk rating[a]	Institutional Investor credit rating[a]	Highest marginal tax rate[a]		
									Individual		Corporate %
	1985	1997	1985–90	1990–96	1985	1995	February 1999	March 1999	% 1998	On income over (dollars) 1998	1998
Mali	8	..	..	..	2.9	1.8	66.5	15.4	..	..	..
Mauritania	..	..	..	..	6.9	3.2		..	..	..	..
Mexico	21	43	6.7	4.9	0.7	1.0	66.3	46.0	35	25,492	34
Moldova	..	..	..	..	..	2.1	54.5	..	..	..	..
Mongolia	..	42	..	..	8.3	2.4	66.3	..	..	..	..
Morocco	15	12	16.8	..	6.0	4.3	72.3	43.2	44	6,203	35
Mozambique	..	..	..	..	9.9	5.4	58.5	17.9	..	..	..
Myanmar	..	..	..	..	..	..	55.0	18.7	..	..	..
Namibia	29	..	..	..	..	2.1	77.8	..	35	16,461	35
Nepal	..	..	..	..	1.1	0.9	..	24.4	..	..	..
Netherlands	69	72	..	..	3.0	2.1	87.8	91.7	60	51,373	35
New Zealand	51	38	..	..	2.0	1.3	77.5	73.1	33	19,922	33
Nicaragua	11	25	..	..	17.4	2.2	47.8	11.6	30	18,083	30
Niger	..	..	5.1	..	0.8	1.2	54.8	..	..	..	..
Nigeria	9	..	..	..	1.5	..	56.3	16.8	25	1,600	28
Norway	68	69	..	..	3.1	2.7	88.3	86.8	28	6,835	28
Pakistan	15	8	..	..	6.2	6.1	53.5	20.4	..	..	..
Panama	17	25	7.6	7.6	2.0	1.4	72.3	39.9	30	200,000	15
Papua New Guinea	16	..	..	..	1.5	1.4	67.0	30.4	47	57,803	15
Paraguay	23	..	4.8	4.5	1.1	1.4	63.0	31.3	0	..	30
Peru	11	36	6.4	5.7	6.7	1.7	66.3	35.0	30	50,036	30
Philippines	7	18	2.3	2.2	1.4	1.5	73.0	43.3	34	12,464	34
Poland	75	62	..	..	10.2	2.3	80.5	56.7	40	14,372	36
Portugal	45	37	15.1	..	2.9	2.6	82.0	76.1	40	34,186	37
Romania	27	50	..	..	6.9	2.5	57.8	31.2	45	3,672	38
Russian Federation	..	..	..	..	..	11.4	49.8	20.0	35	8,587	35
Rwanda	..	..	..	..	1.7	5.2	..	..	..	..	..
Saudi Arabia	..	..	..	..	22.7	13.5	69.0	54.4	0	..	45
Senegal	..	..	6.9	..	2.8	1.6	63.0	21.7	50	20,821	35
Sierra Leone	5	24	..	..	0.8	6.1	29.5	6.3	..	..	..
Singapore	10	8	..	..	5.9	4.7	87.5	81.3	28	238,095	26
Slovak Republic	..	..	..	..	..	3.0	77.8	41.3	42	31,576	40
Slovenia	..	..	..	..	..	1.5	79.5	58.4	..	..	..
South Africa	31	48	14.9	..	3.8	2.2	68.8	45.8	45	20,576	35
Spain	55	66	..	..	2.4	1.6	79.5	80.3	48	69,216	35
Sri Lanka	16	20	..	..	2.9	4.6	63.8	33.3	30	4,862	35
Sweden	64	71	..	..	3.0	2.8	83.5	79.7	31	27,198	28
Switzerland	..	66	..	..	2.4	1.6	87.3	92.7	13	46,382	45
Syrian Arab Republic	..	..	..	..	21.8	7.2	71.5	23.0	..	..	..
Tajikistan	..	..	..	..	..	3.7	..	..	..	..	..
Tanzania	22	..	12.9	..	3.8	1.8	58.8	18.3	35	13,405	30
Thailand	8	7	..	..	4.2	2.5	67.0	46.9	37	84,836	30
Togo	11	..	..	..	2.6	2.3	60.8	16.6	..	..	..
Tunisia	29	29	..	..	3.6	2.0	72.8	50.3	..	..	..
Turkey	41	47	6.5	5.1	4.6	4.0	56.0	36.9	45	59,259	25
Turkmenistan	..	..	..	..	..	1.7	..	..	..	..	..
Uganda	..	..	..	..	2.0	2.3	63.0	20.3	30	4,316	30
Ukraine	..	..	..	..	..	2.9	59.0	17.2	40	10,754	30
United Kingdom	55	56	3.6	2.8	5.1	3.0	81.3	90.2	40	44,580	31
United States	49	60	..	..	6.1	3.8	82.8	92.2	40	278,450	35
Uruguay	43	61	5.0	..	2.9	2.4	73.0	46.5	0	..	30
Uzbekistan	..	..	..	..	..	3.8	..	..	..	..	..
Venezuela	31	48	22.3	..	2.1	1.1	62.8	34.4	..	..	..
Vietnam	..	..	..	..	19.4	2.6	60.3	27.8	50	5,695	25
Yemen, Rep.	..	33	..	..	..	..	62.8	..	..	..	..
Zambia	..	15	32.2	..	..	2.8	59.8	16.1	30	1,212	35
Zimbabwe	37	..	10.8	11.3	5.7	4.0	52.0	26.5	40	3,578	38
World	28 m	32 m			5.2 w	2.8 w	67.7 m	35.3 m			
Low income	..	..					59.3	19.8			
Excl. China & India	..	..					59.0	18.5			
Middle income	23	33					69.5	36.3			
Lower middle income	19	25					67.9	29.2			
Upper middle income	38	49					73.0	42.9			
Low and middle income	..	..					64.0	28.6			
East Asia & Pacific	..	..					67.8	38.0			
Europe & Central Asia	..	..					65.9	33.8			
Latin America & Carib.	23	33					67.0	33.7			
Middle East & N. Africa	..	13					70.5	34.3			
South Asia	16	20					62.8	25.7			
Sub-Saharan Africa	..	..					60.8	18.5			
High income	55	59					83.4	80.8			

a. This copyrighted material is reprinted with permission from the following data providers: PRS Group, 6320 Fly Road, Suite 102, P.O. Box 248, East Syracuse, N.Y. 13057; *Institutional Investor*, Inc., 488 Madison Avenue, New York, N.Y. 10022; PricewaterhouseCoopers, 1177 Avenue of the Americas, New York, N.Y. 10036. Prior written consent from the original data providers cited must be obtained for third-party use of these data.

Table 18. Power and transportation

| Economy | Electric power | | | | Paved roads % of total | | Goods transported by road Millions of ton-km hauled | | Goods transported by rail Ton-km per $ million of GDP (PPP) | | Air passengers carried Thousands |
| | Consumption per capita Kilowatt-hours | | Transmission and distribution losses % of output | | | | | | | | |
	1980	1996	1980	1996	1990	1997	1990	1997	1990	1997	1996
Albania	1,083	904	4	52	..	30	1,195	80	85,396	5,523	13
Algeria	265	524	11	18	67	69	14,000	..	25,161	..	3,494
Angola	67	61	25	28	25	25			..	..	585
Argentina	1,170	1,541	13	18	29	29	..	..	36,412	..	7,913
Armenia	2,729	905	10	38	99	100	1,533	479	..	..	
Australia	5,393	8,086	10	7	35	39	..	..	82,122	..	30,075
Austria	4,371	5,952	6	6	100	100	13,300	16,600	89,362	78,423	4,719
Azerbaijan	2,440	1,822	14	22	..	..	3,287	497	..	..	1,233
Bangladesh	16	97	35	30	7	12	..	..	8,032	..	1,252
Belarus	2,455	2,476	9	16	96	98	22,128	9,065	1,297,626	624,045	843
Belgium	4,402	6,878	5	5	81	80	32,100	42,800	46,189	31,976	5,174
Benin	36	48	220	87	20	20	..	..	..	..	75
Bolivia	226	371	10	12	4	6	..	..	37,118	..	1,784
Botswana	..	..	..	..	32	24	..	..	..	..	104
Brazil	974	1,660	12	17	10	9	..	..	56,068	..	22,012
Bulgaria	3,349	3,577	10	13	92	92	13,823	483	360,291	210,161	718
Burkina Faso	..	..	..	..	17	16	..	..	..	..	138
Burundi	..	..	..	..	18	7	..	..	..	..	9
Cambodia	..	..	..	..	8	8	..	1,200			..
Cameroon	167	171	7	20	11	13	..	..	33,209	34,023	362
Canada	12,329	15,129	9	7	35	35	54,700	71,473	433,765	..	22,856
Central African Republic	..	..	..	..	..	..	144	60	..	..	75
Chad	..	..	..	..	1	1	..	..	..	..	93
Chile	876	1,864	12	9	14	14	..	..	15,882	5,998	3,622
China	253	687	8	7	..	..	..	..	671,824	364,633	51,770
Hong Kong, China	2,167	5,013	11	14	100	100	..	..	..	..	..
Colombia	561	922	16	22	12	12	6,227	..	2,400	..	8,342
Congo, Dem. Rep.	147	130	8	3	..	..	..	..	32,198	..	178
Congo, Rep.	94	207	1	0	10	10	..	..	144,851	..	253
Costa Rica	860	1,349	0	12	15	17	2,243	3,070	..	..	918
Côte d'Ivoire	192	174	7	16	9	10	..	..	15,791	13,486	179
Croatia	0	2,291	..	16	80	82	2,458	470	190,170	86,593	727
Czech Republic	3,595	4,875	7	8	100	100	..	43,088	..	207,099	1,394
Denmark	4,245	6,113	7	5	100	100	9,400	9,400	19,119	14,518	5,892
Dominican Republic	433	608	21	25	45	49	..	..	..	..	30
Ecuador	361	616	14	21	13	19	2,638	3,558			1,925
Egypt, Arab Rep.	380	924	13	0	72	78	31,400	31,500	23,310	..	4,282
El Salvador	293	516	13	13	14	20	..	..	..	..	1,800
Eritrea	..	..	..	..	19	22	..	..	..	..	..
Estonia	3,433	3,293	5	19	52	51	4,510	2,773	516,391	536,100	149
Ethiopia	16	18	8	1	15	15	..	..	2,467	..	743
Finland	7,779	12,979	6	4	61	64	26,300	24,100	99,052	68,994	5,598
France	3,881	6,091	7	6	..	100	137,000	158,200	49,908	39,109	41,253
Georgia	1,910	1,020	16	23	94	94	7,370	98	..	..	152
Germany	5,005	5,596	4	5	99	99	245,700	281,300	..	39,350	40,118
Ghana	426	275	0	0	20	24	..	..	6,811	..	197
Greece	2,064	3,395	7	7	92	92	12,600	12,800	6,395	1,913	6,396
Guatemala	212	364	6	13	25	28	..	..	..	..	300
Guinea	..	..	..	..	15	17	..	..	..	..	36
Haiti	41	34	26	54	22	24	..	..	..	..	..
Honduras	225	350	14	27	21	20	..	..	..	..	..
Hungary	2,335	2,814	10	13	50	43	1,836	770	247,428	104,327	1,563
India	130	347	18	18	47	46	..	..	248,469	176,217	13,395
Indonesia	44	296	19	12	46	46	..	..	8,619	..	17,139
Iran, Islamic Rep.	491	1,142	10	20	..	50	..	..	40,223	..	7,610
Ireland	2,528	4,363	10	9	94	94	5,100	5,500	14,322	9,132	7,677
Israel	2,826	5,081	5	4	100	100	..	..	16,663	11,947	3,695
Italy	2,831	4,196	9	7	100	100	177,900	197,600	20,795	18,420	25,839
Jamaica	482	2,108	17	11	64	71	..	..	..	..	1,388
Japan	4,395	7,083	4	4	69	74	274,444	305,510	11,603	8,664	95,914
Jordan	387	1,187	19	10	100	100	..	..	78,625	47,242	1,299
Kazakhstan	0	2,865	..	15	55	83	44,775	6,481	5,042,201	..	568
Kenya	92	126	16	16	13	14	..	..	75,496	..	779
Korea, Rep.	841	4,453	6	5	72	74	31,841	74,504	40,875	24,826	33,003
Kuwait	4,749	12,808	10	0	73	81	..	..	..	..	2,133
Kyrgyz Republic	1,556	1,479	6	33	90	91	5,627	350	..	..	488
Lao PDR	..	..	..	..	24	14	120	..	..	..	125
Latvia	2,664	1,783	26	47	13	38	5,853	800	1,209,517	1,114,210	276
Lebanon	789	1,651	10	13	95	95	..	..	..	..	775
Lesotho	..	..	..	..	18	18	..	..	..	..	17
Lithuania	2,715	1,785	12	11	82	89	7,019	8,622	915,522	545,100	214
Macedonia, FYR	0	2,443	..	..	59	64	1,708	1,210	..	..	287
Madagascar	..	..	..	..	15	12	..	..	..	..	542
Malawi	..	..	..	..	22	19	..	..	14,881	10,003	153
Malaysia	630	2,078	9	11	70	75	..	..	16,313	9,416	15,118

Note: For data comparability and coverage, see the Technical Notes. Figures in italics are for years other than those specified.

STATES AND MARKETS

| Economy | Electric power | | | | Paved roads % of total | | Goods transported by road Millions of ton-km hauled | | Goods transported by rail Ton-km per $ million of GDP (PPP) | | Air passengers carried Thousands |
| | Consumption per capita Kilowatt-hours | | Transmission and distribution losses % of output | | | | | | | | |
	1980	1996	1980	1996	1990	1997	1990	1997	1990	1997	1996
Mali	..	..	..	..	11	12	..	..	53,882	..	75
Mauritania	..	..	..	..	11	11	..	..	..	..	235
Mexico	846	1,381	11	15	35	37	108,884	165,000	64,884	53,917	14,678
Moldova	1,495	1,314	8	23	87	87	6,305	780	..	..	190
Mongolia	..	..	..	..	10	3	1,871	..	1,324,119	..	..
Morocco	223	408	10	4	49	52	2,638	2,086	72,108	55,523	2,301
Mozambique	370	76	0	0	17	19	..	110	..	..	163
Myanmar	31	58	22	36	11	12	..	..	..	..	335
Namibia	..	..	..	..	11	8	..	..	308,833	139,137	237
Nepal	13	39	29	28	38	42	..	..	..	..	755
Netherlands	4,057	5,555	4	4	88	90	22,900	27,600	12,779	9,751	17,114
New Zealand	6,269	8,420	13	11	57	58	..	..	51,927	..	9,597
Nicaragua	303	256	14	28	11	10	..	..	..	..	51
Niger	..	..	..	..	29	8	..	..	..	..	75
Nigeria	68	85	36	32	30	19	..	..	3,009	..	221
Norway	18,289	23,487	9	8	69	74	7,940	11,838	..	..	12,727
Pakistan	125	333	29	23	54	58	352	84,174	43,586	26,582	5,375
Panama	828	1,140	13	18	32	34	..	..	..	..	689
Papua New Guinea	..	..	..	..	3	4	..	..	..	..	970
Paraguay	233	914	6	7	9	10	..	..	..	..	261
Peru	502	598	13	15	10	10	..	..	7,486	..	2,328
Philippines	353	405	2	17	0	0	..	..	..	..	7,263
Poland	2,470	2,420	10	13	62	66	49,800	95,500	475,103	284,381	1,806
Portugal	1,469	3,044	12	10	..	..	10,900	11,200	13,976	13,598	4,806
Romania	2,434	1,757	6	12	51	51	13,800	22,400	507,379	231,838	913
Russian Federation	4,706	4,165	8	9	74	..	300	138	2,725,816	..	22,117
Rwanda	..	..	..	..	9	9	..	..	..	..	9
Saudi Arabia	1,356	3,980	9	8	41	43	..	..	4,634	4,206	11,706
Senegal	97	103	11	16	27	29	..	..	51,209	..	155
Sierra Leone	..	..	..	..	11	8	..	..	..	..	15
Singapore	2,412	7,196	5	4	97	97	..	..	..	..	11,841
Slovak Republic	3,817	4,450	8	6	99	99	4,180	3,779	..	297,426	63
Slovenia	4,089	4,766	8	6	72	83	3,440	1,775	142,879	112,529	393
South Africa	3,213	3,719	8	8	30	42	..	..	430,594	337,153	7,183
Spain	2,401	3,749	9	9	74	99	151,000	186,700	22,427	15,984	27,759
Sri Lanka	96	203	15	17	32	40	19	30	5,926	..	1,171
Sweden	10,216	14,239	9	7	71	77	26,500	31,200	127,826	103,299	9,879
Switzerland	5,579	6,919	7	7	..	..	10,400	13,000	..	..	10,468
Syrian Arab Republic	354	755	18	0	72	23	..	..	48,075	29,655	599
Tajikistan	2,217	2,292	7	12	72	83	..	..	..	..	594
Tanzania	50	59	14	12	37	4	..	..	77,466	91,623	224
Thailand	279	1,289	10	9	55	98	..	..	14,869	..	14,078
Togo	..	..	..	..	21	32	..	..	..	..	75
Tunisia	379	674	12	11	76	79	..	..	58,795	53,343	1,371
Turkey	439	1,161	12	17	..	25	..	139,789	30,838	17,747	8,464
Turkmenistan	1,720	1,020	12	11	74	81	..	..	..	..	523
Uganda	..	..	..	..	..	..	..	..	12,582	11,567	100
Ukraine	3,598	2,640	8	10	94	95	79,668	20,532	2,109,937	1,411,737	1,151
United Kingdom	4,160	5,198	8	9	100	100	136,300	153,900	17,191	..	64,209
United States	8,914	11,796	9	7	58	61	1,073,100	1,439,532	360,699	361,911	571,072
Uruguay	977	1,605	15	20	74	90	..	..	10,455	16,125	504
Uzbekistan	2,085	1,657	9	9	79	87	..	..	..	..	1,566
Venezuela	2,037	2,498	12	20	36	39	..	..	..	..	4,487
Vietnam	50	177	18	19	24	25	..	..	13,526	16,352	2,108
Yemen, Rep.	59	99	6	26	9	8	..	..	..	..	588
Zambia	1,016	560	7	11	17	..	..	..	73,728	56,426	235
Zimbabwe	990	765	14	7	14	47	..	..	274,759	196,429	654
World	1,576 w	2,027 w	8 w	8 w	39 m	44 m					1,389,943 s
Low income	188	433	12	12	17	19					103,110
Excl. China & India	155	218	14	19	17	18					37,945
Middle income	1,585	1,902	9	12	52	51					238,360
Lower middle income	1,835	1,771	8	11	54	51					102,609
Upper middle income	1,188	2,106	10	13	52	47					135,751
Low and middle income	633	886	9	12	29	30					341,470
East Asia & Pacific	260	724	8	9	24	12					143,204
Europe & Central Asia	2,925	2,795	8	11	77	83					46,014
Latin America & Carib.	854	1,347	12	16	22	26					76,275
Middle East & N. Africa	483	1,162	10	9	67	50					37,484
South Asia	116	313	19	19	38	41					22,445
Sub-Saharan Africa	444	439	9	10	17	16					16,049
High income	5,783	8,121	8	6	86	92					1,048,473

Table 19.   Communications, information, and science and technology

Economy	Daily newspapers 1996	Radios 1996	Television sets 1997	Telephone main lines 1997	Mobile telephones 1997	Personal computers 1997	Internet hosts Per 10,000 people January 1999	Scientists and engineers in R&D Per million people 1985–95	High-technology exports % of mfg. exports 1997	No. of patent applications filed[a] 1996 Residents	No. of patent applications filed[a] 1996 Nonresidents
	Per 1,000 people										
Albania	34	235	*161*	23	1	..	0.30	..	1	1	18,761
Algeria	38	239	*67*	48	1	4.2	0.01	..	22	48	150
Angola	12	54	91	5	1	0.7	0.00	..	..	..	..
Argentina	123	677	289	191	56	39.2	18.28	671	15	..	..
Armenia	*23*	5	*218*	150	2	..	1.01	..	..	162	20,268
Australia	297	1,385	638	505	264	362.2	420.57	3,166	39	9,196	34,125
Austria	294	740	496	492	144	210.7	176.79	1,631	*24*	2,506	75,985
Azerbaijan	*28*	20	*211*	87	5	..	0.21	..	..	165	16,470
Bangladesh	9	50	*7*	*3*	*0*	..	..	..	*0*	70	156
Belarus	*174*	290	314	227	1	..	0.70	2,339	..	701	20,347
Belgium	160	792	510	468	95	235.3	162.39	1,814	23	1,356	59,099
Benin	2	108	*91*	6	1	0.9	0.02	177	..	..	..
Bolivia	55	672	*115*	69	15	..	0.78	250	9	17	106
Botswana	27	155	*27*	56	*0*	13.4	4.18	..	..	5	56
Brazil	40	435	316	107	28	26.3	12.88	168	18	2,655	29,451
Bulgaria	253	531	*366*	323	8	*29.7*	9.05	..	..	318	22,235
Burkina Faso	1	32	6	3	0	0.7	0.16	..	..	..	..
Burundi	3	68	10	3	0	..	0.00	32	..	1	4
Cambodia	..	127	124	2	3	0.9	0.06	..	..	..	..
Cameroon	7	162	*81*	5	0	*1.5*	0.00	..	3	..	..
Canada	159	1,078	708	609	139	270.6	364.25	2,656	25	3,316	45,938
Central African Republic	2	84	5	3	0	..	0.00	55	*0*	..	..
Chad	0	249	*2*	1	0	..	0.00	..	..	..	..
Chile	*99*	354	233	180	28	54.1	20.18	..	19	189	1,771
China	..	195	270	56	10	6.0	6.00	350	21	11,698	41,016
Hong Kong, China	800	695	412	565	343	230.8	122.71	98	29	41	2,059
Colombia	49	565	217	148	35	33.4	3.93	..	20	87	1,172
Congo, Dem. Rep.	3	98	*43*	*1*	0	..	0.00	..	..	2	27
Congo, Rep.	*8*	124	8	*8*	*0*	..	0.00	..	*16*	..	..
Costa Rica	91	271	403	169	19	..	9.20	..	*14*	..	..
Côte d'Ivoire	16	157	61	9	2	3.3	0.16	..	..	..	..
Croatia	114	333	*267*	335	27	*22.0*	12.84	1,978	19	259	356
Czech Republic	256	806	447	318	51	82.5	71.79	1,159	13	623	24,856
Denmark	311	1,146	568	633	273	360.2	526.77	2,647	27	2,452	72,151
Dominican Republic	52	177	*84*	88	16	..	5.79	..	23	..	..
Ecuador	70	342	294	75	13	*13.0*	1.26	169	12	7	354
Egypt, Arab Rep.	38	316	*127*	56	0	7.3	0.31	458	7	504	706
El Salvador	48	461	*250*	*56*	7	..	1.33	19	16	3	64
Eritrea	..	101	11	6	0	..	0.00	..	..	..	..
Estonia	173	680	479	321	99	15.1	152.98	2,018	24	12	21,144
Ethiopia	2	194	5	3	0	..	0.01	..	*0*	3	..
Finland	455	1,385	534	556	417	310.7	1,058.13	2,812	26	3,262	61,556
France	218	943	606	575	99	174.4	82.91	2,584	*31*	17,090	81,418
Georgia	..	553	*473*	114	6	..	1.27	..	..	289	21,124
Germany	311	946	570	550	99	255.5	160.23	2,843	26	56,757	98,338
Ghana	14	238	109	6	1	1.6	0.10	..	..	..	33
Greece	*153*	477	466	516	89	44.8	48.81	774	12	434	52,371
Guatemala	31	73	126	41	6	*3.0*	0.83	99	13	2	102
Guinea	..	47	41	3	0	0.3	0.00	..	..	..	..
Haiti	3	55	*5*	8	0	..	0.00	..	..	3	6
Honduras	55	409	*90*	37	2	..	0.16	..	4	10	126
Hungary	189	697	436	304	69	49.0	82.74	1,033	39	832	24,147
India	..	105	69	19	1	2.1	0.13	149	*11*	1,660	6,632
Indonesia	23	155	134	25	5	8.0	0.75	..	20	40	3,957
Iran, Islamic Rep.	24	237	148	107	4	*32.7*	0.04	521	..	..	..
Ireland	153	703	*455*	411	146	241.3	148.70	1,871	62	925	52,407
Israel	291	530	321	450	283	186.1	161.96	..	33	1,363	12,172
Italy	104	874	483	447	204	113.0	58.80	1,325	15	8,860	71,992
Jamaica	64	482	*323*	*140*	*22*	4.6	1.24	8	*67*	..	..
Japan	580	957	708	479	304	202.4	133.53	6,309	38	340,861	60,390
Jordan	45	287	43	70	*2*	8.7	0.80	106	*26*	..	..
Kazakhstan	30	384	*234*	108	*1*	..	0.94	..	..	1,024	20,064
Kenya	9	108	19	8	0	2.3	0.23	..	11	15	39,034
Korea, Rep.	*394*	1,037	341	444	150	150.7	40.00	2,636	*39*	68,446	45,548
Kuwait	376	688	*491*	227	116	82.9	32.80	..	4	..	..
Kyrgyz Republic	13	115	44	76	*0*	..	4.04	703	*24*	126	20,179
Lao PDR	4	139	4	5	1	*1.1*	0.00	..	..	..	..
Latvia	246	699	*592*	302	31	7.9	42.59	1,189	15	197	21,498
Lebanon	141	892	354	179	135	31.8	5.56	..	..	..	..
Lesotho	7	48	*24*	10	*1*	..	0.09	..	..	2	37,043
Lithuania	92	292	*377*	283	41	*6.5*	27.48	..	21	101	21,249
Macedonia, FYR	19	184	*252*	204	6	..	2.56	..	..	53	18,934
Madagascar	4	192	*45*	3	0	1.3	0.04	11	2	7	20,800
Malawi	*3*	256	*2*	4	*0*	..	0.00	..	*3*	3	39,031
Malaysia	163	432	166	195	113	46.1	21.36	87	*67*	..	..

Note: For data comparability and coverage, see the Technical Notes. Figures in italics are for years other than those specified.

STATES AND MARKETS

Economy	Daily newspapers 1996	Radios 1996	Television sets 1997	Telephone main lines 1997	Mobile telephones 1997	Personal computers 1997	Internet hosts Per 10,000 people January 1999	Scientists and engineers in R&D Per million people 1985–95	High-technology exports % of mfg. exports 1997	No. of patent applications filed[a] 1996 Residents	Nonresidents
Mali	1	49	10	2	0	0.6	0.00	..	..	..	..
Mauritania	1	150	89	5	0	5.3	0.06	..	..	..	..
Mexico	97	324	251	96	18	37.3	11.64	213	33	389	30,305
Moldova	59	720	302	145	1	3.8	1.17	1,539	9	290	20,245
Mongolia	27	139	63	37	1	5.4	0.08	943	2	114	20,882
Morocco	26	241	160	50	3	2.5	0.20	..	27	90	237
Mozambique	3	39	4	4	0	1.6	0.08	..	8	..	..
Myanmar	10	89	7	5	0	..	0.00	..	..	..	..
Namibia	19	143	32	58	8	18.6	15.79	..	..	..	..
Nepal	11	37	4	8	0	..	0.07	..	0	..	..
Netherlands	305	963	541	564	110	280.3	358.51	2,656	44	4,884	61,958
New Zealand	223	1,027	501	486	149	263.9	360.44	1,778	11	1,421	26,947
Nicaragua	32	283	190	29	2	..	1.47	214	38	..	..
Niger	0	69	26	2	0	0.2	0.02	..	..	..	..
Nigeria	24	197	61	4	0	5.1	0.03	15	..	..	..
Norway	593	920	579	621	381	360.8	717.53	3,678	24	1,550	25,628
Pakistan	21	92	65	19	1	4.5	0.23	54	4	16	782
Panama	62	299	187	134	6	..	2.66	..	14	31	142
Papua New Guinea	15	91	24	11	1	..	0.25	..	..	..	..
Paraguay	50	182	101	43	17	..	2.18	..	4	..	..
Peru	43	271	143	68	18	12.3	1.91	625	10	52	565
Philippines	82	159	109	29	18	13.6	1.21	157	56	163	2,634
Poland	113	518	413	194	22	36.2	28.07	1,299	12	2,414	24,902
Portugal	75	306	523	402	152	74.4	50.01	1,185	11	105	71,544
Romania	..	317	226	167	9	8.9	7.42	1,382	7	1,831	22,139
Russian Federation	105	344	390	183	3	32.0	10.04	3,520	19	18,138	28,149
Rwanda	0	102	..	3	0	..	0.00	24	..	..	..
Saudi Arabia	59	319	260	117	17	43.6	0.15	..	29	27	810
Senegal	5	141	41	13	1	11.4	0.21	..	55	..	..
Sierra Leone	5	251	20	4	0	..	0.03	..	..	..	..
Singapore	324	739	354	543	273	399.5	210.02	2,728	71	215	38,403
Slovak Republic	185	580	401	259	37	241.6	33.27	1,821	15	201	22,865
Slovenia	206	416	353	364	47	188.9	89.83	2,544	16	301	21,686
South Africa	30	316	125	107	37	41.6	34.67	938	..	..	..
Spain	99	328	506	403	110	122.1	67.21	1,210	17	2,689	81,294
Sri Lanka	29	210	91	17	6	4.1	0.29	173	..	50	21,138
Sweden	446	907	531	679	358	350.3	487.13	3,714	34	7,077	76,364
Switzerland	330	969	536	661	147	394.9	315.52	..	28	2,699	75,576
Syrian Arab Republic	20	274	68	88	0	1.7	0.00	..	1	..	..
Tajikistan	20	..	281	38	0	..	0.12	709	..	32	19,570
Tanzania	4	278	21	3	1	1.6	0.04	..	..	..	..
Thailand	65	204	234	80	33	19.8	3.35	119	43	203	4,355
Togo	4	217	19	6	1	5.8	0.24	..	..	..	..
Tunisia	31	218	182	70	1	8.6	0.07	388	11	46	128
Turkey	111	178	286	250	26	20.7	4.30	261	9	367	19,668
Turkmenistan	..	96	175	78	0	..	0.55	..	..	66	18,948
Uganda	2	123	26	2	0	1.4	0.05	..	..	..	38,497
Ukraine	54	872	493	186	1	5.6	3.13	3,173	..	3,640	22,862
United Kingdom	332	1,445	641	540	151	242.4	240.99	2,417	41	25,269	104,084
United States	212	2,115	847	644	206	406.7	1,131.52	3,732	44	111,883	111,536
Uruguay	116	610	242	232	46	21.9	46.61	688	8	25	182
Uzbekistan	3	452	273	63	0	..	0.10	1,760	..	914	21,088
Venezuela	206	471	172	116	46	36.6	3.37	208	10	182	1,822
Vietnam	4	106	180	21	2	4.6	0.00	308	..	37	22,206
Yemen, Rep.	15	64	273	13	1	1.2	0.01	..	0	..	..
Zambia	14	121	80	9	0	..	0.31	..	..	6	93
Zimbabwe	18	96	29	17	1	9.0	0.87	..	6	30	181
World	.. w	380 w	280 w	144 w	40 w	58.4 w	75.22 w				
Low income	..	147	162	32	5	4.4	0.17				
Excl. China & India	13	133	59	16	1	..	0.23				
Middle income	75	383	272	136	24	32.4	10.15				
Lower middle income	63	327	247	108	11	12.2	4.91				
Upper middle income	95	469	302	179	43	45.5	19.01				
Low and middle income	..	218	194	65	11	12.3	3.08				
East Asia & Pacific	..	206	237	60	15	11.3	1.66				
Europe & Central Asia	99	412	380	189	13	17.7	13.00				
Latin America & Carib.	71	414	263	110	26	31.6	9.64				
Middle East & N. Africa	33	265	140	71	6	9.8	0.25				
South Asia	..	99	69	18	1	2.1	0.14				
Sub-Saharan Africa	12	172	44	16	4	7.2	2.39				
High income	286	1,300	664	552	188	269.4	470.12				

a. Other patent applications filed in 1996 include those filed under the auspices of the African Intellectual Property Organization (75 by residents, 20,863 by nonresidents), the African Regional Industrial Property Organization (10 by residents, 20,347 by nonresidents), the European Patent Office (38,546 by residents, 48,068 by nonresidents), and the Eurasian Patent Organization (39 by residents, 18,055 by nonresidents). The original information was provided by the World Intellectual Property Organization (WIPO). The International Bureau of WIPO assumes no liability or responsibility with regard to the transformation of these data.

Table 20.   Global trade

Economy	Merchandise exports Millions of dollars		Mfg. % of total		Exports of commercial services Millions of dollars		Merchandise imports Millions of dollars		Mfg. % of total		Imports of commercial services Millions of dollars	
	1983	1998[a]	1983	1997	1983	1997	1983	1998[a]	1983	1997	1983	1997
Albania	..	135	..	99	13	52	..	650	..	..	22	93
Algeria	12,480	9,380	1	4	649	..	10,399	9,080	71	63	2,251	..
Angola	1,822	4,222	..	..	129	226	983	2,332	..	..	628	1,738
Argentina	7,836	25,227	16	33	1,405	2,941	4,504	31,402	75	88	2,026	6,104
Armenia	..	235	..	..	..	..	..	875	..	..	..	..
Australia	20,113	55,949	15	27	3,954	18,360	21,458	64,678	69	80	6,735	18,385
Austria	15,427	61,717	85	89	9,343	29,213	19,423	68,260	71	81	5,662	28,371
Azerbaijan	..	545	..	..	..	..	..	1,075	..	..	..	..
Bangladesh	725	3,778	66	..	164	266	2,165	6,710	41	..	329	1,184
Belarus	..	7,016	..	..	..	..	..	8,509	..	..	..	..
Belgium[b]	51,939	171,703	68	76	9,589	33,431	55,313	158,843	58	74	9,119	31,606
Benin	67	195	..	..	43	..	318	613	..	..	83	..
Bolivia	755	1,103	1	16	95	180	577	1,983	70	81	229	379
Botswana	635	2,942	..	..	84	145	735	2,261	..	..	186	339
Brazil	21,899	50,992	39	53	1,648	6,765	16,801	60,980	34	74	3,734	17,612
Bulgaria	12,140	4,275	..	61	1,059	1,308	12,290	4,980	..	50	598	1,153
Burkina Faso	58	327	10	..	..	..	291	735	53	..	..	..
Burundi	80	86	..	..	..	..	182	121	..	..	..	..
Cambodia	15	330	..	..	..	150	180	660	..	..	..	182
Cameroon	976	1,860	..	8	408	242	1,224	1,358	..	63	703	485
Canada	76,749	214,298	51	62	8,284	29,290	64,789	205,038	73	80	11,869	35,944
Central African Republic	80	174	..	33	11	..	77	232	..	60	91	..
Chad	105	202	..	..	..	..	157	240	..	..	..	..
Chile	3,830	14,895	7	14	756	3,592	3,085	18,828	48	73	1,116	3,854
China	22,151	183,757	55	85	2,466	24,516	21,323	140,165	70	77	1,840	30,063
Hong Kong, China[c]	22,454	174,145	89	93	6,267	38,179	24,409	188,745	73	87	3,696	23,209
Colombia	3,001	10,890	18	30	819	4,053	4,963	15,840	70	79	1,214	4,171
Congo, Dem. Rep.	1,131	530	..	..	..	..	470	460	..	..	..	..
Congo, Rep.	640	1,600	9	..	71	45	648	550	79	..	715	553
Costa Rica	873	4,066	26	23	264	1,490	988	4,676	66	85	249	1,135
Côte d'Ivoire	2,090	4,183	11	..	376	577	1,839	2,817	57	52	919	1,186
Croatia	..	4,541	..	72	..	3,994	..	8,383	..	73	..	1,972
Czech Republic	..	26,360	..	85	..	7,033	..	28,820	..	79	..	5,305
Denmark	16,053	47,047	55	61	5,018	15,105	16,266	45,795	60	73	4,425	14,936
Dominican Republic	785	903	20	..	451	2,071	1,471	4,716	40	..	292	956
Ecuador	2,348	4,133	1	8	297	689	1,487	5,496	84	71	469	1,089
Egypt, Arab Rep.	3,215	3,908	12	38	2,955	9,096	10,275	13,600	63	62	2,509	5,813
El Salvador	735	1,263	21	39	127	276	892	3,112	61	67	238	354
Eritrea	..	..	..	..	..	..	..	..	..	..	..	..
Estonia	..	3,208	..	65	..	1,314	..	4,750	..	71	..	649
Ethiopia[d]	..	551	..	..	119	318	..	1,100	..	..	220	378
Finland	12,518	42,360	74	83	2,489	7,097	12,826	31,945	59	73	2,429	8,180
France	94,943	307,031	70	76	33,380	80,269	105,907	287,210	56	76	24,694	62,086
Georgia	..	195	..	..	..	..	..	1,095	..	..	..	..
Germany[e]	169,417	539,689	84	86	23,285	74,722	152,877	466,619	..	68	34,714	118,144
Ghana	1,158	1,550	0	..	35	152	1,248	1,680	28	..	91	395
Greece	4,413	9,709	48	51	2,812	9,224	9,500	23,470	52	72	1,304	4,196
Guatemala	1,159	2,550	24	31	43	542	1,126	4,619	74	68	244	627
Guinea	488	730	..	..	..	70	267	1,000	..	..	..	204
Haiti	166	133	..	..	..	..	441	606	..	..	..	..
Honduras	672	1,580	9	20	80	328	803	2,417	67	72	154	359
Hungary	8,770	22,940	61	46	583	4,825	8,555	25,820	59	66	447	3,634
India	9,148	33,210	52	73	3,167	8,679	14,061	42,850	53	51	3,622	12,277
Indonesia	21,152	48,840	6	42	546	6,792	16,352	27,420	62	73	4,228	16,214
Iran, Islamic Rep.	19,950	13,150	..	..	478	743	18,320	13,000	..	..	4,110	2,899
Ireland	8,592	63,252	62	80	1,092	6,020	9,159	43,681	67	79	1,351	15,032
Israel	5,108	23,282	80	92	2,671	8,338	9,574	29,130	59	76	3,136	10,867
Italy	72,877	240,869	85	89	17,435	71,729	79,808	213,995	41	67	13,570	70,146
Jamaica	718	1,352	14	26	520	1,428	1,494	3,025	49	65	384	1,146
Japan	146,965	387,965	96	95	19,560	68,136	126,437	280,531	21	54	33,540	122,079
Jordan	580	1,750	46	..	1,102	1,717	3,036	3,910	54	..	911	1,241
Kazakhstan	..	5,410	..	..	..	833	..	4,300	..	..	..	1,081
Kenya	876	2,053	15	25	359	764	1,334	3,273	52	64	295	731
Korea, Rep.	24,446	133,223	91	87	3,662	25,439	26,192	93,345	51	61	3,369	29,037
Kuwait	11,504	9,700	19	4	679	1,513	7,373	8,200	83	80	2,896	4,302
Kyrgyz Republic	..	605	..	38	..	..	..	835	..	48	..	..
Lao PDR	41	359	..	..	..	..	150	648	..	..	..	..
Latvia	..	1,812	..	61	..	1,027	..	3,189	..	62	..	637
Lebanon	691	716	..	..	..	..	3,661	7,060	..	..	..	..
Lesotho	31	170	..	..	23	..	485	980	..	..	30	..
Lithuania	..	3,755	..	60	..	1,020	..	6,025	..	66	..	850
Macedonia, FYR	..	..	..	..	..	..	..	..	..	..	..	..
Madagascar	263	215	9	36	40	253	387	477	61	73	122	280
Malawi	229	530	6	..	29	..	311	760	71	..	128	..
Malaysia	14,130	73,275	25	76	1,743	14,868	13,198	58,540	70	82	3,872	17,363
* Taiwan, China	25,094	109,890	89	96	2,342	17,021	20,308	104,240	51	73	3,626	24,112

Note: For data comparability and coverage, see the Technical Notes. Figures in italics are for years other than those specified.

GLOBAL LINKS

Economy	Merchandise exports Millions of dollars 1983	1998[a]	Mfg. % of total 1983	1997	Exports of commercial services Millions of dollars 1983	1997	Merchandise imports Millions of dollars 1983	1998[a]	Mfg. % of total 1983	1997	Imports of commercial services Millions of dollars 1983	1997
Mali	165	518	..	..	28	62	353	811	..	..	154	324
Mauritania	292	448	..	..	20	19	240	380	..	..	170	197
Mexico	25,559	117,505	37	80	3,749	11,214	10,896	128,940	96	83	4,300	11,813
Moldova	..	680	..	..	..	..	..	1,075	..	..	..	..
Mongolia	560	418	..	10	55	47	852	443	..	65	43	87
Morocco	2,006	7,295	40	35	774	2,203	3,592	10,270	44	48	476	1,267
Mozambique	132	200	..	20	..	..	636	760	..	66	..	..
Myanmar	378	866	..	..	56	..	268	2,053	..	..	70	..
Namibia	846	1,400	..	..	..	356	921	1,600	..	..	..	494
Nepal	94	402	41	77	107	795	464	1,716	63	32	83	216
Netherlands	64,684	198,212	49	67	13,133	48,529	61,652	184,148	52	68	13,824	43,812
New Zealand	5,414	12,114	20	29	1,315	3,905	5,333	12,501	68	82	1,749	4,893
Nicaragua	429	610	8	33	36	124	826	1,553	66	67	101	229
Niger	299	268	..	..	..	..	324	424	..	..	..	..
Nigeria	10,357	10,360	0	..	402	786	12,254	9,900	54	..	2,211	4,694
Norway	17,997	39,645	29	23	6,988	14,256	13,497	36,193	74	77	7,102	14,460
Pakistan	3,077	8,370	63	86	668	1,463	5,329	9,170	51	52	847	2,413
Panama	321	712	9	18	976	1,382	1,412	3,097	60	71	517	1,154
Papua New Guinea	813	2,142	2	..	62	436	1,120	1,697	50	..	314	747
Paraguay	269	1,021	7	17	134	..	546	3,050	62	65	149	..
Peru	3,015	5,550	8	15	649	1,447	2,548	10,050	60	61	892	2,190
Philippines	4,890	29,330	52	85	1,516	15,130	7,977	31,960	60	74	1,598	14,073
Poland	11,580	26,300	64	72	1,990	8,969	10,600	48,020	52	77	1,783	5,681
Portugal	4,599	23,503	72	84	1,427	7,523	8,240	35,082	50	73	1,131	6,148
Romania	10,160	8,295	..	79	727	1,398	7,640	11,820	..	67	726	1,998
Russian Federation	..	73,900	..	23	..	13,898	..	59,500	..	46	..	19,082
Rwanda	121	88	..	..	18	42	279	299	..	..	86	151
Saudi Arabia	45,861	38,800	..	9	4,151	4,484	39,197	23,700	84	73	16,424	13,927
Senegal	618	924	..	..	200	364	1,025	1,189	..	..	253	405
Sierra Leone	119	17	25	..	17	71	160	91	37	..	40	79
Singapore[c]	21,833	109,846	49	84	7,733	30,379	28,158	101,496	55	82	3,747	19,422
Slovak Republic	..	10,665	..	76	..	2,151	..	12,965	..	60	..	2,062
Slovenia	..	9,120	..	90	..	2,032	..	10,100	..	76	..	1,439
South Africa	18,508	26,322	18	43	2,669	4,882	15,813	29,268	63	64	3,360	6,050
Spain	19,734	109,037	69	69	11,252	43,570	29,193	132,789	37	68	4,825	24,264
Sri Lanka	1,066	4,770	28	..	282	850	1,820	5,970	55	..	396	1,270
Sweden	27,446	84,455	77	78	6,191	17,584	26,098	67,637	63	76	6,166	19,462
Switzerland	25,592	78,741	91	93	8,230	25,615	29,192	80,017	73	84	4,625	14,132
Syrian Arab Republic	1,923	3,916	15	10	384	1,366	4,542	3,900	46	68	698	1,302
Tajikistan	..	560	..	..	..	..	..	725	..	..	..	..
Tanzania	364	674	..	9	106	460	832	1,454	..	64	162	706
Thailand	6,368	53,575	31	71	1,733	15,619	10,287	41,800	60	77	1,845	17,126
Togo	163	237	25	..	58	..	282	373	58	..	112	..
Tunisia	1,850	5,746	44	78	921	2,427	3,107	8,333	64	75	483	1,014
Turkey	5,728	26,140	46	75	1,917	19,193	9,235	46,400	43	72	1,073	8,085
Turkmenistan	..	650	..	..	..	..	..	1,015	..	..	..	..
Uganda	372	557	..	..	..	..	377	1,312	..	..	..	..
Ukraine	..	12,825	..	..	..	4,937	..	14,746	..	..	..	2,268
United Kingdom	91,619	272,692	63	83	27,060	91,928	100,080	316,077	65	81	20,962	71,265
United States	205,639	682,977	65	80	51,040	231,896	269,878	944,586	60	78	39,590	152,448
Uruguay	1,045	2,848	29	37	255	1,465	788	3,842	41	76	455	903
Uzbekistan	..	3,940	..	..	..	..	..	4,205	..	..	..	..
Venezuela	13,937	17,200	2	11	1,035	1,290	6,419	15,600	67	69	2,636	5,213
Vietnam	616	8,980	..	..	..	..	1,526	11,015	..	..	..	..
Yemen, Rep.	701	2,481	..	..	..	..	3,101	1,901	..	..	..	..
Zambia	836	901	..	..	79	..	851	807	..	..	321	..
Zimbabwe	1,135	2,508	..	27	124	..	1,205	3,092	..	77	409	..
World	**1,757,216 t**	**5,414,844 t**	**66 w**	**78 w**	**356,892 t**	**1,326,312 t**	**1,755,569 t**	**5,358,567 t**	**57 w**	**73 w**	**377,843 t**	**1,307,618 t**
Low income	88,785	334,896	42	75	10,869	51,538	102,719	295,254	63	71	21,228	85,092
Excl. China & India	..	..	..	..	5,457	18,068	..	..	..	..	17,369	44,337
Middle income	410,520	953,662	41	64	57,320	230,847	381,036	1,018,458	60	71	87,836	247,297
Lower middle income	..	329,691	..	..	27,570	101,056	205,214	370,345	..	..	35,868	103,897
Upper middle income	225,563	622,990	48	72	30,088	130,233	184,578	647,211	60	73	51,234	143,661
Low and middle income	493,984	1,288,084	42	66	68,072	282,785	482,412	1,313,145	61	71	108,707	332,063
East Asia & Pacific	97,271	537,234	52	78	12,292	105,518	101,854	411,054	62	73	17,773	128,602
Europe & Central Asia	..	249,450	..	51	..	77,726	..	309,720	..	64	..	59,655
Latin America & Carib.	99,355	270,876	25	50	14,268	44,471	74,429	337,406	63	77	21,329	63,390
Middle East & N. Africa	118,705	103,782	..	16	14,926	30,412	123,259	113,156	68	..	38,488	36,039
South Asia	14,868	50,743	53	75	4,457	12,396	25,032	67,304	52	52	5,329	17,494
Sub-Saharan Africa	49,231	84,706	12	..	6,603	13,026	51,878	86,534	59	..	14,347	25,133
High income	1,274,830	4,124,433	72	81	288,345	1,043,005	1,278,838	4,040,845	56	74	271,116	977,279

a. WTO 1998 figures are based on preliminary estimates made in early 1999; for many countries, the estimates are based on incomplete preliminary data and are subject to revision. b. Includes Luxembourg. c. Includes reexports. d. Data prior to 1992 include Eritrea. e. Data prior to 1990 refer to the Federal Republic of Germany before unification.

Table 21. Aid and financial flows

Economy	Net private capital flows (Millions of dollars)		Foreign direct investment (Millions of dollars)		External debt Total (Millions of dollars)		Present value % of GNP	Official development assistance Dollars per capita		% of GNP	
	1990	1997	1990	1997	1990	1997	1997	1990	1997	1990	1997
Albania	31	47	0	48	349	706	22	3	51	0.5	6.7
Algeria	−424	−543	0	7	27,877	30,921	65	10	8	0.4	0.6
Angola	237	−24	−335	350	8,594	10,160	206	29	37	3.3	10.2
Argentina	−203	19,834	1,836	6,645	62,233	123,221	38	6	6	0.1	0.1
Armenia	0	51	0	51	41	666	26	1	45	0.1	9.7
Australia	..	..	7,465	8,737	..	..	..	..	..	..	..
Austria	..	..	653	2,354	..	..	..	..	..	..	..
Azerbaijan	..	658	..	650	..	504	10	0	23	0.0	5.0
Bangladesh	70	118	3	135	12,768	15,125	20	19	8	6.9	2.3
Belarus	173	169	7	200	189	1,162	5	18	4	0.5	0.2
Belgium	..	..	..	..	..	..	..	..	..	..	..
Benin	1	3	1	3	1,292	1,624	46[b]	57	39	15.0	10.7
Bolivia	3	812	27	601	4,275	5,247	51[b]	85	92	12.0	9.2
Botswana	77	95	95	100	563	562	9	117	81	4.2	2.4
Brazil	562	43,377	989	19,652	119,877	193,663	23	1	3	0.0	0.1
Bulgaria	−42	569	4	498	10,890	9,858	96	2	25	0.1	2.2
Burkina Faso	0	0	0	0	834	1,297	30[b]	38	35	12.3	15.6
Burundi	−5	1	1	1	907	1,066	58	49	19	24.1	12.6
Cambodia	0	200	0	203	1,854	2,129	52	17	36	13.0	12.1
Cameroon	−125	16	−113	45	6,679	9,293	93	39	36	4.2	5.9
Canada	..	..	7,581	7,132	..	..	..	..	..	..	..
Central African Republic	0	6	1	6	698	885	53	86	27	17.2	9.3
Chad	−1	15	0	15	524	1,026	35	55	31	19.9	14.3
Chile	2,098	9,637	590	5,417	19,227	31,440	43	8	9	0.4	0.2
China	8,107	60,828	3,487	44,236	55,301	146,697	15	2	2	0.6	0.2
Hong Kong, China	..	..	..	..	..	..	..	7	1	0.1	0.0
Colombia	345	10,151	500	5,982	17,222	31,777	27	3	7	0.3	0.2
Congo, Dem. Rep.	−24	1	−12	1	10,270	12,330	215	24	4	10.5	3.2
Congo, Rep.	−100	9	0	9	4,953	5,071	247	104	99	9.9	14.7
Costa Rica	23	104	163	57	3,756	3,548	34	78	−1	4.4	0.0
Côte d'Ivoire	57	−91	48	327	17,251	15,609	141[b]	59	31	7.5	4.7
Croatia	..	2,397	..	388	..	6,842	36	0	10	0.0	0.2
Czech Republic	876	1,818	207	1,286	6,383	21,456	40	1	10	0.0	0.2
Denmark	..	..	1,132	2,792	..	..	..	..	..	..	..
Dominican Republic	130	401	133	405	4,372	4,239	27	16	9	1.7	0.5
Ecuador	183	829	126	577	12,109	14,918	72	16	15	1.7	0.9
Egypt, Arab Rep.	698	2,595	734	891	32,947	29,849	28	104	32	12.4	2.5
El Salvador	8	61	2	11	2,148	3,282	25	68	51	7.4	2.7
Eritrea	..	0	..	0	..	76	4	..	33	..	14.8
Estonia	104	347	82	266	58	658	14	10	44	0.3	1.4
Ethiopia[a]	−45	28	12	5	8,634	10,078	131	21	11	15.8	10.1
Finland	..	..	812	2,128	..	..	..	..	..	..	..
France	..	..	13,183	23,045	..	..	..	..	..	..	..
Georgia	21	50	0	50	79	1,446	20	0	46	0.0	4.7
Germany	..	..	2,532	−344	..	..	..	..	..	..	..
Ghana	−5	203	15	130	3,873	5,982	57[b]	38	28	9.8	7.2
Greece	..	..	1,005	984	..	..	..	4	..	0.0	..
Guatemala	44	166	48	90	3,080	4,086	21	23	29	2.7	1.7
Guinea	−1	−23	18	1	2,476	3,520	65	49	55	10.9	10.1
Haiti	8	3	8	3	889	1,057	21	27	44	5.8	11.8
Honduras	77	124	44	122	3,724	4,698	86	93	51	16.4	7.0
Hungary	−308	2,605	0	2,079	21,276	24,373	52	6	16	0.2	0.4
India	1,872	8,307	162	3,351	83,717	94,404	18	2	2	0.4	0.4
Indonesia	3,235	10,863	1,093	4,677	69,872	136,174	62	10	4	1.6	0.4
Iran, Islamic Rep.	−392	−303	−362	50	9,020	11,816	9	2	3	0.1	0.2
Ireland	..	..	627	2,727	..	..	..	..	..	..	..
Israel	..	..	101	2,706	..	..	..	294	204	2.7	1.2
Italy	..	..	6,411	3,700	..	..	..	..	..	..	..
Jamaica	92	377	138	137	4,671	3,913	90	117	28	7.4	1.8
Japan	..	..	1,777	3,200	..	..	..	..	..	..	..
Jordan	254	61	38	22	8,177	8,234	110	275	104	23.8	6.8
Kazakhstan	117	2,158	100	1,321	35	4,278	19	7	8	0.4	0.6
Kenya	124	−87	57	20	7,056	6,486	49	51	16	14.8	4.6
Korea, Rep.	1,056	13,069	788	2,844	46,976	143,373	33	1	−3	0.0	0.0
Kuwait	..	..	..	20	..	..	..	3	1	0.0	0.0
Kyrgyz Republic	0	50	0	50	4	928	39	5	52	1.1	14.1
Lao PDR	6	90	6	90	1,768	2,320	53	44	71	20.6	19.5
Latvia	43	559	29	521	65	503	8	1	33	0.0	1.5
Lebanon	12	1,070	6	150	1,779	5,036	32	71	58	7.5	1.6
Lesotho	17	42	17	29	396	660	35	83	46	13.9	7.4
Lithuania	−3	637	0	355	56	1,540	15	1	27	0.0	1.1
Macedonia, FYR	..	8	..	15	..	1,542	75	..	75	..	6.9
Madagascar	7	13	22	14	3,701	4,105	85	35	59	13.7	24.3
Malawi	2	1	0	2	1,558	2,206	45[b]	59	34	28.8	13.7
Malaysia	769	9,312	2,333	5,106	15,328	47,228	48	26	−11	1.1	−0.3

Note: For data comparability and coverage, see the Technical Notes. Figures in italics are for years other than those specified.

GLOBAL LINKS

	Millions of dollars				External debt		Present value % of GNP	Official development assistance			
	Net private capital flows		Foreign direct investment		Total Millions of dollars			Dollars per capita		% of GNP	
Economy	1990	1997	1990	1997	1990	1997	1997	1990	1997	1990	1997
Mali	−8	15	−7	15	2,467	2,945	73[b]	58	44	20.5	18.7
Mauritania	6	2	7	3	2,096	2,453	169	122	102	25.8	23.9
Mexico	8,253	20,533	2,634	12,477	104,431	149,690	37	2	1	0.1	0.0
Moldova	0	257	0	60	39	1,040	52	2	15	0.3	3.5
Mongolia	28	16	2	7	350	718	49	134	99	..	26.7
Morocco	341	1,303	165	1,200	24,458	19,321	53	44	17	4.2	1.4
Mozambique	35	37	9	35	4,653	5,991	135[b]	76	58	45.6	29.6
Myanmar	153	180	161	80	4,695	5,074	..	4	1	..	..
Namibia	..	..	29	137	..	..	..	91	102	5.0	5.0
Nepal	−8	12	6	23	1,640	2,398	25	23	19	11.8	8.3
Netherlands	..	..	12,352	9,012	..	..	..	..	..	..	..
New Zealand	..	..	1,735	2,650	..	..	..	..	..	..	..
Nicaragua	21	157	0	173	10,708	5,677	244[b]	101	90	39.0	22.7
Niger	9	−12	−1	2	1,726	1,579	56[b]	52	35	16.5	18.6
Nigeria	467	1,285	588	1,539	33,440	28,455	72	3	2	1.0	0.5
Norway	..	..	1,003	3,545	..	..	..	..	..	..	..
Pakistan	182	2,097	244	713	20,663	29,664	38	10	5	2.7	1.0
Panama	127	1,443	132	1,030	6,678	6,338	88	42	47	2.0	1.5
Papua New Guinea	204	143	155	200	2,594	2,272	41	109	78	13.5	7.8
Paraguay	67	273	76	250	2,104	2,052	20	14	24	1.1	1.3
Peru	59	3,094	41	2,030	20,064	30,496	45	19	20	1.3	0.8
Philippines	639	4,164	530	1,222	30,580	45,433	51	20	9	2.9	0.8
Poland	71	6,787	89	4,908	49,366	39,889	27	35	17	2.4	0.5
Portugal	..	..	2,610	1,713	..	..	..	..	..	..	..
Romania	4	2,274	0	1,215	1,140	10,442	29	11	9	0.6	0.6
Russian Federation	5,562	12,453	0	6,241	59,797	125,645	27	2	5	0.0	0.2
Rwanda	6	1	8	1	712	1,111	33	43	75	11.6	32.0
Saudi Arabia	..	..	1,864	−1,129	..	..	..	3	1	0.0	0.0
Senegal	42	44	57	30	3,732	3,671	56	112	49	14.9	9.7
Sierra Leone	36	4	32	4	1,151	1,149	89	18	27	9.1	16.0
Singapore	..	..	5,575	8,631	..	..	..	−1	0	0.0	0.0
Slovak Republic	278	1,074	0	165	2,008	9,989	48	1	13	0.0	0.3
Slovenia	..	..	..	321	..	..	..	..	49	..	0.5
South Africa	..	3,610	..	1,725	..	25,222	19	..	12	..	0.4
Spain	..	..	13,984	5,556	..	..	..	..	..	..	..
Sri Lanka	54	574	43	430	5,863	7,638	35	43	19	9.2	2.3
Sweden	..	..	1,982	9,867	..	..	..	..	..	..	..
Switzerland	..	..	4,961	5,506	..	..	..	..	..	..	..
Syrian Arab Republic	18	69	71	80	17,068	20,865	114	58	13	6.0	1.2
Tajikistan	0	20	0	20	10	901	34	2	17	0.4	5.0
Tanzania[c]	5	143	0	158	6,447	7,177	77	48	31	30.3	13.9
Thailand	4,399	3,444	2,444	3,745	28,165	93,416	61	14	10	0.9	0.4
Togo	0	−6	0	0	1,275	1,339	59	74	29	16.4	8.4
Tunisia	−122	903	76	316	7,691	11,323	58	48	21	3.3	1.1
Turkey	1,782	12,221	684	805	49,424	91,205	43	21	0	0.8	0.0
Turkmenistan	..	847	..	85	..	1,771	59	2	2	0.1	0.4
Uganda	16	179	0	180	2,583	3,708	31[b]	42	41	16.2	12.8
Ukraine	369	1,419	0	623	551	10,901	21	6	4	0.3	0.4
United Kingdom	..	..	32,518	37,007	..	..	..	..	..	..	..
United States	..	..	47,918	93,448	..	..	..	..	..	..	..
Uruguay	−192	632	0	160	4,415	6,652	32	17	17	0.7	0.3
Uzbekistan	40	435	40	285	60	2,760	11	3	6	0.3	0.5
Venezuela	−126	6,282	451	5,087	33,170	35,541	41	4	1	0.2	0.0
Vietnam	16	1,994	16	1,800	23,270	21,629	78	19	13	4.2	4.1
Yemen, Rep.	30	−138	−131	−138	6,345	3,856	56	37	23	9.3	7.3
Zambia	194	79	203	70	7,265	6,758	136	62	65	16.0	16.7
Zimbabwe	85	32	−12	70	3,247	4,961	52	36	29	4.2	4.1
World	.. s	.. s	192,662 s	400,394 s	.. s	.. s		14 w	11 w	1.4 w	0.7 w
Low income	14,819	88,685	5,732	59,509	473,398	669,626		15	11	4.3	2.9
Excl. China & India	4,840	19,551	2,083	11,922	334,380	428,525		..	..	..	..
Middle income	28,091	210,049	18,697	103,786	998,783[d]	1,645,941[d]		13	9	1.0	0.5
Lower middle income	..	..	..	..	..	..		13	10	1.5	0.9
Upper middle income	..	..	..	..	..	..		10	5	0.3	0.1
Low and middle income	42,910	298,734	24,429	163,295	1,472,181[d]	2,315,567[d]		14	11	1.5	0.9
East Asia & Pacific	18,720	104,257	11,135	64,284	286,061	654,551		6	4	1.0	0.5
Europe & Central Asia	7,695	49,875	1,097	22,314	221,028	390,579		19	15	0.9	0.5
Latin America & Carib.	12,411	118,918	8,188	61,573	475,366	703,669		12	13	0.5	0.5
Middle East & N. Africa	622	7,899	2,711	5,240	182,399	192,378		45	19	2.3	1.0
South Asia	2,174	11,110	464	4,662	129,899	154,946		5	3	1.5	0.8
Sub-Saharan Africa	1,288	6,674	834	5,222	177,428	219,445		40	26	10.7	5.0
High income	..	..	168,233	237,099	601[e]	1,034[e]		..	..	..	..

a. Data prior to 1992 include Eritrea. b. Data are from debt sustainability analyses undertaken as part of the Heavily Indebted Poor Countries (HIPC) Debt Initiative. Present value estimates for these countries are for public and publicly guaranteed debt only. c. GNP data refer to mainland Tanzania only. d. Includes data for Gibraltar not included in other tables. e. Data refer only to Malta.

Table 1a. Key indicators for other economies

Economy	Population Thousands 1998	Surface area Thousands of sq. km 1996	Population density People per sq. km 1998	Gross national product (GNP) Millions of dollars 1998[b]	Gross national product (GNP) Avg. annual growth rate (%) 1997–98	GNP per capita Dollars 1998[b]	GNP per capita Avg. annual growth rate (%) 1997–98	GNP measured at PPP[a] Millions of dollars 1998	GNP measured at PPP[a] Per capita (dollars) 1998	Life expectancy at birth Years 1997	Adult illiteracy % of people 15 and above 1997	Carbon dioxide emissions Thousands of tons 1996
Afghanistan	25,761	652.1	40	..	..	..[c]	..	..	..	45	67	1,176
American Samoa	63	0.2	315	..	..	..[d]	..	..	..	..	..	282
Andorra	65	0.5	144	..	..	..[e]	..	..	..	..	..	..
Antigua and Barbuda	67	0.4	152	555	2.1	8,300	1.2	631	9,440	75	..	322
Aruba	94	0.2	495	..	..	..[e]	..	..	..	..	..	1,517
Bahamas, The	294	13.9	29	..	3.0	..[e]	1.4	3,073	10,460	74	4	1,707
Bahrain	641	0.7	929	4,912	2.1	7,660	–1.3	8,787	13,700	73	14	10,578
Barbados	266	0.4	618	2,096	2.5	7,890	2.2	3,257	12,260	76	..	835
Belize	236	23.0	10	615	0.8	2,610	–1.8	927	3,940	75	..	355
Bermuda	63	0.1	1,260	..	..	..[e]	..	..	..	..	..	462
Bhutan	759	47.0	16	..	..	..[c]	..	..	..	61	..	260
Bosnia and Herzegovina	..	51.1	..	..	..	..[g]	..	..	..	..	..	3,111
Brunei	314	5.8	60	..	..	..[e]	..	..	..	76	10	5,071
Cape Verde	412	4.0	102	437	4.5	1,060	1.7	1,216[f]	2,950[f]	68	29	121
Cayman Islands	36	0.3	138	..	..	..[e]	..	..	..	..	..	282
Channel Islands	149	0.3	478	..	..	..[e]	..	..	..	78	..	..
Comoros	531	2.2	238	196	1.0	370	–1.5	787[f]	1,480[f]	60	45	55
Cuba	11,103	110.9	101	..	..	..[g]	..	..	..	76	4	31,170
Cyprus	753	9.3	82	..	..	..[g]	..	..	..	78	4	5,379
Djibouti	653	23.2	28	..	..	..[g]	..	..	..	50	..	366
Dominica	74	0.8	98	222	0.2	3,010	0.2	291	3,940	76	..	81
Equatorial Guinea	432	28.1	15	647	36.0	1,500	32.5	1,900	4,400	50	20	143
Faeroe Islands	42	1.4	42	..	..	..[e]	..	..	..	..	..	630
Fiji	827	18.3	45	1,745	–4.2	2,110	–5.7	2,962	3,580	73	8	762
French Guiana	163	90.0	2	..	..	..[e]	..	..	..	..	..	920
French Polynesia	228	4.0	62	..	..	..[e]	..	..	..	72	..	561
Gabon	1,181	267.7	5	4,664	5.7	3,950	3.2	7,865	6,660	52	..	3,690
Gambia, The	1,216	11.3	122	413	5.0	340	2.0	1,743[f]	1,430[f]	53	67	216
Greenland	56	341.7	0	..	..	..[e]	..	..	..	68	..	509
Grenada	96	0.3	283	305	1.6	3,170	0.9	454	4,720	72	..	161
Guadeloupe	431	1.7	255	..	..	..[d]	..	..	..	77	..	1,513
Guam	149	0.6	271	..	..	..[e]	..	..	..	77	..	4,078
Guinea-Bissau	1,161	36.1	41	186	–28.9	160	–30.4	872	750	44	66	231
Guyana	857	215.0	4	660	–1.5	770	–2.6	2,302	2,680	64	2	953
Iceland	274	103.0	3	7,675	5.1	28,010	4.1	6,256	22,830	79	..	2,195
Iraq	22,347	438.3	51	..	..	..[g]	..	..	..	58	..	91,387
Isle of Man	73	0.6	122	..	..	..[d]	..	..	..	..	..	..
Kiribati	85	0.7	117	101	15.2	1,180	12.6	297	3,480	60	..	22
Korea, Dem. Rep.	23,171	120.5	192	..	..	..[g]	..	..	..	63	..	254,326
Liberia	2,969	111.4	31	..	..	..[c]	..	..	..	47	52	326
Libya	5,330	1,759.5	3	..	..	..[d]	..	..	..	70	24	40,579
Liechtenstein	32	0.2	200	..	..	..[e]	..	..	..	..	..	..
Luxembourg	427	2.6	161	18,587	4.2	43,570	3.0	15,962	37,420	76	..	8,281
Macao	455	0.0	22,763	..	..	..[e]	..	..	..	78	8	1,407
Maldives	262	0.3	874	323	..	1,230	..	..	..	67	4	297
Malta	378	0.3	1,180	3,564	4.1	9,440	3.4	5,138[f]	13,610[f]	77	9	1,751
Marshall Islands	62	0.2	310	..	–4.4	1,540	..	..	..	..	..	..
Martinique	397	1.1	374	..	..	..[e]	..	..	..	79	3	2,023
Mauritius	1,159	2.0	571	4,288	4.5	3,700	3.5	10,899	9,400	71	17	1,744
Mayotte	126	0.4	315	..	..	..[d]	..	..	..	..	..	..
Micronesia, Fed. Sts.	113	0.7	155	203	–3.1	1,800	–4.8	..	..	67	..	..
Monaco	32	0.0	1,600	..	..	..[e]	..	..	..	..	..	..
Netherlands Antilles	213	0.8	266	..	..	..[e]	..	..	..	75	4	6,430
New Caledonia	206	18.6	11	..	..	..[e]	..	..	..	73	..	1,751
Northern Mariana Islands	70	0.5	140	..	..	..[c]	..	..	..	..	..	..
Oman	2,322	212.5	11	..	..	..[d]	..	..	..	73	33	15,143
Palau	19	0.5	32	..	..	..	..	..	..	71	..	245
Puerto Rico	3,857	9.0	435	..	..	..[d]	..	..	..	75	7	15,806
Qatar	742	11.0	67	..	..	..[e]	..	..	..	74	20	29,121
Reunion	687	2.5	275	..	..	..[e]	..	..	..	75	14	1,561
Samoa	176	2.8	62	180	1.8	1,020	0.5	607	3,440	69	..	132
São Tomé and Principe	142	1.0	148	40	2.5	280	0.2	192	1,350	64	..	77
Seychelles	79	0.5	175	507	–1.3	6,450	–2.5	827	10,530	71	..	169
Solomon Islands	415	28.9	15	311	–7.0	750	–9.7	862[f]	2,080[f]	70	..	161
Somalia	9,076	637.7	14	..	..	..[c]	..	..	..	47	..	15
St. Kitts and Nevis	41	0.4	113	250	3.7	6,130	3.7	324	7,940	70	..	103
St. Lucia	160	0.6	263	546	3.7	3,410	3.0	738	4,610	70	..	191
St. Vincent and the Grenadines	113	0.4	290	274	2.3	2,420	1.6	463	4,090	73	..	125
Sudan	28,347	2,505.8	12	8,221	5.0	290	2.7	38,602	1,360	55	47	3,473
Suriname	413	163.3	3	685	2.7	1,660	2.4	..	..	70	..	2,099
Swaziland	988	17.4	57	1,384	1.8	1,400	–1.3	3,540	3,580	60	23	341
Tonga	99	0.8	137	167	–1.0	1,690	–1.8	381	3,860	70	..	117
Trinidad and Tobago	1,317	5.1	257	5,835	6.3	4,430	5.5	8,854	6,720	73	2	22,237
United Arab Emirates	2,671	83.6	32	48,666	–5.7	18,220	–8.9	52,659[f]	19,720[f]	75	25	81,843
Vanuatu	182	12.2	15	231	2.1	1,270	–0.4	574[f]	3,160[f]	65	..	62
Virgin Islands (U.S.)	118	0.3	348	..	..	..[e]	..	..	..	77	..	12,912
West Bank and Gaza	2,673	6.2	411	..	..	..[g]	..	..	..	71	..	..
Yugoslavia, FR (Serb./Mont.)	10,640	102.2	104	..	..	..[g]	..	..	..	72	..	..

a. Purchasing power parity; see the Technical Notes. b. Calculated using the World Bank *Atlas* method. c. Estimated to be low income ($760 or less). d. Estimated to be upper middle income. ($3,031 to $9,360). e. Estimated to be high income ($9,361 or more). f. The estimate is based on regression; others are extrapolated from the latest International Comparison Programme benchmark estimates. g. Estimated to be lower middle income ($761 to $3,030).

Technical Notes

hese technical notes discuss the sources and methods used to compile the 149 indicators included in this edition of Selected World Development Indicators. The notes follow the order in which the indicators appear in the tables.

Sources

The data published in the Selected World Development Indicators are taken from *World Development Indicators 1999.* Where possible, however, revisions reported since the closing date of that edition have been incorporated. In addition, newly released estimates of population and gross national product (GNP) per capita for 1998 are included in table 1.

The World Bank draws on a variety of sources for the statistics published in the *World Development Indicators.* Data on external debt are reported directly to the World Bank by developing member countries through the Debtor Reporting System. Other data are drawn mainly from the United Nations and its specialized agencies, from the International Monetary Fund (IMF), and from country reports to the World Bank. Bank staff estimates are also used to improve currentness or consistency. For most countries, national accounts estimates are obtained from member governments through World Bank economic missions. In some instances these are adjusted by staff to ensure conformity with international definitions and concepts. Most social data from national sources are drawn from regular administrative files, special surveys, or periodic census inquiries. The Data Sources section following the Technical Notes lists the principal international sources used.

Data consistency and reliability

Considerable effort has been made to standardize the data, but full comparability cannot be assured, and care must be taken in interpreting the indicators. Many factors affect data availability, comparability, and reliability: statistical systems in many developing economies are still weak; statistical methods,

coverage, practices, and definitions differ widely; and cross-country and intertemporal comparisons involve complex technical and conceptual problems that cannot be unequivocally resolved. For these reasons, although the data are drawn from the sources thought to be most authoritative, they should be construed only as indicating trends and characterizing major differences among economies rather than offering precise quantitative measures of those differences. Also, national statistical agencies tend to revise their historical data, particularly for recent years. Thus, data of different vintages may be published in different editions of World Bank publications. Readers are advised not to compile such data from different editions. Consistent time series are available on the *World Development Indicators 1999 CD-ROM.*

Ratios and growth rates

For ease of reference, the tables usually show ratios and rates of growth rather than the simple underlying values. Values in their original form are available on the *World Development Indicators 1999 CD-ROM.* Unless otherwise noted, growth rates are computed using the least-squares regression method (see "Statistical methods" below). Because this method takes into account all available observations during a period, the resulting growth rates reflect general trends that are not unduly influenced by exceptional values. To exclude the effects of inflation, constant-price economic indicators are used in calculating growth rates. Data in italics are for a year or period other than that specified in the column heading—up to two years before or after for economic indicators, and up to three years for social indicators because the latter tend to be collected less regularly and change less dramatically over short periods.

Constant-price series

An economy's growth is measured by the increase in value added produced by the individuals and enterprises operating in that economy. Thus, measuring real growth requires estimates of GDP and its components valued in constant prices. The World Bank collects constant-price national accounts series in national currencies and recorded in the country's original base year. To obtain comparable series of constant-price data, it rescales GDP (and value added) by industrial origin to a common reference year, currently 1995. This process gives rise to a discrepancy between the rescaled GDP and the sum of the rescaled components. Because allocating the discrepancy would give rise to distortions in the growth rate, the discrepancy is left unallocated.

Summary measures

The summary measures for regions and income groups, presented at the end of most tables, are calculated by simple addition when they are expressed in levels. Aggregate growth rates and ratios are usually computed as weighted averages. The summary measures for social indicators are weighted by population or subgroups of population, except for infant mortality, which is weighted by the number of births. See the notes on specific indicators for more information.

For summary measures that cover many years, calculations are based on a uniform group of economies so that the composition of the aggregate does not change over time. Group measures are compiled only if the data available for a given year account for at least two-thirds of the full group, as defined for the 1987 benchmark year. As long as this criterion is met, economies for which data are missing are assumed to behave like those that provide estimates. Readers should keep in mind that the summary measures are estimates of representative aggregates for each topic and that nothing meaningful can be deduced about behavior at the country level by working back from group indicators. In addition, the weighting process may result in discrepancies between subgroup and overall totals.

Table 1. Size of the economy

Population is based on the de facto definition, which counts all residents, regardless of legal status or citizenship, except for refugees not permanently settled in the country of asylum, who are generally considered part of the population of the country of origin. The indicators shown are midyear estimates (see the technical note for table 3).

Surface area is a country's total area, including areas under inland bodies of water and coastal waterways.

Population density is midyear population divided by land area. Land area is a country's total area excluding areas under inland bodies of water and coastal waterways. Density is calculated using the most recently available data on land area.

Gross national product (GNP) is the sum of value added by all resident producers, plus any taxes (less subsidies) not included in the valuation of output, plus net receipts of primary income (employee compensation and property income) from nonresident sources. Data are converted from national currency to current U.S. dollars by the World Bank *Atlas* method (see "Statistical methods" below). **Average annual growth rate of GNP** is calculated from constant-price GNP in national currency units. **GNP per capita** is GNP divided by midyear population. It is converted into current U.S. dollars by the *Atlas* method. **Aver-**

age annual growth rate of GNP per capita is calculated from constant-price GNP per capita in national currency units. **GNP measured at PPP** is GNP converted to U.S. dollars by the purchasing power parity (PPP) exchange rate. At the PPP rate, one dollar has the same purchasing power over domestic GNP that the U.S. dollar has over U.S. GNP; dollars converted by this method are sometimes called international dollars.

GNP, the broadest measure of national income, measures total value added from domestic and foreign sources claimed by residents. GNP comprises gross domestic product (GDP) plus net receipts of primary income from nonresident sources. The World Bank uses GNP per capita in U.S. dollars to classify economies for analytical purposes and to determine borrowing eligibility. When calculating GNP in U.S. dollars from GNP reported in national currencies, the World Bank follows its *Atlas* conversion method. This involves using a three-year average of exchange rates to smooth the effects of transitory exchange rate fluctuations. (See "Statistical methods" below for further discussion of the *Atlas* method.) Note that growth rates are calculated from data in constant prices and national currency units, not from the *Atlas* estimates.

Because nominal exchange rates do not always reflect international differences in relative prices, table 1 also shows GNP converted into international dollars using PPP exchange rates. PPP rates allow a standard comparison of real price levels between countries, just as conventional price indexes allow comparison of real values over time. The PPP conversion factors used here are derived from the most recent round of price surveys conducted by the International Comparison Programme, a joint project of the World Bank and the regional economic commissions of the United Nations. This round of surveys, completed in 1996 and covering 118 countries, is based on a 1993 reference year. Estimates for countries not included in the survey are derived from statistical models using available data.

Rankings are based on 210 economies and include the 78 economies with sparse data or populations of less than 1.5 million from table 1a. Range estimates for GNP and GNP per capita have been used to rank many of these 78 economies—such as Liechtenstein and Luxembourg, which rank first and second respectively for GNP per capita.

Table 2. Quality of life

Growth of private consumption per capita is the average annual rate of change in private consumption divided by the midyear population. (See the definition of private consumption in the Technical Note to table 13.) The distribution-corrected growth rate is 1 minus the Gini index (see the Technical Note to table 5) multiplied by the annual rate of growth of private consumption. Improvements in private consumption per capita are generally associated with a reduction in poverty, but where the distribution of income or consumption is highly unequal, the poor may not share in the improvement. The relationship between the rate of poverty reduction and the distribution of income or consumption, as measured by an index such as the Gini index, is complicated. But Ravallion and Chen (1997; see Data Sources) have found that the rate of poverty reduction is, on average, proportional to the distribution-corrected rate of growth of private consumption.

Prevalence of child malnutrition is the percentage of children under age 5 whose weight for age is less than minus 2 standard deviations from the median of the reference population, which is based on children from the United States, who are assumed to be well nourished. Weight for age is a composite indicator of both weight for height (wasting) and height for age (stunting). Estimates of child malnutrition are from the WHO.

Under-5 mortality rate is the probability that a child born in the indicated year will die before reaching age 5, if the child is subject to current age-specific mortality rates. The probability is expressed as a rate per 1,000 children.

Life expectancy at birth is the number of years a newborn infant would live if patterns of mortality prevailing at its birth were to stay the same throughout its life.

Age-specific mortality data such as infant and child mortality rates, along with life expectancy at birth, are probably the best general indicators of a community's current health status and are often cited as overall measures of a population's welfare or quality of life. The main sources of mortality data are vital registration systems and direct or indirect estimates based on sample surveys or censuses. Because civil registers with relatively complete vital registration systems are fairly uncommon, estimates must be obtained from sample surveys or derived by applying indirect estimation techniques to registration, census, or survey data. Indirect estimates rely on estimated actuarial ("life") tables, which may be inappropriate for the population concerned. Life expectancy at birth and age-specific mortality rates are generally estimates based on the most recently available census or survey; see the Primary data documentation table in *World Development Indicators 1999*.

Adult illiteracy rate is the percentage of persons aged 15 and above who cannot, with understanding, read and write a short, simple statement about their everyday life. Literacy is difficult to define and to measure. The definition here is based on the concept of functional literacy: a person's ability to use reading and writing skills effectively in the context of his or her society. Measuring literacy using such a definition requires census or sample survey measurements under controlled conditions. In practice, many countries estimate the number of illiterate adults from self-reported data or from estimates of school completion rates. Because of these differences in method, comparisons across countries—and even over time within countries—should be made with caution.

Urban population is the share of the population living in areas defined as urban in each country.

Access to sanitation in urban areas is the percentage of the urban population served by connections to public sewers or household systems such as pit privies, pour-flush latrines, septic tanks, communal toilets, or other such facilities.

Table 3. Population and labor force

Total population includes all residents regardless of legal status or citizenship, except for refugees not permanently settled in the country of asylum, who are generally considered part of the population of their country of origin. The indicators shown are midyear estimates. Population estimates are usually based on national censuses. Intercensal estimates are interpolations or extrapolations based on demographic models. Errors and under-

counting occur even in high-income economies; in developing countries such errors may be substantial because of limits on transportation, communication, and the resources required to conduct a full census. Moreover, the international comparability of population indicators is limited by differences in the concepts, definitions, data collection procedures, and estimation methods used by national statistical agencies and other organizations that collect population data. The data in table 3 are provided by national statistical offices or by the United Nations Population Division.

Average annual population growth rate is the exponential rate of change for the period (see "Statistical methods" below).

Population aged 15–64 is a commonly accepted measure of the number of people who are potentially economically active. In many developing countries, however, children under age 15 work full or part time, and in some high-income economies many workers postpone retirement past age 65.

Total labor force comprises people who meet the definition established by the International Labour Organization (ILO) for the economically active population: all people who supply labor for the production of goods and services during a specified period. It includes both the employed and the unemployed. Although national practices vary, in general the labor force includes the armed forces and first-time jobseekers but excludes homemakers and other unpaid caregivers and workers in the informal sector. Data on the labor force are compiled by the ILO from census or labor force surveys. Despite the ILO's efforts to encourage the use of international standards, labor force data are not fully comparable because of differences among countries, and sometimes within countries, in definitions and methods of collection, classification, and tabulation. The labor force estimates reported in table 3 were calculated by applying activity rates from the ILO database to the World Bank's population estimates to create a labor force series consistent with those estimates. This procedure sometimes results in estimates that differ slightly from those published in the ILO's *Yearbook of Labour Statistics*.

Average annual labor force growth rate is calculated using the exponential end-point method (see "Statistical methods" below).

Females as a percentage of the labor force shows the extent to which women are active in the labor force. Estimates are from the ILO database. These estimates are not comparable internationally because in many countries large numbers of women assist on farms or in other family enterprises without pay, and countries use different criteria to determine the extent to which such workers are to be counted in the labor force.

Children aged 10–14 in the labor force is the share of that age group that is working or seeking work. Reliable estimates of child labor are difficult to obtain. In many countries child labor is illegal or officially presumed not to exist and is therefore not reported or included in surveys or recorded in official data. Data are also subject to underreporting because they do not include children engaged in agricultural or household activities with their families.

Table 4. Poverty

Survey year is the year in which the underlying data were collected.

Rural population below the national poverty line is the percentage of the rural population living below the rural poverty line determined by national authorities. **Urban population below the national poverty line** is the percentage of the urban population living below the urban poverty line determined by national authorities. **Total population below the national poverty line** is the percentage of the total population living below the national poverty line. National estimates are based on population-weighted subgroup estimates from household surveys.

Population below $1 PPP a day and **Population below $2 PPP a day** are the percentages of the population living at those levels of consumption or income at 1985 prices, adjusted for purchasing power parity.

Poverty gap at $1 PPP a day and **Poverty gap at $2 PPP a day** are calculated as the average difference between the poverty line and actual income or consumption for all poor households, expressed as a percentage of the poverty line. This measure reflects the depth of poverty as well as its prevalence.

International comparisons of poverty data entail both conceptual and practical problems. Different countries have different definitions of poverty, and consistent comparisons between countries using the same definition can be difficult. National poverty lines tend to have greater purchasing power in rich countries, where more generous standards are used than in poor countries.

International poverty lines attempt to hold the real value of the poverty line constant between countries. The standard of $1 a day, measured in 1985 international prices and adjusted to local currency using PPP conversion factors, was chosen for *World Development Report 1990: Poverty* because it is typical of poverty lines in low-income economies. PPP conversion factors are used because they take into account the local prices of goods and services that are not traded internationally. However, these factors were designed not for making international poverty comparisons but for comparing aggregates in the national accounts. As a result, there is no certainty that an international poverty line measures the same degree of need or deprivation across countries.

Problems can arise in comparing poverty measures within countries as well as between them. For example, the cost of food staples—and the cost of living generally—are typically higher in urban than in rural areas. So the nominal value of the urban poverty line should be higher than the rural poverty line. But it is not always clear that the difference between urban and rural poverty lines found in practice properly reflects the difference in the cost of living. For some countries the urban poverty line in common use has a higher real value—meaning that it allows poor people to buy more commodities for consumption—than does the rural poverty line. Sometimes the difference has been so large as to imply that the incidence of poverty is greater in urban than in rural areas, even though the reverse is found when adjustments are made only for differences in the cost of living.

Other issues arise in measuring household living standards. The choice between income and consumption as a welfare indicator is one. Incomes are generally more difficult to measure accurately, and consumption accords better with the idea of a standard of living than does income, which can vary over time even if the standard of living does not. But consumption data are not always available, and when they are not, there is little choice but to use income. There are still other problems. Household survey questionnaires can differ widely, for example in the number of distinct categories of consumer goods they identify. Survey quality varies, and even similar surveys may not be strictly comparable.

Comparisons across countries at different levels of development also pose a potential problem because of differences in the relative importance of consumption of nonmarket goods. The local market value of all consumption in kind (including consumption from a household's own production, particularly important in underdeveloped rural economies) should be included in the measure of total consumption expenditure. Similarly, the imputed profit from production of nonmarket goods should be included in income. This is not always done, although such omissions were a far bigger problem in surveys before the 1980s than today. Most survey data now include valuations for consumption or income from own production. Nonetheless, valuation methods vary: for example, some surveys use the price at the nearest market, whereas others use the average farmgate selling price.

The international poverty measures in table 4 are based on the most recent PPP estimates from the latest version of the *Penn World Tables* (National Bureau of Economic Research 1997; see Data Sources). However, any revisions in the PPP conversion factor of a country to incorporate better price indexes can produce dramatically different poverty lines in local currency.

Whenever possible, consumption has been used as the welfare indicator for deciding who is poor. When only household income is available, average income has been adjusted to accord with either a survey-based estimate of mean consumption (when available) or an estimate based on consumption data from national accounts. This procedure adjusts only the mean, however; nothing can be done to correct for the difference between the Lorenz (income distribution) curves for consumption and income.

Empirical Lorenz curves were weighted by household size, so they are based on percentiles of population, not of households. In all cases the measures of poverty have been calculated from primary data sources (tabulations or household data) rather than existing estimates. Estimates from tabulations require an interpolation method; the method chosen is Lorenz curves with flexible functional forms, which have proved reliable in past work.

Table 5. Distribution of income or consumption

Survey year is the year in which the underlying data were collected.

Gini index measures the extent to which the distribution of income (or, in some cases, consumption expenditure) among individuals or households within an economy deviates from a perfectly equal distribution. The Gini index measures the area between the Lorenz curve (described in the technical note to table 4) and a hypothetical line of absolute equality, expressed as a percentage of the maximum area under the line. As defined here, a Gini index of zero would represent perfect equality, and an index of 100 would imply perfect inequality (one person or household accounting for all income or consumption).

Percentage share of income or consumption is the share that accrues to deciles or quintiles of the population ranked by income or consumption. Percentage shares by quintiles may not add up to 100 because of rounding.

Data on personal or household income or consumption come from nationally representative household surveys. The data in the table refer to different years between 1982 and 1997. Footnotes to the survey year indicate whether the rankings are based on income or consumption. Distributions are based on percentiles of population, not of households. Where the original data from the household survey were available, they have been used to directly calculate the income or consumption shares by quintile. Otherwise, shares have been estimated from the best available grouped data.

The distribution indicators have been adjusted for household size, providing a more consistent measure of income or consumption per capita. No adjustment has been made for differences in the cost of living in different parts of the same country because the necessary data are generally unavailable. For further details on the estimation method for low- and middle-income economies, see Ravallion (1996; see Data Sources).

Because the underlying household surveys differ in method and in the type of data collected, the distribution indicators are not strictly comparable across countries. These problems are diminishing as survey methods improve and become more standardized, but strict comparability is still impossible. The income distribution and Gini indexes for the high-income economies are directly calculated from the Luxembourg Income Study database. The estimation method used here is consistent with that applied to developing countries.

The following sources of noncomparability should be noted. First, the surveys can differ in many respects, including whether they use income or consumption expenditure as the living standard indicator. Income is typically more unequally distributed than consumption. In addition, the definitions of income used in surveys are usually very different from the economic definition of income (the maximum level of consumption consistent with keeping productive capacity unchanged). Consumption is usually a much better welfare indicator, particularly in developing countries. Second, households differ in size (number of members) and in the extent of income sharing among members. Individuals differ in age and in consumption needs. Differences between countries in these respects may bias distribution comparisons.

Table 6. Education

Public expenditure on education is the percentage of GNP accounted for by public spending on public education plus subsidies to private education at the primary, secondary, and tertiary levels. It may exclude spending on religious schools, which play a significant role in many developing countries. Data for some countries and for some years refer to spending by the ministry of education of the central government only and thus exclude education expenditures by other central government ministries and departments, local authorities, and others.

Net enrollment ratio is the number of children of official school age (as defined by the education system) enrolled in primary or secondary school, expressed as a percentage of the number of children of official school age for those levels in the population. Enrollment data are based on annual enrollment surveys, typically conducted at the beginning of the school year. They do not reflect actual attendance or dropout rates during the school year. Problems affecting cross-country comparisons of enrollment data stem from inadvertent or deliberate misreporting of age and from errors in estimates of school-age populations. Age-sex structures from censuses or vital registration systems, the primary sources of data on school-age populations, are commonly subject to underenumeration, especially of young children.

Percentage of cohort reaching grade 5 is the share of students enrolled in primary school who eventually reach fifth grade. Because tracking data for individual students are not available, aggregate student flows from one grade to the next are estimated using data on average promotion, repetition, and dropout rates. Other flows, caused by new entrants, reentrants, grade skipping, migration, or school transfers during the school year, are not considered. This procedure, called the reconstructed cohort method, makes three simplifying assumptions: that dropouts never return to school; that promotion, repetition, and dropout rates remain constant over the entire period in which the cohort is enrolled; and that the same rates apply to all pupils enrolled in a given grade, regardless of whether they previously repeated a grade.

Expected years of schooling is the average number of years of formal schooling that a child is expected to receive, including university education and years spent in repetition. It may also be interpreted as an indicator of the total educational resources, measured in school years, that a child will require over the course of his or her "lifetime" in school.

Data on education are compiled by the United Nations Educational, Scientific, and Cultural Organization (UNESCO) from official responses to surveys and from reports provided by education authorities in each country. Because coverage, definitions, and data collection methods vary across countries and over time within countries, data on education should be interpreted with caution.

Table 7. Health

Public expenditure on health consists of recurrent and capital spending from government (central and local) budgets, external borrowings and grants (including donations from international agencies and nongovernmental organizations), and social (or compulsory) health insurance funds. Because few developing countries have national health accounts, compiling estimates of public health expenditure is complicated in countries where state, provincial, and local governments are involved in health care financing. Such data are not regularly reported and, when reported, are often of poor quality. In some countries health services are considered social services and so are excluded from health sector expenditures. The data on health expenditure in table 7 were collected by the World Bank as part of its health, nutrition, and population strategy. No estimates were made for countries with incomplete data.

Access to safe water is the percentage of the population with reasonable access to an adequate amount of safe water (including treated surface water and untreated but uncontaminated water, such as from springs, sanitary wells, and protected boreholes). In urban areas the source may be a public fountain or standpipe located not more than 200 meters from the residence. In rural areas the definition implies that household members do not have to spend a disproportionate part of the day fetching water. An "adequate" amount of safe water is that needed to satisfy metabolic, hygienic, and domestic requirements, usually about 20 liters per person per day. The definition of safe water has changed over time.

Access to sanitation is the percentage of the population with disposal facilities that can effectively prevent human, animal, and insect contact with excreta. Suitable facilities range from simple but protected pit latrines to flush toilets with sewerage. To be effective, all facilities must be correctly constructed and properly maintained.

Infant mortality rate is the number of infants who die before reaching 1 year of age, expressed per 1,000 live births in a given year (see the discussion of age-specific mortality rates in the technical note to table 2).

Contraceptive prevalence rate is the percentage of women who are practicing, or whose sexual partners are practicing, any form of contraception. It is usually measured for married women aged 15–49 only. Contraceptive prevalence includes all methods: ineffective traditional methods as well as highly effective modern methods. Unmarried women are often excluded from the surveys, and this may bias the estimate. The rates are obtained mainly from demographic and health surveys and contraceptive prevalence surveys.

Total fertility rate is the number of children who would be born to a woman if she were to live to the end of her childbearing years and bear children in accordance with current age-specific fertility rates. Data are from vital registration systems or, in their absence, from censuses or sample surveys. Provided that the censuses or surveys are fairly recent, the estimated rates are considered reliable. As with other demographic data, international comparisons are limited by differences in data definition, collection, and estimation methods.

Maternal mortality ratio is the number of women who die during pregnancy or childbirth, per 100,000 live births. Maternal mortality ratios are difficult to measure because health information systems are often weak. Classifying a death as maternal requires a cause-of-death attribution by medically qualified staff, based on information available at the time of death. Even then, some doubt may remain about the diagnosis in the absence of an autopsy. In many developing countries, causes of death are assigned by nonphysicians and often attributed to "ill-defined causes." Maternal deaths in rural areas often go unreported. The data in table 7 are official estimates from administrative records, survey-based indirect estimates, or estimates derived from a demographic model developed by the United Nations Children's Fund (UNICEF) and the WHO. In all cases the standard errors of maternal mortality ratios are large, and this makes the indicator particularly unsuitable for monitoring changes over a short period.

Table 8. Land use and agricultural productivity

Land under permanent crops is land cultivated with crops that occupy the land for long periods and do not need to be replanted after each harvest, excluding trees grown for wood or timber. **Irrigated land** refers to areas purposely provided with water, including land irrigated by controlled flooding. **Arable land** includes land defined by the Food and Agriculture Organization (FAO) as land under temporary crops (double-cropped areas are counted once), temporary meadows for mowing or for pasture, land under market or kitchen gardens, and land temporarily fallow. Land abandoned as a result of shifting cultivation is not included.

The comparability of land use data from different countries is limited by variations in definitions, statistical methods, and the quality of data collection. For example, countries may define land use differently. The FAO, the primary compiler of these data, occasionally adjusts its definitions of land use categories and sometimes revises earlier data. Because the data thus reflect changes in data-reporting procedures as well as actual changes in land use, apparent trends should be interpreted with caution.

Agricultural machinery refers to wheel and crawler tractors (excluding garden tractors) in use in agriculture at the end of the calendar year specified or during the first quarter of the following year.

Agricultural productivity refers to agricultural value added per agricultural worker, measured in constant 1995 U.S. dollars. Agricultural value added includes that from forestry and fishing. Thus interpretations of land productivity should be made with caution. To smooth annual fluctuations in agricultural activity, the indicators have been averaged over three years.

Food production index covers food crops that are considered edible and that contain nutrients. Coffee and tea are excluded because, although edible, they have no nutritive value. The food production index is prepared by the FAO, which obtains data from official and semiofficial reports of crop yields, area under production, and livestock numbers. Where data are not available, the FAO makes estimates. The index is calculated using the Laspeyres formula: production quantities of each commodity are weighted by average international commodity prices in the base period and summed for each year. The FAO's index may differ from those of other sources because of differences in coverage, weights, concepts, time periods, calculation methods, and use of international prices.

Table 9. Water use, deforestation, and protected areas

Freshwater resources consists of internal renewable resources, which include flows of rivers and groundwater from rainfall in the country and river flows from other countries. Freshwater resources per capita are calculated using the World Bank's population estimates.

Data on freshwater resources are based on estimates of runoff into rivers and recharge of groundwater. These estimates are based on different sources and refer to different years, so cross-country comparisons should be made with caution. Because they are collected intermittently, the data may hide significant variations in total renewable water resources from one year to the next. These annual averages also obscure large seasonal and interannual variations in water availability within countries. Data for small countries and countries in arid and semiarid zones are less reliable than those for larger countries and countries with more rainfall.

Annual freshwater withdrawals refers to total water withdrawals, not counting evaporation losses from storage basins. It also includes water from desalination plants in countries where these are a significant source of water. Withdrawal data are for single years between 1980 and 1997 unless otherwise indicated. Caution is advised in comparing data on annual freshwater withdrawals, which are subject to variations in collection and estimation methods. Withdrawals can exceed 100 percent of renewable supplies when extraction from nonrenewable aquifers or desalination plants is considerable or when there is significant reuse of water. Withdrawals for agriculture and industry are total withdrawals for irrigation and livestock production and for direct industrial use (including withdrawals for cooling thermoelectric plants), respectively. Withdrawals for domestic uses include drinking water, municipal use or supply, and use for public services, commercial establishments, and homes. For most countries sectoral withdrawal data are estimated for 1987–95.

Access to safe water refers to the percentage of people with reasonable access to an adequate amount of safe drinking water in their dwellings or within a convenient distance of their dwellings. Information on access to safe water, although widely used, is extremely subjective, and such terms as "adequate" and "safe" may have very different meanings in different countries, despite official WHO definitions. Even in industrial countries, treated water may not always be safe to drink. Although access to safe water is equated with connection to a public supply system, this does not take account of variations in the quality and cost (broadly defined) of the service once connected. Thus cross-country comparisons must be made cautiously. Changes over time within countries may result from changes in definitions or measurements.

Annual deforestation refers to the permanent conversion of forest area (land under natural or planted stands of trees) to other uses, including shifting cultivation, permanent agriculture, ranching, settlements, and infrastructure development. Deforested areas do not include areas logged but intended for regeneration or areas degraded by fuelwood gathering, acid precipitation, or forest fires. Negative numbers indicate an increase in forest area.

Estimates of forest area are from the FAO's *State of the World's Forests 1997,* which provides information on forest cover as of 1995 and a revised estimate of forest cover in 1990. Forest cover data for developing countries are based on country assessments that were prepared at different times and that, for reporting purposes, had to be adapted to the standard reference years of 1990 and 1995. This adjustment was made with a deforestation model designed to correlate forest cover change over time with certain ancillary variables, including population change and density, initial forest cover, and ecological zone of the forest area under consideration.

Nationally protected areas refers to totally or partially protected areas of at least 1,000 hectares that are designated as national parks, natural monuments, nature reserves, wildlife sanctuaries, protected landscapes and seascapes, or scientific reserves with limited public access. The indicator is calculated as a percentage of total area. For small countries whose protected areas may be smaller than 1,000 hectares, this limit will result in an underestimate of the extent and number of protected areas. The data do not include sites protected under local or provincial law.

Data on protected areas are compiled from a variety of sources by the World Conservation Monitoring Centre, a joint venture of the United Nations Environment Programme, the World Wide Fund for Nature, and the World Conservation Union. Because of differences in definitions and reporting practices, cross-country comparability is limited. Compounding these problems, the data available cover different periods. Designating land as a protected area does not necessarily mean, moreover, that protection is in force.

Table 10. Energy use and emissions

Commercial energy use refers to apparent consumption, which is equal to indigenous production plus imports and stock changes, minus exports and fuels supplied to ships and aircraft engaged in international transportation. The International Energy Agency (IEA) and the United Nations Statistical Division (UNSD) compile energy data. IEA data for nonmembers of the Organisation for Economic Co-operation and Development (OECD) are based on national energy data that have been adjusted to conform with annual questionnaires completed by OECD member governments. UNSD data are compiled primarily from responses to questionnaires sent to national governments, supplemented by official national statistical publications and by data from intergovernmental organizations. When official data are not available, the UNSD bases its estimates on the professional and commercial literature. The variety of sources affects the cross-country comparability of data.

Commercial energy use refers to domestic primary energy use before transformation to other end-use energy sources (such as electricity and refined petroleum products). It includes energy from combustible renewables and waste. All forms of commercial energy—primary energy and primary electricity—are converted into oil equivalents. To convert nuclear electricity into oil equivalents, a notional thermal efficiency of 33 percent is assumed; for hydroelectric power, 100 percent efficiency is assumed.

GDP per unit of energy use is the U.S. dollar estimate of real gross domestic product (at 1995 prices) per kilogram of oil equivalent of commercial energy use.

Net energy imports is calculated as energy use less production, both measured in oil equivalents. A minus sign indicates that the country is a net exporter of energy.

Carbon dioxide emissions measures those emissions stemming from the burning of fossil fuels and the manufacture of cement. These include carbon dioxide produced during consumption of solid, liquid, and gas fuels and from gas flaring.

The Carbon Dioxide Information Analysis Center (CDIAC), sponsored by the U.S. Department of Energy, calculates annual anthropogenic emissions of carbon dioxide. These calculations are derived from data on fossil fuel consumption, based on the World Energy Data Set maintained by the UNSD, and from data on world cement manufacturing, based on the Cement Manufacturing Data Set maintained by the U.S. Bureau of Mines. Each year the CDIAC recalculates the entire time series from 1950 to the present, incorporating its most recent findings and the latest corrections to its database. Estimates exclude fuels supplied to ships and aircraft engaged in international transportation because of the difficulty of apportioning these fuels among the countries benefiting from that transport.

Table 11. Growth of the economy

Gross domestic product is gross value added, at purchasers' prices, by all resident and nonresident producers in the economy plus any taxes and minus any subsidies not included in the value of the products. It is calculated without deducting for depreciation of fabricated assets or for depletion or degradation of natural resources. Value added is the net output of a sector after adding up all outputs and subtracting intermediate inputs. The industrial origin of value added is determined by the International Standard Industrial Classification (ISIC), revision 2.

The **GDP implicit deflator** reflects changes in prices for all final demand categories, such as government consumption, capital formation, and international trade, as well as the main component, private final consumption. It is derived as the ratio of current- to constant-price GDP. The GDP deflator may also be calculated explicitly as a Laspeyres price index in which the weights are base-period quantities of output.

Agriculture value added corresponds to ISIC divisions 11–13 and includes forestry and fishing. **Industry value added** comprises the following sectors: mining (ISIC divisions 10–14), manufacturing (ISIC divisions 15–37), construction (ISIC division 45), and electricity, gas, and water supply (ISIC divisions 40 and 41). **Services value added** corresponds to ISIC divisions 50–96.

Exports of goods and services represents the value of all goods and market services provided to the rest of the world. Included is the value of merchandise, freight, insurance, travel, and other nonfactor services. Factor and property income (formerly called factor services), such as investment income, interest, and labor income, is excluded, as are transfer payments.

Gross domestic investment consists of outlays on additions to the fixed assets of the economy plus net changes in the level of inventories. Additions to fixed assets include land improvements (fences, ditches, drains, and so on); plant, machinery, and equipment purchases; and the construction of buildings, roads, railways, and the like, including commercial and industrial buildings, offices, schools, hospitals, and private dwellings. Inventories are stocks of goods held by firms to meet temporary or unexpected fluctuations in production or sales.

Growth rates are annual averages calculated using constant-price data in local currency. Growth rates for regional and income groups are calculated after converting local currencies to U.S. dollars at the average official exchange rate reported by the IMF for the year shown or, occasionally, using an alternative conversion factor determined by the World Bank's Development Data Group. Methods of computing growth rates and the alternative conversion factors are described under "Statistical methods" below. For additional information on the calculation of GDP and its sectoral components, see the technical note to table 12.

Table 12. Structure of output

Gross domestic product represents the sum of value added by all producers in the economy (see the technical note to table 11 for a more detailed definition and for definitions of **agriculture**,

industry, manufacturing, and **services value added**). Since 1968 the United Nations' System of National Accounts (SNA) has called for estimates of GDP by industrial origin to be valued at either basic prices (excluding all indirect taxes on factors of production) or producer prices (including taxes on factors of production, but excluding indirect taxes on final output). Some countries, however, report such data at purchasers' prices—the prices at which final sales are made—and this may affect estimates of the distribution of output. Total GDP as shown in this table is measured at purchasers' prices. GDP components are measured at basic prices.

Among the difficulties faced by compilers of national accounts is the extent of unreported economic activity in the informal or secondary economy. In developing countries a large share of agricultural output is either not exchanged (because it is consumed within the household) or not exchanged for money. Financial transactions also may go unrecorded. Agricultural production often must be estimated indirectly, using a combination of methods involving estimates of inputs, yields, and area under cultivation.

The output of industry ideally should be measured through regular censuses and surveys of firms. But in most developing countries such surveys are infrequent and quickly go out of date, so many results must be extrapolated. The choice of sampling unit, which may be the enterprise (where responses may be based on financial records) or the establishment (where production units may be recorded separately), also affects the quality of the data. Moreover, much industrial production is organized not in firms but in unincorporated or owner-operated ventures not captured by surveys aimed at the formal sector. Even in large industries, where regular surveys are more likely, evasion of excise and other taxes lowers the estimates of value added. Such problems become more acute as countries move from state control of industry to private enterprise because new firms go into business and growing numbers of established firms fail to report. In accordance with the SNA, output should include all such unreported activity as well as the value of illegal activities and other unrecorded, informal, or small-scale operations. Data on these activities need to be collected using techniques other than conventional surveys.

In sectors dominated by large organizations and enterprises, data on output, employment, and wages are usually readily available and reasonably reliable. But in the service sector the many self-employed workers and one-person businesses are sometimes difficult to locate, and their owners have little incentive to respond to surveys, let alone report their full earnings. Compounding these problems are the many forms of economic activity that go unrecorded, including the work that women and children do for little or no pay. For further discussion of the problems encountered in using national accounts data see Srinivasan (1994) and Heston (1994) in Data Sources.

Table 13. Structure of demand

Private consumption is the market value of all goods and services, including durable products (such as cars, washing machines, and home computers), purchased or received as income in kind by households and nonprofit institutions. It excludes purchases of dwellings but includes imputed rent for owner-occupied dwellings. In practice, it may include any statistical discrepancy in the use of resources relative to the supply of resources.

Private consumption is often estimated as a residual, by subtracting from GDP all other known expenditures. The resulting aggregate may incorporate fairly large discrepancies. When private consumption is calculated separately, the household surveys on which a large component of the estimates is based tend to be one-year studies with limited coverage. Thus the estimates quickly become outdated and must be supplemented by price- and quantity-based statistical estimating procedures. Complicating the issue, in many developing countries the distinction between cash outlays for personal business and those for household use may be blurred.

General government consumption includes all current spending for purchases of goods and services (including wages and salaries) by all levels of government, excluding most government enterprises. It also includes most expenditure on national defense and security, some of which is now considered part of investment.

Gross domestic investment consists of outlays on additions to the fixed assets of the economy plus net changes in the level of inventories. For the definitions of fixed assets and inventories see the technical note to table 11. Under the revised (1993) SNA guidelines, gross domestic investment also includes capital outlays on defense establishments that may be used by the general public, such as schools and hospitals, and on certain types of private housing for family use. All other defense expenditures are treated as current spending.

Investment data may be estimated from direct surveys of enterprises and administrative records or based on the commodity flow method, using data from trade and construction activities. The quality of public fixed investment data depends on the quality of government accounting systems, which tend to be weak in developing countries; measures of private fixed investment—particularly capital outlays by small, unincorporated enterprises—are usually very unreliable.

Estimates of changes in inventories are rarely complete but usually include the most important activities or commodities. In some countries these estimates are derived as a composite residual along with aggregate private consumption. According to national accounts conventions, adjustments should be made for appreciation of the value of inventories due to price changes, but this is not always done. In economies where inflation is high, this element can be substantial.

Gross domestic saving is the difference between GDP and total consumption.

Exports of goods and services represents the value of all goods and services (including transportation, travel, and other services such as communications, insurance, and financial services) provided to the rest of the world. Data on exports and imports are compiled from customs returns and from balance of payments data obtained from central banks. Although data on exports and imports from the payments side provide reasonably reliable records of cross-border transactions, they may not adhere strictly to the appropriate valuation and timing definitions of balance of payments accounting or, more important, correspond with the change-of-ownership criterion. (In conventional balance of payments accounting, a transaction is recorded as oc-

curring when ownership changes hands.) This issue has assumed greater significance with the increasing globalization of international business. Neither customs nor balance of payments data capture the illegal transactions that occur in many countries. Goods carried by travelers across borders in legal but unreported shuttle trade may further distort trade statistics.

Resource balance is the difference between exports of goods and services and imports of goods and services.

Table 14. Central government finances

Current tax revenue comprises compulsory, unrequited, nonrepayable receipts collected by central governments for public purposes. It includes interest collected on tax arrears and penalties collected on nonpayment or late payment of taxes. It is shown net of refunds and other corrective transactions.

Current nontax revenue includes requited, nonrepayable receipts for public purposes, such as fines, administrative fees, or entrepreneurial income from government ownership of property, and voluntary, unrequited, nonrepayable current government receipts other than from governmental sources. This category does not include grants, borrowing, repayment of previous lending, or sales of fixed capital assets or of stocks, land, or intangible assets, nor does it include gifts from nongovernmental sources for capital purposes. Together, tax and nontax revenue make up the current revenue of the government.

Current expenditure includes requited payments other than for capital assets or for goods or services to be used in the production of capital assets. It also includes unrequited payments for purposes other than permitting the recipients to acquire capital assets, compensating the recipients for damage or destruction of capital assets, or increasing the financial capital of the recipients. Current expenditure does not include government lending or repayments to the government, or government acquisition of equity for public policy purposes.

Capital expenditure is spending to acquire fixed capital assets, land, intangible assets, government stocks, and nonmilitary, nonfinancial assets. Also included are capital grants.

Overall deficit/surplus is current and capital revenue and official grants received, less total expenditure and lending minus repayment.

Goods and services expenditure comprises all government payments in exchange for goods and services, including wages and salaries.

Social services expenditure comprises expenditure on health, education, housing, welfare, social security, and community amenities. It also covers compensation for loss of income to the sick and temporarily disabled; payments to the elderly, the permanently disabled, and the unemployed; family, maternity, and child allowances; and the cost of welfare services such as care of the aged, the disabled, and children. Many expenditures relevant to environmental protection, such as pollution abatement, water supply, sanitation, and refuse collection, are included indistinguishably in this category.

Data on government revenues and expenditures are collected by the IMF through questionnaires distributed to member governments, and by the OECD. In general, the definition of government excludes nonfinancial public enterprises and public financial institutions (such as the central bank). Despite the

IMF's efforts to systematize and standardize the collection of public finance data, statistics on public finance are often incomplete, untimely, and noncomparable. Inadequate statistical coverage precludes the presentation of subnational data, making cross-country comparisons potentially misleading.

Total central government expenditure as presented in the IMF's *Government Finance Statistics Yearbook* is a more limited measure of general government consumption than that shown in the national accounts because it excludes consumption expenditure by state and local governments. At the same time, the IMF's concept of central government expenditure is broader than the national accounts definition because it includes government gross domestic investment and transfer payments.

Central government finances can refer to one of two accounting concepts: consolidated or budgetary. For most countries central government finance data have been consolidated into one account, but for others only budgetary central government accounts are available. Countries reporting budgetary data are noted in the Primary data documentation table in *World Development Indicators 1999*. Because budgetary accounts do not necessarily include all central government units, the picture they provide of central government activities is usually incomplete. A key issue is the failure to include the quasi-fiscal operations of the central bank. Central bank losses arising from monetary operations and subsidized financing can result in sizable quasi-fiscal deficits. Such deficits may also result from the operations of other financial intermediaries, such as public development finance institutions. Also missing from the data are governments' contingent liabilities for unfunded pension and insurance plans.

Table 15. Balance of payments, current account, and international reserves

Goods and services exports and **goods and services imports** together comprise all transactions between residents of a country and the rest of the world involving a change in ownership of general merchandise, goods sent for processing and repairs, nonmonetary gold, and services.

Net income refers to compensation earned by workers in an economy other than the one in which they are resident, for work performed and paid for by a resident of that economy, and investment income (receipts and payments on direct investment, portfolio investment, other investment, and receipts on reserve assets). Income derived from the use of intangible assets is recorded under business services.

Net current transfers consists of transactions in which residents of an economy provide or receive goods, services, income, or financial items without a quid pro quo. All transfers not considered to be capital transfers are current transfers.

Current account balance is the sum of net exports of goods and services, income, and current transfers.

Gross international reserves comprises holdings of monetary gold, special drawing rights, reserves of IMF members held by the IMF, and holdings of foreign exchange under the control of monetary authorities. The gold component of these reserves is valued at year-end London prices ($589.50 an ounce in 1980 and $287.80 an ounce in 1998).

The balance of payments is divided into two groups of accounts. The current account records transactions in goods and services, income, and current transfers. The capital and financial account records capital transfers; the acquisition or disposal of nonproduced, nonfinancial assets (such as patents); and transactions in financial assets and liabilities. Gross international reserves are recorded in a third set of accounts, the international investment position, which records the stocks of assets and liabilities.

The balance of payments is a double-entry accounting system that shows all flows of goods and services into and out of an economy; all transfers that are the counterpart of real resources or financial claims provided to or by the rest of the world without a quid pro quo, such as donations and grants; and all changes in residents' claims on, and liabilities to, nonresidents that arise from economic transactions. All transactions are recorded twice: once as a credit and once as a debit. In principle, the net balance should be zero, but in practice the accounts often do not balance. In these cases a balancing item, called net errors and omissions, is included in the capital and financial account.

Discrepancies may arise in the balance of payments because there is no single source for balance of payments data and no way to ensure that data from different sources are fully consistent. Sources include customs data, monetary accounts of the banking system, external debt records, information provided by enterprises, surveys to estimate service transactions, and foreign exchange records. Differences in recording methods—for example, in the timing of transactions, in definitions of residence and ownership, and in the exchange rate used to value transactions—contribute to net errors and omissions. In addition, smuggling and other illegal or quasi-legal transactions may be unrecorded or misrecorded.

The concepts and definitions underlying the data in table 15 are based on the fifth edition of the IMF's *Balance of Payments Manual*. That edition redefined as capital transfers some transactions previously included in the current account, such as debt forgiveness, migrants' capital transfers, and foreign aid to acquire capital goods. Thus the current account balance now more accurately reflects net current transfer receipts in addition to transactions in goods, services (previously nonfactor services), and income (previously factor income). Many countries still maintain their data collection systems according to the concepts and definitions in the fourth edition. Where necessary, the IMF converts data reported in earlier systems to conform with the fifth edition (see the primary data documentation table in *World Development Indicators 1999*). Values are in U.S. dollars converted at market exchange rates.

Table 16. Private sector finance

Private investment covers gross outlays by the private sector (including private nonprofit agencies) on additions to its fixed domestic assets. When direct estimates of private gross domestic fixed investment are not available, such investment is estimated as the difference between total gross domestic investment and consolidated public investment. No allowance is made for the depreciation of assets. Because private investment is often estimated as the difference between two estimated quantities—domestic fixed investment and consolidated public investment—private investment may be undervalued or overvalued and subject to errors over time.

Stock market capitalization (also called market value) is the sum of the market capitalizations of all firms listed on domestic stock exchanges, where each firm's market capitalization is its share price at the end of the year times the number of shares outstanding. Market capitalization, presented as one measure used to gauge a country's level of stock market development, suffers from conceptual and statistical weaknesses such as inaccurate reporting and different accounting standards.

Number of listed domestic companies is the number of domestically incorporated companies listed on stock exchanges at the end of the year, excluding investment companies, mutual funds, and other collective investment vehicles.

Interest rate spread, also known as the intermediation margin, is the difference between the interest rate charged by banks on short- and medium-term loans to the private sector and the interest rate offered by banks to resident customers for demand, time, or savings deposits. Interest rates should reflect the responsiveness of financial institutions to competition and price incentives. However, the interest rate spread may not be a reliable measure of a banking system's efficiency, to the extent that information about interest rates is inaccurate, that banks do not monitor all bank managers, or that the government sets deposit and lending rates.

Domestic credit provided by the banking sector includes all credit to various sectors on a gross basis, with the exception of credit to the central government, which is net. The banking sector includes monetary authorities, deposit money banks, and other banking institutions for which data are available (including institutions that do not accept transferable deposits but do incur such liabilities as time and savings deposits). Examples of other banking institutions include savings and mortgage loan institutions and building and loan associations.

In general, the indicators reported here do not capture the activities of the informal sector, which remains an important source of finance in developing economies.

Table 17. Role of government in the economy

Subsidies and other current transfers includes all unrequited, nonrepayable transfers on current account to private and public enterprises and the cost to the public of covering the cash operating deficits on sales to the public by departmental enterprises.

Value added by state-owned enterprises is estimated as sales revenue minus the cost of intermediate inputs, or as the sum of these enterprises' operating surplus (balance) and their wage payments. State-owned enterprises are government-owned or -controlled economic entities that generate most of their revenue by selling goods and services. This definition encompasses commercial enterprises directly operated by a government department and those in which the government holds a majority of shares directly or indirectly through other state enterprises. It also includes enterprises in which the state holds a minority of shares, if the distribution of the remaining shares leaves the government with effective control. It excludes public sector activity—such as education, health services, and road construction and maintenance—that is financed in other ways, usually from the government's general revenue. Because financial enterprises are of a different nature, they have generally been excluded from the data.

Military expenditure for members of the North Atlantic Treaty Organization (NATO) is based on the NATO definition, which covers military-related expenditures of the defense ministry (including recruiting, training, construction, and the purchase of military supplies and equipment) and other ministries. Civilian-related expenditures of the defense ministry are excluded. Military assistance is included in the expenditure of the donor country. Purchases of military equipment on credit are recorded at the time the debt is incurred, not at the time of payment. Data for other countries generally cover expenditures of the ministry of defense; excluded are expenditures on public order and safety, which are classified separately.

Definitions of military spending differ depending on whether they include civil defense, reserves and auxiliary forces, police and paramilitary forces, dual-purpose forces such as military and civilian police, military grants-in-kind, pensions for military personnel, and social security contributions paid by one part of government to another. Official government data may omit some military spending, disguise financing through extrabudgetary accounts or unrecorded use of foreign exchange receipts, or fail to include military assistance or secret imports of military equipment. Current spending is more likely to be reported than capital spending. In some cases a more accurate estimate of military spending can be obtained by adding the value of estimated arms imports and nominal military expenditures. This method may understate or overstate spending in a particular year, however, because payments for arms may not coincide with deliveries.

The data in table 17 are from the U.S. Arms Control and Disarmament Agency (ACDA). The IMF's *Government Finance Statistics Yearbook* is a primary source for data on military spending. It uses a consistent definition of defense spending based on the United Nations' classification of the functions of government and the NATO definition. The IMF checks data on defense spending for broad consistency with other macroeconomic data reported to it, but it is not always able to verify their accuracy and completeness. Moreover, country coverage is affected by delays or failure to report data. Thus most researchers supplement the IMF's data with independent assessments of military outlays by organizations such as ACDA, the Stockholm International Peace Research Institute, and the International Institute for Strategic Studies. However, these agencies rely heavily on reporting by governments, on confidential intelligence estimates of varying quality, on sources that they do not or cannot reveal, and on one another's publications.

Composite ICRG risk rating is an overall index taken from the *International Country Risk Guide* and based on 22 components of risk. The PRS Group's *International Country Risk Guide* collects information on each component, groups these components into three major categories (political, financial, and economic), and calculates a single risk assessment index ranging from 0 to 100. Ratings below 50 indicate very high risk and those above 80 very low risk. Ratings are updated monthly.

Institutional Investor credit rating ranks, from 0 to 100, the probability of a country's default. A high number indicates a low probability of default. *Institutional Investor* country credit ratings are based on information provided by leading international banks. Responses are weighted using a formula that gives more importance to responses from banks with greater world-wide exposure and more sophisticated country analysis systems.

Risk ratings may be highly subjective, reflecting external perceptions that do not always capture a country's actual situation. But these subjective perceptions are the reality that policymakers face in the climate they create for foreign private inflows. Countries not rated favorably by credit-risk rating agencies typically do not attract registered flows of private capital. The risk ratings presented here are not endorsed by the World Bank but are included for their analytical usefulness.

Highest marginal tax rate is the highest rate shown on the schedule of tax rates applied to the taxable income of individuals and corporations. The table also presents the income threshold above which the highest marginal tax rate applies for individuals.

Tax collection systems are often complex, containing many exceptions, exemptions, penalties, and other inducements that affect the incidence of taxation and thus influence the decisions of workers, managers, entrepreneurs, investors, and consumers. A potentially important influence on both domestic and international investors is the tax system's progressivity, as reflected in the highest marginal tax rate on individual and corporate income. Marginal tax rates on individuals generally refer to employment income. For some countries the highest marginal tax rate is also the basic or flat rate, and other surtaxes, deductions, and the like may apply.

Table 18. Power and transportation

Electric power consumption per capita measures the production of power plants and combined heat and power plants less distribution losses and their own use. **Electric power transmission and distribution losses** measures losses occurring between sources of supply and points of distribution, and in distribution to consumers, including pilferage.

The IEA collects data on electric power production and consumption from national energy agencies and adjusts those data to meet international definitions, for example, to account for establishments that, in addition to their main activities, generate electricity wholly or partly for their own use. In some countries self-production by households and small entrepreneurs is substantial because of their remoteness or because public power sources are unreliable, and these adjustments may not adequately reflect actual output.

Although power plants' own consumption and transmission losses are netted out, electric power consumption includes consumption by auxiliary stations, losses in transformers that are considered integral parts of those stations, and electricity produced by pumping installations. Where data are available, consumption covers electricity generated by all primary sources of energy: coal, oil, gas, nuclear, hydroelectric, geothermal, wind, tide and wave, and combustible renewables. Neither production nor consumption data capture the reliability of supplies, including the frequency of outages, breakdowns, and load factors.

Paved roads are roads that have been sealed with asphalt or similar road-building materials. **Goods transported by road** is the volume of goods transported by road vehicles, measured in millions of metric tons times kilometers traveled. **Goods transported by rail** measures the tonnage of goods transported times

kilometers traveled per million dollars of GDP measured in PPP terms. **Air passengers carried** includes passengers on both domestic and international passenger routes.

Data for most transportation industries are not internationally comparable, because unlike demographic statistics, national income accounts, and international trade data, the collection of infrastructure data has not been standardized internationally. Data on roads are collected by the International Road Federation (IRF) and data on air transportation by the International Civil Aviation Organization. National road associations are the primary source of IRF data; in countries where such an association is absent or does not respond, other agencies are contacted, such as road directorates, ministries of transportation or public works, or central statistical offices. As a result, the compiled data are of uneven quality.

Table 19. Communications, information, and science and technology

Daily newspapers is the number of copies distributed of newspapers published at least four times a week, per thousand people. **Radios** is the estimated number of radio receivers in use for broadcasts to the general public, per thousand people. Data on these two indicators are obtained from statistical surveys by the United Nations Educational, Scientific, and Cultural Organization (UNESCO). In some countries, definitions, classifications, and methods of enumeration do not entirely conform to UNESCO standards. For example, some countries report newspaper circulation as the number of copies printed rather than the number distributed. In addition, many countries impose radio license fees to help pay for public broadcasting, discouraging radio owners from declaring ownership. Because of these and other data collection problems, estimates of the number of newspapers and radios vary widely in reliability and should be interpreted with caution.

Television sets is the estimated number of sets in use, per thousand people. Data on television sets are supplied to the International Telecommunication Union (ITU) through annual questionnaires sent to national broadcasting authorities and industry associations. Some countries require that television sets be registered. To the extent that households do not register some or all of their sets, the number of registered sets may understate the true number of sets in use.

Telephone main lines counts all telephone lines that connect a customer's equipment to the public switched telephone network, per thousand people. **Mobile telephones** refers to users of portable telephones subscribing to an automatic public mobile telephone service using cellular technology that provides access to the public switched telephone network, per thousand people. The ITU compiles data on telephone main lines and mobile phones through annual questionnaires sent to telecommunications authorities and operating companies. The data are supplemented by annual reports and statistical yearbooks of telecommunications ministries, regulators, operators, and industry associations.

Personal computers is the estimated number of self-contained computers designed to be used by a single person, per thousand people. Estimates by the ITU of the number of personal computers are derived from an annual questionnaire, supplemented by other sources. In many countries mainframe computers are used extensively, and thousands of users may be connected to a single mainframe computer; in such cases the number of personal computers understates the total use of computers.

Internet hosts are computers connected directly to the worldwide network; many computer users can access the Internet through a single host. Hosts are assigned to countries on the basis of the host's country code, though this does not necessarily indicate that the host is physically located in that country. All hosts lacking a country code identification are assigned to the United States. Because Network Wizards (the source of these data at http://www.nw.com) changed the methods used in its Internet domain survey beginning in July 1998, the data shown here are not directly comparable with those published last year. The new survey is believed to be more reliable and to avoid the problem of undercounting that occurs when organizations restrict download access to their domain data. Nevertheless, some measurement problems remain, and so the number of Internet hosts shown for each country should be considered an approximation.

Scientists and engineers in R&D is the number of people trained to work in any field of science who are engaged in professional research and development activity (including administrators), per million people. Most such jobs require completion of tertiary education.

UNESCO collects data on scientific and technical workers and R&D expenditure from its member states, mainly from official replies to UNESCO questionnaires and special surveys, as well as from official reports and publications, supplemented by information from other national and international sources. UNESCO reports either the stock of scientists and engineers or the number of economically active persons qualified to be scientists and engineers. Stock data generally come from censuses and are less timely than measures of the economically active population. UNESCO supplements these data with estimates of the number of qualified scientists and engineers by counting the number of people who have completed education at ISCED (International Standard Classification of Education) levels 6 and 7. The data on scientists and engineers, normally calculated in terms of full-time equivalent staff, cannot take into account the considerable variations in the quality of training and education.

High-technology exports consists of goods produced by industries (based on U.S. industry classifications) that rank among a country's top 10 in terms of R&D expenditure. Manufactured exports are those commodities in the Standard International Trade Classification (SITC), revision 1, sections 5–9 (chemicals and related products, basic manufactures, manufactured articles, machinery and transport equipment, and other manufactured articles and goods not elsewhere classified), excluding division 68 (nonferrous metals).

Industry rankings are based on a methodology developed by Davis (1982; see Data Sources). Using input-output techniques, Davis estimated the technology intensity of U.S. industries in terms of the R&D expenditure required to produce a certain manufactured good. This methodology takes into account direct R&D expenditure by final producers as well as indirect R&D expenditure by suppliers of intermediate goods used in producing the final good. Industries, classified on the basis of the U.S. Standard Industrial Classification (SIC), were ranked according to

their R&D intensity, and the top 10 SIC groups (as classified at the three-digit level) were designated high-technology industries.

To translate Davis's industry classification into a definition of high-technology trade, Braga and Yeats (1992) used the concordance between the SIC grouping and the Standard International Trade Classification (SITC), revision 1, classification proposed by Hatter (1985). In preparing the data on high-technology trade, Braga and Yeats considered only SITC groups (classified at the four-digit level) that had a high-technology weight above 50 percent. Examples of high-technology exports include aircraft, office machinery, pharmaceuticals, and scientific instruments. This methodology rests on the somewhat unrealistic assumption that using U.S. input-output relations and trade patterns for high-technology production does not introduce a bias in the classification.

Number of patent applications filed is the number of documents, issued by a government office, that describe an invention and create a legal situation in which the patented invention can normally only be exploited (made, used, sold, imported) by, or with the authorization of, the patentee. The protection of inventions is limited in time (generally 20 years from the filing date of the application for the grant of a patent). Information on patent applications filed is shown separately for residents and nonresidents of the country. Data on patents are from the World Intellectual Property Organization, which estimates that at the end of 1996 about 3.8 million patents were in force in the world.

Table 20. Global trade

Merchandise exports shows the f.o.b. (free on board) value, in U.S. dollars, of goods provided to the rest of the world. **Merchandise imports** shows the c.i.f. (cost plus insurance and freight) value, in U.S. dollars, of goods purchased from the rest of the world. **Manufactured exports and imports** refers to commodities in SITC sections 5 (chemicals), 6 (basic manufactures), 7 (machinery), and 8 (miscellaneous manufactured goods), excluding division 68 (nonferrous metals) and group 891 (arms and ammunition). **Commercial services** comprises all trade in services, including transportation, communication, and business services, excluding government services, which comprise services associated with government sectors (such as expenditures on embassies and consulates) and with regional and international organizations.

Data on merchandise exports and imports are derived from customs records and may not fully conform to the concepts and definitions contained in the fifth edition of the IMF's *Balance of Payments Manual.* The value of exports is recorded as the cost of the goods delivered to the frontier of the exporting country for shipment—the f.o.b. value. Many countries collect and report trade data in U.S. dollars. When countries report in local currency, the value is converted at the average official exchange rate for the period. The value of imports is generally recorded as the cost of the goods when purchased by the importer plus the cost of transport and insurance to the frontier of the importing country—the c.i.f. value. Data on imports of goods are derived from the same sources as data on exports. In principle, world exports and imports should be identical. Similarly, exports from an economy should equal the sum of imports by the rest of the world from that economy. But differences in timing and definition result in discrepancies in reported values at all levels.

The data in this table were compiled by the World Trade Organization (WTO). Data on merchandise trade come from the IMF *International Financial Statistics Yearbook*, supplemented by data from the COMTRADE database maintained by the United Nations Statistical Division and from national publications for countries that do not report to the IMF. Data on trade in manufactures come from the COMTRADE database. Where data were not available from the WTO, World Bank staff estimated the shares of manufactures using the most recent information available from the COMTRADE database. Wherever available, WTO reports merchandise trade data on the basis of the general system of trade, which includes goods imported for reexport. Two economies, Hong Kong (China) and Singapore, with substantial levels of reexports are noted in the table. Goods transported through a country en route to another are not included. Data on trade in commercial services are drawn from the IMF Balance of Payments database, supplemented by national publications from countries that do not report to the IMF.

Table 21. Aid and financial flows

Net private capital flows consists of private debt and nondebt flows. Private debt flows include commercial bank lending, bonds, and other private credits; nondebt private flows are foreign direct investment and portfolio equity investment. **Foreign direct investment** is net inflows of investment to acquire a lasting management interest (10 percent or more of voting stock) in an enterprise operating in an economy other than that of the investor. It is the sum of equity capital flows, reinvestment of earnings, other long-term capital flows, and short-term capital flows as shown in the balance of payments.

The data on foreign direct investment are based on balance of payments data reported by the IMF, supplemented by data on net foreign direct investment reported by the OECD and official national sources. The internationally accepted definition of foreign direct investment is that provided in the fifth edition of the IMF's *Balance of Payments Manual*. The OECD has also published a definition, in consultation with the IMF, Eurostat (the Statistical Office of the European Communities), and the United Nations. Because of the multiplicity of sources and differences in definitions and reporting methods, more than one estimate of foreign direct investment may exist for a country, and data may not be comparable across countries.

Foreign direct investment data do not give a complete picture of international investment in an economy. Balance of payments data on foreign direct investment do not include capital raised in the host economies, which has become an important source of financing for investment projects in some developing countries. There is also increasing awareness that foreign direct investment data are limited because they capture only cross-border investment flows involving equity participation and omit nonequity cross-border transactions such as intrafirm flows of goods and services. For a detailed discussion of the data issues see volume 1, chapter 3, of *World Debt Tables 1993–94*.

Total external debt is debt owed to nonresidents repayable in foreign currency, goods, or services. It is the sum of public, publicly guaranteed, and private nonguaranteed long-term debt,

use of IMF credit, and short-term debt. Short-term debt includes all debt having an original maturity of one year or less and interest in arrears on long-term debt. **Present value of external debt** is the sum of short-term external debt plus the discounted sum of total debt service payments due on public, publicly guaranteed, and private nonguaranteed long-term external debt over the life of existing loans.

Data on the external debt of low- and middle-income economies are gathered by the World Bank through its Debtor Reporting System. World Bank staff calculate the indebtedness of developing countries using loan-by-loan reports submitted by these countries on long-term public and publicly guaranteed borrowing, along with information on short-term debt collected by the countries or from creditors through the reporting systems of the Bank for International Settlements and the OECD. These data are supplemented by information on loans and credits from major multilateral banks and loan statements from official lending agencies in major creditor countries, and by estimates from World Bank country economists and IMF desk officers. In addition, some countries provide data on private nonguaranteed debt. In 1996, 34 countries reported their private nonguaranteed debt to the World Bank; estimates were made for 28 additional countries known to have significant private debt.

The present value of external debt provides a measure of future debt service obligations that can be compared with such indicators as GNP. It is calculated by discounting debt service (interest plus amortization) due on long-term external debt over the life of existing loans. Short-term debt is included at its face value. Data on debt are in U.S. dollars converted at official exchange rates. The discount rate applied to long-term debt is determined by the currency of repayment of the loan and is based on the OECD's commercial interest reference rates. Loans from the International Bank for Reconstruction and Development and credits from the International Development Association are discounted using a reference rate for special drawing rights, as are obligations to the IMF. When the discount rate is greater than the interest rate of the loan, the present value is less than the nominal sum of future debt service obligations.

Official development assistance (ODA) consists of disbursements of loans (net of repayments of principal) and grants made on concessional terms by official agencies of the members of the Development Assistance Committee (DAC) and certain Arab countries to promote economic development and welfare in recipient economies listed by DAC as developing. Loans with a grant element of more than 25 percent are included in ODA, as are technical cooperation and assistance. Also included are aid flows (net of repayments) from official donors to the transition economies of Eastern Europe and the former Soviet Union and to certain higher-income developing countries and territories as determined by DAC. These flows are sometimes referred to as "official aid" and are provided under terms and conditions similar to those for ODA. Data for aid as a share of GNP are calculated using values in U.S. dollars converted at official exchange rates.

The data cover bilateral loans and grants from DAC countries, multilateral organizations, and certain Arab countries. They do not reflect aid given by recipient countries to other developing countries. As a result, some countries that are net donors (such as Saudi Arabia) are shown in the table as aid recipients.

The data do not distinguish among different types of aid (program, project, or food aid; emergency assistance; peacekeeping assistance; or technical cooperation), each of which may have a very different effect on the economy. Technical cooperation expenditures do not always directly benefit the recipient economy to the extent that they defray costs incurred outside the country for salaries and benefits of technical experts and for overhead of firms supplying technical services.

Because the aid data in table 21 are based on information from donors, they are not consistent with information recorded by recipients in the balance of payments, which often excludes all or some technical assistance—particularly payments to expatriates made directly by the donor. Similarly, grant commodity aid may not always be recorded in trade data or in the balance of payments. Although estimates of ODA in balance of payments statistics are meant to exclude purely military aid, the distinction is sometimes blurred. The definition used by the country of origin usually prevails.

Statistical methods

This section describes the calculation of the least-squares growth rate, the exponential (end-point) growth rate, the Gini index, and the World Bank's *Atlas* methodology for calculating the conversion factor used to estimate GNP and GNP per capita in U.S. dollars.

Least-squares growth rate

Least-squares growth rates are used wherever there is a sufficiently long time series to permit a reliable calculation. No growth rate is calculated if more than half the observations in a period are missing.

The least-squares growth rate, r, is estimated by fitting a linear regression trendline to the logarithmic annual values of the variable in the relevant period. The regression equation takes the form

$$\ln X_t = a + bt,$$

which is equivalent to the logarithmic transformation of the compound growth equation,

$$X_t = X_o (1 + r)^t.$$

In this equation, X is the variable, t is time, and $a = \log X_o$ and $b = ln (1 + r)$ are the parameters to be estimated. If b^* is the least-squares estimate of b, the average annual growth rate, r, is obtained as $[\exp(b^*) - 1]$ and is multiplied by 100 to express it as a percentage.

The calculated growth rate is an average rate that is representative of the available observations over the entire period. It does not necessarily match the actual growth rate between any two periods.

Exponential growth rate

The growth rate between two points in time for certain demographic data, notably labor force and population, is calculated from the equation

$$r = \ln (p_n/p_1)/n,$$

where p_n and p_1 are the last and first observations in the period, n is the number of years in the period, and ln is the natural logarithm operator. This growth rate is based on a model of continuous, exponential growth between two points in time. It does not take into account the intermediate values of the series. Note also that the exponential growth rate does not correspond to the annual rate of change measured at a one-year interval which is given by $(p_n - p_{n-1})/p_{n-1}$.

The Gini index

The Gini index measures the extent to which the distribution of income (or, in some cases, consumption expenditure) among individuals or households within an economy deviates from a perfectly equal distribution. A Lorenz curve plots the cumulative percentages of total income received against the cumulative percentage of recipients, starting with the poorest individual or household. The Gini index measures the area between the Lorenz curve and a hypothetical line of absolute equality, expressed as a percentage of the maximum area under the line. Thus a Gini index of zero represents perfect equality, where an index of 100 percent implies maximum inequality.

The World Bank employs a numerical analysis program, POVCAL, to estimate values of the Gini index; see Chen, Datt, and Ravallion (1993; see Data Sources).

World Bank Atlas *method*

In calculating GNP and GNP per capita in U.S. dollars for certain operational purposes, the World Bank uses a synthetic exchange rate commonly called the *Atlas* conversion factor. The purpose of the *Atlas* conversion factor is to reduce the impact of exchange rate fluctuations in the cross-country comparison of national incomes.

The *Atlas* conversion factor for any year is the average of a country's effective exchange rate with the G-5 countries (or alternative conversion factor) for that year and those for the two preceding years, after adjusting for differences in rates of inflation between the country and the G-5 countries. A country's effective exchange rate is an average of its exchange rates with a selection of other countries, usually weighted by the country's trade with those countries. The G-5 (Group of Five) countries are France, Germany, Japan, the United Kingdom, and the United States. A country's inflation rate is measured by its GNP deflator. The inflation rate for the G-5 countries is measured by changes in the SDR deflator. (Special drawing rights, or SDRs, are the IMF's unit of account.) The SDR deflator is calculated as a weighted average of the G-5 countries' GDP deflators in SDR terms. The weights are determined by the amount of each currency included in one SDR unit. Weights vary over time because the currency composition of the SDR and the relative exchange rates for each currency both change. The SDR deflator is calculated in SDR terms first and then converted to U.S. dollars using the SDR-to-dollar *Atlas* conversion factor.

This three-year averaging smooths annual fluctuations in prices and exchange rates for each country. The *Atlas* conversion factor is then applied to a country's GNP. The resulting GNP in U.S. dollars is divided by the country's midyear population for the latest of the three years to derive its GNP per capita. When official exchange rates are deemed to be unreliable or unrepresentative during a period, an alternative estimate of the exchange rate is used in the *Atlas* formula (see below).

The following formulas describe the computation of the *Atlas* conversion factor for year *t*:

$$e_t^* = \frac{1}{3}\left[e_{t-2}\left(\frac{p_t}{p_{t-2}} \middle/ \frac{p_t^{S\$}}{p_{t-2}^{S\$}}\right) + e_{t-1}\left(\frac{p_t}{p_{t-1}} \middle/ \frac{p_t^{S\$}}{p_{t-1}^{S\$}}\right) + e_t \right]$$

and for calculating GNP per capita in U.S. dollars for year *t*:

$$Y_t^{\$} = (Y_t / N_t) / e_t^*$$

where e_t^* is the *Atlas* conversion factor (units of national currency to the U.S. dollar) for year *t*, e_t is the average annual exchange rate (units of national currency to the U.S. dollar) for

year *t*, p_t is the GNP deflator for year *t*, $p_t^{S\$}$ is the SDR deflator in U.S. dollar terms for year t, $Y_t^{\$}$ is the *Atlas* GNP in U.S. dollars in year *t*, Y_t is current GNP (local currency) for year *t*, and N_t is the midyear population for year *t*.

Alternative conversion factors

The World Bank systematically assesses the appropriateness of official exchange rates as conversion factors. An alternative conversion factor is used when the official exchange rate is judged to diverge by an exceptionally large margin from the rate effectively applied to domestic transactions of foreign currencies and traded products. This is the case for only a small number of countries (see the primary data documentation table in *World Development Indicators 1999*). Alternative conversion factors are used in the *Atlas* method and elsewhere in the Selected World Development Indicators as single-year conversion factors.

Data Sources

ACDA (Arms Control and Disarmament Agency). 1997. *World Military Expenditures and Arms Transfers 1996*. Washington, D.C.

Ahmad, Sultan. 1992. "Regression Estimates of Per Capita GDP Based on Purchasing Power Parities." Policy Research Working Paper 956. World Bank, International Economics Department, Washington, D.C.

———. 1994. "Improving Inter-Spatial and Inter-Temporal Comparability of National Accounts." *Journal of Development Economics* 4:53–75.

Ball, Nicole. 1984. "Measuring Third World Security Expenditure: A Research Note." *World Development* 12(2):157–64.

Bos, Eduard, My T. Vu, Ernest Massiah, and Rodolfo Bulatao. 1994. *World Population Projections 1994–95*. Baltimore, Md.: Johns Hopkins University Press.

Braga, C.A. Primo, and Alexander Yeats. 1992. "How Minilateral Trading Arrangements May Affect the Post-Uruguay Round World." World Bank, International Economics Department, Washington, D.C.

Chen, Shaohua, Gaurav Datt, and Martin Ravallion. 1993. "Is Poverty Increasing in the Developing World?" Policy Research Working Paper. World Bank, Washington, D.C.

Council of Europe. Various years. *Recent Demographic Developments in Europe and North America*. Strasbourg: Council of Europe Press.

Davis, Lester. 1982. *Technology Intensity of U.S. Output and Trade*. Washington, D.C.: U.S. Department of Commerce.

Eurostat (Statistical Office of the European Communities). Various years. *Demographic Statistics*. Luxembourg.

FAO (Food and Agriculture Organization). 1997. *State of the World's Forests 1997*. Rome.

———. Various years. *Production Yearbook*. FAO Statistics Series. Rome.

Happe, Nancy, and John Wakeman-Linn. 1994. "Military Expenditures and Arms Trade: Alternative Data Sources." IMF Working Paper 94/69. International Monetary Fund, Policy Development and Review Department, Washington, D.C.

Hatter, Victoria L. 1985. *U.S. High-Technology Trade and Competitiveness*. Washington, D.C.: U.S. Department of Commerce.

Heston, Alan. 1994. "A Brief Review of Some Problems in Using National Accounts Data in Level of Output Comparisons and Growth Studies." *Journal of Development Economics* 44:29–52.

ICAO (International Civil Aviation Organization). 1998. *Civil Aviation Statistics of the World: 1997*. ICAO Statistical Yearbook. 22nd ed. Montreal.

IEA (International Energy Agency). 1998a. *Energy Statistics and Balances of Non-OECD Countries 1995–96*. Paris.

———. 1998b. *Energy Statistics of OECD Countries 1995–96*. Paris.

IFC (International Finance Corporation). 1998. *Emerging Stock Markets Factbook 1998*. Washington, D.C.

ILO (International Labour Organization). Various years. *Yearbook of Labour Statistics*. Geneva: International Labour Office.

———. 1995a. *Labour Force Estimates and Projections, 1950–2010*. Geneva.

———. 1995b. *Estimates of the Economically Active Population by Sex and Age Group and by Main Sectors of Economic Activity*. Geneva.

IMF (International Monetary Fund). 1986. *A Manual on Government Finance Statistics*. Washington, D.C.

———. 1993. *Balance of Payments Manual*. 5th ed. Washington, D.C.

———. Various years. *Direction of Trade Statistics Yearbook*. Washington, D.C.

———. Various years. *Government Finance Statistics Yearbook*. Washington, D.C.

———. Various years. *International Financial Statistics Yearbook*. Washington, D.C.

Institutional Investor, 1999. New York. (March).

IRF (International Road Federation). 1998. *World Road Statistics 1998*. Geneva.

ITU (International Telecommunication Union). 1998. *World Telecommunication Development Report*. Geneva.

Luxembourg Income Study. LIS database. http://lissy.seps.lu/index. htm.

National Bureau of Economic Research. 1997. *Penn World Tables Mark 5.6*. http://nber.harvard.edu/pwt56.html.

OECD (Organisation for Economic Co-operation and Development). 1989. *Geographical Distribution of Financial Flows to Developing Countries*. Paris.

———. 1997a. *National Accounts 1960–1995*. Vol. 1, *Main Aggregates*. Paris.

———. 1997b. *National Accounts 1960–1995*. Vol. 2, *Detailed Tables*. Paris.

———. 1998. *Development Co-operation: 1997 Report*. Paris.

PRS Group. 1999. *International Country Risk Guide*. February. East Syracuse, N.Y.

PricewaterhouseCoopers. 1998a. *Corporate Taxes: A Worldwide Summary*. New York.

———. 1998b. *Individual Taxes: A Worldwide Summary*. New York.

Ravallion, Martin. 1996. "What Can New Survey Data Tell Us about the Recent Changes in Living Standards in Developing and Transitional Economies?" World Bank, Policy Research Department, Washington, D.C.

Ravallion, Martin, and Shaohua Chen. 1997. "Can High-Ineqaulity Developing Countries Escape Absolute Poverty?" *Economic Letters* 56: 51–57.

Srinivasan, T.N. 1994. "Database for Development Analysis: An Overview." *Journal of Development Economics* 44(1):3–28.

UNCTAD (United Nations Conference on Trade and Development). Various years. *Handbook of International Trade and Development Statistics*. Geneva.

UNESCO (United Nations Educational, Scientific, and Cultural Organization). Various years. *Statistical Yearbook*. Paris.

UNICEF (United Nations Children's Fund). 1999. *The State of the World's Children 1999*. Oxford, U.K.: Oxford University Press.

UNIDO (United Nations Industrial Development Organization).1996. *International Yearbook of Industrial Statistics 1996*. Vienna.

United Nations. 1968. *A System of National Accounts: Studies and Methods*. Series F, no. 2, rev. 3. New York.

———. 1985. *National Accounts Statistics: Compendium of Income Distribution Statistics*. New York.

———. 1997. *World Urbanization Prospects: The 1996 Revision*. New York.

———. Various years. *Energy Statistics Yearbook*. New York.

———. Various issues. *Monthly Bulletin of Statistics*. New York.

———. Various years. *National Income Accounts*. Statistics Division. New York.

———. Various years. *Statistical Yearbook*. New York.

———. Various years. *Update on the Nutrition Situation*. Administrative Committee on Coordination, Subcommittee on Nutrition. Geneva.

———. Various years. *Population and Vital Statistics Report*. New York.

U.S. Bureau of the Census. 1996. *World Population Profile 1996*. Washington, D.C.: U.S. Government Printing Office.

WHO (World Health Organization). Various years. *World Health Statistics*. Geneva.

———. Various years. *World Health Statistics Report*. Geneva.

WHO and UNICEF. 1996. *Revised 1990 Estimates on Maternal Mortality: A New Approach*. Geneva.

World Bank. 1993a. *Purchasing Power of Currencies: Comparing National Incomes Using ICP Data*. Washington, D.C.

———. 1993b. *World Debt Tables 1993–94*. Washington, D.C.

———. 1998. *Global Development Finance 1998*. Washington, D.C.

———. 1999. *World Development Indicators*. Washington, D.C.

World Resources Institute, UNEP (United Nations Environment Programme), and UNDP (United Nations Development Programme). 1994. *World Resources 1994–95: A Guide to the Global Environment*. New York: Oxford University Press.

World Resources Institute, in collaboration with UNEP (United Nations Environment Programme), and UNDP (United Nations Development Programme). 1998. *World Resources 1998–99: A Guide to the Global Environment*. New York: Oxford University Press.

Classification of Economies by Income and Region, 1999

| Income group | Subgroup | Sub-Saharan Africa | | Asia | | Europe and Central Asia | | Middle East and North Africa | | Americas |
		East and Southern Africa	West Africa	East Asia and Pacific	South Asia	Eastern Europe and Central Asia	Rest of Europe	Middle East	North Africa	
Low-income		Angola Burundi Comoros Congo, Dem. Rep. Eritrea Ethiopia Kenya Lesotho Madagascar Malawi Mozambique Rwanda Somalia Sudan Tanzania Uganda Zambia Zimbabwe	Benin Burkina Faso Cameroon Central African Republic Chad Congo, Rep. Côte d'Ivoire Gambia, The Ghana Guinea Guinea-Bissau Liberia Mali Mauritania Niger Nigeria São Tomé and Principe Senegal Sierra Leone Togo	Cambodia China Indonesia Korea, Dem. Rep. Lao PDR Mongolia Myanmar Solomon Islands Vietnam	Afghanistan Bangladesh Bhutan India Nepal Pakistan	Armenia Azerbaijan Kyrgyz Republic Moldova Tajikistan Turkmenistan		Yemen, Rep.		Haiti Honduras Nicaragua
Middle-income	Lower	Djibouti Namibia South Africa Swaziland	Cape Verde Equatorial Guinea	Fiji Kiribati Marshall Islands Micronesia, Fed. Sts. Papua New Guinea Philippines Samoa Thailand Tonga Vanuatu	Maldives Sri Lanka	Albania Belarus Bosnia and Herzegovina Bulgaria Georgia Kazakhstan Latvia Lithuania Macedonia, FYR[a] Romania Russian Federation Ukraine Uzbekistan Yugoslavia, Fed. Rep.[b]		Iran, Islamic Rep. Iraq Jordan Syrian Arab Republic West Bank and Gaza	Algeria Egypt, Arab Rep. Morocco Tunisia	Belize Bolivia Colombia Costa Rica Cuba Dominica Dominican Republic Ecuador El Salvador Guatemala Guyana Jamaica Paraguay Peru St. Vincent and the Grenadines Suriname
	Upper	Botswana Mauritius Mayotte Seychelles	Gabon	American Samoa Korea, Rep Malaysia Palau		Croatia Czech Republic Estonia Hungary Poland Slovak Republic	Isle of Man Turkey	Bahrain Lebanon Oman Saudi Arabia	Libya	Antigua and Barbuda Argentina Barbados Brazil Chile Grenada Guadeloupe Mexico Panama Puerto Rico St. Kitts and Nevis St. Lucia Trinidad and Tobago Uruguay Venezuela
Subtotal:	157	26	23	23	8	26	2	10	5	34

Classification of Economies by Income and Region, 1999 *(continued)*

| Income group | Subgroup | Sub-Saharan Africa | | Asia | | Europe and Central Asia | | Middle East and North Africa | | Americas |
		East and Southern Africa	West Africa	East Asia and Pacific	South Asia	Eastern Europe and Central Asia	Rest of Europe	Middle East	North Africa	
High-income	OECD			Australia Japan New Zealand			Austria Belgium Denmark Finland France Germany Greece Iceland Ireland Italy Luxembourg Netherlands Norway Portugal Spain Sweden Switzerland United Kingdom			Canada United States
	Non-OECD	Réunion		Brunei French Polynesia Guam Hong Kong, China[c] Macao New Caledonia N. Mariana Islands Singapore Taiwan, China		Slovenia	Andorra Channel Islands Cyprus Faeroe Islands Greenland Liechtenstein Monaco	Israel Kuwait Qatar United Arab Emirates	Malta	Aruba Bahamas, The Bermuda Cayman Islands French Guiana Martinique Netherlands Antilles Virgin Islands (U.S.)
Total:	211	27	23	35	8	27	27	14	6	44

a. Former Yugoslav Republic of Macedonia.
b. Federal Republic of Yugoslavia (Serbia/Montenegro).
c. On July 1, 1997, China resumed its sovereignty over Hong Kong.

Source: World Bank data.

For operational and analytical purposes, the World Bank's main criterion for classifying economies is gross national product (GNP) per capita. Every economy is classified as low-income, middle-income (subdivided into lower-middle and upper-middle), or high-income. Other analytical groups, based on geographic regions and levels of external debt, are also used.

Low-income and middle-income economies are sometimes referred to as developing economies. The use of the term is convenient; it is not intended to imply that all economies in the group are experiencing similar development or that other economies have reached a preferred or final stage of development. Classification by income does not necessarily reflect development status.

This table classifies all World Bank member economies with populations of more than 30,000. Economies are divided among income groups according to 1998 GNP per capita, calculated using the World Bank *Atlas* method. The groups are: low-income, $760 or less; lower-middle-income, $761–$3,030; upper-middle-income, $3,031–$9,360; and high-income, $9,361 or more.

Index

References to boxes are noted by *b*, to figures by *f*, and to tables by *t*.

Afghanistan, emigration, 38
Africa. *See also* North Africa; Sub-Saharan Africa; *specific countries*
  authoritarian governments, 46
  banking crisis, 37*f*
  biodiversity, 43
  civil society and political parties, 122
  decentralization of government, 45–46, 123
  demographic shifts, 44
  foreign direct investment, 72
  infectious diseases, 26
  life expectancy, 26, 26*f*
  macroeconomics, 16
  trade, 51
  urbanization, 47, 47*f*, 48*f*, 130, 130*b*
  water scarcity, 28*b*
  WTO membership, 57*f*
Aging population, 1, 29, 35, 36*b*, 38
Agreement on Sanitary and Phytosanitary Measures, 64
Agriculture, 27–28
  chart by country, 244–45, 250–53
  crop variations, 42
  environmental issues, 89*f*, 93
  food supplies. *See* Food shortage
  GDP percent, 28, 47
  map of changing crop yields, 89*f*
  trade, 6, 61, 63–64, 63*f*
  water scarcity and, 29*b*
AIDS, 26, 27*b*
Air pollution. *See also* Environmental issues
urban areas, 141, 150, 151*b*
Albania, poverty reduction, 111
Algeria, natural resources preservation, 102
Alliance of Small Island States (AOSIS), 99
Alphons, K.J., 144
Andean Community trade, 53
Antarctica, 8, 88*b*, 90, 95
Antibiotics, 27*b*
Antidumping laws, 6, 34, 58–59, 60*f*, 60*t*, 61*f*
Antitrust issues, 6, 52, 59
AOSIS (Alliance of Small Island States), 99
Aquaculture, 92*b*
Arab Republic of Egypt. *See* Egypt
Arbitration. *See* Dispute resolution
Argentina
  antidumping laws, 58
  banking sector, 74, 76*f*, 77
  budgetary constraint on local governments, 124

capital account convertibility, 71
  decentralization of government, 45*t*, 113–14
  foreign direct investment, 37, 73*f*
  government structure, 116*t*
  investment treaties, 72
  private infrastructure, 144
  tax sharing, 118, 118*b*
  trade reform, 56*f*, 59*f*
Armenia, government structure, 115
ASEAN (Association of Southeast Asian Nations), 85
Asia. *See also* Central Asia; East Asia; South Asia; *specific countries*
  biodiversity, 43
  bond market, 133
  chart by region and income, 290–91
  child labor, 62*b*
  trade in services, 65
  urbanization, 47, 47*f*, 48*f*
Association of Southeast Asian Nations (ASEAN), 85
Australia
  antidumping laws, 58
  immigration trends, 38–40
  public services and horizontal equity, 110

Balance of payments, chart by country, 258–59
Balance of power, 111–14
Bangladesh
  banking sector, 24
  decentralization of government, 45*t*
  flooding due to climate change, 42, 87, 99–100, 100*f*
  government structure, 116*t*
  infant mortality, 142, 142*t*
  life expectancy, 26*f*
  trade reform, 56*f*
Bank for International Settlements. *See* Basle Accords
Banking Regulations and Supervisory Practices Committee. *See* Basle Accords
Banking sector
  competition, 35
  deposit insurance, 76–77
  developing countries, 7, 35, 70, 73–79
  diversification, 75–79
  financial contagion, 74, 75*b*
  foreign banks. *See* Foreign banks

foreign currency deposits and liability, 80
  government incentives to reduce risk-taking, 77
  loan screening, 77
  municipal development funds (MDFs), 134
  private incentives to reduce risk-taking, 77
  reform, 77–78
    case study of Hungary, 158, 160–63, 161*b*
    regulation, 75–79
    rural women, loans to, 24
    subnational issues, 77
    subordinated debt and, 77
Bankruptcies, 74
  municipal, 133–34
Barbados, components and parts exports, 66, 66*t*
Basle Accords, 7, 32, 37–38, 78
Biodiversity, 8, 32, 42–43, 90, 93–94, 102–5
  chart by country, 222–23
Block grants, 118
Bolivia
  Andean Community trade, 53
  life expectancy, 26*f*
  local governments, 111, 122
  water pollution, 140–41
Bond market, 133
Bosnia and Herzegovina, decentralization of government, 108, 109*b*
"Brain drain" from developing countries, 38–39
Brazil
  antidumping laws, 58
  banking sector, 37*f*, 76*f*
  biodiversity, 43
  components and parts exports, 66, 66*t*
  decentralization of government, 45*t*, 113–14, 158, 163–66, 163*b*
  educational reforms, 23
  firms from and international debt, 70, 71*f*
  foreign direct investment, 37, 72, 73*f*
  government structure, 33, 116*t*, 153
  import-substitution policies and, 2, 13
  localization economies, 127
  politics, 44, 122
  state debt, 119, 124, 133, 164–65
  taxes, 117
  technology exports, 59*f*

trade in services, 65
urbanization issues, 131, 145–46,
    149–50, 153
Britain. *See* United Kingdom
Building codes, 144

Cameroon and forests' biological resources,
    93
Canada
    antidumping laws, 58
    biodiversity, 43
    bond market, 133
    chart by region and income, 290–91
    decentralization issues, 114
    GATT case for offering industrial
        incentives, 136
    government structure, 116*t*
    immigration trends, 38–40
    public services and horizontal equity,
        110
Capital account liberalization, 79–81
Capital flows. *See* International capital
    flows
Carbon dioxide emissions, 8, 41–42, 42*f*,
    87, 90, 93. *See also* Climate change
    chart by country, 248–49, 272
    economic growth and, 20
    global attempts to control, 97–102
    trading mechanisms, 101
Caribbean. *See* Latin America
CDF. *See* Comprehensive Development
    Framework (World Bank)
Central Asia. *See also specific countries*
    chart by region and income, 290–91
    decentralization of government, 45
    energy consumption, 101*f*
    poverty, 25*f*
    trade in services, 34*f*
    urbanization, 47*f*, 48*f*
CFCs. *See* Chlorofluorocarbons
Child labor, 62*b*
    chart by country, 234–35
Child mortality, 19*f. See* Infant mortality
Chile
    banking sector, 37*f*, 76*f*, 77
    decentralization of government, 123
    disincentives for short-term capital
        inflows, 79
    political participation and civil society,
        122
    telephone service, 24
    trade reform, 56*f*
China
    aging population, 36*b*
    carbon dioxide emissions, 42
    components and parts exports, 66*t*
    decentralization of government, 46,
        108*b*, 111–12, 113*b*
    development strategy, 2, 16–17
    diaspora, 39–40, 40*b*
    environmental issues, 90

foreign direct investment, 37, 72, 73*f*
investment treaties, 72
ozone depletion, 96
rapid economic growth, 2, 16–17
social welfare, 152
technology exports, 59*f*
total suspended particulates (TSPs),
    141–42
urbanization issues, 130–31, 141
Chlorofluorocarbons (CFCs), 8, 42, 94*b*,
    95–97
Cholera, 143
CITES (Convention on International
    Trade in Endangered Species), 103,
    104*b*
Civil society and accountability of local
    governments, 122
Climate change, 41–42, 41*f*, 87, 94,
    103–5. *See also* Carbon dioxide
    emissions
    chart by country, 222–23
    global attempts to control, 1, 8, 30, 32,
        97–102
    map of changing crop yields, 89*f*
Coal production subsidies, 90–91
Colombia
    Andean Community trade, 53
    banking sector, 76*f*
    decentralization of government, 45*t*,
        108, 114, 116*t*, 123
    FINDETER program, 134
    trade, 52
    violence, 145, 151–52
Communications
    chart by country, 266–67
    institutions providing
        telecommunications, 24
    technological advances, 4, 29–30
    trade via electronic communication, 33
Community resources, 50
Competition
    antitrust issues, 6, 59
    banking sector, 35
    economic growth and, 17*b*
    trade, 52, 59
    water supply, 148
Components and parts exports, 33, 65–67,
    66*t*
Comprehensive Development Framework
    (CDF) (World Bank), 20, 21*b*, 173
Consumption, chart by country, 238–39
Contraceptive use, chart by country,
    242–43
Convention on Biological Diversity, 8, 43,
    88, 94, 94*b*, 102–3
Convention on International Trade in
    Endangered Species (CITES), 103,
    104*b*
Coral reef protection, 103
Corruption, 17*b*, 21*b*
    World Development Reports, 22*b*

Costa Rica
    capital account convertibility, 71
    Certified Trading Offsets (CTOs), 104
    National Biodiversity Institute (INBio),
        103
Côte d'Ivoire, 37*f*, 52, 148
Crime. *See* Violence
Croatia, components and parts exports, 66*t*
CTOs (Certified Trading Offsets), 104
Cultural differences
    Comprehensive Development
        Framework and, 21*b*
    decentralization of government and, 109*b*
    loss of, 1
Currency crises, 73–75, 75*b*
Czech Republic
    banking crisis, 37*f*
    bond market, 133
    components and parts exports, 66, 66*t*
    environmental issues, 94*b*
    government structure, 115
    municipal development funds (MDFs),
        134
    trade reform, 58

DAC (Development Assistance Committee
    of the OECD), 20
Dam projects of World Bank, 18, 18*b*
Decentralization of government, 4, 4*f*,
    8–10, 28, 32–33, 43–44, 107–24. *See
    also* Subnational governments
    balance of power, 111–14
    block grants, 118
    case study of Brazil, 158, 163–66, 163*b*
    chart by country, 216–17
    civil society and, 122
    data indicators, 213–14
    devolution of powers, as, 108*b*
    elections, 121–23
    ethnic diversity and, 109*b*
    executive power, 114
    fiscal issues, 115, 117–19, 123
    incentives for national and subnational
        cooperation, 114
    large democracies, 45, 45*t*
    legislative allocations and regional
        interests, 113
    local administration, effectiveness, 122
    political parties, 122
    political stability and, 107–8
    poverty reduction and, 109–11
    public service performance and, 108–9
    regional influence on national
        government, 113
    resource control, 117–19
    sequencing of events, 123
    shared functions, 115, 117
    smaller countries, 45
    structures and functions of subnational
        governments, 114–21
    taxation, 117–19, 118*b*

Decentralization of government—*continued*
  threat to macroeconomic stability, 111
  transfers of revenues, 117–18
  transition policies, 123–24
Deconcentration and central governments,
  108*b*
Deforestation. *See* Forests and deforestation
Democracies
  increase in number of, 9*f*
Democracies, increase in number of, 8–9,
  9*f*, 28, 43, 43*f*
Demographic shifts
  Africa, 44
  aging of population, 29, 35, 36*b*
  immigration's effect, 38
  Middle East, 44
  urbanization, 46–47, 47*f*
Deposit insurance, 76–77
Derivative instruments, 34
Desertification, 8, 87, 88*b*
Developing countries. *See also specific*
    countries
  antidumping complaints, 61*f*
  banking sector, 7, 35, 70, 73–75, 76*f*
  biodiversity, 43, 102
  child labor, 62*b*
  climate change, 42
  emigration of skilled workers, 38–39
  environmental issues, 88, 96, 100
  exchange rates, 71
  financial reform, 69–85
  foreign direct investment in, 37, 38*t*,
    69–75, 73*b*
  foreign investment by, 72
  GDP per capita, 14
  gender-based discrimination, 19–20
  international capital flows, 7*f*. *See*
    International capital flows
  macroeconomics and, 16, 111*f*
  municipal development funds (MDFs),
    134
  poverty, 26
  public services, 144–55
  subnational debts, 120*t*
  subnational expenditures, 111
  trade growth, 5–6, 5*f*, 33, 51–53, 52*f*,
    59, 64–65
  urbanization, 10–11, 10*f*, 46, 47*f*, 142,
    144–55
Development Assistance Committee
    (DAC) of the OECD, 20
Development policy, 2–4, 13–30, 172–74
  future outlook, 24–30
  government intervention, effect, 15–16
  government's role, 2, 13
  guidelines proposed for, 3
  interdependence of policies, 2–3, 13–14,
    173
  investment correlated with growth, 15, 15*f*
  objectives of sustainable development, 2,
    13, 18–21

past experiences as starting point, 14–18
  processes' and institutions' importance,
    3, 11, 14
  sustainable development agenda, 28, 28*b*
  urbanization and, 49–50
Diasporas, 39, 40*b*, 66
Diseases, 26, 27*b*, 141–43. *See also* Health
  issues
Displaced workers, 6
Dispute resolution
  investment agreement provisions, 82
  trade complaints, 54–55, 61
Distribution of income or consumption,
  chart by country, 238–39
Diversification of banking sector, 75–79
Diversity. *See* Cultural differences
Dollarization, 80
Drugs, 27*b*, 103

East Asia. *See also specific countries*
  aging population, effect, 36*b*
  authoritarian governments, 46
  economic downturn, 13, 16, 17*b*, 32,
    35–37, 74, 75*b*
  economic growth, 2, 11, 14–16, 17*b*, 48
  energy consumption, 101*f*
  export subsidies and, 2
  poverty, 25, 25*f*
  return of emigrants, 39
  technology exports, 56
  trade in services, 34*f*
  trade reform and foreign investment, 81
  urbanization, 47*f*, 48*f*
Eastern Europe. *See also specific countries*
  decentralization of government, 45
  economic problems, 17*b*
  housing, 146
  land use, 134
  life expectancy, 26, 26*f*
Economic growth
  chart by country, 250–51
  urbanization and, 125–38, 126*f*
Economy
  chart by country, 230–31, 250–59
  chart by region and income, 290–91
  government's role, chart by country,
    262–63
Ecuador
  Andean Community trade, 53
  genetic material and biodiversity, 103
Education, 11, 16, 26
  chart by country, 240–41
  child labor and, 62*b*
  Comprehensive Development
    Framework and, 21*b*
  DAC goal, 20
  decentralization of Mexican education,
    124
  East Asia, 16
  foreign direct investment and, 81
  health outcomes and, 19

information and technology revolution,
    effect, 29–30
  institutional reforms, 23
  social capital and, 18*b*
  trade liberalization and, 59, 67
  vocational training, 137
  World Development Reports, 22*b*
Egypt
  environmental issues, 97
  investment treaties, 72
  trade reform, 56*f*, 65, 157–60, 159*b*
Elections. *See* Decentralization of
    government; Subnational
    governments
Electronic commerce, 33, 65
Emerging market funds, 75*b*
Emissions. *See* Carbon dioxide emissions
Employment issues
  child labor, 62*b*
  displaced workers, 6
  labor conditions, 60
  labor costs, 137
  labor force, chart by country, 234–35
  trade liberalization, 59, 67
  unemployment, 49–50, 137*b*
  urbanization and, 128, 150–52
Endangered species. *See* Biodiversity
Energy. *See also* Environmental issues
  chart by country, 248–49, 264–65
  Comprehensive Development
    Framework and, 21*b*
  consumption patterns, 100, 100*f*, 101*f*
  falling costs of renewable energy, 98*b*
  research, 98
  subsidies, effect on environment, 90–91
  World Bank projects, 18, 18*b*, 98*b*
Entrepreneurship on municipal level,
  136–38
Environmental issues, 1, 8, 20, 30, 32,
    40–43, 87–105, 88*b*. *See also*
    Biodiversity; Carbon dioxide
    emissions
  chart by country, 222–23, 244–49
  Comprehensive Development
    Framework and, 21*b*
  DAC goal, 20
  data indicators, 215
  fishing and overfishing, 91, 92*b*
  institutions that provide physical services
    and, 24
  international measures needed, 93–94
  lead pollution, 141
  population growth and, 27–28
  protected areas, chart by country,
    246–47
  subsidies to industries, effect, 90–91
  sustainable development agenda and, 28,
    28*b*
  taxation to pay for damage, 91
  trade and, 67, 104*b*
  treaties and conventions, 90, 94–97, 104*b*

urbanization and, 141
World Development Reports, 22*b,* 90, 96*b*
Equity issues. *See* Gender equality;
    Inequality
Ethiopia
    decentralization of government, 45*t,*
        108, 109*b*
    government structure, 116*t*
    population growth, 44
    tax sharing, 117
Europe. *See also specific countries*
    agricultural trade disputes, 63
    antidumping laws, 58
    capital account convertibility, 71
    chart by region and income, 290–91
    coal production subsidies, 90–91
    energy consumption, 101*f*
    executive power, 114
    municipal development funds (MDFs),
        134
    poverty, 25*f*
    social partnerships, 137*b*
    trade in services, 34*f*
    urbanization, 47*f,* 48*f*
Exchange rates, 71
Executive power, 114
Exports. *See* Trade

Finance. *See also* Banking sector;
    Investment; Taxation
    chart by country, 256–57
Financial contagion, 74, 75*b*
Financial flows, 6–7, 7*f,* 34–38. *See also*
    International capital flows
    chart by country, 270–71
    developing countries and, 69–85
    institutionally managed funds, 71, 71*f*
Financial integration of world, 1, 69–75
Fishing and overfishing, 8, 91, 92*b*
    chart by country, 222–23
Food shortage, 1, 13, 27–28, 64
    chart by country, 232–33
    food stamps and food distribution, 23–24
Foreign aid, 73*b*
    chart by country, 270–71
Foreign banks, 35, 74, 78–79
Foreign direct investment, 6, 7*f,* 36–38,
        37*f,* 38*t,* 69–75
    attracting, 81–84
    chart by country, 270–71
    net flows to developing countries, 70*f,*
        73*b*
    regional foreign investment agreements,
        83–84
    service industries, 72
Forests and deforestation, 90, 93–94
    chart by country, 246–47
Framework Convention on Climate
    Change, 8, 88, 94*b,* 102
France
    government structure, 116*t*

land use in urban areas, 135*b*
    private infrastructure, 143–44
    vocational training, 137
Fund managers' methods to avoid spread of
    financial crises, 75*b*

GATS. *See* General Agreement on Trade in
    Services
GATT. *See* General Agreement on Tariffs
    and Trade
GDP. *See* Gross domestic product
GEF. *See* Global Environment Facility
Gender equality, 19–20, 26
    CDF goal, 21*b*
    DAC goal, 20
    education, chart by country, 240–41
    labor force, chart by country, 234–235
    World Development Reports, 22*b*
General Agreement on Tariffs and Trade
    (GATT), 5, 51, 53, 55
    antidumping actions, 60*t*
    environmental rulings by dispute panel,
        104
    subsidies and incentives, 136
    trade reform, commitment to, 35*f*
General Agreement on Trade in Services
    (GATS), 65, 82
Germany
    banking sector, 76*f*
    coal production subsidies, 91
    decentralization issues, 114
    government structure, 116*t*
    immigration trends, 38–40
    legislative representation, 113
    public services and horizontal equity, 110
    taxes, 117
Global Biodiversity Assessment (UNEP),
        102
Global commons, 87–105. *See also*
    Environmental issues
Global environment. *See* Climate change
Global Environment Facility (GEF), 8, 43,
        94*b,* 98*b,* 102
Global integration, 17*b*
Global production networks and
    international trade, 51, 65–67, 66*t*
Global warming. *See* Climate change
Globalization, 173–74. *See also*
    Supranational issues
    advantages and disadvantages, 4–5
    defined, 2
    factors contributing to, 4
    financial markets, 34–38
    partnerships and institutions required, 3
    trade and, 51–68. *See also* Trade
    trend of, 31
    urban challenges and, 140
Government finances. *See also* Taxation
    chart by country, 256–57
Government intervention and economic
    growth, 15–16, 20, 21*b*

Governmental institutions, 23
    World Development Reports, 22*b*
Great Britain. *See* United Kingdom
Greenhouse gases. *See* Climate change
Gross domestic product (GDP)
    agriculture and, 28, 47
    chart by country, 250–57
    growth rate, 15, 15*f*
    per capita, 14, 14*f,* 16
Gross national product (GNP), key
    indicator for economy, chart by
    country, 272
Growth of the economy. *See* Economic
    growth

Health issues
    chart by country, 242–43
    Comprehensive Development
        Framework and, 21*b*
    expenditures on, 19
    improvements, 26
    infectious diseases, 26, 141–43
    information and technology revolution,
        effect, 29–30
    institutions and sectoral issues involving,
        24
    social capital and, 18*b*
    trends, 27*b*
    urban growth and, 141
    World Development Reports, 22*b*
Hedge funds, 34
HIV. *See* AIDS
Homeless people, 48
Honduras
    components and parts imports, 66
    life expectancy, 26*f*
Hong Kong. *See also* China
    components and parts exports, 66, 66*t*
Horizontal equity and public services,
        110
Housing, 10–11, 48
    affordable housing, 139, 141*f,* 144–46
    chart by country, 220–21
    prices, 135
Human capital. *See* Education; Life
    expectancy
Human needs and development, 1, 3
    development services provided by
        institutions, 23–24
Human rights, 1, 43
Hungary
    banking reform, 158, 160–63, 161*b*
    firms from and international debt, 71*f*
    government structure, 115
    trade reform, 56*f,* 58

IBPGR (International Board for Plant
    Genetic Resources), 42
ICSID (International Centre for Settlement
    of Investment Disputes), 82
Illiteracy, chart by country, 232–33, 272

ILO (International Labour Organization),
   62*b*
IMF. *See* International Monetary Fund
Import-substitution policies, 13
Imports. *See* Trade
INBio (National Biodiversity Institute
   (Costa Rica)), 103
Income insurance, 50. *See also* Social
   welfare
Income tax. *See* Taxation
Incomes
   distribution of income, chart by country,
      238–39
   map of world, 229
   rich vs. poor countries, 14–15, 14*f*
India
   air pollution, 141
   antidumping laws, 58
   banking sector, 76*f*
   citizens' report cards, 153, 154*b*
   corruption, 144–45
   food supply, 13
   government structure, 115, 116*t*
   health issues in urban areas, 143
   industrial challenges, 49
   investment projects, 83
   legislative representation, 113
   local governments, 46, 109, 110*b*
   ozone depletion, 96
   politics, 44
   power projects, 98*b*
   taxes and revenues, 117–18
   trade, 52, 56, 59*f*
   urbanization issues, 131–32, 136, 141,
      145, 153, 154*b*
   within-state equity, 110
Indonesia
   banking sector, 37*f*, 76*f*, 80
   Clean Rivers program, 24
   components and parts imports, 66
   environmental issues, 93
   foreign direct investment, 72, 73*f*
   health status, 19
   Kampung Improvement Programs
      (KIPs), 146
   land use, 147*b*
   life expectancy, 26*f*
   trade reform, 56*f*
   transportation, 136
   urbanization issues, 130–31, 141, 146,
      147*b*, 149
   within-state equity, 110
Industrial countries. *See also specific countries*
   aging population, 36*b*
   antidumping complaints, 61*f*
   energy-related issues, 100, 100*f*, 101*f*
   foreign direct investment stock, 38*t*
   government structure, 116*t*
   infrastructure, 132
   institutionally managed funds invested
      abroad, 71, 71*f*

subnational debts, 120*t*
subnational expenditures, 111
trade in services, 34*f*
trade reform, 56, 58
urbanization, 47*f*
Industrial sector, 51, 65
   chart by country, 250–53
Inequality. *See also* Gender equality
   decentralization of government and,
      109–11
   economic growth and, 15
   horizontal equity, 110
   income inequality and import increases,
      59
   within-state equity, 110–11
Infant mortality, 19–20, 19*f*, 26, 48, 142,
   142*t*
   chart by country, 232–33, 242–43
Infectious diseases, 26, 27*b*. *See also* Health
   issues
Inflation, 30
Information
   chart by country, 266–67
   economic value, 4
   revolution in, 29–30
Infrastructure. *See also* Privatization; *specific*
   type of service
   publicly financed, 132–33
   World Development Reports, 22*b*
Institutionally managed funds and financial
   flows, 71, 71*f*
Institutions, 3–4, 11, 21–24, 23*b*, 174
   governmental, 23
   human development services, 23–24
   infrastructure and physical services, 24
   national, 32
   subnational, 32–33, 46
   supranational, 32
Integrated Framework for Trade and
   Development in the Least-Developed
   Countries (World Bank), 56, 58*b*
Intergovernmental Panel on Climate
   Change (IPCC), 94, 97
International Board for Plant Genetic
   Resources (IBPGR), 42
International capital flows, 6, 7*f*, 35, 70–73
   benefits of liberalization, 75
   chart by country, 270–71
International Centre for Settlement of
   Investment Disputes (ICSID), 82
International Convention for the Prevention
   of Pollution from Ships, 94*b*
International Covenant on Civil and
   Political Rights, 43
International Development Law Institute
   (Rome), 83
International Labour Organization (ILO),
   62*b*
International Monetary Fund (IMF), 7
   banking standards memorandum of
      understanding, 78

International trade. *See* Trade
Internet, 4*f*, 33
   chart by country, 266–67
Investment, 2. *See also* Foreign direct
   investment
   attracting foreign investment, 81–84
   capital flows. *See* International capital
      flows
   chart by country, 270–71
   East Asia, 17*b*
   economic growth correlated with, 15,
      15*f*
   foreign direct investment, 7*f*
   foreign portfolio investment, 6, 7*f*, 70*f*
   urban growth and capital investment,
      132–34
IPCC (Intergovernmental Panel on Climate
   Change), 94, 97
Iran
   decentralization of government, 45*t*
   government structure, 116*t*
Ireland and social partnerships, 137*b*
Irrigation. *See* Water
Italy
   government structure, 116*t*
   legislative representation, 114
   vocational training, 137

Jamaica
   capital account convertibility, 71
   food stamps, 23–24
Japan
   aging population, effect, 36*b*
   banking sector, 76*f*
   coal production subsidies, 90
   foreign banks in U.S., 79
   foreign investments by Japanese firms,
      81
   government structure, 116*t*
   ozone depletion, 97
   rapid economic growth, 2
Jordan
   housing, 146
   taxes, 117

Kazakhstan and life expectancy, 26*f*
Kenya
   decentralization of government, 45*t*
   gender-based discrimination, 20
   government structure, 116*t*
   trade reform, 56*f*
Knowledge, 1. *See also* Information
Korea, Republic of
   aging population, 36*b*
   antidumping laws, 58
   banking sector, 37*f*, 76*f*
   central government's loss of authority,
      44
   components and parts exports, 66*t*
   decentralization of government, 45*t*
   government structure, 116*t*

industry's dispersal, 129*b*, 131–32
investment treaties, 72
localization economies, 127
trade, 52
training of skilled workers, 39
urbanization, 48
Kuznets, S., 15
Kyoto Convention, 42, 94, 99*b*, 101, 104

Labor issues. *See* Employment issues
Land use, 134–36, 135*b*, 138*b*, 147*b*, 151
chart by country, 244–45
Latin America. *See also specific countries*
biodiversity, 43
bond market, 133
capital account convertibility, 71
chart by region and income, 290–91
debt crisis, 16, 32, 111
decentralization of government, 45, 109,
111, 123
emigration of skilled workers, 39
energy consumption, 101*f*
environmental issues, 94*b*
executive power, 114
health care expenditures, 19
industrial challenges, 49
international capital flows, 74
investment treaties, 72
poverty, 25, 25*f*
services provided through partnerships,
145
trade, 51, 56
trade in services, 34*f*
training needs, 49
urbanization, 47*f*, 48*f*
Latvia and government structure, 115
Lead pollution, 141
Legal frameworks, necessity of, 17*b*, 21*b*, 23
Legislative allocations and regional
interests, 113
Lewis, A., 15
Life expectancy, 11, 16, 19, 26, 26*f*, 48
chart by country, 232–33, 272
DAC goal, 20
demographic shift, 29
Living conditions in cities. *See*
Urbanization
Loans from banks. *See* Banking sector
Local governments. *See* Subnational
governments
Localization. *See also* Subnational
governments
advantages and disadvantages, 5
defined, 2
economies, 127
factors contributing to, 4
partnerships and institutions required,
3–4
trend of, 31–33, 43–46, 173–74
urban challenges and, 140
Long-term foreign investment, 7, 70, 81

Macedonia and banking crisis, 37*f*
Macroeconomics
African countries and, 16
Comprehensive Development
Framework and, 21*b*
developing countries and, 16
East Asia and, 16, 17*b*
investment reform, 84–85
stability, 1, 3, 16, 33
stability and decentralization of
government, 111
World Development Reports, 22*b*
Madagascar and government structure, 115
Malawi and government structure, 115
Malaysia
banking sector, 37*f*, 74, 76*f*
components and parts exports, 66*t*
foreign direct investment, 72, 73*f*
government structure, 116*t*
land use, 135
trade, 59*f*
vocational training, 137
Manufacturing. *See* Industrial sector
Marine pollution, 88*b*
Marine Stewardship Council, 92*b*
MDFs (municipal development funds), 134
Medical care. *See* Health issues
Memorandum of understanding, banking
standards, 78
Mercado Común del Sur (MERCOSUR),
83
Merck and Company, funding of Costa
Rican National Biodiversity Institute
(INBio), 103
MERCOSUR (Mercado Común del Sur),
83
Mexico
antidumping laws, 58
banking crisis, 35, 37*f*, 74, 75*b*, 79–80
banking sector, 76*f*
components and parts trade, 66, 66*t*
decentralization of government, 45, 45*t*,
113, 124
energy projects with World Bank, 102
firms from and international debt, 70, 71*f*
foreign direct investment, 37, 72, 73*f*, 82
government structure, 116*t*
political participation and civil society,
122
tax sharing, 118*b*
trade, 52, 56*f*
Middle East. *See also specific countries*
chart by region and income, 290–91
decentralization of government, 45
demographic shifts, 44
energy consumption, 101*f*
foreign direct investment, 72
life expectancy, 26*f*
poverty, 25*f*
trade in services, 34*f*
urbanization, 47*f*, 48*f*

MIGA (Multilateral Investment Guarantee
Agency), 83*b*
Migration trends, 38–40
Military expenditures, chart by country,
262–63
Millennium Round, 6, 34
Monopolies. *See* Antitrust issues
Montreal Protocol, 8, 32, 95, 96*b*, 104*b*
Morocco
decentralization of government, 45*t*
trade, 52
Mortality rates. *See* Infant mortality; Life
expectancy
Mozambique and government structure,
116*t*
Multilateral Investment Guarantee Agency
(MIGA), 83*b*
Multinational corporations, 35, 37
foreign direct investment, 69–70, 72, 81
trade policies and, 66, 81
Municipalities. *See* Urbanization

NAFTA (North American Free Trade
Agreement), 82–83
National governments
policy trends, 32
privatization and, 108*b*
regional influence on, 113
types of, 4
urbanization and, 130–32
Natural resources protection, 91. *See also*
Biodiversity; Fishing and overfishing;
Forests and deforestation
chart by country, 246–47
international investment and, 72–73
Nepal
agriculture, 28
decentralization of government, 45*t*
government structure, 116*t*
New Zealand, antidumping laws, 58
NGOs. *See* Nongovernmental
organizations
Nicaragua, components and parts exports,
66, 66*t*
Nigeria
decentralization of government, 45*t*
infrastructure failure, 49
Nongovernmental organizations (NGOs),
3–4, 43
civil society and, 122
environmental role, 96, 96*b*
housing assistance, 146
public service providers, as, 145
sewerage systems, 149
North Africa. *See also specific countries*
chart by region and income, 290–91
decentralization of government, 45
energy consumption, 101*f*
poverty, 25*f*
trade in services, 34*f*
urbanization, 47*f*, 48*f*

North American Free Trade Agreement
    (NAFTA), 82–83

OECD. *See* Organisation for Economic
    Co-operation and Development
Oman and life expectancy, 26*f*
Organisation for Economic Co-operation
    and Development (OECD), 20, 94, 96
Ozone depletion and treaties, 8, 32, 42,
    94–97, 95*f*

Pacific. *See* East Asia
Pakistan
    government, 45*t*, 46, 113, 116*t*
    infrastructure failure, 49
    job training, 137
    sewerage systems and Orangi Research
        and Training Institute, 149, 153,
        168–69
    urban conditions, 141*f*, 147, 158,
        166–69, 167*b*
Participatory politics. *See* Decentralization
    of government
Partnerships, 3–4, 40
    Comprehensive Development
        Framework and, 21*b*
    cross-border partnerships with firms in
        developing countries, 72
    urban services, 139, 145
Patents, chart by country, 266–67
Pension assets. *See* Aging population
Persistent organic pollutants, 87, 88*b*
Peru
    Andean Community trade, 53
    governmental authority, 46
Pharmaceutical drugs, 27*b*, 103
Philippines
    Community Mortgage Program, 146
    components and parts trade, 66, 66*t*
    decentralization of government, 45, 45*t*,
        111
    government structure, 116*t*
    trade reform, 56*f*
    urban poverty program, 151
    vehicle emission inspections, 150, 151*b*
    water pollution, 141
Poland
    biodiversity project, 102
    bond market, 133
    decentralization of government, 45, 45*t*,
        123
    foreign direct investment, 37
    government structure, 116*t*
    trade reform, 58
Polio, 26
Political parties, 122
Political pluralism. *See* Decentralization of
    government
Political rights, 1, 43–44
Pollution. *See* Air pollution; Environmental
    issues; Sewerage

Poor countries. *See also* Developing
    countries
    growth of incomes, 14–15, 14*f*
    water scarcity, 29*b*
Popular participation in government, 43.
    See also Democracies
Population growth
    urban areas, 128*f*, 130*f*, 140
    world-wide, 1, 27
Poverty reduction, 1, 24–26, 25*f*. *See also*
    Food shortage
    chart by country, 236–37
    child labor and, 62*b*
    Comprehensive Development
        Framework and, 21*b*
    DAC goal, 20
    decentralization of government and,
        109–11
    economic growth and, 15
    local government's responsibility, 11
    social capital and, 18*b*
    urban areas and, 49–50, 142–43,
        150–52
    World Development Reports, 22*b*
Power projects. *See* Energy
Power projects of World Bank, 18*b*
Private sector finance, chart by country,
    260–61
Privatization, 18, 18*b*, 143–45, 153
    foreign direct investments and, 82
    local governments and, 122, 142
    national governments and, 108*b*
    "self-provision," 145
    water supply, 143–44, 147–48, 153
Production networks and international
    trade, 51, 65–67, 66*t*
Productivity
    output, chart by country, 252–53
    trade and, 52
Public services
    decentralization of government, 108–10
    developing countries, 144–55
    horizontal equity, 110
    shift to private sector. *See* Privatization
    urban areas, 139–44

Quality of life. *See* Urbanization

Regional economic development, 137*b*
Regional foreign investment agreements,
    83–84
Regional trade arrangements (RTAs), 53,
    54*b*, 54*f*, 56, 66
Reproductive health services
    Comprehensive Development
        Framework and, 21*b*
    DAC goal, 20
Republic of Korea. *See* Korea, Republic of
Responsive processes and development, 1, 3
Retirement age, 36*b*
Revenue sharing, 118*b*

Reverse migration, 39
Rich countries, growth of incomes, 14–15,
    14*f*
Rio Earth Summit, 8, 42, 88, 90, 102
Roads. *See* Transportation
Romania, decentralization of government,
    45*t*
RTAs. *See* Regional trade arrangements
Rules. *See* Institutions
Rural development
    case study of Tanzania, 158, 169–72,
        170*b*
    Comprehensive Development
        Framework and, 21*b*
    institutional structures and, 24
    social capital and, 18*b*
    vs. urban growth, 10, 28, 130, 140. *See
        also* Urbanization
    World Development Reports, 22*b*
Russian Federation
    biodiversity, 43
    bond market, 133
    decentralization of government, 45, 45*t*,
        108–9, 123, 123*b*
    economic problems, 16, 17*b*, 44
    government structure, 33, 116*t*, 123
    housing, 146
    life expectancy, 26, 26*f*
    ozone depletion, 97
    politics and elections, 44, 113
    private enforcement of laws, 44
    social problems, 44

Sanctions
    biodiversity protections, 103
    trade violations, 60, 62*b*
Sanitary and phytosanitary regulations, 64
Sanitation. *See* Sewerage
Saudi Arabia, foreign direct investment,
    73*f*
Savings
    East Asia, 17*b*
    pension assets. *See* Aging population
Science. *See* Technology
Services sector
    chart by country, 250–55
    economic growth in, 29–30
    economic value, 4
    foreign direct investment, 72
    trade, 6, 33, 34*f*, 64–65, 64*f*
        chart by country, 268–69
Sewerage
    chart by country, 220–21, 232–33,
        242–43
    Comprehensive Development
        Framework and, 21*b*
    urban areas and, 11, 49, 140, 140*b*, 142,
        148–49
Sex equality. *See* Gender equality
Short-term foreign investment, 7, 69–70,
    79

Singapore
    capital account convertibility, 71
    components and parts exports, 66*t*
    foreign direct investment, 73*f*
Slovak Republic, government structure, 115
Slovenia, components and parts exports, 66*t*
Slums. *See* Housing
Smallpox, 26
Social capital, 18, 18*b*, 22
    urbanization and, 49
Social welfare, 1, 50, 150–52
Socially inclusive processes and
    development, 1, 21*b*
SODECI, 148
"Sourcing," 33
South Africa
    antidumping laws, 58
    bond market, 133
    decentralization of government, 45, 45*t*,
        107, 108*b*
    firms from and international debt, 71*f*
    government structure, 116*t*
    legislative representation, 113
    trade reform, 56*f*
    urban management, 145
South America. *See also specific countries*
    Andean Community trade, 53
    chart by region and income, 290–91
South Asia. *See also specific countries*
    diaspora, 40, 40*b*
    emigration of skilled workers, 39
    energy consumption, 101*f*
    health care expenditures, 19
    poverty, 25, 25*f*
    trade, 51
    trade in services, 34*f*
    urbanization, 47*f*, 48, 48*f*
Soviet Union. *See now* Russian Federation
    economic growth, 15–16
    land use, 134, 135*b*
    urbanization issues, 130–31
Spain
    government structure, 116*t*
    legislative representation, 114
Sri Lanka
    government structure, 119
    health care expenditures, 19
    housing programs, 146
Stock markets, 84
Sub-Saharan Africa. *See also specific
        countries*
    agriculture, 28
    chart by region and income, 290–91
    diaspora, 40
    emigration of skilled workers, 39
    energy consumption, 101*f*
    energy projects of World Bank, 18, 18*b*
    health care expenditures, 19
    life expectancy and education, 11, 16
    politics, 44
    poverty, 25, 25*f*

trade in services, 34*f*
urbanization, 47*f*, 48, 48*f*
water scarcity, 29*b*
Subnational governments, 3, 8–11, 32–33,
    44–46. *See also* Decentralization of
    government
    accountability, 121–23
    banking sector, 77
    central regulation of, 119, 121
    debts and borrowing controls, 119, 120*t*,
        124
    electoral rules, 121–22
    expenditures, 111*f*, 118
    foreign direct investments, 82, 83*b*
    horizontal equity, 110
    incentives for national and subnational
        cooperation, 114
    personnel issues, 119, 121
    structures and functions, 114–21
    taxes and revenues, 112*f*, 117–19, 118*b*,
        123
    within-state equity, 110–11
Subsidies
    chart by country, 262–63
    coal production, 90–91
    export, 2
    municipalities giving to overseas
        industries, 136
Supranational issues, 3, 5–8, 32

Taiwan (China)
    banking sector, 76*f*
    components and parts exports, 66, 66*t*
    computer industry investments in
        Europe and U.S., 40*b*
    trade, 52
    training of skilled workers, 39
Tanzania and urban-rural synergies, 158,
    169–72, 170*b*
Tariffs. *See* Trade
Taxation
    chart by country, 256–57, 262–63
    decentralized governments, 117–19, 123
    environmental taxes, 91
    horizontal equity and, 110
    international investment, 72
    international trade profits, 66–67
    location choices for businesses, 137
    subnational and local taxes, 112*f*,
        117–19, 118*b*, 123
    tax sharing, 117, 118*b*
Technology
    chart by country, 266–67
    innovations, 1, 29–30, 33
    trade, 56, 59*f*, 81
Telecommunications. *See* Communications
Thailand
    air pollution, 141
    banking sector, 37*f*, 75*b*, 76*f*, 79–80
    components and parts trade, 66, 66*t*
    decentralization of government, 45*t*

firms from and international debt, 70,
    71*f*
foreign direct investment, 72
government structure, 116*t*
land use, 135
poverty, 25
urban transportation problems, 141
The Theory of Economic Growth, 15
Trade, 51–68. *See also* General Agreement
        on Tariffs and Trade (GATT); World
        Trade Organization (WTO)
    agriculture, 6, 61, 63–64
    benefits of liberalization, 52–53
    chart by country, 250–51, 254–55,
        258–59, 268–69
    competition, 52, 59
    components and parts exports, 33,
        65–67, 66*t*
    developing countries, 51–53, 52*f*
    dispute resolution, 54–55, 61
    employment issues, 59, 67
    environmental issues, 67, 104*b*
    final goods production, 52–53
    growth, 5–6, 5*f*
    import-substitution policies, 2, 13
    Integrated Framework for Trade and
        Development in the Least-Developed
        Countries (World Bank), 56, 58*b*
    production networks, 65–67, 66*t*
    productivity and, 52
    reduction of trade barriers, 55
    reform, 33–34, 53–54, 56–61, 56*f*
        case study of Egypt, 157–60, 159*b*
    foreign investments and, 81–82
    regional trade arrangements (RTAs), 53,
        54*b*, 54*f*, 56, 66
    sanctions, effectiveness, 60, 62*b*
    services. *See* Services sector
    "sourcing," 33
    subsidies, 2
    tariff binding, 55, 63, 63*f*
    tax implications, 66–67
    technology exports, 59*f*
    transparent trade policy regimes and, 55
    trends, 33–34, 51–68
    urban growth and, 67, 131, 136
    World Development Reports, 22*b*
Training. *See* Education
Transition economies
    subnational debts, 120*t*
    subnational expenditures, 111*t*
    subnational taxes, 112*f*
Transportation
    chart by country, 220–21, 264–65
    Comprehensive Development
        Framework and, 21*b*
    reduced costs, 4
    urban areas, 11, 136–37, 149
Treaties
    environmental, 90, 94–97, 95*f*, 104*b*
    foreign investors' rights, 72, 83

TSPs (total suspended particulates), 141–42
Tuberculosis (TB), 27*b*, 141
Turkey
  bond market, 133
  government structure, 116*t*, 119
  return of emigrants, 39
  trade, 52
  urbanization issues, 145

Uganda
  decentralization of government, 45*t*, 108, 108*b*
  government structure, 116*t*
  life expectancy, 26*f*
Ukraine
  decentralization of government, 45, 45*t*
  economic and social instability, 44
  government structure, 116*t*
Unemployment, 49–50, 137*b*, 150, 152*b*. *See also* Employment issues
United Kingdom
  government structure, 116*t*
  health status, 19
  municipal development funds and bonds, 134
  Non-Fossil Fuel Obligation (NFFO), 98*b*
  pension assets, 35
  private provision of basic services, 143
United Nations (UN)
  Convention on the Law of the Sea (UNCLOS), 88*b*
  Convention to Combat Desertification, 88*b*
  Environment Programme (UNEP), 42, 88*b*, 96*b*, 102, 105
  environmental issues, 42, 92*b*, 104*b*
  Global Shelter Strategy for the Year 2000, 146
  Human Rights Committee, 43
United States
  aging population, 35, 36*b*
  antidumping laws, 58
  banking sector, 76*f*
  bond market, 133
  carbon dioxide emissions, 42, 97
  chart by region and income, 290–91
  decentralization issues, 114
  executive power, 114
  government structure, 116*t*
  immigration trends, 38–40
  institutionally managed funds invested abroad, 71, 71*f*
  metropolitan areas, 130
  pension assets, 35
  state marketing offices overseas, 136
  taxes, 117
Urbanization, 10–11, 10*f*, 28–29, 46–50, 125–55
  agglomeration economies, 126–27

chart by country, 218–19, 232–33
citizens' report cards, 153, 154*b*
data indicators, 214
definitions of terminology, 127*b*
dynamics of city formation, 128–30
economic analysis, importance of, 138*b*
economic growth and, 125–38, 126*f*
entrepreneurship on municipal level, 136–38
housing. *See* Housing
land use. *See* Land use
living conditions, 139–55
  case study of Pakistan, 158, 166–69, 167b
  chart by country, 220–21, 232–33
  data indicators, 214–15
local policies for economic growth, 132–38
municipal bankruptcies, 133–34
municipal bonds, 133
municipal development funds (MDFs), 134
national government's role, 130–32
population and size of cities, 128*f*, 130*f*, 140
poverty. *See* Poverty reduction
production site choice, 131
public services, 139–44
rural-urban linkages, 127, 128*b*
  case study of Tanzania, 158, 169–72, 170*b*
sanitation issues. *See* Sewerage
systems of cities, 127–28
trade and, 67, 131, 136
transportation issues, 11, 136–37, 149–50
water issues. *See* Water
Uruguay Round, 52, 55–56, 61, 63–65, 63*f*
Utilities. *See* Public services
Uzbekistan and poverty reduction, 111

Value added tax (VAT). *See* Taxation
Venezuela
  Andean Community trade, 53
  banking sector, 74, 76*f*
  capital account convertibility, 71
  decentralization of government, 45*t*
  government structure, 116*t*
  political participation and civil society, 122
Vienna Convention for the Protection of the Ozone Layer, 95
Vietnam
  taxation and horizontal equity, 110
  urbanization issues, 130–31, 141, 150
  water supply, 148, 148*b*
Violence, 48, 142, 151–52

Wages, 60, 62*b*, 137
Waste disposal. *See* Environmental issues

Water
  chart by country, 220–21, 242–43, 246–47
  Comprehensive Development Framework and, 21*b*
  partnerships with community organizations, 148, 148*b*
  private providers of public water supply, 143–44, 147–48, 153
  scarcity, 1, 28, 29*b*
  urban areas, 11, 140*f*, 143–44, 146–48
Welfare. *See* Social welfare
Women. *See* Gender equality
World Bank
  banking standards memorandum of understanding, 78
  Comprehensive Development Framework, 20, 21*b*, 173
  energy projects in Mexico, 102
  foreign investment role, 83*b*
  Integrated Framework for Trade and Development in the Least-Developed Countries, 56, 58*b*
  projects and successful development, 17–18, 18*b*
World Development Reports since 1990, 20, 22*b*, 90
World Trade Organization (WTO), 5–6, 32, 51
  African membership, 57*f*
  antidumping actions, 60*t*
  benefits of, 53–56
  developing countries' representation, 55–56, 57*f*
  dispute resolution, 54–55, 61
  environmental ruling, 104
  labor conditions, 60
  number of member countries, 6*f*, 33, 35*f*, 53
  reduction of trade barriers, 55
  regional trade arrangements and, 54*b*
  scope of, 53*f*
  tariff binding, 55
  Trade Policy Review Mechanism, 55
  trade reform, 53–54
  transparent trade policy regimes and, 55
WTO. *See* World Trade Organization

Yemen and life expectancy, 26*f*
Yugoslavia
  tax sharing, 117
  trade reform, 58

Zambia
  government structure, 115
  life expectancy, 26*f*
  local governments, 109
Zimbabwe
  environmental issues, 97
  life expectancy, 26*f*
Zoning, 134

DISTRIBUTORS OF WORLD BANK GROUP PUBLICATIONS

Prices and credit terms vary from country to country. Please consult your local distributor before placing an order.

ARGENTINA
World Publications SA
Av. Cordoba 1877
1120 Buenos Aires
Tel: (54 11) 815 8156
Fax: (54 11) 815 8156
E-mail: wpbooks@infovia.com.ar

AUSTRALIA, PAPUA NEW GUINEA, FIJI, SOLOMON ISLANDS, VANUATU, AND SAMOA
D.A. Information Services
648 Whitehorse Road
Mitcham 3132
Victoria, Australia
Tel: (61 3) 9210 7777
Fax: (61 3) 9210 7788
E-mail: service@dadirect.com.au
URL: www.dadirect.com.au

AUSTRIA
Gerold and Co.
Weihburggasse 26
A-1010 Wien
Tel: (43 1) 512 47310
Fax: (43 1) 512 473129
E-mail: buch@gerold.telecom.at

BANGLADESH
Micro Industries Development Assistance
Society (MIDAS)
House 5, Road 16
Dhanmondi R/Area
Dhaka 1209
Tel: (880 2) 326427
Fax: (880 2) 811188

BELGIUM
Jean de Lannoy
Av. du Roi 202
1060 Brussels
Tel: (32 2) 538 5169
Fax: (32 2) 538 0841
E-mail: jean.de.lannoy@infoboard.be

BOSNIA AND HERZEGOVINA
Book Trading Company "Sahinpasic"
Marsala Tita 29/II
71000 Sarajevo
Tel: (387 71) 64 48 56
Fax: (387 71) 64 48 56
E-mail: tajib@btcsahinpasic.com
URL: www.btcsahinpasic.com

BRAZIL
Publicacões Tecnicas Internacionais Ltda.
Rua Peixoto Gomide, 209
01409 Sao Paulo, SP
Tel: (55 11) 259 6644
Fax: (55 11) 258 6990
E-mail: postmaster@pti.uol.br
URL: www.uol.br

CANADA
Renouf Publishing Co. Ltd.
5369 Canotek Road
Ottawa, Ontario K1J 9J3
Tel: (613) 745-2665
Fax: (613) 745-7660
E-mail: order.dept@renoufbooks.com
URL: www.renoufbooks.com

CHINA
Chinese Corporation for Promotion and
Humanities
15, Ding Hui Dong Li, Kun Lan Hotal
Haidian District 100036
Beijing
Tel: (86 10) 88117711
Fax: (86 10) 88129871
E-mail: wangjiang99@yahoo.com

China Book Import Centre
Ms. Zhou Rui
P.O. Box 2825
Beijing

China Financial & Economic Publishing
House
8, Da Fo Si Dong Jie
Beijing
Tel: (86 10) 6401 7365
Fax: (86 10) 6401 7365

COLOMBIA
Infoenlace Ltda./An IHS Group Company
Calle 72 No. 13-23 - Piso 3
Edificio Nueva Granada
P.O. Box (A.A) 34270
Santafé de Bogotá, D.C.
Tel: (57 1) 255 8783
Fax: (57 1) 248 0808
E-mail: infoenlace@gaitana.interred.net.co

CÔTE D'IVOIRE
Centre d'Edition et de Diffusion Africaines
(CEDA)
04 B.P. 541
Abidjan 04
Tel: (225) 24 6510
Fax: (225) 25 0567
E-mail: info@ceda-ci.com
URL: www.ceda-ci.com

CYPRUS
Center for Applied Research
6, Diogenes Street, Engomi
P.O. Box 2006
Nicosia
Tel: (357 2) 59 0730
Fax: (357 2) 66 2051
E-mail: ttzitzim@sting.cycollege.ac.cy

CZECH REPUBLIC
USIS, NIS Prodejna
Havelkova 22
130 00 Prague 3
Tel: (42 2) 2423 1486
Fax: (42 2) 2423 1114
E-mail: pospisilovaj@usiscr.cz
URL: : www.usiscr.cz

DENMARK
Samfundslitteratur
Rosenoerns Alle 11
DK-1970 Frederiksberg C
Tel: (45 35) 351942
Fax: (45 35) 35 7822
E-mail: ck@sl.cbs.dk
URL: www.sl.cbs.dk

ECUADOR
Libri Mundi—Libreria Internacional
Juan Leon Mera 851
P.O. Box 17-01-3029
Quito
Tel: (593 2) 521606
Fax: (593 2) 504209
E-mail: librimu1@librimundi.com.ec

CODEU
Ruiz de Castilla 763, Edif. Expocolor
Primer piso, Of. #2
Quito
Tel: (593 2) 507-383
Fax: (593 2) 507-383
E-mail: codeu@impsat.net.ec

EGYPT, ARAB REPUBLIC OF
Al Ahram Distribution Agency
Al Galaa Street
Cairo
Tel: (20 2) 578 60 83
Fax: (20 2) 578 68 33

The Middle East Observer
41, Sherif Street
Cairo
Tel: (20 2) 392 6919
Fax: (20 2) 393 9732
E-mail: mafouda@meobserver.com.eg
URL: www.meobserver.com.eg

FINLAND
Akateeminen Kirjakauppa
P.O. Box 128
FIN-00101 Helsinki
Tel: (358 9) 121 4418
Fax: (358 9) 121 4435
E-mail: akatilaus@akateeminen.com
URL: www.akateeminen.com

FRANCE
Editions Eska; DJB/Offlib
12, rue du Quatre-Septembre
75002 Paris
Tel: (33 1) 42 86 56 88
Fax: (33 1) 42 60 45 35
E-mail: offilib@offilib.fr
URL: www.offilib.fr

GERMANY
UNO-VERLAG
Poppelsdorfer Allee 55
D-53115 Bonn
Tel: (49 228) 949020
Fax: (49 228) 217492
E-mail: unoverlag@aol.com
URL: www.uno-verlag.de

GHANA
Epp Books Services
Post Office Box 44
TUC
Accra
Tel: (233 21) 778843
Fax: (233 21) 779099
E-mail: epp@africaonline.com.gh

GREECE
Papasotiriou S.A.,
International Technical Bookstore
35, Stournara Str.
106 82 Athens
Tel: (30 1) 364 1826
Fax: (30 1) 364 8254
E-mail: gprekas@papasotiriou.gr

HAITI
Culture Diffusion
Mr. Yves Clément Jumelle
5, Rue Capois
C.P. 257
Port-au-Prince
Tel: (509) 23 9260
Fax: (509) 23 4858

HONG KONG, CHINA; MACAU
Asia 2000 Ltd.
Sales & Circulation Department
302 Seabird House
22-28 Wyndham Street, Central
Hong Kong, China
Tel: (852) 2530 1409
Fax: (852) 2526 1107
E-mail: sales@asia2000.com.hk
URL: www.asia2000.com.hk

HUNGARY
Euro Info Service
Margitszgeti Europa Haz
H-1138 Budapest
Tel: (36 1) 350 80 24; 350 80 25
Fax: (36 1) 350 90 32
E-mail: euroinfo@mail.matav.hu

INDIA
Allied Publishers Ltd.
751 Mount Road
Madras 600 002
Tel: (91 44) 852 3938
Fax: (91 44) 852 0649
E-mail: allied.mds@smb.sprintrpg.ems.
vsnl.net.in

INDONESIA
Pt. Indira Limited
Jalan Borobudur 20
PO Box 181
Jakarta 10320
Tel: (62 21) 390 4290
Fax: (62 21) 390 4289

IRAN
Kowkab Publishers
P.O. BOX 19575-511
Tehran
Tel: (98 21) 258 3723
Fax: (98 21) 258 3723
E-mail: kowkabpub@tavana.net

Ketab Sara Co. Publishers
P.O. Box 15745-733
Tehran 15117
Tel: (98 21) 8716104
Fax: (98 21) 8712479
E-mail: ketab-sara@neda.net.ir

IRELAND
Government Supplies Agency
4-5 Harcourt Road
Dublin 2
Tel: (353 1) 661 3111
Fax: (353 1) 475 2670
URL: www.opw.ie/govt.htm

ISRAEL
Yozmot Literature Ltd.
P.O. Box 56055
3 Yohanan Hasandlar St.
Tel Aviv 61560
Tel: (972 3) 5285 397
Fax: (972 3) 5285 397

R.O.Y. International
P.O. Box 13056
Tel Aviv 61130
Tel: (972 3) 649 9469
Fax: (972 3) 648 6039
E-mail: royil@netvision.net.il
URL: www.royint.co.il

Palestinian Authority/Middle East
Index Information Services
P.O.B. 19502 Jerusalem
Tel: (972 2) 6271219
Fax: (972 2) 6271634

ITALY
Licosa Libreria Commissionaria Sansoni
S.P.A.
Via Duca di Calabria 1/1
50125 Firenze
Tel: (39 55) 645 415
Fax: (39 55) 641 257
E-mail: licosa@ftbcc.it
URL: www.ftbcc.it/licosa

JAMAICA
Ian Randle Publishers Ltd
206 Old Hope Road
Kingston 6
Tel: (876) 927 2085
Fax: (876) 977 0243
E-mail: irpl@colis.com

JAPAN
Eastern Book Service (EBS)
3-13 Hongo 3-chome, Bunkyo-ku
Tokyo 113
Tel: (81 3) 3818 0861
Fax: (81 3) 3818 0864
E-mail: orders@svt-ebs.co.jp
URL: www.svt-ebs.co.jp

KENYA
Legacy Books
Loita House
P.O. Box 68077
Nairobi
Tel: (254 2) 330853
Fax: (254 2) 330854
E-mail: legacy@form-net.com

Africa Book Service (E.A.) Ltd.
Mr. Talat Lone
Quaran House, Mfangano Street
P.O. Box 45245
Nairobi
Tel: (254 2) 223 641
Fax: (254 2) 330 272

KOREA, REPUBLIC OF
Dayang Books Trading Co.
International Division
954-22, Bangbae-Dong, Socho-ku
Seoul
Tel: (82 2) 582 3588
Fax: (82 2) 521 8827
E-mail: dico3@chollian.net

Eulyoo Publishing Co., Ltd.
46-1, Susong-Dong
Jongro-Gu
Seoul
Tel: (82 2) 734 3515
Fax: (82 2) 732 9154
E-mail: eulyoo@chollian.net

LEBANON
Librairie du Liban
P.O. Box 11-9232
Beirut
Tel: (961 9) 217 944
Fax: (961 9) 217 434
E-mail: hsageh@cyberia.net.lb
URL: www.librairie-du-liban.com.lb

MALAYSIA
University of Malaya Cooperative
 Bookshop, Limited
P.O. Box 1127, Jalan Pantai Baru
59700 Kuala Lumpur
Tel: (60 3) 7565 000
Fax: (60 3) 755 4424
E-mail: umkoop@tm.net.my

MEXICO
INFOTEC
Av. San Fernando No. 37
Col. Toriello Guerra
14050 Mexico D.F.
Tel: (52 5) 624 2800
Fax: (52 5) 624 2822
E-mail: infotec@rtn.net.mx
URL: www.rtn.net.mx

Mundi-Prensa Mexico, S.A. de C.V.
c/Rio Panuco, 141 - Colonia Cuauhtemoc
06500 Mexico DF
Tel: (52 5) 533 56 58
Fax: (52 5) 514 67 99
E-mail: 1015245.2361@compuserve.com

NEPAL
Everest Media International Services (P.)
 Ltd.
GPO Box 5443
Kathmandu
Tel: (977 1) 416 026
Fax: (977 1) 224 431

NETHERLANDS
De Lindeboom/Internationale
 Publikaties b.v.
M.A. de Ruyterstraat 20A
7482 BZ Haaksbergen
Tel: (31 53) 574 0004
Fax: (31 53) 572 9296
E-mail: lindeboo@worldonline.nl
URL: home.worldonline.nl/~lindeboo

NEW ZEALAND
EBSCO NZ Ltd.
Private Mail Bag 99914
New Market
Auckland
Tel: (64 9) 524 8119
Fax: (64 9) 524 8067
E-mail: WGent%ess-nz.ebsco@iss.
 ebsco.com

Oasis Official
P.O. Box 3627
Wellington
Tel: (64 4) 4991551
Fax: (64 4) 499 1972
E-mail: oasis@actix.gen.nz
URL: www.oasisbooks.co.nz

NIGERIA
University Press Plc
Three Crowns Building Jericho
Private Mail Bag 5095
Ibadan
Tel: (234 22) 411356
Fax: (234 22) 412056
E-mail: suike@hotmail.com

PAKISTAN
Oxford University Press
5 Bangalore Town, Sharae Faisal
P.O. Box 13033
Karachi 75350
Tel: (92 21) 446307; 449032; 440532
Fax: (92 21) 4547640;449032
E-mail: usmanm@oup.net.pk

Pak Book Corporation
Aziz Chambers 21
Queen's Road
Lahore
Tel: (92 42) 636 3222; 636 0885
Fax: (92 42) 636 2328
E-mail: pbc@brain.net.pk

Mirza Book Agency
65, Shahrah-e-Quaid-e-Azam
Lahore 54000
Tel: (92 42) 7353601
Fax: (92 42) 576 3714
E-mail: merchant@brain.net.pk

PERU
Editorial Desarrollo SA
Apartado 3824
Ica 242, OF. 106
Lima 1
Tel: (51 14) 285 380
Fax: (51 14) 286 628

PHILIPPINES
International Booksource Center, Inc.
1127-A Antipolo St.
Barangay, Venezuela
Makati City
Tel: (63 2) 896 6501
Fax: (63 2) 896 6497

POLAND
International Publishing Service
Ul. Piekna 31/37
00 677 Warsaw
Tel: (48 2) 628 6089
Fax: (48 2) 621 7255
E-mail: books%ips@ikp.atm.com.pl
URL: www.ipscg.waw.pl/ips/export

PORTUGAL
Livraria Portugal
Apartado 2681
Rua Do Carmo 70-74
1200 Lisbon
Tel: (351 1) 347 4982
Fax: (351 1) 347 0264

ROMANIA
Compani De Librarii Bucuresti s.a.
Str. Lipscani nr. 26, sector 3
Bucharest
Tel: (40 1) 313 9645
Fax: (40 1) 312 4000

RUSSIAN FEDERATION
Izdatelstvo << Ves Mir >>
Moscow 101831
Tel: (7 95)917 8749
Fax: (7 95)917 9259
E-mail: ozimarin@glasnet.ru
URL: www.vesmir.tsx.org

**SINGAPORE; TAIWAN, CHINA,
MYANMAR; BRUNEI**
Hemisphere Publishing Services
Golden Wheel Building
41 Kallang Pudding Road, #04-03
Singapore 349316
Tel: (65) 741 5166
Fax: (65) 742 9356
E-mail: info@hemisphere.com.sg

SLOVENIA
Gospodarski vestnik Publishing Group
Dunajska cesta 5
1000 Ljubljana
Tel: (386 61) 133 83 47
Fax: (386 61) 133 80 30
E-mail: repansekj@gvestnik.si
URL: www.gvestnik.si/EUROPA/index.htm

SOUTH AFRICA, BOTSWANA
For single titles:
Oxford University Press Southern Africa
P.O. Box 12119
N1 City 7463
Cape Town
Tel: (27 21) 595 4400
Fax: (27 21) 595 4430
E-mail: oxford@oup.co.za

For subscription orders:
International Subscription Service
P.O. Box 41095
Craighall
Johannesburg 2024
Tel: (27 11) 880 1448
Fax: (27 11) 880 6248
E-mail: iss@is.co.za

SPAIN
Mundi-Prensa Libros, s.a.
Castello 37
28001 Madrid
Tel: (34 91) 436 37 00
Fax: (34 91) 575 39 98
E-mail: libreria@mundiprensa.es
URL: www.mundiprensa.es

Mundi-Prensa Barcelona
Consell de Cent No. 391
08009 Barcelona
Tel: (34 3) 488 3492
Fax: (34 3) 487 7659
E-mail: barcelona@mundiprensa.es

SRI LANKA, THE MALDIVES
Lake House Bookshop
P.O. Box 244
100, Sir Chittampalam Gardiner Mawatha
Colombo 2
Tel: (94 1) 32 104
Fax: (94 1) 432 104
E-mail: LHL@sri.lanka.net

SWEDEN
Wennergren-Williams Informations Service
 AB
P.O. Box 1305
S-171 25 Solna
Tel: (46 8) 705 9750
Fax: (46 8) 27 0071
E-mail: mail@wwi.se

SWITZERLAND
Librarie Payot S.A.
Service Institutionnel
Côtes-de-Montbenon 30
1002 Lausanne
Tel: (41 21) 341 3229
Fax: (41 21) 341 3235
E-mail: institutionnel@payot-libraire.ch

ADECO Van Diermen Editions Techniques
Ch. de Lacuez 41
CH-1807 Blonay
Tel: (41 21) 943 2673
Fax: (41 21) 943 3605

THAILAND
Central Books Distribution Co. Ltd.
306 Silom Road
Bangkok 10500
Tel: (66 2) 233-6930-9
Fax: (66 2) 237-8321

**TRINIDAD & TOBAGO AND
THE CARIBBEAN**
Systematics Studies Ltd.
St. Augustine Shopping Center
Eastern Main Road
St. Augustine
Tel: (868) 645 8466
Fax: (868) 645 8467
E-mail: tobe@trinidad.net

UGANDA
Gustro Limited
P.O. Box 9997
Madhvani Building
Plot 16/4, Jinja Road
Kampala
Tel: (256 41) 251467
Fax: (256 41) 251468
E-mail: gus@swiftuganda.com

UKRAINE
LIBRA Publishing House
Ms. Sophia Ghemborovskaya
53/80 Saksahanskoho Str.
252033, Kiev 33
Tel: (7 44) 227 62 77
Fax: (7 44) 227 62 77

UNITED KINGDOM
Microinfo Ltd.
P.O. Box 3, Omega Park
Alton
Hampshire GU34 2 PG
Tel: (44 1420) 86 848
Fax: 44 1420) 89 889
E-mail: wbank@ukminfo.demon.co.uk
URL: www.microinfo.co.uk

The Stationery Office
51 Nine Elms Lane
London SW8 5DR
Tel: (44 171) 873-8372
Fax: (44 171) 873-8242
E-mail: chris.allen@theso.co.uk
URL: www.tsonline.co.uk

VENEZUELA
Tecni-Ciencia Libros, S.A.
Sr. Luis Fernando Ramirez, Director
Centro Cuidad Comercial Tamanaco
Nivel C-2
Caracas
Tel: (58 2) 959 5547
Fax: (58 2) 959 5636
E-mail: lfrg001@ibm.net

ZAMBIA
University Bookshop, University of Zambia
Great East Road Campus
P.O. Box 32379
Lusaka
Tel: (260 1) 252576
Fax: (260 1) 253952
E-mail: hunene@admin.unza.zm

ZIMBABWE
Academic and Baobab Books (Pvt.) Ltd.
4 Conald Road
Graniteside
P.O. Box 567
Harare
Tel: (263 4) 755 035
Fax: (263 4) 759 052
E-mail: Academic@Africaonline.Co.Zw